La Nijinska

Bronislava Nijinska, 1953.

Photo by Serge Lido, inscribed to "dear, charming Mariusha Fredericksz," 1953. Collection of Marie Nugent-Head.

La Nijinska

Choreographer of the Modern

LYNN GARAFOLA

OXFORD
UNIVERSITY PRESS

Oxford University Press is a department of the University of Oxford. It furthers
the University's objective of excellence in research, scholarship, and education
by publishing worldwide. Oxford is a registered trade mark of Oxford University
Press in the UK and certain other countries.

Published in the United States of America by Oxford University Press
198 Madison Avenue, New York, NY 10016, United States of America.

CIP data is on file at the Library of Congress
ISBN 978-0-19-760390-1

DOI: 10.1093/oso/9780197603901.001.0001

1 3 5 7 9 8 6 4 2

Printed by Sheridan Books, Inc., United States of America

To Eric Foner and Daria Rose Foner
with love

Contents

Acknowledgments

La Nijinska: Choreographer of the Modern was made possible through the generosity of numerous individuals and institutions. First and foremost I want to thank the John Simon Guggenheim Memorial Foundation and the Dorothy and Lewis B. Cullman Center for Scholars and Writers for their fellowship support, and Columbia University's Harriman Center for translation assistance. Second, I wish to acknowledge my debt to the numerous archivists and librarians who opened their collections to me. This book is the first to draw extensively on the Bronislava Nijinska Collection, housed in the Music Division of the Library of Congress. Elizabeth Aldrich, the Library's former Curator of Dance, was unwavering in her enthusiasm and unstinting in her support during the early stages of the project, when the collection had yet to be fully catalogued; I am deeply grateful to her, as I am to her successor, Libby Smigel. I am equally grateful to Jane Pritchard, the Curator of Dance at the Victoria and Albert Museum, who was ever-generous in guiding me to documents concerning Nijinska's activities in England and to newly acquired Nijinska costumes, designs, and memorabilia. I am indebted to Irina Klyagin for locating sources at Harvard University's Houghton Library and to Norton Owen for guiding me to material at Jacob's Pillow. I owe a special debt of gratitude to Linda Murray, Curator of the New York Public Library's Jerome Robbins Dance Division, and to her colleagues and staff, who provided critical help during the pandemic when the library was closed to outsiders. As always, I am indebted to the late Elizabeth Souritz of Moscow for her inspiration and help in too many ways to list; I am equally grateful to her daughter Irina Gruzheva; her colleagues Georgy Kovalenco and Sergei Konaev, who led me to crucial information and sources; and especially Vyacheslav V. Ivanov, for publishing Nijinska's earliest extant writings in the Russian journal *Mnemozina*.

I take this opportunity to express my thanks to Rachel Atman of the Carnegie History center in Bryan, Texas, for access to the Ana Ludmilla Gee Collection; Robert Davis, Librarian for Russian, Eurasian, and East European Studies, Columbia University; Sari Mariia Harjanne and the staff of the Carina Ari Library, Stockholm; Evgenia Iliukhina, Curator of the Larionov-Goncharova Collection, Tretiakov Gallery, Moscow; Sergei Laletin, St. Petersburg State Museum of Theatre and Music; Anne Meadmore, Royal Ballet School, London; Michelle Potter, Inaugural Curator of Dance, National Library of Australia; Karen S. Raines, Special Collections, University of California, Riverside; John Neumeier and Dr. Hans-Michael Shäfer, Stiftung John Neumeier, Hamburg; Jonathan Gray, Editor, *Dancing Times*; Oliver Halsman Rosenberg of the Philippe Halsman Archive; Anna-Marie Holmes; Peter Kayafas, Eakins Press Foundation; Nadine Stadler, George Kirsta Collection, University of Salzburg; the staff of the Teatro Colón Library, Buenos Aires; and Heidy Zimmermann, Paul Sacher Stiftung, Basel. This book is much the richer because of their generosity.

Third, I express my gratitude to the numerous colleagues who have shared their knowledge, thoughts, and research with me: in Argentina, Professor Susana Tambutti, Universidad Nacional de Buenos Aires, and Paulina Antacli, Universidad Nacional de Córdoba, for helping me understand the world that Nijinska inhabited in Buenos Aires; in Brazil, Arnaldo Leite de Alvarenga and Beatriz Cerbeno, for underscoring the importance of Maria Olenewa, and Tatiana Leskova, for sharing her memories of Nijinska; in Poland, Maria Dworakowska, Polish Theater Institute, Warsaw, critic and curator Jadwiga Grabowka Majewska, and musicologist Małgorzata Komorwoska, for guiding me to written and visual sources elucidating Nijinska's experience with the Polish Ballet; Sue Lonoff de Cuevas for sharing material and information about the Marquis de Cuevas; Marie Nugent-Head for allowing me to publish the portrait of Nijinska inscribed to her aunt; Patrizia Veroli and Carmelo A. Zapparrata for Nijinska's engagements in Italy; art historian Anthony Parton of the University of Durham for sharing his thoughts about Natalia Goncharova as well as showing me her little-known portrait of Nijinska; George Jackson, for material about Nijinska's ill-fated season at the Vienna Staatsoper; the Ukrainian theater scholars Virlana Tkacz and Irena R. Makaryk for reading Chapter 2 and making many helpful suggestions; Russian art historians John Bowlt and Nicoletta Misler, for sharing their vast knowledge of the early Soviet avant-garde; John A. Goodman, for ongoing discussions about André Levinson; Alex Kirsta, daughter of the artist and designer George Kirsta, for explaining her father's long relationship with Nijinska; José Reynoso for directing me to Margarita Tortajada Quiroz's books about the history of twentieth-century dance in Mexico; Idoia Murga Castro, for documents from the Salvador Dalí archives in Spain; Renee Renouf, for recounting her meeting with Nijinska in the 1960s; Natasha

Tower for sharing Nijinska's letters to her grandmother, Nina Sirotinine; Laurie Kaden, for helping me access the papers of Nijinska's dancer Joyce Berry; Ann Hutchinson Guest, for her reminiscences of Nijinska at Jacob's Pillow; Sergey Belenky, for alerting me to Russian sources I would not otherwise have known about; Cheryl Forrest, for sending me a copy of her book with Georgia Snoke about Roman Jasinski and sharing her research with me; Carlos Carvajal, for his reminiscences of Nijinska in the Grand Ballet du Marquis de Cuevas; and my London friends and colleagues Millicent Hodson, Stephanie Jordan, Stacey Prickett, Tamara Tomic-Vajagic, and especially Geraldine Morris, who spent hours talking to me about working with Nijinska in the 1960s. Finally, I wish to thank my colleagues at Columbia University's Harriman Institute for their encouragement and willingness to answer questions about early Soviet cultural life, and to my former colleagues in the Barnard College Dance Department, especially Katie Glasner, for sharing thoughts about choreography and the experience of women in the ballet world.

I owe a profound debt of gratitude to my translators. First and foremost, I wish to thank Dina Odnopozova, who deciphered hundreds of pages to bring Nijinska's diaries and letters and those of her numerous correspondents to English life, cheerfully answering last-minute calls for a quick translation or for explanation of a grammatical point. For Nijinska's letters in Polish to her mother I am grateful to Tom Agnessi and his class of translation students at the University of Lviv, and to Eliza Cushman Rose for translating most of the materials relating to Nijinska's involvement with the Polish Ballet. Sofya Deak and Larissa Babji provided summaries and translations of Ukrainian documents; Sandra Chiritescu, Sophie Schweiger, and Sven Beckert helped with German-language documents and press. Maria Cook's translation assistance at a very early stage of the project was invaluable. I also wish to thank Jayne Cosson for her research assistance and Thom Lloyd for photographing papers relating to the defection of Serge Lifar's brother Leonid in Kiev's Cheka Archives.

The last chapter of La Nijinska was completed during the Covid-19 pandemic, when I was fortunate to "meet," virtually, more than a dozen former students of Kathleen Crofton at the Center Ballet of Buffalo. This was the last group of dancers to learn and perform several of Nijinska's ballets, and their love for her, expressed in Zoom and FaceTime interviews, long emails, clippings, and scans of personal photographs, sustained me during weeks of lockdown in New York.

Warm thanks to my agent, Sandy Dijkstra, who believed in this project from the start. Thanks, too, to my editor, Norman Hirschy, and to the entire Oxford University Press team, especially project manager Jeremy Toynbee, production editor Leslie Johnson, and copy editor Timothy DeWerff. All are heroes in this time of Covid.

Finally, I wish to thank Elizabeth Kendall and Margo Jefferson for their friendship and inspiration, and our many wonderful discussions about Nijinska, ballet, and women.

This book is dedicated to my daughter, Daria Rose Foner, an arts scholar in her own right, and to my husband, Eric Foner, my first reader and torchbearer.

Transliteration and Russian Names

Russian names are transliterated according to the Library of Congress system, except where a generally accepted Western variant exists. Hence, "Nijinska" rather than "Nizhinskaia," "Exter" rather than "Ekster," and "Fokine" rather than "Fokin." Soft signs have been eliminated in the body of the text but retained in the notes. Although "Kyiv" is now the accepted name of the Ukrainian capital, I have used its Russian name, "Kiev," which is how Nijinska always referred to it.

Preface

La Nijinska: Choreographer of the Modern is the first book-length study of ballet's premier female choreographer and a pioneer of the modern tradition in ballet. Overshadowed in life and legend by her brother Vaslav Nijinsky, Bronislava Nijinska had a far longer and more productive career, choreographing more than sixty original works in addition to dozens of dances in operas. She was an architect of twentieth-century neoclassicism who experienced the transformative power of the Russian Revolution and created her greatest work under the continuing influence of its avant-garde. Many of her ballets rested on the probing of gender boundaries, a mistrust of conventional gender roles, and the heightening of the ballerina's technical and artistic prowess. A key figure of Russia Abroad, she contributed to the many diasporic or émigré companies, including her own short-lived ensembles, that dotted the ballet landscape of the interwar years. Through her career as a freelance choreographer, she also played a crucial role in the international dissemination of ballet modernism. She was also a remarkable dancer in her own right with a bravura technique and powerful stage presence that enabled her to perform an unusually broad repertory. Finally, she was the author of an acclaimed volume of memoirs in addition to a major treatise on movement, although little of what she wrote was published in her lifetime. Her career sheds new light on the modern history of ballet and of modernism more generally, recuperating the memory of lost works and forgotten artists, many of them women. But it also reveals the sexism pervasive in the upper echelons of the early and mid-twentieth-century ballet world with which Nijinska and others had to reckon.

Remarkably, no biography of Nijinska has been written until now. Her *Early Memoirs*, published posthumously in 1981, translated and heavily edited by her daughter, Irina Nijinska, and Jean Rawlinson,[1] reveals her young self through a lovingly re-created biography of her brother: we meet the protagonists of her life through his, as if it was only as a minor character in the grand narrative of his life that she could insist upon her own posterity. The book ends before she choreographed her first dances and drafted her first treatises, leaving few clues about the long career that followed. Telling the story of this career has been no easy task. Her nomadic life unfolded on three continents, leaving traces in Polish, Ukrainian, Russian, Spanish, English, Italian, German, and French. Her journey began in Russia, ended in California, and, despite her productivity, left only a handful of works in living repertory. Nijinska kept all her unpublished writings after she emigrated— the letters, diaries, essays, memoirs, treatises, and choreographic notes that chart her inner life as an artist—along with the programs, press clippings, music scores, costumes, and designs that document her public one. However, her collection long remained in private hands, off-limits to scholars. Not until it was sold to the Library of Congress in the late 1990s (and processed more than a decade later) did it become possible to write a full account of Nijinska's life and assess the full scope of her accomplishments along with the struggles, hardships, and tragedies she encountered.

Born in Minsk, the capital of Belarus, on December 27, 1890 (Old Style), Nijinska was the third and youngest child of Tomasz Nijinsky and Eleonora Bereda, Polish dancers who spent the better part of their careers performing in opera houses and city theaters throughout southern and western Russia. Reflecting her parents' peregrinations, Stanislav was born in Tiflis (today Tbilisi) in 1886 and Vaslav in Kiev in 1889. It was an enchanted childhood as they moved from city to city, learned their letters in Polish and Russian, listened to balalaikas playing at sunset along the Volga, and began their training as dancers. Like all idylls, it came to an end. In 1897, just before Nijinska turned seven, a new partner stole her handsome father away from his wife. Deserting his family to live with her, Tomasz left behind a wound in his daughter's heart that would never heal. By then, Eleonora and her children were living in St. Petersburg, where she was determined they would attend the city's famed Imperial Ballet School. Stanislav had fallen behind, but Vaslav was admitted to the School in 1898, followed two years later by Bronislava. The course was eight years, and when she graduated in 1908, she became a member of the corps de ballet of the Maryinsky Theater, home to the Imperial Ballet and Imperial Opera.

However, it was as a member of Serge Diaghilev's newly formed Ballets Russes, which she joined at its outset in 1909 and as a full-time member in 1911, that Nijinska experienced the artistic awakening to which she owed her future as a choreographer. She danced in all of Michel Fokine's innovative ballets and took a prominent role in Vaslav's experimental works. Nijinska's body was the clay on which her brother molded his first landmark ballet, *L'Après-midi d'un Faune* (1912), and its controversial successor, *The Rite of*

Spring (1913). She learned how hard it was to invent movement and to make the body move in unfamiliar ways, but also that making ballets was something she wanted to do. Diaghilev, however, demurred. If this was what she wanted, she would have to do it on her own.

Nijinska returned to St. Petersburg in 1914 and spent the next seven years in Russia and Ukraine doing just that: making dance. Separated from her brother, caught up in the revolutionary moment, she became a key figure of the choreographic avant-garde. In Moscow in 1918 she drafted her first treatise, "The School and Theater of Movement," which revealed her profound disillusionment with ballet of the late Imperial period; her vision of a new, abstract art; and her goal of creating "intelligent, committed" artists rather than "professional" dancers trained, as she had been, for nothing but stage performance. In Kiev in 1919 she opened the School of Movement, which became the center of her artistic explorations. Here, in an atmosphere of what Ukrainian scholars Virlana Tkacz and Irena R. Makaryk have called "jubilant experimentation,"[2] she choreographed her first abstract works, trained and rehearsed her first company of dancers, and worked with avant-garde theater directors and painters, including the artist Vadim Meller, who created powerful images of her dancing.

Nijinska left Kiev in 1921. During their years of separation, Vaslav had become mentally ill, and it was hoped that her presence would snap him back to health. It didn't, and so, with a mother and two children to support, she rejoined the Ballets Russes. Diaghilev welcomed her back both as a dancer and, this time, as a choreographer, the first woman to serve him in that capacity. He used Nijinska—as he had once used her brother—to transform the repertory by exploring new facets of modernism, including early examples of neoclassicism. During the next four years, Nijinska created eight ballets and contributed dances to a dozen operas. Many were collaborations with composers of the French modernist group known as "Les Six" and visual artists from the elite ranks of international modernism. She choreographed two ballets to scores by Stravinsky—the biting satire *Le Renard* (1922) and her masterwork, *Les Noces* (1923), which brought to the Western stage the abstract architectural forms and impersonal human masses of post-Revolutionary constructivism, leading some critics to denounce the work as "Bolshevik." Yet from the start *Les Noces* was also recognized as a milestone, one of "the handful of great ballets that can sustain comparison with the finest achievements in any medium."[3] With all the women dancing on pointe, *Les Noces* was a key work in the emergence of ballet neoclassicism. This was also true of *Les Biches* (1924), a ballet of sexual ambiguity set among the era's "Bright Young Things" in which Nijinska as the Hostess wore ropes of pearls inspired by Chanel but danced the bravura steps of a man. She created several male roles for herself, and even performed her brother's part in *L'Après-midi d'un Faune*. Those years with Diaghilev catapulted her to the elite ranks of twentieth-century ballet, earning her a privileged place in the history of ballet modernism.

In achieving this kind of recognition as a ballet choreographer, Nijinska was a rarity. There was no shortage of women who choreographed in the ballet idiom, but few worked for elite institutions or enjoyed the privilege of authorship. Ballerinas might become teachers, but few added choreography to their other duties. By contrast, late nineteenth-century music halls and cabarets welcomed women as choreographers, even if this wasn't a term they used. At London's Empire Theatre, the Viennese-born Katti Lanner ruled the boards for nearly twenty years, while across the Channel at the Folies-Bergère, her colleague and sometime rival Madame Mariquita choreographed scores of ballets during roughly the same period. By the early twentieth century, even the Paris Opéra had hired a woman—Madame Stichel—to take charge of the company. Women also choreographed for their students. This was another "minor genre" of ballet-making open to women even at schools affiliated with elite institutions, although nearly always choreography was folded into their identity as teachers. Nijinska was certainly aware of these female practices: her own mother had found work staging dances in operettas, and Nijinska had danced in several ballets by her teacher Klavdiia Kulichevskaia. However, as Nijinska surely knew, dances choreographed by women seldom outlived their original production, coalesced into a repertory, or earned their makers recognition as choreographers. By admitting her into the elite circle of Ballets Russes choreographers, Diaghilev rescued Nijinska from these semi-visible female practices, extolling the merit of her work and insisting upon its place in a modernist succession.

In 1925, Nijinska left the Ballets Russes and embarked on a career as a freelance choreographer. Over the next forty-five years she worked with numerous companies, creating new ballets and reviving older ones, in addition to staging the works of other choreographers. At great personal expense and largely on credit, she formed two short-lived companies for which she choreographed some of her most personal works. The first, which Diaghilev did his best to shut down, reunited her with the celebrated painter Alexandra Exter, fresh from Soviet Russia, who made the splendid costume designs. The second, which culminated in a version of *Hamlet* (1934) in which she played the title role, left her bankrupt and her entire stock of scenery and costumes impounded, thanks to the chicanery of a shady Russian impresario. She spent several seasons at the Teatro Colón in Buenos Aires, where she contributed decisively to the professionalization of the ballet company and the modernization of its repertory.

In 1928, Nijinska was engaged by Ida Rubinstein to form a ballet troupe. Exotically beautiful and immensely wealthy, Rubinstein had originated roles in Diaghilev's *Cléopâtre* and *Schéhérazade*. Decamping from the Ballets Russes, she established herself as an independent producer, commissioning elaborate multidisciplinary works with high-profile collaborators in which she invariably starred. Trained as an actress and celebrated for her gestural expressiveness, Rubinstein now determined to become a classical ballerina. This desire certainly complicated Nijinska's task as choreographer, but it gave her the means to form a company that included two future choreographers— David Lichine and the great Frederick Ashton—and scores of talented youngsters, many supporting impoverished émigré families, a transnational community bonded by sweat and devotion to art. Thanks to Rubinstein, Nijinska added to her growing repertory Stravinsky's *Le Baiser de la Fée* (1928), two ballets by Ravel—*Bolero* (1928) and *La Valse* (1929)—and *The Swan Princess*, a Russian legend inspired by Pushkin.

Nijinska was always on the move. She worked virtually non-stop between 1919, when she founded the School of Movement, and 1972, when she died with a contract in hand to stage *Les Biches* in Dusseldorf. Always short of money, ever on the lookout for jobs, she worked with companies in Buenos Aires, Warsaw, Brescia, Paris, London, Chicago, Buffalo, Vienna, and Rome. The studio was her laboratory, and she unfailingly began the day teaching class before rehearsing and choreographing. She left her mark on generations of dancers, including celebrated ballerina-muses such as Alicia Markova, Irina Baronova, Alexandra Danilova, and Rosella Hightower, all of whom paid warm tribute to the impact of her coaching. And then they scattered, seeding far-flung companies, while her own dances, nearly all created for short-lived ensembles, disappeared. As she approached her eightieth birthday, she felt that nothing remained of her passage through decades of ballet history.

Nijinska's career deserves attention not only because of her accomplishments as a choreographer, teacher, and dancer, but also because it challenges the familiar grand narrative of twentieth-century ballet history in the West, which begins with Diaghilev's Ballets Russes, continues in the 1930s and 1940s with the Ballets Russes de Monte-Carlo directed by Colonel Wassily de Basil and the Ballet Russe de Monte Carlo[4] led by S. J. or Sergei Denham, and culminates in the Royal Ballet and New York City Ballet. The vast majority of ballet books focus on some aspect of these companies— their genesis, year-to-year chronicle, repertory, style, critics, aesthetic orientation, and stellar artistic personnel. Building on one another, they reinforce the teleologies and myths surrounding each company while insisting upon the centrality of its works to the ballet canon. This narrative is as notable for what it excludes as for what it encompasses. With the exception of Diaghilev's Ballets Russes, Nijinska had only limited access to these companies and none at all to the New York City Ballet (apart from training a few of its early stars). Yet she worked constantly. Her life fleshes out the history of the interwar years, with its numerous ensembles claiming the "Ballet Russe" name (including her own company, "Les Ballets Russes de Bronislava Nijinska") and others (such as the Polish Ballet and the Teatro Colón) espousing the aesthetics of ballet modernism although lying far from its European centers. It spotlights the many companies headed by women—Carina Ari, Ida Rubinstein, Vera Nemchinova, Alicia Markova, Catherine Littlefield, Marie Rambert, to say nothing of Nijinska's own ensembles—all of which, with the partial exception of Ballet Rambert, mostly lie beyond the notice of existing historiography. And it reveals how the post–World War II national model, typically supported by state subsidy, all but erased multinational companies from the historical record.

Nijinska's works significantly alter our understanding of abstraction in twentieth-century ballet, a subject dominated by the great corpus of works choreographed by George Balanchine beginning in the 1940s and Léonide Massine's "symphonic" ballets of the 1930s, with Fokine's *Chopiniana/Les Sylphides* (1908–1909) and Fedor Lopukhov's *Dance Symphony* (1923) as precursors. Yet Nijinska was central to this history. Beginning with her lost works of the Kiev years, she choreographed both plotless and semi-plotless ballets as well as modernist narratives, offering a highly original approach to ballet aesthetics, composition, and technique. At the same time her work complicates the notion that the shift away from demi-caractère to classical styles in the post-Diaghilev period was mainly the work of Balanchine and Frederick Ashton. Actually it was Nijinska who began to explore the variety and abundance of classical forms as early as the 1920s. Approaching the *danse d'école* through the prism of modernism not only gave her choreography its distinctive flavor but also expanded the lexicon and syntax of classical technique, above all in the area of female virtuosity.

Nijinska first came to the United States in 1934, when she choreographed the dances in Max Reinhardt's pioneering film of *A Midsummer Night's Dream*. She returned in 1939 at the outset of World War II, part of a wave of stateless Russian dancers en route to their second diaspora. Settling in Southern California, she began to work with a group of gifted young dancers, including Betty Marie (later Maria) Tallchief and Syd (later Cyd) Charisse. She traveled frequently to New York, where she contributed works to (American) Ballet Theatre and Sergei Denham's Ballet Russe de Monte Carlo, only to find herself undercut by muscle-flexing Americans or Russians who had sunk roots in the United States. She formed a long-term relationship with Ballet International, founded in New York in 1944 by the Marquis de Cuevas, who later relocated it to Monte Carle and then Paris and renamed it. In the Grand Ballet's Franco-Russian-American atmosphere, Nijinska, who never learned to speak English fluently, felt at home. But in the postwar dance capitals of New York and London, she dropped from sight and memory of her works faded—transnational has-beens in an era of national canons.

During the most creative part of her career, Nijinska was widely recognized as a "truly great artist," in the words of Ted Shawn.[5] By the early 1960s, however, Nijinska's ballets had all but disappeared from the stage. Hence, the significance of the revivals of *Les Biches* in 1964 and *Les Noces* in 1966 by Britain's Royal Ballet, now directed by her former dancer Frederick Ashton. These splendid productions, which were filmed, notated, and maintained in repertory, were crucial to the survival of these ballets and to the solidifying of Nijinska's reputation. This recuperative effort was reinforced by the publication in 1981, nine years after her death, of *Early Memoirs*, and the restaging of *Les Noces* that year in California by the Oakland Ballet. Five years later, the exhibition *Bronislava Nijinska: A Dancer's Legacy*, which opened in New York and then traveled to San Francisco, showcased for the first time her collaboration with Alexandra Exter, while challenging the widespread belief that Balanchine was the sole progenitor of ballet neoclassicism. However, little scholarship on Nijinska followed.

The Nijinska who emerges in the pages of her surviving Kiev diary is emotionally fragile but utterly committed to her students and what she calls her "creativity." Emigration transformed her. A woman in what was universally considered a man's job, she learned to be ruthless. She drove her dancers mercilessly, working them morning to night, compelling them to

enter her imaginative world and collaborate wholeheartedly in the creation of new work—a phenomenon far closer to the kind of relationship
that existed between Mary Wigman or Martha Graham and their dancers
than between ballet masters and dancers at institutions like the Maryinsky
or the Paris Opéra. She gave few interviews and trusted only her family
and a small circle of intimates. She was paranoid, often with good reason,
and her rudeness was legendary. She made decisions she came to regret,
stubbornly refused to compromise, and was often her own worst enemy.
Nothing came easy to her; again and again she had to prove herself, starting
from scratch even when she was a respected professional (still the case for
many women choreographers in ballet), and the carapace she developed
was partly a response to the misogyny she encountered in most quarters
of the ballet world. Her accomplishments were repeatedly disparaged, her
works misrepresented, and her presence both as a dancer and a choreographer slighted or ignored. Promises of work fell through. Her body was fair
game. Jean Cocteau compared her "sturdy legs" to a "pickaxe or a carpenter's
plane," while Arnold Haskell, in his influential book *Balletomania* (1934),
all but ignored her as a choreographer, while claiming she was "the only ugly
dancer to find fame."[6] More often than not she remains on the sidelines of
her own history, willfully unremembered or diminished by the accurate but
demeaning sobriquet "Nijinsky's sister."

In the few interviews she gave, Nijinska scrupulously avoided personal
matters. However, she left a trove of writings that reveal the woman behind
her public mask. This is especially true of her diaries from the late 1920s and
1930s. Here is the story of her love, mute, unspoken, hidden from all but a
single close friend, for the great Russian basso Fedor Chaliapin. Nijinska had
met him in the spring of 1911 in Monte Carlo, and he singled her out, telling
Diaghilev that she was very gifted. Nothing happened between them, but
like the Muse's fatal kiss in *Le Baiser de la Fée*, their encounter marked the
dawn of her creative self-awareness, the moment of her birth as an artist and
a woman.

Nijinska's unconsummated and unrequited "love" allowed her to assert an
identity that did not come easily to women in ballet. Men had not done well
by her. Her father had abandoned her, followed by her brother, Diaghilev, and
her first husband, Alexander Kochetovsky. Her second husband, Nicholas
Singaevsky, adored her. But he was no replacement for any of Nijinska's failed
fathers, and she never imagined him folding her in his arms or kissing her
tenderly as she dreamed again and again of Chaliapin doing.

But perhaps her obsession with Chaliapin wasn't about him at all, but a measure of the guilt she felt in pursuing her "path" or "destiny" as an independent creative artist. In Nijinska's case the guilt was compounded because of her family, and especially her children, who were mainly raised by their grandmother, assisted by family friends, as their mother left for weeks and months at a time, always putting her career first. Nijinska's voice in her diaries insists upon a "femininity" belied by the objectivity of her ballets and by her increasingly authoritarian behavior in the studio. Nothing could be more different from Nijinska's public persona than the intensely emotional "I" of the diaries, where her ambition, assertiveness, potency, and strength lay safely concealed under cover of extreme subjectivity.

The 1930s were a time not only of great economic precarity for Nijinska but also of personal tragedy. Her mother died in 1932, and her sixteen-year-old son three years later in a car accident. The first books about her brother, filled with inaccuracies, appeared, and their "revelations" about his relationship with Diaghilev left her profoundly disturbed, even as they relegated her to the sidelines. Meanwhile, a struggle was taking place over Diaghilev's legacy and the consolidation of the Ballets Russes canon. Here, again, Nijinska lost out, as this canon, as defined by the de Basil company, centered on the pre-World War I ballets by Fokine and—as a nod to the company's English audience—Massine's early ballets. In other words, this was a "canon" that eliminated all of Nijinska's works for Diaghilev, as well as Balanchine's, and all of Stravinsky's ballets for Diaghilev composed after *Petrouchka*—a canon eviscerated of modernism. Far more egregiously than Diaghilev, de Basil used Nijinska, sabotaging her company in 1934, dangling promises of commissions that fell through, and unceremoniously dumping her when she had served his purpose. Leon Woizikovsky, a leading Polish dancer with the Diaghilev company, also did his best to toss her out of the Diaghilev "family," while undermining her position both with de Basil and with the organizers of the Polish Ballet, whose directorship he assumed once Nijinska was out of the way. Ballet politics was dirty and shot through with sexism.

Unlike many émigrés, Nijinska never turned against the Soviet Union, a stance that earned her the enmity of critics such as André Levinson, who attacked her again and again for not fleeing Russia immediately after the Revolution and, instead, establishing a school and company under its auspices. One senses her nostalgia for Russia in *Les Noces* (1923), *Variations* (1932), and *Pictures at an Exhibition* (1944) and in the floodgate of ancestral memories that opened when she visited Belovezh, a former Romanov hunting lodge on Poland's border with Belarus, where she stood, for the first time in sixteen years, on Russian soil. "How great my heart feels here!" she wrote in her diary.[7] When Soviet ballet companies began touring abroad during the Cold War, she sought out Galina Ulanova and Yuri Grigorovich in the hope of staging *Les Noces* at the Bolshoi Theatre, and in 1970 she taught her brother's *L'Après-midi d'un Faune* to members of the Kirov Ballet, a project, however, that never reached the stage. In the 1960s she enjoyed an epistolary friendship with the Leningrad ballet historian Vera Krasovskaya that spanned several years. And during the same decade, she renewed contact with former students from the School of Movement, several of whom were now artists living in Moscow, discovering through their letters her own younger self, full of passion for her art and buoyed by the love and admiration of her dancers.

I have tried to tell the story of this remarkable woman and artist not only through her own words but also through those of her contemporaries. I have quoted liberally from reviews to suggest what her lost ballets looked like, how a variety of critics responded to them, and how their responses reflected social and political as well as cultural concerns. I have incorporated the recollections, published as well as unpublished, of generations of dancers who worked with her, thereby adding another set of voices to the narrative. And I have made extensive use of her voluminous correspondence—letters she saved and the drafts of letters she sent—which reveal her capacity for friendship, especially with women. Above all, I have tried to re-create the contexts in which she worked to understand how her art was shaped simultaneously by the cataclysmic events of the twentieth century and the often egregious operation of sexism. Finally, I have sought to show how looking at twentieth-century ballet history through the lens of this unique artist makes that world appear different, revealing female critics, choreographers, ballet masters, and directors long expunged from the master narrative of ballet history, especially in its Anglo-American variant. The almost complete absence today of female choreographers from the major ballet companies has lately become a topic of investigation and complaint. Nijinska's career shows that women are certainly capable of being first-rate choreographers, but also reveals the barriers that have held them back.

The book that follows is the story of a major artist who was also a woman. It begins not at the start of Nijinska's biological life or in her childhood—so wonderfully evoked in *Early Memoirs*—but at the quickening that took place when she joined Diaghilev's Ballets Russes and set off on her path as an artist.

These years of apprenticeship, in which Nijinska was both constrained because of the social limitations she experienced as a woman and privileged because of the presence of her brother, prepared her to grasp the opportunities
made possible by the Russian Revolution. The story begins in St. Petersburg,
as Bronislava Fominichna Nizhinskaia, known as Bronia to her friends
and Nijinska to posterity, made ready to take her place on the stage of the
Maryinsky Theater, the very conventional start of a most unconventional life
and career.

1

Nijinska's Apprenticeship

In 1908, wearing a tea-rose lace gown and carrying a bouquet of yellow roses, Bronislava Fominichna Nizhinskaia graduated from St. Petersburg's Imperial Ballet School. She was seventeen and, now, with all six of her classmates, she left the school's cloistered precincts for the blue-halled Maryinsky Theater, home of Russia's foremost ballet troupe. She had been a good student, with excellent marks in her academic classes, and had received the "white dress" awarded to the senior girl who showed the greatest promise. Already, the press had noticed her. Only months before she graduated, the *Petersburg Gazette* commended her "good plastique and expressive mime," noting that she "produced a very good impression" when she danced.[1] Still, for all her gifts she wasn't obvious ballerina material. "Overall, this year's output is quite weak," Vladimir Teliakovsky, director of the Imperial Theaters, observed in his diary after her graduation performance. Four students, including Nijinska, had received the highest grade of twelve, but "not one," in his opinion, deserved it.[2] Nevertheless, an official Maryinsky debut was scheduled, and on June 1, fulfilling her mother's dream, Nijinska became an Artist of the Imperial Theaters.

Thus began Nijinska's choreographic apprenticeship. At the School she had mastered the building blocks of the *danse d'école*, the steps and codes of behavior that ballet choreographers have used and transformed over the centuries. Now she would extend that knowledge to the repertory of ballets for which the Maryinsky was famed, not only ones like *Swan Lake* (1895), *Giselle* (1841/1884), *The Sleeping Beauty* (1890), and *La Bayadère* (1877) that later generations would hail as classics, but also ones that disappeared over time except from the memory of their dancers. Although Nijinska ultimately rejected many of the Maryinsky's artistic practices, its repertory would become her stock-in-trade, an inheritance on which she drew throughout her life. She began her career in the corps de ballet, dancing mainly in operas and as a substitute in ballet performances. Dancers were expected to know their roles in advance, so Nijinska, aiming to be letter-perfect, learned the choreography she didn't know from friends a few years ahead of her. She spent her free time watching rehearsals, absorbing like a sponge the works by Marius Petipa, the Maryinsky's long-serving ballet master-in-chief, and his assistant Lev Ivanov that made up most of the repertory. Even more than the ballets themselves, she was fascinated by the breadth of Petipa's choreographic invention, the irrepressible fantasy of his solos, especially for women, and the masterful design of his grand ensemble dances. She saw all the era's stars, falling in love with Anna Pavlova's poetic lyricism and Olga Preobrajenska's sparkle but caring little for Mathilde Kschessinska's show-stopping bravura. "I was absorbed, captivated by the Dance," Nijinska later wrote, "the interpretation, the movement, the correlation of music and dancing."[3]

Nijinska's progress through the Maryinsky ranks was slow but steady. During her first year she was cast in her first named role, Hebe in *The Awakening of Flora* (1894), a one-act Petipa ballet sometimes used to try out new dancers.[4] She received her first promotion (and salary increase) at the start of the 1909–1910 season, when she moved from the second to the first line of the corps, and another the following year, when she became a coryphée, dancing in groups of four or six, a sign that she was being groomed as a soloist. By October 1910 she was earning 900 rubles a year.[5] With each promotion came more work. During the 1909–1910 season she appeared in sixteen ballets and two operas, dancing a total of sixty-one performances; one highly visible role was Silver, in the Precious Stones pas de quatre in *The Sleeping Beauty*. In the fall of 1910, while still appearing in thirty-four ballets and eleven operas, other roles were added to her repertory, including one of the Cygnets in *Swan Lake* and the Goddess Dew in *The Awakening of Flora*, where she scattered bits of silver paper from a shell representing a horn of plenty.[6]

In *Early Memoirs*, Nijinska reveals her profound discontent with the Maryinsky's "oppressive and stifling" atmosphere and absence of artistic leadership. Petipa had stepped down in 1904, leaving a vacuum that the new ballet master Nikolai Legat could hardly hope to fill. She complained about his interminable rehearsals for the revival of *Le Talisman* (1889), a Petipa ballet in four acts and six scenes, and his own equally old-fashioned five-act ballet *The Blood-Red Flower* (1907). She criticized how rehearsals were conducted, singling out both Legat and the company's chief *régisseur* or rehearsal director, Nikolai Sergeyev. Unlike Nijinska, who would take a physically active part in rehearsals even in her mid-seventies, Legat and Sergeyev demonstrated nothing to the dancers and completely ignored what she called "the artistic interpretation." In rehearsing the corps de ballet, they demanded only that steps were correct and fell "on the musical beat"; that legs lifted and lowered identically and lines were straight; and that dancers remained glued to their spots on stage. Soloists, who rehearsed separately, were exempt from this military-style discipline. But even if they were allowed to change a step or two, they danced "traditionally," discouraged from venturing into new interpretative terrain. As Nijinska viewed it, "Nobody was concerned with artistic direction, for neither Legat nor Sergeyev were . . . genuine artistic leaders of the ballet."[7]

Nijinska was particularly incensed at Sergeyev's efforts to impose uniformity. She relates an incident during a rehearsal for the Precious Stones quartet, when Sergeyev reprimanded her for jumping higher than the others during the coda. "All four of you must jump to the same height!" he cried. Nijinska protested that she couldn't regulate her jumps to fit the other three, since it was impossible to guess how high they were going to jump. "All my jumps," she declared, "correspond absolutely to the musical beat, and that is the only way I can assess my elevation." Sergeyev threatened to replace her but never made good on his threat.[8] In fact, Nijinska had an enormous jump, which many envied and often compared to a man's.

However stultifying Nijinska found the Maryinsky's artistic atmosphere, she loved the camaraderie among the dancers. At the School she formed attachments that lasted for decades, even surviving the Soviet-émigré divide. Near the end of her life she begged Vera Krasovskaya, the Leningrad ballet historian, to send regards to "everyone who studied with me at the Theatre Academy and remembers me as I remember all of them."[9] Nijinska was particularly close to Lubov Tchernicheva, who was in the same class, helping her with her studies and even with her love letters. Ludmilla Schollar, who graduated in 1906, was another schoolmate who became a close friend, and as with "Luba," their friendship outlived the dislocations of emigration. Although the School existed to train professional dancers, it did not discourage students from more intellectual pursuits. Nijinska became something of a bookworm, devouring Tolstoy and Dostoyevsky. Ironically, considering her dislike of Sergeyev, Nijinska turned out to be the best student in his "Theory" class, mastering the Stepanov system of notation that was used to record the Maryinsky repertory. The year before Nijinska graduated she was called upon to demonstrate a notated pas de quatre to be danced at the annual School performance, an analytic skill that presaged her later attempts to record the choreography of her own ballets, although she never employed Stepanov notation.[10]

However hard-working and observant, Nijinska harbored a stew of emotions that she found difficult to control. In March 1907 a schoolgirl scrap brought her to the attention of top administrators. "The Inspectrice of the Theater School came to tell me that two pupils, graduating next year, were fighting," Teliakovsky recorded in his diary. "Moussia" Dobroliubova, in an argument with Nijinska during the tension-filled weeks before the annual student performance, "hit the latter on the cheek. Both these girls have grades of 12 for behavior, and until this time they were in good standing. Subsequently, a reconciliation took place. This is why it was decided to reduce Dobroliubova's grade for behavior from 12 to 6 and to take away her leave until the end of the season."[11] According to Nijinska, Moussia, a friend for more than a decade, stole up from behind and slapped her, accusing her of lying about her role in the performance. "Everything inside me was burning," Nijinska wrote in *Early Memoirs*. "I could not forget the incident. . . . I had been called a liar, and in front of all the students and the governess too." Unlike Moussia, Nijinska did receive a coveted solo. But she was "sick with hurt," attributing this to her "Polish pride," which made her "oversensitive to insult, often to the point of injury." Although Moussia was punished, Nijinska was incensed that the governess did not take the miscreant publicly to task or make her apologize.[12] Nijinska's response is a troubling anticipation of the sudden, inexplicable furies she later visited on so many dancers and colleagues. Her Imperial Theaters dossier records another incident—this one reported by a police officer on duty at the Maryinsky in September 1910—that revealed a similar combination of hostility and aggrievement, especially toward authority. In this incident, which took place during a rehearsal, Nijinska pulled—apparently intentionally—at the curtain in the doorway of a makeup room, causing the rod to fall and injuring her face. Medical attention was required.[13] In her memoirs she passes over the incident entirely.

***

My Brother Vatsa was Nijinska's own title for the volume published after her death as *Early Memoirs*. In a way her title was a more accurate reflection of the book, dominated by her brother's looming presence and the compelling narrative of his life, fragmenting and partly effacing her own. Two years older than his sister, Nijinsky left a deep imprint on her development as a dancer and choreographer as well as on her ideas of artistic creation. He was a rare phenomenon—a classical male virtuoso in an art dominated by women. His talent was a gift from God, an accident of his genetic blueprint. He worked hard; he was disciplined; he was blessed; and he was favored. When he graduated into the Maryinsky, he was hailed by critics as a Wunderkind. Ballerinas vied to dance with him, and balletomanes noted the dates of his performances. Within St. Petersburg's hothouse ballet world, Nijinsky was a rising star even before he left school.

Today, Nijinsky is remembered as an icon of modernity, superlative performer, innovative choreographer, pioneer of sexual openness, and genius who succumbed to madness. A less flattering picture emerges from examining his relationship with his sister. To be sure, there was much they shared. She had the same jump, the same stocky frame; she too, in time, grew into a charismatic performer. She was also a girl. She lived among the whispers of aunts and discovered the sorrows of the unfavored. Like so many little sisters, Nijinska adored her brother. He was her elder, but close in age, a dancer who sensed early on, as she did, that they belonged to a tribe of artists. She was intensely loyal to him, a helpmate who wrote his essays and did his math problems so he wouldn't fail, who went without so he could have more. Her body was the clay for his first choreographic experiments and the secret sharer of his ideas. He was the lodestone of her art, and even years later when she wrote the manuscript that became *Early Memoirs* in the 1960s, she remained his passionate advocate, blind to his imperfections. No word of anger crosses her lips, no admission of thwarted ambition, no hint of usurped identity: in her eyes he can do no wrong, and she is ever in his debt.

In *Writing a Woman's Life*, the feminist literary scholar Carolyn Heilbrun comments about the traditional genre of female autobiography, "above all other prohibitions, what has been forbidden to women is anger, together with the open admission of the desire for power and control over one's life (which inevitably means accepting some degree of power and control over other lives)."[14] Nijinska's relationship with her brother was far more complicated than she made out in *Early Memoirs*. Reading between the lines, one discerns not only hidden currents of anger but also a far less flattering picture of Nijinsky as a brother and colleague. Nijinsky used his sister to further his own ends, discarded her when expedient, and behaved at times with cruelty, even deepening the rupture with their father, whom he rejected but she continued to adore. He failed to acknowledge her choreographic aspirations and erased her from two of his ballets. A prodigy he may have been, but he was also self-absorbed and vain.

When Tomasz Nijinsky decamped in 1897, Eleonora found what work she could staging dances in operettas or teaching. However, the money was never enough to make up for the loss of the family breadwinner. With her children she moved from apartment to apartment, spent summers in the country, skimped on food, clothing, and health care. Suffering and sacrifice were a way of life that Eleonora accepted in order for her children to become Artists of the Imperial Theaters. It was a hard lesson, but Nijinska learned it well. Her mother's example of quiet heroism would become her model, after she too was abandoned by a philandering husband. Like Eleonora, she became the family breadwinner, both mother and father to her children, the dutiful daughter who supported her beloved "Mamusia"—her Mummy—until she died, who struggled to reconcile her artistic ambitions with the need to put food on the table. The daily practice of frugality is a recurring theme of *Early Memoirs*.

Vaslav, by contrast, "loved good and elegant things," Nijinska wrote.[15] By his senior year at school he had become quite the dandy, shopping on the Nevsky Prospect for clothes that came from London. He wore fine leather shoes and had his uniforms specially tailored, while his food preferences ran to *millefeuilles*, foie gras, and fresh fruit. Eleonora could only do so much. Prince Lvov, the handsome, wealthy scion of an old noble family and secretary to the Minister of Communications, took Nijinsky under his wing during the latter's first year at the Maryinsky. Lvov was generous; he made it possible for Nijinsky to study privately with Enrico Cecchetti, and took him to plays, concerts, and sporting events. He also indulged his craving for luxury, antici- pating, as Bronislava put it, "Vaslav's material needs in such a way that Vaslav never had to ask him for assistance"; Nijinsky could repay him later.[16] Once Vaslav and Bronislava were both working, the family moved to a large, com- fortable apartment at 13 Bolshaia Konniushennaia Ulitsa in the heart of fash- ionable Petersburg. Here Nijinska had a room of her own, the first time she enjoyed the luxury of privacy, and she had saved up to decorate it. By contrast, her brother had two rooms, a study and a bedroom, which Lvov furnished for him. A large wardrobe stood along one wall, and "all along another, standing in a row, were at least twelve pairs of elegant shoes, all made to order by the renowned master shoemaker, Korokevitch, on Bolshaya Morskaya Ulitsa."[17] Nijinsky also acquired a piano, a Bluthner, brought specially from Germany. After years of privation, he had become a sybarite.

Lvov also endeared himself to Eleonora and her daughter, treating them with "courtesy, respect, and kindness"; in fact, the chapter about Lvov in

Nijinska's original Russian typescript bore the title "Prince Lvov, Friend of Our Family."[18] When Eleonora was sued by creditors, Lvov paid off her debts, which included months of back rent and long overdue tradesmen's bills. He plied her with gift boxes filled with caviar, salmon, cheeses, and foie gras, and offered Bronislava his grandmother's collection of old Venetian and Valenciennes laces as a birthday present. He took all three of them out to dinner and entertained them at his home. And, with Eleonora's blessing, Lvov invited Vaslav to spend the summer of 1908 at his villa on the islands near St. Petersburg.[19]

Before long, people began to gossip. Liaisons between female dancers and wealthy men were common, although few dancers were as brazen as Kschessinska, with her entourage of Grand Dukes. Anna Pavlova had lovers as well as a protector (Victor Dandré, a minor aristocrat and member of the Duma), as did the future pedagogue Agrippina Vaganova.[20] So, too, did some of the company's young men. Although the upper echelons of tsarist society were "remarkably tolerant of 'deviant' sexual behaviour," homosexuality was officially a crime. The law was not always enforced, "but convictions did occur—even among the upper crust."[21] The revolution of 1905 ushered in a decade of unprecedented freedom of speech and press, and for the first time, as the literary scholar Simon Karlinsky has written, "Russia's gay writers could step out of their closets."[22] Gay dancers of the Maryinsky, however, occupied a very public stage and also existed as dependents of the Court, with all that this implied in terms of proximity to the Imperial family; even if a number of Grand Dukes were gay, discretion remained the order of the day.[23]

Nijinsky, however, seems to have been unusually open about his relationship with Lvov, with gossip even reaching the director of the Imperial Theaters. "It turns out," wrote Teliakovsky in May 1908, "that the young dancer Nijinsky has become terribly rich. He has rented for himself a big apartment, all decorated with diamonds and precious stones, and [is] big friends with M. Benckendorff and Prince P. Lvov. From them, they say, [he gets] his money."[24] As the young dancer began to receive principal roles, a situation that kindled envy and resentment, rumors spread that he was cast only because Lvov was footing the bill for new costumes; others said that "Vaslav was unable to love a woman." Rumors even reached Nijinska at the school, but she "was still childishly innocent and did not understand what was being insinuated."[25] Whatever she understood or failed to understand, the situation was troublesome, not least because mother and daughter appeared to condone the relationship and certainly profited from it. Vaslav's behavior drew Nijinska into the web of prostitution that remained a part of Maryinsky life until the Revolution. She herself rejected that life; she took no part in the trade of sexual favors, sought no one to lobby on her behalf or deliver her into the lap of luxury. She would make her own way, without patronage or influence.

Her brother chose a different path. By 1908 he was actively in pursuit of Serge Diaghilev, and by the fall of that year, as plans moved forward for a ballet season in Paris, the impresario had succumbed. Lvov faded from the scene (but not before Diaghilev tapped him for a contribution to his newest venture). Diaghilev, of course, had far more to offer Nijinsky than his erstwhile protector. Indeed, as Nijinsky became central to Diaghilev's personal life, he also become essential to his lover's artistic plans. The repertory that Diaghilev now set about fashioning for Paris increasingly centered on him and would transform the Russian virtuoso into an international star. Fervent in his pursuit of Diaghilev and an eager recipient of his largesse, Nijinsky was hardly "the passive observer later observers claimed him to be."[26]

Through all this, Nijinsky remained deeply devoted to his mother. With respect to his sister, now grown up and a fellow professional, his devotion waxed and waned. Thus, in 1909, when Diaghilev began signing up dancers for the coming Paris season, Nijinsky initially refused to advocate for her. Rubbing it in, he told her that Diaghilev did not intend to engage her because she was "too 'set'" in her ways as a classical dancer and thus unsuited to "the new style of ballets he planned to present"—a lame excuse, since Fokine, the choreographer of those ballets, had just cast her in *Chopiniana*. Eleonora protested; Nijinsky refused to budge: "I will not extend any favoritism for Bronia in the ballet just because she is my sister." Only when Eleonora countered that many of those signed up by Diaghilev enjoyed the "protection or favoritism of the balletomanes" did he relent, and Nijinska's contract arrived the following day.[27] In Paris, surrounded by friends of Diaghilev (to whom he pointedly did not introduce her), he invited her nowhere and saw her only at teatime with Eleonora. Only when he came down with typhoid at the end of the season and had to spend a month convalescing in his hotel room did the easy comradeship of earlier years return.[28]

Again and again, Nijinsky goaded his sister to excel. When Fokine cast her as the Butterfly in *Carnaval* (1910), the choreographer sketched her solo, then left it to her to flesh out. In fact, it was Nijinsky, who was also in the ballet, who coached her, breaking down the choreography, speeding up the tempo, and explaining how to harmonize the skimming footwork with the fluttering of her arms while navigating the semi-circular stage. She was up half the night working out the details, and the next morning—the day of the performance—she rehearsed for hours on her own.[29] From this experience Nijinska learned how to transform a role without changing the actual steps, how to invest it with expression and make it her own. She also learned that mastery resulted not so much from inspiration as from analysis, hard work, and drive, and that pain was the price of excellence.

Pain was evident in other brother-sister interactions. In 1906 the mother of one of Bronislava's classmates asked Nijinsky to teach her daughter privately during the summer. He agreed, so long as Nijinska could take the class as well. Although her friend was by far the weaker dancer, it was Nijinska who bore the brunt of his criticism. He would not allow her to wear blocked shoes, but insisted that she wear soft men's slippers, even when dancing on full pointe. Oblivious to the physical and psychological pain he was inflicting, Vaslav made her repeat everything not once or twice, but innumerable times. In jumps he wanted her to feel the floor and use the entire foot in take-off and landing, which improved her elevation along with the strength and elasticity of her arch and enabled her to do double and triple pirouettes and sixteen fouetté turns, all on full pointe. "Those two months of Vaslav's classes," Nijinska later wrote, "were full of dancing discoveries and were to lay the foundation for the development of my technique and dancing achievements."[30] But by his example, he also taught Nijinska a way of exerting authority and enforcing discipline that bordered on the sadistic, even if she was a willing victim. This, too, was a lesson she would not forget.

It was because of her devotion to her brother that Nijinska severed her relationship with the Imperial Theaters. In January 1911, for a Maryinsky performance of *Giselle*, instead of wearing the regulation costume for the first act, he donned the shorter, more revealing tunic for the Diaghilev production. The Dowager Empress was in the audience, along with two grand duchesses and a pair of grand dukes from Kschessinska's entourage. After the first act, the Dowager Empress dispatched Grand Duke Sergei Mikhailovich backstage "to find out," as Teliakovsky recorded in his diary, "what costume Nijinsky would wear in the next act, because if it was the same one, she and the Grand Duchesses would have to leave."[31] Nijinsky ignored the warning. When he emerged from his dressing room, he bowed to no one in particular, then, barely concealing his anger, flung open his cloak to reveal the offensive costume for Act II. Grand Duke Sergei was livid. But Nijinsky went on to give an electrifying performance, demonstrating "not only his phenomenal lightness and rare gift of flexibility, but also his complete *understanding* of classical ballet style." For the anonymous reviewer of *Rech'* he allowed one to glimpse "the classical dance of an era when it was a real art, when its forms were a living means of art-making, not a petrified, alien, immature cliché. . . . [E]verything that surrounded Nijinsky seemed by comparison a powerless and counterfeit art."[32] Backstage a more tawdry drama played out. Nijinsky was summoned to the offices of the Imperial Theaters and fired, although he was told that if he immediately wrote an apology, he would probably be reinstated. He was also offered the prospect of a better contract. He turned down both offers and left the Imperial Theaters. Lamented *Rech'*: "How could the administration dare to insult this most distinguished artist, to sacrifice his self-esteem and artistic qualities. . . . There is no one who can measure up to [Nijinsky's] greatness."[33]

Eleonora was heartbroken. She was even more upset when her daughter also resigned. "In view of the dismissal of my brother, Vaslav Nijinsky, from service in the Imperial Theaters," Nijinska wrote to the St. Petersburg Office of the Imperial Theaters on February 15, "I request the Office to remove me from the list of artists of the Imperial ballet troupe."[34] Within a week her resignation was official. Teliakovsky was unhappy to see her go. She had made rapid progress and was starting to dance solo roles. He told Alexander Krupensky, who headed the St. Petersburg office of the Imperial Theaters, to "have a talk with her," but she refused to budge.[35] Eleonora remonstrated with her. "Vaslav is already famous," she argued, "and so he can easily return and be accepted back into the Imperial Theatres whenever he chooses. But what will become of you?" She then appealed to her daughter's professional pride. At the Maryinsky, Nijinska had already achieved a degree of recognition whereas in the Diaghilev company, she was still a member of the corps. Moreover, "Diaghilev had declared, 'I cannot have two geniuses of the dance from one family!'" which Eleonora understood, wrongly, to mean there was no future for her daughter in his company. What mattered now, Nijinska told her mother, was "to work and live in a real, contemporary art—our ballet . . . and also to work with Vaslav."[36] Before long, she had left for Monte Carlo and the start of a full-time career with the Ballets Russes.

***

In 1909, while continuing to dance at the Maryinsky, Nijinska had joined the summer touring ensemble that in two years' time would become the Ballets

Russes. It was a momentous step. She was eighteen, a good dancer, hard-working and ambitious, and it was time, as her mother argued, "for her to work in new ballets and go forward."[37] She had seen a fair amount of Fokine's early choreography, and that winter, before Diaghilev introduced his ballets to Paris, she had danced in *Chopiniana* at the Maryinsky. "The impression of this performance . . . has remained forever in my memory," she wrote in *Early Memoirs*:

> For the first time I could clearly comprehend the true art in Dance and Ballet. Something was revealed to me; something was born in me and became the basis of my creative work, to influence all my artistic activity.[38]

In the years that followed, Nijinska would appear in virtually all of Fokine's works for the Ballets Russes. She danced both classical and character parts, reveling in the way he used free movement and expressive gesture to infuse those idioms with a personal sensibility and modern feeling. However, it was only when Diaghilev formed his year-round company in 1911 that Nijinska's career took off. In Monte Carlo, where the Ballets Russes gave its first official performances, she was now one of two lead Wilis in *Giselle*, one of two "big" swans in *Swan Lake*, and one of three Odalisques in *Schéhérazade* (the trio was later remounted by Fokine as a role for Nijinska alone). Another role that came her way was the Mazurka in *Les Sylphides* (she also occasionally danced the Waltz), and for the first time as a Ballets Russes dancer a solo role was choreographed on her—the Bacchante in Fokine's *Narcisse* (1911). She was also one of two Street Dancers in his *Petrouchka* (1911), to a new and exciting score by Igor Stravinsky. By 1912 she had advanced to lead roles in *The Polovtsian Dances* and several other ballets, including *Petrouchka* (Ballerina), *Cléopâtre* (Ta-Hor), a role she danced in bare feet rather than pointe shoes, and *Giselle* (Myrtha), in all of which she shared the limelight with her brother, while continuing to dance any number of secondary roles.[39] This is the repertory of a dancer who was adept at both classical and character work, a dancer of powerful physicality and daring, with a taste for meaty roles and strong characterizations and the ability to transform herself in performance.

As her repertory grew, critics began to single her out. They called her "exuberant" and "dynamic," "a miracle of rhythm and suppleness," even "very beautiful," which must have gratified her no end, and included her among the "constellation" of company "stars" and audience favorites.[40] *Le Dieu Bleu* (1912) may not have amounted to much (one critic dismissed

Reynaldo Hahn's score as "Hindu music Paris style"), but Nijinska's intoxicated Bayadère, flying across the stage with "speed and lightness," opened critical eyes to her rapidly developing gifts. Robert Brussel, who had followed Diaghilev's activities since his first Paris concert in 1906, announced to readers of *Figaro* that Nijinska was "on her way to becoming a star," while a colleague wrote in a front-page column a week later that "with her technique and her virtuosity, Nijinska recalled the greatest ballerinas of all times."[41] She danced at special events, such as the "*causerie*" that Robert Brussel gave at the Théâtre *Fémina* in 1912, where she, Nijinsky, Karsavina, and Maria Piltz, the "most celebrated dancers of Mons. Serge de Diaghilew's troupe," led a performance of *Les Sylphides*, and the following year, at the Russian Embassy in Paris, where the same cast (except for her brother) performed with a chorus of Russian singers from the Maryinsky to raise money for the Red Cross.[42] In London, where the Ballets Russes gave its first performances in 1911, she acquired an admirer in the *Daily Mail*'s music critic Richard Capell, who commended her "enchanting" Mazurka in *Les Sylphides* and exquisite flutter across the stage to Schumann's "Papillons" and, the following year, her "superb, delirious dance of a bacchante" in *Narcisse*. "M. Nijinsky's role is the most elaborate of those in which he has been seen here," he wrote, "and the performance is curious and wonderful. But . . . [i]t is Mlle. Nijinska's bacchanalian dance that chiefly lingers in one's memory."[43] Stravinsky, who attended numerous Ballets Russes performances during this period, was also impressed by her. "Karsavina and Nijinsky are worthy of their profession," he told readers of the *Petersburg Gazette* in October 1912. "But, besides Karsavina, I should mention Nijinskaya, sister of the famous dancer. She has been phenomenally successful since she left the Imperial Theaters. She is extremely talented, a fascinating ballerina, fully the equal of her brother. When she and her brother dance, the others pale by comparison."[44]

Nijinska loved taking part in Fokine's rehearsals for *Schéhérazade* and *Firebird*, which he choreographed for the 1910 season. It was "a most wonderful experience," she later wrote, "the inner joy of striving to attain perfection in the dance."[45] Attaining that perfection did not come easily. In *Early Memoirs* she recounts the challenge of making her body pliant and expressive, of ridding it of "dance habits formed in the old classical school [to] achieve a new balance [and] a new freedom."[46] In Monte Carlo, she caught the eye of the celebrated basso Fedor Chaliapin, who told Diaghilev to pay more attention to her, insisting that she was very "gifted." Chaliapin came to rehearsals, took her driving in his car, and after performances to the Café de

Paris. His encouragement, she wrote, "helped me so much. It created in me an awareness of myself. . . . I am inspired to new creativity."[47]

When she first went out with Chaliapin, who was married, a notorious womanizer, and nearly twice her age, friends always accompanied them. She had been brought up very strictly; she had never flirted or had a boyfriend. Now she fell head over heels in love. Chaliapin called her his "pure angel," and she danced for him alone; he was her "Genius."[48] Vaslav tried talking to her, but she wouldn't listen; anyway, there was more than a touch of jealousy in his attitude toward Chaliapin, the sun around whom his sister's every thought now revolved. Diaghilev stepped in, and together with Vaslav, persuaded Tamara Karsavina, the company's senior ballerina, to "have a word" with Nijinska: Chaliapin was a man of the world, with a reputation, and young ladies weren't safe with him. So, Nijinska and Chaliapin were separated. Apart from a chaste kiss or two, nothing had passed between them. However, Nijinska was no longer intact. That spring in a Monte Carlo scented by lilacs, she lost her virginity as an artist. Chaliapin opened her emotionally, penetrating to the very source of her creative being. And, as her diaries attest, he remained a continuous presence in her emotional life, an inspiration that endured for decades as she pursued what she called her "creativity."

Chaliapin was one of the "sacred monsters" of Nijinska's world. So, too, were her brother and Anna Pavlova. She wrote about the two as Olympian deities, uniquely paired in talent and transforming what they danced into something sublime. More than any other dancers, they embodied her ideas about movement; even when performing conventional steps and poses, they subordinated them into a continuous flow, melding music and movement into a single, celestial harmony. Pavlova never danced *Giselle* with Nijinsky in Russia. However, they rehearsed it for months in 1909, and Nijinska along with other members of the Maryinsky company watched. In the celebrated pas de deux in the second act, she writes, Giselle was not a "living girl, but rather the phantom of Albrecht's thoughts and imagination; she is the Giselle of whom he is aware in another world, the world beyond existence." Pavlova, Nijinska continues, "barely touches the ground with her *pointe* . . . ; her *arabesque*, fragile in the perfection of its line, flutters; every moment of her airy dance whispers of another, unearthly world, and of her love, conquering even eternal sleep."[49] Nijinska would never dance this way. Even in roles she took over from Karsavina, her brother's regular partner, she eliminated the *belle femme*, so that in Nijinska's hands, Karsavina's porcelain Ballerina doll became a handcrafted, fairground double of Nijinsky's Petrouchka.

It was through her brother that Nijinska first gleaned the possibility of making dances of her own. When Vaslav returned to Petersburg from Venice in 1910, he was bubbling with ideas. "Bronia," he announced, "what I am about to tell you nobody must know. For the new season in Paris I am staging a ballet. It is called *L'Après-midi d'un Faune* and has music by Debussy." "What about Fokine? Does he know about this?" Nijinska asked. No, and for now he didn't need to know. "I will sketch on you the whole ballet, and Sergei Pavlovich [Diaghilev] and Bakst will look at it. If it is good, then Sergei Pavlovich will speak to Fokine about my production."[50]

In the weeks that followed, the family sitting room became a studio, as Nijinsky developed the movement for his role as the Faun on his sister. She became his model and his muse, his body's imperfect but necessary double in this new undertaking. For though Diaghilev and Bakst may have chosen the music for his new ballet and determined the general style—"archaic" rather than "classical" Greek—neither was a dancer or a choreographer. Nijinsky did have a bit of choreographic experience: he had created the dances for an amateur performance of a children's opera, *Cinderella*, with music by Boris Asafiev.[51] But *Faune* was in a different league entirely. Like the dances of Isadora Duncan and the sisterhood of female recitalists, it was created not from a lexicon of codified steps but from movements generated by the choreographer's own body. "Sometimes," Nijinska wrote, "we spend the whole evening sitting and lying on the floor. Vaslav creates his role of the Faun, modeling on me each pose and movement, as if from clay. We rehearse fully absorbed in our work."[52] What she called "the new technique of his ballet"—"every movement, position of the body, and expression of each choreographic movement"—he seemed to capture immediately, while she struggled with it. "I rehearse the male role of the Faun, Nijinsky's own part," she wrote, "and naturally I cannot grasp it all immediately and fully assimilate the choreography. I am 19 years old—it is hard for me to express all the nuances and shades of the Faun's character." Tempers sometimes flared, and as always Nijinsky was a harsh taskmaster. "Perhaps our work is even harder and more nerve-wracking," she wrote, "because we are brother and sister. Sometimes in our rehearsals, he lacks patience with me, but Vaslav is always demanding, not only now in his own creation, but in each of my dance performances." But, she adds, "I learn so much from him."

Indeed, she learned a great deal—that movement invention was a creative search, stemmed directly from corporeal experiment, and constituted the originality of a work and a choreographer's unique style. She also learned techniques for conducting this search, including something akin to improvisation, at least on the part of the choreographer; just as important, she learned that as a dancer one had to submit, be willing to serve as the vehicle for somebody else's vision. She learned, too, that this was hard work: decades later she told a journalist that she had "watched her brother create his ballets and . . . marvelled that anyone was capable of doing anything so difficult."[53] Finally, she learned that it was possible to generate new movement without abandoning the morning ballet class, as Duncan and other recitalists insisted, that the corporeal training of the *danse d'école* could serve as the foundation on which to build a living new art.

Faune was not produced in 1911. The sketches that Nijinska danced for Diaghilev did not impress him; he found the style severe and was disturbed by the absence of conventional dance movements. Nijinsky's debut as a choreographer was postponed. In December 1911, while vacationing in Bordighera, Nijinsky had worked on his sister's role, but it was only the following month in Berlin that Diaghilev gave him the go-ahead to begin rehearsals with the Nymphs. Ida Rubinstein, for whom he had intended the role of the Chief Nymph, took one look at the choreography and withdrew. The others had trouble moving from pose to pose while maintaining the bas-relief form. When "official" rehearsals began in Monte Carlo in spring, it took ninety practice sessions for the cast to execute the "whole choreographic material," as Nijinska put it, "not only exactly as he saw it but also according to his artistic interpretation." Although Nijinsky as a dancer had freely altered roles to inflect them with his own sensibility, as a choreographer, he demanded absolute conformity: "Each position of the dance, each position of the body down to the gesture of each finger, was mounted according to a strict choreographic plan." The dancers, outwardly compliant, inwardly resisted: "We feel as though we are carved out of stone," they told Nijinska.[54]

She was his intermediary and his translator. When words failed him, as they often did, she spoke for him and helped him break down the choreography so the dancers could absorb it. When he began to sketch the choreography for a new work, *Jeux* (1913), to a commissioned score by Debussy, she again served as his clay, along with one of her friends, Alexandra Wassilievska, a Polish dancer with whom she was often paired and who was now standing in for Tamara Karsavina, who would actually dance the ballet with Nijinska. The style of *Jeux* was very different from *Faune*'s. Instead of moving in an archaic frieze, the dancers performed conventional ballet steps and even wore pointe shoes. However, they only danced on three-quarter pointe; their feet were in parallel, their fingers clenched, and their arms held stiffly in half-circles, so that the ballet seemed to build on an abstraction of line and curve, not unlike the images of the era's cubists.

Totally different again was *Le Sacre du Printemps* or *The Rite of Spring*. This would be Nijinsky's great production of 1913, a ballet that vanished after a season to become a legend, a work remade so many times by so many choreographers that it became part of a canon of memory. In November 1912, while the company was performing at the Kroll Theater in Berlin, Nijinsky began to work with Nijinska on the "Danse Sacrale," in which the Chosen Maiden dances herself to death. By then, Nijinsky had received Stravinsky's handwritten orchestral score for the dance. Michel Steiman, the company's rehearsal pianist and sometime conductor, transposed the music as he played. In a letter to the Soviet ballet historian Vera Krasovskaya written in 1967, Nijinska described the intensity and exhilaration of those rehearsals:

Nijinsky listened to the music . . . several times through to the end, then began to repeat it in parts, and when he had gotten it by heart, as I did as well, began to choreograph. Nijinsky possessed great musicality and a great musical memory.

Vaslav, in this part of his choreography, did not delineate the rhythm of the musical bars and did not resort to counting them out. After listening to the music, he let himself be inspired by it and followed, in his composition, his perceptions of the music and its "breath." The rhythm of the movements, like the pas themselves invented by Vaslav for this solo, were complex and unfamiliar to me; rehearsing them with me, Vaslav danced himself, dem- onstrating the dance to me. My work with my brother proceeded quickly and easily, perhaps because I saw and grasped and precisely performed, with respect both to the dance and the music, every movement and faith- fully reflected their inner rhythm. Vaslav did not explain anything in words; he only said that the solo was the Maiden's ritual, sacrificial dance. I saw that in her primitive sacrificial dance, the maiden was dancing in a frenzy, her harsh, forceful, elemental movements seemed to engage the heavens in battle, to defend the earth against a threatening sky; she falls down in a trance, and at the end, in her frenzy, must kill herself by dancing. No one had ever used any of the movements invented by Nijinsky for the choreog- raphy; they were unfamiliar, but I was taken by them. I imagined overhead a dark, threatening sky . . . in expectation of an approaching hurricane—and it s᷍emed to me as though that hurricane must soak up my body in order to save the earth. I saw that Vaslav was satisfied with his work and mine—his face looked happy, and he said to me: "Only you, Bronia, can perform this dance, no one else."[55]

In addition to everything else she did for him, Nijinska also calmed her brother's furies. Fokine had left the company at the end of the 1912 Paris season, and with him gone, the pressures on Nijinsky mounted exponentially. He was now responsible for staging all of the company's new ballets, while continuing to dance in virtually every performance. The tantrums multiplied, and increasingly Diaghilev called upon her to mollify him. *The Rite of Spring* added to Nijinsky's woes. Although the dancers were familiar with Stravinsky's music for *Firebird* and *Petrouchka*, *The Rite* was so complex they could not rely on the ear to follow the melody of the music but had to count. Nijinska recalled that corps rehearsals were exhausting and on several occasions led to protests that "required intervention from Diaghilev himself, primarily to calm Nijinsky." Nijinsky failed to understand that movements he performed with ease were beyond the ken of the average dancer, and when this was pointed out, he "would get angry" and accuse the dancer of "sabotage."[56]

Further chaos resulted from what Nijinska disparagingly calls the "Dalcroze System," a system of physicalizing rhythm developed by the Swiss music pedagogue Emile Jaques-Dalcroze. Like most of the company's experiments, eurhythmics was taken up with enthusiasm by Diaghilev, who thought it might help Nijinsky with Stravinsky's score. During the 1912 German tour, he took Nijinsky, Nijinska, and a few others to visit the new Dalcroze Institute at Hellerau. Nijinska was fascinated by the lighting effects that Adolphe Appia had achieved in the specially designed studio-theater, but dismayed by the eurhythmics demonstration, and appalled to learn that Diaghilev had hired someone to teach eurhythmics to the company. It was unnecessary, she told him; the company had no problem dealing with complicated scores, and besides, the Dalcroze people couldn't dance. Nijinska certainly had a point. When choreographing her solo as the Chosen Maiden, her brother had managed quite well with the music simply by listening to it again and again. However, when Nijinsky returned to the choreography in 1913, he took a Dalcroze approach, "'graphically' render[ing] each musical note by a physical movement" and "counting the beats aloud."[57] The effort to visualize Stravinsky's rhythmically complex score caused havoc. More than forty dancers were on stage in the first tableau. They had to hold themselves in a knock-kneed stance they found anathema and maintain that position while stamping, jumping, trembling, and shaking, all the while registering different rhythms in different parts of the body. Nijinsky refused to move ahead until the dancers had mastered all the movement. The compositional process slowed to a snail's pace, and weeks had to be cleared of other rehearsals so the company could devote itself full-time to the ballet.

The months in Monte Carlo and Germany when *Jeux* was sketched and the "Danse Sacrale" choreographed marked the zenith of Nijinska's artistic collaboration with her brother. By early 1913 it had begun to fray. After a few *Rite of Spring* rehearsals in London, she ceased to be called and noticed, to her dismay, that Marie Rambert, the eurhythmics teacher hired by Diaghilev, had supplanted her as Nijinsky's helpmate. Rambert now sat with him at rehearsals, reviewing the score, and stayed on to sketch out the movements for the next rehearsal. Rambert spoke Russian and Polish (as well as various other languages) and thus could act, as Nijinska had before her, as an intermediary with the dancers. None of this boded well for Nijinska. Her brother was avoiding her, whether because he had fallen for Rambert's ideas or for Rambert herself (she certainly was in love with him).[58]

Nijinska was one of the company's leading dancers, yet Diaghilev began taking roles away. For the Covent Garden season in February 1913 he hired Sofia Fedorova to replace her as Ta-Hor in *Cléopâtre* and, for the London and Paris seasons, in *The Polovtsian Dances*. He hired Nijinska's old friend Ludmilla Schollar to share her roles in *Les Sylphides* and other ballets. When Nijinska demanded to know why he had replaced her with Fedorova during the Covent Garden season, Diaghilev replied, "'I need a *ballerina* for the London Season!'" This prompted Nijinska to recall a conversation not long before, when he had asked her to dye her hair red and "'dress more like a *ballerina*.' But I had refused. I felt that dyed red hair would make me look like a [clown] and what concerned me about my appearance was how I looked onstage, not how glamorous I could make myself for a social event."[59] For Diaghilev, however, the ballerina was an icon of femininity offstage as well as on. The public, he said, "wanted *ballerinas* with sweet and pretty faces," and Nijinska, however glamorous she may have appeared on stage, was anything but sweet and pretty.[60] Her refusal to play along didn't help her career.

Nijinska was also stung by the way her brother and Diaghilev had wrecked her romance with Chaliapin, even if they were right to do so. She knew, too, that Nijinsky did not approve of her decision to marry Alexander Kochetovsky, a character dancer from the Bolshoi who was a company soloist, considering him a rival for his sister's affections. "He almost felt he was losing a comrade," Nijinsky's wife Romola later wrote. "He did not hide this feeling, but expressed it to Bronia, who bitterly reproached him with the fact that she could not be constantly with him, so she might as well get married."[61] Nijinska herself had second thoughts, and her mother was dead-set against her marrying a fellow dancer, as she had done. (Eleonora turned out to be right: "Sasha," like Tomasz Nijinsky, had an eye for the ladies and eventually decamped.) Nijinska, however, decided to go ahead, and on July 2, 1912, she was married at the Registry Office in the District of St. Giles, London. Two weeks later, on July 15, the couple was married a second time in the Russian Orthodox chapel in the Russian Embassy. Nijinska wore her tea-rose lace graduation gown, with the diamond and ruby pin that Prince Lvov had given her. Diaghilev stood in for her father and led her to the altar, while Nijinsky, as best man, held the heavy gold crown above her head. The two hosted a supper for the newlyweds at the Savoy Hotel, and Vaslav gave her a thousand francs as a present. Diaghilev's gift, she told his biographer Richard Buckle, was a ring set with sapphires and diamonds.[62]

Nature now intervened. In mid-January 1913, Nijinska became pregnant, although it wasn't until March that her condition was confirmed. Her mother, who had danced virtually until giving birth, knew all about the hazards of pregnancy. In order to avoid a miscarriage, she insisted that Nijinska tell her brother, so that he would allow her to "mark" rather than dance full out during the strenuous rehearsals for *The Rite of Spring* in April, when the company would be performing in Monte Carlo, and also to have a replacement ready if she had to cancel performances. The news enraged Nijinsky. He threatened her husband with physical violence and screamed that Nijinska was sabotaging his work; he refused to listen to reason when Eleonora explained that it was only natural for a married woman to get pregnant. Now estranged from his sister, he pulled her out of *Jeux*, replacing her with Ludmilla Schollar, and out of *The Rite of Spring*, replacing her with Maria Piltz, to whom she had to teach the role of the Chosen Maiden.[63]

As Ballets Russes playbills reveal, Nijinska continued to dance throughout the spring and summer seasons that followed her brother's blow-up; she didn't stop until the company disbanded in August for a short holiday and she had entered her seventh month. In Monte Carlo she performed a number of physically demanding roles, including Myrtha in *Giselle*, the Mazurka in *Les Sylphides*, Papillon in *Carnaval*, and the lead Polovtsian Girl in *Prince Igor*, and she usually appeared in two of an evening's three ballets; sometimes

she was cast in all three. On April 27, barely a month before the premiere of
The Rite of Spring, she was one of the two "big" swans in the second act of
Swan Lake, led the czardas in Act III, then performed the exotic Ta-Hor in
Cléopâtre—a stylistic tour de force that she seemed to relish. In Paris she lost
several of her best roles. However, she continued to dance solo parts in addition to corps roles, and she still usually appeared in two ballets a night, including her brother's *L'Après-midi d'un Faune*. Indeed, at the first, memorable
performance of *The Rite of Spring*, she danced with him in the evening's curtain raiser, *Les Sylphides*, even though she had been removed from the role of
the Chosen Maiden. During the company's month-long season in London at
the Theatre Royal Drury Lane that opened on June 25, she took part in every
performance but one, and at the closing performance on July 25, she actually
danced in all four ballets—*Schéhérazade*, *L'Après-midi d'un Faune*, *Thamar*,
and *Les Sylphides*.[64] Nijinska mentions none of this in *Early Memoirs*.

The "Danse Sacrale" was an unusually taxing role, and it is certainly
possible that Nijinska would have had to withdraw from at least some
performances of *The Rite of Spring*, especially by the London season when
she entered her sixth month. However, *Jeux* appears to have been no more
challenging than the mazurka in *Les Sylphides*, which she danced throughout
the London season. Taking her out of ballets to which she had contributed so
much was yet another instance of the cruelty that appeared time and again in
Nijinsky's behavior toward his sister. Again and again he seemed to be pun-
ishing her female body—because it was weaker than his, couldn't do what
his could do, because it was different from his, biologically and culturally,
because it defied him in his hour of greatest need. He also seemed to be chas-
tising her for betrayals of the heart—for her adoration of Chaliapin, for her
marriage to Kochetovsky, for wanting a love life of her own, for becoming a
mother.

In the aftermath of her failed romance with Chaliapin, Nijinska
approached Diaghilev with a proposition. "I was still young," she told Marc
Semenoff, a Russian émigré journalist in 1932, "but I felt myself capable of
composing a ballet myself. Unfortunately, I was only a woman, and Diaghilev
made me understand that 'two chefs cannot work together in close union of
vision and direction.'"[65] Here, perhaps, lay the real danger posed by this talented, headstrong, and immensely intelligent young woman. She threatened
to become her brother's choreographic competitor, and as such jeopardized
the erotic-creative relationship on which Diaghilev had partly founded the
Ballets Russes. Nijinsky may have been an extraordinary dancer, but he was

also the instrument of Diaghilev's imagination; it was through Nijinsky that Diaghilev could leave his mark on ballet, wrest it into the modern world, and exert his creative powers as a producer. This kind of relationship, iterations of which appear throughout Diaghilev's life, was not one that Nijinska could hope to share with him. However, as her brother's choreographic apprentice, she learned not only how to experiment but also how this was done in the elite sphere of high art, how reputations were made and patrons cultivated, and how necessary a man like Diaghilev was to the enterprise. Through her brother she also learned what she had missed, first, by being a woman, and second, by choosing to conduct her life outside the haut monde to which he now belonged. In a powerful rejection of the world in which Nijinsky chose to live, Nijinska chose the tribe of her parents, artists and artisans of the dance. Even more than the stage, the studio would become the mainstay of her life and the utopian source of her imagination. Both her husbands would be dancers, along with her daughter and most of her friends. But the permanent company she longed to have would always elude her, and she never found a voice, other than her own, to speak to the world on her behalf.

***

When the Ballets Russes season in London ended, Nijinska and Kochetovsky returned to Russia, first to Moscow, where she met her mother-in-law (Kochetovsky's father was dead), and then to St. Petersburg, where the couple moved in with Eleonora.[66] Nijinsky, meanwhile, had sailed with the Ballets Russes to South America, its first tour outside Europe. Diaghilev intended to accompany the troupe, as his name—along with Nijinsky's—appears on the list of passengers who embarked for Argentina on the SS *Avon* on August 15. The company boarded in Southampton, Nijinsky in Cherbourg, but without Diaghilev.[67] The two had been arguing steadily, and Nijinsky's behavior, exacerbated by Diaghilev's apparent loss of faith in him as a choreographer, had grown increasingly unpredictable. Nijinska recounts a conversation with Diaghilev before she left London in which he told her that he planned to drop both *Jeux* and *The Rite of Spring* and that further ballets along these lines put the company at grave financial risk with audiences and presenters. He also told her that he was negotiating a contract with Covent Garden for the following year with the obligation to produce two new ballets, both by Fokine, including *The Legend of Joseph*. This disturbing news Diaghilev was afraid to impart to Nijinsky; he wanted Nijinska to do it. Nijinska spoke to her brother, who, predictably, blew up, blaming Diaghilev for myriad crimes against art and for becoming a "theatrical lackey."[68]

Even before Nijinsky sailed for South America, Nijinska implies, Diaghilev had decided to part with her brother and remain in Europe, although the presence of his name on the manifest suggests the decision was sudden. In any event, Nijinsky sailed without him and in Buenos Aires married the Hungarian socialite Romola de Pulszky. When news of Nijinsky's marriage reached St. Petersburg, Eleonora was devastated. So was Diaghilev. Nijinska alone welcomed the news of her brother's marriage. "Now," she later wrote, "everything that Vaslav had felt in his heart against my marriage would disappear."[69] She looked forward to meeting Romola and becoming close to her, a sister. Married now, Nijinsky would rejoin the dancing tribe of their family. Only days later, on October 7, Nijinska gave birth to her daughter Irina. Vaslav wired congratulations from Rio de Janeiro, and her friend Ludmilla Schollar pinned an ikon of St. Michael the Archangel to the baby's crib.

Meanwhile, Nijinsky was fired by Diaghilev. Both Nijinska and her husband remained under contract to the Ballets Russes, however, and Diaghilev was anxious to retain them, Nijinska above all, since she was clearly developing into a major artistic force. She, of course, wanted to quit, out of loyalty to her brother and anger at what she perceived as Diaghilev's machinations. By January 1914, however, Nijinska had been six months without work; her savings were gone, and when Diaghilev rang to invite her and Sasha to have dinner with him at the new, ultra-luxurious Hotel Astoria, her indignation melted. "Diaghilev still had over me the same magical strength and power to make me respect his command," she later wrote.[70] The repast was sumptuous, and Diaghilev was at his most charming.

> All during dinner Sergei Pavlovitch continued to assure me that I had always been very dear to him, that he loved me as if I were his daughter, and that I was equally dear to him as an artist. I felt that Diaghilev's feelings were stronger towards me now than in the past, as though he saw in me a part of Vaslav. I could also feel how painful for him had been the break with Vaslav. He told me how hurt he had been, how insulted he had felt.[71]

Turning on all his charm, he begged her to rejoin the company. "Reliable sources" had told her that Fokine had demanded her dismissal along with Nijinsky's. But Diaghilev had balked; she was already under contract. Now he assured Nijinska that if she rejoined the company in Prague she would retain all her roles, even though Fokine was claiming several of them for his wife Vera Fokina. The evening, which turned out to be the last time she saw Diaghilev until 1921, ended with a scene so fantastic it might have come from a Russian novel:

> When we parted he embraced me several times, and as he helped me on with my fur coat he looked deep into my eyes. Suddenly he took my *botiki* [felt overboots] from the hall porter, and as gallantly as a youth he bent on one knee to help me put them on. That was too much for me. I took my *botiki* from him and gave them to Sasha. I hugged Sergei Pavlovitch and said, "All right, I shall come to Prague!"[72]

However, when Nijinska arrived, she discovered that Fokina was now to dance the role of Ta-Hor, which she had never danced before and was part of Nijinska's repertory. When a telegram arrived from Nijinsky asking her to leave the Ballets Russes and go to work for him, at a huge yearly salary of 80,000 francs, she did not hesitate. She said that her contract with Diaghilev was broken, as "certain agreements had not been kept." She knew her worth, and her brother awaited. So she took her leave of the Ballets Russes.

***

As word of Nijinsky's dismissal spread, he began to receive "propositions from every side," as he wrote to Stravinsky.[73] Among them was an offer from London's Palace Theatre, and it was this offer that he talked about with Nijinska when she and Kochetovsky arrived in Paris from Prague. The contract, he told her, was for eight weeks (only four, according to the London press), required Nijinsky to present a fifty-minute program, and paid £1,000 a week, a generous sum at a time when most people earned about fifty pounds a year, although out of this he had to bear all the production costs, administrative expenses, and salaries. He was to appear in the ballets that had made him famous, with scenery and costumes by the artists who had designed them, and with the support of a "picked ballet from St. Petersburg and Moscow." The contract also spelled out the repertory: *Les Sylphides*, *Le Spectre de la Rose*, and *Carnaval*, all ballets by Fokine, plus a "new rhapsody by Liszt, which has not yet been performed in London."[74]

In an interview with the *Times*, Nijinsky explained that these works had all been "rearranged, so as to give his own impression of their themes, and not that of any other *maître de ballet*." He also noted that the scenery had been redesigned by Boris Anisfeld, and the music for *Les Sylphides* reorchestrated by Maurice Ravel. The costumes were new as well.[75] Always so insistent on exactitude in the performance of his own works, Nijinsky made light of revising Fokine's. As he explained to his sister,

> these ballets can hardly be credited solely to Fokine. *Les Sylphides . . .* is as much a creation of Benois as of Fokine. *Le Spectre de la Rose* is Théophile Gautier, Bakst, and Nijinsky. . . . As for *Carnaval*, that is entirely Bakst's ballet; Harlequin, I created that role myself, not Fokine. . . . *You*, Bronia, created Papillon.[76]

To some extent, Nijinsky was right: everyone owns a piece of a collaborative work. However, stealing from Fokine was different from borrowing from Petipa. Fokine's ballets did not come from the stock of "old" ballets; they were newly invented, the work of a single individual, and identified with Diaghilev's "Western" repertory, even if the dancers and choreographer were Russian and the ballets had originated in St. Petersburg. How ironic that Nijinsky, having so recently crossed the threshold of choreographic modernism, should act like an old-style ballet master circulating versions of somebody else's works.

By the time Nijinska reached Paris in late January, her brother had chosen the repertory. However, that was about all he had done. Although the opening of the Saison Nijinsky was little more than a month away, no dancers had been hired, no costumes or scenery commissioned, and with one exception no arrangements made for the music. The undertaking, Nijinska thought, was "pure folly."[77] She went with her brother to see Maurice Ravel, and together they chose the pieces of Chopin music for Nijinsky's new version of *Les Sylphides*, which the composer had agreed to orchestrate for the Palace Theatre's relatively small orchestra. She then set off with Kochetovsky for Russia to hire dancers. As she explains in *Early Memoirs*, this was no easy task. Experienced dancers were unwilling to leave the Bolshoi or Maryinsky for an eight-week foreign engagement in mid-season, and few private studios offered ballet training at a professional level. At Lydia Nelidova's studio in Moscow, she found a former Diaghilev dancer named Boni, and two other dancers, Tarasova and Kozhukhova, and in St. Petersburg Anatole Vilzak's sister Valentina (or Valia, as she called her), who was still a student. They all now embarked on the two-day trip to London, arriving on February 20, which left only ten days to rehearse for the opening on March 2. Four Russian men, "very good dancers," in Nijinska's opinion, joined the company in London, along with four women. She was surprised how easy it was to "find good ballet artists in London," considerably easier than in Russia. Three of the four newcomers were English, so their names were hastily Russified— Johnson became Ivanova, Doris, Darinska, and Jacobson, Yakovleva. It was hardly a company of "Leading Members of the Imperial Russian Ballet," as the season's advertising proudly announced.[78]

Up to now Nijinska had had little to do with the day-to-day running of a ballet company. She had watched rehearsals because she was interested in learning the choreography and in observing the nuts and bolts of the dance-making process. She had assisted Fokine in restaging *Firebird* and taught her brother's "Danse Sacrale" to another dancer, but such assistance was on an ad hoc basis, not part of her formal responsibilities. As for hiring, casting, scheduling, and teaching, all critical to the operation of a dance company, these responsibilities belonged to management. In big companies they were divided up. Ballet masters conducted rehearsals, and teachers gave class, while choreographers produced new dances. The functions often overlapped, and most people also continued to perform. Other responsibilities lay in the hands of an artistic director, who made all the major repertory and production decisions, commissioned artistic personnel, engaged stars, and took part in casting principal roles.

At the Imperial Theaters this was the territory of an all-male army of bureaucrats, who recorded promotions, infractions, salary increases, and requests for domestic as well as foreign passports. In the Ballets Russes things were different. The company was relatively small, with headquarters wherever Diaghilev happened to alight. He made the decisions and held the purse-strings, even when the purse was empty. He had backers, patrons, advisors, assistants, old friends, and hangers-on—another mostly male group—and in Sergei Grigoriev a company manager of genius who maintained discipline and repertory standards, though dancers, choreographers, and teachers came and went over the years. In chamber-sized companies, such as Nijinska's parents', responsibilities were shared: everyone did a bit of everything, including women. This was also the case of the Saison Nijinsky, although in *Early Memoirs* Nijinska is careful to keep the spotlight on her brother.

Once the season started on Monday, March 2, Nijinsky danced every night and two matinées a week; the first week a third was added "to give an opportunity to those living in the provinces to utilise the Thursday excursions."[79]

In the early 1910s the Diaghilev company seldom gave more than four performances a week, even on tour. The physical strain on Nijinsky must have been immense. "Morning, noon, and night, practically every day since his arrival in London," a company member told a reporter, "M. Nijinsky has been rehearsing new dances and ballets."[80] In addition to dancing, choreographing, and rehearsing, he had to handle the administrative side of the company, although in this he was helped by Kochetovsky, who spoke some English, and by Faustin Zenon, a Russian living in London, who spoke French and English well, and had worked for other Russian performing arts groups. In the weeks leading up to the season's opening, Zenon shuttled between London and Paris, bringing costumes (from the prestigious firm of Maison Muelle) as well as music, including the scores for *Faune* and *Jeux*, which at some point Nijinsky considered staging.[81]

Although Nijinsky put in "two and a-half hours of vigorous exercise" every morning before leaving his hotel (as he told a reporter),[82] it is likely that his sister gave a more traditional class to the dancers she had so recently chosen. Even more important, she served as her brother's ballet master or répétiteur. "I assured Vaslav," she wrote in an unpublished note, "that I would rehearse everybody and teach them the repertory."

> Vaslav staged the dances, and I "trained" the artists and rehearsed them. . . . Vaslav would come only for the final "refinement," to "clean" the work. . . . Here my talent at rehearsing was revealed for the first time: we achieved an artistic performance with this very raw material in a very short time.[83]

In the studio, then, Nijinska pretty much took charge. She understood instinctively how to use discipline to make up for the inexperience of the dancers and intensive practice to mold them into a unified ensemble, something she would do again and again during the next fifty years. How well she succeeded may be judged by the reviews. Wrote G. H. M. in the *Manchester Guardian*, "it has to be said that the ballet which supports him has all the accomplishment and finish of the Russians we have already seen, and that in the last movement, particularly, of the Chopin Fantasy they dance with exquisite rhythm and grace."[84]

As the Palace headliner, the Saison Nijinsky was widely reviewed. Nijinsky was no stranger to the critics who wrote about him, and many reviews draw explicit comparisons between his program at the Palace and his appearances with the Diaghilev company. The consensus was that he was as good as ever, but that the framework had changed: "he came," in the words of one critic, "as a single star separated from a constellation which we know."[85] There was criticism of the changes he had introduced into *Les Sylphides*, especially Anisfeld's "exotic vegetation" (*Times*), "too new and assertive for the lovely purity of the ballet" (*Observer*). The critic for the *Daily Telegraph*, on the other hand, admired the fresh setting, "an impressionist picture of trees and foliage of delicate, ethereal tints, palest greens and indefinable blues, the whole silvered by a crescent moon."[86] Nijinska herself marveled at the freshness of the choreography. "There was nothing borrowed from Fokine," she wrote in an unpublished note. "Not only was the composition of the ballet new, but even individual pas were Vaslav's original finds." She thought that the music was "exquisitely orchestrated" by Ravel.[87]

Nijinsky was the season's star and invariably referred to in the listings as "the famous Premier Danseur." However, Nijinska was his ballerina, with second billing. In the Diaghilev company they had seldom danced together. Now, as his partner, she had finally taken Karsavina's place as his on-stage love object. In *Les Sylphides* she danced the pas de deux with him; in *Le Spectre de la Rose* she conjured him from a dream; in *Carnaval* she was his Columbine.[88] Nijinska did not suffer from the comparison. In fact, many reviews never mentioned Karsavina at all. "The best thing" in *Les Sylphides*, wrote the critic for the *Times*, "was M. Nijinsky's personal performance, combined with the aerial dancing of his sister, Mlle Nijinska." In *Le Spectre de la Rose*, "Mlle. Nijinska, as the young girl, expressed the tenderness of her dream of first love with a delicate mastery which no artist could, in our opinion, have surpassed."[89] Another critic thought she "was as good or nearly as good as Karsavina"; others described her as Nijinsky's "wonderful little sister," accomplished and charming, supporting him with "grace, assurance, and . . . finish."[90]

Much to Nijinsky's dismay, the Palace's managing director Alfred Butt wanted a Russian dance on the program, claiming this was what the public expected. According to Nijinska, her brother flew into a rage, slapped Butt, then did two or three movements from a Ukrainian squat dance, screaming, "Is this what you want to see from Nijinsky?" before Kochetovsky, who was there because he spoke English, grabbed Nijinsky by the arms and calmed him.[91] In the end, on Thursday of the second week, the company premiered a "revised version" of another popular Fokine work, *The Polovtsian Dances* from Borodin's opera *Prince Igor*. With a total of six dancers, this new

Danse Polovtsienne was tailor-made for Nijinska and for Kochetovsky. In *Early Memoirs*, Nijinska makes a point of saying how "beautifully" Nijinsky had mounted the number, adding that it was conceived for herself and the company's four male character dancers. Her admirer Richard Capell singled her out in the *Daily Mail*, although he missed the "crowd of warriors, maidens, and youths" of the original version.

> The new version has no little gorgeousness of colour and movement and gives opportunities to Mlle. Nijinska, whose suggestion of savage passion is wonderful, and to the gifted M. Kotchetovsky [*sic*]. But to those who had not seen the original all the fury of these dances must have seemed meaningless.[92]

Nijinska did not necessarily share this view, and over the next several years she would restage the work, tinkering with the choreography to shift the focus from the Polovtsian Chief (as in the Fokine version) to the Polovtsian Girl (as in the Saison Nijinsky one). Unlike other favorite roles, the Polovtsian Girl belonged to what might be called Nijinska's personal repertory. She danced versions of the role for years, growing with it and transforming it, using it as a yardstick to map changes in her personal performance style. Her mother hated it. "Bronia," she told her, "don't dance the Polovtsian Dances so fiercely—it always seems to me you are going to die."[93] Nijinska's Polovtsian Girl threw conventional femininity to the winds. She was a force from the steppes, a girl who ruled a tribe of men, powerful and triumphant, like the Chosen Maiden.

A crowded, enthusiastic house greeted the opening performance of the Saison Nijinsky. In the first row Diaghilev watched like a hawk, his arms tightly crossed, his fists clenched to hide his stubby fingers. He did not applaud. He had done all he could to undermine the season, ordering Bakst and others not to collaborate with Nijinsky and suing Nijinska for breach of contract, so that she missed the dress rehearsal. Sir George Lewis, a well-known attorney, filed a countersuit, claiming that Diaghilev was guilty of breach of contract because Fokine had taken away all her leading roles; the judge ruled in her favor, thus enabling her to dance on opening night. The next day, doubtless at Diaghilev's instigation, Fokine demanded that *Spectre* be taken off the program. Nijinsky chose not to comply.[94]

At the start of the third week, Nijinsky began running a high fever. He was exhausted, his patience at an end, and he was arguing with Kochetovsky, who reproached him for failing to "show respect" toward Nijinska. Rehearsals ended in tears.[95] On Monday, March 16, Nijinsky sent word that he could not dance owing to what the *Times* described as "a sudden and severe indisposition," but since the announcement came after the show had already started, the company carried on, giving a performance "that was much appreciated," even if "condensed."[96] Nijinsky missed the next two performances as well, at which point Butt canceled the remainder of the season. Speculation followed about the hastiness of his action and also about the cause of Nijinsky's illness. A dancer told the *Evening News* that Nijinsky was so absorbed in his work that he forgot to eat and would sometimes fast all day; he was also having trouble sleeping. The *Manchester Guardian* ran a long article demanding a fuller explanation of why "a break of three nights in the appearance of a renowned artist like Nijinsky could be 'detrimental to the success of the engagement,' more especially as he was about to begin the more popular numbers of his repertory." The *New York Times* wrote that he was "in a state of complete nervous prostration" and "may never dance again," which suggests some kind of breakdown.[97]

Thus, the Saison Nijinsky came to an abrupt and unhappy end. The sets, costumes, and music were hastily packed and sent to storage, a temporary arrangement, except that World War I intervened, and they were eventually sold for nonpayment of warehouse fees. Nijinsky paid the dancers a month's salary (although they had only performed for a little over two weeks) and, for those who lived in Russia, their return fare. Nijinska and her husband decided to stay in London in the hope of securing future engagements. Nothing materialized on the professional front. Moreover, Romola, Nijinsky's wife, did not improve on further acquaintance. Nijinska had little use for a lady who lunched, while Romola couldn't understand why her husband and his sister wouldn't join her in the afternoon for a leisurely meal. There were language problems: Nijinska spoke only Russian and Polish, while Romola, although fluent in French, German, and English as well as her native Hungarian, spoke neither. She also sensed that Nijinska didn't like her. "She seemed to resent everything that happened and blame it on me," Romola wrote in her biography of Nijinsky. "She isolated herself behind a screen of ice which I could never penetrate."[98] For Nijinska, her sister-in-law was another intruder on her relationship with her brother, but unlike Marie Rambert, one with little sympathy for his art. She blamed Romola for allowing Nijinsky to sign a contract with a music hall and failing to read the fine print.[99] Above all, Nijinska saw her sister-in-law as an outsider, unwilling to join the tribe of artists that was the siblings' birthright.

The Saison Nijinsky marked the end of Nijinska's apprenticeship. Despite its unhappy dénouement, for the first time she understood what it took to run a company, even a small one, and also that she had untapped gifts as a ballet master and répétiteur. Although Nijinsky may have reproached Diaghilev for sacrificing art for money, the Ballets Russes was one of the few organizations of the prewar era willing to underwrite choreographic exploration, even when this entailed numerous hours in the studio. This was not the case of the Maryinsky, as Nijinska well knew, or of the commercial stage. Nijinska may not have been as dead set as her brother against the music hall stage before the Palace engagement; after all, her parents had made their living as popular entertainers. However, after that engagement, she avoided the commercial theater like the plague, even during the 1920s and 1930s, when numerous ballet choreographers found it a welcome source of income. Only at times of great economic hardship—after the Revolution, when she and Kochetovsky danced at a Moscow cabaret, and after she emigrated, when she and a partner danced at a Vienna music hall—did she overcome her profound distaste for commercial work.

Not long after the season ended, Nijinsky left with Romola for Vienna, where their daughter Kyra was born in June. Nijinska and Kochetovsky saw the couple off, and in April returned to St. Petersburg, where Eleonora and Irina, now five months old, awaited them. Nijinska would never see her brother dance again or see him compos mentis. As the train sped across Central Europe during that fabled spring of 1914 before the Great War changed everything, she could not have imagined what lay ahead.

2

Amazon of the Avant-Garde

Nijinska was happy to be back in St. Petersburg. It was the first spring she had spent in the city since 1908, her first white nights since joining Diaghilev. In *Early Memoirs* she evoked the city's beauty, imagining a carriage ride down the Nevsky Prospekt, along the Embankment, and across the bridges, savoring the columned grace of Theater Street and the memory of strolls with Vaslav in the Summer Garden. Home was now 39 Angliiskii Prospekt, a corner building off the Griboiedova Canal, within walking distance of the Maryinsky. The family had moved there in 1912, and it was here that Nijinska lived with her mother, husband, and daughter Irina until they all left for Kiev in 1915. In late June 1914 a letter arrived from Nijinsky announcing Kyra's birth, followed by a cable asking Kochetovsky to come to London to help negotiate future engagements. Oblivious to the momentous events unfolding in the Balkans, Kochetovsky boarded a packet boat to London, only to find that Nijinsky had just left. Kochetovsky spent a few days in the British capital, then boarded what turned out to be the last train through Germany before the border with Russia was closed. By August 2 the unthinkable had happened: Europe had gone to war.[1]

London had whetted Nijinska's appetite for teaching. She sensed that a vital connection existed between daily practice in the studio and the molding of dancers for the stage, that training an artist's mind was as important as training the body, and that the making of a new choreographic culture began in the studio. In Petrograd (as Petersburg had been renamed), she began giving a class to about a dozen women, including Valentina Vilzak, who had danced in the Palace Theatre season. With Nijinsky under house arrest in Budapest and Austria-Hungary at war with Russia, engagements abroad were out of the question. So Nijinska and Kochetovsky looked for work at home. They found jobs for the 1914–1915 season at Narodny Dom—the People's House of the Emperor Nicholas II (to give the theater complex its full name)—which offered opera and drama performances at popular prices. Despite the war, Petrograd's theaters were in full swing. Thirty-five operas were given at Narodny Dom alone during the 1914–1915 season. They ran the gamut from French and Italian warhorses to more than a dozen Russian operas, both "classics" and works by living composers. For a dancer who had spent nearly five years with the Diaghilev company, Narodny Dom was definitely a comedown. The ballet troupe was small and opportunities limited, and few seemed to strive for "contemporary artistic perfection."[2] Petrograd newspapers routinely covered Narodny Dom performances but seldom mentioned the dancers.

By the end of Nijinska's engagement at Narodny Dom the press began to notice her. In May 1915 the magazine *Teatr i iskusstvo* (Theater and Art) singled her out in a divertissement that accompanied the opera *Lakmé*: "the spirited Mme Nijinska brilliantly performed the 'Bacchanale' to the music of Glazunov with Mons. Kochetovsky"—surely a version of Fokine's celebrated concert number for Anna Pavlova and Mikhail Mordkin. In June a review of *Faust* praised her again: "But the heroes of the show were Mons. Kochanovskii (Mephistofeles), whose voice captivates with its bel canto, and Mme. Nijinska (the young ballerina), whose grace and dances provoked rapture in 'Walpurgis Night.'"[3]

During that first year back in Russia, Nijinska choreographed what she called her "first composition,"[4] which became part of the concert repertory that she and Kochetovsky were building. Among her papers is a playbill for one of their concerts—a "Grand Evening of Vocal Music and Ballet"—that almost certainly dates from the couple's early years in Kiev, when the two toured in southern Russia.[5] Most were divertissements they had previously danced at Narodny Dom. One was a number called either *La Tabatière* ("The Snuffbox") or *The Doll*, to music by Liadov, which Nijinska danced for years. There was *Autumn Song*, to Tchaikovsky, a solo that decades later she taught Alicia Markova, and for Kochetovsky, a *Trepak* to Rubinstein and a dance of the Crimean Tatars called *Haytarma*, to Spendiarov. Finally, there was the *Polovtsian Dances*, which they now performed as a duet, with costumes after Anisfeld's designs for the Palace Theatre season. Made for them in Petrograd, these costumes and Nijinska's *Snuffbox* dress, after one of Bakst's designs for *The Fairy Doll* (1903), became part of their growing stock of theatrical material, which also came to include a considerable music library.[6]

Opportunities in Petrograd were limited, and in search of greener pastures as well as a venue where they would have a freer hand to amass the capital for an independent company, the couple accepted an engagement at the Kiev City Theater for the 1915–1916 season. Kochetovsky was hired as a dancer and ballet master, Nijinska as his première danseuse—just like her parents

during the happy years of their partnership. Kochetovsky had to be in Kiev
for pre-season rehearsals no later than August 20, 1915, so the couple packed
up, put the piano, furniture, seven trunks, and two suitcases in storage, and
with Eleonora and Irina, now almost two, set off. His salary was 400 rubles
a month for roughly six months, although the contract could be extended.[7]
Except for a ten-month interlude in Moscow, the remainder of Nijinska's
Russian life would center in Kiev.

Eleonora deplored the move. She had spent years dancing on Russia's provincial stages, given birth to Vaslav in Kiev and to Bronislava in Minsk, and
endured great hardship to put them through school in the Russian capital. To
her dismay, both had left the Imperial Ballet and subsequently the Diaghilev
company; now her stubborn, gifted daughter was dragging her back to the
provinces. Yet Kiev was far from the backwater Eleonora made it out to be.
A city of "breathtaking beauty," with "glittering onion-domed hilltop mon-
asteries, wooded ravines, and spectacular vistas,"[8] the Ukrainian capital was
culturally and socially heterogenous and on its way to becoming a major
modernist center.[9] The Belle Epoque had left its mark on the upper city,
where modern hotels and grand apartment buildings sprouted at the turn
of the century. The newly rebuilt Kiev City Theater, a huge edifice in French
Renaissance style that opened to the public in 1901, was an expression of
bourgeois confidence and ease. The theater and its neighborhood would become the heart of Nijinska's life in Kiev.

In terms of ballet, though, Eleonora was right: as at Narodny Dom, the
ballet troupe at the Kiev City Theater chiefly existed to take part in opera
productions. But the couple had grander ambitions. Kochetovsky's contract
specified that he was to "stage . . . ballets, divertissements, and also classical
and character dances in operas."[10] Within six weeks of taking up their duties,
one of the city's major papers, *Poslednie novosti* [Latest News], noted the
enormous interest that the ballet divertissements had aroused, chiefly because of the "participation of the new prima ballerina Mme. B. Nijinska." The
anonymous critic went on to praise the *Valse Badinage* (to music by Liadov),
which she performed with elegance and "exceptional choreographic humor"
to a packed house.[11] Other divertissements staged by Kochetovsky that year,
almost certainly with help from Nijinska, were the *Bacchanale*; Snowflakes
from *The Nutcracker*, presumably after Lev Ivanov's choreography; and a
piece called *Dreams* to the music of Berlioz.[12] She made a big splash in the
opera *Carmen*, with the *Kiev Theatrical Courier* writing that the "best thing
in the show were the dance episodes of the fourth act with the scintillating,

ardent, and virtuosic prima ballerina B. Nijinska at its center."[13] After the success of these first performances, Nijinska later wrote, "the public esteemed and loved us. . . . Our artistic authority in the . . . theater also rose, which was very important for our aspirations."[14]

At the same time, according to the Ukrainian ballet historian Iurii Stanishevskyi, the new directors "began actively propagating the latest achievements in Russian choreography."[15] With a newly enlarged corps of twenty-four dancers, including three women (Valentina Vilzak, the former Ballets Russes dancer Susanna Puare, and Elena Zhabchinskaia) from Nijinska's class in Petrograd,[16] Nijinska and Kochetovsky offered the Kiev audience a sampling of Fokine's new repertory—*Egyptian Nights*, *Ball in Crinolines*, *In the Moor's Room* (based, respectively, on *Cléopâtre*, *Carnaval*, and Scene 3 of *Petrouchka*), and *The Polovtsian Dances*.[17] The exotic *Egyptian Nights* seems to have enjoyed the greatest success. Writes Stanishevskyi:

> The unusual choreography, which imaginatively combined . . . stylized "Egyptian" movements with classical dance impressed the Kiev audience, and Nijinska's passionate, energy-infused dancing in the role of . . . Tahor was captivating in its emotional power and restraint. Her love-heated duet with Amoun (Kochetovsky), her pained and sorrowful dance before Cleopatra, and the . . . bacchanalia (which had to be repeated more than once by popular demand) were particularly successful.[18]

Artistically, this first season represented a milestone in Kiev, where the Diaghilev repertory was all but unknown. It also established Nijinska as a star with a following. Finally, it inspired the couple to plan "something serious," as Nijinska explained to a school friend, Alexandra Fedorova. "Next season they will even design new scenery for the ballets."[19] Instead of following up successes with adaptations of other Diaghilev works or a full production of *Petrouchka*, they decided to stage *The Little Humpbacked Horse*, with Nijinska dancing the ballerina role of the Tsar Maiden. Even in 1916, this was an old ballet. First choreographed in 1864 by the French choreographer Arthur Saint-Léon, it was one of very few ballets in the Imperial repertory with a Russian theme. The Kiev production was based on Alexander Gorsky's version, except for the technically difficult part of the Tsar Maiden, which retained Petipa's older choreography. Given the company's modest resources, Kochetovsky made cuts and significantly reduced the number of divertissements, but the production and its realization even earned plaudits from Fokine, when he passed through Kiev on a concert tour.[20] In setting the ballet on the Kiev company, Nijinska and Kochetovsky may have wanted to capitalize on the growth in domestic touring by stars from Moscow and Petrograd—a phenomenon already well advanced in the dramatic theater, and a reason for Kiev's growing dynamism as a theatrical center.[21] Tamara Karsavina, for instance, danced in the Kiev production some three months after its premiere, although neither she nor her partner, Kasian Goleizovsky, was greeted with much enthusiasm.[22] Ballet's growing popularity stoked local ambitions. In May 1916 the Kiev correspondent of *Teatr i iskusstvo* reported that "among several local ballet artists, the idea has arisen to create in Kiev a ballet theater along the lines of the capital's Imperial Theaters."[23] Although unmentioned, Nijinska and Kochetovsky must have been among those artists.

For dancers the situation was considerably worse in Kiev than at Narodny Dom. As Nijinska reminisced:[24]

The Kiev [City] Theater was supposed to be the best one, but it was still a provincial theater. Our first impression was that it was a "dream from the theatrical past." The orchestra was excellent and . . . [t]he chorus . . . sang well. There was no stage direction to speak of: the director only pointed out the entrances. . . . The artists rehearsed and agreed among themselves how to sing their arias and act. . . . [Semen] Evenbakh was in charge of stage sets. . . . [W]hen sets were needed for our small ballets and for *The Little Humpbacked Horse*, Evenbakh brought two big albums with numbered photographs each showing a separate detail of a stage set: wings, backdrops, a palace, trees, riverbanks with bushes, a lake; winter—summer—autumn. "Choose [what you need]," he told us. "Write down the numbers, and then tell me what number to put where."

Nijinska and her husband worked as a team. They shared everything—even the choreography seems to have been a joint affair—and they had to fend pretty much for themselves. Together, they built a repertory, music library, and costume collection that became part of their growing capital, assets of an independent company along the lines of the Ballets Russes but choreography-driven and dancer-controlled. Nijinska's recollections offer a glimpse of practices outside the subsidized realm of Russia's state theaters, where dancers and ballet masters were often expected to furnish their own

costumes, music, and even orchestrations. "We tried to make every performance as good as possible," she wrote.

> We ordered all our personal costumes at our own expense—some
> were made after the sketches by [Léon] Bakst, [Alexandre] Benois, and
> [Nicholas] Roerich. . . . We obtained all the orchestral music. By the end
> of our Kiev tenure we had accumulated quite a big library of scores and
> orchestral parts . . .—*Schéhérazade, Islamey, Swan Lake, The Polovtsian
> Dances.* . . . The orchestra score for . . . *The Little Humpbacked Horse* was
> copied from the Imperial Theaters.

As was true throughout the early twentieth-century opera world, dancers
were second-class citizens:

> Prior to our arrival . . . the ballet artists . . . were not allowed in the
> Foyer. . . . The chief conductor didn't conduct the orchestra when a ballet
> was performed; he turned it over to the second conductor. Little by little
> the attitude toward ballet among the opera artists changed dramatically.
> Several would go through their roles with me. It must be said that the public
> and the critics received us very well and esteemed us from the start.

Unsurprisingly, the cultural level of the dancers was low, and Nijinska felt
called upon to instruct them in the basics of their profession:

> Little by little during the opera season . . . I tried to educate . . . the ballet art-
> ists. We did a lot of things that were new for Kiev, in opera divertissements
> and little ballets, and we managed to teach [the artists] not only how to
> dance, but how to do it artistically, and also how to wear costumes and
> make-up appropriately.

Nijinska's efforts did not go unnoticed. Her benefit performance in January
1917, at which she danced *The Little Humpbacked Horse*, was a triumph.
The stage was covered with flowers, and there seemed no end to the gifts.
Among the ovations was one "by her comrades" in recognition of her success
in raising the standard of "ballet art in our theater" during "two seasons of
much effort and work," as one critic wrote. The reviews were ecstatic.[25]
By the start of the 1917–1918 season, however, the couple must have felt it
was time to move on. New opera productions at the Kiev City Theater were at

a standstill, and even Nijinska and Kochetovsky did not stage anything new but merely supervised the existing ballet repertory. The couple was "working mainly for drama and variety theaters, and in their own choreographic studio"—activities that Nijinska omits from her notes and reminiscences— just as she passes over her teaching of expressive movement (plastique) and dance to music, drama, and opera students. There is evidence that she broke her contract with the theater, that Kochetovsky was called up, and that the two were parting in more ways than one.[26] (Nijinska alluded to this tele- graphically in her autobiographical outline: "I see clearly my conjugal life. Break."[27]) And, in all likelihood, she was feeling creatively restive.

***

In August 1917 Nijinsky wrote to his sister asking her to join him in Spain. His life, he tells her, is about to change. When his contract with Diaghilev ended in October, he wrote, "I want to organize my own troupe. . . . Competent people have advised me and will run the business side, but I alone will con- duct the artistic side. My work and that of the artists will be guaranteed by them so that they will earn, and the artists and I will have the opportunity to present work of real art." Now he tells her what she must do:

> You should be with me. It will be easier for you and for me because you will be working with me, and besides you are my sister, and I am your loving brother. We will leave Mama with Irina and Kyra and a governess together in my *dacha* in Switzerland. Once they are settled, it will be easier for us to work, and you will be able to see Sasha from time to time.[28]

With her mother and four-year-old daughter, Nijinska left for Moscow seeking passports and visas for the three of them to join Nijinsky in Spain. However, by the time they arrived, the Bolsheviks had come to power. Elena Malinovskaia, who assumed control of Moscow's newly nationalized, former Imperial Theaters in January 1918, issued the passports, but the French and Spanish consulates denied Nijinska's request for visas.[29]

Although the middle and upper classes were fleeing Moscow for Kiev (a way station for most to emigration), Nijinska stayed put. Kochetovsky was still off the scene, although they remained in touch. On January 3, 1918, she sent him New Year's greetings from Moscow (he was in Kiev) and asks whether he has received her postcards. She couldn't get to Petrograd because there were no tickets. She should get her passport in a few days. She can take 2,000 rubles with her, double the fixed amount of 1,000. She has found good people to help. Someone named Rzsokhina has said that she could arrange a tour of city theaters in Finland and Sweden, and also a very good contract in Vladivostok, except that letters can't get through. She bumped into Margarita Froman, who related that in America Vaslav had made the stupendous sum of $4,500 a week and that his life with Romola was "bad." Then she turns to more personal matters.

> The chaos in my soul is like that in my daily life. With all my heart I wish to be with you, to believe that you can be different, the way my heart sees you; it is hard to be without you because only with you can my faith in you be reborn; without seeing you I know I will lose you through my doubt. Oh, if I could only feel that . . . I have succeeded in creating in you and in me [the truth] that my soul weeps for. . . . How much I want to bring you to the new life.[30]

Later that month Kochetovsky was in Moscow, and he and Nijinska were reconciled. Instead of returning to Kiev, now the capital of an independent Ukraine, they found well-paying jobs dancing at the Yar, a once celebrated cabaret with the finest restaurant in Moscow.[31] During her conversation with Malinovskaia, Nijinska relates, Elena Konstantinovna asked why she wanted to leave "the Soviets." Nijinska explained that it was essential for her to be with her brother, take part in his choreographic researches, and expand her own understanding of dance, ballet, and theater. "There is no need to go abroad," Malinovskaia responded. "Write to Nijinsky and tell him to come to Moscow. All that you have told me is exactly what we need here. . . . Meantime you shall be reorganizing the Government Ballet in the Bolshoi Theatre." The conversation had certainly taken an unexpected turn. "I am flattered . . . but I cannot accept," Nijinska told her. "In art one cannot create and make something new out of something old. What is needed in the theater is new material in the ballet." Malinovskaia: Well, then, find young people. Nijinska: What about the Government artists? Malinovskaia: Let them sell apples in the street. "As it is, we are getting rid of the former Imperial Theaters. The proletariat does not need them." Nijinska would not be persuaded. "All I was interested in was to be with Vaslav and to work by his side."[32]

Assuming that this conversation did take place (there is no record of it in Malinovskaia's voluminous archives), once Kochetovsky was back on the scene, the couple may have decided to stay in Moscow rather than go abroad. After all, no love was lost between the two men, and Nijinsky had excluded Kochetovsky from his invitation. In March the Commissariat of the Third Station of the Meshchanskaia District certified that Kochetovsky and his wife, Bronislava Fominichna Kochetovskaia, were permanent Moscow residents living at 66/68 Meshchanskaia Street. Most likely Kochetovsky's mother and sisters lived there as well, with the newcomers crowding into the family apartment.[33] By April, Nijinska was pregnant.

For Nijinska the months in Moscow proved a transformative experience. It was here that she developed a "passion for the ideas of Leo Tolstoy," became "acquainted with philosophy," and explored "new ideas on the creation of the Artist."[34] A possibly aspirational list suggests the breadth of her reading— works by Plato, Oscar Wilde, Aristotle, Erasmus, Marcus Aurelius, Cesare Lombroso, Byron, and Nietzsche, and several books about theater and toys.[35] And she started to write.[36] The Bronislava Nijinska Collection at the Library of Congress holds multiple versions of her treatise "Movement and the School of Movement." One was published in 1930 in the German dance journal *Schrifttanz*, a somewhat different one in Nancy Van Norman Baer's 1986 exhibition catalogue *Bronislava Nijinska: A Dancer's Legacy*.[37] A foot-note in the *Schrifttanz* version refers to an even earlier work, *The School of Movement (Theory of Choreography)*, published in Kiev in 1920, although a copy of this has yet to be found. In all likelihood, this lost version grew out of the manuscript she called "The School and Theater of Movement 1918," scrawled on more than 100 pages of a "Common Exercise Book." Here, and in a second notebook labeled "B. Nijinska 1918," she laid out her vision of a new kind of dance and dance artist.[38]

The rambling manuscript that Nijinska began writing in Moscow reveals her profound disillusionment with ballet of the late Imperial period. "After finishing the Imperial Ballet School, I spent three years on the Imperial stage and left it without ever having seen any genuine art," she declared.[39] Her chief criticism of Russia's "old" ballet, exemplified by the works of Marius Petipa, was its emphasis on the virtuoso technique originating in Italy that had transformed ballet into a display of female bravura dancing. "The art of dance is no longer an art," she asserted, "it is acrobatism in various forms" (43). Instead of expanding the palette of movement, ballet masters "took the basic movements . . . and started to . . . complicate them" (34), adorning them with tricks like fouetté turns and "lifts with the female dancers in the most unnatural poses" (45). As a consequence, "genuine, pure dance was forgotten;

everything was now built upon the 'school,' and exercises were passed off as dance. All expression disappeared" (44 insert).

By now, Nijinska had grown sharply critical of Fokine, an erstwhile hero through whose works she had honed her own artistic identity. She decries the influence of Isadora Duncan, which led him to reject technique and embrace only the "beauty of form." Seeking to bring greater "truth" and "accuracy of style" to ballet, enriching it with "real-life movements," he ended up imitating "movements we know from other art forms" (13–14). Although Fokine received the brunt of her criticism, Nijinska also mentions Alexander Gorsky, a Moscow choreographer who worked along similar lines at the Bolshoi and, like Fokine, fell under Duncan's spell:

> They understood that something was ... wrong in choreography. ... So they looked to history, ... and everything turned out to be very clear. Tutus were wrong. If it's Greece, there should be chitons. As for high legs and turns on pointe: the bas-reliefs show something very different. ... (I used to be among the admirers of the new style and was so carried away that I even created in it.) ... And, so, in the new "choreographic dramas" and "choreographic tableaux" they try to replicate the "real" Egypt or Greece, the 1840s, and Romanticism. And the better the imitation, the greater their delight, because it differs absolutely from the old classical dance. (30–33)

Nijinska calls the "seemingly 'new' dances" "a corpse of the old art" (47).

The new art, by contrast, was exemplified by contemporary painting. Nijinska writes at length about this, and it is clearly the source of her most cogent ideas, the spark that lit her imagination. Nijinska's language echoes uncannily that of Kazimir Malevich, who argued for "the supremacy of pure feeling in creative art" and for the need to abandon the objective world. "Pictorial art," wrote Nijinska,

> must cast aside the naturalism that enchains it. ... In an artist's canvas we should feel ... the power of his idea and ... the mood he seeks to convey. ... We don't need images of a human body or flowers, [n]o matter how they are painted. ... I want to approach a picture and see only a symphony of colors. (19–21)

She drew analogies with movement, viewing the use of color and line in contemporary painting as a model for a new kind of dance. "One must use movement like drawing, like colors. All colors are beautiful; all lines are beautiful" (16). And elsewhere: "Every movement is a sound in our future symphony" (17).

Language such as this, equating expression in one art with that in another, makes clear Nijinska's absorption of the symbolist idea of synaesthesia. She does not cite her sources, but the idea circulated widely in the early years of the twentieth century. It was accepted as an article of faith by members of Diaghilev's early circle. Similar ideas also circulated in the literature influenced by Emile Jaques-Dalcroze, whose theories of gesture and their correlation with rhythm enjoyed wide currency among progressive-minded theatrical directors and theorists. Nijinska does not mention Dalcroze, but she is clearly intrigued by the theoretical possibilities of Dalcrozian thought generally—the idea of the artist as a transformative agent, the belief in gesture as a synthesizing force and in rhythm, Dalcroze's core idea about the music-dance relationship.[40] However, instead of a tight connection between the two, Nijinska pleaded for the independence of the dance. Why, she asked, "does choreography depend on music? Why is the choreographer always subject to the composer, illustrating the music instead of creating" (38)? Voicing an idea embraced by modern dance choreographers of the 1920s and 1930s, Nijinska argued for writing the music of a dance after—rather than before—it was choreographed, and ideally from a choreographic score. This, she explained, would free both the choreographer and the composer—the choreographer, because he no longer had to "force" his work into an ill-fitting piece of music; the composer, because he no longer had to create a "danceable" score (39). The choreographer would thus "come to a complete understanding with the composer," enabling them to create a truly "unified work" (40).

A strong utopian current runs through Nijinska's treatise. Again and again she equates "creativity" and "spirit," seeking, like Malevich, to "[abort] all reminiscences of the material world" and "speak in a cosmic language."[41] "The future," she exults, "is the triumph of the spirit. In art the spirit alone must shine in everything" (11). For Nijinska, spirit—*dukh*—has the potential to transform society at large, to create a new man and a revolution of the cultural order as dramatic as the political changes taking place around her. "Only when the spirit merges into culture will there be happiness. . . . If the spirit is highly developed, one won't need the framework of socialism" (10). This is the sole reference to the revolutionary events transforming the Russia she knew, as piece by piece the tsarist state was dismantled and a new, unknown country struggled to be born. No wonder the idea of transformation was uppermost in Nijinska's mind, the need to awaken the individual to a realization of his own spiritual potential—the "divine spark" and "beauty" that existed in everyone (8–9). In her longing for transformation on a well-nigh universal scale and in the cosmic aspiration of her thinking, however roughly expressed, one senses the appeal of ideas associated with theosophy and P. D. Uspensky's fourth dimension, so popular among artists of the late Imperial period.[42]

This belief in the spiritual dimension of art only heightened Nijinska's disgust for the meretriciousness of the ballet world. Intoxication with fame, celebrity, and the cult of the new was turning ballet into a marketplace, with dancers transformed into "salesmen" (48), "lackeys" (51), "speculators" (57), "cocottes" (51)—some of the choicer terms Nijinska reserved for artists who compromised and sold out. ("Cocottes" was also the word Nijinsky used in his diary for prostitutes.)[43] "Nobody wants just to create" (29). Again and again, she returns to her vision of the new "educated" dancer, an artist who "truly loves her art" and uses it to "convey profound meaning." "I want our art to become equal to the other arts as it used to be in ancient Greece" (57).

The treatise ends with Nijinska's credo—her wish list for the future. The list is too long to quote in its entirety, but the individual statements, like the slogans of the day, have a naked power. One can imagine them on the walls of the studio she had used the treatise to conceptualize, urging on the dancers as they sweated through class, prodding them to discover their own "divine spark" (8) and the "spiritual pleasure" (2) of art.

> I want the art of dance to live again.
> I want senseless acrobats to become creators again.
> I want cocottes of art to disappear. . . .
> Professionals should be destroyed. . . .
> A creator should live only through his creation . . . not the intoxication
> of . . . the crowd. . . .
> If creativity is my need, then my happiness is in creativity. (94–95)

***

A catalyst for this remarkable burst of creative and intellectual activity was almost certainly the artist Alexandra Exter. Like Nijinska, she spent the war years in Kiev, although the two first met in Moscow in 1917. Exter was at the height of her creative powers, a leading member of the Russian avant-garde. She had recently launched a spectacular career as a stage designer with the director Alexander Tairov's Kamerny Theater in Moscow. Indeed, what brought Exter to Moscow in the fall of 1917 was Tairov's production of *Salomé*, a version of Oscar Wilde's play in which she and the director did away with wings, painted backdrops, and scenic illusions, replacing them with platforms, stairs, curtains, and costumes that not only moved with the performers but were also fundamentally abstract.[44] Her vision of a fully kinetic stage clashed with the painterly approach of the colorists associated with the early Ballets Russes. Exter demanded that movement infuse all aspects of the production. "Free movement," she asserted, "is the fundamental element of the theatrical act."[45]

In *Notes of a Director* (1921), Tairov laid out a number of ideas that echo Nijinska's theoretical approaches and emerging choreographic practice: the idea of "synthetic theater," "fus[ing] *organically* the various scene arts . . . to produce a single *monolithic* work" (54); the idea of "*emotional form*," or "form saturated with creative emotion" (52); the need for a "new *master-actor*," trained in the multiple disciplines of drama, ballet, and opera (54). Finally, he underscored the importance of rhythm: "This is the first and chief requirement," he wrote (87).[46] Movement was incorporated into every aspect of Tairov's theater, just as it was highlighted by Nijinska in her theoretical writings and in the name of her school ("School of Movement"). Movement, she declared, was the primary element in dance, what "gives life to dance" and "enables the dance to affect the spectator. Rhythm lives only in movement."[47]

No matter how exhilarating, life in Moscow was harrowing. In his diary, later published as *Cursed Days*, the writer Ivan Bunin recorded scenes, images, and impressions that must have been all too familiar to Nijinska during the harsh winter months of 1918: once prosperous members of society selling their belongings on street corners; Bolsheviks with revolvers in their belts; potholes in the filthy streets; demonstrations, banners, and posters of a newly visible proletariat; terrible cold and hunger, as fuel grew scarce and the daily bread ration fell below a quarter of a pound.[48] In April the anarchists took to the streets, terrorizing the city and committing murder, robbery, and arson, until they were gunned down and arrested by the Cheka, which lit bonfires in the streets burning their literature.[49] Several times Nijinska collapsed in the street from exhaustion.[50] It was hard to eat for two in a starving city. So, like Bunin and so many others, the Nijinska-Kochetvosky family decided to head south. By mid-October 1918 the couple was back in Kiev, where food was more plentiful and where Nijinska would be in a "friendly atmosphere"—as she put it—to "begin" her new work.[51]

**

When Nijinska returned to Kiev, the city was alive with political and cultural change. The Russian Revolution had destroyed the monarchy but also hastened the collapse of the Russian Empire by unleashing long-suppressed nationalisms. Massive rallies took place, leading to the creation of the Central Rada (as the Ukrainian Parliament was called) and subsequently the Ukrainian National Republic. To counterbalance the influence of Russian culture, the new government proclaimed national-cultural autonomy for minorities, which included Poles as well as Jews and Ukrainians. Ukrainian and Jewish literary and artistic expression experienced a renaissance, and organizations like the Kultur-Lige, which promoted Yiddish culture, and the Molodyi or Young Theater, which performed classic and experimental plays in Ukrainian, flourished.[52] The columns of *Teatr i iskusstvo* record the day-to-day changes taking place in the city's theatrical life—the pressures for Ukrainian-language theater, the appearance of Jewish theater groups, and the growing number of theaters presenting programs of "miniatures" or "small forms," variety, farce, and even "adult" fare. Crowded with refugees from Moscow and Petrograd, the city had a thriving music and theater scene that included Tairov's Kamerny Theater, Nikita Balieff's "Bat Theater" from Moscow, director Nikolai Evreinov at the Grand Miniature Theater, and both a ballet studio and a ballet company headed by Mikhail Mordkin installed at the City Theater.[53] Asked about the goals of contemporary Ukrainian art at the All-Ukrainian Congress of the Representatives of Art Organizations, Exter responded, "Having as much free art as possible and as little provincialism as possible."[54]

In Kiev, Nijinska gravitated to Exter's studio. A center of the "jubilant experimentation"[55] that characterized the Revolutionary era in the city, the studio was a gathering place for artists, such as Vadim Meller, Simon Lissim, Nissan Shifrin, Boris Aronson, and Pavel Tchelitchev, who would revitalize stage design in Russia and abroad. It had become what the Exter scholar Georgy Kovalenko describes as a "creative club," open to everyone, with a production department that accepted commissions for stage design and graphic projects, and weekly lectures by writers, directors, actors, and critics who had fled to Kiev from Moscow and Petrograd that were sometimes announced in the press. Kievans also gave talks, including the poet Benedikt Livshits (whom Nijinska came to know quite well) and Nijinska herself.[56] What an education those lectures must have been, and how much it must have meant for her to be recognized for what she was in the process of becoming, a theorist of a new dance art.

However, Exter's days in Kiev were numbered: by mid-January 1919 she had fled to Odessa to escape the approaching Bolsheviks. She returned to Kiev in 1920 and in May (when the Poles had temporarily occupied the city) reopened her studio. Many of her old friends had gone, but Vadim Meller and his wife Nina Genke (also an artist) remained; she also met up with the theater director Les Kurbas. "They told her," Kovalenko writes,

> that the only interesting thing in town was a set of productions being staged by Bronislava Nijinska's *School of Movement*. And not only the productions themselves, but everything that took place at this "school." . . . Nijinska's . . . performances struck Exter . . . with their strong-willed direction, with their unusual choreographic language, and with their . . . expressiveness. But most of all she was struck by [their] adherence . . . to many of the principles of contemporary plastic arts—or at least those to which Exter herself subscribed.[57]

Exter was thus at hand during the months leading up to the opening of Nijinska's School of Movement, and during the six-month period in 1920 that overlapped with the creation of Nijinska's first abstract works. The two did not formally collaborate. (They did so later after both had emigrated.) However, as Nijinska explained to the art critic Andrei B. Nakov in the early 1970s, Exter "often came to my studio and saw my work there. . . . I discussed my projects with her, but . . . [a]t that time I worked with the artists Vadim Meller and Nissan Shifrin."[58] A note from Exter, one of the few private communications that accompanied Nijinska into emigration, suggests that a project may have been in the offing, but that the choreographer demurred, perhaps fearing the impact of Exter's formidable artistic personality. The note is dated 1920, when Exter was back in Kiev:

> I came by to tell you that I decided to go to Moscow and then come back to work with you. Only if you need me, of course. I'm excited about working with you. . . . Bronislava Fominichna, I will write to you from Moscow and will await your decision regarding my return.[59]

In another letter, written shortly after she emigrated, Exter fondly recalled their days in Kiev, adding that when she was working in Moscow, she "talked a lot about you to [Konstantin] Stanislavsky. He dreamed of inviting you and your studio to Moscow."[60]

***

On February 10, 1919 (New Style), Nijinska opened her studio at 21 Fondukleevskaia Street, only a few doors away from Exter's at number 27 and just across the street from the City Theater, soon to be nationalized and renamed the Karl Liebnicht National Opera Theater. The building was elegant: Prince Trubetskoy and members of the wealthy Vichnevsky family had residences there, and the studio, possibly in a converted ballroom, had high ceilings and even a chandelier. (Nijinska herself lived in a rambling six-room apartment at 17 Bolshaia Podvalnaia in an Art Nouveau neighborhood on the other side of the theater.)[61] She called her studio the School of Movement, *Shkola dvizhenii* in Russian, and it opened only three weeks after the birth on January 20 of her second child, Lev, or Levushka, as he was familiarly known.[62] The name of the school came from the title of her 1918 treatise, and the choice of language was significant: Nijinska's school was about "movement," not "ballet" or even "dance."

In fact, Nijinska's curriculum differed significantly from that of other ballet schools. It offered no pointe, partnering, or variations classes, that is, classes designed to instill mastery of ballet technique beyond an elementary level while teaching the codified forms of ballet repertory. Instead, its course of study was intended to develop a well-rounded, contemporary dancer, interested in creating dances as well as developing corporeal skill. In 1919 there were eleven students each in the beginning, intermediate, and advanced classes; by 1920 the number had jumped to twenty in each group, including eight boys. Classes began at 9 in the morning and lasted until 11 at night, with all three groups meeting together in the evening.[63] In addition, the School offered movement classes for actors and opera singers. After years of watching singers and observing how they correlated gesture with sound, she developed a system of movements that helped the many singers who came to her for lessons to "open" and amplify their voices.[64]

Nijinska's 1918 treatise, in which she envisioned the School, laid out a curriculum embracing both practical and theoretical subjects. Classical dance led the practical side, followed by character dance, style in movement, mime and expression, and free movement. In other words, along with the mechanics of movement, students learned how to generate and manipulate it, while developing compositional or choreographic strategies. The theoretical subjects included music and theory of music, aesthetics, history of art and theater, ethics, "discussions" (never spelled out), drawing and painting, and the recording of dances in notation.[65] This was not a curriculum likely to produce ballet professionals. But then the Nijinska of the Moscow and Kiev years had no interest in training professionals in the conventional sense; she wanted to educate her students in the art of dance as a contemporary practice. Few of the students had dance backgrounds; most were art or gymnasium students or aspiring actors who gravitated to Nijinska's studio in the creative explosion that followed the Revolution: they were cultured in a way that music-hall or opera-ballet dancers weren't. Some went on to professional dance careers, including Anna ("Niusia") Vorobieva, her "best student" who danced for Nijinska in the West and became the ballerina of the Sofia Opera, and several men—Yanek Khoer [Jan/Jean Hoyer], Cheslav Khoer [Tcheslaw Hoyer], Zhenia [Eugène] Lapitsky [Lapitzky], and Sergei [Serge/"Seriozha"] Ung[u]er—who joined the Ballets Russes and also danced in her later companies. Many became visual artists, including a group of Moscow women who renewed contact with Nijinska in the late 1960s.[66] However, despite the emphasis on education, performance remained uppermost in Nijinska's mind, and within a year of its founding, the studio gave its first public performances, with a repertory of her own original works or adaptations by her of existing ones. Here, one sees very clearly Nijinska's affinity with the era's "free dancers," for whom choreographic invention at least partly depended on developing new corporeal techniques.

In March 1919, Nijinska wrote to her brother in Switzerland. Only the draft survives; the letter itself went astray. She tells him that it has been over a year since she has heard from him, although a letter has come from Romola's mother, urging Nijinska to join him in Switzerland. However, everything has changed, she writes.

> We are locked in again, and there is no chance for us to escape. . . . I am not going to write about the things we have been through—it will take too long and worry you, but we have gotten used to everything and exist knowing that there is only today to live. We have a newborn son, Levushka, who is already six weeks old. Despite these difficult times I am happy that I was able to give birth to a child, and I am even happier that I have a son.

She is also happy about what she calls her "spiritual life," what she has come to understand about art, and the School of Movement.

> I am now fully preoccupied with the school that I have established, which brings no monetary profit . . . but . . . many of the things I need for my happiness and for the important undertaking I have started. The main goal of the school is to create an entirely new breed of dancers . . . for whom art is an essential need and an expression of their spiritual state. . . . There exists a school of "classical dance," but I have a school from which every human movement emanates. . . . I am in charge of the school's entire curriculum, except for the theory of music. I spend five hours a day at the school, running home to feed Levushka, and the rest of the time I prepare for courses. My school is the "program" of my life.[67]

***

On February 3, 1919—a week before the School opened its doors—the Bolsheviks took Kiev, bringing to an end both the Ukrainian National Republic and its experiment in multi-ethnic democracy. Martial law was declared, and Nijinska, like those who chose to remain in the city, found herself swept up by political events beyond her control. Nijinska devoted herself to teaching, the creation of her first works to shake off Fokine's influence, and securing a position for herself and her school in the changing political climate. According to Marina Kurinnaia, "she allied herself with the Soviet regime and was fairly active in supporting its reform of the region's theater (possibly with the aim of preserving her own ballet studio)." In February 1919, Nijinska "became a member of the Central Committee for the Nationalization of the Kiev Opera and a member of the City Art Soviet"—possibly SARABIS, the Art Workers Union she mentions in her notes. "She took part in concerts and formed the First Mobile Concert Troupe to introduce Red Army men to art in Kiev."[68] She must have joined in spirit if not in deed the artists of Exter's former studio, including her friends Meller and Shifrin, who transformed the streets of Kiev into a carnival of modern art on May Day 1919, covering buildings and streetcars with posters and banners.[69] It was a thrilling time to be a young artist. "Every kind of art began to flourish," recalled the film director Grigory Kozintsev: "Innumerable committees . . . discussed projects for producing all the great classical plays of the world, for organizing popular festivals, and for decorating the squares in honour of the first of May. Theatre studios and art studios proliferated. Everyone took to art with passion, and with passion people taught it."[70]

By contrast with Nijinska's earlier projects, the School was very much her own. Her name was writ large on the opening announcement, and she taught all the important subjects, while Kochetovsky taught character dance and was available to stage dances for schools. Maybe he was bored; maybe he felt that his wife was turning into one of those "Amazons" transforming the landscape of the Soviet visual arts and theater design, working all hours, serving on committees, and generally neglecting him.[71] In any event he began to stray, and in the summer of 1919 she threw him out. She had an "ungovernable temper and . . . was extremely jealous," he told the author of a wildly unreliable biography written years later when he had settled in Texas. Suspecting an affair, Nijinska walked into his dressing room unannounced, found the other woman there, and scratched him from the face to the waist, drawing blood.[72] He took off for Odessa (which the Bolsheviks had occupied in April) and didn't write for weeks. Then in July he landed a job as ballet master at the Odessa City Theater and started getting concert work. There was only one snag: he needed music. So, on July 25, 1919, he swallowed his pride and wrote her a long, rambling letter. He can't imagine working without her and still hopes for a miracle. He misses the children, and when he looks at her photograph, something "tightens in his throat." Then he comes to his real purpose.

> Bronichka, please find a way . . . to send me musical scores, the more the better. Most importantly, "The Little Humpbacked Horse" [which he had agreed to stage] and folk dances. . . . Everyone here is looking forward to your tour. I assured them that you will come . . . as soon as we stage the ballets and fix communication. Bronichka, please send the scores with someone trustworthy; otherwise I will run aground.

Finally, he promises to turn over a new leaf. "I've lived only for myself until now; it is terrible to admit it, but it's true." He pleads with her to forgive him.[73] There is no indication that Nijinska ever sent him the music, went to Odessa, or forgave him. He never saw his son again and his daughter only after she had settled in California in the 1940s. As for Nijinska, she was now the sole support of her family and the sole director of the enterprise they had dreamed of building together.

Late in 1919, Nijinska returned to the big stage. She had agreed to mount *The Little Humpbacked Horse* at the Kiev City Theater and dance her old role of the Tsar-Maiden. She hated the prospect of doing it and only agreed because of the money—10,000 rubles for the staging and 4,000 for each performance. Like *The Nutcracker* today, *The Little Humpbacked Horse* was a popular ballet, and the theater wanted it for Christmas. She had been invited by the entire "comradeship," although she feared that when rehearsals started, some of the old-timers—like the Polish ballet master Anton Romanovsky, whom she and Kochetovsky had replaced in 1915—would stir up trouble. "I don't know how I'll manage," she wrote to Nina, a former student who had just left for Odessa and emigration. "I will rehearse from 10 in the morning to 2 [at the theater], then go to the School. I don't know how soon . . . I can do my own work."[74] She talks excitedly about a new group of solos—she calls them "my sad nocturnes"—that she wants to "take . . . to the stage." Otherwise, she is despondent. "For two days now the city has been empty," she writes. "Everything closes at 5; everything dies. . . . They are surrendering the city," which probably refers to the retaking of Kiev by the Red Army on December 17. (The "White" forces of General Anton Denikin had seized the Ukrainian capital from the Bolsheviks the previous September.)[75] Civil war was raging, and by the time it ended in 1920, Kiev had changed hands more than a dozen times.

Despite the devastation, it was a busy time for Nijinska. In her diary, she mentions that Nissan Shifrin was doing the scenery and costumes for *Petrouchka* (December 29, 1919); she also mentions him on lists of students, artists, and friends associated with the School of Movement.[76] Jewish, like so many of Exter's students, Shifrin was active in the Kultur-Lige's Art Section and designed scenery and costumes for the organization's theatrical studio, one of several where Nijinska taught.[77] In a 1973 interview, Shifrin recalled that at the beginning of 1920 one of the city's Jewish theaters decided to organize "a concert—a children's New Year's party." "One of the numbers was a scene from Stravinsky's ballet *Petrouchka* staged by the wonderful ballerina Bronislava Nijinska. I did the decorations." Petrouchka was played by her student Jan (Yanek) Hoyer, while another student, Sergei (Seriozha) Unger, played the Moor. She thought both were superb. *Petrouchka* led to another project with Shifrin: *Egyptian Nights*. Nijinska had previously staged the ballet with Kochetovsky; now she was doing her own version. By February she was in rehearsals, and Shifrin happily immersed in the study of ancient Egypt. But nothing came of the project.[78]

Nijinska started keeping a diary when she was eighteen.[79] By 1919 it was a habit. On December 27 of that year she began a fresh notebook. Nijinska's plain, straightforward prose ushers us into an inner life far from explosions, shattered glass, and shellfire, where the pursuit of a utopian vision of art in the studio was as empowering as the struggle of ideologies taking place in the streets.

27 December (Old Style) 1919, Kiev:

> It's my birthday. I woke up tired: all night I was sewing the costume, painting, and embroidering. It's not a "new" costume, but made from what I had. Still, it [came out] very well. . . . The students at my school are so touching. Everybody celebrated my birthday. I knew they loved me, but still it was very moving. . . . To please them I danced several new sketches. Some I danced very badly—I don't have the necessary new technique yet, plus I'm not used to the stiff new costume. The ones that didn't come out right I danced again, and the second time it was better, clearer. . . . As always, I couldn't sleep after my dances.[80]

The return to professional stage work in 1920—or "theater," as Nijinska called it, with all its negative connotations of "dust" and money—was a rude shock. As she wrote after a performance in early January: "There was no good pianist for me, and everything went so badly. No inspiration, no creativity. I felt like I was in a marketplace" (5 January 1920). During the weeks that followed, Nijinska took part in a number of concert performances—or "choreographic evenings," as they were called. The programs have not survived, but brief mentions appeared in the press. Most seem to have been solo rather than group concerts, with Nijinska drawing on the repertory she had been developing since 1914.

That winter a major change occurred in the status of the School of Movement. On February 1 the school performed for a "commission," and although Nijinska never gets more specific, this was clearly an official body, because afterward "they offered to subsidize the school" and "started to fuss over me" (1 February 1920). Five days later the School gave its first public performance. "The audience liked the whole thing very much," she commented in her diary (6 February 1920). A repeat performance at the Merchants Assembly Hall, a popular venue for classical music concerts, was a "huge success. Everybody was there" (7 February 1920). During the third week of February, Nijinska and the School were busy performing at clubs around Kiev for the "Week for the Front and Transport"—a reminder of the civil war that continued to rage in south Russia and Ukraine.[81] Although Nijinska doesn't say, the subsidy probably entailed food and firewood as well as performance opportunities. She planned more ambitious works—Scriabin's *Poem of Ecstasy*, Mussorgsky's *Night on Bald Mountain* (which she ultimately choreographed for Diaghilev), and a piece called *Firework* [Feierverk] (10 February 1920).

Another big performance was given on June 4 at the former City Theater. Outside, the Bolshevik forces were closing in on the Poles, who had occupied the city since May and would evacuate it a week later. With its familiar numbers—*Demons*, the Chopin *Sketches*, a suite of dances from the second act of *Swan Lake*, excerpts from *Petrouchka* and the *Polovtsian Dances*, and concluding with an unfinished sketch to Liszt's Twelfth Rhapsody—Nijinska's program must have seemed like a breath of normalcy.[82] She recorded the occasion in her diary:

> The day before yesterday was my performance: my children danced the *Sketches* and Liszt's *Twelfth Rhapsody*. So much energy, so much joy, so much me in it (6 June 1920).

Wrote a critic for the newspaper *Kievskii den'* [Kiev Day]:

> Mme. Nijinska is still as good as before: her interpretations of *The Doll* and *Petrouchka* are excellent. Her studio has also made great progress since it performed at the Merchants' Assembly Hall. A large audience (which today is a rare event) loudly cheered the artist. In the audience were representatives of the American Red Cross—Major B[ruce] Muhler (Vice President of the American Red Cross in Poland), Captain Ch[arles] Phillips, and Lieutenant Hall.[83]

According to Marina Kurinnaia, the School of Movement had a showing two or three times a month at the chief city theater. They performed with "invariable success" and "enjoyed the greatest popularity and authority."[84]

***

In addition to working with Nissan Shifrin during her years in Kiev, Nijinska also collaborated with the artist Vadim Meller. Older than Shifrin, he too was a member of Exter's studio, and like Nijinska had spent several years in Western Europe. Meller and his wife, Nina Genke (whose sister Margarita was married to Shifrin), became good friends of Nijinska, and they corresponded with her after she left Kiev.[85] Much of the iconographic evidence of Nijinska's activity in Kiev comes from Meller's images of her. Usually identified as costume designs, these large, striking paintings hung in Nijinska's studio, saturating it with impressions of her new dances as interpreted by a modernist artist.

Like Meller's images, the solos that Nijinska began to choreograph for herself in 1919 were highly stylized and semi-abstract. In her diary she seldom refers to them by title, but generically as *eskizy*—"sketches" or "studies"— sometimes identifying them by the composer of the music. Like Isadora Duncan and a generation of female recitalists, Nijinska used the solo form to find her individual voice as an artist, give form to her creative strivings, and tap into her subjectivity. In January 1920 she began work on a Japanese samurai solo that she had wanted to do for a long time. The dance was inspired by Japanese prints, although what she was after was not the re-creation of their style, but "a deep understanding" of it. The challenge, given the prevailing shortages, was getting felt "to make big thick sandals so the feet would seem almost cubic" (2 January 1920).

One of Meller's most spectacular images of her depicts a figure with the bellicose gesture and weight of a samurai. Called *Fear*, the work represents her body as an interplay of angles and curves, sculptural in its volume, with an oval for her head, platform clogs for feet, and triangles shooting from her center. The emphasis is on movement—a foot lifted in the middle of a heavy stamping motion, an arm extended straight from the shoulder like a sword. The torso presses along the diagonal, even as it remains anchored in a deep, angular plié. The colors are deep, and the surrounding blackness creates a feeling of menace. Other images are lighter. In *Mephisto Valse* she stands in semi-profile, with her face looking left and her body facing right, a stance that creates both a twist in the upper body and the bas relief effect that Alexandra Smirnova-Iskander remembered years later. This effect, evident in Nijinska's oldest extant ballet, *Les Noces*, recalls the two-dimensionality of her brother's *L'Après-midi d'un Faune*, just as the weighted movement in *Fear* invokes the primitivism of his *Sacre du Printemps*. Again the body seems caught in motion, swiveling back as the right leg pushes forward, underscoring the drama of the directional shift. As in other Meller designs, panels mask the upper body—geometric pieces in sunset yellows and sky blues, possibly the colors of a layered tunic, although dressmaking notes are absent.

In Kiev, Nijinska changed not only what she danced but how she danced. She abandoned whatever ballerina aspirations she may once have harbored.

"I am not a . . . ballerina," she wrote to Diaghilev after an altercation in the early 1920s, not even a "second-rate ballerina." But, she added, speaking of herself in the third person, "Nijinska is an exceptional talent, something special."[86] That something special emerged during her years in Kiev. Uncoupling sex and gender, she transformed their representation both in performance and in choreography. In her 1918 treatise, Nijinska argued that all movements, even those deemed "ugly and unaesthetic," could be beautiful if "dressed in creativity." Just as tellingly, they were not gender-specific:

> I don't want the conventions of "proper" and "improper" to exist for the female dancer. Every movement, if it's new, is a find. So we should do somersaults, headstands, climb trees, jump, clown. Every movement is a sound in our future symphony.[87]

In early 1920 when she contemplates doing the *Polovtsian Dances*, she imagines staging it "as Vatsa did" (2 January 1920), referring to Nijinsky's 1914 version, in which the Polovtsian Girl danced alone surrounded by men. However, Nijinska's conception of the central figure—a role intended for herself—accentuates female power and eroticism. "She walks, dances above them," she wrote. "They are beneath all the time—timid, devoted, scared, desirous, hot and numb in front of her, big and strong" (2 January 1920). The conception looks back to the Chosen Maiden's solo in *Le Sacre du Printemps* and forward to the central conceit of *Bolero* (1928), a ballet that she later choreographed for Ida Rubinstein and also danced herself. Abandoning the extremes of gender embedded in pre-Revolutionary ballet, she created a new female hero—powerful, unsexed, Uranian—a woman who danced alone. It was this new woman whom Meller captured in his images and whom her friends remembered long after she left for the West.[88]

During Nijinska's years in Kiev, ideas for new works often came to her in dreams. "Creativity is 'splashing,' giving life, driving away sleep," she noted at one point (29 December 1919). And a few days later, "Last night I woke up as if from an electric shock. New thoughts and feelings were filling me. It seemed I would see something new again and go further" (2 January 1920). In May, "All of a sudden I was awakened while I was creating, and I saw that everything was foreign" (25 May 1920). Again, almost a year later: "Something is flickering in my ill brain. Is it delirium or is something creative being born? Where am I flying to?" (2 April 1921). The first time she mentioned *Firework* [Feierverk]—a title reminiscent of Stravinsky's *Feu d'artifice*, although she doesn't mention a composer—she imagined a background of "frantically changing colors" (13 January 1920). A month later she described the ballet to one of her students:

> Pati sat with me for the second day until 6 in the morning. I told her about my Firework. I invented the orchestra. I recounted it absolutely clearly. I want everything to move like a mechanism across the eyes. There is a dim light, and a background that is constantly changing, and by changing it somehow reveals now the hands, now the feet. Shafts of light, a fury of movement in the music, the scenery, the light. The bodies on top spill down. . . . In the orchestra, brasses, woodwinds, and double basses. (10 February 1920)

She also told Pati about *Poem of Ecstasy*, which began in darkness, with a stream of floating light and a group of massed dancers moving forward on a diagonal. Blackness, splashes of gold, a sigh—"Further I still don't know." She thought about eliminating the human figure, using only color, light, and sound, or possibly a dark panel (an idea not unlike Giacomo Balla's futurist light show to Stravinsky's *Fireworks* for the Ballets Russes a few years earlier), but also imagined bodies inching forward caught like spiders in a web (10 February 1920). She saw the movement in *Mephisto Valse* as aerial rather than heavy (unlike the *Rhapsody* sketches). The ballet opens in darkness, with Mephisto appearing in a flash of blinding light. The dancers come to life, but not by their own volition. Everything happens because of Mephisto. He brings life, light, and bewitchment (1 September 1920). Nijinska spent most of September 1920 working on the new ballet. By the end of the month, she noted in her diary,

> [t]he sketch for the Mephisto scenery is almost ready. It's not yet what I want. I've never painted in oil; I'm not good at holding brushes. [But] the idea of what I want to achieve is already a lot. A real artist, a master, will understand what I want. . . . A sketch in pencil already exists also. (26 September 1920)

Meller ultimately designed the ballet. However, Nijinska had a very clear idea of what she wanted, and here, as on many other occasions, sketched it out. Some drawings may represent choreographic ideas, especially the movement of groups through space. Others look like constructivist doodles. The visual aspect of her imagination and her ability to collaborate with painters on an equal footing because she understood the language of color and visual form gave her work from the beginning an artistic unity that transcended the purely choreographic. She was an artist of the theater, not simply a dancemaker, and she controlled everything that took place in her "house."

Although solos were the driving force of Nijinska's creativity during these years, she also choreographed group works. Several were scenes from Fokine ballets, such as *Petrouchka*, *Egyptian Nights*, and the *Polovtsian Dances*. In addition, she staged excerpts from the nineteenth-century repertory, including ensemble dances from the second act of *Swan Lake* (with a "variation" to interpolated music by Chopin performed by Anna Vorobieva and a male dancer named Griunvald), *The Little Humpbacked Horse*, and the Puss in Boots number from *The Sleeping Beauty*, again set to the music of Chopin (instead of Tchaikovsky) and titled *Masks*.[89]

She also choreographed a number of original group works. Among the earliest and most important was *Demons*, a work for five women intended to produce "the sensation of standing before an enormous insect."[90] She first mentions the piece in late January 1920 when she was absorbed in the final preparations for the first school concert where it almost certainly premiered. (By the following June a critic included it among the program's "familiar" dances.[91]) In her diary she allowed herself a rare moment of praise. "My Demons are so good," she wrote. "Everybody was enthusiastic" (27[?] January 1920). The ensemble was quite large. Oleg Stalinskii remembered it as being divided into two groups that moved with "intertwined bodies" and created the effect of "winding worms."[92] In a later interview with the French critic Fernand Divoire, Nijinska spoke at length about *Demons*, emphasizing its rejection of mimetic expressivity in favor of dance gesture. "Emotion," she told him,

> is in the rhythm, in the lines of the gestures, not in the grimace.... The mass must not be a collection of individuals, but must form one thing endowed with *one* life. In this choreographic mass, one should be able to give birth to as many nuances as exist in the musical mass of an orchestra. Each group has a life; together the groups exist in harmony like notes of the music. And each group places its note in the overall composition.[93]

The large-scale work Nijinska choreographed to Liszt's Twelfth Rhapsody marked an even greater breakthrough than *Demons*. In her diary she described it as "completely abstract" (27 April 1920), in line with her dictum "there should be no 'librettism' in theater" (14 March 1921). (Or, as she expressed it elsewhere, "In a genuine ballet the libretto in its entirety is expressed through movement and not through miming or imitating words with gestures."[94]) The dance was first performed on June 4, 1920, as *Unfinished Sketch to Liszt's Twelfth Rhapsody* and danced by "all the students of the School of Movement."[95] More provocative was *Mephisto*, also to music by Liszt, which provoked a scandal when it was performed at the former City Theater. The work, she wrote, was accused of "bolshevism"; it had "no grace"; it wasn't ballet—attacks that made her feel "very cheerful" (11 November 1920). In *Mephisto* as in *Rhapsody* and *Marche Funèbre* (a work to Medtner that was never publicly performed), her goal was the unity of music and movement.[96]

What gave her greatest pleasure was work—creative work (29 August 1920). "I don't need the fame of theater productions," she wrote. "I just need to go on and not stop" (15 May 1920). In fact, the outstanding theme of her diary is creativity. It is the great aspiration of these years, what drives and sustains her, and day by day she tracks it, along with the dreams and visions that feed it. It is her only happiness, and when it falters, she compares its absence to death. There is barely a word about her family, although she lived with her mother and two children, or her husband, or even her brother, until she receives word of his illness. Unlike her later writings, which emphasize her foiled efforts to rejoin him and insist that the School of Movement was intended only "to train dancers . . . able to understand Nijinsky's new choreography," Nijinska's diary acknowledges very clearly her own artistic needs, goals, and desires.[97]

With the students of her School, Nijinska developed close personal and artistic relationships. They were creative extensions of herself, the instruments of her imagination. "It feels so good when they throw themselves like colors on canvas and do what I want and express what I want," she wrote (13 January 1920).

> If only I could pour all my creativity and power into them. If only I could give them everything I have so they could live better and stronger lives in art than I. . . . They all are dear to me like children. I make plans, but I feel that I could never leave them for a single day. (27 December 1919)

Her students adored her. They sat up all night listening to her visions and took care of her when she was sick. They chopped her firewood, took out the trash, hauled water from the yard, and cleaned the changing room. They worked with her all day, every day, and in the evenings. Most of Nijinska's students came from middle-class backgrounds. Nadia Shuvarskaia was the daughter of a gynecology professor and surgeon at Kiev's Alexandrovskaia Hospital; Nina ("Blue") had a medical background and later married the son of the eminent Petersburg physician Dr. V. N. Sirotinin; "Pati" (Kleopatra Grigorievna Zhakhovskaia-Chukhmanenko) graduated from the Smolny Institute and became a painter; Frania Miatelnikova was related to the Pasternak family; Carolina (Lina) Khaskhelis was raised in a musical family, while her sister, the School's regular pianist, graduated from the Kiev Conservatory. But the exceptional circumstances, a combination of hunger, idealism, and revolutionary ideology, made equals of privileged and unprivileged alike. People shared what little they had and dreamed of a better future. As the composer Arthur Lourié recalled, "There was no bread, and art took its place."[98] The School of Movement was the model for the companies that Nijinska would mother and befriend throughout her career—her first Western company, the Theatre Choréographique [sic], the Ida Rubinstein Ballet, Théâtre de la Danse, Polish Ballet, Center Ballet of Buffalo, and others. But they never quite lived up to the original, with its single-minded devotion to Nijinska, art, and the idea of creativity. Nothing could ever duplicate those terrible but immensely thrilling times.

By 1921, Nijinska later wrote, the whole School was receiving monthly rations in addition to small salaries:

I received a giant . . . academic ration, almost three poods. . . . I remember transporting it in winter on a little sled, with somebody's help—it was impossible to lift: a half pood of flour, millet, buckwheat, beans, and salt; 1½ of tobacco (I didn't smoke then), matches, sugar, 2 arshins of grey calico (from which I sewed Levushka's first little pants).

In addition, I was entitled to firewood. . . . Three giant frozen logs, about two fathoms long, lay for a long time in the dining room/library. . . . Finally, someone got his hands on a big saw. . . . It was freezing cold in the house, . . . so this firewood was a real treasure.[99]

***

With hindsight, Nijinska marveled at the possibilities opened by the Revolution. "Everyone who wanted to work and had the desire to create something new in art received every possible help from the new government."[100] But as she discovered, creative independence came at a personal cost. In 1920 and 1921 many entries allude to illness. She fears she has cancer (29 January 1920), that she needs an operation (29 March 1920), that her health is getting worse and worse (21 February 1921), that she may die. She recognized a connection between her creative life and her illness, and dreamed that one day she would be "strong and powerful" (17 April 1921). Although she never complained, the long hours Nijinska worked, the desperate shortages of food, firewood, and water, the birth of her second child, the fighting that went on relentlessly until 1920—all had to have taken a toll on her physical health.[101]

Mikhail Bulgakov's novel *The White Guard* suggests the bloodshed and cultural violence of the period when Kiev became a battleground where Bolsheviks, Ukrainian nationalist forces, and "White" armies made up of Imperial loyalists and foreign troops struggled and died.[102] An eyewitness recalled that Exter worked "all day long during frequent bombings of Kyiv, to the accompaniment of hissing and roaring artillery blasts."[103] This was even truer of Nijinska, who never fled the city, except that the blasts permanently impaired her hearing, leaving her intermittently deaf. In an autobiographical fragment she recalls being desperately ill and that her students would take turns sitting with her:

> I knew [Nadia Shuvarska] better than others because during the last month before my departure she was "on duty" beside me—assigned by the "secret council" I didn't know about then; later I found out it consisted of . . . Pati, Nina Vasilievna [the School secretary], and other students. . . . It was decided that the students of the School should shoulder part of my chores in order to ease my work. They established an order: the boys were to bring 2–3 buckets of water from the yard (in winter the pipes froze, and no water could come upstairs), chop firewood in the kitchen . . . , and take out the trash . . . ; the girls were to clean the room where they changed. I wasn't very happy about Nadia's "duty" . . . because after a whole day of classes—from 9 a.m. till 11 p.m. . . . I liked to be alone. During that time I had bouts of appendicitis . . . horrible pains and fevers up to 40 degrees. I couldn't bring myself to have an operation. There were already shortages of many medicines, and Dr. Epstein didn't insist too much either as he considered an operation in the existing conditions to be almost hopeless. Nadia's "duty" was the most difficult. . . . At night, woken up by strong pains, I would see Nadia sitting

on a chair at the foot of my bed. When the bouts were very acute, she would drip two drops of opium, which Dr. Epstein had prescribed for me, into a liquor glass. Then she would sit at the foot of the bed, stroke my feet, put her head on them, and cry bitterly.[104]

***

Although she was circumspect when speaking of private matters, her diaries and autobiographical fragments allow a glimpse into the life of Nijinska the woman. Unlike the other theater collectives in Kiev, Nijinska's studio was preeminently a community of women—of healers, students, and surrogate daughters. Although she is seldom alone, she often complains of loneliness, her need for a "friend." There are mentions of women to whom she is drawn, such as the historical novelist Olga Forsh, who was then living in Kiev (13 June 1920). Her affection for Nina Lipskaia, a student who emigrated with her family to Serbia, settled in Paris and subsequently in New York, was intense, and when Nina left, Nijinska was disconsolate. "Why isn't Nina with me?" she wrote in her diary.

> Is she thinking about me? Will we see each other ever again? Was it as difficult for her to part with her family as it was to part with me? I re-read my letter to her and remembered so vividly the time when she was with me. . . . She is a rare person for me, maybe my only possible friend, but everything is being taken away from me. . . . The only thing I have left is the knowledge of what love and a true faithful feeling is. (25/7 January 1920)

The relationship had all the signs of what Lillian Faderman has called "an ideal romantic friendship";[105] not only was it passionate, but it also involved the sharing of Nijinska's most intimate secrets, the tapping of her creative powers, and the creation of her first original dances. At this critical turning point in Nijinska's life, when she felt betrayed as a woman by her philandering husband and vulnerable as an artist just finding her way, she sought love, consolation, and support from other women.

***

Although the School of Movement remained the focus of Nijinska's energies, she also worked with the avant-garde stage directors Les Kurbas and

Marko Tereshchenko. Multilingual and Vienna-educated, Kurbas was the founder of the Young Theater (Molodyi Teatr), a company dedicated to performing serious drama in Ukrainian. He was both a nationalist and a modernist, and like Alexander Tairov he viewed movement as integral to his vision of a new theater and to his theory of actor training. Although no correspondence between them survives, references to Kurbas appear in Nijinska's notes, especially in connection with her student Nadia Shuravska, who later choreographed his production of *Gas* (1923).[106]

When Nijinska returned to Kiev in 1918, the Young Theater was immersed in the study of movement. Kurbas had invited Mikhail Mordkin, who was then staging *Giselle* and other repertory staples at the City Theater and had also opened his own studio, to give classes in expressive movement (or "plastique") to the actors of the Young Theater.[107] Valentina Chistiakova, who later married Kurbas, was more of a dancer than an actress in 1918. "Fate led me in Kiev in 1918 to the shared premises of two artistic collectives," she reminisced in the early 1990s.

In the morning the premises were rented by M. M. Mordkin for the classes of his dance studio; then we, his students, our lesson finished, left the hall, where the actors of the Young Theater led by Les Kurbas replaced us.[108]

Presumably, it was after Mordkin's departure that Kurbas invited Nijinska to work with him. As theater scholar Virlana Tkacz points out, a number of ties existed between the two, including shared studio space and students with experience with both studios.[109] Chistiakova recalled an encounter between the Nijinska and Kurbas groups during a rehearsal for *Oedipus Rex*:

In one of the rehearsals of the Chorus (we were rehearsing on stage, as Nijinska's students were still working in the big lobby), I suddenly caught sight of my friends from the ballet studio—as from this lobby they could slip into the auditorium—who were watching the rehearsal with enthusiasm; but chiefly, of course, they were watching me, the "traitor," as they nicknamed me, when they learned about my joining the Young Theater.[110]

Artistically, the parallels between Kurbas and Nijinska were striking. Both had spent years abroad and considered themselves European artists. Both lived by a credo of formal innovation and continuous creative search. Both shared a belief in the power of movement to communicate meanings that lay beyond the realm of words. Both celebrated the ensemble and explored the different ways it could be used. Both believed in transforming rather than following the libretto, even when dealing with musical or theatrical classics, using it as a vehicle to impose a vision on the production as a whole. And both believed in the theater as a theatrical rather than a literary phenomenon. In 1927, long after Nijinska had emigrated abroad, Kurbas paid tribute to her influence on "dance and expressive movement ['plastique'] in the Ukraine," while simultaneously lamenting the absence of students, teachers, and performers to carry on her legacy.[111]

Finally, for both, rhythm was the underlying principle of movement. It was central to Nijinska's practice, evident above all in *Les Noces*, although her theorizing of it is surprisingly vague. In the earliest published version of her treatise "On Movement and the School of Movement," she states simply, "Rhythm lives only in movement."[112] She told the French journalist Jean Rollot in 1932:

> For me, dance is a rhythm. You know what rhythm is in music. Well, dance rhythm and music rhythm are not the same. Dance, music: two sisters with a "single" existence. Two separate rhythms. The same thing in one harmony.[113]

Nijinska opened her treatise with the bald statement that "Movement is the principal element of dancing." Then follows a series of analogies: "Just as sound is the material of music, and color is the material of painting, so movement constitutes the material of dance.[114] Kurbas, in 1921, stated just as baldly that "the basis of theatre [is] movement, not words."[115]

Nijinska also worked with Marko Tereshchenko, one of several talented stage directors nurtured by the Young Theater. Parting ways with Kurbas in 1920, Tereschenko opened an experimental theater-studio for proletarian youth called the All-Ukrainian Central Studio Drama Group, or Centro-Studio for short. To staff its music, painting, dance, drama, literature, and vocal departments, the new institution assembled the best of the city's artistic and pedagogical "forces," including Nijinska.[116] In March 1921 the studio was renamed the All-Ukrainian State Studio and recognized as a Higher Arts School, with an Arts Soviet whose members included Tereshchenko, Meller, Nijinska, the stage director Aleksei Smirnov, and the composer Anatolii Butskoi, "under the direction of comrade Levitskii,"[117] the People's Commissar of Enlightenment. Two months later, the name changed again, and the studio became the Mikhailichenko Theater. On May 11, less than a month after Nijinska left Kiev, it made its debut with *The First Building of the New World*. Directed by Tereshchenko, with ensemble scenes staged under the influence of Nijinska's choreography (although her name for obvious reasons was dropped from the credits), this eminently political work depicted the struggle between capitalists and the proletariat.[118]

As the subject of its first production makes clear, Centro-Studio (to use its original name) was committed like Proletkult to the idea that socialist culture should be proletarian and collective. Theater, as an inherently collective art, was a central concern, and Proletkult clubs throughout Russia "searched for a mass theater to express the needs of the working class."[119] Rather than the creation of virtuoso performers, the task of the proletarian theater was to provide "an outlet for the creative artistic instinct of the broad masses." Mass spectacles "offered an aesthetic equivalent to the revolution in politics."[120]

Centro-Studio was for everyone. Anyone who wanted to act or dance or sing could take classes, and nobody would turn them away. In his 1935 memoir the Ballets Russes and Paris Opéra Ballet star Serge Lifar recalls stumbling accidentally upon a class at Nijinska's studio in 1921. When he returned, smitten by what he described as the "marvelous harmony between music and . . . bodies made divine by rhythm,"[121] she refused to admit him. Lifar was devastated. However, since she also taught classes at the Centro-Studio, he applied to Max Steiman, the conductor of the City Opera orchestra, whom many claimed was a Communist and thus regarded by the Soviets with a favorable eye. Steiman told Lifar not to worry, "We shall force this bourgeois ballet mistress to work with you."[122] Centro-Studio made Lifar's career possible, but by the time he came to write his memoir, he and his ghost writer, the Pushkin scholar Modeste Hofmann,[123] treated the vast proletarian experiment—to say nothing of the workers, village lads, young ladies, and famished intellectuals whom Lifar describes as his classmates—with contempt.

> The teachers understood better than anyone the absurdity of their situation. They knew perfectly well that they were wasting their time teaching peasants and young ladies . . . and to be on the safe side they taught them nothing, being on a perpetual slowdown.
>
> Madame Nijinska had been beside herself when she was snatched from her school and forced to teach these animals ["fauves"], since for her Centro-Studio was nothing more than a vast menagerie. At the hour scheduled for

her class, she appeared with the majesty of a queen, surrounded by a suite composed of "her" students. Some days she wore tights and showed off her legs and the plasticity of her body. The rest of the time, she made the animals stand, showing them how to lift their leg at the barre in the traditional way. Sometimes they risked exercises in the center . . . , to the great joy of Madame Nijinska's students who laughed at their pitiful awkwardness.[124]

Nijinska nowhere describes the Centro-Studio students as "animals" or mocks their technical limitations: these are Lifar's words or, more correctly, those of his amanuensis, expressing a view shared by the more extreme anti-Soviet émigrés, such as the Zinaida Gippius/Dmitrii Merezhkovsky circle to which Lifar's brother, Leonid Lifar, belonged.[125] However, Nijinska's clear preference for her own students must have been a source of friction with her more ideological colleagues. In an institution that celebrated the amateur and espoused the idea that creative expression was open to all, her emphasis on corporeal skill must have struck some as a form of elitism. In concert performances on behalf of Centro-Studio she used her own students rather than those of the new school. Tereshchenko, in his memoirs, recounts an incident that could well have had repercussions:

> In Kiev there was a conference of workers. . . . Attending this conference was the People's Commissar for Education, G. F. Grinko, from Kharkov. The conference lasted three days, and at its conclusion the participants wanted to see the work of Centro-Studio. . . . They began with a poetry reading, and then Nijinska's studio performed. It showed its well-known ballet *Demons* with the participation of Nijinska herself. After the ballet, singers appeared, and at the end fragments of our work were shown. Two departments occupied the central part of the concert—Nijinska's studio and the fragments of our works.[126]

Tereshchenko's use of movement was a weapon in a culture war waged on two fronts—against the emotional residue of symbolism and for a theater of action. Indeed, the title of the short book he published in Ukrainian in 1921, *The Art of Performance*, can also be translated as *The Art of Action* (*Mystetstvo diistva*). With respect to Nijinska, at least some of his thinking fell on fertile ground. In a long, rambling diary entry in mid-March 1921, she expresses the hope that Chaliapin, a recurring figure in her diary, will respond to the letter that someone has just hand-carried for her to Moscow, so that she can write back and share her thoughts about theater.[127] She imagines working with him to create a new "vocal theater." She is fed up with traditional opera (just as she had been with ballet) and calls for a new school to replace it. Words should be eliminated either by deleting the text or ignoring it, shifting the focus to the music. Vocal theater, she declares, should be a theater of action, not of "personalities" (15 March 1921).

Organized dance movement was sufficiently important to Tereshchenko that Centro-Studio, which had published his own manifesto in its recently inaugurated series "Theatrical Advisor," almost certainly intended to publish what Nijinska refers to in her diary early in 1921 as her "book on Movement" (8 January 1921). Other Centro-Studio publications include Grigorii Gaevskii's *The Task of the Director*, Vladimir Sladkopevtsev's *Introduction to Mime-Drama*, and Alexander Zacharov's *Art of the Actor*, all published in Kiev between 1920 and 1923.[128]

In Nijinska's papers there exists what may well be an early sketch of this lost book.[129] Unlike her 1918 treatise, it is purely theoretical. Movement, she asserts in the very first line, is now coming to be understood as the core element of dance rather than "plastika" or *plastique* and gesture. "Movement is Life," she declares. Without it, the dancer—or "artist," as she prefers—is a corpse, with the gestures and "plastique" of a "painted doll." Movement is the creative "essence" of the dancer's work. It is what animates form, which she describes as a kind of edifice or a containing vessel, into which the artist "pours life." Technique, by contrast, serves as the corporeal "armature" or "skeleton" of the dance, which comes alive through the exertions and "counter-pressures" of movement. Poses and pauses should be thought of as "journeys," always moving, always in transit, rather than as static "stops."

Again and again she resorts to metaphors to explain what she means by movement. It is a "thread" that stretches through an entire performance, a path, a flow, a breath, a stream. "See how it flows, quiet and straight, slides under, overflows, spreads, already runs in surges and suddenly changes its pressure, thickens, and in its slow might breaks everything it encounters." It is movement, too, that "infects" the spectator, absorbing him into its unceasing stream, an idea that anticipates what in the 1930s the American dance critic John Martin termed "metakinesis"—the ability, as Susan Manning explains, "of one body to sense another body and to reexperience physically sensations projected by that other body."[130]

Along with movement, Nijinska's second key idea is "action." By this she means everything that transpires in a performance, which, like the individual artist, only comes alive through movement. Hence, her emphasis on "Common Movement," a universalizing element that she equates with Action. A work, she writes, may offer the individual opportunities to display his or her "personal form" or expression. However, the artist is always "part of the whole," subordinate to a larger entity, while the group as a unit "submits to a single Movement-Action." In her theorization, movement is so powerful that it absorbs and even renders the body that creates it invisible.

Although no direct connection appears to exist between them, a number of Nijinska's ideas resonate with those of the Central European dance theorist Rudolf Laban, who published his first important theoretical work *Die Welt des Tänzers* (The Dancer's World) in Stuttgart in 1920. Among these ideas is what Laban calls the kinesphere, the "reach space" immediately surrounding the body.[131] Nijinska evokes this when speaking of the "atmosphere" that "enfolds the dancer." "Around the dancer there cannot be empty space," she asserts. "The force of movement . . . creates a world around the dancer." Another idea the two seem to share is what Laban terms "effort," the "inner impulse" from which movement originates and the "link between mental and physical components of movement."[132] Like him, she is interested in "counter-movements" or "counter-pressures," akin to what he theorizes as opposing effort elements. Finally, the two shared a broad, general consensus about movement itself. As the Laban scholar Valerie Preston-Dunlop writes, "He saw movement as the common denominator of all things: rhythm, oscillation, pulsation, tension and relaxation, attraction and repulsion, stability and mobility, circling, swinging—the fundamentals shared by humans and their environment. Position and stillness were for him illusory, for all is in flux and change."[133]

However, the two were also very different. Laban was a born theorist, fascinated by the mapping, categorizing, and analysis of movement. Nijinska, a creative artist, was chiefly interested in performance and choreography, and the relationship between the two. Unlike Laban, she accepted the *danse d'école*, although she felt it had to be treated in a contemporary way. She almost always used trained dancers, and her goal was to create intelligent, dynamic, and versatile performers. The difference between the two is also evident in their diagrams. Whereas Nijinska's are dynamic and full of movement, spilling into space, Laban's are static, contained, and logical.

Nijinska never spoke of either Kurbas or Tereshchenko publicly after she left Soviet Russia. In her notes the references to Tereshchenko are both cryptic and disturbing. She calls him one of the "'All-Ukrainian' ministers of art," the others being Meller and herself, and links all three of them to the opening of Centro-Studio. In another note, again in connection with Centro-Studio, she calls him "one of the theater 'ministers,' also [an] art [minister]— not a value," which she underscores.[134] On Christmas Eve 1920 she draws a snake with peacock feathers, labels it "MARK" (or MAPK, in Cyrillic letters), then recounts a dream in which she is a young man at a riverbank intent on proving the "legitimacy" of her ideas to an older, wiser self, a ragged God's fool who compels her emotional and intellectual submission. Clearly, she had deeply ambivalent feelings toward him. But she also harbored ambivalent feelings toward the new Soviet state, which supported her creative work but also integrated her into the emerging arts bureaucracy. Among the School of Movement's most enthusiastic supporters was the theater critic Samuil ("Angelo") Margolin, in her words the "most active . . . member" of the All-Ukrainian Art Commissariat established by the Commissariat of Enlightenment, and a founder of the Kultur-Lige's theater section. About her relationship in Kiev with the new Soviet powerbrokers, Nijinska maintained a discreet silence once she returned to the West.

***

In April 1920, Nijinska received a letter from her brother's wife "Romushka." Written in awkward Russian on stationery from the Steinhof Sanatorium in Vienna, it relayed the troubling news of Vaslav's mental illness and the doctors' conviction that the presence of his sister and mother was essential for his recovery.

> That is why I <u>earnestly</u> beg you to liquidate your school immediately and come to Vienna with your mother and children. You do not have to worry about the future, because I will help you with everything. I will . . . send someone to the Polish or Rumanian border to . . . meet you; it is impossible to [send someone] to Kiev.
> So . . . proceed to one of those borders and wire me immediately, so that I can get you. Make sure that you have enough food for the trip from Kiev to the border and while you wait for my trusted emissary. After you cross the border, I will take care of everything.[135]

Nijinska was devastated. She may not have thought much about her brother in the past few years, but that he should fall victim to mental illness, as had her older brother Stanislav, was terrible to contemplate. "How life mocks me!" she wrote in her diary. "Everything was being built for him, to give to him, to help him. And now everything is gone" (7 April 1920).

It would, however, be more than a year before Nijinska left Kiev. It was not an easy decision. Although the original ending of *Early Memoirs* presents a straightforward escape narrative climaxing in her reunion with Vaslav,[136] the diaries tell a more complicated story. Much as Nijinska may have wanted to join her brother, she found it difficult to pick up and leave. In part, this was because of the contradictory and usually erroneous reports that reached her about his condition. Vaslav is not ill (25 May 1920); he has died in New York (16 March 1921); he is alive and dancing in Paris (24 March 1921); he is alive but incurably ill in a psychiatric clinic (27 March 1921). But there were other reasons, and these had to do with her creative work and the School. "I'm in a creative mood," she writes three weeks after Romola's letter:

> Liszt's *Rhapsody*. It's good. Completely abstract. It holds me here even more. It's hard to leave. In Europe there will be a new life again; I'll have to build everything from scratch. Here I have everything already. (27 April 1920)

In June, after the premiere of her *Unfinished Sketch to Liszt's Twelfth Rhapsody*:

> I need to leave, but it's impossible to leave. (6 June 1920)
>   I couldn't leave; it would be too painful to lose the School. . . . Intuitively I feel that I need to go, but to my brain it seems absurd. (13 June 1920)

During the summer of 1920 a darker note appears in her diaries. The Polish-Soviet War was raging across Ukraine, briefly raising the hope that she could leave on a Polish military train.[137] She feels lost, lonely, ill, useless; she can't do anything creatively; one of her students has drowned. On July 31, Nijinska went to the train station but found she couldn't leave.

Work absorbed her during the fall, and she was clearly elated by the reception of *Rhapsody* and her Chopin sketches and the recognition from the authorities that followed. On November 27, the entry ends in mid-sentence, and Nijinska later penciled in, "Pages torn out before the Bolsheviks [came]." In her autobiographical outline she recalls the Bolsheviks searching the house, looking for guns in her son's crib, and, later, visits by the Cheka (as the secret police was then known) to the School.[138] She doesn't recount these incidents in her notes, but she mentions other encounters with the Cheka.

One involved her student Anna (Niusia) Vorobieva, who had been arrested as a "state criminal":

> I remember how Nina Vas[ilievna] accompanied me in my efforts to free Niusia from arrest, how we both went to the Kiev Cheka secretariat during the period of horrible terror. Efforts like these were far from safe.... [They] meant you sympathized with her.[139]

On February 11, 1921, Nijinska recorded in her diary that it was the School's second anniversary and that she felt that her students had been with her all her life. But she was also angry and frightened. She had wanted to go to Minsk but was denied a pass.

> They shut me in a cage, listen to my songs, and think they are the songs of a free bird. I don't have anywhere to go, and everything here is dear to me, but why is my garden shut? ... Do they really need to watch us?

What had happened to prompt this outburst? Had the Cheka stepped up its surveillance? Threatened her? Had she intended to escape, and the Cheka had gotten wind of it? Was she now regarded as a flight risk? It wasn't paranoia on her part to imagine that she might be arrested. The Cheka was exceptionally active in Ukraine and during the era of what came to be known as the Red Terror exceptionally brutal. Women and children were not spared. According to George Leggett, "There are accounts of women being tortured and raped before being shot . . . and many cases of children between the ages of 8 and 16 being imprisoned [and] executed."[140]

In late February—just two days after an open rehearsal of her new Medtner work—Nijinska decided against traveling to Kharkov, now the capital of the Ukrainian Socialist Soviet Republic: "I absolutely can't leave my children alone," she wrote in her diary. "Something terrible might happen, and I'll never see them again. . . . But I need to be with Vatsa. My health is getting worse and worse; I feel it when I'm not creating" (21 February 1921). Again, various scenarios suggest themselves. She was going to Kharkov to apply for an exit visa, perhaps to appeal to Levitskii, the People's Commissar of Enlightenment, the one high official mentioned in her notes.[141] There was no question of leaving through Kharkov, which (unlike Minsk) was nowhere near the Polish or Lithuanian border. It seems clear that she feared being arrested.

But otherwise everything was going well. She was overwhelmed with work and the School was flourishing:

> I work physically all day long. I'm never alone. I even create now during given hours. I'm not complaining. I want to work, but I need to change the pace of work. (16 March 1921)

Then only five days later comes an astonishing entry:

> [T]he School as it is now should be destroyed. Probably I will start it again later, but in a completely different way. I can't pretend any longer that I teach and create when everything is doomed. . . . Why am I afraid of tomorrow? (21 March 1921)

There was good reason. The next day, she writes,

> The School is destroyed. It's ruined. (22 March 1921)

She was shattered. "What do I have left?" she asked. "My babies and my mother" (23 March 1921). Her students gathered round, asking her what to do; some began to look for new places. Teaching, she wrote, is a waste of energy; even a small piece of choreography is better than forcing her creative vision on others.

Although there had been many reasons to leave Kiev, the one that finally impelled her to do so seems to have been the "torment of losing the School" (7 April 1921). Long after she had learned that her brother was ill, the School held her. It had given her a new life and an identity of her own as a modernist artist. It was her child, the home of her imagination, a community of friends and devoted followers, the catalyst and expression of her creativity. In the weeks that followed she quietly made plans to leave. On April 19 she recorded her last diary entry in Kiev: "This morning I felt this notebook was foreign and belonged already to the past. . . . Here probably my first part will end" (19 April 1921). And then with her mother and two children she boarded a train for Volochisk, ostensibly to check conditions at the local theater, but in reality to head for the Polish border. After inspecting the theater, she was smuggled by train to the town of Proskurov. Actors from the former Alexandrinsky Theater in Petrograd had a "wagon-salon" car to themselves, and they agreed to take her, while the conductor hid her mother and children in his compartment. In Proskurov, a town savaged in 1919 by a po-grom conducted by the Ukrainian People's Army, Chekists were everywhere. Nijinska had brought with her a considerable sum of old tsarist rubles, which she used to bribe "K.," who then bribed the border guards. As they pretended to sleep, the family waded across the Southern Bug River to Poland. K., how-ever, had kept most of their belongings, although Nijinska convinced him to retrieve her theatrical costumes. The following day, May 10, the family re-ceived Polish registration cards and travel permits for Warsaw.[142]

A new life lay ahead. She could hardly know what form it would take or where it would lead or how it would build upon the life she had put be-hind her. She had left Western Europe as her brother's helpmate. Now, after seven years and a lifetime of experiences that he would never share, she had returned. She wrote to Diaghilev: "Now I know that . . . I can do many things."[143]

3

Back from the Future

When Nijinska arrived in Poland, her thoughts turned almost immediately to Diaghilev. He had been her brother's lover and the man who stood in for her father when she married, the indefatigable champion of new creative paths in ballet. Diaghilev was also her artistic director, the "boss" who had both promoted her career as a dancer and thwarted her aspirations as a choreographer. She knew him personally, as few Ballets Russes dancers did, and had experienced multiple sides of his personality. She knew how generous he could be and how unpredictable; she had seen him flatter, charm, and weep. But few knew more about ballet than Diaghilev, and Nijinska, however complicated her feelings, respected him totally. He had given meaning to her life and the credo by which she lived. "I perceived this truth from Diaghilev," she later wrote. "One can live only in art and for art."[1]

Full of conflicting emotions, Nijinska wrote to Diaghilev only days after her arrival in Poland. She had last seen him in January 1914, when he charmed her into returning, albeit temporarily, to the Ballets Russes. Since then so much had happened, so much she wanted him to know.

> I have just come from Russia and hasten to fulfill my old wish to express my profound gratitude for everything I received from you that has made me the artist I am today. I long to see you and share with you my creative joys and achievements. Soon I go to Vienna to see Vaslav.[2]

The very thought of Diaghilev seemed to lift the malaise of the last weeks in Kiev. "The need to create is flooding all my veins," she wrote in her diary on May 21:

> Pregnancy with creativity is making me heavy and sick. . . . I want to see Diaghilev; he is my ninth month; he could become the midwife of my creativity. He could become the father of my child.

Meanwhile, she sat in Warsaw, waiting for her Polish passport. She went to see Stanislaw Drobecki (Drubetskii or Drobetsky in Russian), an Austro-Pole from Lemberg who had worked as one of Diaghilev's administrators when the Ballets Russes toured North America. Now living in the Polish capital, he alerted his former employer of the arrival of dancers fleeing Russia and helped them get their papers. "B. Nijinska is in Warsaw with her mother and children," Drobecki wrote on May 25 to Diaghilev's trusty régisseur, Sergei Grigoriev. "She is on her way to Vienna . . . and sends greetings." Nijinska added a hasty note to Grigoriev's wife, Lubov Tchernicheva, a close friend since their school days in St. Petersburg. "Luba, . . . I have just fled Russia, after a thousand adventures. Now I go to Vienna and Vatsa. . . . I kiss you and send my regards to Sergei Leonidovich and to your mother, and kiss your little son."[3]

After all the rumors about Nijinsky's condition, Romola's telegram with the good news that "Vatsa is alive and well" (15 May 1921) must have cheered the refugees as they made their way to Vienna. The visit had all the makings of a happy family reunion, with the two sets of cousins—Bronislava's Irina and Levushka and Vaslav's Kyra and Tamara—finally getting to meet. What transpired in the Austrian capital was anything but happy. Romola met them at the train station, and the next day Nijinska and her mother went to the Steinhof Sanatorium. In her diary Nijinska recorded the heartbreaking encounter:

> I'm in Vienna. Vatsa is very ill. . . . He recognizes neither me nor our mother; he says we are strangers. . . . I don't know if he will ever get well, but everything inside him is perfectly clear to me. He lost himself in his visions and forgot the way back. (2 June 1921)

Unlike her brothers, Nijinska had found the way back. No matter how lonely or sad, she would continue on the path she had chosen. By withdrawing from her life, Nijinsky had released her as an artist, allowing her finally to go her own way. She vowed:

> I will finish all his work and expand whatever I can. I will return to "my own" work as the continuation of Vaslav's art. Vaslav will rejoice wherever he is—on earth or in heaven. Everything I do is worthy of Great Art. Now there will be more, and it will be better. (2 June 1921)

In Vienna, Nijinska's relationship with Romola quickly soured. Eleonora, who had moved into the Sanatorium (which had a well-appointed wing for private patients) to be near her son, accused Romola of misappropriating Vaslav's once considerable savings. There were terrible scenes, and at one point Romola even threatened to have Eleonora herself committed.[4] Nijinska doesn't write about this incident in her diary. However, she was appalled by another suggestion of Romola's—that she start some kind of enterprise they would market to the public under "Vatsa's name." A bitter argument ensued, but Nijinska stuck to her guns. She would not commercialize Nijinsky's name. By then she was utterly disillusioned with Romola:

> My God, what a marriage Vaslav had. I know he is a tyrant, a despot, but he has a big, kind heart. Romola is completely different. Vaslav wanted only art, to work for art. . . . How endlessly he agonized about not being understood in anything. (7 June 1921)

Initially, Romola had agreed to support Bronislava and her family. However, as the relationship with her sister-in-law worsened, Romola withdrew her support. Nijinska now found herself overwhelmed by money problems. Her son, Levushka, became ill, but she didn't have money for a doctor (8 June 1921). And then came the hotel bill—25,000 kronen. Where was the money to come from? Romola refused to pay a penny, so Nijinska resorted to selling off what little they had left—small icons, jewelry, her mother's things. The 6,000 kronen she received for these last remaining treasures was only a drop in the bucket of her debts. She found the world increasingly incomprehensible and in her diary wondered whether life in Europe had "strangled" Vatsa as it seemed to be strangling her (30 June 1921).

Again, her thoughts turned to Diaghilev, which infuriated Romola, who insisted that her sister-in-law have nothing to do with him. In desperation, Nijinska cabled him in London, where the Ballets Russes was performing: "I want to work with you. Please arrange my departure from Vienna immediately."[5] She followed this with a long letter that began conventionally enough, but went on to convey ideas percolating in Kiev and other Soviet avant-garde centers. Art news trickled slowly from Soviet Russia, so Diaghilev must have read with mounting interest what Nijinska wrote. Still, artistic radicalism had to have shocked him, especially her assault on the proscenium stage and use of painted scenery—practices he never abjured—as well as the statement that corporeal movement was the "material" of a new action-based theater.

> My relations with Vaslav's wife are broken. We left Russia, like everyone else, with nothing. My children, my mother, and I are in a dire situation. I must find something quickly and begin working.

My first thought, of course, was you. I sent you a telegram but have not received an answer. I won't and can't undertake anything without hearing from you. . . . I have completed several compositions. . . . I seek "new" movements, "new" forms of decor and costume, and I am sick of the theatrical "box." We must create Theater itself, not ballet. Bodily movement is the material-means of this new Theater.

We must destroy "theater" as a background for the display of dancers in a painted "box."

Everything in theater must be action. . . .

Working with you was my greatest joy. I must see you, even if I haven't worked with you since I was your "child."[6]

Finally, on July 2, a telegram arrived from Diaghilev (3 July 1921). Announcing that she would start work on September 15, he told her to meet him in Venice, where for years he had spent the late summer. She wrote back immediately:

I am thrilled to work with your company. It is essential that we see one another. However, I don't know how to arrange it. I no longer have any money to make the trip. Perhaps I can arrange a concert in Venice (a suite of dances and sketches to the music of Chopin, Scriabin, and Prokofiev). . . . If it becomes impossible for me to go to Venice, would you please write to me in detail about what you would do with me in your company and if I have something like a contract? It is essential to know this very soon if possible in order to organize my family life—to be free to work. I want so much to know what is being done and thought in your theater, and who is working with you. In Russia, we had information, but it was very limited.[7]

The same day she received Diaghilev's telegram, Nijinska signed a lucrative six-week contract with the Moulin-Rouge, one of Vienna's biggest music halls. She never breathed a word afterward about the Moulin-Rouge, which she considered demeaning, even though she was a headliner and performing her own repertory. Much as she hated the experience, it was exhilarating to dance after a dry spell of several months. Her opening was a big success, with flowers and applause, and she was elated by the *Polovtsian Dances* (2 August 1921), which she danced with Vladislav Karnecki, stepping in for Kochetovsky. She also performed *The Doll*, her old solo to the music of Liadov. Residez-Atelier, a studio that specialized in theater subjects, photographed her wearing Vaslav's old *Papillon* costume, "futurized" with hand painting and accessorized with hand-painted tights, which suggests that she performed at least one other number, possibly *Fear*.[8] Even if Nijinska's inner life remained in turmoil, financially things were looking up. She bought smart new clothes for the children and took them to a photographer, where they posed—Irina in a pleated dress, with a big bow in her hair, and Levushka in a suit with short pants. Smiling for the camera, they look happy and well fed—not like refugees from Kiev.[9] Meanwhile she waited for Diaghilev to contact her. "God grant," she wrote, "we can come to an agreement so I can begin to work there" (10 August 1921).

Even before she learned that Diaghilev would be mounting *The Sleeping Beauty*, she feared that he was turning away from the experimentalist path he had pursued with her brother and during World War I with Léonide Massine, who had replaced Nijinsky in Diaghilev's affections and as the object of his creative mentorship. In her negotiations with him she tried to stipulate conditions but came to believe that she had "no chance," that Diaghilev again doubted her talents.[10] "Maybe," she mused in her diary,

> I should find a place here in Vienna and open a studio. Everything I need will come out of it. But everything requires money, and I don't have it. This is the problem. (28 July 1921)

Ironically, Vienna, with its modern dance studios and ballet traditions, would have been far more welcoming of Nijinska's brand of choreographic and technical experiment than Paris turned out to be.[11]

Nijinska spent almost four months in Vienna before rejoining the Ballets Russes. It was not a happy introduction to postwar life in the West. She endured penury, created no new dances, and performed every evening for six weeks in a music hall. She took part in a single concert performance—for the Relief Committee of Russian Organizations in Vienna for the Hungry in Russia—where she danced two of her Moulin-Rouge numbers, *The Doll* and *The Polovtsian Dances*, in which she was partnered again by Karnecki.[12] If before she left Russia (as she always referred to Ukraine), she had gone hungry and felt the tightening of the political noose, now she experienced the first wave of nostalgia for her old life. True, it was "hard, enormous, scary, dark, and bloody" (3 July 1921). But everybody "share[d] the same fate," and "her lot was better than many others" (23 July 1921).

In an essay published in the *Dancing Times* in 1937, Nijinska recalled her shock at returning to the Ballets Russes in 1921 and discovering that her first assignment was working on a revival of *The Sleeping Beauty*, which Diaghilev had renamed *The Sleeping Princess*. To be sure this was the most significant production of Petipa's ballet since its premiere in St. Petersburg in 1890, the first to touch the Western imagination and the first to craft the ballet for a twentieth-century audience. In London, where *The Sleeping Princess* ran for three months, it left a huge impression, although most critics turned up their noses at the old-fashioned spectacle and its Tchaikovsky score. Audiences dwindled after a time, but for those who made a habit of returning, it was a continuous feast, with multiple casts of the finest Russian dancers in the West. Many had recently emigrated; others, like Olga Spessivtzeva, had yet to sever their ties with the Soviet Union. For the critic André Levinson, who abhorred the country's new Bolshevik masters, the revival of the ballet—with its former Imperial ballerinas and theme of monarchy reborn—signified, even in a London music hall, nothing less than the rebirth of Petersburg's refined, aristocratic ballet culture. "The great revolutionary tempest [had] swept away centuries of civilisation," he wrote in his introduction to a sumptuous volume of Bakst's designs for the ballet.

> Yet such is the force of a living tradition, that the debris of the illustrious Imperial Ballet survived, and one saw young dancers . . . dancing the part of Aurora before a turbulent audience thronged with Red Guards. . . . All this heroic loyalty to the art of dancing, to its honour and to the ideal aspirations of the great "Petipa style," represents so much ineffectual beauty in the midst of hideous, implacable reality. *The Sleeping Princess* sleeps in a dying land—a sleep from which there can be no awakening.
>
> It was at this moment, when the destiny of the Russian ballet had seemingly run its course, that Diaghilev appeared, and called upon Bakst to bring Aurora back to life.[13]

Nijinska viewed the ballet—and the project of reviving it—very differently. "Diaghileff's idea in producing the *Sleeping Princess*," she wrote in the mid-1930s,

> seemed to me the negation of the fundamental "religion" of the ballet as he conceived it, and of his searching towards the creation of a new ballet. It was just at that time that I returned to his company as a choreographer. I started

my first work full of protest against myself. I had just come back from Russia in revolution, and after many a production of my own over there, the revival of the *Sleeping Princess* seemed to me an absurdity. . . . Naturally what I wanted and what I strove for was a return to the former tendencies of Diaghileff's ballet (tendencies which did become his tradition) in which I had been brought up from my early youth, so as to realise new life, new paths and a new technique in ballet composition.[14]

Nijinska had lost touch with the Ballets Russes in 1913. Thus, she did not see the 1914 season that introduced the young Bolshoi dancer Léonide Massine to the public, nor did she take part in his choreographic apprenticeship or Diaghilev's encounter with the cubo-futurist avant-garde during the war years. These were the twin pillars of Diaghilev's new modernist repertory. Fokine's ballets continued to be performed, usually in their original dress, but new commissions went to artists who had experienced the revolution of Cubism. To be sure, visual magic was always crucial to the success of the Ballets Russes. What changed over the years was the aesthetic behind that magic—broadly symbolist before World War I, cubo-futurist during the war and post-Armistice years, and eclectic during the 1920s when multiple expressions of international modernism passed through the repertory. Nijinska's years as a Ballets Russes choreographer coincided with the opening moment of the third phase. But they began with *The Sleeping Princess*, when Diaghilev for the last time turned to Léon Bakst, the companion of his youth, to design a production that tapped their common memories.

In reviving the ballet, Diaghilev was less concerned than Levinson with the historic destiny of Russian ballet. He had long harbored mixed feelings about Petipa's work, dismissing his last fully produced ballet, *The Magic Mirror* (1903), as "boring, long, complicated, and pretentious"[15] and *The Sleeping Beauty* as an "interminable" Franco-Italian *féerie*.[16] It was Stravinsky who persuaded Diaghilev of the ballet's merits. The two spent the spring of 1921 traveling in Spain, and it was here, after playing the score "over and over" that Diaghilev experienced a change of heart.[17] "The time I saw Diaghilev the most enthusiastic," wrote Stravinsky more than thirty years later,

was when—feeling that the moment had at last arrived when he could give to the public a composer whom he had never ceased to love—he produced in London, with unprecedented splendor, Tchaikovsky's ballet *The Sleeping Princess*. I never saw him work with such ardor and love! After long and painstaking preparation, in which I also took an active part, the ballet was finally produced with a brilliant cast . . . and with magnificent sets and costumes designed by Bakst.[18]

Diaghilev seems to have kept the idea of staging *Beauty* even from his régisseur, Sergei Grigoriev. In his memoirs, Grigoriev remembered the revival idea coming up almost by accident:

It happened that a musical play called *Chu Chin Chow* was then running in its third year at His Majesty's Theatre. Diaghilev was amazed at the possibility of such an enormous run, and one day he said to me half jokingly how much he wished he could discover a ballet that would run for ever—that would be happiness!

Diaghilev kept returning to the subject and eventually said he had thought of the "ideal solution"—*The Sleeping Beauty*. Grigoriev agreed it was an excellent plan.[19]

Petipa's ballet was light years away from *Chu Chin Chow*—a musical spectacular based on *Ali Baba and the Forty Thieves*—that opened in 1916 and closed in the summer of 1921. Could anyone really think—let alone a master showman like Diaghilev—that the West End audience that loved *Chu Chin Chow* would take to heart a four-act ballet celebrating France's *grand siècle*? Surely, it was with the Paris Opéra in mind that he took the risky decision to stage *Beauty* in the first place. More than any other ballet in the Russian repertory, *Beauty* paid tribute to French art and a vanished theatrical patrimony, the resurrection of which Jacques Rouché had made a goal of his programming since becoming director of the Opéra in 1915.[20]

In October 1921, less than a month before *The Sleeping Princess* opened in London, Rouché formally agreed to a month-long engagement of the Ballets Russes at the Opéra the following spring. There were to be seventeen performances, and Diaghilev promised "in addition to the usual repertory," three new works—*The Sleeping Beauty*, which would open and close the season, and Stravinsky's *Noces Villageoises* (as *Les Noces* was then known) and one-act opera buffa *Mavra*. Diaghilev would receive a generous performance fee of 14,000 francs, and the pleasure of returning to the most illustrious theater of Western Europe. Rouché, for his part, promised that for the duration of the contract no Russian dancers could perform at the Opéra without Diaghilev's consent. Exceptions were made for Ida Rubinstein, Fokine, and "Mme. Kschessinska," although in the end only Rubinstein in *Artémis Troublée*, a classical interlude designed by Bakst, actually appeared.[21] Even before the contract with Rouché was signed, word had leaked to the press that the Ballets Russes was rehearsing the "most lavish and sensational" spectacle that Diaghilev had ever presented to the French public—a celebrated, classical Russian work, with the original, lovingly preserved Petipa choreography, and it would be performed in Paris the following May.[22] *Beauty* was to be the star balletic attraction in the Opéra's programming for the Molière tercentenary.

As the pages of *Comoedia* make abundantly clear, Paris in 1922 was swept up in Molière fever. Hardly a day passed without notice of a play, concert, exhibition, opera, or lecture honoring not only the celebrated playwright but also the world of his contemporaries, including his most distinguished patron, Louis XIV. Petipa's French birth, his brother Lucien Petipa's long years of service at the Paris Opéra, and the impassioned Francophilia of *Beauty*'s original producer, designer, and librettist, Prince Ivan Vsevolozhsky, a former member of the Russian legation in Paris—all this contributed to *Beauty* being a singular expression of the Gallic idea.[23] Vsevolozhsky had set the opening scenes in the reign of Henri IV and the later ones in that of Louis XIV. Diaghilev pushed forward the dates, so that *The Sleeping Princess* spanned the whole of the *grand siècle*, invoking the splendor of French court culture under Louis XIV and his successor, both as an image of national greatness and a symbol of cultural regeneration. If *Skating Rink*, produced by the Ballets Suédois in January 1922, celebrated the sights, sounds, and movements of working-class Paris life, *Beauty* celebrated a highly traditional and politically conservative idea of French glory. The more conservative segment of the Russian émigré community proved highly receptive to such thinking. Among those invited by *Comoedia* to contribute an essay on Molière was Dmitrii Merezhkovskii, a Russian poet, novelist, literary critic, religious philosopher, and former associate of Diaghilev's journal *Mir iskusstva*. Now living in exile, Merezhkovsky turned his essay on "Molière and Russia" into an anti-Soviet screed, crying at one point, "I am Russian, and it is with Lenin that I have suit—Lenin, who has killed Russia, my Mother, and who would kill even your mother, France."[24]

Thus, *The Sleeping Beauty* held particular resonance for "Russia Abroad," as the historian Marc Raeff calls the million or so people who poured out of Russia after 1917, the first wave of exiles in a century of diasporas.[25] Many were soldiers, the remnants of the White armies evacuated by their international supporters. They were joined by aristocrats, a segment of the intelligentsia, and a broad spectrum of the middle class. Although the former Imperial Theaters continued to function, they lost performers and backstage personnel to the West, including most of the Maryinsky's leading ballerinas. Somewhere between 120,000 and 150,000 Russians settled in France, many in Nice and its environs, where a large aristocratic colony of Russians had existed since the nineteenth century. However, the capital of Russia Abroad was Paris. It was here that magazines, newspapers, and literary journals were published; writers, poets, and former political figures congregated; and re-tired Imperial ballerinas set up studios and displaced impresarios' opera companies. Parents sent their children to Russian music schools and Russian summer camps, and their daughters to Russian ballet schools—even people who once shuddered at having a dancer in the family. They went to Russian churches and to performances by Russian artists, even as mothers eked out a living in the garment industry and fathers in the car factories that ringed Paris or by driving the proverbial taxis. Artists designed clothing for Russian shops and made posters for Russian artists' balls, while émigré stars like Fedor Chaliapin and Anna Pavlova sang and danced for Russian charities.[26]

Both Stravinsky and Diaghilev belonged to this émigré world, although they had settled abroad before the Revolution, spoke French fluently, and were identified with the modernism many émigrés associated with the Soviets. Both had lost friends and family in the Revolution. Diaghilev's half-brother Valentin had joined the Red Army, but his two oldest sons had fought with the Whites; by 1921 both were dead. In Petrograd, Diaghilev's beloved stepmother, after surviving surgery, died of cancer and semi-starvation.[27] Added to the experience of personal loss was that of exile. By the end of 1921, those who had elected to live abroad, like Diaghilev and Stravinsky, had be-come stateless, deprived by Soviet decree of their citizenship.[28] Their self-chosen status was now a permanent condition; there was no going home. Stravinsky alluded to the resulting sense of cultural loss in the essay he wrote for *The Sleeping Princess* souvenir program, which took the form of an open letter addressed to Diaghilev:

> It gives me great happiness to know that you are producing that masterpiece "The Sleeping Beauty," by our great and beloved Tchaikovsky. It makes me doubly happy. In the first place, it is a personal joy for this work appears to me as the most authentic expression of that period of our Russian life which we call the "Petersburg Period," and which is engraved upon my memory

with the morning vision of the Imperial sleighs of Alexander III, the giant Emperor and his giant coachman, and the immense joy that waited me in the evening, the performance of "The Sleeping Beauty."

It is, further, a great satisfaction to me as a musician. . . .

For Stravinsky, *Beauty* was the supreme example of Tchaikovsky's "great creative power" and also his "profound" Russianness, which Stravinsky identified with the composer's melodic eloquence and "living" rather than "archeological" approach to the past. "I warmly desire," Stravinsky concluded, "that your audiences . . . may feel this work as it is felt by me, a Russian musician."[29] The music critic Ernest Newman may have accused Diaghilev of insincerity in professing admiration for the "banality" of Tchaikovsky's music in *The Sleeping Princess*, but its dirge of cultural exile was lost on him: only Russians heard the ballet's lament.[30]

This was the world Nijinska entered when she left Vienna in September 1921 to rejoin the Ballets Russes.[31] Diaghilev's old friend Walter Nouvel, who was now the company's business manager, was deputized to conduct the contract negotiations. He appeared in late August and spent a whole day talking to her, then wrote a long letter to Diaghilev.

> As a dancer, she thinks she is stronger and more technical than ever. . . . But what interests her most of all is choreographic creativity or "composing," . . . and this is the principal reason she wants to join you. What she told me about her work in Kiev testifies to the seriousness and advanced nature of her initiatives and searches. . . . She considers her creativity a continuation and development of Vatsa's choreography, but with unique features . . . for example, the absence of plots, culture of the body and movement. In a letter it's hard to explain everything, but it appears to me that what she is doing is indisputably interesting and full of talent. . . . To understand somewhat her artistic development let me say that in her room are two sketches by Kiev cubists, but she considers cubism obsolete and inclines now to the "round." . . . She was very interested in and questioned me about new trends in French painting. All this makes me wonder whether she is not the dream choreographer you need.[32]

Dream choreographer or not, Nijinska was also "very ugly, especially her mouth and teeth," Nouvel wrote, although the one-time dandy was apparently relieved that her body was "thin."[33]

The two also spoke about Nijinsky and whether there was any chance of his dancing again. Nouvel reported:

> Vatsa seems incurable. One doctor says the situation is hopeless; others that he may recover sometime, but when—who knows. Bronia views the situation skeptically, but nevertheless does not lose hope. . . . Today Bronia will try to get permission for me to see him, but she is not sure if she can manage it. His condition now is difficult, more cheerful when Bronia comes, but his mother, for instance, he apparently doesn't recognize. In other words we can't count on him.[34]

Nouvel's conversations with Nijinska culminated in a contract signed on August 30. Covering an eleven-month period beginning September 1, it called for her to be paid 5,000 francs a month as well as first-class travel expenses. (Nouvel had first offered 3,000 francs; she demanded 6,000, citing the high cost of living and the family she had to support.) The contract also specified that she had to attend the daily class given by the teachers "designated by management," a bitter pill for someone who had been teaching for years.[35] Although she was supposed to be in London by September 1, she arrived late, held up by her Moulin-Rouge engagement. Leaving her mother and children behind in Vienna, she traveled to Paris, where she received her visa, and from there to London, where she arrived by September 20.[36] There she found the company hard at work with Nicholas Sergeyev, the Maryinsky's chief régisseur, or rehearsal director, from 1903 to 1918.[37] Diaghilev had found him living in Paris with the notated scores of numerous Maryinsky ballets—he had helped himself to them when he emigrated—and hired him to stage The Sleeping Beauty, his first major commission in the West.[38]

Sergeyev certainly knew the ballet well. He had rehearsed it for nearly two decades and supervised its first major revision in 1914. But reproducing it on a company of dancers not necessarily familiar with Petipa's style and less than fully convinced of the ballet's merits proved a challenge. Moreover, as a répétiteur, Sergeyev had serious flaws. At the Maryinsky, Nijinska recalled in an essay written in the late 1960s for a Soviet volume about Petipa, Sergeyev "devoted all his attention to obtaining unassailable dance lines."

> The corps de ballet did its best—it danced with all its might—but without reflecting the nuances of the music, only the snapping of Sergeyev's fingers

beating time. If it happened that in a solo the dance phrase did not coincide with the musical phrase, he didn't notice.[39]

No love was lost between Sergeyev and the dancers he snapped to attention. In fact, he seems to have been universally despised and regarded both as an "intriguer" (as ballet historian Natalia Roslavleva calls him) and as a spy for the Maryinsky management.[40] Many also regarded him as incompetent. Ninette de Valois, who worked with Sergeyev in the 1930s, when he set core works of the late Imperial repertory on the young Sadler's Wells company, echoed these complaints. Sergeyev was "unmusical to a degree bordering on eccentricity," she wrote in her memoir *Come Dance with Me*. For no apparent reason, he would "pencil out a bar of music," which Constant Lambert, the company's musical director, would restore during the lunch break, while de Valois "extend[ed] some small choreographic movement to cover Mr. Lambert's tracks."[41] Even more astonishing, given his long experience, Sergeyev lacked a sense of choreographic style. When he staged Fokine's *Polovtsian Dances*, André Levinson was incensed to discover that nothing remained of the choreographer except his name on the program. Sergeyev, he wrote, was merely "a talentless subaltern . . . who has never arranged anything himself but is reduced to signing the works of others."[42]

In London, Nijinska wrote her first diary entry on September 20. By then she had spent time with Larionov and Natalia Goncharova, seen their designs, and had her first glimpse of Goncharova's sketches for *Les Noces*. However, much of the long entry concerns Stravinsky. Nijinska knew his prewar ballets well. She had danced in the original productions of *Firebird* and *Petrouchka*, and was initially cast as the Chosen Maiden in *Sacre*. In Kiev she had staged scenes from *Petrouchka* at the City Theater as well as for members of the School of Movement. However, she seemed unaware of Stravinsky's post–*Rite of Spring* work, and among the modern composers she had used in Kiev, he is noticeably absent. "Stravinsky has arrived," she wrote.

Sergei Pavlovich considers him a genius. He is a very prominent musician. I need to listen to more of him now. Many years have passed.

She goes on to describe their efforts to shape the *Beauty* score:

Sergei Pavlovich and Stravinsky are putting the music of *The Sleeping Princess* "into shape." They are making cuts and emphasizing the best [parts]. At first I thought this wasn't right. Why does Stravinsky touch somebody else's [work] and add himself (like a taste)? Later I realized it was very good. A five-act ballet can't all be "good Tchaikovsky"; out of tiredness he produces a lot of rubbish. So it's very "kind" of the [younger] composer to toss out what is unnecessary and to elevate the genuine Tchaikovsky. (20 September 1921)

This "reshaping" took place with rehearsals already underway. Observing the initial results of Sergeyev's efforts must have convinced Diaghilev that the Maryinsky version had to be adapted—not simply "reproduced"—for the modern eye and ear. In the weeks ahead, Diaghilev, with the assistance of Stravinsky, Nijinska, and Bakst, produced not only the first version of the ballet conceived for a Western public, but also the first version designed to meet the expectations of a twentieth-century one. In her study of *The Sleeping Princess*, the musicologist Maureen Gupta enumerates some of the changes that Diaghilev and Stravinsky introduced into the score:

> Overall, the musical changes instigated by Diaghilev and carried out by Stravinsky shortened the performance by about half an hour. . . . The most extensive musical cuts were in the long, narrative scenes: No. 4 Finale, in which Carabosse arrives and announces her curse; No. 5 Scène, in which the condemned knitters are pardoned by the King; and No. 9 Finale when Aurora discovers the spindle and the kingdom falls into one hundred years of sleep. Diaghilev accomplished the deletions of mime and pantomime, in large part, through excision of repeated musical phrases or sections within larger bodies of music. . . . Diaghilev also shortened . . . several of the elaborate ensemble dances. These included the Garland Dance and the music for the *corps* during the Vision Scene.[43]

Not all of Diaghilev's musical changes entailed cuts. To accommodate an extra fairy in the Prologue, he interpolated the Sugar Plum Fairy's variation from *The Nutcracker*, which the Lilac Fairy now performed, while Lilac's variation was performed by a new fairy, the Fairy of the Mountain Ash. He wanted ten-year-old Lillian Alicia Marks to dance still another fairy variation, but scotched that idea when she came down with diphtheria.[44] From *Swan Lake* he borrowed the variation that Prince Charming danced in the Wedding pas de deux (the latter was absent from Sergeyev's score). He also restored the Hunting Dances long excised from Act II.[45] Diaghilev's edits magnified the presence of dance throughout the ballet while reducing its considerable narrative "padding." Although *The Sleeping Princess* was the longest ballet seen on the London stage in decades, it was more concentrated, compact, and varied than its Maryinsky predecessor.

***

The company Nijinska returned to was very different from the one she had left. To be sure, there were familiar faces—Lubov Tchernicheva, her husband Sergei Grigoriev, the company's tireless *régisseur*, Ludmilla Schollar and her husband Anatole Vilzak, Lydia Sokolova (the company's first English dancer), Lydia Lopokova, the "baby ballerina" of 1910, Nijinska's estranged husband, Alexander Kochetovsky, and her future one, Nicholas Singaevsky. But her mother and her children were in Vienna, and, as she prepared to take over rehearsals and undertake her first choreography on this unfamiliar company, she felt not only lonely but also deeply alienated from her "material." She found the dancers remote and uncurious, indifferent to the project at hand—unlikely to become active participants in her creative efforts. Nijinska had already shown her mettle as a dancer, and according to Anton Dolin, a young English recruit, she was already teaching company class. Now she had to stand before the dancers in the army drill hall on Chenies Street where they rehearsed, and impose her authority as a choreographer and as a rehearsal director—the first time in the history of the Ballets Russes that a woman did so. She approached her first choreographic assignment with trepidation and self-doubt. "I don't know how I will be," she wrote in her diary:

> All these people are of a different "composition"; it's quiet in their brains. And they don't need anything. . . . Everyone wears a cardboard crown and is afraid to drop it. . . . Tomorrow, apparently, I'll have to stage [choreograph]. It's unfortunate I have to do it like this, at once, not yet knowing the [human] material. It would be good to rehearse them in things they already know, so they would get to know me. I can do something only with material that believes in me. (2 October 1921)

Those first rehearsals broke the ice, and the dancers began talking to her. They had thought she was "mad," she wrote on October 9. "They confessed they were afraid of me and thought I was ill like Vatsa," a fear that Nijinska herself had shared since learning of his illness. But they also thought she was crazy because she "perceive[d] everything differently." Although several of the dancers had escaped the Revolution, none had experienced its transformative power or discovered untapped creative powers in the chaos that followed. Unlike Nijinska, none had questioned the very basis of their art or struggled to make the transition from performer to choreographer. Even if she had fled the Soviet Union, she still carried its taint of artistic radicalism. Making art, making new art, mattered to her, whereas for most émigré Russian dancers, a paying job was more important.

> When I talk about movement or dance, they become frightened. . . . To me it seems I say normal things, but they are scared by the intensity. There is nobody who understands. All the dancers are "good and beautiful"—but these are the qualities of a department store like . . . Galeries Lafayette in Paris. (9 October 1921)

The dances Nijinska choreographed for *The Sleeping Princess* followed Diaghilev's plan. She began with "Bluebeard" and "Schéhérazade," new divertissements that he had decided to interpolate into the Wedding Act. "Bluebeard" was set to the music of "Tom Thumb" and "Schéhérazade" to the "Danse Arabe" (Coffee) music from *The Nutcracker*.[46] She also started work on the Hunting Dances. Although she was not "reproducing" Petipa's choreography, as Sergeyev had, she viewed the movement she was creating as neither "genuine" nor fully her "own" (9 October 1921). In the "choreography" entry in *Ballet Alphabet*, Lincoln Kirstein distinguishes between "different levels of creation." "Choreography," he writes,

> may be interpretative or decorative, or more importantly, inventive and creative. To "interpret" or illustrate music, or to decorate a stage with period revivals, however charming, is less interesting than the creation of lyric drama where dancing . . . can be preeminently an arrangement of ideas particularly suitable to expression in dance terms.[47]

"Interpretative" or "decorative" work was for the most part the traditional approach to choreography. Even Petipa devoted much of his energy to reviving, revising, and re-touching existing works—a category that included ballets such as *Paquita*, *Le Corsaire*, and *Giselle*. For lesser lights this was standard practice; it was expected of them, like staging the dances in operas. Both required invention and imagination, but within a clearly under tood system of constraints. Rethinking a dance or transforming its style was out of the question. Rather what was needed was an act of creative mimicry—choreographing new material in the style of another artist.

It turned out that Nijinska was rather good at this, and in quick succession she choreographed a number of other dances for the production. The one with the longest life was "Innocent Ivan and His Brothers," a lively Russian character number with squat steps and tumbling—the kind of dance her father and husband excelled at—set improbably to the music of the coda of the Wedding pas de deux. She probably had a hand in "The Porcelain Princesses," an interpolated divertissement to the "Danse Chinoise" (or Tea) music from *The Nutcracker*. And she must have done some work on the Precious Stones pas de quatre, which, minus its first (Gold) and third (Sapphire) variations, became a quartet for Colombine (Silver), Pierrette (Diamond), and their partners, Harlequin and Pierrot, respectively. According to the souvenir program, she produced both the "Dances" and "Aurora's Variation" in the Vision Scene, one of the ballet's expressive high points, which she must have extensively rechoreographed. Finally, she was responsible for the "Action-Scenes," meaning that she staged everything that wasn't specifically choreographed, such as "the mass episodes" for Carabosse's entrance, Aurora's scene with the spindle, and her awakening.[48] She had to get the dancers on- and offstage, position the supers—the Lords, Ladies, Pages, and Servants who added human density to the scene—and smooth over the extensive choreographic cuts.

She also had to accommodate the reductions in cast necessitated by Diaghilev's company of sixty or so dancers, compared to the more than two hundred of the pre-Revolutionary Maryinsky. (The Garland Waltz, for instance, went from seventy-two dancers, including twenty-four children, in the original production to thirty-two dancers and no children in the revival.)[49] In fact, Nijinska's choreography became the glue holding the ballet together as well as the palimpsest through which the West discovered Petipa's masterwork. Her achievement elicited praise from the former St. Petersburg ballet critic André Levinson, a newcomer, like Nijinska, to the West. Speaking of the "correspondence" among Bakst's "sparkling" colors, Levinson wrote that her ensembles against the background of Bakst's imposing decors attained "even pathos. Such is the final scene of the first act where the prostrate courtiers mount in a vermillion wave toned with emerald toward the cradle of the princess and the royal couple in blue velvet and ermine, with a group of Negroes in black and gold as a contrast."[50]

Slow to praise, Diaghilev liked what he saw in the studio.[51] To be sure, the detailed choreographic plan was his, so the general outcome was hardly a surprise. However, Nijinska had worked quickly, quietly establishing her authority and subordinating her own needs to those of the production as a whole. Diaghilev, for his part, was "very helpful":

> He describes everything [in detail], so I just have to complete "the order." Everybody here is amazed at how fast I'm working. Only is it really work? When I start doing my own work, I'll move forward very slowly, just like everybody else. *The Sleeping Princess* belongs to the past, so the technique for it already exists. Whereas when you do your own work, you need to [invent] . . . new laws . . . and . . . technique. (13 October 1921)

By early October, Sergeyev's rehearsal period was two-thirds over. Nijinska thought the ballet was doomed. "If I get to rehearse the whole of *Sleeping Princess*," she wrote,

> maybe it will turn out all right. As it is now, it will definitely fail. Everybody is bored. They need to be energized. (2 October 1921)

Sergeyev's contract ended on October 17. With only two weeks left to opening night, Nijinska took over rehearsals. Cyril W. Beaumont, the writer, publisher, and bookshop owner who enjoyed Diaghilev's confidence, attended many rehearsals on the semi-lit stage of the Alhambra Theatre during those October weeks. In the stalls he glimpsed Diaghilev, Stravinsky, Bakst, and occasionally Sergeyev, whom he describes as "short, spare, grizzled, and grim of expression."[52] A grey-haired pianist, Mrs. Lucas, played near the prompt corner. The dancers clustered in groups—the women in pink tights, shoes, short skirts, and, to ward off the cold, sweaters and knitted leg warmers, the men in close-fitting black breeches, white shirts and socks, and black shoes.[53]

> Sometimes the rehearsals would concentrate on an *ensemble*, when the main body of dancers would swirl into long sinuous lines, combine into one throbbing mass, divide, form circles, revolve, then dash from sight. The proceedings were directed by Nijinska. In her dark practice clothes, with her pale features and straw-coloured hair, she seemed like a goddess as she stood near the footlights, bending this plastic, infinitely responsible

material to her will, staying it, urging it on, guiding it through evolution after evolution with dramatic gestures of her white arms, faintly luminous in the half light.[54]

With her galvanizing presence, Nijinska infused the choreography with the rhythm and dynamic energy of her own work.

Arriving in the West, she had imagined that Diaghilev would welcome and support her creative ambitions. She had witnessed firsthand the role he had played in the gestation of her brother's work, and she imagined him doing the same for hers. Unlike her brother, she came to him with a repertory of solos and abstract group works that revealed a high degree of original invention, as well as experience in staging and adapting existing ballets. Diaghilev, Nijinska, and Nijinsky: linked by bonds of love and family, they were an odd Oedipal trio. He was her father in absentia, but he loved her because of her brother, because she was touched by the same genius, because she came, as he said, from the same "stable as Nijinsky."[55] In Warsaw, when the "need to create" returned with full force, she had imagined Diaghilev at her side assisting at the birth of her creative offspring. During the unhappy months in Vienna she had yearned to show him her work—the solos she had created after establishing the School of Movement as well as the more ambitious group works she had choreographed or planned. But Diaghilev kept putting her off, and one may well speculate why. The nineteenth-century composers she had used belonged to his company's past, to ballets like *Les Sylphides* (Chopin), *Carnaval* and *Papillons* (both Schumann), and at least two of her brother's projects that had failed to materialize (Liszt). Of the modern composers whose music she had used, only Prokofiev interested Diaghilev. Moreover, how could she be a Diaghilev artist if she had found her distinctive creative voice on her own? "Bronia," he once told her, "it is a pity that you already know everything about ballet," meaning that unlike her predecessors Nijinsky and Massine, she was already formed as an artist.[56] Finally, Nijinska was independent and headstrong, qualities, according to his biographer Sjeng Scheijen, that Diaghilev "found hard to appreciate in a woman."[57]

Throughout the early months in London, Nijinska kept hoping that he would produce her work.

On October 9:

Now I'm afraid to lose Sergei Pavlovich's trust by doing *The Sleeping Princess*, and then I won't be able to do my own, genuine [work]. It all distresses me. Of course an artist reveals himself sooner or later. I can't wait to do my sketches.

The following day:

> Why isn't [Diaghilev] . . . anxious to display Nijinska the Artist? It must be for some purely "commercial" [reason]. Later it will be hard for him to announce me. . . . I stage dances for this production, but nothing for myself. (10 October 1921)

She never performed her sketches. Instead, Diaghilev kept testing her, adding to her responsibilities, seeing how she coped with them. Unlike her brother or Massine, who were chosen, Nijinska had to earn Diaghilev's respect; she had to prove herself worthy of his creative mentorship. (This is still the case for women in elite ballet companies. As choreographer Rosie Kay complained to the *Dancing Times*, "Men get promoted on potential and women only advance on their past track records.")[58] Whatever new work Nijinska produced had to bear Diaghilev's creative stamp, which meant sweeping her dances from Kiev under the carpet, hiding them as if they did not exist.

Nijinska's diary offers a rare glimpse of Diaghilev's commanding presence in the studio. In Larionov's drawings or in the sketches of Picasso and Cocteau, he sits on the sidelines, portly, middle-aged, leaning on a walking stick, out of place among the slim, young dancers. Yet it was Diaghilev who energized them. His eagle eye, trained by years of rehearsals, classes, and performances, saw who was working hard and who was slacking off, who had the stuff of greatness. Although Nijinska initially feared his presence, especially when she was choreographing, she soon came to appreciate its effect on the dancers. "When he is present, everything always seems to go well," she wrote in her diary (2 October 1921).

As well as rehearsing and partly rechoreographing *The Sleeping Princess*, Nijinska danced four roles in the ballet—the Fairy of the Humming Birds in the Prologue; Pierrette in Act III (a role she shunned as the season went on); the Lilac Fairy, which she alternated performing with Lydia Lopokova and Lubov Egorova; and Princess Florine in the Blue Bird pas de deux. Although the Fairies were technically "classical" roles and Pierrette and Florine "character" ones, she treated them all as material to be molded and personalized by the dancer. During her years in Kiev, Nijinska's whole approach to dancing had changed, and now she sought to apply her new expressive technique to the material at hand. Choreographically, she changed nothing. But she danced the choreography in a way that set her apart from the others. "I'm such a different dancer," she wrote,

> that even the dancers don't know if it's good or bad, but it hypnotizes them. . . . They say about me: why am I re-inventing these Petipa variations when they are already choreographed? But I'm not inventing anything. I'm dancing with my whole body, not just with my legs. (10 October 1921)

Returning to the company, "the Theater I grew up in," as she called it, confirmed the distance she had traveled since 1913. She felt that she was "a really great dancer," although Diaghilev said that she had " 'unlearned' to dance" in the intervening years, which prompted a wave of self-doubt in Nijinska, as Diaghilev must have known it would (2 October 1921).

Nijinska received good notices for her dancing. Critics lamented that she had too little to do; others commented on her fascinating and compelling personality.[59] Philip J. S. Richardson in the *Dancing Times* praised her versatility:

> In the part of the "Lilac Fairy," I have to date seen Lydia Lopokova, Lubov Egorova and Madame Nijinska, and the last-named appeals to me as the most versatile dancer of the entire company. Her technique in her classical numbers is beyond reproach . . . and her mime and personality in the demi-caractère dances most convincing. The latter is best seen when she dances as "Pierette" [*sic*] in the first of the "Fairy Tales" in the last act.[60]

Vogue, in a long and mostly unfavorable review of the ballet, singled her out: "Nijinska, *folle* from the hips upward and flinging herself with a delicious *abandon* in two directions at once, provided an occasional grotesque excitement."[61] As photographs of her as the Fairy of the Humming Birds reveal, she used makeup less to enhance her features than to make them strange, lengthening her eyes, pursing her lips, making her face an extension of the insect-like antennae sprouting from her headpiece.[62] (Nijinska's "striking" makeup reminded her friend Nina Moiseevna of "old Polish icons."[63]) She used her upper body with freedom and in dynamic contrast with her legs; abandoning classical restraint, she infused the choreography with modern rhythm. In a sense this most "feminine" choreography became the first of the grotesque roles that Nijinska would fashion for herself in the next three years, the first of her Diaghilev assignments to offer a critique of ballet's conventional representation of femininity. On programs she dropped her first name (as she had done earlier at the Moulin-Rouge) and signed her choreography as Nijinska or La Nijinska. In the history of the Ballets Russes she was the only dancer to do this.

Much later, Nijinska wrote a brief reminiscence, probably intended as a chapter in a volume of memoirs, about returning to the Ballets Russes and working on *The Sleeping Princess*. At this point, her chief concern was to document her full contribution to the work, since at the time, she explains, she had stipulated that her "name not appear in the company's programs for the [overall] restaging of the ballet, but only for the composition of individual dance numbers, so as not to be taken in my very first work as a choreographer of the old school."[64] She stated that Diaghilev and Bakst "had specially invited [her] to [work] under their guidance to rescue [the ballet] from all that was old and alien in the Maryinsky Theater [production]," and that together with Stravinsky all three "labored" to that end. "Every evening," she wrote,

> we met at the Savoy Hotel [where Diaghilev was staying] and conferred about how to "clean up" *The Sleeping Beauty* and present the *Beauty* in her. It must be said that there were pearls of Petipa's choreography in [the ballet], but for a long period in its life, supervision of the ballet was unenlightened, and it was spoiled in many ways.

She claims that by the time she arrived in London, the ballet had been "diligently restored" by Sergeyev. However, when Diaghilev and Bakst saw his work in rehearsal, "they decided that it was impossible to show such a *Sleeping Beauty* in London . . . , [and that] I, together with Diaghilev, Bakst, and Stravinsky was to 'restore' and 'renew' the entire [ballet] from the beginning, and most importantly, create all the mise-en-scènes."

She then goes on to discuss her transformation of the role of the Lilac Fairy—something that histories of the ballet, written as they tend to be from a Russian perspective, generally ignore.

> The role of the Lilac Fairy was re-created by me in its entirety. In Petersburg, in my time, the Lilac Fairy was performed by [Marie Petipa], the no longer young daughter of Marius Petipa. In appearance and character she did not

blend in with the other fairies. She did not wear dancing slippers but heeled shoes, and from her shoulders fell a long train carried by six little pupils of the Theater School (I was among them). She carried a long [staff] with a bouquet of lilies at the end, and . . . reminded me of a Grande Dame, imperious mistress of the action, and even then I did not like her, although outwardly she was considered beautiful. I created the Lilac Fairy entirely on pointe; [I made her] a fairy-tale, unreal, benevolent fairy, who moves around the stage on pointe like a cloud.

Nijinska also transformed the choreography of Petipa's fairy "Violente,"[65] now renamed the Fairy of the Humming Birds and popularly known as the "Finger" variation. Petipa had described the role as *échevelée*—"disheveled" or "tempestuous" (as Wiley prefers)—her gift being that of temperament or power. However, as Giannandrea Poesio points out, the variation has a number of Italian precedents, including one in Manzotti's 1881 spectacle ballet *Excelsior*, in which Light "dances with pointed fingers to convey Alessandro Volta's discovery of electricity."[66] Vera M. Krasovskaya describes the variation, as she knew it in Russia, as a dance "built . . . on a sharp alternation of movements. The arms tense, with index fingers stretched out and pointing, they cut through the air like flashing lightning."[67] When Nijinska arrived in London, all the solo parts, except for the Violente, had been cast. The variation, she writes,

was considered quite unsuccessful at the Maryinsky in Petipa's version. This dance I completely re-created as a variation on Petipa's theme all in spiral movements of the hands and body. . . . Diaghilev and Bakst were ecstatic over it. . . . This variation is still performed . . . as part of Petipa's choreography for *The Sleeping Beauty*, even though it was wholly created by me.[68]

This was the "Finger" variation that Nijinska taught Ninette de Valois in 1923. However, it was only when de Valois showed the variation to Olga Preobrajenska, the former Imperial ballerina with whom she was studying in Paris, that she realized how different it was from the original. After a moment of dead silence, "Preo" grimly commented, "'*Bizarre, très bizarre.*'"[69] De Valois herself preferred Nijinska's "infinitely more interesting development" of the solo. "Do not just point," Nijinska had told her. "Make a spiral movement with your whole arm." Diaghilev, too, according to de Valois, preferred Nijinska's "modern arrangement" to the traditional one and later asked de Valois to teach it to someone else.[70]

In 1935, Nijinska herself taught it to Irina Baronova, a "baby ballerina" of the De Basil Ballet Russe. The only major choreographic change, Baronova wrote in her memoirs, was the running entrance from the wings, entering downstage rather than from the top left, sweeping past the footlights and circling to center stage; the steps that followed were the same. However, the execution was "totally different." From the waist up, the body and shoulders were in constant movement, "the arm movements rounded, elbows slightly raised, the jumps long rather than high." On the semi-dark stage, with Nijinska singing and shouting, the ordinary had become extraordinary— "vibrant, unusual, fascinating."[71] Although the role was not so personal to Nijinska that she could not pass it on, its conceptualization was indebted to her particular character as a dancer: choreography and embodiment overlapped to a far greater degree than usually happens in ballet. This kind of imaginative transformation is what she learned from her brother's performances as the Blue Bird, and also from his coaching of her as Papillon in Fokine's ballet *Carnaval* (another role passed on to de Valois)—the metamorphosis of an image without altering the pattern or basic choreography of a role.[72]

The Sleeping Princess opened in London on November 9, 1921. The first night was a technical disaster. When Carabosse appeared at the end of Act I to cast her spell, "the 'machine' worked badly, and the cactus which began to spring up round the enchanted castle refused to become the luxuriant crop . . . it should have been," while in the Vision Scene "the mists . . . got caught up on the scenery when they ought to have descended."[73] Diaghilev broke down and sobbed.[74] Critics called the ballet a bore, a vulgar dress parade, a "superior pantomime," a rambling "procession of scenes and dances . . . without meaning," "straightforward old-style ballet-dancing," and the "suicide of the Russian Ballet" (the latter by Diaghilev's arch-enemy, the music critic Ernest Newman who wrote for the *Sunday Times*).[75] Nijinska relates none of this in her diary. In fact, she ignores completely the twice-postponed opening, the disasters of the first night, the mixed reception, the words of praise for herself, and the card addressed "To my returned Bronia" that Diaghilev sent her for the premiere, presumably with flowers.[76] For six weeks, from October 19 to November 19, she leaves off writing, and when she resumes, she says next to nothing about the ballet.

What she writes about instead is what she views as the artistic bankruptcy of the entire Diaghilev enterprise. She does not mince words:

Diaghilev's "Theater": a horrifying degradation of everything I expected to find here. It has turned into a brothel that "displays" beautiful female dancers. I'm not sure anybody is interested in creative accomplishments. . . . My sense of being unneeded . . . [is] destroying me. . . .

Everything here is totally retrograde. I never hear that so-and-so is a good or a bad artist, only that someone jumps well or turns well. . . . It's no better here than at a "City Opera Theater."

What use is it all? . . . Nobody needs art anymore, only something that draws an audience. . . .

What madness in me: I'm still looking for creativity. I still want something!

Someone said that the only thing left in Europe is Industry. If only that were true. In reality, there is only rot. . . . One should only do what one loves. One mustn't sell one's creativity. God give me strength. I want to go back to Russia so much. (29 November 1921)

Around this time Nijinska seems to have tried to force Diaghilev's hand. In her archives is the penciled draft of a letter to Diaghilev alluding to some kind of "scandal." The specifics are lost, but reading between the lines, one senses that Nijinska had insisted on recognition of her gifts as a performer. "I naturally can't stand creating scandals," she wrote,

but I recognize that in recent years I have picked up some bad habits, and I want you to forgive them. . . . I am not a second-rate ballerina (behind Lopokova and Tchernicheva), and I am not even on the same level as they are. Nijinska is an exceptional talent, something special. I promise not to demand "ballerina" jobs, but whenever I dance, the company sings about me in front of the public and the press.[77]

On November 30 she seems to have reached a dangerous breaking point:

I walk and cry and can't cope with myself. I don't know what I live for. I don't know how to live. Everything is broken: my children are far away, and Vatsa is gone. . . . My unbearable love and my crazy creativity don't have any outlet. Fedor [Chaliapin] appears in my dreams and ruined hopes. Madness gains on me.

The next entry, on December 2, suggests that the "scandal," whatever this may have been, had passed:

It seems that I am recovering. . . . Everything I deserve will come. No need to worry about "recognition." Why do I need it? I can always earn enough for my children. I must arrange my life so that I can do what I think should be done, even if only on a small scale. Everything will be fine. Maybe all this happened because I tried to accomplish something by "politicking," whereas [in the past] I have always . . . relied only on my own talent.

Whatever may have happened, Diaghilev continued to hold her in high regard. With a salary of 5,000 francs a month, she was the third-highest paid member of the company.[78] In fact, he was delighted with her. As he wrote to the composer Francis Poulenc in mid-November, "I am happy to tell you that I now have an admirable new *maître de ballet*—Nijinsky's sister, la Nijinska, who works wonders."[79] Two years later Poulenc and Nijinska would collaborate on *Les Biches*.

Nijinska had married her husband on the rebound from her failed romance with Chaliapin. Now both converged on London. After leaving Russia, Kochetovsky made his way to Paris and danced for the Chauve-Souris, the émigré cabaret directed by Nikita Balieff that had successfully transplanted itself from Moscow. He joined the Ballets Russes during rehearsals for *The Sleeping Princess*. Nijinska's relationship with Kochetovsky was distant but friendly, and within a few weeks of her arrival they agreed to divorce, although it wasn't until 1924, when she was making plans to marry her second husband, that Nijinska actually filed the papers. However, she felt attracted to him, and they continued to see one another, despite the fact that he was seeing someone else. When he came to say goodbye before leaving for New York with the Chauve-Souris, he seemed eager for some kind of reconciliation even though his girlfriend was pregnant:

Sasha came by before leaving for America. It was as if all the past was resurrected: it was possible for me to kiss him and hold his head. . . . [But] it's impossible for me to be with him. The days . . . before his departure assured me of that, but . . . he was still thinking about . . . marriage. While . . . a woman is expecting his baby, he is . . . kissing my feet. . . . [T]he story repeats itself, the one that happened to me when I was little. Father and his other family. . . . [But] I know that nothing would work out; he would leave again for another life, and I would feel even more disgusted by everything. (25 January 1922)[80]

Kochetovsky left for New York, where he scored something of a hit. Arthur Hornblow in *Theatre Magazine* was fascinated by his "marvelous conception" of a "clown issuing from the lights of the arena into the silence and loneliness of his dressing room," a pantomime expressing his "fate and life and hopes and despairs."[81] Although their lives now followed separate paths, Nijinska kept the clipping, as though it held special significance for her. In fact, it seems to foreshadow one of her most poignant roles, Pedrollino, the tragic Chaplinesque clown of *Les Comédiens Jaloux* (1932). As this modern-day Pierrot, Nijinska wore what became her rehearsal uniform—a loose jacket, loose pants, and soft ballet shoes. "She's plump, her oval face is paper-white," wrote Michel Mok in the *New York Post* after watching her rehearse *La Fille Mal Gardée* for Ballet Theatre's 1940 season, "and because she wears a . . . smock, . . . sailor pants, . . . and . . . white cotton gloves she reminds you of Auguste—shy, awkward, blundering Auguste—the traditional clown of the French circus."[82] In her adoption of this persona one senses a current of feeling linking her to her ex-husband, a suggestion of a shared artistic identity, something that hinted at a creative journey they had begun as a couple.

Apart from Kochetovsky, the Ballets Russes included two other men with claims on Nijinska's heart. The first was Vladislav Karnecki, who joined the Ballets Russes in London, almost certainly at Nijinska's behest and possibly traveling with her from Vienna. In an unpublished note, Nijinska wrote that in 1915, when the city of Lvov was taken by Russian troops, Karnecki—or Karnetskii, as Nijinska called him,

found himself in Kiev as an Austrian refugee. He went to Kochetovsky at the City Opera Theater and asked for work. I remember asking him: Does he know how to dance? "Oh, yes, ballroom dances and a very good tango." "This is something for the Opera," Kochetovsky and I chuckled. . . . Kochetovsky . . . then went to Bagrov, the Director, requesting that he take him on as a ballet dancer (in the ballet, including Kochetovsky, there were only five men). Bagrov agreed. So Karnetskii began his ballet [career]. He was very hardworking and quickly made a success of his dances.[83]

Although unmentioned in her diary, Karnecki had spent the last several months partnering her at the Moulin-Rouge. He was handsome with dark curly hair and a touch of her father's rakish charm. Nijinska cast him in the Garland Waltz and the Hunt scene and as one of the three Ivans in the lively character number "Innocent Ivan and His Brothers" that stole the show[84]—a sign she may have had a soft spot for him and her feelings were reciprocated.

Also in the company was another "pupil" from Kiev, Nicholas Singaevsky. Like many of her students, he was educated. A childhood friend of the writer Mikhail Bulgakov (of *The White Guard* and *The Master and Margarita* fame), he had studied law at Imperial Moscow University and St. Vladimir's University in his native Kiev, although he probably didn't complete his degree. Tatiana Lappa, the writer's first wife, recalled him as a handsome man, tall and lean, who dreamed about studying ballet but became a cadet to defend the city against the Ukrainian nationalist forces of Simon Petliura.[85] How he gravitated to the School of Movement is a mystery; he appears on Nijinska's Kiev lists, but apart from noting (erroneously) that he left in May 1920, she says nothing about him. In fact, he spent less than a year at the School before emigrating. Passing through Warsaw, he posed for the Leo Forbert Studio, first as a "barefoot" dancer à la Duncan, then as a soulful Pierrot.[86] He danced briefly with the Ballets Russes in 1919, spent the 1920–1921 season at the Grand Theater in Poznan, then rejoined the Ballets Russes in Monte Carlo in April 1921.[87] In 1924 she would marry him, although he was nearly five years her junior.

Finally, there was Chaliapin. As always, he remained at arm's length. Like Nijinska, he had spent the post-Revolutionary years in the Soviet Union, and although long identified as a political radical, he too ran partly afoul of Russia's new rulers. In the autumn of 1921, after an absence of seven years, Chaliapin returned to sing in England. Traveling under Soviet auspices, he gave five famine relief concerts, including two in London. Nijinska was among the thousands crowding the huge Albert Hall on October 5. The audience was "enthralled," wrote Herman Klein in the *Musical Times*, as Chaliapin performed "group after group of 'selected arias'—all sung in the unfamiliar Russian language, not one of them advertised or announced by name beforehand."[88] Nijinska, too, was overwhelmed, although she had long since rejected the Stanislavskian aesthetic to which Chaliapin subscribed. "He is as colossal an artist as he was," she wrote in her diary.

> True, he had to "please" the audience—to apologize for his Bolshevist "sins." . . . But he is closer to me as a person than as an artist. Even though I don't know a bigger artist than Chaliapin. (9 October 1921)

Nijinska doesn't explain what his "Bolshevist sins" were, nor do the reviews that appeared in the *Times*, *Observer*, and *Manchester Guardian*. However, in *Man and Mask*, a memoir published in emigration, he recalled the catcalls that had greeted him in Estonia, where he first sang abroad after the Revolution, and being taken for a Bolshevik simply because he came from Soviet Russia. (Of his London concerts, all he recalled was turning over half his English royalties to the Soviet ambassador.[89]) Still, conservatives may well have attacked his Soviet loyalties, and Nijinska, troubled by her own mixed feelings for the country she had recently fled, was identifying with what she perceived as his victimization. Certainly, she continued to see him as a beacon—the memory of his love coupled with the aphrodisiac of his presence remained tied in her mind to the flow of her own creativity. Now she was bereft: "Having lost my love I also lost the ability to create," she wrote three days before 1921 drew to a close. But she cut out a photo of him for her scrapbook, with the legend, "London, October 1921, returned to Europe from Soviet Russia."[90]

A month later, in one of the diary's last entries, she describes returning alone at night to her dingy hotel room, with its narrow bed, wash stand, and framed photo of the singer on the fireplace, and experiencing, as she wrote, "a crazy longing for Dance!"

> In the deep, soft armchair [my] body comes to life and quietly sings in a whisper. Then the room is forgotten. . . . [My] body, elated, flexes every little vein; it ties itself into a knot; the growing slowness increases the pleasure. . . . Then all of a sudden a dance of the face only—eyes and mouth . . . A slow prelude is repeated many times, and each time there is something to add; again and again—until I lose consciousness and under- standing, until everything is drunk off. . . . Then, quietly, a nocturne begins. Jewel-like lace turns into stormy protest and ends in torment. . . . Everything

is forgotten—ecstasy is dancing in a two-meter space of my own. (27 January 1922)

The Sleeping Princess received 114 performances in London, surely a ballet record. However, about halfway through the run, receipts began to drop off. On February 4, to a cheering house, the company danced its last performance. Lydia Lopokova made a curtain speech announcing they would soon return, although it would be nearly three years before that happened. Then, the company scattered. Diaghilev had already gone to Paris, and the Alhambra impounded the sets and costumes. Nijinska left for Vienna and her family.

4

Where Is Home?

After a short stay in Vienna, Nijinska joined Diaghilev in Paris in early April 1922. Diaghilev had been there for well over a month, lying low in an aerie at the Hôtel Continental and eating the *plat du jour* at a nearby workingmen's restaurant.[1] He had fled London even before *The Sleeping Princess* ended, borrowing money to pay his most pressing debts but failing to lift a finger to save the scenery and costumes of the ballet from being impounded by the Alhambra Company Limited, which had paid for them. When it became clear that audiences and receipts were diminishing, it was suggested that he alternate performances of the ballet with evenings of repertory. But Diaghilev was adamant. He had taken a gamble and intended to play to the end. So the company scattered, and *The Sleeping Princess* became a memory.

A less resilient producer might have thrown in the towel, imagining that in the increasingly straitened circumstances of the postwar period—without free-spending Russians to help balance the books—a ballet company along the lines of the Ballets Russes was an inconceivable luxury. Moreover, Diaghilev was under contract to present *The Sleeping Beauty* (in France the ballet reverted to its original title) at the Paris Opéra. But Diaghilev seemed to revel in extreme situations of this kind, as if the dynamics of near disaster and providential rescue gave life a stimulating edge of danger, pushing him to come up with solutions that people felt compelled to accept. He may have been a "great *charmeur*," as he had told his stepmother nearly thirty years before,[2] but he was also a brilliant con man.

After *The Sleeping Princess*, the company became appreciably smaller. The youngest and least experienced dancers (such as Anton Dolin and Errol Addison) were dropped, and a number of senior dancers departed. Olga Spessivtzeva headed back to Petrograd (where she would star in Fedor Lopukhov's first Soviet revival of *The Sleeping Beauty*), while Lydia Lopokova, Lydia Sokolova, Leon Woizikovsky, and several others remained in London, where they danced for a time with Massine, landed jobs at the London Coliseum, and appeared in the musical comedy *Phi-Phi*.[3] However, a still substantial company of fifty or so dancers converged on Monte Carlo for ten days of rehearsal and a short season before opening in Paris on May 18. Serge Grigoriev summed up the situation laconically: "We were overwhelmed with work."[4]

Meanwhile, Diaghilev came up with a repertory plan to satisfy the Opéra. This involved creating a forty-minute divertissement of the most striking dances from *The Sleeping Princess* and mounting a mini-Stravinsky festival consisting of two short new works—*Le Renard*, a "burlesque ballet with song," and *Mavra*, a "comic opera in one act"—and two major revivals— Fokine's *Petrouchka* and Massine's version of *The Rite of Spring* (1920). Nijinsky's *L'Après-midi d'un Faune* (revived for the first time in Paris since 1913), Massine's *Contes Russes* and *Soleil de Nuit* or *Midnight Sun*, and several Fokine favorites—*Carnaval* (1910), the *Polovtsian Dances from "Prince Igor"* (1909), *Schéhérazade* (1910), and *Le Spectre de la Rose* (1911)—completed the repertory of the nearly four-week season.[5]

Jacques Rouché, the director of the Paris Opéra, accepted the substitution of *Le Renard* for *Les Noces villageoises* (which the original contract had called for and which Diaghilev, after briefly rehearsing, had put off); both, after all, were new Stravinsky works. *Beauty*, however, was another matter. "[I]n place of *The Sleeping Beauty*, a grand, evening-long ballet, you propose giving a fragment of the work, *The Marriage of the Sleeping Beauty*," he complained.

> You understand how receipts can be affected by substituting a one-act ballet inserted in a program of old ballets for a brilliant spectacle composed of a single, entirely new work. I had counted on a profitable success, *The Sleeping Beauty* being already known here thanks to the stir created by its numerous London performances, its magnificent production, Bakst's numerous sets and costumes, and the quality of its interpreters.

"The solution you propose," he ended, "offers nothing but disadvantages."[6]

In the end Rouché acceded, and the Ballets Russes played its last long season at the Palais Garnier. For Nijinska, that season—and the two weeks that followed at the Théâtre Mogador when *Chout*, *The Good-Humoured Ladies* (1917), and *Les Sylphides* (1909) were added to the repertory—was pivotal to her development as an artist and to her position in the consolidating canon of ballet modernism. It confirmed her membership in ballet's "apostolic succession" (in Lincoln Kirstein's phrase) and in the modernist tradition created by Diaghilev that included Fokine, her brother, Massine, and George Balanchine. It established her as a choreographer equally at home in classical and contemporary styles, someone conversant with the legacy of Russia's dance past but harboring her own creative ideas about movement. It revealed her singular, dynamic presence as a performer and her inclination for roles that crossed gender boundaries. Finally, it marked her as an outsider in a French ballet world grown increasingly conservative. The experimentalist who had once dreamed of dancing in Kiev's Andreevskaia Church[7] had become a hard-working, highly productive, and respected ballet professional, albeit one still attuned to the modern.

***

Aurora's Wedding, as *The Marriage of the Sleeping Beauty* was titled in English, was one of Nijinska's most felicitous compositions. It became one of Diaghilev's most popular ballets and a staple of the Ballets Russes companies that sprang up after his death, remaining in active repertory until the 1960s. Along with the second act of *Swan Lake* and *Giselle, Aurora's Wedding* allowed Western audiences of the interwar years to glimpse the repertory of the Imperial Ballet. In the 1930s, the Sadler's Wells company, under the direction of Ninette de Valois, would embark on a project to recuperate what were perceived to be the masterworks or "classics" of that repertory. But until then, and long afterward for audiences outside England, *Aurora's Wedding* was as close as people came to experiencing *The Sleeping Beauty*.

Pretty much everything about the new project was recycled. The scenery and most of the costumes were by Alexandre Benois for *Le Pavillon d'Armide* (1909), a ballet set in the eighteenth century and long unperformed, with additional costumes by Natalia Goncharova. The ballet retained key dances from *The Sleeping Princess*: the first part consisted of the Polonaise from Act III, the "Pas de Sept of the Maid of Honour and Their Cavaliers" from the Prologue (with the seven fairy variations), and dances for the Duchesses, Countesses, and Marquesses, and the Farandole from the Hunt Scene. The "Fairy Tales" followed—"Florestan and His Sisters," "Puss in Boots," "The Blue Bird," "Little Red Riding Hood," "Bluebeard," "The Siamese Butterfly" (a new addition), "Schéhérazade," "The Porcelain Princesses," "The Three Ivans," "Princess Aurora and Prince Charming (Pas de Deux)"—the whole concluding with a Mazurka. Here was *The Sleeping Beauty*, viewed through the prism of *The Sleeping Princess*, with its narrative content removed and its virtuosity enhanced: at the Paris premiere, in good nineteenth-century fashion, the ballerina Vera Trefilova interpolated into the final pas de deux the thirty-two fouetté turns from *Swan Lake* moving forward down the Opéra's raked stage. Critic André Levinson, who knew both versions well, described *Aurora's Wedding* as a "long fragment or . . . succinct summary" of the Petersburg original, a "vast divertissement" stripped of drama.[8] As such, it was kin to the semi-plotless works produced by experimental choreographers of Russia's post-Revolutionary years, a repertory to which Nijinska herself had contributed and that would be significantly enriched the following year by Fedor Lopukhov's *Dance Symphony: The Creation of the Universe* and by Nijinska's own *Les Noces*. *Aurora's Wedding* may have lacked the strong point of view and the individual choreographic voice of these fully modernist works, but to the extent that it extracted a pure dance work (albeit one with narrative overtones) from a nineteenth-century story ballet, it anticipated Balanchine's neo-Imperial abstractions of the late 1940s, especially *Theme and Variations* (1947), with its many allusions to *The Sleeping Beauty*.

Aurora's Wedding charmed French critics. "Never," wrote Louis Laloy in *Comoedia*, "has a princess marrying the prince of her dreams been so fêted, even in the theater, with such brilliance and wit, as fairies come to mix with the court ladies and one after another the most marvelous tales pass before the eyes of the happily awakened bride, so light in the arms of Prince Charming."[9] Adolphe Jullien, in *Le Journal des Débats*, rhapsodized over the "sumptuous setting, with scenery and disguises of great richness, imagined by Alexandre Benois and recalling the splendors of ballets of the seventeenth century, when [Jean-Baptiste] Lully reigned."[10] The composer André Messager, in *Figaro*, dismissed Tchaikovsky's music as a "bibelot . . . evoking an abolished era," but expressed admiration for the work as a whole:

> The staging, scenery, and costumes offer a charming spectacle; the ensembles are arranged with that ingenuousness, neatness, and variety of invention that characterizes the Ballets Russes; the dances or variations (a little too abundant) are danced by soloists of first order, and the whole is a treat for the eyes.[11]

Messager's views with respect to Tchaikovsky were echoed by many critics—his music was vulgar, mannered, unoriginal, and the least Russian imaginable—even as they expressed pleasure in everything else. Thus, Jean Poueigh in *Carnet de la Semaine*, after announcing that "all the glosses, however peremptory or ingratiating, will never succeed in persuading me to accept Tchaikovsky's music as good," described the ballet as a "visual feast," with sumptuous costumes and "dances, stunning in their disciplined fantasy . . . [and] dazzling spatial patterns."[12] Finally—and how this must have galled Diaghilev—some critics mentioned the ballet in the same breath as *Artémis Troublée*, in which Ida Rubinstein, his first Cleopatra, now dazzling in a tutu designed by Bakst, had made her debut in pointe shoes at the Paris Opéra only days before the start of the Ballets Russes season.[13]

Many critics commented favorably on the combination of traditionalism and modernism, noting that the original ballet had been choreographed by a Frenchman, Marius Petipa, born in Marseille. (The French connection was emphasized in the playbill, with a credit that read "Classic ballet by Marius Petipa, French choreographer [1822–1910] represented on the centenary of his birth.")[14] Few realized what deep cuts had been made in his choreography, since French ballets, even those of several acts, never occupied a full evening but were always programmed with an opera. However, even if critics did not appreciate how radically *Aurora's Wedding* differed from its Petersburg ancestor, they did remark upon the touches of modernity in the production, the combination, in Levinson's words, of "old things of great beauty" and "some highly ingenious recent inventions."[15] Louis Laloy, for instance, noted "the modern taste of the staging" and how it added "much that was picturesque" to the original costumes, adding,

> I strongly doubt that they would rival in the vibrant harmony of color those of Mme Goncharova, just as the *entrées*, so brief and yet so expressive, of Bluebeard between two of his women, Puss in Boots, Little Red Riding Hood, the Chinese with their fans, Scheherazade held captive by her wild brothers, the three Ivans, and finally this sketch of a Cambodian . . . are certainly greatly indebted to Mme Nijinska.[16]

Indeed, far more than later versions of *Aurora's Wedding*, the ballet that critics saw on opening night belonged to Nijinska. The dances for the Hunt Scene were hers, as were most of the Fairy Tales and Pierre Vladimirov's variation as Prince Charming. Onstage, she was one of seven "Ladies of Honor" dancing her revamped "Finger Variation"; then in the divertissement, she donned male attire and a mask to perform "Puss in Boots" (to Ludmilla Schollar's White Cat), and, after another costume change, she became a "Siamese Butterfly," a solo that was probably a cousin of her brother's *Danse Siamoise* from 1910. Cuts, however, began once the company left the Paris

Opéra for a follow-up season at the Théâtre Mogador. In the Hunt Scene, the Countesses disappeared, in the Fairy Tales both "Florestan and His Sisters" and "The Siamese Butterfly," Nijinska's own solo, and she was bumped from "Puss in Boots" by Stanislas Idzikovsky. In other words, she gave up—or had to give up—the gender-crossing or gender-ambiguous roles that had complicated the nineteenth-century world of Petipa's *Sleeping Beauty*. After Nijinska left the company, further cuts were made, and most of these involved her choreography. By 1928 "The Marquesses" were gone, and only "The Three Ivans" was credited to Nijinska. Everything else, according to the program, was Petipa's.[17]

Aurora's Wedding was only one of the season's new ballets in which Nijinska crossed gender boundaries. In *Le Renard*, Stravinsky's "burlesque ballet with song," she was the Fox to Stanislas Idzikovsky's Cock, Jean Jazvinsky's Goat (or Ram in the original Russian libretto), and Michel Fedorow's Cat, one of a male barnyard quartet, albeit a character who donned female garb to charm the cock of the walk. The ballet grew out of Stravinsky's fascination with popular Russian theatrical forms and experiments in the staging of word, music, and movement that peaked during World War I, when he completed the work in Switzerland. "*Le Renard*," the program note read,

is a "burlesque story that is played and sung" with actors who are on stage and singers who are in the pit.

The actors do not speak; the singers speak for them. The Cock and the Fox are the principal characters.

The Fox, disguised as a nun, seizes the Cock, but is put to flight by the Cat and the Goat. They dance for joy.

The Fox reappears disguised as a vagabond. He offers sweets to the Cock and seizes him again. He plucks him. But the Cat and the Goat save the Cock and slit his tormentor's throat. They dance for joy and exit the stage as they entered it.[18]

Originally, Stravinsky had envisaged the players as "clowns, dancers, or acrobats, preferably on a trestle stage, with the orchestra behind them."[19] The work that Nijinska staged in 1922 was considerably more conventional, although with only four dancers, four singers, and four instrumentalists, it was certainly spare for a Diaghilev production. In fact, it would be hard to imagine a more incongruous setting for this twenty-minute work than the Paris Opéra, with its huge proscenium stage and sumptuous auditorium. The space must have swallowed the unassuming tale, with its burlesque action and dialogue ("Oh . . . he pulls me by the tail, he pulls me by the tail," wails the Cock when the Fox first grabs him) and the playful anthropomorphic modernism of Mikhail Larionov's costumes. For Nijinska's Fox, he designed a slinky plaid skirt and Russian peasant shoes, to which he added a fox snout and a bushy foxtail and, when she became a nun, the veil and surplice of an Orthodox habit. The Goat, in shades of yellow and brown, wore a Russian peasant blouse, along with horns and a beard, while the Cock, in officer garb, sported a tail and beaked headpiece. Larionov's wintry backdrop, in muted blues and browns, depicted a traditional Russian farmyard, covered in snow, with a ladder and a perch for the Cock. It was based on a sketch by Diaghilev himself, testifying to his active engagement in the creative process.[20]

Most critics couldn't make heads or tails of the story. They carped about the "puerile and rustic French," the "bizarre" and "curious" music (although some admired its "new and ingenious effects"), and the exasperating "silliness" of the project as a whole.[21] Gérard d'Houville, writing in *Le Gaulois*, registered only disappointment:

> We remember that before the war, *The Rite of Spring*, that bizarre and beautiful thing, a sort of barbaric prophecy of Bolshevik rule, was booed and hissed, while giving rise to endless discussions and controversy. . . . Now, today, we accept with a kind of passivity *Le Renard*, which is not really amusing as dance and is certainly weak and grating as music.[22]

Only Louis Laloy, writing in *Comoedia*, expressed genuine enthusiasm for Stravinsky's music.[23]

By contrast, almost everyone praised the cast. Laloy spoke of Nijinska's "indefatigable vivacity" as the Fox and Idzikovsky's "extremely witty" Cock. The choreography was acrobatic, with a strong dose of the grotesque, a combination that fit Stravinsky's theme like a glove but struck at least one critic, Ravel's future biographer Roland-Manuel, as "vulgar and coarse."[24] However, Diaghilev loved the work and finally engaged Nijinska as the company's official choreographer.[25] Stravinsky had warm memories of the production and for her contribution to it. "Nijinska had admirably seized the spirit of its mountebank buffoonery," he wrote in his autobiography.

> She displayed such a wealth of ingenuity, so many fine points, and so much satirical verve that the effect was irresistible. She herself, playing the part of *Renard*, created an unforgettable figure.[26]

Stravinsky paid several visits to Monte Carlo where *Le Renard* was choreographed and, pleased with what he saw in the studio, asked Nijinska to direct the "plastic movement" of his opera buffa *Mavra*, which premiered a few weeks after *Le Renard*. "She had marvelous ideas," he recalled, "which were unfortunately balked by the inability of the singers to subject themselves to a technique and discipline in the practice of which they were unversed."[27] To Stravinsky's intense disappointment, *Mavra* sank without a trace, probably because only Russian speakers understood it and appreciated its satiric humor.

During the long 1922 spring-summer season that opened in Monte Carlo on April 25 and ended in Ostend on August 10, Nijinska danced every performance. She appeared in two or three ballets and displayed a versatility unmatched by any of her peers and exceeded only by her brother in the years before *The Rite of Spring*. She reclaimed the Fokine roles she had abandoned on leaving the company in 1914—the Mazurka in *Les Sylphides*, Ta-Hor in *Cléopâtre*, the Odalisque in *Schéhérazade*, the Ballerina in *Petrouchka*, the Polovtsian Girl in *Prince Igor*. At the same time she added several new roles to her repertory. One was the Buffoon in *Chout*, to Prokofiev's first score for the Ballets Russes, which Thadée Slavinsky, jointly with Larionov, had choreographed in 1921 (and in which Slavinsky had starred). This was another male role with a cross-dressing element, another burlesque tale from the inexhaustible source of Russian folklore.[28] Although the ballet had fallen flat its first season, Nijinska reanimated it. She danced it for the first time after the company moved to the Mogador, on a program with *Les Sylphides*, *L'Après-midi d'un Faune*, and *Schéhérazade*, in all of which she danced—a tour de force that *Figaro* called "a form of genius."[29] The expatriate American critic Florence Gilliam, a Ballets Russes enthusiast and a friend of both Larionov and Goncharova, attributed much of the ballet's success to Nijinska, "who in the part of the chief Buffoon is a marvel of spontaneous humour reinforced with an amazing comic gift in pantomime."[30] Nijinska also ventured into Massine territory. In his repertory she found another comic role, Kikimora, inspired by Russian folk tales. Nijinska must have loved the role of the wicked spirit who vanquishes and kills the story-telling Cat: it was earthy and Russian and allowed for yet another of the metamorphoses that were rapidly becoming one of her artistic trademarks, calling for a mask-like makeup that all but concealed her face. Lydia Sokolova had originated the role; Nijinska now inherited it. However, Nijinska never mentioned Kikimora in any of her writings, and she never breathed a word about another Massine role that she inherited from Sokolova—the Chosen Maiden in his *Rite of Spring*.

Her silence is not hard to explain. Loyalty to her brother was a cornerstone of her character, and he was an inalienable part of her identity. It is quite possible that in 1922 she tried to convince Diaghilev to revive Nijinsky's *Rite of Spring*. True, it had been almost a decade since the ballet had been performed, and most of the original dancers had gone. However, Nijinska had watched the work grow in rehearsals, and with her profound knowledge of Nijinsky's style and her own experience as a choreographer she could easily have filled in the gaps that remained. She may also have considered "correcting" certain sections, above all those in which he had "graphically" rendered, as she wrote in *Early Memoirs*, "each musical note by a physical movement,"[31] bringing the ballet as a whole in line with the style of Nijinsky's original choreography for the Chosen Maiden. Although telegraphic, Nijinska's book outline of the 1930s suggests that she did contemplate reviving her brother's *Rite*, but that attacks by the critic André Levinson and opposition to Nijinsky's works within the company caused the effort to fail.[32] Florence Gilliam's remark in a review of the Massine *Rite* that "the earlier Nijinsky version . . . has the reputation of being dominated by the museum spirit"[33] suggests that Diaghilev had put it about that Nijinsky's work represented a choreographic dead end.

Because Massine's *Rite* in 1922 was a revival rather than a new work, it received few reviews. Of the daily critics only Levinson, who was seeing it for the first time, covered it. In his weekly column in *Comoedia*, he compared it to Nijinsky's *Rite of Spring* as he remembered it from 1913. Levinson was a die-hard conservative; as a critic he upheld the "old ballet" of the late Imperial period, and he loved its ballerinas. Fokine was anathema, along with most of Diaghilev's productions: modernism, Levinson despised. Now, after everything that had transpired since 1913, he recalled Nijinsky's ballet—and the pandemonium it had caused—with nostalgia, even as he insisted that Stravinsky's music "defi[ed]" all efforts at plastic (i.e., choreographic) realization and that "Nijinsky's rhythmic formalism caused the work to abort." However, he loved the opening of the second tableau, a scene "perfumed with lyricism," where "the young girls, shoulder to shoulder, circle[d] with all the angelic preciosity of Byzantine saints." He went on to describe Maria Piltz as Nijinsky's Chosen Maiden:

And I see again Maria Piltz, facing with serenity a tumultuous house. . . . A sudden convulsion hurtles her numbed body, rigid as a cadaver, laterally into space. Under the savage force of the rhythm, she shakes and clenches in an ecstatic and jerky dance. And this primitive hysteria, grotesque and terrible, enthralls and overwhelms the distraught spectator.[34]

Of Nijinska as the Chosen Maiden in the Massine version of the dance Levinson was of two minds:

> Mlle. Nijinska is dramatic from the first moment: immobile, the left elbow resting on the right palm, the cheek tilted on the other palm in a movement familiar to the Slavic woman, she is the very image of anguish. Then, she dances. Yet this dance, vehement, but supple and loose, with great turning jumps that rage like a whirlwind, do not attain the terrible shaking that made the graceful body of Maria Piltz, already ossified by the death that threatens her, so lamentable.[35]

Here as elsewhere, Levinson weighs Nijinska's merits against the conventionally "feminine" attributes of a lyrical ballerina. Thus, in his review of *Petrouchka*, he comments:

> Mlle. Nijinska plays the Ballerina accenting to excess the grotesque side, with the enthusiasm that she brings to everything. But she does not efface from my memory the porcelain figure of [Tamara] Karsavina as the Ballerina, with her adorably stupid smile and her beautiful eyes empty of soul.[36]

He takes a similar rhetorical approach in his review of *Aurora's Wedding*:

> Next to [Vera] Trefilova, limpid as a scherzo of Mozart, Nijinska, a powerful and strange dancer, inebriated with rhythm, who sniffs the music like a drug, breaks and clenches herself in crazy arabesques, vies in speed with the most breathless prestos of the orchestra.[37]

"Powerful" and "strange"—Nijinska's self-representation did not sit well with Levinson. He wanted his dancing women to be feminine, melting with grace and vulnerability. To be sure, a nineteenth-century ballerina was no shrinking violet, even if she died onstage with regularity. However, Nijinska upset ballet's conventions of heteronormativity. In the range of roles she danced and in her willingness to discard what queer theorist Judith Halberstam calls "femininity and its accessories," Nijinska had become an early model of Halberstam's concept of "female masculinity," despite being a heterosexual woman in an art identified with femininity.[38]

Unlike Levinson, Florence Gilliam saw Nijinska on her own terms rather than as a ballerina *manquée*. In *Gargoyle*, the "little magazine" she had founded with her husband Arthur Moss and for which she wrote regularly about dance and theater, Gilliam related that Nijinska's performance as the Chosen Maiden had left her nearly speechless:

> Of *Sacre du Printemps* it is very difficult for me to write, such is the over-whelming dynamism of the strange complicated rhythms, the primitive ecstasies of that prehistoric spring festival, reaching its climax in the racking macabre quality of La Nijinska's spasmodic gyrations in the dance of the virgin chosen for sacrifice—a more complete embodiment of a Strawinsky music abstraction than I had thought humanly possible.[39]

The following year, when Sokolova returned to the Ballets Russes, Gilliam analyzed how her more "feminine" interpretation of the Chosen Maiden differed from Nijinska's. "La Nijinska," she wrote in *Theatre Arts Monthly*, "danced the role with terrible macabre intensity."

> Sokolowa [*sic*] . . . makes the part more voluntary, more spiritual, more ex-alted. She is less the victim and more the martyr. La Nijinska's was a dance of spasmodic, hysterical terror in the face of an inevitable fate; Sokolowa's is rather the fanatic ecstasy of the dervish who dances until overtaken by un-consciousness or death.[40]

Although the choreography of the ballet was Massine's, Nijinska's Chosen Maiden must have incorporated elements from the version choreographed by her brother. This, after all, had been designed for her own body, and like her brother, she subscribed to the belief that a dancer's creativity lay in the personalizing of a role, transforming it into an ideogram of his or her distinctive personality. However, when Diaghilev decided to revive Nijinsky's *L'Après-midi d'un Faune*, unseen in Paris since 1913, Nijinska became her brother, embodying the role sketched on her years before.

According to Irina Nijinska, it was Diaghilev's idea for her mother to dance the Faun after watching with admiration as she taught the role to Leon Woizikovsky.[41] But Woizikovsky left the Ballets Russes after the financial debacle of *The Sleeping Princess*, and Nijinska stepped in. The revival was mentioned in all the advance press, both that Nijinska was staging the ballet and that she would be dancing the role of the Faun.[42] However, because this was a revival, coverage was perfunctory. Levinson devoted a long paragraph to the ballet's history, praised Lubov Tchernicheva as the Chief Nymph, and thanked Nijinska for "re-remembering her brother so piously."[43] In fact, only Florence Gilliam seems to have *looked* at Nijinska and tried describing her in performance, again for the English-speaking readership of *Gargoyle*:

> *L'Après-midi d'un Faune* is a remarkable achievement for La Nijinska. Her facial and bodily makeup, the non-human quality of every attitude, the beauty of her movements confined to a single plane, the intensity which she reads into the whole episode . . . constitute a memorable second to her brother's original creation.[44]

Was the critical brotherhood bothered by the revelation of a female body in the Faun's painted unitard? A drawing by Larionov of Nijinska rehearsing in the studio shows a slight, girlish figure with short hair, no bosom, and weight in the thighs. But the physical proportions of all the figures, including Diaghilev, who watches from the sidelines, are out of whack.[45] *Faune* was performed eleven times during the Opéra-Mogador season, and on the tour that followed in Geneva, San Sebastián, Brussels, Bordeaux, Antwerp, and Liège, and in the spring of 1923 in Monte Carlo and Lyon. It was clearly anything but an embarrassment and a role that Nijinska relished dancing. Even when Woizikovsky returned to the Ballets Russes in 1923, she held on to it. Not until the following year did she relinquish it to him.[46]

Diaghilev admired Nijinska, so much so, according to his biographer Arnold Haskell, that he said, "If I had a daughter, I would like one with such gifts."[47] But he didn't want a daughter. He wanted a lover-son—a Vaslav, not a Bronia. Indeed, he once told her "how unhappy he was that he could not have his own son," and that he loved Nijinsky and later Massine "like his own sons."[48] But reminding him of Vaslav had its drawbacks. "Poor Bronislava had no luck with Diaghilev," Stravinsky told Robert Craft. Her "sex, looks, and name were against her." "[H]er face was bony and interesting, instead of doll-like," and she looked like her brother; she was even "shaped like him. . . . It pained Diaghilev . . . that this person who dared look like Nijinsky was a woman."[49] Although Diaghilev certainly did not refrain from dalliances during the first two years of Nijinska's tenure and briefly entertained the idea of hiring Alexander Sakharoff, a Munich-bred concert dancer,[50] he lacked an in-house lover on whom to build the new repertory. So Nijinska built it on herself, although she knew it was only a matter of time before a young man edged her from the spotlight.

The reviews make clear that Nijinska was the charismatic presence of the 1922 season. However, she wasn't the company's ballet master (even if she did the work of one),[51] and she was hardly a star of the magnitude of her brother or Massine or even Tamara Karsavina, who arrived with much fanfare for a gala appearance toward the end of the Mogador season. In the souvenir program there were no sketches of her by Picasso or any of the designers of the season's new works, only a single photograph in *The Sleeping Princess*. Although she must have been present at the supper party that followed the premiere of *Le Renard* where Marcel Proust and James Joyce famously met, there is no record of it,[52] nor did she rate a mention in the program for the preview performance of *Mavra* hosted by Diaghilev at the Hôtel Continental, although she was the opera's stage director.[53] She did take part in the "Fête de l'Eté," organized by the Comité France-Amérique on June 23 at the magnificent Hôtel de Roquelaure on the Boulevard Saint-Germain, where she performed a national dance alongside stars of the Paris Opéra, Natalia Trouhanova, and Ruth Draper, who mimed "The Girl of the Far West."[54] She also seems to have talked to her first Western journalist, which, given her limited French at this time, was quite an achievement. On May 1, in an article mostly devoted to the former Bolshoi dancer Alexandra Balashova, Jean Bernier, a novelist who had contributed to the company's 1921 souvenir program, devoted the last three paragraphs to presenting Nijinska's quite radical ideas about costume:

> The dance costume imagined by Nijinska is not simply decorative.
> It participates in the choreographic action by its structure and its cut, fitting itself to the movements of the dancer and reveals their character.
> Here, imperfectly summarized, are the key ideas of Mlle. Nijinska, ballet mistress and stage director, whose conceptions are so new and so bold that they will only be seen when she has her own theater and troupe.[55]

One may well imagine Diaghilev's chagrin at reading this. "Any insubordination was insufferable to him," Nijinska later wrote.[56] Not only had she failed to toe the company line, she had also dared to articulate a personal point of view. Finally, and how terrible this must have been for Diaghilev with his "taste for everything fashionable,"[57] she had made his decorative aesthetic seem old-fashioned. Needless to say, this was Nijinska's first and last interview of 1922.

During those months in Monte Carlo and Paris, she had choreographed two new works, added a half-dozen roles to her repertory, and infused the company with new energy and discipline. She had also earned a salary that enabled her to support not only herself but also her mother and children in Vienna. Yet she was not happy. Success had come at the price of sacrificing her own creative pursuits. She wanted to go home, to a place where she could live and work independently. But she no longer knew where that was.

***

Although Nijinska left off writing her diary in February 1922, she was a prolific letter writer. At this time in her life, she seldom kept copies of her own letters. But she carefully saved the ones she received, allowing us to glimpse what others sensed at this crucial juncture of Nijinska's life—a woman artist seeking to balance her responsibilities to the Ballets Russes with her own creative needs, her professional ambitions with her craving for love, her yearning for Russia with her desire to settle permanently in the West. Even if secondhand, these letters offer an alternative narrative of her early life in emigration, before a carapace of toughness hid the vulnerability of her Russian self.

Nijinska received her first letter from Kiev in November 1921. It was from Pati and the School, and it touched her to the quick. As she wrote in her diary:

> It all comes back to me again. How much happiness my work with them brought. They are waiting for me, dreaming of working with me. . . . I don't know how, but I will return to them. (30 November 1921)[58]

Between 1921 and 1924, Nijinska kept up a lively correspondence with friends, colleagues, and former students in Soviet Russia. Letters flew back and forth, even if they took several weeks to arrive and followed Nijinska from one forwarding address to another. Many were long and chatty. They kept her abreast of escalating prices, the death of loved ones, the latest arrests, and who had died in prison. They told her about marriages, love affairs, and domestic squabbles, who had fallen ill from typhus, moved to the country, left for the West, lost a baby, or succumbed to depression.

Many letters concern Nijinska's old apartment at 17 Bolshaia Podvalnaia Street in Kiev. Located only a few blocks from the former City Theater, her apartment had turned into something of a communal dwelling shared by former students and desired by former friends. "As one can see from many letters," Nijinska commented on a note slipped into the sheaf of letters from the soprano Nina Moiseevna Gorkina Stefanovich, Levushka's godmother,

> there was a battle for my apartment going on: who would move into it? Nina Moiseevna and Nina Genrikhovna [Meller] were on one side, and Pati and Nadia [Shuvarska] on the other. I was on Pati's side: she was a close friend of mine, . . . was poor, and didn't have an apartment, while Nina Moi[seevna] and Nina Genri[khovna] had their own apartments, but wanted mine, a better one. It had six rooms, two servants' rooms, a bathroom, a kitchen, 3,000 volumes of books, furniture, sheets, a big music library, etc. And a wonderful grand piano, a "Bechst[ein]."[59]

The School of Movement's chief accompanist, Nikolai Sherman, would claim the Bechstein (and eventually take it to Moscow), and despite all of Nina Moiseevna's efforts to keep Nijinska's music library together and send it to her, it remained in Kiev, where it was scattered by looters in the aftermath of a fire in Nina's apartment building in 1941. Nina and her husband did manage to preserve the volume of antique Japanese prints that Nijinska had bought in London in 1914. However, the Ministry of Foreign Trade refused to authorize its export, fearing the Japanese writing was possibly seditious, so the album traveled with them to the Siberian city of Krasnoyarsk, where they were evacuated during World War II, then to Kharkov, and back to Kiev.[60]

Before leaving Kiev, Nijinska had made arrangements to ensure the continuity of her work. She entrusted her classes at the School of Movement to Nadia Shuvarska and Evgenii ("Zhenia") Lapitsky and those at Centro-Studio to Anna ("Niusia") Vorobieva. The decision, she wrote in an unpublished note, was based on their "pedagogical talent and knowledge of my dancing method."[61] But as Nina Moiseevna gently reminded her in February 1922,

> there is no School; there is only a group of your students who study with Zhenia . . . at his home. . . . All your students are in Kiev, but they have nothing in common, even your ideas haven't bound them together. Only Zhenia Lap[itsky] is faithful to you and your ideas. . . . He received an offer to study in Moscow, and Cen[tro]-St[udio] asked him to become head of the choreographic department. But Zhenia lives solely with the idea of joining you, no matter how long he has to wait. (21 February 1922)

Nijinska's departure precipitated a crisis among her students. Her "senior" students (as Nina Moiseevna called the older group) began to go their separate ways. Several moved on to professional careers. Tina Bergman joined the Railway Opera Theater. Lena Krivinskaia performed numbers like Debussy's "Golliwog's Cake-Walk" at "miniature" or variety-style theaters around Kiev. Others studied acrobatics and aerial work. Nadia Shuvarska taught movement classes for actors at the Shevchenko Theater and Les Kurbas' Berezil studio in addition to choreographing for him. Even her student and (in Nina Moiseevna's phrase) "vehement admirer" Viktorov, a tenor, made good: after a successful debut at the Bolshoi, he was invited to sing with the troupe.[62]

Nijinska responded to Nina Moiseevna's assertion that the School was no more by firing off a letter to Lina Khaskelis. On March 12, as Nijinska relaxed with her family in Vienna, "the group of Zhenia, the boy" responded:

Dear Bronislava Fominchna!
We just finished our class and decided to stay and write a letter to you. The School exists. There are three groups, and everybody is free to choose with whom to study—with Zhenia, Niusia [Vorobieva], or Nadia. We started regular classes in autumn. In summer there was a break due to lack of space. To our joy, in spring the number of students will reach over 20. . . . Zhenia's classes are very strict and good. . . . We have all advanced technically. . . . 3–4 students from Centro-Studio attend our classes and are very devoted to our common work. Dear Bronislava Fominichna, everything we do is done only to be with you and continue the work you have begun.[63]

Nina Moiseevna felt that it was wrong for Nijinska to keep them dangling. In March she wrote:

I see your students often. . . . They . . . whimper and cry, and "Bronichka" is on their lips at all times. They await your return, living on rumors that you have parted with Diaghilev and are now in Vienna, on your way back to Kiev. . . . Write to them whatever you want, but you need to cure them, not keep stirring them up. (30 March 1922)

Nearly a year after her departure neither Nijinska nor core members of her former studio had given up hope of working together again.

By August 1922, Nijinska had made up her mind to reconstitute the School of Movement in Vienna, where she was living when she wasn't traveling with the Ballets Russes. For several months her sister-in-law Romola had been making inquiries in New York and elsewhere, and although her efforts failed to identify a sponsor, they seem to have spurred Nijinska to action.[64] Whether she was preparing to break with Diaghilev is unclear. She certainly needed the salary, although his company's future looked bleak that August as his dancers, including Singaevsky, waited in Paris—unpaid and without contracts—for news of future performances. Moreover, after nearly a year with Diaghilev, Nijinska remained unhappy with her position and anxious to resume her own creative work with dancers she had formed and who believed in her. In a note she refers to a letter to an unnamed Kiev corre- spondent, in which she wrote about Diaghilev and the "necessity of leaving him."[65] Anton Muravin, who had danced with her at the City Theater and helped organize the School of Movement, was one of several correspondents who expressed dismay at how much work she had to do for Diaghilev; in- stead, he admonished, she should be devoting all her energy to her own work, which he hoped she would resume soon.[66]

Initially, she confided her plan to Nina Moiseevna and Lapitsky, who then contacted the dancers. "Everyone is getting ready to leave," Lapitsky wrote in early August.[67] Nina, with her eye for detail, conveys the excitement gener- ated by the move. "Dear Bronichka," she wrote on September 10:

> your students are so dedicated to you and your work—a recent episode demonstrated it. At 12 midnight I communicated to Zhenechka [Lapitsky] that I had a letter from you. . . . And imagine, on the second day 30 people came from everywhere . . . to find out who were the lucky ones who would see you soon. . . . At that meeting it became clear that everybody . . . could join you. . . . They sent a telegram to you the same day. . . . So, we are all waiting for letters from you. I understand perfectly well that you can't write to everyone individually, given how full of activity your life is now, . . . but I fear that once you have all your students with you you'll never write to me. . . . I simply love you very much, and when I don't hear from you, I feel I'm dying.

On September 11, Lapitsky wrote to Nijinska that he was ready to leave and that his father and sisters had blessed him. As her assistant, Nijinska in- tended to appoint Nadia Shuvarska. A confidante of Nijinska's later days in Kiev, Nadia (like Lapitsky) was chosen by her to continue classes at the School of Movement, and, like her mentor, Nadia had choreographic ambitions.

On October 16, she wired Nijinska, "I can leave immediately." Another telegram on the same date from Serezha Unger stated: "I am ready to go with Nadia. What should I do?"[68] However, when Nadia and Unger told Nina Moiseevna they were planning to leave the next day with Niusia Vorobieva and Alexandra Stashkevich, even though they had hardly any money, Nina told them to stay put until Nijinska sent for them, as she was touring and always on the move. Nina then took Nadia aside and told her that Nijinska had written that she wasn't to come until later. This was a lie, but Nina was convinced that Nadia would be more trouble than she was worth, and others, including Lapitsky and Meller, agreed. Nadia never left Russia.

Meanwhile, against all odds, Diaghilev had put together an autumn tour. Singaevsky, who had spent the previous weeks of an unpaid vacation strolling in the Bois de Boulogne and bemoaning his idleness, announced the good news to Nijinska on August 30.[69] Rehearsals were to begin in Paris on September 4, with performances in San Sebastián beginning four days later; then back to France and dates in Bayonne and Bordeaux, followed by a short season in Geneva and three weeks of performances in Belgium, the last on November 1. The company's prospects now brightened. Diaghilev and his patron the Princesse Edmond de Polignac (née Winnaretta Singer, the sewing machine heiress) had convinced her nephew by marriage, who had married the heiress to the Principality of Monaco, to persuade the Société des Bains de Mer (which ran both the celebrated Casino and the Monte Carlo Opéra) to sign the Ballets Russes for a six-month residency at the Théâtre de Monte-Carlo. So in November 1922 the Ballets Russes—along with its sets, costumes, and other paraphernalia—decamped for the Riviera. On November 26 the company danced its first performance in Monte Carlo under the new arrangement.[70]

By then, Romola had left Vienna, and with Vaslav now in Paris, there was no reason for Nijinska to stay in the Austrian capital.[71] So, she and her family headed south, and plans for reviving the School of Movement fell through.

When Nijinska left Kiev, did she imagine that she would never return? She had walked away from a home, a place in the new Soviet avant-garde, and a thriving studio that had provided the human material for her experiments. There were things she had pawned in Petrograd that may have belonged to her mother or possibly to her brother, along with her apartment in Kiev; it all disappeared, along with her books and music, letters and diaries, as though history had conspired to undo everything she had struggled to create. Although her students clung to the hope that she would return,

Nina Moiseevna urged her to remain in the West, and was distraught by early rumors that she wanted to return to Russia (21 February 1922). "Bronichka, my dear, your return is out of the question" (30 March 1922). She talks about her "successful" godson, Levushka, and says that when she sees him smiling with his sister Irochka in the pictures Nijinska has sent her, she finds it "hard to believe they ever lived in Sovdepiya," a derogatory word for the Soviet Union; they look so "completely foreign." Nijinska, she notes with approval, has filled out.

> The photo of you in *The Sleeping Princess* is adorable! I noticed that your neck bones are not visible anymore, and your arms have become plumper. Thank God, you have put on weight. (29 April 1922)

However, at the end of 1922, when it became clear that the plans to reconstitute the School in Vienna had fallen through, Nina broached the idea of Nijinska returning to Russia. Not to Kiev, but to Moscow, where many of their mutual artist friends had relocated and where her School would be supported.

> My dear, tell me, have you thought about coming back to Russia . . . ? A whole pilgrimage to Moscow has started: Felix Mikhailovich [Blumenfeld], Gustav Genr[ikhovich Neuhaus], the Shifrins, etc.—so many Kievans. . . . Everybody says that if you were in Moscow now, you could just work for yourself, with your School. . . . There is a housing crisis in Moscow, but for your work you could get a whole mansion, and the rest would also be taken care of by the Government. . . . Vadim Georgevich [Meller] is going to go to Moscow in the spring; he is thinking about talking to certain people there about you, of course only after knowing your thoughts on this matter. By the way, [Nikolai] Sherman visited Kiev. He is now director of the Moscow Philharmonic. He also says that if you came back, a lot would be done for you. . . . You need "bricks" for your work, and I think that nowhere else will you find such "bricks" as here, in Russia. Your students still live on the idea of being with you. (21 December 1922)

Muravin, too, urged her to consider returning to Russia. Far more than Nina Moiseevna, he was upset that she had abandoned her plan to reopen the school, although given her extensive travel schedule he understood why. In any case, he believes she would enjoy greater support for her school in

Russia, where "all artistic forces," even beginners starting their search in "left-wing art," are being supported by the People's Commissariat for Education. Goleizovsky is one such example: even though much of his work seems absurd to Muravin, "they seized on him," and now Moscow is proud of him, and he has been invited to give several performances in Petersburg. There is also a lot of talk about Foregger, whom Nijinska knows. Muravin talked about Nijinska with a patron, and he said that if she worked in Russia she would have a colossal influence on all new art, not to mention that she would be provided with everything she needed for her work (21 November 1922).

One can only imagine how tempting this must have been. But none of her autobiographical fragments comment upon the possibility of reopening her school in Moscow, which suggests that she never really considered it. No doubt this had something to do with her role as family breadwinner. Life may have been hard in the capitalist West, but it was easier to feed a family there than in a socialist country plagued by famine. It is also possible that she felt that things were looking up for her professionally, that the work she was doing compensated for Diaghilev's "coldness," the "plots" and slights she experienced from members of his company and entourage, and the sometimes harsh criticism she received in the press.[72] Her mother and children were now at hand for six months of the year, and by early 1923 several of her former students had joined the Ballets Russes.

When Nijinska made plans in 1922 to reconstitute the School of Movement in Vienna, she certainly viewed it as an independent entity and a vehicle for the expression of her own creativity. However, she also seems to have considered it a stepping stone to the Ballets Russes, just as she had viewed her Kiev studio as training dancers for her brother's future company. Presumably, she discussed this with Diaghilev, who was always in need of dancers, although the memoir literature and her notes are silent on the point. She did confide in Singaevsky, who became her lover in early August, and it was probably his support that gave her the confidence to go ahead with her plans. However, Singaevsky felt that Diaghilev treated dancers "outrageously" and that she—they—had a moral obligation to warn her students. On August 21, he wrote to her in Vienna, where she had rejoined her family while Diaghilev scrambled around Europe looking for engagements:

[L]et me, Bronia, tell you my opinion about the students. I believe that you can give them to Diaghilev only if going abroad and working here is a matter of principle for them . . . because with Diaghilev one can have neither security nor confidence. He would probably look at them, choosing those he can exploit more easily. I believe they should know this, in order to lessen our own responsibility.[73]

Diaghilev was interested in her students, but only the men. Male dancers were particularly hard to find outside Russia, and most of the "weaker" dancers he had just trimmed from the company were men who needed to be replaced.[74]

Not long after the autumn tour got underway, Nijinska sent for her five best men, "the boys," as she called them. "We all agree to your proposal," wrote Serge Unger on September 19,

> Otherwise, we cannot exist. . . . We can and will go hungry, but . . . we are used to it. . . . Even your students from Centro-Studio, who worked only a little with you, are devoted to our work. For example, Seriozha ("little") Lifar dreams of being with you. . . . Life in Kiev is dreary.[75]

By October 20, Jan and Czeslaw Hoyer were in Warsaw. (Because they were Polish, it was relatively easy for them to emigrate.) However, the others— Unger, Lapitsky, and Lifar, along with the uninvited Lina Khaskelis—were still waiting in Kiev. Unger wrote to Nijinska:

> We met on Monday, October 16, to leave, and suddenly Nina Moiseevna received the letter describing Diaghilev's present situation. Despite that I still want to be with you. No obstacle scares me. . . . We suffocate in Kiev. There is no work. We think only of being with you.[76]

The Russian group finally made it out. But bad luck continued to dog them. By the time they got to Warsaw, they were out of money and all they could afford was a flophouse where they slept on chairs in a room with ten other men and had to clear out by morning. They barely ate.[77] On December 9 one of the Hoyers telegraphed Diaghilev at the Hôtel Continental in Paris that Unger, Lifar, and Lipitsky had been robbed, and begged him to send money and papers or they couldn't leave.[78] Meanwhile, Stanislaw Drobecki, Diaghilev's eyes and ears in Warsaw, had second thoughts about the bedraggled group and urged Diaghilev to come to Poland before engaging them. Diaghilev decided against it. On December 13, he wired Drobecki 1,500 francs, but there were still problems with papers. The one who found himself in the direst straits was Lifar. On December 19 he wrote to Nijinska, thanking her profusely for allowing him "to go with the boys to you, in Monte Carlo." He was robbed twice and is now broke, he tells her:

> the first time they took all my money, clothes, and possessions, so I had to go back home; the second time only my possessions. But thanks to Seriozha [Unger], who helped me, I was able to get to Warsaw. Here . . . I counted on support from certain acquaintances of mine, but they've gone bankrupt and can't help me.

Now he begs her to tell him what to do next.

> I appeal to you again. . . . Can I go to you and work with Diaghilev, without burdening you, on the same terms as the others, or not? (If not, it will mean I have to go back home and forget about ballet altogether, because my family won't allow me to continue my studies.)[79]

As telegrams flew back and forth about money and documents, Nijinska had one last request: would Diaghilev get a visa for Lina as well as the "boys"? As she explained to Walter Nouvel, "This young girl helped the boys during the trip, and her relations even lent them money for the trip from Rovno to Warsaw." Lina received her visa; money was sent to the "boys," although, as Unger explained, it wasn't enough: they had had to pay a fine for illegally crossing the border and a lawyer to get them a permit to stay in Warsaw, plus train fares had doubled.[80]

By the time they reached Monte Carlo the group had been traveling for over two months. They were out of practice and physically weak. Unsurprisingly, when they were put through their paces, as Grigoriev later wrote,

> we were disappointed to find them very weak and inexperienced. The best of the party was E[ugene] Lapitsky. The worst was a boy named Serge Lifar. When Diaghilev first saw them soon after their arrival, he made a face, and remarked that they seemed hardly worth the trouble and expense involved in bringing them so far to join us.[81]

As the company's ballet master, Nijinska must have been the one who put them through their paces. No doubt she, too, was disappointed by the poor showing of her former students. In her unpublished notes she gives the exact date of the group's arrival in Monte Carlo (the only specific date she gives in all her autobiographical notes), but says nothing about the "audition" that followed. However, she singles out Lapitsky, describing him as the "best student of the School of Movement, a very serious artist, with a great pedagogical talent." He was devoted to her and, until his untimely drowning in 1931, followed her everywhere—from Kiev to the Ballets Russes to her own independent company, the Teatro Colón, the Ida Rubinstein company, and the Opéra Russe à Paris. He recorded her classes for years (although his notes seem to have disappeared) and, as a performer, stood out, as she wrote, "for his absolutely exact musical and choreographic rendering."[82] With Lapitsky, Singaevsky, and the "boys" at her side, Nijinska had laid the foundation for a company of her own inside the Ballets Russes.

**

Even though Nijinska's letters have disappeared, we hear her voice through the words of others. This is especially true of Nina Moiseevna's letters, which reflect years of shared memories and intimacies. Roughly the same age, both were artists, Nina a coloratura soprano with a long career ahead of her when they met during World War I and one of the very few of Nijinska's Kiev correspondents to use the familiar form of address. She addresses Nijinska as "my little dove," "my darling Bronichka," always using the diminutive, a sign of their closeness. She tells her about her newfound marital happiness and wishes the same for Nijinska. "Dear Bronichka," she wrote in her very first letter, "I ask God that the day will come when you stop saying and thinking: 'I'm not waiting for anything,' 'I don't need anything'" (21 February 1922). Her first marriage had broken up, probably because he had taken up with another woman—a situation that paralleled Nijinska's relationship with Kochetovsky. Nijinska had counseled divorce, and now Nina congratulates her on deciding to do the same, even if she doesn't want to get married (21 December 1922).

Strangely, Nijinska makes no mention of her affair with Singaevsky. Yet he adored her, decanting his passion in letters written when they were apart. "Bronia, I love you to tears, to pain," he wrote in the spring of 1922, "I love you more than life, more than my own life, my dear beloved Bronia, I kiss the soles of your feet."[83] He buys her perfume and dreams about her and is jealous of her children when she visits them during the company's August break ("You had to leave, I should have understood it"[84]). He builds up her confidence: "Stay calm, believe in yourself," he tells her."[85] Often she doesn't write him for days, and sometimes she pushes him away. He goes to a fortune teller, and the cards say that she is "cheating" on him, although he doesn't believe it, and assures her that he is faithful.[86] He wants her to need him. "I will only feel good when . . . I can do more than just love you, when I can also do things for you. I have always wanted it, . . . but you think otherwise. . . . If only you fell in love with me, Bronitchka."[87] But Nijinska was keeping a tight rein on her emotions. Singaevsky may have touched her heart and flattered her intellect but he failed to ignite her imagination.

In nearly every letter, Nina tells her friend how much she misses her. "The first snowdrops have appeared, and the bright spring sun makes me miss you," she writes in 1922.

> Together with Misha I went to the Andreevskaia [Saint Andrew's] Church, and we discovered that a lot has been destroyed in your "domain." . . . I walked along all those streets you and I used to wander together accompanied by the murmur of brooklets, and then Kiev became dear to me. And I miss you! (30 March 1922)

As the months since Nijinska's departure lengthened into years, it must have become clear to Nina and the others left behind that Russia Abroad was now Nijinska's home. The two women never saw each other again.

Had Nijinska written the book that she outlined in the 1930s, using these letters to document her years in Kiev, it would have been very different from the one she actually wrote three decades later. For one thing, it would have focused on what *she* had accomplished rather than on what she was preparing to do for her brother. For another, it would have demonstrated beyond the shadow of a doubt that her students were devoted to *her* and not to him. In fact, in the extensive collection of letters at the Library of Congress, Nijinsky is noticeable by the virtual absence of references to him. Occasionally, one of her older colleagues—Nina Moiseevna or Anton Muravin usually—asks after him, sometimes reporting a rumor about his death, but their questions make it clear that Nijinska, however much she may have been haunted by her brother's fate, seldom talked about him. Finally, the letters indicate Nijinska's profound unhappiness at her experience in the Diaghilev company and how anxious she was to pursue her own work with her own dancers. Given the decimation of the Soviet avant-garde in the late 1920s and 1930s, Nijinska was fortunate to stay in the West. But one can only wonder how different her work might have been had she reopened her studio in the Moscow of the 1920s, allowing her once again to choreograph in an environment free of commercial pressures and the tyrannical figure of "Big Serge," in an avant-garde arts community to which she belonged by language and birthright and because, like her peers, she had experienced the Revolution's transformative power.

Fig. 1 Nijinska at the Imperial Ballet
School, 1908.

Fig. 2 Nijinska in *Chopiniana*,
Maryinsky Theater, 1908.

Fig. 3 Nijinska in her graduation
finery, 1908.

Fig. 4 Nijinska at the time of her graduation, 1908.

Fig. 5 Nijinska (third from left), with Adolph Bolm (left), Ludmilla Schollar, Valerian Svetlov, and others in Monte Carlo, spring 1911.

Fig. 6 Nijinska as the Street Dancer in *Petrouchka*, 1911.

Fig. 7 Nijinska and her daughter Irina, St. Petersburg, 1914.

Fig. 8 Nijinska and her brother in *L'Après-midi d'un Faune,* 1912.

Fig. 9 Maurice Ravel (left), with Nijinsky and Nijinska in Paris, 1914.

Fig. 10 Alexandra Exter, 1910s.

Fig. 11 Nina Moiseevna (left), Alexander Kochetovsky, Pavel Gorkin, and Anton Muravin outside the Kiev City Theater, 1916.

Fig. 12 Nijinska's handwritten announcement of the School of Movement, 1919.

Fig. 13 *Demons*, as sketched by Nijinska, 1920.

PROGRAMME

LA NIJINSKA
Chorégraphe des Ballets Russes.

Fig. 14 "La Nijinska" in *The Sleeping Princess*, 1921.

Fig. 15 Nijinska in Kikimora in *Contes Russes*, 1922.

Fig. 16 Nijinska (standing left) in the Prologue of *The Sleeping Princess*, 1921.

Fig. 17 Mikhail Larionov, Nijinska rehearsing her brother's role in *L'Après-midi d'un Faune*, 1922.

Fig. 18 Nijinska as the Polovtsian Girl, London, 1924.

Fig. 19 Eleonora Bereda Nijinsky,
Vienna, 1922.

Fig. 20 Nijinska and her son Léon,
spring 1924.

Fig. 21 Eugene Lapitzky, mid-1920s.

Fig. 22 Serge Unger, mid-1920s.

Fig. 23 & 24 Felia Doubrovska
as the Bride in *Les Noces* and
rehearsing with the Diaghilev
company, London. 1926

Figs. 25 & 26 Natalia
Goncharova, female and male
group, *Les Noces,* 1923.

Fig. 27 Portrait-postcard inscribed by Francis Poulenc to Nijinska 1923.

Fig. 28 Nijinska as the Hostess in *Les Biches*, 1924.

Fig. 29 *Le Train Bleu*, London, 1924.

DIAGHILEFF INTRODUCES NEW BALLETS.

The Production of "Les Noces" and "Romeo and Juliet" by the Russian Ballet at His Majesty's

"A RENDERING IN SOUND AND VISION OF THE PEASANT SOUL": TWO SCENES, TAKEN DURING AN ACTUAL PERFORMANCE, FROM THE NEW BALLET, "LES NOCES." IN THE PICTURE ON THE RIGHT IS SEEN ONE OF THE FOUR COMPOSER-PIANISTS WHO APPEAR ON THE STAGE DURING THE BALLET TO SUPPLEMENT THE ORCHESTRA

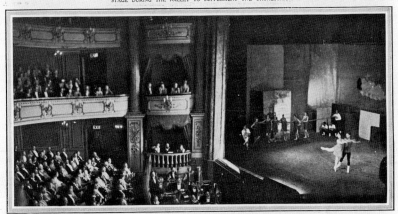

THE STAGE AND STALLS AT HIS MAJESTY'S THEATRE DURING A PERFORMANCE OF "ROMEO AND JULIET"

Special SPHERE pictures

TWO SCENES FROM THE NEW BALLET, "ROMEO AND JULIET," WHICH DEPICTS THE REHEARSAL OF A BALLET IN A DANCING ACADEMY

The production of *Les Noces* by the Russian Ballet at His Majesty's Theatre has aroused a storm of criticism and excited comment. This is one of the new ballets in the "new style." Many of the critics at the first night were frankly hostile, and Mr. H. G. Wells, in consequence, dashed into the fray in defence of M. Diaghileff and *Les Noces*. According to him the ballet is "a rendering in sound and vision of the peasant soul"; certain it is that *Les Noces* is in keeping with the latest tendencies of the Russian Ballet, inasmuch as it departs very radically from the sweet, flowing music and graceful airy dancing to which M. Diaghileff owed his initial and greatest success in England. *Romeo and Juliet*, the second ballet pictured above, is more "understandable" by the average man. It depicts a scene in a dancing academy, where a rehearsal is in progress. During the rehearsal, two lovers appear and carry on a flirtation. The two lovers in this ballet are Madame Karsavina and M. Serge Lifar.

Fig. 30 *Les Noces* and *Romeo and Juliet*, London, 1926.

Fig. 31 Nijinska in a grotesque role.

Fig. 32 Nijinska (lower right) and members of Theatre Choréographique in *Touring*, 1925.

Fig. 33 Nijinska in *Petrouchka*, Opéra Russe à Paris, 1930.

Fig. 34 Nijinska (front) and members of Theatre Choréographique in Alexandra Exter's costumes for *Holy Etudes*, 1925.

Fig. 35 Nijinska, Nicholas Singaevsky (to her right), and members of Theatre Choréographique outside "Caleb Foxwell Breeches Maker" on tour in England, 1925.

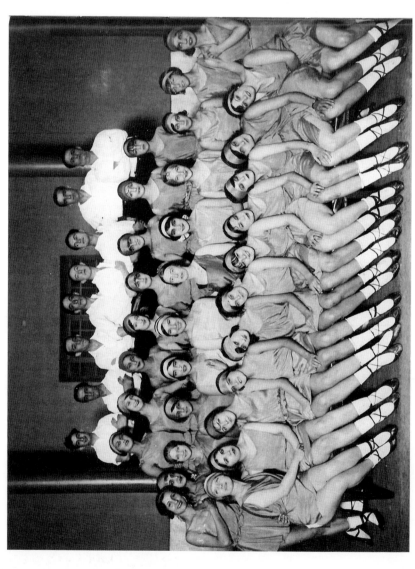

Fig. 36 Nijinska (center) surrounded by dancers of the Teatro Colón, 1926–1927.

5

Les Noces

In November 1922 the Ballets Russes settled for the winter in Monte Carlo. After an August layoff that left many dancers stranded without pay and a seven-week tour in September and October, it must have been wonderful to say goodbye to trains, one-night stands, and uncertain salaries.[1] A playground for the rich, Monte Carlo was the jewel of the Riviera, with mild winters, blue skies, and hillsides dotted with villas. With fresh fish and fruit all year round, Monte Carlo must have seemed like nirvana to Eleonora when she arrived with her grandchildren.

The Ballets Russes was hardly a stranger to Monte Carlo. The company danced there often, usually in April during the last crucial weeks of rehearsal before the Paris season, when most new works were unveiled. The financial debacle of *The Sleeping Princess* left a big gap in the yearly round of performances that not even Diaghilev could fill. Now, with the Société des Bains de Mer engaging the Ballets Russes from November to the following May, the company had six months of guaranteed support. The advantage of the "scheme," as Grigoriev explains in his memoirs, was twofold: it gave the company employment throughout the winter and Diaghilev "ample time to devise new productions" and polish old ones.[2] The atmosphere of crisis lifted.

There was one obstacle to the plan: the Monte Carlo opera house already had a ballet company. Unfazed, Diaghilev made an "interim agreement," as he explained to Grigoriev, to work "*with* the Italians," meaning with Georges Belloni, the company's ballet master, and his mostly Italian and French dancers. Russians at the beck and call of Italians, Grigoriev asked incredulously. "Oh, *you'll* have to deal with *them*! laughed Diaghilev.... I'll be behind the scenes!"[3] As Grigoriev—with Nijinska and the Ballets Russes dancers— did their best to make the arrangement work, Diaghilev schemed. Belloni and his dancers had to go.

For Russians of Nijinska's generation, the "old ballet" meant Petipa's ballet, the body of work, both original and inherited, that he had choreographed or rechoreographed during his half-century at the helm of St. Petersburg's Imperial Ballet. They knew next to nothing about contemporary Western ballet, even after scores of them settled in the West, and, like Diaghilev, acted as if it didn't exist. But it did: ballets like *Coppélia* (1870), *La Korrigane* (1880), and *Les Deux Pigeons* (1886), all originally produced at the Paris Opéra; *Au Japon* (1902), a "grand ballet" to music by the Casino's music director Louis Ganne first staged by Carlo Coppi at the Alhambra Theatre, London; *Au Temps Jadis* (1905), a ballet-opera inspired by the history of Monaco, with music by Justin Clérice and choreography by Giorgio Saracco; and ballets from operas that were performed independently such as the celebrated "Witches' Sabbath" from Charles Gounod's *Faust* and the Dance of the Hours from Amilcare Ponchielli's *La Gioconda* (1876). In 1922–1923 all these works were "arranged" by Belloni for performance in Monte Carlo. Belloni also restaged ballets of his own choreographed over a career that began in Milan and included stints at La Scala, Grand-Théâtre in Bordeaux, Grand Théâtre du Capitole in Toulouse, the amphitheater in Béziers, and the Casino de Paris. His works were simultaneously highbrow and lowbrow, crossing boundaries from opera house to variety stage. Together they constituted a repertory that circulated from theater to theater in versions adapted by in-house ballet masters; in an era before the widespread use of film or notation, these journeymen choreographers and their dancers were the chief keepers of choreographic memory and repertory.[4] This Franco-Italian tradition would soon be swept away by the tidal wave of Russian émigré talent and need.

For Nijinska, this repertory was not simply the "old ballet"; it was old-fashioned opera-house ballet without the academic or classical status to which the Petipa repertory could lay claim. Like Grigoriev, she fell in with Diaghilev's scheme. However, she found it disheartening. As she reported to Walter Nouvel—or Valechka, as she called him—in late December: "All our performances in Monte Carlo are so sad, so it is better not to write about it. I work with the troupe every day. They eagerly attend my class and work well."[5] Belloni, in fact, was unexpectedly pleased with the more than proficient Ballets Russes dancers when he put them through their paces. But something entirely different now lay on the horizon.

For years *Les Noces* had been in the Ballets Russes pipeline, announced, promised in contracts, and then put off to another season. The idea for the ballet came to Stravinsky shortly before the premiere of *The Rite of Spring*, and in many ways it remained a close relation of Nijinsky's masterwork, transformed by a decade of upheavals. Choreographers had come and gone, along with orchestrations and sets of designs for costumes and scenery. The ballet was in Diaghilev's contract with Jacques Rouché in 1921; with a new Stravinsky score, it promised to be the season's modernist *clou* in stark contrast to *The Sleeping Beauty*. *Beauty* was dropped early on, but Diaghilev continued to cling to *Les Noces*. Over lunch at Prunier's in March 1922 he told Nijinska that he wanted her to choreograph the new ballet. After the bleak months in London making dances *après* Petipa and improvising in a rented Bloomsbury room, the news "burst upon [her] like a ray of sunlight." After lunch she went with Diaghilev to Stravinsky's Pleyel studio where for the first time she heard him play the music of what became her most memorable work. "The music of *Noces* astounded me," she wrote many years later,

> overwhelming me with its disturbing rhythm. *Les Noces* seemed to me to be deeply dramatic, interspersed with occasional splashes of joyousness and true feeling of Russia. At that moment I saw the picture of *Les Noces* and my choreographic line for the ballet.[6]

After this transcendent experience, Diaghilev took her to the studio of the ballet's designer Natalia Goncharova. On the artist's long work table were dozens of costume sketches, presumably of the painter's Northern spring series, "admirably drawn, magnificent colors, theatrical and sumptuously Russian." It was definitely not how Nijinska imagined the ballet, and in no uncertain terms she announced this to Diaghilev. The costumes were magnificent, but they belonged in a Russian opera, not a ballet: in her view the dance costume was a functional garment that took part in the choreographic action and followed the movement of the dancer's body, which these costumes did not. Moreover, they did not "respond" to Stravinsky's music. However, Diaghilev had approved the designs, as had Stravinsky. Miffed, Diaghilev took back his offer. Years later, Nijinska recalled Diaghilev telling her, "And so, Bronia, I shall not let you direct *Les Noces*."[7]

As her diary attests, Nijinska learned about *Les Noces* within days of arriving in London. By then she had seen two of Goncharova's sketches for *Liturgie*, which she liked (unlike Picasso's costume designs for *Le Tricorne*, which she thought were "just bad"). Then, after a couple of sentences about the retrograde nature of theater after the corpses and battles of World War I, she mentions *Les Noces*. "How good it would be if nobody braided the hair in *Les Noces*—nobody needs that. So theater falls into kitsch or laughter . . . so it can appeal to the 'boulevard.'"[8] This kind of information can only have come from Diaghilev or Stravinsky, and given that both were in London working on *Beauty*, they must have described the action to her.[9] In an interview with the dance writer Françoise Reiss, Nijinska describes in nearly identical terms her reaction to Stravinsky's libretto. "When I create a ballet," she told Reiss in the early 1950s,

> I read the poem, then I forget about it entirely in order to re-compose it in choreographer's language.
>
> When I had in my hands Stravinsky's libretto for *Les Noces*, I said to Serge Diaghilev that I would not and could not stage it in this form. "Well, Bronia, don't stage it," he responded. But after a while he changed his mind: "Do what you want." He had confidence in me because he understood that I felt the subject. Then I re-thought and re-dreamed it entirely. I explained each scene in my way, choreographically.[10]

Two decades earlier, in 1936, when Nijinska revived *Les Noces* for the post-Diaghilev Ballets Russes company of Colonel Wassily de Basil, she spoke in an interview with the *New York Times* critic John Martin about the interrelated problem of the ballet's libretto and design:

> "I have been asked many times why I have chosen to stage Stravinsky's 'Les Noces' against a mood and background of black and white rather than in the hilarious spirit of conventional peasant folklore. I debated this point with Diaghileff for a whole year before he consented to my interpretation. . . . The wedding of two innocent peasants, unknown to each other until their wedding night, and the cruel attendance that is danced upon their sacred relations, are of the nature of tragedy and are so treated. To interpret the libretto as the merrymaking of Russian peasants against a pictorial background of sheer exuberance and unalloyed joy would serve to defeat the inherent tragedy."[11]

The ballet was briefly rehearsed in 1922, then canceled. "Am certain that Bronia will never put *Noces* on in a month," Stravinsky wired Diaghilev from Monte Carlo on April 24.[12] Not that the composer, who had yet to complete the orchestration, was ready to move into production. After a week of rehearsals it became clear that nobody would be ready for Paris, and so *Les Noces* was put on hold again.

Although the company's balance sheet remained dismal, the 1922 season reestablished the Ballets Russes as a viable Paris enterprise. In the months that followed, Diaghilev continued to underscore the company's French identity through his personal presence (as when he attended, along with a crowd of notables, Proust's funeral—complete with military honors—in Paris)[13] and by realigning the company artistically, tuning it to the heartbeat of Paris. On March 6, 1923, he was in the audience for the Paris debut of Alexander Tairov's Kamerny Theater, one of the most adventurous of Russia's dramatic ensembles. In *Comoedia*, André Levinson published a long and unusually sympathetic preview of the Soviet company, describing its innovative stage sets by artists such as Alexandra Exter and its splendid actors who were simultaneously "tragedians, buffoons, and strolling players, disciplined executants and casual improvisers." Above all, Levinson emphasized that this was a company of the future, "conceived during the war . . . and toughened in the revolutionary storm," coming "to do battle for the advent of a new theatrical order."[14]

Nijinska did not attend the premiere with Diaghilev. She was in Monte Carlo, teaching class and rehearsing the dancers (especially, one imagines, her former students from Kiev, who had to be worked into the repertory) for the month-long Monte Carlo season that opened on April 17. However, in an unpublished essay, she recalls how worried Diaghilev was by the Kamerny's season, whose radical vision threatened to expose the tired aesthetics of the Ballets Russes, and to what lengths he had gone to "spoil" Tairov's success with influential members of the first-night audience:

> Imagine, Bronia, in the first intermission Picasso declared that this company was the best that he had seen, and Cocteau was dashing everywhere and shouting that this was a "completely new path" for theater, that everything Tairov does . . . is better than anything we have seen till now. In other words, we must reject the Ballets Russes and follow Tairov's Kamerny Theater. All my comments were drowned among the raptures. You can imagine what I went through! During the second intermission I took Picasso's arm and suggested to him that he was mistaken. During the third intermission Picasso declared that Tairov's theater was on a false road. . . . Now, Tairov's theater no longer exists for Paris. Cocteau can dash and prattle as much as he wants, but he will not save Tairov.[15]

What better way to prove the continued artistic vitality of the Ballets Russes than to bring *Les Noces* to the stage as Nijinska had imagined it?

By March 27, 1923, three weeks after the Kamerny's debut in Paris, company rehearsals were underway.[16] By then Nijinska had studied the score and had questions about the reprise in rehearsal 1. Diaghilev relayed these to Stravinsky, who replied on March 27 that "It was a piece of cake"— although the Russian idiom he used involved a steamed turnip—"and any decent musician can tell you what fragment should be repeated." He gave her tempo markings, and told her that if anything wasn't clear, she should read the letter to her pianist, a woman, "who will surely understand it, as S[ergei] P[avlovich] says she has finished or at least studied at the Moscow Conservatory." Despite the caustic tone, he ended on a conciliatory note, "I hope to see you soon and work together on *Svadebka*," using the ballet's Russian title.[17]

Once rehearsals began, the dancers were at it six days a week. Days were long in the Diaghilev company. They began with class, which Nijinska now taught, dressed as always in a blue tunic,[18] followed by two or three rehearsals, depending on whether the company was performing. On matinee days, the second rehearsal took place from 9 to 11 at night.[19] During April, there were *Noces* rehearsals every day, often but not always in the 2:30–5 P.M. slot. Sometime in mid-April, Stravinsky appeared, with Vera Soudeikina, his lover, in tow. According to Robert Craft, Vera was playing the "role of the Bride" but "was obliged to withdraw because of illness."[20] In fact, all the ballet's female roles required pointework, which only a dancer with far greater training than Soudeikina could do. In a work that rested upon the "common expression" of the mass, it is inconceivable that Nijinska would have tailored her choreography to accommodate the limitations of an amateur.[21]

At the end of April the number of daily rehearsals doubled. By then, the company was in performance mode, first in Monte Carlo, then in Lyons and Montreux. On June 1 the dancers arrived in Paris, and in the days leading up to the gala opening on June 13 at the Gaîté-Lyrique they practically lived in the theater, where class began at 9 A.M.[22] Tempers were short. The theater, which nobody liked, stood at the northern edge of the Marais, the center of the garment industry, far from fashionable precincts to the west. Classes were held, Lydia Sokolova tells us, "in a long, bleak room at the top of the building, with a bar down one side."[23] According to Grigoriev, it was "next to impossible to find anywhere to stay." The cost of living had risen "uncomfortably," and the company demanded an increase of salary.[24] The morning music rehearsals were shrill and chaotic, with Stravinsky hurling orders and the conductor Ernest Ansermet displaying "the patience of a shepherd."[25] Upstairs, critics looked in on the dancers. In *Comoedia*, Louis Laloy marveled at the boldness and power of Nijinska's "moving constructions," the likes of which had "never been seen on the stage."[26] Edouard Beaudu, a journalist writing for *L'Intransigeant*, observed a rehearsal of *Les Noces*, led by Nijinska. "Human clusters balance, break up, rejoin, leap or crouch, or simply bend into a harmonious whole," he wrote.

> The fierce music of Stravinsky electrifies all these young and sensitive beings, devoted only to the cult of Dance, which torments them visibly, commands them, projects them alone or in groups to the places assigned by Nijinska, who has arranged this powerful entertainment.[27]

By now, some of these "young and sensitive beings" wanted to strike. They were tired; they wanted more money; they had danced non-stop for months; even on Easter they rehearsed. A number of dancers threatened to resign. But, as Grigoriev drily noted, "this was not . . . the way to approach Diaghilev."

> His reply was to call the whole company together and explain that he was not in a position to pay them more. He added that if those who were dissatisfied should resign, he would quite understand. But no-one did so.[28]

As a sop or reward for their hard work, the entire company was invited to an *audition privée* of the music at the Princesse de Polignac's two days before the opening. This was highly unusual; nearly always, such events were attended only by Diaghilev and his intimates, along with titled music lovers, composers, patrons, and "friends" of the company. According to Jacques Brindejont-Offenbach, who covered the event for *Le Gaulois*, Diaghilev dedicated what he called the "150th and next-to-last rehearsal of . . . Stravinsky's new score" to the Princesse as an expression of gratitude for her loyal patronage.[29] The number was probably not too far from the mark, if rehearsals began on March 27, and doubled as the premiere approached. With so much unison work, above all in the fourth tableau, rehearsals must have been long, arduous, and exhausting, with everyone dancing "full-out" at every run-through. According to Grigoriev, the dress rehearsal was a disaster when it was discovered that the two double pianos the music called for could not fit into the orchestra pit along with the timpani, four solo singers, and Vasily Kibalchich's Russian chorus. Eventually, the pianos seem to have been placed on the side of the stage, near the proscenium.[30] Although Nijinska's response is unrecorded, she could not have been happy with this solution, since it significantly reduced the space for dancing.

Like many Stravinsky works conceived during the 1910s, *Les Noces* was sung. Stravinsky himself wrote the text, about a peasant wedding set in old Russia, gradually transforming what he had initially conceived as a divertissement-style work with comic elements into a scenic ritual and tragedy, a ballet-cantata fusing music and movement. His quest for "ethnographically reliable and unmediated sources" of folk music led him to some of the earliest transcriptions from phonographic field recordings of Russian wedding songs and wedding and funeral laments, as well as to what the musicologist Margarita Mazo has called the "phonemic approach" to word-setting.[31] This meant, in the words of a critic paraphrasing Stravinsky, that the "words do not combine to make logical sense [but] are arranged . . . according to their sonorous and rhythmic potential."[32] The folk wedding ritual, as Mazo describes it, consisted of more than a dozen episodes. Stravinsky "singled out the key personnages [sic], their behavior, their characteristic gestures, and the most important episodes that support the ritual's progress."[33] In *Expositions and Developments*, one of his conversation books with Robert Craft, Stravinsky stressed the "ritualistic" essence of *Les Noces*. However, he also insisted upon its modernist character, linking its use of language to *Ulysses*, published only a year before the ballet's premiere. Both works, he explained, "are trying to *present* rather than to *describe*."[34]

Stravinsky went on to discuss the impersonality of the characters, their interchangeability, the fact that they existed as types rather than as unique individuals:

> Individual roles do not exist in *Les Noces*, but only solo voices that impersonate now one type of character and now another. Thus, the soprano in the first scene is not the bride, but merely a bride's voice; the same voice is associated with the goose in the last scene. Similarly, the fiancé's words are sung by a tenor in the grooming scene, but by a bass at the end. . . . Even the proper names in the text such as Pelagai or Saveliushka belong to no one in particular. They were chosen for their sound, their syllables, and their Russian typicality.[35]

In March 1921, Nijinska had envisioned in her diary a new form of opera, a "theater of action" with the texts crossed out and the focus shifted to the music, declaring, "There should be no 'librettism' in theater."[36] In an interview with the Polish-born critic Waldemar George in 1922, she said much the same thing: "The dance, 'done into choreography,' is endowed with an emotional power that can easily do without a scenario."[37] She reiterated this idea in an article published in the *Dancing Times* in 1937 applying it explicitly to *Les Noces*:

> In my theatre of 1920 in revolutionary Russia my first works ... were ... ballets "without libretti." Diaghileff did not sympathise with the idea. . . . [I]n spite of this, with great efforts, I was able to carry my ideas of the form of the ballet as I conceived them into my productions with Diaghileff. These ballets of mine did not merely renounce the stylisations which Diaghileff's ballets were fostering, but they also carried out the negation of the literary libretto, having a pure dance form for their foundation and moulding this into a new species of composition. *Noces* was the first work where the libretto was a hidden theme for a pure choreography; it was a choreographic concerto.[38]

The work had four episodes: At the Bride's House, At the Bridegroom's House, The Departure of the Bride, and, finally, The Wedding Feast.[39] In the first, eight women dance with the Bride's eight-foot-long braids, winding them around her neck as if strangling her. In the second, eight men surround the groom with lusty if highly stylized folk dances. The wedding party leaves the stage in the third, as the Bride's mother laments the loss of her daughter. Finally, in the fourth, the guests carouse while the newlyweds are sent to bed by their parents. There is no actual scenario, only a handful of stage directions. Many of these occur in quick succession before the lament at the end of the third tableau. Here, as the Bride leaves home, Stravinsky wanted to clear the stage of revelers, have the mothers slip back on opposite sides of the stage as the two solo female voices sing "child of my womb; come back" (rehearsal 84). In the last tableau the stage directions seem left over from an earlier, more literal version: a couple is chosen to warm the marriage bed; the newlyweds kiss; they are made to lie down; the bedroom door closes; the parents keep watch outside.[40] Nijinska followed only the most general of these directions. In her choreography for the fourth tableau nobody warms the bed, and the newlyweds never kiss, while in the third, the Bride is the sole object of her mother's lament, a moment when you can hear a pin drop in the audience. As for Stravinsky's sung text, this Nijinska ignores almost entirely. Its images of nightingales and matchmakers, rings of gold, leaning stems of flowers, white swans a-swimming, a father who sells his daughter for drink, and ribald guests from afar find no echo in her choreography, which drives forward propulsively like the rhythms of Stravinsky's score, shorn of folklore and the picturesque, as plain as Goncharova's drab, uniform costumes.[41]

In the fourth tableau, snatches of raucous dialogue warn the Bride what to expect: "You, sow the flax," "You, ask her for your shirts," "Be in the cellar and the attic," "From morning to night, be up, be up and on your feet," "Supervise the help," "Be up and on your feet," "Chop the wood," "The wood," "After that," "Smack," "Love her," "Like your soul," "Love her like your soul," "Shake her like a plum tree" (rehearsal 98–100). None of these images found their way into Nijinska's choreography. Yet they resonate throughout the ballet and offer a key, like the mother's lament, to the core meaning of the staged work, as viewed through the lens of its choreographer. Nijinska never referred to her as such (although a number of contemporary critics made the connection), but her Bride is an artistic cousin of Nijinsky's female victim in *The Rite of Spring*. Both are chosen and compelled to serve; each enacts a ritual she cannot escape. To be sure, the Bride's plight is comparatively benign: unlike the Chosen Maiden, she does not die a violent death. But she still remains a communal victim, her body used, abused, and violated. As Nijinska wrote in her reminiscence of the ballet:

> I saw a dramatic quality in . . . the fate of the bride and groom, since the choice is made by parents to whom they owe complete obedience—there is no question of *mutuality of feelings*. The young girl knows nothing at all about her future family nor what lies in store for her. Not only will she be subject to her husband, but also to his parents. It is possible that after being loved and cherished by her own kin, she may be nothing more in her new, rough family than a useful extra worker, just another pair of hands. The soul of the innocent is in disarray—she is bidding good-bye to her carefree youth and to her loving mother. . . . From the very beginning I had this vision of *Les Noces*.[42]

In the final lines of the text Stravinsky celebrates the first passionate embrace of the newlyweds. It takes one aback to read it, since onstage, to the tolling of bells and with the slowness of a familiar ritual, the dancers assemble a complex human pyramid—a gendered architecture built from the blocs of same-sex figures that appear earlier in the ballet. At the center stands the column of "braided" female heads from the end of the first tableau (an image that reappeared in Balanchine's *Mozartiana*), surmounted now by a new

Bride-to-be, while men fan out on either side and prostrate themselves. At the last moment, the new Groom-to-be is hoisted to the apex of the pyramid. Then the curtain falls. What has just transpired is not a unique event, but a ritual that repeats itself again and again.[43]

Nothing could be further from the eroticism of Stravinsky's concluding text (rehearsal 131–134), with its images of a feather mattress and well-smoothed sheets, and under them, hidden, "curly headed Khvetis"—one of Stravinsky's names for the Groom—the "sparrow" who has "found its nest" and "holds his mate tight." "He has taken his Nastasiushka in his arms . . . has taken her in his arms, has pressed her to his heart. . . . Well, my darling, my sweetheart, flower of my days, honey of my nights, honey of my nights, flower of my life, I shall live with you the way people are supposed to live, so that the others envy us, so that we make them envious." *Les Noces* was two ballets, one by the composer, an impatient lover, the other by a daughter and spurned wife, who never made love to the love of her life. Few people realized that *Les Noces* arrived onstage cleansed of desire and erotic love. Stravinsky's text appeared in none of the season's publications, and in any event, most of the audience didn't know Russian. Like Nijinska, they responded to the tragic power of the music, heightened by the implacable drive of the choreography. For Jacques Copeau, the French avant-garde stage director, *Les Noces* was the only work of the previous decade that suggested "the possibility of a renewal of tragedy."[44]

Like the music, the choreography builds on structural blocks.[45] Its movement vocabulary came from the *danse d'école* but also from the lexicon of Russian national dance forms. Thus the skittering of the women rests on bourrées and pas couru, some of ballet's oldest steps, while the squat steps of the men evoke a Ukrainian hopak. But nothing is quite right: the women may be on pointe, but they never turn out; the men jump, but never hover in the air. Instead, they hug the ground, hunched over even in jumps with fists to their ears, like dumb beasts of burden. Much of the work is in unison, and often it appears mechanical, with every gesture and every element of a gesture performed with equal weight and occupying an equal unit of time. Large blocks of movement are repeated, not exactly, but with enough identical elements to create the impression of a monolith, as at the end of the second tableau where repeats of the wheeling runs and jumps build to a powerful climax. There are a number of religious allusions—right hands that touch the heart as in the Orthodox sign of the cross, although the gesture is never completed; bodies that bow and lie prostrate on the floor, although there is no church and no icons to pray to, only a community as blind to human need as that of *The Rite of Spring*. Like Stravinsky's music, Nijinska's choreography is profane or secular rather than religious.

In her interview the previous year with Waldemar George, Nijinska had reaffirmed her belief in the enduring value of the *danse d'école*, calling it the "indispensable armature of the art." But she also told him that she refused to limit her choice of movements to the "so-called classical vocabulary," augmenting, as he put it, "both the initial alphabet and the number of expressive signs that follow from it." Nijinska also insists, he wrote,

> on the organic character of her art. . . . Space is its domain. Rhythmic movement is its principal function. The human body is its tool. Hence, the practice of gymnastics, athletics, and acrobatics can become for the dancer a valuable addition so long as he can turn it to good account and use it for scenic ends.[46]

Some of that language would come back to haunt her.

The 1923 season at the Gaîté-Lyrique was short. There were eight performances, crammed into nine days, beginning on June 13 with a gala for Russian charities in France under the patronage of the former Grand Duchess Marie, a gathering, *Vogue* remarked, of "Tout Paris" and "Tout Etranger," because of the numerous foreigners in the audience.[47] The premiere of *Les Noces* was a triumph, and Stravinsky, Nijinska, and Goncharova all took bows.[48] Tickets sold quickly, and a rumor circulated that the season would be extended.[49] It wasn't, but should have been, for it offered an almost unimaginable embarrassment of riches. *Les Noces* figured on every program, and on two, it was performed back to back with Massine's *Rite of Spring*. With two all-Stravinsky evenings and five performances pairing *Les Noces* with a second Stravinsky work (*Petrouchka* and *Pulcinella* were also danced), the season offered a dazzling homage to the composer so closely identified with the Ballets Russes. Moreover, with two performances each of *Chout* (Prokofiev) and *Contes Russes* (Liadov) and three of *The Polovtsian Dances* (Borodin), it was a profoundly Russian season. (Only *Parade* anticipated the French direction in which Diaghilev was already steering the 1924 repertory.) A number of critics spoke of the company's "rebirth"; *Vogue*'s J. L., who had followed Diaghilev's enterprises since 1908, thought it was possibly the "most glorious" of all his seasons.[50] Grigoriev, in his laconic way, wrote that "it even reminded us of our triumphs of 1909."[51]

Stravinsky's score for *Les Noces* received the lion's share of attention. All the music reviewers wrote about it, as did any number of *gens de lettres*, and it was also covered in the foreign, expatriate, and émigré press. Whether liked or disliked, it was not easily dismissed. It was a major new score by a major composer, possibly the outstanding composer of his age. Wits made light of it. Paul Souday called it a "strange hubbub" that ended up giving him a headache, Gustave Bret an "implacable, turbulent, and precise sound factory." Paul Veber thought it was fun "the way taking the veil is," Gustave de Pawlowski that it was a little like "a wedding in Salpêtrière," the Paris hospital for the mentally ill, while Adolph Aderer, striking a nationalist note, wondered when somebody would revive "a pretty French ballet with a minuet, gavotte, or pavane."[52] Several critics commented upon the fact that the text was in Russian, which they couldn't understand.[53]

Like the score, the choreography could not be ignored, and this, for the most part, was viewed with admiration. Wrote Georges Auric, a composer, critic, and one of the ballet's four pianists, in *Les Nouvelles littéraires*:

> Mlle. Nijinska's choreography unfolds in groups, plastic masses, dances, stamps, and jumps that is not inspired by a dramatic action; it is not a commentary on words or scenes with which, nevertheless, it melds in the most unforgettable way. Hence, its great independence and the pure emotion that overwhelms us.[54]

Louis Schneider, writing in *Le Matin* as well as the *New York Herald*, extolled Nijinska's choreography even more than Stravinsky's music. "The groups are grace itself," he told his French readers, "their plastic poses, almost geometric, are of a harmony and eurhythmy that will no doubt be imitated but not surpassed. The black and white costumes, against a background of the same colors, . . . create the impression of a lunar ceremony. All this is a very refined art."[55] For the composer-critic Paul Dukas, *Les Noces* was a strange and powerful work, perhaps "the strangest and most powerful we have ever seen and heard" from the Russians. "As a spectacle, it shatters all laws, defeats all classifications, and stands wholly and deliberately apart from all . . . known ballets. . . . This wedding is the funeral song of the saddest Humanity."[56]

Boris de Schloezer, a Russian émigré critic who reviewed music for *La Revue musicale* and *La Nouvelle Revue française*, and went on to write books about Stravinsky and Scriabin and translate Russian classics such as Tolstoy's *War and Peace*, was even more enthusiastic, hailing *Les Noces* as

"Stravinsky's most perfect work" and its realization as "the most important artistic event" of recent years. "*Les Noces*," he wrote in France's most prestigious literary journal, "is a milestone in the development of music and scenic art, for Nijinska's choreography, the culmination of a long series of efforts and researches, is worthy of the brilliant music that inspired it."[57] That milestone, he went on to explain, lay in the relationship of music and dance. In *Les Noces*,

> music is at the root of things; the dance is inspired and penetrated by it, but soon detaches itself to develop according to its own nature. There is an intimate correlation between the dance and the music, but not in the particular, not in the detail. . . . What links [them] is rhythm. However, on the rhythm furnished by the music, Nijinska constructs her own plastic edifice with . . . freedom. . . . What Nijinska does . . . is classicism in the broad sense, in the true sense of the word, which designates not such and such movements or poses, but a certain conception of the dance, which is reduced to an ideal of absolute autonomy and can be realized in a hundred different ways.[58]

Equally overwhelmed was the music critic Emile Vuillermoz, the author of books about Debussy and Fauré, and an early writer on film. "On a stage without scenery," he wrote in *Excelsior*,

> transformed into a vast cinematographic screen, moves a simplified humanity, black and white, as if born from a projector. With studied awkwardness, learned stiffness, and fixed expressions, these artificial marionnettes execute bold, curious evolutions, slide, parade, entwine, and construct strange architectures with their docile bodies. They mime the ceremonies of a popular wedding—sad, mechanical, machine-like, burlesque, and moving . . . like life itself! These two humble destinies are brutally pushed toward one another by every dark, irresistible force of social discipline. Before us, the choreography dismantles, piece by piece, the machinery of family and civilization. It is a terrible and unforgettable spectacle.[59]

The critic Roland-Manuel, a student, friend, and future biographer of Maurice Ravel, wrote in his season review that the Ballets Russes had "come magnificently alive again" with *Les Noces*. Brushing aside the witticism that the ballet was unlikely to encourage bachelors to marry, he emphasized that

Stravinsky's new work was a "poignant tragedy." "An immense melancholy hovers over everything," he wrote in *L'Eclair*.

> An implacable fatality bows the old parents, leads the onlookers' games and even the guests' traditional jests. These actors of an everyday drama borrowed from popular imagery appear here like schematized, living expressions of the inexorable mechanism that rules the actions, even to their loves.[60]

Only *Comoedia*, the daily theatrical newspaper, went out of the way to censure *Les Noces*. The music review went to Raymond Charpentier, rather than Louis Laloy, who had long championed Stravinsky's music, possibly because he had written a preview of the new work. A conductor, minor composer, and sometime music director of the Comédie-Française, Charpentier went on the attack in his first sentence, with Stravinsky's continuous reinvention of himself and the snobbery of his adoring public his real targets. "Mons. Igor Stravinsky, who has the ear of a very important clan," he began,

> can exhibit at his leisure endeavors such as *Les Noces*; he astonishes none of the declared partisans of progress or, rather, of "transformism" in art. Indeed, the majority of that public . . . accepts unconsciously even . . . the risk of falling into [his] carefully concealed ambush. . . . Thus the opinion of those who call themselves "the elite" is made: after perhaps stupid but active or fierce resistance, it ends up adopting someone, with the terms of its continuing admiration no longer being subject to any measure.[61]

Charpentier admits that in *Les Noces* Stravinsky achieves "extremely powerful effects." But if, like the author, you are fond of "sentimentality" in music and of nineteenth-century works like *Tosca*, *Mignon*, or *Werther*, then you are bound to be "cruelly struck by the scarcely disguised hammering" of Stravinsky's new work.[62]

As was usual in *Comoedia*'s coverage of dance works, André Levinson's review of the choreography came last. In this first of several reviews, he criticized the choreography because of its exact translation of Stravinsky's musical rhythms and what he perceived as the regimented, impersonal, and gymnastic quality of its movement:

> The very peculiar choreography, which owes something to the stadium and to the parade ground is by Mlle Nijinska, sister of the illustrious dancer.

Moreover, she has taken inspiration from one of the most debatable elements in the first version of *The Rite of Spring—the mechanical reproduction of rhythm*. Arranged in columns or in symmetrical figures, tightly linked to one other, the performers walk each note and *tap* each accent with a simultaneous, uniform, and insistent movement. . . . In the guise of a finale, Mlle Nijinska arranges her regimented and mechanized personnel in an immobile three-part grouping, a kind of *practicable* built of living flesh.[63]

This critique is virtually identical to what Levinson wrote about *The Rite of Spring* in the St. Petersburg newspaper *Rech* back in 1913 and reiterated five years later in *Ballet Old and New*; in Nijinsky's ballet, he wrote, "shamans and possessed . . . walk[ed] the notes" in a "tedious demonstration of rhythmic gymnastics."[64] Now it was Nijinska's tapping, impersonal masses who walked Stravinsky's notes, in a world ruled not by nature but by firing squads and communal spectacles. Of course, the French didn't know the prehistory of Levinson's critique, and they probably didn't realize its underlying political animus. This he made crystal clear in a review for the Russian émigré newspaper *Poslednie novosti*:

The style of Mme. Nijinska . . . is connected to the rhythmic practice of Dalcroze, which was born at the same time as the delirious ideology of the Soviet "mass" theater. It is a method of "theatricalization of life," which allows an entire Red Army division to be involved in the show as well as crowds of working-class people. Elementary rhythm, performers without personality, automatized motions (the so-called "biomechanics" of Meyerhold) make such choreography look like machinery: mechanical, utilitarian, industrial. This is electrification applied to ballet. There is no connection between this choreographic "Marxism" and Stravinsky's work.[65]

Two days after his initial *Comoedia* review, Levinson devoted his weekly dance column to the present state of the Ballets Russes. Furious at what he called Diaghilev's "itching for destruction" and "mania for vivisection," his unwillingness to revive *The Sleeping Beauty* and hire yesteryear's Russian glories in emigration, Levinson manages to trash just about everything and everyone he mentions. Then he gets to *Les Noces*. He has now seen it four times and awaits the concert version, the work's "true place," although

Stravinsky, to Levinson's chagrin, apparently thought otherwise. "Is it the fever of theatrical success," Levinson asked,

> that presses the great musician to immolate his work, fully sufficient in itself, on the boards of the stage? Does he not see his inspiration diminished by this false "exteriorization"? Can he endure without anguish Mlle. Nijinska's "marxist" choreography, which levels the art of the dancer by debasing it? I close my eyes and before me rises the great voice of eternal Russia, the immense respiration of its "black soil." And I shudder at the phrases of the recitative.[66]

Then, to conclude, he turns his wrath on Nijinska:

> A soloist much appreciated by the Imperial Theaters, Diaghilev's temporary ballet mistress, was noticed for . . . [her] agility and musicality in *Carnaval*. Then she replaced Karsavina in *Petrouchka*, making the best of her naturally strange face and exaggerating the burlesque side of the character. Last year we saw her take the place—with a casualness that borders on impiety—of her illustrious brother in *Faune*. In *Aurora's Wedding* we saw her lead the grand adagio, where she distorted Petipa's work with exaggerated and invented preparations. A mediocre if vigorous performer, a good musician, a dancer inclined to the grotesque . . . because of her natural shortcomings, a vivid mime but hysterical and tense in her delivery, having passed through the collectivist reveries of the Soviets and Swiss theories of physical culture—this is the artist to whom Diaghilev has entrusted the fate of his . . . *Ballets Russes!*[67]

The year before, Levinson had commended Nijinska for the "piety" of her revival of *Faune* and praised *Aurora's Wedding* for returning Petipa to France. Now, he sees her body—grotesque, hysterical, distorted, unfeminine—infected with the virus of Bolshevism. Abandoning all semblance of critical decorum, he turns vicious, personal, and misogynous. She is a "pedantic and stubborn vampire," who has sucked "all the blood and all the life" from the movement sources of her choreography. Elsewhere he says that she has "castrated" them, "schematizing" them virtually beyond recognition. She is "hysterical" (as so many women were diagnosed in the nineteenth century), physically "strange," and "tense." Finally, she has dared to claim the particle of "nobility, genius, or infamy" and reinvent herself as La Nijinska.[68] For Levinson, gender and political prejudice reinforced one another.

The morning that Levinson's second *Comoedia* review appeared, Sébastien Voirol sat down and wrote Nijinska an apology for his "confrère." A critic, poet, playwright, and translator as well as the author of a "simultaneous" poem inspired by *The Rite of Spring*, Voirol wrote to her on the letterhead of "Art et Liberté," an "association for the affirmation and defense of modern works." "My regret is great," he began, "at the moment I do not have a column in which to express my thought."

> André Levinson is almost a friend although I have only met him recently. But his article this morning deserved the riposte of a colleague. It is supremely unjust . . . for you, let us not speak about it . . . for the Nijinska who had the intelligence and personality to adapt choreographically a powerful and substantial work. . . . Where are the ballet masters able to do even a fraction of that?

He signed himself "your most sincere admirer and friend."[69]

Boris de Schloezer was another critic who felt that Levinson had gone too far, although he never mentions him by name. In *Zveno*, an émigré literary journal, he took pains to refute the connection with Dalcroze that Levinson had made so much of, insisting, instead, on Nijinska's original and highly creative approach to the synthesis of music and movement. In *Les Noces*, Schloezer argued, these two systems

> are connected through *rhythm* as opposed to meter. (In Dalcroze's paradigm, meter is what is transformed into dance.) In *Les Noces*, the metrical divisions of dance and music do not coincide systematically, but rhythm gives pulse to the orchestra and charts a trajectory for the movement. The movement itself is constructed by Nijinska completely freely, without relation to the music.
>
> The choreography of *Les Noces* is a reflection of the whole musical image in Nijinska's creative imagination. From that image Nijinska has intuitively conceived an image that is generally connected to the music as its whole, but never coincides in the details.
>
> Obviously, this is a purely subjective approach: Nijinska has experienced Stravinsky's music in this particular way; another choreographer could

experience it differently. But this is the meaning of an artist's creation—to transform his personal, subjective experience into a common, generally valid, universal, and non-transient one.[70]

Although Schloezer had refuted the Dalcroze argument, Levinson failed to budge. In "Stravinsky and the Dance," first published in 1923 in *La Revue musicale* and the following year in *Theatre Arts Monthly*, he wrote that Nijinska brings "a hollow image of life, mechanical and bloodless," to the score, while her choreography recalls "nothing so much as the athletic stadium or the drill grounds." Groups "reproduc[e] the rhythm"; they stand in double file like "soldiers of a firing squad." At the end, "Mlle. Nijinska," as Levinson persists in calling her, although she was married and in her mid-thirties, "herd[s] her cowed company into . . . a sort of practicable . . . constructed with flesh and blood or an apotheosis of exhibition gymnastics."[71] In the opening chapter ("Grandeur and Decadence of the Ballets Russes") of *La Danse d'aujourd'hui* (1929), he inserts a whole paragraph from one of his 1923 reviews, including one of his choicer phrases about "Mlle. Nijinska's 'marxist' choreography . . . level[ing] the art of the dancer by debasing it."[72] In the next chapter ("Stravinsky and Theatrical Dance"), an updated version of the Stravinsky essay, he repeats the whole *Noces* section and then some.[73] As late as 1931, in a review of Nijinska's *Etude*, he hammered away. "On an arbitrarily shrunken base of the *danse d'école*, she constructs a style of her own composed of three elements: *classicism*—but reduced into simplified and frozen patterns; *Germanism* (melding the individual into the group and replacing harmony with order); *Sovietism*," although Levinson adds that he means by this "an attitude of the spirit," not politics.[74]

Critics listened to Levinson. By June 27 when Henry Malherbe came to write his second review of the 1923 Ballets Russes season, he had picked up on Levinson's unfounded Dalcroze critique. "The dancers move with exactitude on each rhythm," Malherbe wrote in *Le Temps*. "One can say that each note of *Les Noces* is translated by a movement and finds an arbitrary choreographic equivalent."[75] Maurice Brillant, in the August issue of *Le Correspondant*, found the dancers stamping "on every *beat* of the score" and in the choreography "a little bit of 'eurythmics' and those gymnastics à la Dalcroze that [he] could never really confuse with dance."[76] Even Florence Gilliam in a season review for *Theatre Arts Monthly* thought the ballet's "rhythmic and plastic mode . . . owes something to Dalcroze."[77]

How refreshing then to read Fernand Divoire, a poet, critic, and dance writer who had lost his heart to Isadora Duncan. An admirer of Dalcroze, he nevertheless linked Nijinska's "new conceptions of the dance" to the Futurist-influenced experiments in "vocal simultaneism" of Henri-Martin Barzun and a number of other French writers, who viewed polyphony and simultaneity as means of eroding the boundary between art and life. "It would be interesting," Divoire wrote, "to see . . . a collaboration between the two simultaneisms of spoken voices and gestures. Both have the same end: the balanced use of human masses."[78] Enormously impressed by the company's newfound "homogeneity," Divoire sought Nijinska out, interviewing her about "her achievements and her projects." She told him that her goal was to "represent not life but the rhythm of life," and to do so only by using "dance elements" or gestures. "The emotion is in the rhythm and in the lines of the gestures." She explained that the choreographic mass was not a collection of individuals but an entity endowed with a single life, capable of giving birth to "as many nuances" as an orchestra.[79] She also told him that she had worked out many of these ideas in *Demons*, a work she had choreographed in Kiev. At that, Nijinska later wrote, Diaghilev hit the ceiling. " 'How could you say that, Bronia?' he shouted. For a long time he could not forget my 'blunder' and looked at me with an unfavorable eye." Everything, she added, "had to originate" with him.[80]

Despite Levinson, *Les Noces* brought Diaghilev his greatest artistic success of the 1920s. Ten days later, the *Fête Merveilleuse* in Versailles marked the apogee of his company's social success. Paris had no shortage of gala entertainments, and many had a retrospective theme. However, nothing quite matched the *Fête Merveilleuse*. The high point of a campaign to raise money for Louis XIV's palace, whose condition (*Figaro* explained) "worsens from day to day," this unique event was intended to "resuscitate the Grand Siècle" itself.[81] It was the brainchild of Gabriel Astruc, the music impresario who had built and lost the Théâtre des Champs-Elysées and presented Diaghilev's most celebrated prewar seasons. Astruc enlisted Diaghilev to create an entertainment as unforgettable as the surroundings—the Hall of Mirrors, transformed into a theater for the night; the Marble Court, a temporary car park; the Queen's Bedchamber, her Guard Room, the Royal Dining Hall, the Peace Room, Coronation Room, and other extraordinary galleries through which everyone passed on their way to the Hall of Battles, where a Candelabra Supper began at midnight. The dancers spent three days rehearsing at Versailles. Lydia Sokolova remembered the brilliant sunshine, the carpenters hammering away, and dressing in the Sun King's own bed-chamber, with his wig and death mask on the wall. On the day of the dress rehearsal, Grigoriev wrote, the dancers in full costume, including makeup and wigs, could be seen strolling through the gardens.[82]

The core of the performance was *Aurora's Wedding*. However, Diaghilev now divided it up, arranging the dances into two "*entrées*" ("Entrée of the Gentlemen and Ladies of the Court" and "Entrée of the Fairytales") and inserting between them unrelated vocal numbers and dances recycled from other works. In this way, with flair, imagination, and a half-dozen new costumes, he re-created the structure if not the actual content of a seventeenth-century court ballet. Among the unrelated dances were the divertissements from Massine's *Le Astuzie Femminili* (1920), now retitled the "Entrée of the Ballet of the Queen of Naples"; the Dance of the Buffoons from Fokine's *Le Pavillon d'Armide* (1909), which became the "Entrée of the King's Fools"; and the pavane from *Las Meninas*, Massine's 1916 Velásquez-inspired ballet, now fitted out with new choreography by Nijinska and called the "Entrée and Pavane of the Spanish Infantas."

Music by Lully opened the performance: at the end, as Daniel Vigneau of the Opéra-Comique sang Rameau's "Hymn to the Sun," Louis XIV himself appeared in all his grandeur, wearing a mantle of blue and ermine thirty-five meters long that unrolled slowly and solemnly as he ascended the grand mirrored staircase of the stage. The visual setting was equally stunning. Juan Gris, in his first commission for Diaghilev, had decorated the platforms and stairs that formed a multi-tiered performance structure with garlands, scrolls, and other motifs that not only simulated the surrounding glitter but mirrored and multiplied them.[83] More than a thousand people crammed the gallery. Despite the high price (300 francs) people were begging for seats, even for places with little or no view; an American lady offered to pay 6,000 francs for a ticket. (At the time Diaghilev's corps dancers earned about 800 francs a month.) More than 300,000 francs were raised for restoration of the palace. Pierre-Plessis, one of the lucky journalists to attend the event, sat down at midnight to write his story, unable to contain his excitement. "Versailles is reborn," he told his readers. "Three men have performed this miracle: Henry Lapauze [the palace curator], Gabriel Astruc, and Serge de Diaghilew. May the shade of the Sun King thank them!"—a sentiment that must have endeared the author to Diaghilev.[84] Hubert Morand, equally overwhelmed, quoted Madame de Sévigné about a fête she had attended nearly 300 years before, "All is grand, all is magnificent, and the music and the dance are perfection."[85]

Although the *Fête Merveilleuse* was a unique performance, it anticipated the repertory for which Diaghilev was now laying the groundwork. It was French, looked back to the Grand Siècle, yet had its feet in the artistic present. When the company broke up for a six-week summer holiday on July 1, Nijinska got down to work on her new assignments.

6

Les Biches

Nijinska must have had mixed emotions contemplating the season that lay ahead. *Les Noces* had proven her worth as a choreographer, but it did little to bolster her position with Diaghilev. If anything, the shift in his artistic priorities, already well underway, undermined her authority. Never again would she enjoy the creative freedom she had experienced in *Les Noces* or bask in Diaghilev's undivided support. She must have regarded his new orientation with mixed feelings. She was a Russian artist, a modernist artist, indifferent to the retrospective charms of the French classical past and no doubt apprehensive at the prospect of collaborating with artists whose work was unfamiliar and who spoke only French. It was hard to avoid the conclusion that her days as a Diaghilev choreographer were numbered. She had seen Fokine come and go; even her brother, Diaghilev's great love, had been ruthlessly discarded. The growing insecurity of her position was coupled with the increasing burden of her responsibilities.

During the year that began in July 1923, Nijinska choreographed four original ballets, touched up a number of others, and staged the dances for at least nine operas. This non-stop activity, in which she bore the full choreographic burden of Diaghilev's contractual arrangement with Monte Carlo, turned her into a master craftsman, while adding to the body of works comprising her stock-in-trade. Like Massine before her and Balanchine, who followed her as Diaghilev's in-house choreographer, Nijinska emerged from her years with the Ballets Russes a citizen of the West. Whatever the downside of that experience, it gave her an identity that made it possible for her both to earn a living and to continue developing as a creative artist. For Nijinska and so many other émigrés, the Ballets Russes was a haven, protecting its members from a hostile world, and, because of the stature they enjoyed as Diaghilev artists, a passport to that world. Thanks to Diaghilev, Nijinska acquired an elite status within the international arts community.

When the company returned to Monte Carlo in October 1923, Diaghilev's star was at its zenith. The contracts he had signed made him a leading cultural player in the diminutive principality. Belloni was gone, and with him the old Franco-Italian repertory, although the seasonal round and the number of performances remained much the same as the previous year. For the dancers this meant six months of uninterrupted work, for Diaghilev that they were at his sole beck and call. Five weeks of "Ballets Classiques," featuring the ex-Maryinsky ballerina Vera Trefilova in Diaghilev's abbreviated version of *Swan Lake*, opened the season on November 23. A month-long "Festival Français" began on New Year's Day, followed by a six-week season of grand opera and another month-long Ballets Russes season interspersed with the occasional opera. Then the company headed west to Barcelona and north to the Netherlands, finally entraining in mid-May for Paris and the "Grande Saison d'Art" at the Théâtre des Champs-Elysées celebrating the 1924 Olympics.

For Diaghilev the year's high point was the Festival Français, the crux of a plan to insert himself—through the latest metamorphosis of his company's repertory—into an elite French discourse on cultural identity viewed through the prism of the Grand Siècle. Diaghilev had no interest in reconstructing the past with exactitude; he sought, instead, to experience its recovered objects through a modern sensibility. To accomplish this, he enlisted artists of the School of Paris and composers associated with the group known as Les Six, while relying on Nijinska for choreography. As a strategy, retrospective modernism was not new; it first appeared during the war years to "update" period material. *The Good-Humoured Ladies* (1917), *Le Tricorne* (1919), *La Boutique Fantasque* (1919), and *Pulcinella* (1920) exemplified the genre: set, respectively, in Goldoni's Italy, France of the Belle Epoque, Andalusia under the Napoleonic occupation, and eighteenth-century Naples, they were neither pompous nor self-important, with scores based on older music and designs by modern artists. All were choreographed by Massine, and revealed the speed, angularity, and full-body stylization that characterized his early work, inspired by futurism and film, eighteenth-century dance manuals, and new theories of body mechanics. Irony was a critical element of the genre.

Unlike these predecessors, the cycle of retrospectivist operas and ballets that Diaghilev now set out to produce were all French, and all in some way invoked the Grand Siècle. To be sure, only the music by Montéclair for the ballet *Les Tentations de la Bergère ou l'Amour vanqueur* actually dated to the period. The operas—Gounod's *Philémon et Baucis* (1860), *La Colombe* (1860), and *Le Médecin malgré lui* (1858), and Chabrier's *Une Education manquée* (1879)—all came from the mid-nineteenth century, while the ballet *Les Fâcheux* had a new score by Georges Auric. However, two of the works

were inspired by comedies by Molière and two others by tales of his contemporary, the fabulist La Fontaine. With their light touch and amatory themes,
they were the antithesis of nineteenth-century grand opera, with its historicism, high-mindedness, and theatrical pageantry. Thus, in *Une Education
manquée* (sometimes translated as "an incomplete education") a teenage
bride and groom wonder what to do on their wedding night; in *Philémon et
Baucis* Jupiter makes an aging couple young again and falls in love with the
wife, who thwarts him by begging to be restored to old age. Nothing could be
further from war, revolution, and social upheaval, the transformative events
of Nijinska's recent past, than these charming trifles. Diaghilev's new aesthetic turn must have seemed an unforgivable retreat from the contemporary.

Diaghilev had long been drawn to the eighteenth century. In his huge
1905 exhibition of Russian historical portraits, obscure eighteenth-century
artists, including many serf painters, figured prominently. Retrospectivism
was a key theme of his magazine *Mir iskusstva*, and among its contributors,
none embraced the arabesques and artifice of the rococo with greater ardor
than Alexandre Benois, whom Diaghilev now enlisted to design as well as
direct *Philémon et Baucis* and *Le Médecin malgré lui*. Richard Taruskin has
lamented what he terms Diaghilev's postwar *"reprise de contact* with the
aristocratic *Mir iskusstva* values from which the Ballets Russes had sprung,"
and how the "old *barin*" carried Stravinsky along with him.[1] In any event
the Festival Français turned out to be a flop. The French may have been dazzled by the Fête Merveilleuse, and there did exist a coterie audience for lost
French musical goodies,[2] but Diaghilev's cosmopolitan audience had little
interest in such forgotten gems. Only one of the operas, *Une Education
manquée*, outlived the season in Monte Carlo, and this was dropped after its
second Paris performance.

For Diaghilev, however, the journey into the byways of the French musical past turned into a passion. He spent hours at the Paris Opéra library,
studying scores by Auber, Hérold, Rameau, Halévy, Mouret, Mondonville,
Destouches, and others; he consulted authorities and had numerous pages
copied from old music books. He jotted down titles and dreamed up the most
incongruous pairings: modernist artists such as Larionov for Le Sueur's *Fête
à la cour des Miracles* (1803), Kisling for Bizet's *Jeux d'Enfants*, Vlaminck for
Méhul's *La Dansomanie* (1800), and Derain for Adam's *Giselle* (1841).[3] (Like
most people of his time, Diaghilev identified ballets by their composers, not
their choreographers.) None of these projects came to fruition. "I'm very
happy *Namouna* isn't happening," Nijinska confessed to Diaghilev in July

1923, after he had abandoned yet another retrospective project. "If only the music were different!"[4]

Although *Les Noces* must have left Nijinska creatively drained, Diaghilev had rushed into rehearsals of *Les Tentations de la Bergère*, intending to produce it at Versailles. But with barely a week between the end of the Gaîté-Lyrique season and the *Fête Merveilleuse*, there wasn't time to conjure up a new ballet from scratch, and Diaghilev quickly replaced *Tentations* with *Aurora's Wedding*. In July, when the company scattered for vacation, Nijinska took a working holiday and started on the new ballet.[5] The story was simple: a pretty shepherdess is wooed by a marquis, but the king blesses her union with the shepherd she loves. Major roles were already cast, including the shepherdess, either Vera Nemchinova (who ultimately played the role) or Olga Spessivtseva (whom Diaghilev was trying, unsuccessfully, to woo back to the Ballets Russes). The stage action, too, was largely set. The six Marquises, Diaghilev wrote on July 22, enter before the peasants and "join the general dance when Apollo appears." The three Counts dance "a charming passepied"; the four Barons "dance the same thing as the Marquises." The letter makes clear Diaghilev's extensive involvement in planning the ballet's action. The vision was his, the choreographer an artisan charged with the steps.[6]

The company returned to Paris from vacation on August 15 and spent the first few days of the six-week rehearsal period trying to patch together *Le Pavillon d'Armide* and *Narcisse*, both long out of repertory. Nijinska arrived with Diaghilev, and on August 21 rehearsals began in earnest for *Tentations*; they continued, according to Kremnev's log, for the next six weeks, usually after lunch, while mornings were set aside for other works, after the required 9 A.M. company class. The heat in Paris was stifling, Grigoriev remembered, and the dancers were "half exhausted." But Diaghilev "insisted" they go on, until the ballet was "ready," and by the time the company left Paris for Geneva, it was.[7]

Juan Gris, commissioned to design *Tentations* the previous spring, was already in Monte Carlo when Nijinska arrived there with the company on October 24. Although Diaghilev was very interested in Gris, his biographer and dealer Daniel-Henry Kahnweiler was appalled at how Diaghilev treated the artist:

Gris made an exact model of his set, done to scale, and did a large number of pastels and water-colours for the costumes. I was astonished at the ease or rather mastery of it all. Diaghilew used to come and discuss with him.

I was frequently present during those talks, and I must admit that I can imagine nothing more demoralising. Diaghilev, with an air of friendly charm,
would scrap, or at least modify, all Gris' original ideas.[8]

Like the ballet's choreographer, the visual artist was reduced to executing
Diaghilev's ideas.

Gris found Monte Carlo "as boring as a sanatarium." Every day he went
to the scene-painters' studio to see, as he told Kahnweiler, "that they do not
make stupid mistakes." Gris was also having trouble with *La Colombe*, another
opera Diaghilev had also asked him to design. In early December, when the
scenery was hung in the theater, it turned out that the colors "were nothing
like those of the design."[9] He wrote to Kahnweiler on December 20: "I *must*
escape soon from this centre of incompetence and hysterics."[10] Surrounded
by Russians—"eccentrics of one sort or another," he called them—he had yet
to succumb to what Cocteau famously called the "red-and-gold disease."[11]

Compared to the operas, *Les Tentations de la Bergère* turned out to be a
gratifying experience. Gris doesn't actually say anything about his interaction
with Nijinska in the weeks leading up to the premiere, but he was impressed
by her professionalism. "The Montéclair ballet has been a great success," he
told Kahnweiler.

> I had to take a curtain call, and Nijinska says that she has never seen such a
> complete harmony. But Oh! How frantic I was during the last days. Except
> for Nijinska, who takes her work seriously, and Diaghilew who knows his
> job, nobody uses his brains or foresees anything. . . . I cannot wait to get
> away from this infuriating *milieu*.[12]

Of course, *Tentations* was not the only ballet Nijinska was choreographing
for the Festival Français. No sooner had she arrived in Monte Carlo than
she started work on *Les Biches*—"The Does" is one translation—her most
important Diaghilev-era creation after *Les Noces* and one that remains
in repertory. The music was by Francis Poulenc, a member of the Les Six,
the group of young French composers taken up by Jean Cocteau after the
war and championed in *Cock and Harlequin*, a manifesto of the new music
published in 1918.[13] Diaghilev was strongly influenced by Cocteau's theories
and, according to Darius Milhaud, another Les Six composer, was "distinctly
attracted by the amusingly direct art personified by Poulenc and Auric."[14]
In May 1921, after hearing Poulenc's music for *Le Gendarme Incompris*, a

play by Cocteau and Raymond Radiguet, Diaghilev commissioned the composer to write a ballet score for him.[15] "Mon cher ami," Diaghilev wrote from London the following November:

> As I told you, this ballet interests me a great deal, and the details you give me about it seem very amusing. . . .
>
> Before the Christmas holidays I hope to come to Paris, and I will be very curious to see and hear what you have done.[16]

More than two years would elapse before Poulenc's ballet became a reality. In the meantime he became a Ballets Russes insider. In 1922 he went to see *Mavra* at the Paris Opéra and was one of the work's few enthusiasts. He attended the Karsavina Gala at the Théâtre Mogador, going on to a "gay" supper at the Princesse de Polignac's with Picasso, Stravinsky, and Diaghilev, and after the revival of *Chout*, reported to Milhaud that Nijinska was "very good" as the Buffoon.[17] Years later Poulenc memorialized the impresario: "Dear, irreplaceable Diaghilev, you were the wonder of my 20-year-old self, not only because you gave me your confidence and esteem, but because I owe to you my most violent aesthetic shocks."[18]

Once the Mogador season was over, Diaghilev, Poulenc, and Nijinska went to see "Mother Bongard," Poulenc's nickname for the well-known fashion designer Germaine Bongard, the ballet's librettist who was to design the costumes as well. They talked for two hours, and not even Diaghilev's fabled powers of persuasion convinced her to let them use her libretto while dropping her designs for the costumes. "She kept everything," the composer told Milhaud. "Perhaps we will do a suite of dances without a libretto."[19] A few days later they visited the painter Marie Laurencin, who agreed to do the sets and costumes. Poulenc would later say that Diaghilev "betrothed" him to Laurencin, as he coupled so many composers and visual artists, whose likenesses and maquettes dominated the season's "Programme Officiel."[20] *Les Biches*, Poulenc declared, is "absolutely Marie Laurencin."[21] In the days following their meeting a crucial decision was made. "There will be no subject," Poulenc reported to Stravinsky, "but simply dances and songs. I am delighted by this decision."[22] Nijinska must have been as well. Indeed, after the Bongard libretto was abandoned, she must have argued vigorously against replacing it, although Poulenc's support was probably crucial in getting Diaghilev to agree to the idea. For Nijinska, *Les Biches* was a "pure dance" work, a descendant of those first plotless ballets she had choreographed in Kiev, and a progenitor, with *Les Noces*, of a long series of choreographic abstractions.

As *Les Biches* took shape, Poulenc kept his friends abreast of its progress. To Milhaud, in August, "*Les Biches* will be a very clear, solid, and classical ballet."[23] To Charles Koechlin, in September, "I am working hard on my ballet *Les Biches*, which I'm passionate about."[24] He sent a full report to Diaghilev later that month. He had finished the Introduction, the song for three men, the solo for the star ("very *dansante* and andantino"), and the Rag-Mazurka. "Tell Nijinska that from now on she can think in terms of frenetic movements in three tempi."[25] By January 1923, Diaghilev had scheduled *Les Biches* along with Auric's *Les Fâcheux* and an untitled Satie ballet (never realized) to premiere the following December in Monte Carlo.[26] Holed up in Nazelles in the Loire Valley where he was staying with friends, the composer made a flying visit to Paris in June to see *Les Noces*, which he called "immense" and "brilliant," then retreated to his family's country home in Nogent-sur-Marne to finish *Les Biches*.[27] "Excuse my silence," he wrote to Milhaud at the end of July,

> but I work the whole day on *Biches*, which I am finishing. I . . . have finally found the "Chanson dansée," which is a sort of game in the middle of the ballet. It is leaping, fierce, and charming. Marie has started the set. She has made an adorable costume for the star dancer—a short dress, very sweeping, very low-cut, in grey-white tulle, covered with rose moiré panels, a pancake hat with aigrettes of the same color.[28]

By early August, the score was finished. Overjoyed that Diaghilev liked it, Poulenc asked him to have Boris Kochno write or telephone "the *exact* date of Nijinska's arrival in Paris," so he could meet her.[29] Back in Nazelles, he orchestrated the ballet. "Cher Ansermet," he wrote to the conductor Ernest Ansermet in October:

> A thousand excuses for my silence. . . . I am in the thick of orchestrating *Les Biches*. It's a big score: 27 minutes of very rapid music. Diaghilev is happy. I think it is good. In any case I put my heart in it and whatever skill I have. . . . I am orchestrating from the manuscript and the Russians have the only copy.[30]

It was this copy that Nijinska used when she began staging *Les Biches* at the end of October in Monte Carlo. By early November the composer was there, recording changes in red ink on the score. The number of men went from four to three, and instead of two there were now four women soloists. The idea of inserting a solo for Lubov Tchernicheva in the Rondeau was dropped, and the setting was changed: in the score it "represented a forest in summer," closer to the rustic settings of eighteenth-century fêtes galantes than to Laurencin's fashionable salon.[31]

According to Boris Kochno, Diaghilev had feared that Nijinska might be "unresponsive to the Latin charm" of Poulenc's score. However, once he got to Monte Carlo, he was pleasantly surprised. As he wrote to Kochno,

> Here everything is going along much better than I had expected. Poulenc is enthusiastic about Bronia's choreography, and they get along excellently together. The choreography has delighted and astonished me. But then, this good woman, intemperate and antisocial as she is, does belong to the Nijinsky family.[32]

As for Poulenc, he was thrilled. "The choreography of *Les Biches* is . . . *ravishing*," he wrote to Milhaud.[33] To the composer Henri Sauguet he was even more enthusiastic. "The choreography of *Les Biches* is a masterpiece. It's ravishing from beginning to end and everything that I wanted."[34] Writing to Diaghilev in December, he could barely contain his excitement about Nijinska's solo for Vera Nemchinova as the Girl in Blue (whom Poulenc calls the "Star") and her choreography for the blue sofa:

> Highness, you cannot imagine what you have missed for the last two days. When Nemchinova's dance is finished—and what a marvel—they start the game. I must say that as madness it surpasses anything one could imagine. Nijinska is *a genius*. Listen to this: having decided that the sofa is a "star," just as she herself is, she is making it dance throughout the game!!! Grigoriev asked the Casino for the loan of a magnificent sofa, and they fell to work (in an entirely proper fashion, naturally).
>
> I shan't try to describe to you what happens. In a "presto" movement, the women take sitting positions, leap into the air, fall onto the tufted cushions, roll over on their backs (although the two men are straddling the sofa back), and then they drag the poor sofa . . . in all directions. When, in the middle section, the music calms down, the Star and Vilzak bounce onstage. Thereupon

the Girls turn the sofa (its back is now to the audience) into an observatory, their heads popping up over the back and then dropping out of sight; when the game resumes . . . the two men quickly turn the sofa around, and there are the two women lying down in a position that, thinking of Barbette, I can only describe as head-to-tail. . . . At rehearsals, I laugh until I cry.[35]

Poulenc was not alone in admiring Nijinska's choreographic fecundity during these pressured weeks. "Nijinska was completely in her element," remembered Lydia Sokolova.

She improvised and invented steps and dances at such speed that the girls found it impossible to follow her; demonstrations and explanations would develop into an uproar. Silence would then be called for, and the whole thing would begin again. The ballet seemed to take shape overnight.[36]

With "at least 72 rehearsals or close to 250 hours of work" (as Poulenc calculated), it was hardly overnight.[37] But the atmosphere in the studio was electric. During rehearsals for the pas de deux, "all the dancers insisted on watching," he told Kochno, a sure sign of their admiration for the choreography.[38] Poulenc turned out to be a real flirt, charming the "girls" while having a fling with one of the "boys."[39]

Unsurprisingly, a gay sensibility infuses *Les Biches*. As Christopher Moore notes, "Poulenc's use of a network of rhetorical and stylistic devices that simultaneously conceal and creatively exploit the secret of his sexual identity reflects the composer's profound engagement with the queer cultural practices of camp."[40] Camp aesthetics, he notes, are evident throughout the ballet, but "cross-dressing, androgyny, and same-sex desire are most apparent in three of the ballet's central scenes: the Woman [Girl] in Blue's 'Adagietto,' the Hostess's 'Rag-Mazurka,' and the 'Petite chanson dansée' featuring two young women."[41] In the opening "Rondeau" a dozen women in salmon-pink flapper dresses slink stylishly on pointe in a salon that Claude Rostand described as halfway between "the Casino and the brothel" and Robert Brussel as "the lobby of a fashion house."[42] Their perambulations are interrupted in the "Chanson dansée" by three brawny athletes in shorts who flex their muscles and display their physiques, a dance, Diaghilev thought, that had "come out extremely well." The dancers—Anatole Wilzak, Leon Woizikovsky, and Nicolas Kremnev—"perform it with bravura," Diaghilev added, "weightily, like three cannon."[43]

Then, the Garçonne appears. Danced by Vera Nemchinova, she was a chic and equivocal figure, a "bachelor girl" and the androgynous center of the ballet's queer universe. Poulenc told a Monegasque journalist before the premiere that the women in *Les Biches* were modern women, "used to Rolls-Royces and pearl necklaces from Cartier" and "pulsating" with "the rhythm of modern life."[44] Moore sees the Garçonne as a camp figure, a man in drag who dons pointe shoes and white gloves. Her costume, a fitted blue tunic over briefs that left her legs fully exposed (albeit covered in sleek white tights), was "practically identical," he suggests, to the costume for the Poet in *Les Sylphides*.[45] She appeared and disappeared, drifting across the stage on pointe, oblivious to all but a powerful magnet for the lead athlete, who follows her off. Louis Schneider called her a *gandin*, a dandy but with the "look of an androgyne."[46] To a dancer who performed the role in the 1960s, Nijinska explained that she was like an "envelope, her exterior neatly folded to contain the information within."[47] André Levinson alone resisted her enigmatic appeal. He found her solo laughable and launched into a tirade against the choreography. Never one to mince words when it came to Nijinska, he declared that a "true spirit of perversity . . . seems to inspire the ballet mistress. She dissects the classical steps with the will of a torturer."[48]

After a playful game of hide-and-seek for two of the "Biches" and the two unattached athletes, the Hostess appears. This was Nijinska's own role, and it was a tour-de-force of petit allegro—brisés, entrechats-quatre, and beats galore—men's steps, repeated over and over, but performed in heeled slippers (all the other women were in pointe shoes). Brandishing a cigarette holder and wearing long ropes of Chanel pearls over a dropped-waist cocktail dress, she reminded some critics of a minor American music-hall diva.[49] She actually mounted the role on a young soloist, Ninette de Valois, the founding director of the company that became Britain's Royal Ballet. Nijinska "plucked" her from the corps and told her that she had to be ready to "show" it to Nijinska so the choreographer could work on it for herself. "Those long evenings spent in the rehearsal room," de Valois recalled many years later, "after the day *corps de ballet* rehearsals—are not easily forgotten."[50]

Nijinska was "irresistible" in the Rag-Mazurka, Sokolova remembered. She danced with two of the men,

which gave an extraordinary picture of a spoilt, capricious woman carrying on a sophisticated flirtation. She flew round the stage, performing amazing contortions of her body, beating her feet, sliding backwards and forwards, screwing her face into an affected grimace, enticing the men and flinging herself in an abandoned attitude onto the sofa. She danced as the mood took her and was brilliant.[51]

Musically, according to Moore, the "Rag-Mazurka" is "as confused about its genre as the Hostess seems to be about her gender." The dotted rhythms may "conjure up the worlds of both mazurka and rag, [but] neither dance is . . . musically maintained." Moreover, the dance abounds in "quirky mixed time signatures," as if the composer "took particular pleasure in queering the Hostess's beat."[52] In fact, this was the section with the greatest number of musical changes on the score, with many cuts and additions to the bass line, although at the start Poulenc writes that "The whole dance must be very rhythmic." In the pages that follow, contemporary allusions abound. A woman "slowly turns . . . like a mannequin modeling dresses," while "shimmy of the legs on pointe" and "little movement of the shoulders, body almost immobile" suggest the choreography's playful relationship with social dances of the day.[53]

The Garçonne and the lead athlete return for the Andantino, a pas de deux in which they go through the motions of balletic love as expressed in the developpés and supported turns of the typical Petipa adagio—but barely exchange a look. As Poulenc explained to Claude Rostand in the 1950s, "In *Les Biches*, it's not a question of love but of pleasure. That's why the *Adagietto* has to be performed without romantic pathos. In this ballet, one does not love for life; one goes to bed!"[54] The "Petite chanson dansée" that follows adds yet another layer of gender ambiguity, a dance for "two inseparable friends"— Sokolova and Lubov Tchernicheva in the original cast—that the composer considered "very secretly Proustian."[55] Sokolova disliked the dance; she thought it was "wrongly conceived and badly constructed" and that Nijinska couldn't have "understood the type of women we were meant to be."[56]

But Diaghilev was sager in this regard. "Don't worry," he told Poulenc. "She will guess without understanding," referring to the dance's Proustian echoes. Nijinska's rendering was "inspired," Poulenc wrote in 1946, "for she understood its intention without really analyzing it," or as he put it elsewhere, it was a "genius full of unconsciousness that made so much audacity possible." She was also, he said, "an extraordinarily pure being."[57] This is an odd statement. To be sure, Nijinska slept with men rather than women, but her relationship with Singaevsky was as yet unblessed by wedlock. She had been the "man" of her family for years, and in Kiev, certainly, had enjoyed close friendships with women, some of which had an erotic component. As for

Diaghilev's immediate circle, how could she *not* be aware of the ebb and flow of its sexual currents? Her brother had been Diaghilev's lover and, before him, Prince Lvov's. She knew Massine's story, and she was now grooming Diaghilev's latest love interest, Anton Dolin, who had joined the company in November 1923, for leading roles and stardom.[58] She was intimate enough with Diaghilev to enjoy his occasional confidences. Late one evening, after a long day of rehearsals, he invited her to have a drink at the Café de Paris, and later they walked and talked until two or three in the morning. "During this time," she wrote in an unpublished reminiscence,

> He talked not only about ballet but also about his personal feelings: how unhappy he was that he could not have his own son and how dear to him were Vaslav and Massine. He loved them like his own sons, and what joy it was to rear them as artists and how proud he was of their ... successes.[59]

It's easy to say that Poulenc and Laurencin, a prominent figure in the 1920s Sapphic world, had "queered" *Les Biches* because of their sexuality. But one can also view the ballet's female figures as projections and critiques of Nijinska's own gendered self—the vulnerable young woman she had been (Girls in Grey), the powerful, "masculine" woman she had become (Hostess), and the romantic ballerina figure she couldn't or refused to be but continued to find appealing (Garçonne). This was not the first time that Nijinska had spotlighted these figures. The Bride and her friends in *Les Noces* belong to the same family as the Girls in Grey just as the Fox in *Le Renard* is a cousin of the Hostess and Nijinska's transformed "Finger" variation in *The Sleeping Princess* a forerunner of the Garçonne. Poulenc's music allowed Nijinska to "queer" the allure of familiar balletic roles while giving her the space to complicate—and enlarge—her repertory of gendered selves.

Les Biches premiered on January 6, 1924. It was a "triumph," Poulenc wrote to Paul Collaer. There were eight curtain calls, something rare in Monte Carlo. "I must confess," he wrote, "that Nijinska's choreography was of such beauty that even the old Englishwoman with a passion for roulette couldn't resist it. It was truly the dance itself."[60] Poulenc could now rest on his laurels. Nijinska, however, had another premiere looming—*Les Fâcheux*, with a score by Georges Auric. According to Juan Gris, rehearsals for the ballet began on December 20, barely a month before the premiere on January 19. Meanwhile, on New Year's Day, 1924, *La Colombe*, the first of the French operas was given, followed by *Le Médecin malgré lui* on January 5, *Philémon et Baucis* on January 10, and *Une Education manquée* on January 17. Except for *Le Médecin malgré lui*, which included a ballet, Nijinska was not closely involved in these productions.

In addition to new works, the Festival Français included a number of older ones. One was Fokine's *Daphnis and Chloë* (1912), which had a marvelous score by Ravel but had gone out of the Ballets Russes repertory in 1914. The ballet was complicated. None of the dancers remembered it, and Jacques Rouché refused to lend Albert Aveline (who had worked with Fokine when he restaged the ballet at the Paris Opéra in 1921) to recall the troublesome passages. Grigoriev managed to resuscitate much of the work from his remarkable memory, while the blanks were filled in by Nijinska, who also choreographed new solos and a pas de deux for Dolin and Lydia Sokolova.[61] The result was a ballet "after Fokine," as the choreography credit read, while Nijinska was listed only as the production's "Ballet Mistress." It must have been her choice not to spell out her contributions. Fokine kept close tabs on his ballets, and he knew that she was changing them. He was especially exercised about *The Polovtsian Dances*. In 1923, during the season that witnessed the triumphant premiere of *Les Noces*, the "first two dances" were attributed to Nijinska and only the "grande danse finale" to Fokine.[62] By the time the ballet opened in London the following year, more than the choreography had changed. According to the *Times*:

> M. Roerich's camp scene . . . is still the same, and much of the choreography is that devised by M. Fokine for the original production. But Mme. Nijinska has remodelled the opening dances for the women, and someone has introduced new ideas to their costumes. One wondered what these women with their seductive undulating movements and their liberal display of bare limbs were supposed to be—surely not the wives and daughters of a hardy warlike race! They seemed to have strayed out of *Scheherazade*.[63]

Fokine, who was in London staging the dances for *A Midsummer Night's Dream* at the Drury Lane Theatre, may have paid a surreptitious visit to the Coliseum to see his celebrated work. Or he may have read about the changes in the *Times* or learned about them from a friend. In any event, he complained to Nijinska. Although his letter does not survive, in her reply Nijinska lays the blame on Diaghilev. "Dear Mikhail Mikhailovich,"

> I regret very much not being able to see you during your last visit to London. Besides the fact that seeing you would have been a pleasure, I wanted to

reassure you that it was not my idea to add two new dances to your master-piece, the *Igor Dances*, esteemed so much by me. S. P. Diaghilev was staging the act of *Prince Igor* with singing, and it was then that I choreographed those dances . . . [which] were added as an introduction to the main part to lengthen the performance. While I was working with . . . Diaghilev, I tried very hard to preserve everything you created, so the news that you are not happy about the *Polovtsian Dances* makes me very sad.[64]

Fokine thanked her for the "detailed description" of her work, ending with an admonishment. "Remaking things done by others is for people inca-pable of creating their own. I hope you will continue doing your own artistic work . . . not under Diaghilev's wing. Only then will it be serious and justi-fied."[65] She received this as she was preparing to form her own company.

***

Although Grigoriev, assisted by Kremnev, rehearsed most of the repertory, Nijinska must have had a hand in rehearsing or at least coaching the male role in *L'Après-midi d'un Faune* that she was now relinquishing to Woizikovsky. In *Swan Lake* she choreographed a new dance for the corps in Act II just be-fore Odette's solo.[66] She also freshened up two Massine ballets: *Las Meninas* (which she had already partly rechoreographed for the Fête Merveilleuse) and the divertissements from *Le Astuzie Femminili*, which was now length-ened "by the addition of new numbers," in Grigoriev's words, and retitled *Cimarosiana*.[67] Again, Nijinska's name does not appear among the ballets' credits. However, in November 1924 Diaghilev told the London *Observer* that Nijinska had "completely altered the finale and . . . added for the four youngest dancers of the company a delightful pas de quatre."[68] (The dancers were Ninette de Valois, Alice Nikitina, Serge Lifar, and Constantin Tcherkas.) The Finale was subsequently retouched by Massine.[69]

Diaghilev had high expectations for *Les Fâcheux*. Auric was his favorite composer of Les Six and the first of the group he commissioned, after hearing his *musique de scène* for a production of the Molière play at the Théâtre de l'Odéon in spring 1921.[70] *Les Fâcheux*, wrote the critic Louis Laloy after the Monte Carlo premiere, was neither "a reconstruction nor an adaptation or a restoration, but a resurrection [of] a tradition that must be dear to us,"[71] "a return" of the classical idea.[72] Boris de Schloezer waxed rhapsodic about the score, calling it a "revelation" that nothing until then had prepared him for and "one of the most significant works . . . since the war in French music."[73] Unlike the plotless *Les Biches*, *Les Fâcheux* had a detailed libretto by Boris Kochno, although one might wonder, as Henry Malherbe did in *Le Temps*, why so fine a writer as Auric, who wrote music criticism for *Les Nouvelles littéraires*, needed this "mysterious literary man."[74] A good-looking youth from a wealthy Moscow family, Kochno was only twenty when he wrote this, his second libretto for Diaghilev (the first was for *Mavra*). Originally hired as a secretary, he was on his way both to making himself indispensable to his mentor and to making a career for himself in the ballet world.[75] For *Les Fâcheux* (which is usually translated as *The Bores*), he dreamed up a libretto, which Auric duly followed, that was heavy on incident and light on dance—a glorified pantomime in which a man on his way to visit his mistress is way-laid by a series of bores.[76]

Once the ballet went into rehearsal, Nijinska and Kochno locked horns. According to Grigoriev:

> Nijinska did not consider Kochno, with whom she was supposed to co-operate, experienced enough to plan a ballet, and was inclined very often to disregard his suggestions. Then, on watching a rehearsal, Diaghilev would not approve what he saw; and this would result in long and heated arguments between him and Nijinska, which would go on and on till rehearsals would have to be cancelled and the dancers sent home. Nijinska would then do her best to carry out Diaghilev's instructions; but this not only wasted a lot of time, it also caused her to lose interest. These disputes were, to my mind, the more regrettable in that the ballet had seemed to me to be progressing quite happily; whereas the interference of Diaghilev and Kochno was not by any means always well directed.[77]

Kochno not only had Diaghilev's ear, but together they concocted all sorts of stage business that she was forced to include. Among their ideas for the Paris version of the ballet was that Dolin, as the Dandy, "should dance a *variation* on 'points' like a ballerina," as Grigoriev wrote, "imagining that this would be strikingly effective."[78] According to Dolin, the company "ridiculed the idea and considered it stupid," the reason he asked Nijinska to rehearse him privately until the dress rehearsal, when their "derision turned to admiration."[79] The press took note, although Gilson MacCormack, the Paris correspondent of the *Dancing Times*, wondered if there weren't "sufficient women in the company for the occasional necessary displays of virtuosity on the pointes."[80] Dolin's solo was not the only instance of gender play. When Stanislas Idzikovsky, on whom Nijinska choreographed the role of Lysander, left the company only hours before the premiere, Nijinska stepped into the breach, donning his costume and winning plaudits for her "brilliant authority" and "delicious" interpretation of yet another "trouser" role.[81]

Braque's designs were another source of contention. According to Kochno, who supervised the execution of the Louis XIV–style costumes, the artist copied the drawings that appeared on the front from seventeenth- and eighteenth-century fashion plates, while the back was a uniform brown. The painter's idea was to make the dancers "disappear" not by leaving the stage but by turning their backs to the audience and thus blending in with the blurry green and brown scenery. However, much to Kochno's annoyance (if he is to be believed), Nijinska ignored Braque's intentions, resulting in what he called a "conventional pantomime."[82]

Critics took a different view. Louis Laloy, who reviewed Les Fâcheux in Monte Carlo, wrote that Braque "was careful not to copy some old decor," yet what rose before one's eyes was an old town with "houses of a vivid brown as if washed by a recent rain, and a horizon of rivers and woods" that showed to advantage "the brilliant costumes . . . imagined and . . . invented . . . for the occasion by a dandy of the era, as they were by an artist of ours."[83] The choreography, he continued, was in a style midway between comedy and ballet. The lovers danced "steps in the most gallant and pure classical style." Elsewhere there was more action than dance, although Laloy clearly enjoyed the Gossips with their "delicious" air of frivolity and the final battle, a "veritable pantomime scene." Louis Schneider, writing in Le Gaulois, also praised the combination of artifice and variety.[84]

Although most critics commended Nijinska for her blending of old and new, Boris de Schloezer thought that she—as well as Braque—could have gone further in transforming their sources. Auric's music," he wrote,

completely transposes the style of a Lully and belongs more to the twentieth century than to the seventeenth: the costumes should have . . . undergone an analogous distortion. I would make a similar reproach to Mme Nijinska's choreography, which abounds in exquisite inventions: Mme. Tchernicheva's dance as Orphise, for example, and Mons. Woizikovsky's as the Card Player. In adapting the old dance movements to the exigencies of the mimed action, . . . Mme Nijinska is afraid to break too openly with the choreographic traditions of the

Grand Siècle; the example of the composer should have prompted her and the painter to greater boldness.[85]

Levinson, as always, found fault. "Nothing," he told *Comoedia* readers, "will lead me to believe that Mlle. Nijinska is the Molière of choreography," as if anyone had suggested she was.[86] "It's not," he continued,

> that she is devoid of all imagination. But she is short-breathed. Most of the interludes start out well. Lysander's saltatory theme or that of the Card Player is witty and appealing. But no development comes to amplify it. Monotony and boredom threaten us. . . . The ballet as a whole as well as each isolated interlude remains thin, sluggish, and empty.

About the only thing he liked, apart from some of the dancers, was the finale. This, he described, with a flourish of historicism, as a "grand ballet" of the seventeenth century, a "coda" of the Milanese masters "renewed by Mlle. Nijinska," as each group of dancers returned to the stage, offered a brief reprise of their respective themes, then melded into a rapid "tutti," on which the curtain fell.[87]

Levinson was much harsher on *Les Tentations de la Bergère*, probably because of its relative authenticity as an eighteenth-century artifact. The music, by Montéclair, dated to the period, and it was "reconstituted" and orchestrated by Henri Casadesus, an expert on eighteenth-century music (although some of the "rarities" he discovered turned out to be his own compositions).[88] There was no program note, and the action of the ballet (as Levinson put it) was "simplicity itself."[89] A Shepherd and a Marquis compete for the affections of a Shepherdess, who prefers the fruits and flowers of the shepherd to the riches of the seigneur. Juan Gris color-coded the twin worlds of the ballet, dressing the peasants in cool green and the courtiers in grey-blue. According to Levinson, Nijinska's choreography evoked only very freely the "dances of long ago." He applauds her decision, believing, as she does, that the dances of Pécour's time would have little theatrical impact. However, her "incomplete knowledge" of eighteenth-century dance, especially its rich tradition of petit allegro, has caused what he calls an "extreme timidity in the choice of means." (When she added and expanded the vocabulary of "beaten" steps for the Paris performances, he described the resulting "monotony" as no less tedious.) He complains about her use of the trap door to raise and lower the king, his dress, his stance, his *grands changements*—all errors of history and taste. Because of such "failures of general culture," he asserts, the ballet enjoyed only a *succès d'estime*.[90]

Of course, Diaghilev had had a considerable hand in working out the ballet, as Levinson must have known. According to Grigoriev, Nijinska based the choreography on classical steps, "guided carefully by Diaghilev as regards details of style."[91] Taken as a whole Grigoriev thought the ballet was "interesting and effective," although the set, with its platforms of various heights, was complicated and cumbersome, and the Montéclair score "rather dull and monotonous."[92] (Louis Schneider, who reviewed the ballet in Paris, put it more positively: "Nothing here to wound the ear.")[93] Sokolova, who found the costumes heavy, "never felt the ballet came to life," since Nijinska "was not really at home in the stilted artificialities of that period.[94] Levinson, by contrast, adored the artifice. In 1925 he published several articles on ballet of the Grand Siècle, including "The Dancers of Lully," which appeared in the January 1925 issue of *La Revue musicale*. Here he displayed his vast erudition, wandering across time and place, combing through the myriad details of history in search of a living tradition that culminated in the ballet he loved.[95] For Nijinska, the past never came alive this way.

Little is known about Nijinska's other choreographic accomplishments that winter. The playbills from Monte Carlo suggest the non-stop pace of assignments (or, as Grigoriev put it, "the composition of innumerable incidental dances"),[96] with the opening of the grand opera season three days after the close of the Festival Français. Some of these assignments were so minor that Nijinska took her name off them: the "Ballet Aérien" in *The Damnation of Faust* (which must have brought back memories of Kiev) and the Seguidilla in *Carmen*. However, plum assignments also came her way in *Manon*, *Tales of Hoffmann*, *Samson et Dalila*, and *Prince Igor*—all operas with substantial dance sequences.[97] For Mussorgsky's *Sorochintsky Fair* she choreographed *Night on Bald Mountain*, which, like *The Polovtsian Dances*, had an independent afterlife, albeit only a brief one with the Ballets Russes. According to Sokolova, who danced the role of the Witch in the ballet version, this was one of Nijinska's "most remarkable creations," a Witches Sabbath conjured up by "a writhing, whirling mass of bodies."[98] De Valois, too, remembered it as a ballet of "outstanding merit." "Time," she wrote in 1937, "has not obliterated from the memory of the writer [its] transitory choreographic brilliance."[99]

From the start of her career as a dancemaker, Nijinska had taught as well as choreographed. When she rejoined the Ballets Russes, she gave up teaching, but when the company was reconstituted in Paris after the debacle of *The Sleeping Princess*, she added company class to her other responsibilities. Nijinska's was a choreographer's class, designed to improve the dancer's technique but even more to inculcate her own choreographic principles and style. "She had theories that she considered we needed to study," Ninette de Valois wrote. "It was not enough for us to accept them just as part of her choreography." De Valois found Nijinska's classes "interesting but difficult." They were strengthening, and "in no time" she noticed an improvement in her elevation. Nijinska was "obsessed with correct breathing and gradually one saw the important relationship between breathing and movement."

> Correct breathing soon became a habit, so much so that it is now difficult to recall the theory involved that she would expound at great length. She taught us a very definite approach to body movement, as intricate as any contemporary dance, but strictly in relation to the classical school.[100]

To prepare Dolin for his debut in *Daphnis and Chloë*, Diaghilev insisted that he have private classes with Nijinska. She had not welcomed his arrival; she thought there was quite enough male talent in the company and certainly no need to add a "foreigner."[101] But since Diaghilev was in love and grooming the young Irishman for stardom, she agreed to give him a private lesson in the afternoon away from the company. Those two-hour classes on the stage of the Beaux Arts Cinema in Monte Carlo cemented a friendship that lasted until Nijinska's death. "To dear Anton, my long time and beloved friend," she wrote toward the end of her life, a testimony even more touching because it was in English, "with best remembrances of our happy days in Ballet."[102] "How deeply I loved her," Dolin wrote in his last volume of reminiscence. "She was my University of the Dance, and her lessons, although hard, were wonderful." She taught him as much in three months as he had learned in the previous three years, and was the first to stress the importance of breathing.[103]

> I remember her explaining more in movements than in words how to hold my breath while my body was suspended in the air and only when it had descended to the ground to expand gradually. She told me, then, how the secret of this had been largely the cause that governed her brother's jump, and that pause in the air which all who have seen him dance remember so well.[104]

She coached Dolin in several roles, including the Poet in *Les Sylphides* and the Blue Bird pas de deux. And she drove him, pushing and cajoling him—as she did all her protégés—to go beyond his comfort zone. In *Divertissement*, a memoir published in 1931, Dolin described her in rehearsal, "pale-faced, tired, her hair unkempt, tied in a bun at the back, black practice dress, hands that express brilliantly the power of speech and movement." Shouting "no," "that's wrong," "not like that," she would spring up, her face lit, to demonstrate, becoming "a different being" as she executed the movements he was to copy.[105]

Dolin left other snapshots of Nijinska dancing. During a rehearsal in Paris, one of the many Picasso attended, his three-year-old son Paulo exclaimed, "Papa, isn't she ever going to come down?"—as Nijinska performed a series of leaps to demonstrate a step she wanted Dolin to do. In the Mazurka of *Les Sylphides*, he wrote, "her movements were so full of poetry and her jump, for a woman, was extraordinary. She did not seem to dance—she moved."[106] Here was a practical demonstration of her theory of movement turned into art.

Nijinska may have been a superb coach and her class may have illuminated her choreography, but some, including Ninette de Valois, questioned its pedagogical value as daily fare. In fact, the founder of the company that eventually became the Royal Ballet regarded it as a mistake. "Two or three times every week, with good conventional Russian School in between, would have been the perfect arrangement," she wrote. "Alone it became wholly woven with her own special approach to choreography." Of course, this was what Nijinska intended. She believed that ballet pedagogy had not kept pace with the choreographic changes of the previous twenty years, that it needed to embrace and incorporate these developments into the traditional class. In theory she probably could have accepted the wisdom of de Valois' argument. However, in practice, given the conservatism of "Russian School" teachers such as Nicolas Legat, it is hard to imagine an amicable relationship between the old and new pedagogy. Finally, Nijinska was desperate to hang on to what she had achieved. Her stubbornness, her unwillingness to compromise, grew out of a sense of impending loss she always carried with her. Although she enjoyed an enviable position, she knew how tenuous it was. She felt surrounded by enemies, people ready to pull the rug from under her feet, to destroy her art and her means of making a living. Dancers complained about her classes. "There was a 'deputation' to Diaghilev," de Valois continued, and one stately lady of the older school told me that she had worn a cold compress on each knee—I presume to heighten the drama of the situation. Diaghilev did not appear to be unduly moved by either the deputation or the cold compresses. I was anyway enjoying this new approach to a class, and realised that it was all closely related to the ballets that we had to execute for her. I was young and looking for new ways of thinking, and I had already begun to feel a deep interest in choreography as opposed to mere execution.[107]

At some point Diaghilev asked Picasso what he thought of Nijinska's "lunatic" class. He told him it was fine. So, Diaghilev, with his enormous admiration for the painter, decided it should stay.[108]

7

Le Train Bleu and Its Aftermath

As 1923 drew to a close, Diaghilev invited Jean Cocteau to join the company in Monte Carlo. With Auric and Poulenc already there, Diaghilev hoped that their presence and the bustle and excitement of the new season would lighten Cocteau's grief at the death of his lover, the novelist Raymond Radiguet. During the next several months Cocteau published articles on *Les Biches* and *Les Fâcheux* in *La Nouvelle Revue française* and *La Revue de Paris*, in addition to contributing to books about those ballets.[1] The Festival Français brought a number of journalists to Monte Carlo, including Maurice Martin du Gard, the editor of *Les Nouvelles littéraires* (for which Auric regularly covered music); Louis Laloy, *Comoedia*'s lead music critic (and a contributor to *Figaro* and other publications); and the newspaper's dance critic, André Levinson, all of whom wrote about the new works.[2] Cocteau, however, was a Diaghilev intimate, admitted backstage like one of the artists. During rehearsal breaks he watched as Dolin practiced what he called his acrobatic "tricks," and the idea for *Le Train Bleu* was born. As Dolin later wrote: "The beginnings of the ballet . . . were inspired almost by chance, and . . . Cocteau's . . . conceited young man on the beach was created from his first impressions of me."[3] Cocteau's idea could not have come at a more opportune moment. Learning that Diaghilev planned to produce *Daphnis and Chloë* in Paris without chorus, Ravel withdrew the performance rights, leaving the impresario without a vehicle to launch his latest protégé.

When the Festival Français ended, Diaghilev and Dolin left for Paris, where Diaghilev signed up collaborators. Among the first to receive an unexpected visit from him was Milhaud. "I was working peacefully," he wrote to a friend on February 10.

> Diaghilev arrived, that snake-charmer shark. . . . He commissioned a Ballet from me with Cocteau for May!! I'm going to try, but I'm not sure I can manage it. Two [ballets] at the same time is a lot.[4]

On February 16 he noted in his diary:

> This ballet for Diaghilev is quite a folly. Music in the manner of Offenbach, Maurice Yvain [a modern operetta composer], and a Verdi-like finale with all the true harmonies *plates d'un bout à l'autre. Pas un syncope.* It is Paris, vulgar, dirty, and sentimental, with many polkas, galops, waltzes, etc. . . . I am a little frightened [of all the work], but I am very amused by the whole adventure.[5]

After signing up Milhaud, Diaghilev took Dolin to see Chanel at her salon in the Rue Cambon. The celebrated couturière, who was designing the costumes for *Le Train Bleu*, ordered the young dancer to strip and don a sleeveless "vest-pants creation" in wool jersey, while she pinned and snipped.[6]

Set "on a beach in 1924"—as the program note read—*Le Train Bleu* was about the sports people played at fashionable resorts such as Deauville. Cocteau's Bright Young Things, whom he called Poules (Chicks) and Gigolos, with their hand-knitted Chanel swimwear, bare legs, rubber bathing caps, and sandals, might have stepped from the stylish pages of *Femina*. There were four main characters: a tennis champion in white with a *bandeau* à la Suzanne Lenglen (Nijinska); a golf player in plus fours with a pipe inspired by the Prince of Wales (Woizikovsky); a bathing-beauty in hot pink named Perlouse (Sokolova); and Beau Gosse (Dolin), a pleasure-bent youth whose acrobatics created a sensation. They, too, belonged to the world depicted in *Femina*, with its young fashionistas who played tennis in perfectly pleated skirts, competed on country club golf links for the "*Femina* Cup," took the wheel of sleek automobiles, exercised to keep fit, and danced the night away.[7] By profession, social background, and choice, Nijinska did not belong to this world, but she had lived in proximity to it for years. According to Boris Kochno, Cocteau made a special copy of the libretto for Nijinska "filled with examples she was to follow in developing the ballet"—a team of acrobatic dancers appearing at Ciro's (a classy Monte Carlo nightspot), images of the Prince of Wales playing golf, slow-motion films of foot races, and so forth.[8]

In fact the libretto dated February–March 1924 in the Nijinska papers hardly differs from the published version, which makes very clear what Cocteau intended.[9] About the music he wrote: "Some scenes must be <u>arranged with the music</u>, others without it or, at least, without a visible relationship between the choreography and the musical rhythm. The dances, gestures, and poses of these last scenes are simply <u>accompanied</u> by the or-chestra, as in films" (2). He demanded a consistent approach to the subject matter. He had "avoided the comic, the burlesque characters, surprises, and plot," he wrote, and expected her to follow suit, using gesture to convey "the 'hidden meanings' and obscenities of the operettas that have inspired these scenes" (11). He concluded with claims about the ballet as a disposable ar-tifact. "The ballet must go out of fashion in a year and remain an image of 1924," he announced. "The ballet must be an article of fashion." "The blue train must . . . be . . . a monument to frivolity. . . . One can deceive artists about what they want or expect, but not people of fashion about fashion" (12).

Nijinska did not respond well to Cocteau's deluge of suggestions. Kochno (and others following him) have attributed this not to the libretto, with its ten scenes, virtual absence of dances, and non-stop flow of mimetic incident, but to Nijinska's mulish determination to ignore the high-life details knitted into Cocteau's imagined ballet. "The personalities and events from which Cocteau proposed that Nijinska draw her inspiration," Kochno wrote,

> belonged to the worldly milieu of the day—a milieu that Nijinska, who led a quiet, secluded life, didn't know and, furthermore, detested. She did not speak French and so could not explain herself to Cocteau or get him to accept her ideas. Although Diaghilev used to intervene, acting as in-terpreter and mediator, their relations from the outset were tense, if not hostile.[10]

Of course, Nijinska's life was far from quiet and secluded. From 9 A.M., when company class began, until 11 P.M., when evening performances or rehearsals ended, she was surrounded by people—dancers, accompanists, rehearsal masters, company administrators—all of whom conducted their business in Russian. This was the professional world of the Ballets Russes, the dancers' world, one to which Cocteau and his protégés did not belong, even if they occasionally fraternized with its artists. Kochno didn't belong to that world either. But Diaghilev was making a place for him there and increas-ingly allowing him to throw his weight around. Diaghilev's inner circle was all-male but largely gay, and however much Cocteau may have believed that art was "born of the copulation between the male element and the female element of which all of us are composed"[11]—an idea to which Diaghilev cer-tainly subscribed—only men, apparently, had the luxury of embracing their other half.

Although Monte Carlo's grand opera season was in full swing, Nijinska left for Paris in mid-February, almost certainly to confer with Cocteau, who had returned to the capital a few weeks before.[12] (Whether she saw Milhaud is unclear; none of his published writings mention her in any capacity, even as the choreographer of his ballet.[13]) The meetings with Cocteau did not go well. "Ask Nijinska how she's feeling about me," he wrote to Diaghilev in late February.

> I am not going to make a move unless I am sure she will listen to me, for ri-
> diculous diplomatic games are useless. I do not insist that my name appear
> on the program as director (although my researches in relation to details of
> the staging have a logical place in my work), but, in exchange, I do insist on
> being listened to.[14]

Some kind of compromise must have been reached. At Dolin's insistence, Nijinska, accompanied by Diaghilev, went to see the acrobatic adagio team of Marjorie Moss and Georges Fontana, who were dancing in Monte Carlo at the Metropole Hotel. Nijinska was impressed by their routine, and the waltz in *Le Train Bleu*, according to Dolin, was to a "great extent inspired by these beautiful dancers."[15]

Rehearsals for *Le Train Bleu* began in earnest in Barcelona, where the company opened in mid-April. "I very much like the first dance," Diaghilev reported to Kochno,

> which is quite gymnastic. I made a long speech to the company, explaining
> just what the word "operetta" means, what Milhaud's music is about, and
> what is, in my view, the plastic problem that this ballet presents. I was lis-
> tened to with devout attention. I think everything will be all right and hope
> that . . . this ballet will be a true expression of ourselves.[16]

All went well until the company reached Paris, where it was due to open at the Théâtre des Champs-Elysées on May 26. The ballet was still unfinished, but with several weeks remaining until its premiere on June 20, the situation was far from desperate, as it was the only new work in rehearsal. Still, as Grigoriev points out, there remained a great deal of "preparatory work" to be done, including the readying of "difficult" ballets such as *The Rite of Spring* and *Les Noces*, untouched for nearly a year. (Ninette de Valois, a new member of the *Noces* cast, remembers her frantic efforts to memorize the ballet as almost driving her "to Bedlam."[17]) Most rehearsals took place in "dark" theaters such as the Théâtre Cora-Laparcerie, where in mid-May an interviewer from *Le Gaulois* caught up with Diaghilev as Nijinska rehearsed *Les Noces* under work lights. Surrounding him was his "staff"—Picasso, Auric, Cocteau, and Dolin, soon to be the "new Nijinsky of the troupe."[18] They were there again a week later, this time with patrons and society friends of the company. Again Nijinska was conducting the rehearsal, this time of *Les Biches*. Wrote the novelist Joseph Kessel:

> Mme. Nijinska sees nothing except her dancers, hears nothing except the lively rhythm of the piano. The magnificent demon that inhabits her seizes her completely. She seems caught up in a spectacle that she herself has arranged, by a harmonious force that she herself has unleashed, and of which she remains, by her will, taste, and instinct, mistress of every section.[19]

The dancers were in their regulation rehearsal clothes, sweating under the work lights, the faces of the men tense with effort, the women "tender" and "expansive." Nothing, wrote the balletomane author, could be more moving than this intimate glimpse of dancers at work. After *Biches*, the company began rehearsing *Le Train Bleu*, with Diaghilev humming the opening measures.

> The music is clear and sparkling. The invention of Jean Cocteau has the sharp eye and color of our time.
>
> Here are beach games, magnificent groups, merry fights, and dives. The movement of bodies evokes the August sun with their freedom and a fashionable beach with their studied elegance.
>
> Suddenly, breaching the groups, an adolescent flies out. He has that strength, that passion, that bold and secret fire one recognizes in great dancers. He leaps, turns, precise, vigorous, and light; he walks on his hands, falls back, gets up, and disappears.
>
> This is Dolin, the new discovery created by Diaghilev with his divining rod.[20]

By now Nijinska was a chain-smoker. The journalist and poet Pierre-Plessis, who observed a rehearsal at the Théâtre Mogador, noted in *Comoedia* that "the cigarette never leaves her lips." In *Les Biches*, its smoke followed the "prodigious speed" of her jumps and turns like a "perfumed wake." Dolin, dreamy in black trunks, had the look of a "Florentine swimmer exiled in Venice," even as Diaghilev adjusted his monocle to watch him. Meanwhile, "Nijinska lit another cigarette."[21]

Not all rehearsals were so amicable. When Cocteau first saw the ballet in Paris, he exploded, according to Kochno. Declaring that Nijinska had ignored his directions,

> Cocteau persuaded her to modify the numbers she had done. When she came to putting the finishing touches on a new version of the ballet, he intervened again and, in highhanded fashion, interrupted rehearsals, and substituted pantomime scenes for dances that Nijinska had created. The atmosphere at rehearsals was highly charged, and, on the verge of the opening, the dancers still did not know whether they should obey Cocteau or Nijinska.[22]

The dress rehearsal was hell. Cocteau was "furious," wrote Dolin, "because this was wrong and that was wrong." Nijinska cried, Dolin cried, and in the remaining hours before the curtain went up, much of the choreography was changed. At Cocteau's insistence, Dolin's role was beefed up, and at the last minute Nijinska invented a new pas de deux for the two of them in a large dressing room. There were costume problems as well. When the dancers came onstage, it turned out that many of Chanel's swimsuits did not fit and had to be altered, while the knitted fabric made it hard to partner (nobody seems to have realized it might be slippery), a problem in Sokolova's duet with Woizikovsky, who had to throw her up spinning into the air, then catch her as she came down, a move that Nijinska probably adapted from acrobatic adagio routines.[23] The set by the sculptor Henri Laurens seems to have made little impression, although the freestanding semi-cubist cabanas marked a partial break with Diaghilev's reliance on traditional painted decor. As if anticipating the ho-hum reception of Laurens' set, Diaghilev persuaded Picasso to allow the company's scene painter, Prince Schervashidze, to enlarge a small watercolor of two women running along a beach for use as a front curtain. Picasso was delighted with the result and dedicated the curtain, his third for the company, to Diaghilev.[24] Accompanied by a commissioned fanfare by Auric, the magnificent new "Ballets Russes Curtain . . . by Picasso," as it was identified in the souvenir program, opened not only the ballet but also the season.[25] The episode was yet another instance of Diaghilev's genius for improvisation, although the curtain's *zaftig* giants could not be more different from the company's increasingly slender women.

Despite the awful dress rehearsal, the premiere of *Le Train Bleu* was a huge success, above all for Dolin. It took place at a charity gala presided over by the Grand Duchess Marie Pavlovna and the Marquise de Ganay that brought high French and international society to the Théâtre des Champs-Elysées. The Marquis de Polignac took three boxes to accommodate a score of guests; the dress circle was resplendent with diamonds.[26] At the supper party that followed the performance, Cécile Sorel, the great actress of the Comédie-Française, planted a kiss on the young man's face, telling him, "My dear Dolin, you were superb!" "Stravinsky kissed me," the new star wrote to his mother. "Nijinska and I kissed, Sokolova and I also. It was a big triumph and I am so happy."[27] Four days later Robert Brussel, who had been writing about Diaghilev's undertakings since 1906, told readers of *Figaro* that "Mons. Anton Dolin has all the qualities of a very great dancer: strength and flexibility, beauty of pose, virtuosity, . . . a theatrical sense, and musical intelligence."[28]

The Diaghilev season at the Théâtre des Champs-Elysées was part of the "Grande Saison d'Art" of the 1924 Summer Olympics, officially known as the Games of the VIII Olympiad, which took place in and around Paris. The Games put swimmers and gymnasts on the front pages of Paris newspapers, while Suzanne Lenglen, the first female tennis celebrity and a Paris native, who was expected to dominate women's singles both at Wimbledon and at the Olympics, captured headlines when illness forced her to withdraw from both. It was the perfect background for *Le Train Bleu*, a ballet celebrating youth and the pleasure of physical exertion, just as the Théâtre des Champs-Elysées, which the Ballets Russes had helped to launch in 1913 but to which it had never returned, was viewed by many as its "true setting."[29] "I left the Ballets Russes once again dazzled," wrote Fernand Gregh in *Les Nouvelles littéraires*. "I know . . . that *Les Biches* has already been given this winter in Monte Carlo and that *Les Noces* was performed for us last year. . . . But it was the whole of the evening that seemed to produce an incomparable feast."[30] The writer Pierre Drieu La Rochelle likened the theater to Babel, where one could study "the formation of a cosmopolitan art," citing as examples two works by the Ballets Suédois—*La Création du Monde*, a "Negro ballet, conceived by a Jewish-French musician, a Swiss-French poet, and a French-French painter," and *Within the Quota*, "an American ballet, imagined by Americans who live in Paris."[31]

Diaghilev's enterprise certainly belonged to this "Cosmopolis," although it was older, more professional, with a wider-ranging repertory, and his audience reached into the upper echelons of Tout-Paris. It was an audience with its own physiognomy, a club of admirers, enthusiasts, and theater people, who returned again and again, despite the high ticket prices, to see a favorite work and sup at a nearby café, offering discreet bravos when Diaghilev and his entourage joined them.[32] The two-month "Saison d'Art" of which the Ballets Russes was a part was organized by the French Olympic Committee under the chairmanship of the Marquis de Polignac and the direction of Jacques Hébertot, who controlled programming at the Théâtre des Champs-Elysées. With the wounds of World War I still fresh, Germans were excluded from both the festival and the games. But otherwise Hébertot cast his net widely. In June there were performances of *The Marriage of Figaro* and *Don Juan*, a Mozart Festival, a cycle of Beethoven works, the Leeds Chorus, a recital by the Polish piano virtuoso Paderewski, all in addition to the Ballets Russes. Diaghilev could not have returned to the Champs-Elysées under more favorable auspices. And, as if to confirm its elite status, the Ballets Russes took part in a Red Cross gala at Au Printemps, the Art Nouveau emporium on the Boulevard Haussmann only steps from the Opéra, where the Festival of Stars climaxed in a performance of *Swan Lake* with Vera Trefilova as Odette. Although the Ballets Russes season spotlighted the modern, the gala program evoked the receding world of St. Petersburg. Meanwhile, the dancers, unpaid and unfed, walked off with soap and hand towels from the changing area.[33]

Compared to Diaghilev's 1923 season, dominated by the premiere of *Les Noces*, the press was divided—not about the continued vitality of the company and its "singularly gifted" *animateur*—but about what one critic called "the increasingly mythic group, Les Six," three of whose members wrote music for the season's new works.[34] On the one hand, Diaghilev was hailed for holding aloft the standard of French music amid an embarrassment of international riches. On the other, he was taken to task for ignoring other living French composers. One critic found "a disconcerting harmonic and orchestral poverty" in *Les Biches*; another thought the "casualness and fairly continuous banality" of Poulenc's score hardly justified the "laudatory epithets" that a "squad of sycophants" had rained upon it. Auric's music for *Les Fâcheux*, despite moments of inspiration, was too sketchy and too long for an audience to sit through; the score had too many false notes and too few ideas, and "hammered the evolutions of the dancers."[35] In *Le Rappel*,

Louis Vuillemin wrote: "Listening to these two very youthful works, one is astonished that their authors have once more been designated . . . masters of modern French music!"[36]

Although "warmly welcomed by the Ballets Russes public," *Le Train Bleu* was also controversial. On the one hand, it was fun, lively, a modern operetta with "easily digestible rhythms and melodies," a sketch full of gaiety and the "physical joy of a troupe of bathers at the seaside." On the other, Cocteau's scenario, even if it displayed style and invention, was taken to task for what some critics perceived as its banality. One disgruntled observer called Milhaud's score "music in pyjamas," drawing attention to the latest fashion in resort wear, "with the oompah-pah of circus music," highlighting the ballet's combination of snobbery and slumming in the domain of circus, music hall, and café-concert.[37] This surrender to the popular—albeit within a setting of privilege—was strongly criticized by André Levinson. Yes, he says, it can be amusing to see the circus ring, dance hall, cinema, and fairground transposed to the grand lyric stage. In the long run, however, "theatrical dance"—by which he really means ballet—"will never be able to live off the music hall. By borrowing from other genres, it will quickly end by ruining itself."[38] Levinson managed a word of praise for the work's two "highlights": the scene in slow motion—one of Cocteau's happiest inventions—and the diving scene.

France had a long tradition of composer-critics, and this certainly contributed to the polarization of the musical fourth estate. Les Six was especially well represented in the press, with Auric emerging in the 1920s as an important critical voice. In 1924 he had a regular column in *Les Nouvelles littéraires* and also wrote on an occasional basis for *La Revue musicale*. Over the years he contributed to "thick" journals (as the Russians would say) as well as newspapers, with his collected writings on music running to no fewer than four volumes.[39] Auric's position as a critic bolstered his reputation as a composer. Unhampered by concern about conflict of interest, he reviewed his friends and his friends reviewed him. He wrote about the Ballets Russes, Ballets Suédois, and Soirées de Paris, productions at the Paris Opéra, and concert series that spotlighted the music of Les Six. For "outsiders," Les Six, its master publicist, and its mascot Erik Satie could easily pass as members of a mutual admiration society. Sly allusions to self-promotion or to what "some of our contemporaries find 'amusing'" were responses to this, as were dismissive remarks, such as Gustave Bret's after the opening-night performance that "musically, the show . . . would have presented only the slightest interest had it not ended with a revival of *Les Noces*."[40]

Cocteau was exceptionally active that year on behalf of his protégés. His articles on *Les Biches* and *Les Fâcheux* anticipated and coincided with the Champs-Elysées season and appeared in books about the two ballets that appeared a few months later. Striking a nationalist pose in the first of these essays, published in the influential *Nouvelle Revue française*, he wrote: "The marches of Beethoven and Wagner are silent. *Les Biches* and *Les Fâcheux* allow me to come back home."[41] Although Cocteau spotlighted the composers and visual artists who contributed to those productions, he talked quite a bit about Nijinska. It was hard to avoid her: after all, she was the choreographer of those ballets and, as such, crucial to their theatrical realization. But he could damn her with faint praise, deny her agency and intellectual awareness, and in other ways belittle her. In *Les Biches*, he asserts, she "attains grandeur without premeditation . . . preserved from this by the absence of a subject and by the apparent lightness of the musical style."[42] Nijinska clipped Cocteau's article and pasted it in one of her scrapbooks. She might have wondered what she and the dancers were doing during the more than 200 hours of rehearsal that it took to stage the ballet. Because they danced, did it mean they didn't think? Was it because they were Russians (although not all were) and, hence, primitive, that they could process information without engaging in actual thought? Was it only her Slavic "nose," as Cocteau declared, that allowed Nijinska to take her place with Poulenc and Marie Laurencin without striking a "false note"?[43] She didn't seem to talk—at least she didn't talk much to him, and he didn't speak Russian—and she didn't go in for parties with fancy people or bother with fashion. So he turned her into a female grotesque, a body machine:

> Mme. Nijinska lives shut up in her work. She never stops. Scarcely does she pause to do her hair or fasten her dress. By dint of jumping, pirouetting, and working her muscles, she ceases to be a worker and becomes a tool. Looking at her sturdy legs, her hair, her angel eyes, one admires her as one would a pickaxe or a carpenter's plane. . . . But her brother's blood runs in her veins—a blood that has wings. She does not try to discover what there is at the back of Poulenc or Laurencin. She is guided by intuition. Without the slightest calculation, and by simply obeying the rhythm, and the exigencies of the frame she has to fill, she is about to create a masterpiece: the Fêtes Galantes of her time.[44]

Cocteau had considerably less to say about Nijinska's contribution to *Les Fâcheux*. In discussing the ballet he focuses mainly on Braque, whose "décor," Cocteau asserts, was on a par with Picasso's for *Parade* and *Pulcinella*, surely an exaggeration. Although Braque seems to have spent most of his time in Monte Carlo in the scene-painting studio, according to Cocteau he was the ballet's "real choreographer" and Nijinska "could only follow him." "The true dance of *Les Fâcheux* was among the beiges, yellows, browns, and greys," he wrote.[45]

Although *Le Train Bleu* was popular with audiences, Cocteau remained unhappy with the choreography. To the writer Louis Gautier-Vignal he confessed, "I find Nijinska's choreography silly, small, and without anything new."[46] Yet numerous reviews speak knowledgeably and highly of her contribution, not only to this but to all the ballets presented that season in Paris.

Boris de Schloezer in *La Nouvelle Revue française* observed the following about her "method":

[I]n *Les Biches* as well as in *Les Fâcheux* she seeks to reform the so-called classical dance, now by introducing certain attitudes and movements characteristic of modern dances, now by assimilating descriptive and expressive gestures into its texture: the dances of Eraste and the Card Player in *Les Fâcheux* are very interesting in this regard: one witnesses *with one's own eyes* the distortion of seventeenth-century classical style on whose frame the choreographer very freely embroiders. There is a danger in this that Nijinska boldly skirts. Almost always she succeeds in melding these diverse elements; but even if she gets it wrong, the path she takes seems so fruitful that we owe it to ourselves to support with all our sympathy the efforts and researches of this artist.[47]

Even *Les Tentations de la Bergère* won plaudits: it was "ravishing," "inspired . . . by the purest tradition."[48] Although Henry Prunières hated the choreography of *Les Fâcheux*, colleagues of his assessed it quite differently. "Let us praise the multiplicity of her invention," urged Jane Catulle-Mendès, "which blends with assiduous ingenuity a choice modern art with traditional, classical inspirations, achieving an overall harmony."[49] Critics singled out Nijinska's "wild *rag-mazurka*" in *Les Biches*: one called attention to its American rhythms, another to its origins on "the banks of the Volga."[50] Her choreography for *Le Train Bleu* won praise even when the libretto was found wanting. "Mme. Nijinska's choreography is so ingenious, so varied," wrote

Louis Schneider, "that this ballet or rather *opérette dansée* becomes something lively, young, fresh, and very agreeable." Robert Brussel summed it up: "The choreography of the very highest value dominates the whole of the performance. Honors go to Mme. Nijinska, whose talent I have never seen more fertile than in *Le Train Bleu*."[51]

Only Fernand Divoire seems to have an inkling of what had gone on backstage. He noted that the ballet was different from what Cocteau had conceived: he wanted "two-minute tableaux, independent of the music like cinema visions; he did not want the music . . . to be danced in order to impose his own personality on the dance," hinting at the frustration he must have felt because he lacked the tools of a choreographer. Divoire found *Le Train Bleu* amusing and "remarkably well danced." He noted, too, groups and figures "where Nijinska finally had a little freedom," especially "a great turning wheel formed by all the dancers."[52] Since Divoire had interviewed Nijinska in the past, it is quite possible that the information about Cocteau's intentions came directly from her.

On July 2, a few days after the Champs-Elysées season ended, Diaghilev met with the company for a pre-holiday pep talk. "Soldiers," he told them, "I am pleased with you." Then he shared his plans for the coming year—a tour of Austria and Czechoslovakia in the fall, five months in Monte Carlo, a season in London, followed by one in Paris, where, as always, he would present his new works. Among them was a ballet by Auric and another by an unnamed Russian composer who was only twenty. Addresses were exchanged, and everyone left for a well-earned rest.[53]

***

Nijinska headed south. When she moved her family to Monte Carlo, she had rented an apartment at 5, rue Bel Respiro, an old gated villa with flowering bushes not far from the center. She had been on the road for almost three months. Levushka was five, Irina going on eleven, and however much she loved them, she was a stranger to them. Eleonora, her own *mamousia*, was as much her children's mother as their grandmother. She lived with them and made sure they did their homework, wiped their tears away, and hugged them when they fell or had bad dreams. In August, Dolin arrived for another round of classes with Nijinska before the company reassembled in September. He had spent much of July with Diaghilev, touring Italy, just as Vaslav had in the years before *The Rite of Spring*. Nijinsky himself was now living with his wife in Paris. One day, with no advance notice to his sister and the dancers of his former company, Romola brought him to a *Train Bleu* rehearsal. Dolin was in the theater, and remembered the hush that came over everybody, as Vaslav walked to the front of the stage and sat down.

> On my right is Ludmilla Schollar, her eyes streaming with tears. On my left Sokolova, her face white. . . . Nijinska comes to me, her eyes wet with tears, her body shaken with emotion, and leaning on my shoulders, with a quivering voice, says, "*Yah ne ma go*" ("I cannot go on") "*Eta tac strashno*" ("It is too awful").[54]

But the drama didn't end there. The free-spending Romola had run through her husband's fortune, and now demanded that others—meaning Diaghilev and Nijinska—shoulder the burden of his care. In early August she wrote to Nijinska insisting that Vaslav and his attendant move in with her immediately: it was her obligation as Vaslav's sister. Nijinska was outraged.

> Please do not remind me of my obligation. Vaslav and I were well educated about the concept of obligation by my mother. I will do anything I can to relieve you of Vaslav. However, four days is too short notice for me to prepare for his arrival. First of all, I have to find a different apartment, . . . a bigger place where Vaslav can have his own room. Second, I have to find the money. You know that I am earning just enough to survive and that from July 1st to October 1st, I will not receive a single franc. Right now, I have only 500 francs at home, and I am supporting my mother, 2 children, a servant, and myself—5 people![55]

She reminded "Roma," as she usually called her sister-in-law, that in 1914 she had terminated a two-year contract with Diaghilev "as soon as Vaslav needed me, and after two weeks my baby, husband, and I were left with nothing. . . . In the same manner I left Kiev and my School."[56]

Even apart from Vaslav's tragic illness and Romola's machinations, Nijinska had much to contend with. The year had left her physically, emotionally, and creatively drained. Since the previous August, she had choreographed non-stop, lived from deadline to deadline, without let-up—always under pressure. Diaghilev seems to have relaxed his grip on her that summer. No projects loomed on the horizon, although two were in the works for the coming spring. Only when they were fully outfitted with scores, libretti, and designs—the choice accoutrements of a Diaghilev production—would she get to see them. As Diaghilev's choreographer, she had one job, and that was to make dances. The reputation of the Ballets Russes depended on her talent and sweat. Yet she had no decision-making power, enjoyed only minimal contact with collaborators, and stood last on the company's production line. *Les Noces*, the great exception, was a happy accident.

The past year had brought her both triumphs and trials. Levinson's attacks, unrelenting and personal, must have caused her to flinch every time she picked up one of his reviews; hurling his jeremiads like thunderbolts, he excoriated both her body and her art. Diaghilev had not stood up for her against Kochno, although the latter was barely out of his teens, or against Cocteau, who insisted she do his bidding and fumed when she stuck by ideas of her own. Like a bad father—like her own father—Diaghilev had withheld his love, while she did everything possible to win it back. She had done her best to make Dolin a star, earning not only the young dancer's respect but also his friendship. But she could not fail to notice that Dolin's days were numbered, that he had other interests, as did Diaghilev, whose eye now alighted on Serge Lifar. He sent the latter to Turin to study with Cecchetti, dressed him to the nines (a sure sign of Diaghilev's interest in someone), and drew Nijinska's ire by announcing that her former pupil would become not only a *premier danseur* but also a choreographer. " 'You are absolutely wrong,' " Lifar claims she told the impresario. " 'Nothing will ever come of Lifar; he not only will never be a *premier danseur*, he will never even be a soloist.' " She even staked a dozen bottles of champagne on it, Lifar says, although such behavior seems totally out of character. In the late 1960s, she told one of her Kiev students that from the time he joined the Ballets Russes, Lifar was her "most vile enemy. Enemy number one. Probably . . . because I refused to see him as . . . a second Nijinsky. Which he wasn't."[57]

Even apart from Lifar, the changes in Diaghilev's entourage must have disturbed Nijinska. Kochno's growing ascendancy did not bode well for the Russian repertory on which Nijinska had cut her eye-teeth or for works, like *Les Noces*, influenced by constructivism and the new Soviet stagecraft. Diaghilev, to be sure, was interested in these post-Revolutionary movements. After witnessing Tairov's performances in Paris, Nijinska wrote, Diaghilev told her he that he was thinking of inviting Meyerhold to take part in "a new ballet experiment." " 'What would you say to this, Bronia?' " he asked her. " 'Excellent,' " she replied, " 'but would Meyerhold like to work with somebody on a production?' "[58] The project never materialized, but by 1924

Diaghilev was being courted by Soviet officials. Although "former Russians turned Parisian" tried to scare him off, as the poet Vladimir Mayakovsky reported to Anatole Lunacharsky, the Soviet Commissar of Enlightenment, "his desire has proved stronger, together with my assurances that in delicacy and grace we surpass the French and that we are more 'businesslike' than the Americans."[59] But the Soviets wouldn't guarantee Kochno, with whom Diaghilev planned to travel, an exit visa, and he canceled the trip.

By midsummer, Nijinska must have had more than an inkling of what was in store for the following year. In April, Auric left for the Auvergne where he hoped to compose most of his second score for Diaghilev, a ballet in two acts and five scenes entitled *Les Matelots* with a libretto by Kochno and designs by a twenty-year-old protégé of Picasso's, Pedro Pruna. It was another comic piece, recalling the plot of *Così fan tutte*, about three sailors disguising themselves to test the virtue and fidelity of their girlfriends.[60] The other big ballet for the 1925 season was *Zéphyr et Flore*. Diaghilev had high hopes for Vladimir Dukelsky, its twenty-year-old Russian composer. Better known today as Vernon Duke, he had arrived in Paris via New York, where his family settled after fleeing Soviet Russia. "Dima" had studied music in Kiev, fallen under the spell of jazz in Constantinople, and made his first money as a composer working for Tin Pan Alley. In spring 1924, symphony in hand, he found his way to Diaghilev, who listened to his music and commissioned a ballet. "Dima" met everyone who was anyone in Diaghilev's Paris that June—Stravinsky, Cocteau, Misia Sert, Coco Chanel, Auric, Poulenc, and others.[61] He attended the company's Stravinsky Gala and was deeply stirred by *Les Noces*, but never watched the dancers at work or exchanged a word with their choreographer. Diaghilev told him what he wanted: a ballet combining "classicism with Russian overtones—tutus with *kokoshniks*." Kochno had selected the story, and Diaghilev had cast it, with Dolin, Lifar, and Alice Nikitina in the principal roles. Kochno and Dukelsky were then sent to the country to work on the libretto and start drafting the music, with letters from Diaghilev arriving almost every day.[62] From the start Nijinska was cut out of the collaboration. It's hard not to see Kochno's hand in this. She had fought with him over *Le Train Bleu* and believed that ballet had no need of libretti, the one contribution he could make. Moreover, it can only have struck her as unfair that Kochno, as the "author" of a ballet, was entitled to a percentage of the royalties. At a time when the choreographer had no such legal claim, Diaghilev was providing him with a small but steady income.[63]

One piece of good news was that Alexandra Exter was in Venice. She had left the Soviet Union in April to take part in the XIV Venice Biennale, a huge exhibition of contemporary art international in scope but organized around national pavilions. It was the first such gathering in which the nascent Soviet Union participated, and Exter had been selected by the high-powered Soviet exhibition committee to take part. The emphasis was on theater art and new work. After a decade-long hiatus, the organizers felt they had to focus on the most significant lines of development, to establish not only that great skill remained in Russia but also that the country was continuing to produce young talent. Four of Exter's abstract paintings hung in the show, along with more than twenty of her designs for recent theater productions and for the film *Aelita*, which opened in Moscow the following September.[64] In addition, Exter painted a magnificent decorative panel, *Venice*, for the pavilion itself. Intended to grace a wall of the second-floor glass corridor, it offered, as the scholar Georgy Kovalenko has said, an almost complete "anthology of the forms and images" of her paintings since 1910, along with others that would emerge in her later Paris work.[65]

Although the Russian Pavilion opened to the public on June 17, Exter waited more than a month to contact Nijinska. By then she had probably been in touch with Diaghilev, who made two trips to Venice that summer—the first in mid-July with Dolin and the second in mid-August with Lifar. On July 19 he told Kochno that "the Bolsheviks are wooing me" and that "the catalogue of their exhibition here starts out with my name."[66] It appears that he also invited Nijinska to Venice, an invitation that within days he rescinded. "Dear Bronislava Foninichna," Exter wrote to Nijinska on July 28:

> I was very happy to hear that you were coming to the Lido as I was hoping to see you and talk to you. But now I have been told that you are not coming, so I decided to write you a few lines, even though I am not sure of the address. I am awfully curious to see your work, to learn about you and your life, and finally I very much want to see you.... Dear Bronislava Fominicha, write to me at 17 Via Dardanelli, Venice, Lido.... I embrace you and eagerly await your letter.[67]

As a later letter makes clear, Exter met with Diaghilev and pressed him to tell her "as much as possible" about Nijinska and her work.[68] It is quite possible that Exter expressed the desire to work with her and proposed that the choreographer join them in Venice to discuss some kind of project. Given the Soviet courtship of Diaghilev and ambitious Soviet plans (in which Exter was involved) for the celebrated Art Deco exhibition the following summer in Paris, an Exter-Nijinska collaboration would be not only politically expedient but also highly marketable. However, something happened in the last week of July that caused Diaghilev to abandon the project and thus keep the two women from meeting in Venice. No doubt the usual suspects had poisoned the atmosphere—Kochno, who was in near daily contact with Diaghilev about *Zéphyr et Flore*, and Lifar, whom Diaghilev stole away from Venice to meet in Milan on July 29, a day after Exter was told that Nijinska wouldn't be coming.[69] It must have been abundantly clear to Diaghilev (as well as Kochno) that an Exter-Nijinska production would have upstaged *Zéphyr* in virtually every way, underscoring its artistic thinness and overall inconsequence. Moreover, unlike Nijinska, whose relationship with Diaghilev had a strong filial dimension, Exter would speak her mind rather than put up with the backstabbing common in Diaghilev's entourage. Finally, Exter, being multilingual (she spoke French as well as Italian), could easily air her grievances in the press.

As soon as she heard from Exter, Nijinska replied. Exter waited until August 15 to write back, explaining that she hoped to be in Paris in mid-September. She asks Nijinska for her address and promises that if she can't get to Paris she will send pictures of her work. "My soul feels joyful at the thought of seeing you. Last year I often thought that I would never again be able to see any of those who left."[70] However, it was not until December 30 that Exter, with Diaghilev's help, arrived in Paris.[71] By then, Nijinska had decided to leave the Ballets Russes.

On September 1 the company assembled in Paris for two weeks of rehearsals before a ten-week tour of Germany. None of the new ballets was given, only proven favorites—Fokine's *Les Sylphides*, *The Polovtsian Dances*, *Schéhérazade*, and *Petrouchka*; and Massine's *Le Tricorne*, *Cimarosiana*, *The Good-Humoured Ladies*, and *Contes Russes*. Of Nijinska's works only *Aurora's Wedding* at least partly bore her signature. It could not have been a happy time for her. On September 6 she started a new diary, shocked into it perhaps by the realization of what lay ahead. "I'll be given two things," she wrote, "*Les Matelots* and *Zéphyr et Flore*: this is my work for the year. I'll pour my life and my form into the emptiness of a libretto."[72]

She doesn't mention that she had made up her mind to remarry. The previous April the Russian Orthodox Church in Western Europe had dissolved her marriage to Kochetovsky, citing his "violation of conjugal fidelity" and

leaving her free to marry in the Church. On August 28, just before she left for
Paris, the Russian Consulate in Nice issued a legal translation of the divorce
certificate. Finally, on October 26, the last day of the company's season at
the Grosse Volksoper, she married Singaevsky in Berlin. For a second time,
Diaghilev gave her away. Dolin, who was one of the witnesses—the other,
unbelievably, was Kochno—later recalled the Russian church where she was
married, and

> the small carpet on which the bride and bridegroom stood and the priest
> asking them questions and blessing them. Then, placing a crown on her
> head and another on his, he blessed them again and they walked twice
> round the church, while Boris and I followed carrying heavy candlesticks.

Afterward, they all had lunch at a hotel.[73] However, as her diary makes clear,
Nijinska did not confide in Singaevsky as she had in Nina Moiseevna or Nina
Lipskaia; however much she leaned on him, he never became the repository
of her dreams, filled the void of her loneliness, or penetrated the recesses of
her creativity. "I'm returning to this notebook as to my best friend, or rather
my only friend," she wrote. "I don't have the good fortune to have a close
friend; my thoughts will cover the pages."[74] For someone who prized her
friendships with women, it comes as a shock that she did not have a single
female witness at her wedding.

Even before the season opened in Paris, rumors were flying about an
English season. On September 22 a notice in the *Daily Mail* announced
the return of the "famous" Russian dancers and also listed the ballets they
would give: interestingly, Nijinska's *Night on Bald Mountain* was included,
although it was later dropped.[75] As word circulated of the company's imminent return to London, where it had enjoyed such triumphs during the immediate postwar years, Dolin found himself adding solo parts to his corps
repertory. In *Les Tentations de la Bergère*, retitled *The Faithful Shepherdess*,
he danced a new duet with Lubov Tchernicheva. His role in *Le Train Bleu*
was again beefed up; the Sunday before the opening he rehearsed all day with
Nijinska, and by the time they were finished, "his legs were a mass of cuts and
bruises."[76] He also learned the Blue Bird pas de deux, which he danced with
Alice Nikitina, now on the fast track to stardom along with Dolin and Lifar.[77]

Excitement ran high in London in anticipation of the company's return.
Lord Rothermere, who had a villa near Monte Carlo and owned the *Daily
Mail*, kept up a drumbeat of advance publicity, including a piece by the

newspaper's veteran music critic, Richard Capell, entitled "Russian Ballet Memories." ("Russian Ballet" was how the company was known in England.) Diaghilev gave his customary long interview to the *Observer*, and after the first night, long clips from ecstatic reviews were published in the *Times*'s theater column.[78] The company was performing at the London Coliseum, a high-end music hall, on a variety bill. There were two programs a day, and a ballet was danced on each. The season opened with a matinee of *Cimarosiana* and an evening performance of *Le Train Bleu*; then the two were switched. Works by Massine and Fokine were gradually added to the programming. In addition to her Tennis Champion in *Le Train Bleu*, Nijinska performed her old roles in *The Polovtsian Dances* and *Les Sylphides*, the season's two Fokine ballets, as well as Kikimora in Massine's *Contes Russes*.

Audiences and critics loved *Le Train Bleu*. Milhaud came from France to conduct the first performance, and bowed at the end, surrounded by the cast and holding hands with Nijinska. There were "twenty-one enthusiastic curtain calls," and Nijinska was given a huge bouquet of flowers.[79] "How jolly it is to have these good people back with us again!" enthused Marcato in the *Evening News*. "Mlle. Nijinska's tennis-racket dance is the great thing of the new ballet," the critic continued. "It is extraordinarily amusing and clever. She is the leading light of the company now."[80] For Eric Blom in the *Manchester Guardian*, the whole ballet was as "refreshing as a breath of sea air and the gentle sting of sunburn." Although he found the dancing a touch too acrobatic, he thought it was "technically the finest thing seen here since the great Russian season at Drury Lane in 1913," high praise indeed, as that season witnessed the first English performances of *The Rite of Spring*. As for Nijinska, she "dances with an almost incredible spirit, and is also responsible for the whole splendid choreography."[81] The anonymous critic of the *Times* also thought Nijinska had made "brilliant use of the various athletic movements, not only of aquatics, but of tennis and golf," while Richard Capell in the *Daily Mail* declared that her "tennis Pas Seul" had "a touch of genius."[82]

Inspired by the ballet's calisthenics theme were articles about how the dancers kept in trim. One journalist, citing "one of Serge Diaghileff's assistants" as his source, described in detail the dancers' average day:

They rise about 8.30. Then at the drill hall in Chenies-street, Tottenham Court-road, from half-past nine to a quarter to eleven they have lessons from Mlle. Nijinska, mistress of the ballet, and from eleven to about one they must rehearse some ballet or other. With two shows to do . . . they have not many leisure moments, and, as well, each artist must practice alone for an hour and a half every day. Practically all the dancers are teetotallers, but their meals are much the same as other people's.[83]

A photograph of the company taking class with Nijinska even appeared in the *Daily Mirror* with the headline, "How the Russian Ballet Dancers Keep Fit."[84]

The *Times* and the *Daily Mail* also dispatched photographers to the Coliseum, and with film now fast enough to take pictures without special lighting, they came away with performance photographs that appeared in numerous publications. *Le Train Bleu* claimed the lion's share of these images, and taken together they reveal quite a lot about Nijinska's choreography— its deployment of space, emphasis on architecture, and use of the platforms and freestanding cabanas of Laurens' stage design. At one point the dancers even build a pyramid, recalling one of Meyerhold's favorite biomechanical exercises. Line drawings and caricatures add to the visual record—a two-page sketch by Hookway Cowles in the *Illustrated London News* shows most of the cast, with Nijinska in her bandeau fingering an outsize tennis racket and two men at the center performing headstands.[85] Einar Nerman, the theater cartoonist of the *Tatler*, poked fun at the style of the ladies' double overarm—or "trudgeon"—stroke, and jested that the ballet introduced "almost every pastime excepting steer-roping."[86] In the *Daily Mirror* the cartoonist William Haselden imagined a "Twentieth Century Ballet for Everyday Use," with color-coordinated activities such as "Le Shoot d'Or," "La Peche Verte," "Le Golf Brun," "Le Renard Rouge," and "Le Hockey Bleu." The caption read: "The return of the delightful Russian Ballet suggests a new form of amusement for country-house parties. The advantage would be that the costumes would be ready to hand."[87]

At the same time, *The Faithful Shepherdess* prompted something like a collective sigh of relief. The ballet was both "enchanting" and "classical," and with its sarabandes and minuets confirmed, as the *Times* put it, that the company's "latest choreographer has not altogether forsaken the old traditions of the ballet for gymnastics and cartwheels, satire and grotesque, however amusing."[88] In the *Dancing Times* the music critic Edwin Evans, probably Diaghilev's closest English intellectual ally, insisted that Nijinska's modernism rested on a bedrock of traditional values. "Those who remember the intricate ingenuity of the Variation danced by La Nijinska in 'The Sleeping Princess,'" he wrote,

> and the part she played in supplementing the choregraphy [sic] of Petipa, will scarcely need to be told of the consequences of her accession to the function of choregraphist [sic] to the Diaghileff Ballet. . . . [I]n the dynasty founded by Fokine each change of ruler has corresponded to a change of direction without loss of the heritage from previous reigns. Under La Nijinska's rule nothing has been lost, but the contact with the tradition has been, not restored, for it was never broken, but strengthened and perhaps made more clearly discernible to the lay onlooker.[89]

After Paris, with its coterie audiences and artistic intrigues and Levinson's ever-fulminating reviews, Nijinska must have relished the warmth of the London public. True, the company was performing in a music hall, but it was giving two ballets a day, six days a week for seven weeks, far more performances than it ever gave in Paris. Audiences turned up for the ballets and left after they were over. They wrote irate letters to the editor demanding why the company couldn't have a season of its own.[90] The critics, too, seemed appreciative of her efforts, alert both to the modernism of her work and to its classicism. Nobody demonized her looks or accused her of Bolshevism: on the contrary, she was acclaimed both as a choreographer and a dancer. Although the more-knowing critics may have mentioned Cocteau, he wasn't there telling her what to do.

However, behind the scenes all was not well. On December 11, Lydia Lopokova had lunch with Sokolova, who told her that Nijinska wanted to leave the troupe. However, it seems unlikely that Nijinska had given notice, since Lopokova goes on to explain that "she has 2 children, [a] mother and [a] husband to support. What a life!"[91] The disappointments of the previous months must have continued to rankle Nijinska—the conflicts over Le Train Bleu, the growing influence of Kochno, the emptiness of her new choreographic assignments, the possibly failed project with Exter, the fact that she had little or no say over the development of new works. Now other actors had appeared on the scene, and although Diaghilev kept her in the dark about his plans, their presence—and gossip about their future—had to have stoked her anxiety, as Diaghilev knew it would; intrigue was second nature to him, and he used it as a weapon. No matter that sixteen years of comity lay behind them, that he had loved her brother, knew her family, and had worked her to the bone when his luck was down. Once they arrived in London, he made plans to replace her.

Russian dancers were common fare in London music halls of the mid-1920s. On October 6, as the Ballets Russes moved through Germany, the Russian State Ballet gave its first performance in London at the Empire. The company, which hailed from the former Maryinsky Theater in the renamed city of Leningrad, had only four dancers—Alexandra Danilova, Tamara Sheversheieff (Gevergeyeva, soon to be shortened to Geva), Nicolai Efimoff (Nicolas Efimov), and George Balanchivadze (soon to be known as Balanchine). The reviews were nothing special, but the group hung on for nearly a month, living near the British Museum.[92] Lopokova went to see them early on and invited them for tea on October 12 along with Nicolas Legat, the former Maryinsky ballet master who had just settled in London. "They were sweet and simple," Lopokova wrote to her future husband, the economist John Maynard Keynes,

> and how much they [would] like to . . . stay here or anywhere without communism: the work they said was better there, but hunger and miserable salaries especially since the N. E. P. end[ed] and also since Lenin's death. They praised my brother [Fedor Lopukhov], but he is so poor what can I do for him? I feel so ashamed to have all these comforts.[93]

When the Empire engagement ended, everyone lost their work permits, so the group went to Paris. Here Diaghilev tracked them down and hastily arranged an "audition, where Balanchine and Geva danced his Scriabin pas de deux, and Danilova a few steps from Fedor Lopukhov's *Firebird*. Diaghilev then asked Balanchine if he could make ballets for operas. The twenty-year-old choreographer didn't know if he could, but said yes anyway and said yes again when Diaghilev asked if he could do them quickly.[94] After some dithering over salaries, Balanchine wired that the group accepted Diaghilev's offer. It was the day before the triumphant opening of the Coliseum season, and the impresario was now in London.[95] On November 30, Lopokova heard from her friend Florrie Grenfell (who heard it at a luncheon for "Serge") that "the 4 Russians from the State theatre are in his troupe."[96] By the week of December 8, all four were in *Prince Igor*, and by January Danilova had danced her first Blue Bird pas de deux with Dolin.[97]

On December 1, Dolin persuaded Diaghilev to audition the fourteen-year-old prodigy Alicia Marks at the studio of her teacher (and Dolin's), Serafima

Astafieva. Nijinska put her through her paces and like the others was aston-ished by her technique. It was arranged that the little girl, soon renamed Alicia Markova, would join the company in Monte Carlo and live with Nijinska and her family.[98] A few days later Diaghilev returned to Astafieva's studio. This time he did so in secret. Besotted with Lifar, he wanted to give his young lover a chance to choreograph as well as star in *Zéphyr et Flore*—the perfect touch for a season celebrating youth. Richard Buckle later learned what happened from Kochno:

> [Alexandra] Tr[o]ussevitch, who sometimes did secretarial work, and whose discretion could be counted on, was invited, with her girlfriend [Vera] Rosenstein, to act as guinea-pigs, along with [C]onstantin Tcherkass. Diaghilev had given Lifar the idea that in the *pas de trois* Flora should remain lifted in the air by the two men, without touching the ground throughout the dance. Lifar managed to get a girl on to his shoulder; he then asked, "What next?" His invention was exhausted. Diaghilev terminated the rehearsal.[99]

Although nothing came of the tryout, it did not long remain a "secret." Nijinska was deeply wounded. Lifar had been her own student; she had brought him out of Russia, given him money, and kept an eye on him during his early days in the company, before he understood how a handsome young man could jump-start a career with Diaghilev. She told Diaghilev that she was resigning; Grigoriev, horrified, did his best to dissuade her, but she replied that his entreaties were useless.[100]

After the fiasco with Lifar, Diaghilev decided to take a closer look at Balanchine's choreography. He scheduled a second tryout, ordering a half-dozen dancers to Astafieva's studio on a Sunday morning. (Sunday was the company's only day off.) "Balanchine was there, young and anxious-looking," Ninette de Valois later wrote.

> He had an engaging charm and a great sense of humour which had made him popular with us, although he had only been with the company for about ten days. . . . For two solid hours we learnt a choreographic conception of his, set to a Funeral March. . . . I worked with a will, for I was as acutely aware as others of his gifts. Just about midday Diaghilev, Kochno and Grigoriev arrived, and we went through our choreographic patterns. . . . I knew that a rumour was circulating . . . that Nyjinska [*sic*] was leaving us quite soon, and that the young Balanchine might become our new choreographer.[101]

During those December days, as rumors flew, Danilova remembered the chilly atmosphere as the dancers, loyal to Nijinska, excluded the newcomers from holiday parties.[102]

Whatever Balanchine's talents, Diaghilev was perfectly aware that he could not rely upon him for all his choreographic needs. Realizing that he had burned his bridges with Nijinska, he decided to make peace with Massine, who was dancing with Vera Trefilova at the Empire. Since leaving the Ballets Russes, Massine had made several attempts to rejoin the company, to no avail. He had toured, danced in revues and on the music-hall stage, and collaborated with the Soirées de Paris. Now, with his back to the wall, Diaghilev agreed to meet the choreographer's "astronomical" demands,[103] and Massine agreed to choreograph *Zéphyr et Flore* and *Les Matelots*. His return along with Nijinska's resignation was first reported in the January issue of the *Dancing Times*. Since the magazine came out at the start of the month, everything must have been settled by Christmas.[104]

Massine had taken her brother's place; now he was usurping hers. But Massine was hardly the only guilty party. All the boys—Diaghilev, Cocteau, Kochno, Lifar, Massine, and even Balanchine (although he had no choice in the matter), everyone except Dolin—wanted her out. She understood that she had lost and lacked both the means and the temperament to fight back. She would not share honors with Lifar or Balanchine or Massine. Sharing, she well knew, was merely Diaghilev's way of eliminating undesirables.[105]

However successful *Les Biches* and *Le Train Bleu*, the events of the previous year had scarred her. With one exception, Nijinska never again worked with Kochno. Or with Auric, Braque, Laurens, or Cocteau. Although she used Milhaud's score for a work inspired by *Le Train Bleu* that she staged in Buenos Aires, she never used any of his other music or resumed contact with him during World War II when both were living in California. Among Diaghilev's numerous French collaborators, only Poulenc remained a member of her artistic "family."

Apart from the works that survived her passage through the company, what was Nijinska's choreographic legacy to the Ballets Russes? Grigoriev thought it lay in a renewed emphasis on classicism. Her style, he wrote, "was nearer to the purely classical than that of her predecessors in our company and may perhaps be best described as 'neo-classical,'"[106] perhaps the earliest application of this term to twentieth-century ballet. This was what de Valois took away as well. Among the Ballets Russes choreographers with whom she worked, Nijinska was the one who revealed "the great tradition of a famous State School."

> She was a *demi-caractère* and character dancer . . . with a great classical knowledge and training. . . . Her class lessons were a great revelation and insight into her choreographic principles, . . . innovations [that] brought forward a new academic classicism of real importance to all in the classroom. With Nijinska it was possible to learn something beyond stage presentation of modern ballet, it was possible to grasp some of its principles and apply them academically.[107]

The London season ended on Saturday, January 10, 1925. *Aurora's Wedding* was the evening's ballet, and the Coliseum was packed, with the audience cheering from the moment the curtain went up. At the end, reported the *Times*, the audience "shouted again and again for the return of the principals. Bouquets of flowers, laurel-wreaths, and horse-shoes tied with British and Russian colours were showered on the leading dancers."[108] The scene that followed was even more extraordinary.

> Led by the orchestra, the audience broke into the singing of "Auld Lang Syne." The curtain fell again, but still the audience refused to leave. Once more the principals stepped before the curtain amid a renewed burst of cheering. Half a dozen times this was repeated, the audience singing, "For they are jolly good fellows." . . . It was not until the announcement . . . that the Ballet w[ould] return in May that any semblance of order could be restored.[109]

Nijinska, however, played no part in the mayhem. In fact, she had danced only twice the preceding week—both times at matinees and both times in *Les Sylphides*—a slap in the face given her position and long history with the company. But Diaghilev could be cruel. His parting gift, she wrote, was a "frank conversation . . . about underwater currents and geniuses," a not-so-subtle reminder that he held all the cards.[110] And so, on January 9, with a bouquet from her "loving students and stage comrades in memory of our work together," Nijinska took her last bow with the Ballets Russes and walked off the Diaghilev stage forever.[111]

8

A Freelance Choreographer

Although her mother and children were in Monte Carlo, Nijinska remained in London and began to teach. She rented a studio at 77 New Oxford Street, just east of Tottenham Court Road, with its Victorian facades and double-decker buses, and placed an ad in the *Dancing Times* seeking "prepared"— or advanced—"pupils who desire tuition in the art of the Dance."[1] Little is known about this teaching experience except that her fees were said to be "very high" and that she was reported to be an "excellent" teacher.[2] Those who gravitated to the new studio probably included the English dancers Joyce Berry and Doris Sonne, who were appearing in Richard Sheridan's comic opera *The Duenna* at the Lyric Theatre, Hammersmith; the former Diaghilev dancer Lydia Krassovska; and Nicholas Singaevsky, Nijinska's new husband—all except Krassovska would be involved with her new choreographic venture.[3] Eugene Lapitzky, Serge Unger, and Jan and Czeslav Hoyer—four of the five young men she had brought out of Kiev—remained with the Ballets Russes, but arranged to join her when Diaghilev's season at the Coliseum ended on August 1.

She had been preparing for months. In her archives is a sketch dated 1924 for a new School of Movement, which she calls "Nijinska's First Conservatory of Theater Dance."[4] She leaves "City" and "Address" blank. In London, where she spent most of the winter of 1925, she tested the waters. On January 17 she cabled Stravinsky, who was in New York, telling him that she had left the Ballets Russes and wondering if he was interested in a cycle of his ballets being performed in America.[5] Three days later she wrote to Morris Gest, the adventurous New York producer who had brought the Chauve-Souris and Stanislavsky's Moscow Art Theater to the United States. After introducing herself, she explains that she feels "oppressed" working in Europe. Would it "interest" him "to organize a ballet [company] in America"?

> I can give quite new repertoires not yet exhibited in Europe—12/15 ballets. Besides the ballets that have been playing in London and Paris, I can supply immediately a company of 40 persons including the leading personages

with names. If a larger number be necessary I can produce same at the required time.[6]

During these early weeks of January she was also in touch with Gabrielle Picabia. The estranged French wife of the avant-garde Cuban artist Francis Picabia, she ran the Paris Press Information Bureau from the Paris apartment she shared with Stravinsky's lover Vera Sudeikina. A trained musician and a familiar figure in Dada circles, Gabrielle had both an interest in performance and a personal link to Stravinsky. "Thank you for your letter," she wrote to Nijinska on January 23.

> To my great regret, I was forced to abandon my plan of going to London. . . . Nevertheless, I want to say immediately how happy I would be if you were to stage [Stravinsky's] *L'Histoire du Soldat* with your dance company. I believe it would be also good if you were to stage *Le Renard*: these two pieces together would form, I believe, a beautiful evening; it is also Stravinsky's wish.[7]

Nothing came of the Stravinsky project, although later in the year Nijinska staged a short work to his "Ragtime" music. Another note from Picabia hinted at additional projects the two women were pursuing. One involved the Metropolitan Opera and the American composer John Alden Carpenter, whose ballet *Skyscrapers* Diaghilev had briefly toyed with producing. The other involved the International Exposition of Modern Industrial and Decorative Arts (or Art Deco Exposition), opening that summer in Paris.[8] Nothing came of these projects either.

By then her sister-in-law had offered her services to Nijinska. Romola was heading to America in search of money and movie fame, and on February 18, in response to a letter from Nijinska, she wrote that she "would like to become your impresario for North and South America."

> I would do everything possible for you—as I did for Vaslav. . . . But to act on your behalf, you need first to send me a letter saying that you appoint me your representative in those countries. Then you need to tell me your program, if you are dancing alone or with students or other artists and something about the terms you would like and the minimum that you would accept as payment per performance. . . . Also the number of performances you could give per week. With your authorization in

hand I will immediately contact competent people, it being understood that I will submit the contracts to you for approval. . . . I have no doubt that you will enable me to earn in proportion. It will be for Vaslav, . . . to give him a calm and well cared-for life. As to [his] health, unfortunately, no change.[9]

Romola also appealed to Gabriel Astruc, Diaghilev's old impresario and producer of the *Fête Merveilleuse* now overwhelmed with preparations for the Art Deco Exposition. In contacting him, Romola had explained that her sister-in-law was looking for a sponsor for the company that she had dreamed of creating since leaving Russia. Did he have any suggestions? In his response Astruc did not mince words:

> I do not see in Paris at this moment, given the business crisis and the general situation, anyone among my acquaintances who might be interested in Mme. Nijinska's undertaking. Your sister-in-law knows the profound esteem I have for her great talent, . . . but as I said above, the times are deplorable and patrons more and more rare. As to finding a person who would take a business interest in this project and advance her funds, I think the thing is completely impossible, and I can only advise her against making any efforts in that direction.[10]

Nijinska would have done well to heed Astruc's advice.

Nijinska remained in London until mid-March, when she gave up her studio and returned with Singaevsky to Paris. They rented an apartment in Neuilly-sur-Seine, the comfortable neighborhood where the family would live for the next decade. "Please don't be nervous," she wrote to her mother, who was still in Monte Carlo with the children. "Just come." Ever bossy, she told Eleonora to "stay calm, [and] keep the children off the platform."

> If the cat runs away, do not let Ira [Irina] rush on the rails to look for him or there will be a disaster. Maybe it would be better to leave the cat with someone in Monte-Carlo, although I would miss it very much. . . . Don't take much in the carriage, but check all the luggage so it won't bother you. It's better to take food with you because . . . there is often no restaurant on these trains. God bless your journey. I am waiting for you, my beloved one.[11]

With "Mamousia" and the children about to join her, Nijinska began to seek work in the French capital. On March 6, Romola wrote on her behalf to Jacques Rouché, the director of the Paris Opéra:

> I am the agent of my sister-in-law as I was once my husband's. I would like to know if you would be interested in having my sister-in-law for some productions at the Opéra. She would be willing to stage new ballets or to stage and dance works of my husband such as *L'Après-midi d'un Faune*, *Jeux*, and *Mephisto Valse*, a work still unknown in Paris—to which I own the rights. I still have two other ballets of my husband, but these could not be staged before the autumn.[12]

On April 3, Romola wrote a second letter to Rouché. "I have spoken to my sister-in-law Mlle Nijinska about our last communication," she began.

> Mlle Nijinska agrees to give a class at the Opéra, with students composed of ballet artists. In Mlle Nijinska's opinion, it is only with professional artists and not with students of "rhythmic gymnastics" that one can obtain a serious result. Two classes a week from 1 1/2 to 2 hours will be indispensable.[13]

By "students of 'rhythmic gymnastics'" Nijinska meant the eurhythmics department founded by Rouché in 1917, one of multiple efforts on his part to modernize dance at the Opéra in the 1910s and 1920s.[14] From the start the new department was a source of contention. André Levinson fulminated against it, as did other tradition-minded critics. "The conflict was no longer between the Italian and the French schools," Léandre Vaillat declared, "or between the French and the Russian schools, but between the academic and the eurhythmic."[15] Whether in response to their criticism, Nijinska's insistence that the section was unnecessary, or his own disappointment at failing to achieve "any interesting result" (as he expressed it in a letter to Emile Jaques-Dalcroze), Rouché closed the section in October 1925.[16] Levinson was elated. "Embracing the beautiful cadences of classicism, the Opéra rejects the idioms of Geneva"—where Dalcroze long taught—"and pidgin-French exoticism."[17]

As Romola told Rouché on April 3, Nijinska didn't care what her class was called—a "character or expressive dance class"—since what counted was the "artistic result." She wanted to teach men as well as women, and she demanded 4,000 francs a month for her services. Since Nijinska planned on being in Paris until the end of July, she was ready to start immediately. As for new works, she was prepared to stage two ballets during the 1925–1926 season, one of which could be an opera-ballet from either *Tannhäuser* or *Prince Igor*.[18] Two weeks later, Romola wrote that she had spoken to Nijinska about a "ballet for Mlle Spessivtseva," who had now left Russia for good and whom Diaghilev was anxious to sign for the Ballets Russes. Yes, Nijinska could choreograph a tutu ballet along the lines that Rouché specified, but he needed to understand that a thirty-minute ballet was "already a grand ballet—in terms of duration." For music she proposed Ravel, but if Rouché wished, she could use another composer.[19] Nothing came of the Ravel idea, but by mid-July *Les Rencontres* by the young French composer Jacques Ibert was underway.[20]

On June 30, only days after the Art Deco Exposition opened, Nijinska made her debut as a Paris Opéra choreographer in *La Naissance de la Lyre*— The Birth of the Lyre—an opera in one act and three tableaux about nothing less than the birth of music. With music by Albert Roussel and a poem by the "learned Hellenist" Théodore Reinach, this ancient idyll in dialogue, song, and choral movement was a testament to Rouché's refined taste and connoisseurship as a director. The reviews were very respectful, but most agreed with Henry Malherbe in *Le Temps* that Reinach's libretto was a work of "pale and cold archeology."[21] In *Comoedia* Levinson devoted a full half-column to the choreography, noting that Nijinska's name "was attached to some of the most aggressive and least felicitous productions of the Ballets Russes." Happily, in this first commission for the Opéra, she "hardly sins through an excess of originality." Rather, she "discreetly reissues certain inventions—and many an error—of Fokine's *Daphnis* and Debussy's *Faune* as arranged by Nijinsky." Levinson admired her groupings and *tableaux vivants*, some of which had "real beauty." He singled out a "graceful and antique" moment when the nymphs took each other by the elbow, and another, when four nymphs posed on the steps of the grotto—rather like the Muses in Balanchine's *Apollo*—"their arms framing their heads in a curve four times repeated, the knees bent by a movement of descent." Finally, he praised her choice of performers—Huguette de Craponne, a dancer with a big jump who had danced the role of Myrtha in the Opéra's revival of *Giselle*, and the "battalion of nymphs" recruited from the ranks of the company's young talents.[22] Philip J. S. Richardson, the editor of the *Dancing Times*, was also impressed by the "intricate and fascinating patterns" of Nijinska's corps work as well as the choreographer's use of *épaulement* and the softness that pervaded the movement.[23] As for Albert Roussel and Théodore Reinach, the day after the premiere they wrote to Rouché thanking him for the "charming and poetic realization" of their work and citing Nijinska among the artists responsible for its near perfection. "From his seat of glory," they wrote, "old Socrates will welcome our homage with a smile." Their letter was subsequently published in *Figaro*.[24]

***

In leaving the Ballets Russes, Nijinska's goal was to form her own troupe, not grapple with an institution like the Opéra, even older and more tradition-bound than the Maryinsky. She wanted to do her own work, not choreograph to somebody else's specifications, and she wanted to work with dancers sympathetic to her aspirations and familiar with her style and technical approach. During the winter of 1925 she must have sketched out the repertory and thought long and hard about the kind of company she wanted. By necessity, it had to be small. With no financial backing, she could not pick and choose her venues: although Nijinska hoped for a London season, her company was launched on what was originally planned as a ten-week tour of English resort towns. Nine dancers in addition to Nijinska made up the troupe—the women Helene Wojcikowska (Antonova), Joyce Berry, Doris Sonne, and Lubov Soumarokova, and the men Eugene Lapitzky, Jan and Czeslaw Hoyer, Serge Unger, and Singaevsky. None could be considered stars. But all were seasoned professionals, and had studied and worked with her. Unlike her brother, a distant figure to his dancers at the Palace Theatre, Nijinska viewed herself as one among equals in a company that foregrounded her choreography. The Theatre Choréographique Nijinska, as she baptized the group, was a collective enterprise, not the vehicle of a singular personality.[25] Although Nijinska had turned thirty-four, retirement from dancing was far from her thoughts, and after a seven-month hiatus, she must have relished getting back onstage again and performing the juicy character roles at which she excelled. At the Paris Opéra she did just about everything but dance.

The repertory that Nijinska began to cobble together in London was designed to be both artistic and entertaining.[26] During her years with the Ballets Russes, she had learned what appealed to audiences and what constituted a varied and professionally assembled program. Nijinska threw out most of her old dances and rebuilt her repertory on the sophisticated wit and musical neoclassicism of Diaghilev's newest repertory. For *Touring* (also called *The Sports and Touring Ballet Review*), she turned to Poulenc, whose "Promenades" (1921), a series of short piano pieces about different modes of locomotion, inspired a ballet with cyclists, horseback riders, aviators, porters, and "a French modiste"—Nijinska's role—"trying to board an omnibus."[27] *Jazz* (or *The Savage Jazz*) was set to another piano piece, Stravinsky's "Ragtime," to which Nijinska created a duet for herself and Lapitzky. *On the Road*, a work of Japanese inspiration about a loving pair ambushed by bandits, had new music by Leighton Lucas, a twenty-two-year-old dancer-turned-conductor and composer.[28] Nijinska had long been interested in choreographing a ballet to excerpts from Bach's Brandenburg Concertos. Now she did so: she called the work, which she tinkered with for years, *Holy Etudes*. She reworked *Night on Bald Mountain* (now called *Night on Bare Mountain*) and as divertissements programmed one of her oldest solos, *The Doll* (now retitled *The Musical Snuff Box*), her familiar Mazurka solo from *Les Sylphides* (rechoreographed as a duet for Lubov Soumarokova and Doris Sonne),[29] her version of the *Polovtsian Dances*, and her "Three Ivans" (now renamed *Trepak*) from *The Sleeping Princess*. Another new piece, "quite the best thing on the programme," in the opinion of the *Bexhill Chronicle*,[30] was *Le Guignol Humoresque*, a comic vignette in Punch-and-Judy style, to music by the nineteenth-century Viennese composer Joseph Lanner. Like Diaghilev, Nijinska sought to balance Russian and Western composers, and use both modern and nineteenth-century music. And she was the first of a long line of twentieth-century ballet and modern dance choreographers to turn to the music of Bach.

To handle the arrangements, Nijinska enlisted Faustin Zenon, identified on playbills as her manager. His past remains a mystery. He was Russian, probably Jewish, lived in London, and dabbled in theatrical management. According to Nijinska, who met him in 1914, when he handled her brother's Palace Theatre season, he was fluent in English and French and "well informed about the business side of the theatre, having been employed by several Russian enterprises performing abroad."[31] When Diaghilev returned to London in 1918, Zenon became something of a factotum, with tasks that included company policeman and claque and possibly less savory dealings involving money.[32] Nijinska had contacted Zenon in 1921 about the sets, costumes, and scores that he had put into storage when the Palace Theatre season ended.[33] She contacted him again in 1925 to manage the London end of her new enterprise. "I have received your letter," he wrote to her from his home in north London on May 28, but I wanted to wait until today for things to work out. I have been trying to persuade people to invest money in your enterprise, but fruitlessly so far, and I don't have this kind of money.[34]

Three weeks later he was able to fill her in on more. "We may have to start in July—2 or 3 weeks in London and the provinces in August and September." She would receive "1/3 of the total house," and he agreed to "provide everything to do with costumes and scenery." However, the costumes he has "aren't enough; you have to take care of this in Paris." He doesn't have the costume for the Faun. "If you can get it from Dolin, that would be great." He advises her against engaging Thadée Slavinsky as "he's a big gossip and can't keep quiet." He reminds her not to forget about the music: they needed "scores for 20 musicians." Finally, and "most important," he tells her, "the dancers must be beautiful."[35] On June 26, Nijinska signed a Memorandum of Agreement with Donald Arthur, "sole proprietor" of Star Attractions in St. Martin's Court, for a "Show of not less than ONE & HALF HOURS duration" commencing "on or about August 4th and to continue until October 24th."[36]

The season Nijinska was planning was quite different from the one that actually took place. It was to include two ballets closely associated with her brother—L'Après-midi d'un Faune and Le Spectre de la Rose—with Anton Dolin, who was about to leave the Ballets Russes, in Nijinsky's roles, and costumes from the Palace Theatre season that Zenon had stashed away and that he and Nijinska now intended to repurpose. Zenon took pains to impress upon Nijinska the need for glamour and stars. He reiterates this in his letter of July 3. "Very important to get Dolin," he writes about the young British dancer, who had become the toast of London and apparently owned Nijinsky's last costume for Spectre. He thanks her for the photographs and publicity, but asks her to bring pictures with the new costumes and press clippings in English with her on July 15. He tells her that the tour starts with three days each in Margate and Harrogate, a day in Scarborough, and a week in Glasgow. He also writes that he has borrowed 100 pounds for her, that this is all he could raise, and that he must repay it in two months. Finally, he raises the issue of work permits. She had requested a visa for herself and for Singaevsky. What about the other performers?[37]

Zenon rented a studio beginning July 15, when Nijinska originally planned to arrive. However, her quest for a visa dragged on, holding up the loan, which depended upon it, and Dolin remained unconfirmed. On July

14, everything was still up in the air. "About the Permit for you and your husband," wrote Zenon,

> it also moves slowly and unsteadily. . . . I . . . went to Gambs and . . . asked him to help speed up the process. . . . After that I visited him twice a day and got the same answer—nothing so far. I think, that is, I suspect that he went to Diaghilev, and I think you need no further explanation—you know Diaghilev's tricks very well.[38]

Gambs was Ernest Ernestovich Gambs, the former vice-consul of the Imperial Russian Government in London and founder, after the Revolution, of the Russian Refugees' Relief and Travel Permit Office. He later told a reporter that he worked "in close touch" with the British Home Office, lending credence to Zenon's suspicions. The latter added that he was taking care of the documents for Antonova, Krassovska, and Stanislaw Zmarzlik. Of these only Antonova, who had Polish nationality through marriage (although she herself was Russian), ended up dancing for Nijinska.[39] But it wasn't until July 22 that Zenon received the "damned" visas. Come at once, he begs her, the studio is waiting.[40]

When Nijinska finally arrived in London, she had only about ten days to rehearse before the first performance in Margate on August 3. The Diaghilev season ended two days earlier, which must have complicated the rehearsal schedule given the amount of new material the dancers had to absorb. But Nijinska had a way with dancers, especially when they were devoted to her. The first leg of the tour took the company south, first to Margate on the Kentish coast, then west to the large seaside resort of Bournemouth, with its lush gardens, famous pier, and grand Victorian hotels. After the second performance in Bournemouth, disaster struck. The Home Office ordered five of the dancers—Jan and Czeslaw Hoyer, Eugene Lapitzky, Sergei Unger, and Lubov Soumarokova—to leave Britain within forty-eight hours under the Aliens Order of 1920, which required all aliens seeking employment to register with the police or face deportation.[41] The five were members of the Diaghilev company, and when the Coliseum season ended, they just stayed on, without renewing or renegotiating their work permits. The ban, which was extensively covered in the regional press, was ignored by the *Times*, while the brief notice in the *Daily Mail* made no mention of Nijinska or the troupe's connection with the Ballets Russes. This, however, was noted in other London newspapers, such as the *Morning Post*, which stated that "M.

Diaghileff . . . made representations to the Home Office, on the ground that permits for the company were issued in his name. Madame Leginska [sic] opposed the representations, with the aid of her theatrical agent, but was unsuccessful."[42]

Clearly, somebody had tipped off the Home Office while Diaghilev was in Italy, holidaying with Lifar. "Diaghilev fights against competition," Nijinska wrote in her autobiographical outline.[43] Ultimately, a compromise was reached, with the Home Office allowing the dancers to remain on British soil for another five weeks. Although this was welcome news and certainly salvaged the tour, it also shaved five weeks off the original eleven-week itinerary. As Laurie Kaden writes: "Where the company had formerly arranged to spend several days and give several performances at many venues, it now planned flying visits and one-night stands."[44] The rationale for the ban was to protect British jobs, but as the *Weston-super-Mare Gazette* pointed out, "that argument is rather discounted by the fact that very few Englishmen go in for ballet dancing, of which the Russians have almost a monopoly."[45]

The failure of the tour and the fact that the company never performed in London must have been a bitter disappointment for Nijinska. Nothing had gone right. She had hoped for a company of thirty, but ended up with one of ten, too small to make much of an impression, while a star like Dolin (whom she had helped immeasurably and who had now left Diaghilev) preferred dancing in *The Punch Bowl Revue* to performing her brother's roles in *Le Spectre de la Rose* and *L'Après-midi d'un Faune*. She had hoped to find a home on the British stage, which had taken so many Russian dancers to heart, but there didn't seem to be room for her. Nobody wanted to invest in her or her dancers or took much interest in new forms of dance (however anodyne). Although the reviews were largely positive and the company's reception warm, Joyce Berry remembered Nijinska "grumbl[ing]" about the tour, disappointed with the small towns and "funny little places" where they performed. The dancers grumbled too, "but we ignored the bad things about it because we were working with Nijinska."[46]

As for Alexandra Exter, who designed simple yet strikingly theatrical costumes for all six of Nijinska's new ballets, what must she have thought? She had just emigrated, although her status remained ambiguous: the Soviets still regarded her as one of their own. Like Nijinska once she left the Ballets Russes, Exter did not find life easy in the West. She may have been a highly respected theater and film designer, but few of her designs ever reached the stage. In part, Georgy Kovalenko explains, this is because French theater of the late 1920s and 1930s was "preoccupied by a different set of questions." But it was also because she never met a director equal to her talent" and because "material factors," above all during the Depression, cut into the production budgets of new plays.[47] Like the dancers, Exter happily joined forces with Nijinska and was photographed observing a rehearsal in the studio.[48] The costumes were built in Paris by Maison Pascaud, a well-regarded costume house, and then altered in London.

Exter's costumes and the designs for them long remained unknown, packed away in Nijinska's attic, until displayed in 1986 at the Cooper-Hewitt Museum in New York. In *Touring*, the accent was on wit and fashion, with a touch of sexual naughtiness. The Horseback Riders wore tuxedo jackets, thigh-high skirts with bustles, top hats, and riding crops; the Cyclists sporting attire; the Porters loose-fitting belted coveralls with caps; Nijinska, as the "Modiste," a blue tailored suit that entered her personal wardrobe. The Japanese-inspired costumes for the Bandits in *On the Road* used wire and padding to distort the body's natural contours, while the Japanese Woman wore a black chenille "fright" wig with a kimono of large black-and-white squares. In *Jazz* the accent was again on geometry, with Courrèges-style shifts that featured either stripes or oversize polka dots and complemented the angularity of the dancers' "eccentric" movement.[49]

The most inventive costumes were for the most abstract of the season's works. In *Night on Bare Mountain* the dancers wore identical long, flowing costumes, grey, hooded, with lengths of fabric stitched to the sleeves. For *Holy Etudes*, Exter designed grey silk pleated tunics, with pink and orange silk capes that hung from light horizontal rods placed across the dancers' backs. (On their heads were halo-like headpieces that recall those worn by Exter's Martians in *Aelita*.) The costumes moved with the dancers; they were dynamic in their own right, but also intended to heighten the effect of the choreography. In *A Night on Bare Mountain* they emphasized the sculptural character of the group, while in *Holy Etudes*, when the dancers turned away from the audience, their capes formed a contrasting background against which the soloists performed. In both works the costumes were all but identical for men and women: Nijinska's daughter, Irina, who turned thirteen in 1925, recalled "jokes among the dancers about not being able to tell" them apart.[50] In *Holy Etudes* they were androgynous heavenly beings, in *Bare Mountain* a mass of restless, turbulent spirits. There was not a tutu in sight, and none of the new works called for pointework. In the absence of sophisticated lighting, Exter's striking use of color was a bright spot in nearly every ballet.

Exter must have been disheartened by the limited scope of the tour, which did nothing to advance her career in the West. A set design for *Holy Etudes* has survived, suggesting that at some point a London season was seriously in the offing and that Nijinska intended to develop the ballet into a more ambitious work. (In her archive is a note referring to the 1925 version as an "Esquisse" or "sketch," with the "ballet" being staged the following year in Buenos Aires.)[51] With its ropes and panels, Exter's design represents an architecture of intersecting planes and asymmetrical lines that conveys a great sense of space and upward movement.[52] Although Exter's design was almost certainly never used, *Holy Etudes* was the 1925 work that remained the longest with Nijinska, as if memorializing the breakthrough moment in Kiev when she discovered that it was possible to choreograph movement that was not only expressive but also abstract.

The Theatre Choréographique gave its last performance on September 19 in Newquay, a fishing port on the Atlantic coast of Cornwall.[53] However, work kept Nijinska in England until September 28, and she lingered for almost another week. On October 6 she wrote to Diaghilev from Paris, saying that she had only "just" received his letter "reproaching" her, presumably for "stealing" his dancers. His accusation was "without foundation," she wrote. "The artists who worked with me are now in Paris. I don't know whether Lapitzky and Unger will return [neither did], although I strongly recommended that they do so."[54]

Meanwhile, she tried to drum up interest in her work in the French capital. There was a performance at the Grand Palais on October 30, shortly before the Art Deco Exposition closed. A second took place at the Opéra on December 3 at a huge charity gala "Dance through the Ages." The Nijinska group danced *The Polovtsian Dances* and *Dances of the Italian Renaissance* ("Holy Sketches") on a program that included dancers from all the major Paris theaters. A global time-trot from Greece to India, Renaissance Italy to Revolutionary France, the show closed with Josephine Baker and *La Revue Nègre*, representing America.[55] But after the gala, Nijinska's company, begun with so much hope, disbanded.

As Nijinska toured the English seaside, Rouché was making plans for the new Opéra season. On September 4 he called Romola to see if Nijinska could stage a short ballet to Jacques Ibert's music, *Les Rencontres*, for an opening in late November. "I promised him," Romola wrote, "that you would try to mount it when <u>you return to Paris the beginning of November</u>, you could do it in two weeks." She thought it was important, she added, "to choreograph from time to time for the Opéra."[56] As it turned out, Rouché had in mind a far more ambitious project than *Les Rencontres*. He wanted Nijinska not only to choreograph and teach, but also to serve as a consultant, advising him (as had the recently deceased Léon Bakst) on dance at the Opéra.[57] Finally, he wanted her to conduct a study of dance at the house, examining over the course of several months, as he explained in a handwritten letter to Romola, "how to transform the school, dance, and music"[58] and even to "to fuse the French classical school and the Russian school," an idea Romola said was "brilliant" and would "revolutionize the art of dance."[59]

When Romola wasn't flattering Rouché, she was doing her best to put him off. She explained that Nijinska was now working with her own company, and "it would be difficult for her to decide." Romola, of course, would try her best to "settle the affair," although if he were flexible on the matter of leaves, a solution was possible. For how long did he want her to engage her? How many ballets would she have to stage? Would the classes she taught be for "artists or children"?[60] At the same time she explained to Nijinska what was going on with Rouché:

> As you know, Monsieur Rouché proposed for you to mount a ballet in autumn. Two days later, he wrote to me offering us still <u>another proposition</u>. He would like to engage you at the Opéra to choreograph ballets and to teach classes according to your ideas . . . to create a center for the art of dance. In short, to make the Opéra an "academy of the Dance." He would agree to give you leaves to be able to go to America or abroad every year. What do you think? I think that 6 months in Paris and 6 months of travel would not be bad. With the right that during the 6 months that you are in Paris you can give performances with your troupe in France—Monte Carlo. What would you ask for 6 months? Rouché wanted to engage Waslaw the same way eleven years ago. The contract was accepted by Watza; it was the war that prevented it. Don't at once refuse. Think, you will have a home and could travel all the same.[61]

From the start, leaves were the sticking point. Although the English tour was a fiasco, Nijinska remained committed to the survival of her company. She seemed fairly sure of a London engagement—the reason she wanted to keep November free—and of an engagement in the United States during the winter. Although Rouché was willing to "tolerate" a November leave, above all for a commitment already made, a leave of two months in the middle of the year, with new ballets in production and a new approach to teaching underway, was "impossible." By now, Romola was also mentioning winter engagements in Germany and Scandinavia, claiming that Nijinska would make up the lost time in spring and summer.[62] Although she wanted her sister-in-law to sign with the Opéra, Romola stuck to her guns. On September 29, as Nijinska lingered in London, she continued to demand 60,000 francs for six months of work. "The question to discuss is the leave," she wrote.

> Even if my sister-in-law refused the Metropolitan and put off the other offer of a tour with her troupe in America for another season, she must fulfill obligations in Germany, Scandinavia, and London. Thus, the months of January–February I must keep free for this work.[63]

None of these engagements panned out, however, and Nijinska went to work for the Opéra.

***

Back in Paris, Nijinska started choreographing *Les Rencontres* and wondered about a second ballet during the two months she would be spending at the Opéra. She also began teaching on a regular basis, giving four classes a week, on Monday and Friday to the "grands sujets," on Tuesday and Saturday to the "petits sujets" and coryphées. She wasn't the only teacher giving regular classes. Carlotta Zambelli, the Italian étoile who had been a fixture at the Opéra for more than thirty years, taught on Tuesday, Wednesday, and Saturday, while her partner, the French-trained Albert Aveline, taught on Monday, Wednesday, and Friday.[64]

Nijinska had welcomed Rouché's proposal to study dance training at the Opéra, and on December 11, after more than two months of teaching and observing classes, she submitted her report. Written by hand in her still shaky French, she commended much of what she had seen during the previous months: the work ethic, drive, and technique of the dancers were all admirable. However, their training was "purely" technical, and their "idea of Dance" extremely limited. They danced, she wrote, "solely with the legs," using their arms and body only for "grace," and they were oblivious of the "form" of the steps they worked to master.

> They have no idea that form can have infinite diversity. That is why it is difficult to give them style, expression, and character. Their School does not teach them to understand the form and subtleties of movement in Dance.
>
> My weekly visits to each class were too few for all that I could teach them. They need more methodical and more frequent work. . . .
>
> The Dance class should contain everything: movement, expression, style, character, rhythm, and complete mechanics—in a word, the technique of a dancer "artist."
>
> This School is the classical School, . . . but the teaching of it should encompass the full experience and richness of that School from the past to our day.
>
> Ballets by contemporary Masters and competitive examinations . . . no doubt contribute a great deal to the dancer's progress, but until the School is completely reorganized, I find it difficult to hope for the appearance of great dancer-artists and choreographers.[65]

Nijinska's report drew on ideas that she had originated in Kiev and would develop in the treatise that she began drafting in the late 1920s and published in the Viennese journal *Schrifttanz* in 1930. Even in Kiev, Nijinska had viewed classical technique as the foundation of professional dance training. At the School of Movement, however, classes in expressive or free movement had enriched the curriculum, emphasizing a creative approach to classically based movement. Now she sought explicitly to divorce her teaching from anything that hinted at eurhythmics and non-classical styles of movement. Instead, she advocated a single classically based class that encompassed, as she explained, both the past and the present of the classical "School," with the "present" subsuming more contemporary approaches. In her treatise she elaborated on this, emphasizing how classical technique had changed over time to accommodate new artistic practices, such as pointework in the aftermath of Romanticism. Although the previous twenty-five years had brought "a revolution in the choreographic art," this revolution was reflected only in works choreographed for the stage. "Schools have learnt nothing from it."[66] Nijinska's class, by contrast, was intended to prepare dancers for the work of modern masters beginning with Fokine. She was less concerned with developing an overall curriculum than with providing a method for extending the range of conventionally trained classical dancers.

Unfortunately, the Opéra's dancers had little interest in expanding their horizons the way Nijinska thought they should. On December 21, exactly ten days after Nijinska submitted her report to Rouché, the dancers struck back. In a letter signed by thirty or so members of the troupe, they stated, first, that they had "nothing to learn from Madame Nijinska that [could] not be taught by [their] current professors." Second, she had used "wounding language about everyone." For this reason, they "refuse[d] to attend her classes," although "Monsieur le Directeur" had made them mandatory.[67] Rouché's response is unrecorded, so Nijinska probably continued to teach at the Opéra until March, when she left for Monte Carlo to stage *Romeo and Juliet* for the Ballets Russes. Anti-émigré feeling was on the rise in the mid- and late 1920s. Nijinska alludes to it in one of her diaries,[68] and in an institution that required most of its personnel to be French, nationalism must have partly accounted for the dancers' ill will. However, Nijinska had a sharp tongue, and as the years passed it became increasingly biting. She had no interest in charming people; if anything, she seemed to go out of her way to alienate them, refusing to meet them halfway, as if compromise meant loss of face and failure. She let fly without thinking of the consequences, and her behavior came back to haunt her.

On November 19, *Les Rencontres*, Nijinska's first ballet for the Opéra, had its premiere. Although slight, the work became an unexpected source of controversy because of Levinson's implacable hatred of modernism, exemplified by Nijinska, and his vision of the Opéra as a temple of classicism, heir to a Maryinsky now lost to the Bolsheviks. *Les Rencontres* appeared on another of Rouché's artfully curated programs, this one featuring two works of lyric theater and music by two recent winners of the Prix de Rome. *Les Rencontres* completed the program. A "small suite in the form of a ballet," it was a very short work, an "ouvrette" one writer called it, only sixteen minutes long, a divertissement to five short piano pieces by Jacques Ibert, orchestrated by the composer at Rouché's behest.[69] For Nijinska it was hardly a plum assignment, almost an afterthought on an evening heavily slanted toward opera, although interest in Ibert, a new voice on the Paris music scene, ran high. The critic-composer Roland-Manuel thought the music was a natural fit for Nijinska; like Poulenc's music for *Les Biches*, Ibert's had a similar air of perversity. "Mme. Nijinska," he wrote,

has sought to make *Les Rencontres* a *concerto* for dance and orchestra. The choreographic element therefore enjoys a certain independence here. It does not slavishly fit the music; it scarcely follows it; it *encounters* it. . . . Mme. Nijinska is too honest an artist to accept flattery. I would lie if I said that she has perfectly realized her entire design, but I would lie no less if I denied the pleasure that the ballet whose steps she arranged has given me. The liberties that she takes with a technique that she does not scorn, this feigned licence and this ironic rigor are in delicious accord with Jacques Ibert's score.[70]

Of course, some critics complained about the decision to orchestrate works conceived for the piano and others to stage works conceived for the concert hall. Still others complained of the ballet's general inconsequence, dismissing it as a "student exercise . . . on a very big stage draped with . . . curtains."[71] But *Les Rencontres* had its defenders, including the many critics who commented on the refinement of the music and the light touches of Nijinska's choreography in response to it.[72] As for the composer, he was thrilled. "There is no greater emotion for a musician," he wrote to Rouché a few days after the premiere, "than to hear his music played for the first time."

This honor and this joy you have brought me in accepting my "Rencontres" and mounting it with a care both artistic and sensitive . . . Please convey my sincere gratitude to Madame Nijinska whose choreographic composition is a model of taste, elegance, and clarity.[73]

Heading the cast was the Opéra's new étoile, the Russian ballerina Olga Spessivtzeva, who had now settled definitively in the West. A great Giselle (she had starred in the Opéra's 1924 revival), a magnificent Odette, and the greatest of Diaghilev's Auroras, she exemplified Maryinsky style at its best. Partnering her was a young Italian-born dancer, Serge Peretti, and surrounding them two young lights of the troupe, Suzanne Lorcia and Gabrielle Rousseau. In this regard at least, Rouché had done well by Nijinska. And it was almost certainly his privileging of Nijinska, both in terms of this assignment and more generally because of his engagement of her in an advisory capacity, that incurred the fury that Levinson unleashed in his review of *Les Rencontres* in *Comoedia*. For one thing, he argues, the work is imitative. The scenario and decor recall Fokine's *Carnaval*, the "endless knitting of pas de bourrées on pointe" his *Les Sylphides*, while the duet for Lorcia and Rousseau is like the Girls in Grey in Nijinska's own *Les Biches*. Echoing sentiments familiar from earlier reviews, he declared that the chance encounter of the protagonists was "treated in a style that is a singular distortion of the *danse d'école*, a 'classical' style that is tight, angular, crippled." As for Spessivtzeva, the "sublime architecture" of whose body he adored, what, he asks, was she doing last night, "decked out in that little straw hat" like a *lorette* of the Second Empire? "Couldn't Giselle have been saved this punishment?" At the end, he goes for the jugular:

> For Mme. Nijinska is incapable of arranging a ballet as I have said from her first effort. I do not question . . . her way of seeing. I question her ability to choreograph. After a long and honorable career as a minor soloist, inclined by the shortcomings of her physique toward the burlesque, a caprice of Mons. de Diaghilew "catapulted" her into a choreographer until the day when his same "good pleasure" brusquely disowned her. *Le roi s'amuse.* Now, since that joke, Mme. Nijinska clings stubbornly to her error. . . . The first theater in the world sanctions this error by entrusting a score and personnel to her questionable skill. This instructive fiasco could be salutary.[74]

Despite the assault, Rouché seemed unwilling to dismiss Nijinska, nor did he appear inclined to embrace the conservative program Levinson advocated or view the Maryinsky as the custodian of ballet traditions compromised or abandoned by the French, which they should now restore under the knowing eye of balletomane émigrés. Rouché must also have been aware of nationalist murmurings at the growing Russian presence within the Opéra. As Adolphe Jullien ended his review of *Les Rencontres*: "And, so, a Russian dancer, Mlle. Spessivtzeva, an Italian dancer, Mons. Peretti, and a Russian choreographer, Mme. Nijinska, have done their best to give us this pleasant score of a winner of the Prix de Rome, M. Jacques Ibert, who is a Frenchman."[75]

Levinson's attack did not go unanswered. In *Les Nouvelles littéraires* the composer-critic Georges Auric used most of his limited space to defend Nijinska and "Rouché's excellent idea" of engaging her. "I have read strong criticisms of Mme. Nijinska's choreography," he wrote. "Shall I confess that they seem too strong to bear all their weight? *Les Rencontres* is a . . . short suite of dances whose scenes could not have been composed with the amplitude of a work of another scale. But I humbly confess to having followed it throughout with interest and pleasure. As it is easy to imagine, Mlle. Spessivtzeva shone with a special brilliance."[76] Roland-Manuel also took pains to answer Levinson, while going out of his way to correct Henry Malherbe, the music critic of *Le Temps*, who echoed Levinson's old canard about Nijinska's choreography being a "note-for-note translation" of the score and fell back on words like "grim," "pedantic," and "hysterical" that Levinson had used to smear *Les Noces*.[77]

Nijinska completed only one additional assignment for Rouché that season, the dances in a revival of Gluck's opera *Alceste*, an eighteenth-century work on a mythological theme with a long history at the Opéra: in 1776 the composer unveiled his reworked version there in the presence of Queen Marie Antoinette herself. The revival was the most recent in a series of works "resurrected" by Rouché, and like *La Naissance de la Lyre* it was steeped in erudition. Nijinska was responsible for the ritual and warrior dances and pantomime, inspired by the "poses depicted on ancient monuments."[78] Her cast this time included members of the recently abolished eurhythmic section, led by Yvonne Franck, a "crossover" dancer equally at home in ballet and "modern" styles, although she seldom worked on pointe. André Messager liked the production overall, although he felt that the dances were the "weakest point of the production." The final divertissement fell "deplorably short," with everybody dancing their part "without a care for his neighbor." "This," he declared, "is unworthy of our National Academy of Dance!"[79] Levinson, in *Comoedia*, should have leapt at the chance to display both his erudition on the subject of the ancient Greek dance (which he viewed as a precursor of classical ballet) and his loathing of Nijinska, her choreography, and the eurhythmic section, but his review, promised at the end of Pierre Maudru's music review, failed for some reason to materialize.[80]

Like all freelancers, Nijinska depended upon a constant flow of work. With *Alceste* behind her, she wrote to Rouché about doing another project for the Opéra, only to be told that he was not mounting any new ballets in February and March, when she was available. "I had thought of giving you a *grand ballet*," he told her, "but the work I had in mind could not go before May 10, and you are leaving in April; therefore I don't have any work for you now."[81]

***

Into the breach stepped Diaghilev, with an unexpected invitation to choreograph a new ballet. As Nijinska knew, he had no compunction about making up with people if he needed them. He had followed her career, "fight[ing] the competition" represented by her small company, then attending the premiere of *Les Rencontres*.[82] Now, according to Sergei Grigoriev, he wanted her to choreograph the first of his company's "English" productions,

Romeo and Juliet. The score by the English composer Constant Lambert was done, as was the libretto, cooked up, like so many others, by Diaghilev and Kochno. "All it amounted to," wrote a disappointed Grigoriev, who had hoped for a little more Shakespeare, "was that, in the first place, the dancers were to be shown rehearsing various incidents from that famous drama, and that, in the second, the two principals playing the 'star-cross'd lovers' were, like them, to elope."[83] An English painter, Christopher Wood, had designed some fussy scenery, which at the last moment Diaghilev replaced with curtains and set pieces by Joan Miró and Max Ernst, surrealists whose show at the Galerie van Leer had just opened in Paris.[84] About the choreography, Diaghilev wondered what Grigoriev thought about having Nijinska do it? Grigoriev considered this an excellent idea.[85] On March 5, in Paris, Diaghilev signed a letter of agreement with his former choreographer. He agreed to pay her 20,000 francs plus travel expenses in exchange for which she was to spend four weeks in Monte Carlo, choreographing *Romeo and Juliet* and rehearsing *Les Noces,* which Diaghilev planned to present in London the following June.[86] It made sense for Diaghilev to engage her for a new ballet since he needed her for *Les Noces.* But her presence was also a signal to Balanchine, and above all Massine, that Diaghilev had no qualms about callously manipulating his choreographers, pitting them against one another and creating rivalries that lasted for decades. He wanted them, when he needed them, in their place.

Romeo and Juliet was another "cocktail" ballet that nobody much liked, although most agreed that it was pleasant enough. A "rehearsal without scenery in two acts," it showed not *Romeo and Juliet* itself, but the "'kitchen' of the work," as Jane Catulle-Mendès put it, "the life of its interpreters, their exercises, the jollity of their leisure moments, the fantasies of their rest time, [and] their flirtations."[87] Opening with what the program note called a "Ballets Russes dance class," it blurred real life with stage fiction, prompting comparisons with Pirandello's *Six Characters in Search of an Author,* acclaimed the previous year in Paris, although the ballet lacked the play's tragic dimension.[88] The action was simple:

> Enter Nikitina and Lifar who notice they are late. Quickly changing into their rehearsal costumes, they start to work. The dancing master teaches them a pas de deux during which, forgetting their steps, they make no secret of their love. Their scandalized comrades separate the lovers and carry them off to the theater where a rehearsal is about to begin.[89]

In the second act the scenes followed in equally quick succession: the Capulet ball where the lovers meet; Romeo's duel with Tybalt; the balcony scene; a scene in which Paris searches for his errant fiancée, and the death scene, which the cast mimics and applauds. The curtain falls, then rises again on an empty stage. Finally, the lovers reappear in flying "kit" and with Juliet poised on Romeo's shoulder, conveyed "their elopement by aeroplane."[90] It was Shakespeare's romantic tragedy viewed through a lens of modernist irony.

Nijinska never explained her approach to the ballet, but according to Boris Kochno, who wrote the libretto and seldom had a good word to say about her, it was all wrong. "She took off from the premise," he wrote many years later,

> that she was choreographing a dramatic work, and, by undertaking simply to substitute gestures for words she repeated for the greater part of the ballet the error she had made with *Les Fâcheux* and foundered in a conventional, realistic pantomime.[91]

Grigoriev, although he had welcomed Nijinska's return, found her choreography "difficult to assess." There was a pas de deux, but otherwise the choreography was negligible, only barre exercises and a great deal of miming.[92] Alice Nikitina, on whom the role of Juliet was created although the premiere in Monte Carlo was danced by Tamara Karsavina, felt that some of the scenes were "really beautiful and full of invention." The most successful, she thought, was the death scene. "Our acting," she wrote, "was entirely directed by Nijinska whose way of presenting the scene was remarkable."[93] Lambert was deeply impressed by Nijinska's use of counterpoint; ten years later he recalled the way she had created an "astonishing choreographic fugue . . . to a purely homophonic passage in the finale."[94] Karsavina, who arrived in Monte Carlo after Nijinska had left and thus did not work directly with the choreographer, found the role of Juliet "clever" but "choreographically insignificant."[95]

André Coeuroy, reviewing the ballet in *La Revue musicale*, disliked most of what he saw: "There are pretty moments like the Andantino for the two lovers and amusing ones in the balcony and death scenes. . . . But despite these excellent details, the whole is dominated by Nijinska's angular, tight, and inhuman bias."[96] Fernand Divoire, long an admirer of Nijinska's, compared the choreography to an "embroidery of modern gesture and pantomime on a perfectly classical foundation," even as he remarked that under Diaghilev's "magic wand" even "revolutionaries become graceful and charming."[97] Across the Channel, Francis Toye in the *Morning Post* praised the "inventiveness" of the rehearsal scenes and felt that "episodes of the play itself were translated into terms of the dance with extraordinary ingenuity. The final flight of the two lovers provided just the right mixture of dancing and the spirit of improvised charade that animates the ballet as a whole."[98]

Levinson was uncharacteristically generous to Nijinska, even acknowledging the "extreme indigence of Kochno's scenario, with its dull and puerile non-sequiturs." He thought there were "episodes of great charm" and that the "short andantino of the two lovers [was] staged with extreme delicacy." He especially liked the "soft curves designed by the arms overhead and the simultaneous movement of the two svelte torsos." Moreover, when Nijinska managed to "escape" what he calls the "nauseating snigger and urge to disparage all that is human—because grimacing irony and disgusted misanthropy seem to be the aesthetic imposed on his world by Serge de Diaghilew—she finds and develops plastic themes not without beauty." Most of all he was taken with Lifar, a "handsome adolescent" who was likely to become the season's "only star."[99] Certainly, Lifar was getting the full Diaghilev star build-up: private classes, orthodontry, plastic surgery, photos by Man Ray, principal roles in virtually every new ballet, and advance press. Writing in *Le Gaulois* before the season opened, Pierre-Plessis described attending a rehearsal of "that extraordinary dancer named Serge Lifar":

> Jumping, whirling, winged as music and as the breeze, he dances until he falls panting with fatigue on the stage. . . . The flame that burns him passes to us; it is the dance! The winged dance![100]

Few such words were spilled over the company's women.

By then, Nijinska was in Buenos Aires. She took no first-night bows, and in London it is amazing how seldom her name appears in the press, although the season opened with *Les Noces* and featured three additional ballets of hers—*Les Biches*, *Aurora's Wedding*, and *Romeo and Juliet*. She knew nothing, too, of the pandemonium that erupted at the Paris premiere of *Romeo and Juliet*, when fifty or so surrealists, incensed by Ernst and Miró's contribution to the ballet, tossed leaflets from the balcony proclaiming that ideas should never be "at the behest of money" or "profit the international aristocracy."[101] Given the Cook's tour crowd at the Théâtre Sarah-Bernhardt with its sleek motorcars and deep pockets, the surrealists' protest wasn't totally off the mark. Nor was she aware of the grumbling among critics about the triviality of the ballet and about the way Diaghilev's new works intentionally pandered to fashion. "Ballet," he told a journalist, "is essentially a modish art. It resembles women's clothes rather than men's. Symphonies and oratorios are like men's clothes—solemn, substantial, and yielding only very gradually to the spirit of change. But an out-of-date ballet is as absurd as a woman's out-of-date hat."[102]

Finally, she knew nothing about the Sturm und Drang behind the scenes as Diaghilev threw out Christopher Wood's designs, brought in Ernst and Miró, and changed her choreography. The day after the first performance (which took place in Monte Carlo), Lambert, who had dedicated the score of *Romeo and Juliet* to Nijinska, sent her a long letter in French detailing the horrors of the days leading up to the premiere. "My dear Madame Nijinska," he wrote:

> I send you the program for the premiere of "Romeo and Juliet," but before I speak about the performance I must tell you about the miserable scandals that have occurred. When I signed the contract, I naturally thought that the decor would be by the good English painter Christopher Wood, as Mons. Diaghilew announced, and that the choreography would remain unaltered. You can imagine my horror when, on my return to Monte Carlo, I learned that Mons. Diaghileff had rejected, without explanation, the charming and well-made decor of the English painter and replaced it with a decor by two painters, Ernst and Miro [*sic*], of such idiocy, inanity, and ugliness that you cannot imagine without seeing it. . . .
>
> Even worse, Mons. Diaghileff has completely spoiled the finale of the first tableau. He has eliminated the dance for three girls and substituted a pas de deux for Romeo and Juliet. It is an incredible insult to an artist like you, and when I saw it I was so furious that I sent you a telegram in Buenos Aires (I hope you received it). I tried to speak to Mons. Diaghileff . . . , but he forbid me to speak about the decor, and when I protested about the choreography, he said, "I have known Mme. Nijinska for twenty years, and I forbid you to speak her name!"[103]

In a letter to his mother written a few days later, Lambert described the "disgraceful changes" Diaghilev had introduced in the choreography,

> altering bits that Nijinska declared she would never be induced to change. For example, at the end of the 1st tableau, instead of the dance of 3 women which Nijinska designed, the lovers (who are supposed to be dragged apart)

return and do a pas-de-deux, with all the rest staring at them. Can you imagine anything more stupid and vulgar?[104]

According to Alexandra Danilova, who was one of the trio of women (the others were Felia Doubrovska and Tamara Geva), Nijinska had choreographed a dance of considerable brilliance, even including *fouettés*, that revealed the technical limitations of Nikitina and Lifar as the lovers. Since Diaghilev was promoting the two as the company's newest stars (although he was well aware of their shortcomings), the trio had to be cut.[105] Karsavina, who had an ailing knee, was probably also anxious to get rid of the *fouettés*. She told Diaghilev that they seemed "utterly unconnected with the whole," thus providing an artistic rationale for him to cut the turning trio.[106]

This was not the end of Diaghilev's choreographic meddling. As Lambert recounted to his mother,

After the Monte-Carlo performance, Kochno came to see me and asked if I had any music for an entr'acte as they thought it would be more "vivante" if there was a passage of dancers from the classroom to the theatre. I was very annoyed at their trying to spoil Nijinska's work anymore, so I said I would give him music for an entr'acte but only on the understanding that not a note of it was to be danced. So they have now added a sort of comic march-past of the characters (without music) in very dubious taste and in a style which is the complete opposite of Nijinska's.[107]

Lambert used much the same language when he wrote to the choreographer after the second Paris performance. As before, he enclosed a program, along with a few reviews, the "most intelligent" in his view being Louis Laloy's. "No doubt you will be amazed at the insertion on the program 'Choreography of the entr'acte by G. Balanchine.'" He then tells her the story he told his mother a few days later. Chivalrously, he tries to soften the blow. "I assure you that I have done everything possible to protect your work, but all alone I can't fight these people."[108]

However, Diaghilev was still not done. In yet another letter, this one written the day after *Romeo*'s London premiere, Lambert describes further cuts. "Another thing is that they have made a cut in the finale," he reported.

I tried to prevent them from doing that, but Mons. Diaghileff said, "If you do not make this cut of 50 measures, I will forbid the dancers from dancing during that time . . . . So not wanting him to spoil the choreography more,

I agreed to this cut. To tell the truth, I am so tired of all these quarrels that I don't have the strength to continue.

Perhaps you think that I have been too intransigent, but I assure you that I don't want to make trouble, I hate it, but I can't bear to see all your beautiful ideas disfigured without saying something.[109]

Nijinska had left the Ballets Russes in anger and with high hopes. The anger no doubt had subsided, but the hopes had to have dimmed. How cold and hard the freelance world must have seemed, with its hand-to-mouth existence and little regular work. She had the freedom to choreograph for herself, a luxury she had not enjoyed since leaving Kiev, but lacked the means to finance it. In Kiev, money may have been scarce, but she had what she needed—dancers, artists, a studio, sympathetic audiences, and performance spaces—to foster her development as a choreographer. Now she needed to fund an entire operation, transform her considerable artistic capital into financial and social capital, and this she could not do. Even as a young Ballets Russes dancer, Nijinska avoided the monied society her brother had entered, preferring the company of her fellow dancers to that of High Bohemia. As an émigré, she pursued a similar course. When she left Diaghilev, she experienced the consequences: few social contacts to press into service, few friends with access to wealthy donors, few journalists willing to publicize her work. So Nijinska was left with all the bills—for the photographs, costumes, studio rentals, salaries, and travel expenses. Even if the dancers rehearsed some of the time for free and Exter worked for nothing, the cost of Theatre Chorégraphique was ruinous. Dunning letters from Zenon followed her until 1929 (when the debt was apparently settled), and some of them are scary. "Esteemed Bronislava Fominichna," he wrote to her on November 26, 1928:

Regarding the money, I don't understand what you want me to do. Mons. Singaevsky promised me many times, and, finally, when I went to Paris, he told me the money would definitely be sent to me on the 15th of this month, and I still haven't received it.

Bronislava Fominichna, as you know and as I have written to you many times, the money I gave you wasn't mine, and now they are violently demanding the money, and I am forced to pay the interest. . . .

What should I do now? I have already pawned my things. . . . That is why I beg you to send the money you owe me, so that I can give it back to Vasilii, who tortures me.[110]

When people can't get credit from reputable sources, they resort to moneylenders, often from their own ethnic group. It took a loan shark named Vasilii to get Theatre Choréographique off the ground, and Nijinska remained in his debt for years.

In addition to paying for everything, Nijinska had to do everything herself. Unlike her brother or Diaghilev, she did not have a Nijinska at hand or a Grigoriev or a Nouvel or even a Kochno—the kind of people who made the Ballets Russes of the 1920s a formidable organization, however mediocre the product sometimes was. She remained friends with Exter and knew a number of Russian émigré artists, but, from the evidence of surviving letters and journals, she seldom swapped ideas with them. Trust was precious, especially in a ballet world rife with competition. Perhaps this was the reason she decided to marry: she needed a man by her side, somebody whose loyalty to her was absolute and who belonged to her family tribe of artists. Although by birth Singaevsky belonged to the intelligentsia, he had traded his world for hers; he had remade himself as a dancer, converted through the power of her imagination, and become her assistant and helpmate, as well as her husband. He was the man who carried her bags and took care of her correspondence, performed minor roles and acted at various times as her agent, interpreter, and manager. In a sense this was what Romola had been to her brother (although once they married, she turned into a lady of leisure). But she also brought him social capital: she could hold her own with bankers and journalists, chatting in several languages, not as a theatrical outsider but as an equal. Singaevsky, by contrast, charmed no one. Rather, he became another of Nijinska's dependents. After leaving the Ballets Russes in 1925, he followed her from job to job, never establishing an identity separate from hers. She mentions him only once in her 1926–27 journal, and it is a tantalizing reference, suggesting that their life together was a source of disappointment, if not unhappiness. "Both times Diaghilev stood in for my father," she writes, meaning that he gave her away when she married. "How hadn't it occurred to me that he brings bad luck to a marriage?"[111] It is unlikely that Nijinska ever contemplated leaving Singaevsky. But she compartmentalized his presence in her life. Even if he never became the interlocutor of her thoughts, when she left for Buenos Aires in 1926, he was, as always, at her side.

9

Globalizing Modernism

It was a long trip from Paris to Buenos Aires. In 1913, on that fateful journey when Nijinsky married Romola at the Iglesia San Miguel Arcángel, the Argentine capital lay more than three weeks from Southampton or Le Havre. The queen city of the River Plate, Buenos Aires was bursting at the seams, with immigrants from Spain, England, Germany, Russia, and especially Italy, the sounds of tango floating from the bars and bordellos along the waterfront, and the wide boulevards of a gracious European city inspired by Haussmann's Paris. In summer, flowers tumbled from balconies, and people sat out in cafés, while the theaters played vaudevilles and zarzuelas imported from Europe.

In 1908, an opera house fit for South America's grandest city opened its doors. Like its predecessor, it was called the Teatro Colón, for Christopher Columbus, and was European to the core.[1] The new Colón took more than twenty years and several European architects to build, and it was magnificent, Italian in style with splendid acoustics and an auditorium that seated 3,500 spectators.[2] Verdi's *Aida* inaugurated the new house, a choice that underscored its Italian orientation and artistic debt to Milan's Teatro alla Scala. Italian influence was just as evident in ballet. In 1883, only two years after its premiere at La Scala, Luigi Manzotti's grand spectacle ballet *Excelsior* was performed by a specially assembled Italian touring company; three years later Hippolyte Monplaisir's *Brahma*, another huge production led by Italians, followed.[3] With no permanent ballet troupe or affiliated school, the Colón imported its ballet masters and ballerinas from Italy and hired corps dancers from local studios.[4]

In 1913 the Ballets Russes made its debut at the Colón, the first of the wave of Russians who would transform ballet at the house. With more than a dozen works from its repertory, including nine by Fokine, Nijinsky's *L'Après-midi d'un Faune*, *Giselle*, an abbreviated *Swan Lake*, and the Blue Bird pas de deux, the season sent shock waves through the city's artistic community and intelligentsia. The company returned in 1917 with another season of forward-looking repertory that included *Firebird* and *Petrouchka*, both to music by Stravinsky, *Faune*, and several of Massine's early ballets. Meanwhile, at the Teatro Coliseo the Anna Pavlova company presented the first of several seasons that revealed another facet of Russian ballet. To those in charge of programming at the Colón it was abundantly clear that ballet was an art form in transition and that its future lay with Russians.

Until 1925 the Colón hired dancers as well as choreographers by the season. That year it established a full-time, permanent ballet company—along with similar troupes of singers and orchestral musicians—as part of a broad effort to raise the theater's artistic profile and professional standards. According to the Colón's historian Roberto Caamaño, the results were dramatic. In less than a decade, all three ensembles acquired the disciplined professionalism of "excellent organizations."[5] At the same time, the Colón made a concerted effort to build a prestige ballet repertory that was not only of high artistic quality but also aligned with recent currents of international modernism. In addition, the Colón sought the services of a "choreographic" director with broad experience in directing dancers, staging repertory, and creating works in keeping with the theater's new mission.

Inevitably, most of the Colón's appointments in the next ten years would come from the ranks of former Ballets Russes choreographers. The first, hired for the 1925 season, was Adolph Bolm, who had left the company in New York in 1917 to pursue a successful choreographic career in the United States. Bolm staged the first of the Colón's prewar Diaghilev works, including *Carnaval*, *The Polovtsian Dances*, *Les Sylphides*, and *Le Spectre de la Rose*, all credited to Fokine, and Bolm's own version of *Petrouchka* (which he had staged at the Metropolitan Opera in 1919 and in which he had danced the title role).[6] However, it was Nijinska, not Bolm, who transformed the Colón and its dancers.

Nijinska arrived in Buenos Aires in late April or early May 1926 and served as the Colón's choreographic director for the 1926 and 1927 seasons.[7] She brought to the job a unique set of qualifications and considerable cultural capital. She was widely recognized as a major choreographer, with an outstanding reputation as a creative artist, a broad knowledge of Diaghilev's modernist repertory, extensive teaching and staging experience, and a gift for developing dancers. In addition, she had spent years choreographing dances and movement for operas. "Nijinska's work," the Argentine critic Enrique Honorio Destaville has written, "left an enduring memory with the audience" and "had far reaching consequences."[8] For Nijinska, it was an appointment from heaven, a fresh start, far from the failures of the previous year. She arrived with her husband and her old friends Anatole Vilzak and Ludmilla Schollar, hired as principal dancers, as was Nijinska herself. The company, she told the management with her usual bluntness, consisted of "nothing but students . . . and there is a lack of principals and men who can dance."[9] But Nijinska was used to teaching students and had a particular gift for teaching men, and she could whip a disparate troupe of dancers into a powerful whole. It's what she had done at the School of Movement and in the wake of *The Sleeping Princess*, when her presence and drive had revitalized the Ballets Russes. Perhaps now, with the backing of the Colón, she could again have a company of her own. And so, speaking French with the odd Russian phrase, she set to work.[10]

Nijinska not only galvanized the dancers but also transformed the Colón's repertory. Bolm had been a charter member of the Ballets Russes and the originator of roles in some of its most memorable ballets. However, he took no part in revamping the Ballets Russes repertory: he danced neither in *The Rite of Spring* nor in Massine's early works. The "prestige" repertory he brought to Buenos Aires was Fokine's, and while this was certainly "modern" compared to the Franco-Italian repertory, it stopped short of the revolution of modernism. Bolm's own choreography, above all in works like *Krazy Kat* (1922), a jazz ballet inspired by George Herriman's comic strip character, may have been a milestone in the development of an American "art" ballet, but its reach was hardly international.

With Nijinska came the shock of European modernism. Two years earlier the journal *Martín Fierro* had called on Argentine artists to embrace the era's "NEW sensibility and NEW understanding" and thus discover in themselves "unsuspected panoramas and new means and forms of expression."[11] Although the journal ignored Nijinska's presence at the Colón (no doubt because she was a woman), this is exactly what she did during her two years there. Thanks to Nijinska, the Colón added new Diaghilev works to its repertory: her brother's *L'Après-midi d'un Faune*, *Le Train Bleu* (renamed *A orillas del mar*), *Night on Bald Mountain*, and *Les Noces*, performed at the Colón only four months after its London premiere.[12] She staged Petipa's Blue Bird pas de deux and *Les Rencontres*, one of her works for the Paris Opéra. She also revived several of her Theatre Choréographique works, including her Bach ballet, *Holy Etudes* (now retitled *Estudios religiosos*), *Le Guignol*, and *On the Road* (as *Momento japonés*), along with various divertissements, among them her chamber version of the *Polovtsian Dances*. She choreographed the dances for several operas, including *La Gioconda* and *La Traviata*, and two new ballets, El "Carillon" Magico, a series of commedia-themed episodes by the modern Italian composer Riccardo Pick-Mangiagalli, and Cuadro campestre (Country Scene), the Colón's first dance work by an Argentine composer (Constantino Gaito).

The following year, 1927, found her just as busy. In addition to reviving Night on Bald Mountain, Holy Etudes, and Les Noces, she restaged Les Impressions de Music-Hall and her own version of Daphnis and Chloë. She also choreographed three premieres: Pomona, to a new score by Constant Lambert; Ala and Lolly, to Prokofiev's Scythian Suite; and La Giara, to music by another modern Italian composer Alfredo Casella. She supervised (and in some cases revised) the Bolm productions of Les Sylphides and Petrouchka. Finally, she contributed dances to several operas, including Stravinsky's Le Rossignol and Rimsky-Korsakov's The Tale of Tsar Saltan, two Russian additions to the lyrical repertory, and a production of Euripedes' tragedy Phaedra.[13]

Nijinska left a deep imprint on the Colón's dance repertory. Musically, this was now dominated by living composers, while visually it bore the distinctive mark of Rodolfo Franco, the Colón's resident designer who created the scenery and costumes for virtually every production. With very few exceptions, the dancers were all members of the Colón's permanent company, and in both Pomona and Daphnis and Chloë the female leads were danced by future Colón ballerinas. In two years Nijinska refocused the repertory, shifting it to the Paris-centered imaginary of the Russian emigration. In so doing she not only expanded the circulation of works produced by the Ballets Russes, but also hastened the consolidation of those works into an international modernist canon.

Operas were programmed in winter at the Colón, ballets and symphony concerts during the spring season, which in 1926 ran from the end of August to November 28. However, the first glimpse of Nijinska's choreography came on June 15, with the premiere of Il "Carillon" Magico, paired with the short opera Cavalleria Rusticana. After a period of intense rehearsal, the first all-ballet program opened on August 29; the second followed on September 21 and the third on October 19, with each of the season's last five performances featuring Les Noces.[14] On the first bill was an expanded version of Holy Etudes, Faune (with Anatole Vilzak in Nijinsky's role and Ludmilla Schollar as the Chief Nymph), and two ballets that highlighted Nijinska's own gifts as a dancer—Le Guignol, a burlesque romance for puppets in which she "obtained a very great and deserved personal success,"[15] and Night on Bald Mountain.

The anonymous critic who wrote for *La Nación* was also taken with *Holy Etudes*, remarking on its stylized choreography and decorative harmonies, simplicity and originality.[16] His counterpart at *La Prensa*, after carping about Joseph Lanner's "vulgar" music for *Le Guignol*, expressed amazement at the "surprising progress" the dancers had made after only four months of work with their new director,

> above all taking into account the unfavorable conditions of their training, [with its] continual change of teachers and long months without study. . . . Bronislava Nijinska has done what she could to remedy these faults, and she has occasionally succeeded, thanks to her dedication and competence.[17]

He went on to praise the Nymphs in *Faune*—all company soloists—but felt that the sculptural choreography of *Holy Etudes* only revealed the poor discipline of the corps. He also commended Rodolfo Franco, who had painted effective backdrops for all four works, "with the greatest simplicity and no less poverty, for at the Colón the decorations are inferior in luxury and material quality to those of any revue."[18]

The second program, which opened three weeks later, was equally varied. It began with *Les Sylphides*, followed by *Cuadro campestre* to music by the Argentine nationalist composer Constantino Gaito. Based on stylized work movements, the ballet had a rural setting, a cast of reapers (led by Nijinska and Vilzak), and a succession of scenes in lieu of a plot—work in the field; repose; dances and loving couples; work resumes; it begins to rain, and the reapers exit.[19] After a symphonic interlude, Nijinska paired a divertissement of Spanish and gypsy dances to snippets of Verdi with her Theatre Choréographique ballet *On the Road*. The evening ended with *A orillas del mar*, a "ballet-sport" that was a version of *Le Train Bleu*. Nijinska reprised her role as the Tennis Champion, casting Vilzak as the sportsman hero and Schollar as the bathing beauty. Lacking a dancer with Anton Dolin's gymnastic skills, Nijinska simply dropped his role of Beau Gosse. A trio of Girls and an ensemble of twenty-four "Bañistas" completed the cast. Nijinska had thrown out most of the libretto's pantomimic detail and eliminated Cocteau's name from the credits.[20] Finally, Nijinska must have felt, it was her ballet.

Reviews of the program were lukewarm. The critic for *La Prensa* felt that Nijinska's choreography for *Cuadro campestre* was often at odds with the "spirit of the music" and was sharply critical of what he called the "heterogeneity" of the musical aspect of the program, which included "pieces unworthy of a theater of the category of the Colón."

> This fundamental flaw was evident in last night's program, which included numbers without symphonic musical merit. . . . We do not deny Bronislava Nijinska's great choreographic gifts, but one must confess that the musical merit of her programs sometimes recalls a variety program at a second-rate music hall.[21]

La Nación took a more positive view. Although its critic dismissed Leighton Lucas's music for *Momento japonés* as an example of "unpleasant modernism," he praised the "fine stylization" of Nijinska's choreography and "the excellent discipline the corps de ballet is acquiring."[22]

The great event of the season was *Les Noces*. It was a huge challenge, not only for the dancers but also for the chorus of singers, who triumphed magnificently, as did the soloists and the four concert pianists.[23] "More than in his other works," wrote the critic of *La Prensa*, "Stravinsky in *Les Noces* uses simple and new expressive means and methods to achieve emotional intensity—who can listen to the solemn and profound last scene without a shiver?"[24] *La Nación* had a lot more to say about the choreography. Nijinska, the newspaper's critic wrote, had animated the work's four tableaux

> with a real display of imagination and good taste. [Her creation] also breaks with many consecrated models of choreography. In lines and groupings that resemble gymnastic exercises and with the same rhythmic sense of the music, the dancers move, form human pyramids that are a miracle of grace, . . . moving on a stage in which a window and a door indicate the houses of the bride and groom and a platform with a door through which a bed appears and before which the final *fiesta* takes place. Meanwhile, from the orchestra pit surge the voices of a prodigiously varied rhythmic orgy that the dry, sharp timbres of the pianos and the drums highlight with extraordinary vigor. And the whole constitutes one of the most beautiful spectacles that we have seen and heard in recent times.[25]

The rest of the program could hardly measure up, although most of the criticism was directed at Jacques Ibert, whose music for *Les Rencontres* was judged to be "elegant, well orchestrated, impersonal, without any craving for novelty, . . . correct, too correct for a young artist."[26]

By the last performance on October 31, Nijinska was desperate to get home. "I work like a machine," she wrote in an undated diary fragment,

> to finish as soon as possible, so that the time passes faster, and I can go back to France. To start my OWN thing there, no matter how difficult it is, to be near my family, to give more time to the children, to work with them, to prepare them for life.[27]

It would be several years before she got to do her "own thing" in France. And despite her wish to spend more time with her family, she returned to the Colón in April 1927 "as teacher and choreographic director" of its permanent ballet company. With a salary of 2,000 pesos a month for seven months (500 more than the previous year), in addition to 4,000 pesos (up from 3,000) as the company's *primera bailarina*, it was an offer she couldn't afford to turn down.[28]

***

Once back in Paris in December 1926, she moved the family to a new apartment at 1 rue du Midi in Neuilly-sur-Seine. With money always a pressing concern, she went back to work for the Opéra, choreographing the dances in *Naïla*, a "lyric tale in three acts" about a pleasure-loving Persian prince who woos and then wearies of a humble girl, who goes mad, recovers her reason when he begs forgiveness, and finally dies in his arms. Jacques Rouché had paired the work with *Les Impressions du Music-Hall*, a ballet with music by Gabriel Pierné and a cast of foxtrot-dancing chorus girls, Dolly Sister look-alikes, a Spanish number, clowns inspired by the Fratellini brothers, a "big-boot" eccentric number for Albert Aveline, inspired by the comedian Little Tich, and a star turn for Carlotta Zambelli, the Opéra's long-reigning Italian *étoile*, wearing a skirt that fell away in petals.[29] It was one of Rouché's typical repasts—tasteful, French, and pleasantly modern.

For Nijinska the assignment was strictly work-for-hire. The idea for *Music-Hall* originated with the composer, who took it to Rouché, who then engaged Nijinska, probably as a replacement for Léo Staats, who had recently decamped to New York's Roxy Theatre.[30] Principal conductor of the Concerts Colonne, Pierné had already composed several ballets, including *Cydalise et le chèvre-pied*, a Zambelli favorite. His musical language was very French—"classical in form and modern in spirit," with a lightness of touch and tendency toward brevity.[31] He wrote out the scenario for Nijinska, and although it was barely legible, she must have liked what she read and the music she eventually heard,[32] as she soon restaged it at the Colón. Pierné was under no legal obligation to share his royalties with Nijinska, yet he agreed to set aside one-third for her in countries covered by the Société des Auteurs Dramatiques, a gesture that must have touched her.[33] After the premiere, he wrote to her about the ballet's "great success," while also thanking her for a "precious and remarkably intelligent collaboration." At the répétition générale, which took place on the afternoon of April 7, 1927, the audience applauded throughout the ballet, he reported, and "all the newspapers were enthusiastic save for *Le Journal* and *Le Matin*, which were very bad," saying that "our artists of the Académie Nationale would never outshine our stars of the Music-Hall."[34]

In fact, most critics were delighted by the ballet, which was witty and amusing, unlike the "lugubrious three acts of *Naïla*," which made *Music-Hall* seem "like a deliverance."[35] Neither an imitation nor a parody of music-hall entertainment, Pierre Lalo explained in *Comoedia*, this ballet "was . . . a transposition of reality into art."[36] André Levinson, of course, had little use for this "choreographic sketch," inspired by the "Cocteau-Satie-Picasso *Parade*." It was "insufficiently stylized," closer to pastiche than parody, "purer but . . . paler than the original." But there was also much to admire, including the "deliciously moving Girls" and clowns who alluded to "familiar themes" and were full of charm, while Zambelli's stage entrance in a dressmaker's box produced the "amused astonishment" one would expect. However delicious her performance, it was not the kind of role he believed she should play. "The illustrious ballerina who dismisses her *danseur* with a kick at one point believes it good to crown several decades of noble success with this tom-foolery, innocent in itself, but hardly compatible with the dignity of her profession and, above all, useless." Quite simply, *Music-Hall* did not belong on the stage of the Palais Garnier.[37] Although Levinson was *Comoedia*'s dance critic, he did not once mention the ballet's choreographer.

He was not alone. A number of critics erased her name from their reviews, even if they spent time describing and even praising her choreography. Only in a review by Jane Catulle-Mendès, the sole woman among the critical brotherhood, does Nijinska receive her due. Wrote Catulle-Mendès in *La Presse*:

> Mme Bronislava Nijinska has arranged the choreography of this unexpected ballet at the Opéra with a great deal of invention and without ever exceeding

the limits imposed by such surroundings. How refreshing to see our stars of the Academy of Dance yield their classical knowledge for the jokes of the music-hall and to fully succeed. Mlle Zambelli has lost none of her nobility and added to her grace. M. Aveline was an extremely funny clown, while . . . Mlle Bourgat . . . wiggled with spirit. In the final ensemble the "Musical Clowns" flawlessly executed a burlesque, twirling movement. The success was considerable from one end of the performance to the other.[38]

During these months in Paris, Nijinska planned the season at the Colón. She wrote to Edition Russe de Musique asking for the scenario of Prokofiev's ballet *Ala and Lolly*.[39] She met a few times with the composer Constant Lambert to talk about *Pomona*, which he was anxious for her to choreograph.[40] She jotted down music for ballets that she may have considered staging, including Bela Bartók's *The Wooden Prince* and two works staged at the Opéra for Ida Rubinstein—Roger-Ducasse's *Orphée*, and Florent Schmitt's *La Tragédie de Salomé*.[41] Clearly, Nijinska was responding to criticism about the quality of her musical choices while thinking of works that reflected the idea of modern lyric theater that Rouché was producing at the Opéra.[42] In Buenos Aires, she had spent hours in the studio and danced in every performance, working virtually non-stop. Now she was choreographing one (very) short ballet and the dances for an opera, and she wasn't performing at all. Although she was edging toward forty, the age when most dancers begin to think about retiring, she was still strong and uninjured, with an appetite for tearing up the stage.

Her idleness weighed on her, and she filled the empty hours with her diary.[43] On January 16, in a long entry, she mused about writing a book about ballet that would simply be about dance—something she had been thinking about for years but hadn't started writing—then confessed that her tongue was "clumsy" and it was only through movement that she could speak. She thought about writing a book about Vaslav in the form of a letter that would enable her to engage and even "doubt" his beliefs. In many entries her mood is black. On February 9 she writes: "Life has withered and people slowly fall into despair. Some shed tears; others gnaw and tear at everything like wolves." On February 22: "I miss the lost past. It was full of everything, the knowledge of what I wanted and endless resources of creative ideas." On March 3 she hit a new low:

To work and only to work—because everything around me is death. Work grinds my sorrow; work makes my wishes and fantasies come true; work gives me the certainty that I have everything I want. Because I know how to want things only in art. It is my passion, my childbirth, my riches, all my pleasure. The day it is taken away from me . . . will be the day my life ends. In the same way that Vaslav's life was over when he was left without art.

Finally, on March 30, a week before *Music-Hall* premiered, Nijinska sailed for Buenos Aires on the SS *Conte Verde*, arriving some two weeks later.[44] "Separation from my family for almost a year," she recorded laconically in her diary, failing to note that her husband, Nicholas Singaevsky, was accompanying her. They would not arrive back in Paris until Christmas.

Another busy season lay ahead. Rehearsals started in May, and she spent the last days of April auditioning dancers. Two were dropped and had to be replaced, resulting in a "fine troupe" of forty-two people, slightly larger than the 1926 company.[45] Men were in short supply, so she had brought along Eugene Lapitzky as her partner and Serge Unger for secondary roles, while Singaevsky danced in the corps. By May 10 she was rehearsing every day. Meanwhile, a problem was developing with the "first dancers" hired by the Colón—Boris Kniaseff and Nina Kirsanova—who were so bad, she told her mother, that just to look at them made her teeth ache. After a meeting with the director, the Colón agreed to dismiss them. "I do not even pity them as human beings," she added, "because they are troublemakers."[46] Nijinska made a number of attempts to secure principal dancers from Europe, including Vera Nemchinova, Felia Doubrovska, and Pierre Vladimiroff, but neither they nor Ludmilla Schollar and Anatole Vilzak were willing to come.[47] So, with the exception of Nijinska herself, the Colón had a company without foreign stars.

In several respects the year's ballet programming was more adventurous than in 1926, revealing a strong curatorial hand. As before, she choreographed a ballet by a contemporary Italian composer that premiered during the opera season—Casella's *La Giara*—while presenting eleven ballet evenings during the Colón's "spring season." *Les Noces* returned to repertory, as did *Holy Etudes* and *Les Sylphides*. She revised *Petrouchka*, staged a new version of Ravel's *Daphnis and Chloë*, and choreographed the dances for Stravinsky's opera *Le Rossignol* and Rimsky-Korsakov's *The Tale of Tsar Saltan*, both directed by Alexander Sanin, whose path would often cross Nijinska's in the next several years. Even if ballet was not featured as prominently during the opera season as the previous year (she told her mother that the opera people were "incredibly jealous"),[48] she received good notices, and subscriptions to all four ballet programs were sold out weeks before the season began, which "really pleased" the Colón's management.[49] By late August more than 60,000 pesos' worth of tickets had been sold, and "the entire city" was talking about the ballet.[50]

The first of the premieres, Constant Lambert's *Pomona*, took place on September 9. A story of seduction and deception from Ovid's *Metamorphoses*, *Pomona* had multiple scenes, a detailed narrative, and mythological subject matter—all of which ran counter to Nijinska's vision of a contemporary ballet. But as Lambert's most recent biographer, Stephen Lloyd, suggests, it may have been her sympathy for Lambert that led her to propose his new project to the Colón.[51] Both, after all, had been badly used by Diaghilev, and Nijinska must have been touched by the composer's loyalty. There had been talk that Anton Dolin, who had left the Ballets Russes, would mount *Pomona* in Paris. But money for the production had fallen through, and by May 20, in response to a cable from Nijinska, Lambert wrote:

> I was enchanted by the idea of production when I thought it would be you doing the choreography, but now I do not regret that the production has been abandoned because, to tell you the truth, I have no confidence in Dolin's taste (his divertissements in London are terrible), and I do not like the idea of *Pomona* being mounted in a week. . . .
>
> I continue to hope that you will mount *Pomona* in Paris. What are your projects now, and is this a possibility?[52]

On July 5, Lambert thanked her for sending a check for £40. He then goes on to report about the Ballets Russes season in London. *Romeo*, he writes, was mounted five times. Unfortunately, cuts were made in the balcony scene and more in the finale and Balanchine's silly entr'acte was added. Still, *Romeo* always has a good success.[53]

Once rehearsals got underway in late July, Nijinska found that she had to supervise pretty much everything connected with the production, including the sets and costumes, which Rodolfo Franco was designing.[54] Despite all her efforts, which included changes in the libretto, the ballet was not a critical success. Lambert's score was considered old-fashioned, its modernism poorly assimilated, "empty and impersonal."[55] "It was saved," wrote the critic of *La Prensa*, "thanks to an elegant and graceful choreography, although without novelty."[56] His colleague at *La Nación* commended the interpretation as well, singling out the principals—Leticia de la Vega in the title role,

Dora del Grande as Diana, and Blanca Zirmaya as Flora—as well as the company as a whole. "Here, as elsewhere, the corps de ballet demonstrated that it is fast becoming a disciplined and homogeneous body, full of talent, capable soon of giving us an ensemble of the first order."[57] The hit of the evening was *Petrouchka*, in which Nijinska as the Ballerina scored a personal triumph. Although Eugene Lapitzky could not efface memories of Adolph Bolm in the title role, Nijinska's staging—credited as a "choreographic revision" of Fokine's original—succeeded in bringing the Shrovetide carnival magnificently to life. Equally inspired was Rodolfo Franco's "handsome" decor.

> With a distinct and personal concept and vision, Franco has illustrated the work in accordance with the coloring of the score: the drop curtains, very original and modern, and the vision of the Russian city, do honor to the young artist and to the theater.[58]

Even if *Pomona* proved too literary for local tastes, Nijinska was elated by how well her opening program was received. "It was our first performance yesterday," she wrote to her mother on September 10:

> The audience was packed with people, and there wasn't a single empty seat. And I have never seen a more stylish audience. There were numerous problems and difficulties before the performance, but the problems were solved, and everything went off well. The performance was a success, and there are many good things written in today's newspapers. All the newspapers sing my praises for *Petrouchka*, especially for the remarkable dancing parts. Zhenia [Lapitzky] danced leading roles in all the ballets and fared well; the same is true for Seriozha [Unger]. . . . So the boys are awfully happy. . . .
>
> I am terribly tired because apart from the dancers there were 50 people from the chorus who took part in *Petrouchka* as supers. They turned out to be difficult to work with. But the performance itself went well. The same program plays tomorrow. But I have already started to rehearse the next program. . . . My costume in *Petrouchka* is stunningly beautiful and far prettier than the Diaghilev one.[59]

Two days later, she told Eleonora that the president of the Republic had attended a matinee and pronounced the performance a delight.[60]

The second program, which premiered on October 11, included *Les Sylphides*, *Petrouchka*, *Ala and Lolly*, and *Les Impressions de Music-Hall*. With two new works, one choreographed from scratch, it was challenging on several counts, from the constant pressure of rehearsals to the absence of administrative support. As she explained to her mother,

> There is no director of ballet here so Kolia helps me with everything. Apart from the ballets he dances in . . . , Kolia writes all the . . . programs and keeps an eye on the costumes and rehearsals. So he works from morning till night. In this short period 5 new ballets, 5 old ballets, and about 20 operas with dancing have been staged.[61]

Music-Hall had turned into a huge production, with an expanded orchestra and cast, an attractive new decor, and handsome costumes.[62] Nijinska had high hopes for the ballet, and she wasn't disappointed. The audience loved it. "The work consists of four numbers," wrote the critic for *La Prensa*, speaking of the music:

> "Chorus of Girls," a pastiche full of irony of the "jazz band" whose sonorities are gracefully evoked by the orchestra; "The Eccentric," an amusing gloss of circus music; "The Spanish Number," of the most conventional Hispanism, which has the merit of parting company with the tambourine of Montmartre; and "Musical Clowns," whose eccentricities are suggested with good taste and very French "wit" in a colorful and picturesque orchestral atmosphere.

The critics noted many felicitous moments in the staging: the arrival of the ballerina star (Aurora Gibellini) in a hat box carried by two grooms, the Bataclan-style sister number performed by Leticia de la Vega and Dora del Grande, Blanca Zirmaya as a Spanish dancer, and the acrobatic antics of the finale. Nijinska had not appeared in the Paris Opéra version of the ballet. Now, she took over Albert Aveline's role as "The Eccentric," yet another in her gallery of male characters, and won praise for it.[63]

Although *Impressions de Music-Hall* was clearly the audience favorite, it was a musical trifle compared to *Ala and Lolly*, the evening's other premiere. Commissioned in 1914 by Diaghilev, who then rejected it, the ballet had a complicated scenario by the Russian poet Sergei Gorodetsky and music by Prokofiev, both later modified by the composer. Because of a mix-up on the publisher's end, the score arrived late, a delay that can only have added to Nijinska's anxieties and very possibly to the mixed reviews of the choreography.[64] As the critic for *La Nación* wrote, "Th[e] music was much liked, more so than the choreography, which although not without novelty and good intentions, did not attain a similar unity in its realization."[65] Nijinska had eliminated the character of Chuzhbog, the evil god of darkness and nemesis of Ala and her knightly hero, transforming the ballet into something along the lines of the *Polovtsian Dances*, another large-scale work that evoked a primitive and barbaric world. *La Prensa*'s critic was more positive. Deeply impressed by the score, he felt that Nijinska had indeed caught its essence and had danced with "vigor and elegance."[66] But this was hardly a ringing endorsement, and she never revisited the work.

For Nijinska, who appeared in all four ballets, the new program was very physically demanding. After the dress rehearsal she wrote to her mother that she had done something to her leg and that it hurt a lot, adding, "I don't know how I am going to dance tomorrow." Trouper that she was, she got through the performance, but the pain was searing, and she thought she had injured either a calf muscle or her Achilles tendon. She went to the doctor the next day and learned to her relief that the injury wasn't serious. However, she didn't have time to rest the leg.[67] The stresses of the season were unremitting, and with a workday that began at 10:30 and ended at midnight, she was bone-tired, as she admitted to her mother in letter after letter. On October 20, she told Eleonora that she still had eight dances to choreograph for "a drama play"—*Phaedra*—and also had to rehearse *Les Noces*.[68]

For the dancers, most of them still in their teens, the demands were beyond anything they had ever experienced. "We were spending the whole day in the theater," Matilde Ruanova, one of three sisters in the company, told the Argentine arts writer Carlos Manso.

> At nine in the morning we were at the Conservatory in white tunics. At 10:15 we had rehearsals with Nijinska and the corps de ballet in pink tunics. The two costumes were obligatory. Discipline at the Colón was very strict. From the rotunda [where rehearsals were held] we went to the stage. All day, every day it was like this—for us there were no Saturdays, Sundays, or holidays. We did not see the light of day; we did everything inside the theater. Our mother looked after us at all times; she brought lunch and made us food. . . . Such was our fervor to study, to develop, to fulfill our vocation.[69]

On October 28 came the last premiere of the season, *Daphnis and Chloë*. This was a ballet that she had revised for Anton Dolin in 1924 and now restaged with Fokine's libretto. Knowing how prickly Fokine could be, Nijinska did not claim the choreography as her own, nor did she ascribe it to Fokine. However, as the ballet's "director of choreography," she must have reshaped it to the talents and needs of a company very different from the Ballets Russes. The music critics were over the moon. They knew their Ravel, but *Daphnis*, with its "ardent lyricism, ample melodic ideas, generous, expressive, and poetic, so authentically French," was new to them. They were thrilled by the "magnificent virtuosity of the instrumentation—diaphanous, luminous, mysterious, or sparkling," and by the "infinitely delicate effects and shadings" of the composer's palette.[70] The work was performed by full chorus (which Diaghilev had often eschewed) and with handsome new settings by Rodolfo Franco. "The interpretation," wrote the critic of *La Nación*, "can be counted among the most successful that we have been offered during the Colón's present ballet season, under the intelligent direction of Bronislava Nijinska, and overall represents a very fine effort that was received with well-deserved applause."[71]

Performances of *Phaedra* followed, and in late November the season's last three ballets. All opened with a repertory work (*Pomona, Holy Etudes*, or *Les Sylphides*) and ended with *Les Noces*, with four or five divertissements sandwiched between them. On November 21, at a gala performance in honor of the mayor of Lima, *Les Impressions de Music-Hall* added to the éclat of the program. The revival of *Les Noces* was a grand occasion, and the critics used it not only to hail the Stravinsky work as a masterpiece but also to register yet again the milestone it represented for the Colón's dancers and chorus. It was a collaborative effort of the first order and a huge success for the conductor, the singers, the four pianists, and Nijinska.[72] Buenos Aires may have been far from the ballet metropoles of Europe, but it was infinitely more receptive to the modernism of *Les Noces* than London.

***

Nijinska was deeply attached to her mother. She wrote to her in Polish, in the untutored intimate language of her childhood, now full of Russianisms, grammatical errors, and usages only they understood. Eleonora was her *mamusia*, the mummy who would always comfort her, the tower of strength who bore every travail and made possible her career as a choreographer. But *mamusia*, who was diabetic, was now ailing, and Nijinska was frantic with worry.[73] She begged her to buy whatever she needed, cable if she needed money, take care of her health. When are you planning to go to Vichy, she asks, so she can send more money for the journey. She has just seen in a newspaper the address of a Russian *pension* there; maybe it will be cheaper. As soon as she arrives, she has to see a doctor to find out which waters she should drink. She wishes *mamusia* had spent more time there and wonders if the treatment brought any relief. What is the diagnosis? What did Dr. Goldenshtein say? She tells her not to think about death, that she will live to a ripe old age. She urges her to write, rues the infrequency of the mails, dependent on steamship schedules, and reports the arrival of letters. Over and over she repeats how much she misses her mother and covers her with kisses.

The children, all but absent from Nijinska's diaries, come into focus in her letters. If they misbehave, she tells Eleonora not to shout at them but just punish them: for instance, don't let them go to the cinema. She's happy to hear they are going to the dentist and can imagine Levka screaming when the dentist pulled out his tooth. The children should spend more time out of doors, not just sit at home in the dark flat; they need sun to stay healthy. The picture of the children that Eleonora sent from Vichy made her very happy, and she carries it with her all the time. If Levushka is writing so well in French, why hasn't he written to her in more than two months? She thinks it's better to send him to the boys' school rather to the other one. She loves them so much and misses them. And Kolia sends them kisses as well.

The other theme of these letters is money. Like so many emigrants who go abroad to work, Nijinska scrimped on herself in order to send funds home. She and Kolia moved from one rented room to the next in search of lodgings that were heated, close to the theater, and inexpensive. She bought two pairs of silk tights, noting they were almost as expensive as in Paris. Pointe shoes cost 100 francs a pair, but since she always wore a new pair on stage it was an unavoidable expense. She bought a spring coat (she didn't have one) and had two dresses made (one black, one brown) that looked really well. A few times she and Kolia spent Sunday afternoon in the country, but otherwise life in Buenos Aires was all work. She took her responsibilities as family breadwinner seriously and was proud of her ability to earn. "This year," she told her mother on June 23, "I have enough money, so don't deny yourself anything." She wired money home almost as soon as she arrived in Argentina: 2,000 francs on May 3; 1,500 on May 20 (she had hoped to send 2,000 but still hadn't been paid her full salary); 5,500 on September 1 (which included 500 francs for Eleonora to buy clothes for herself); 6,000 on September 30 (to cover school fees as well as household expenses).

However much Nijinska scrimped, money was tight because she was paying off debts.

On May 26 Zenon wrote to her from London, begging her to send money:

[T]hey are after me, and I don't know how to extricate myself. Moreover, I have to pay interest, and I am out of work. That is the whole truth. I am in trouble and have spent all I had.[74]

She sent him twenty English pounds, equivalent to more than a thousand pounds in today's money, which he acknowledged. But it was not enough.

I have to pay the interest, and if the debt keeps piling up, I will be stuck with it forever. I am asking you, even begging you to send me the full sum so I can repay Vasilii.[75]

On July 30, along with her monthly stipend to Eleonora, she sent twenty pounds to Savitskii, another creditor. "It makes more than 3 thousand francs," she told her mother,

so I sent 7 thousand francs today. I have already paid Savitskii 8 thousand francs, almost twice as much as I owed him, but he asks to be paid in English pounds, and this way I am paying him *twice* as much as I borrowed, but don't tell this to anyone. As soon as I pay off Savitskii for the costumes I will send money to Nina. This contract is good in the sense of getting out of my debts a little.[76]

On October 10, just before the premiere of the second program, she told Eleonora that she has saved some money and deposited it in a bank, but she still has to pay her London debts.

I have already sent 14 thousand francs, and there is still another 14 thousand to pay back. If it weren't for these debts, all would be fine.[77]

After her difficulties at the Paris Opéra, the Colón was a breath of fresh air. She had a relatively free hand in choosing repertory, dancers who were young and eager, a generous salary, and no competitors: for the first time since the

School of Movement she was in charge of a company that was largely her own creation. In photographs from the period she is surrounded by girls barely out of their teens. Identically clad in tunics, headbands, ballet slippers, and socks, they gaze at her with awe; she is their leader and artistic mother, and they cherish her. She was demanding and strict. "No one dared to contradict her in anything," remembered Angeles Ruanova.

> If we sprained our ankle ... instead of telling us to rest, she would say: "Jump, ladies, jump! . . . ," and, of course, she was right. Only by continuing the exercises and keeping the area moving would the pain go away. But who knew that then?[78]

Maria Ruanova, the sister who went on to an international career, also experienced Nijinska's "tough love" and the drive that lay behind it. "For me," she told Carlos Manso,

> Madame Nijinska, with her discipline, made possible that awareness of dance among us. She was as strict as she was maternal, and she never ever tolerated weakness, even when dancers were in pain or hurt, although then she would go up to them with enormous sweetness.[79]

In Nijinska the members of the Colón's young troupe glimpsed the single-minded discipline and uncompromising determination that separated the professional from the student or recreational dancer.

The veneration that many felt for her is evident in a January 1929 letter from Blanca and Leticia de la Vega, who were then dancing at Rome's Teatro Reale. "Dear Madame Nijinska," they wrote in Spanish,

> you can't imagine how great a desire we have to see you ... and how much we have felt the absence of your direction at the Teatro Colón during the last season, which was so unpleasant for us.
>
> The ballet season was a disaster under the direction of Mr. [Boris] Romanoff [sic]. The public did not accept him as choreographer so nobody came to the Theater; moreover, he was a very bad person; with his intrigues and wickedness he continually tried to hurt people who take a straight line in their behavior and did not approve of his actions, unworthy of a theater like ours; finally, there were so many incidents that the season barely ended; now, happily, everything has changed.[80]

No institution is exempt from politics, let alone an opera house employing hundreds of people and dependent on government funding. Nijinska did her best to keep her head down; she lived in the studio, went from class to rehearsal and rehearsal to performance, and seemed oblivious to everything except her dancers and her work. Charles Lindbergh may have flown across the Atlantic to universal acclaim in May 1927; the *Principessa Mafalda* may have sunk, with scores of casualties, off the coast of Brazil, in October—one would never guess it from Nijinska's letters home or from the very occasional entries in her diary. They seemed to live in a cocoon, she and Kolia, isolated from the world of public events and insulated for the most part from the Colón's politics. Still, she could not remain totally detached. At one point she remarks that the "engagement in intrigues is so high here, they can't even imagine a theater artist . . . occupied only with his own work and interested only in that work."[81]

Initially, Nijinska had anticipated leaving Buenos Aires in November 1927. But the performance dates kept getting changed, and eventually the season was extended to November 27. She spent several weeks frantically looking for a ship that would get her back to Europe in time for Christmas, and finally found the MS *Augustus*. It was a brand-new and very fast Italian liner that would reach Barcelona in only thirteen days. "We are going on the Augustus," she wrote to her children in mid-November. "We leave on December 3rd and will be in Barcelona (Spain) on the 16th and in Paris on the 17th." The 15th, she reminded them, was their Babushka or Granny's birthday.

> She is 70 years old. Don't forget to congratulate her. If I can, I will send you . . . a check so you can get Babushka a present. . . . Praise God that I will soon be with you.[82]

On December 19 she was in Barcelona. It was cold, she wrote in her diary, "winter after the equator." Chaliapin was singing at the Gran Teatre del Liceu, and his presence plunged her into despair. She slept only a couple of hours and then headed with her luggage, train tickets, husband (although she doesn't mention him), and a magazine to the station. The cold chilled her to the bone.[83]

Nijinska's time at the Colón was a critical moment in her continuing development as a choreographer. It gave her the opportunity to revisit a number of her old works and to invent several new ones, independent of Diaghilev and with the human and artistic capital to work on a large scale. It was a good job, but she was unwilling to commit to it on a long-term basis. It was too far away from her family and the heartland of the Russian diaspora she called home. "I dream of the moment I will be back home with you," she wrote to her mother in September. A few days later, returning to the theme, she added, "There is no way I am going to sign a contract here next year. . . . I will stay in Paris and maybe the Lord will help to earn there what is necessary for our family."[84] And so she settled in for the next several years in Paris. One by one her Colón ballets disappeared, remembered only by her dancers. But in terms of the Colón's long-term goals she had succeeded brilliantly. In two years she had created a modern, professional ballet ensemble unrivaled until the 1940s anywhere in the Americas.

10

Les Ballets de Madame Ida Rubinstein

Once back in Paris, Nijinska fell ill. Not until March did she feel like her old self.[1] By then a new project was underway, one that paid well and promised to bolster her position in Paris. This was Les Ballets de Madame Ida Rubinstein, a company founded by a celebrity patroness, who asked Nijinska to direct it.

Born in 1883 in Kharkov to a wealthy Jewish family,[2] orphaned and raised in St. Petersburg, enamored of the arts, and inspired by Isadora Duncan, Ida Lvovna Rubinstein danced briefly but unforgettably for the Ballets Russes. She was a discovery of Fokine, who used her icy, exotic looks to create the legendary temptresses of *Cléopâtre* (1909) and *Schéhérazade* (1910) as well as the *Salomé* (1908) that scandalized St. Petersburg. In 1911 she struck out on her own, commissioning genre-defying spectacles on which she spared no expense and in which she always starred. *The Martyrdom of Saint Sebastian* was the first and most memorable; with its perfumed beauty, stellar collaborators, and transvestism (Rubinstein herself played the saint associated with gay men), it made her a star in her own right and a patron of the first magnitude.

Her productions offered a gallery of larger-than-life stage figures, characters imbued with the mystique, as one of her friends rhapsodized, of an "ancient Amazon" who had hunted lions in Africa, kept monkeys as pets, wore pyjamas of cloth of gold in her desert tent, and commissioned works of poetry and music from her "jewels"—Debussy, Ravel, Gide, Valéry, Honegger, Milhaud, Claudel, and a host of other French artists.[3]

As a performer, Rubinstein defied easy categorization. She trained as an actress but dreamed of becoming a concert dancer along the lines of Maud Allan. Fokine was her first ballet teacher. Later she studied with Rosita Mauri, a former *étoile* of the Paris Opéra trained at La Scala. Still, as nearly every critic pointed out, she was not a ballet dancer. Tall, thin, and angular (Cocteau called her "the great ibex of the Jewish ghetto"),[4] with long, expressive arms and a pliant torso, Rubinstein was the antithesis of the traditional ballerina. Yet, in 1921, at the age of thirty-eight, she posed for the photographer James Abbe as an Anna Pavlova look-alike in pointe shoes and a long

Romantic tutu.[5] Rubinstein actually danced on pointe in *Artemis Troublée* (1922), a one-act mythological ballet conceived by Bakst for the Paris Opéra, and at a few charity performances even assayed Pavlova's signature solo, *The Dying Swan*.[6] What was it about Pavlova that so obsessed Rubinstein? Her iconic status or the outward trappings of a ballerina role that Rubinstein could only inhabit imaginatively?

In 1928, Rubinstein decided that the time had finally come to live her dream. She turned to Alexandre Benois to create not simply a ballet for her but a whole company, staffed by Russians and offering a platform for the young generation of émigré talent emerging from the Paris studios of former Maryinsky ballerinas. Benois was an old Petersburger, deeply cultured and cosmopolitan, a painter, stage designer, book illustrator, critic, editor, and historian of art, who brought to the stage the fantasy and imagination of a *passéiste*, someone who delighted in the past. His designs for *Les Sylphides* and *Petrouchka* have never been bettered, and it was at his behest that Diaghilev staged *Giselle* in 1910. Benois spent the war and post-Revolutionary years in Russia, where he sat on the repertory committee of the former Maryinsky Theater, designed the country's first stagings of *Petrouchka*, and served as curator of Old Masters at the Hermitage from 1918 to 1926, when he and his family emigrated. However, he was already spending long periods of time abroad. In 1924, for the Paris Opéra, he designed the first French production of *Giselle* since the 1860s. He was the art director of Abel Gance's cinematic epic *Napoleon*, which received its gala premiere at the Opéra in 1927, and designer of two other productions that year—Rimsky-Korsakov's opera *Le Coq d'Or* and Rubinstein's *L'Impératrice aux Rochers*. By the late 1920s, Benois had made a place for himself in high French theatrical culture.

He also stood at the nerve center of the émigré arts and theater community. Nina Tikanova, the dancing daughter of a literary and artistic émigré family, recalled how much she and her brother, the future ballet critic André Shaikevitch, "adored going to Alexandre Benois' 'Tuesdays,'" weekly receptions that dated back to Petersburg days and "now gathered under the welcoming eye of his wife, Anna Karlovna, and their daughter Atia, many friends and personalities.... I was by far the youngest of all the guests, and I didn't dare mingle in the discussion, but I listened to the talk with delight."[7] Benois was a charming, generous, and warm-hearted host, and in the spring of 1928 he told Tikanova about his involvement in a new enterprise, a "ballet company created by Ida Rubinstein and endowed with exceptional financial means."[8]

In 1927, Benois recorded in his diary the many evenings he spent with Rubinstein listening to the gifted, conservatory-trained pianist Marcelle

Atoch. First they listened to her play the Schubert-Liszt "Soirées de Vienne," selections from which became *La Bien-Aimée* (The Beloved), a ballet set in the Romantic period. Then they moved on to Bach, whose French Suites inspired *Les Noces de Psyché et de l'Amour* (The Wedding of Psyche and Cupid), a mythological ballet conceived in eighteenth-century style. They listened to Debussy, and in July, when Rubinstein's garden was blue with hydrangeas, to Ravel's *Tombeau de Couperin*.[9] Ravel would figure in the new enterprise with *La Valse*, which Rubinstein was the first to produce in a major venue, and *Bolero*, which she commissioned. Benois also had a hand in shaping Stravinsky's score for *Le Baiser de la Fée* (The Fairy's Kiss), based on themes of Tchaikovsky. "Do you like the idea of fixing up Uncle Petya's music and making something new of it?" Benois asked the composer.[10] Rubinstein's largesse ($6,000) made the idea extremely attractive, and of the fourteen musical sources that Benois proposed Stravinsky ended up using more than half.[11] In addition to his contributions as Rubinstein's "idea" man and inhouse scenarist, Benois designed all the productions.

Although Rubinstein had the final say about repertory, the new enterprise more closely reflected Benois' retrospectivist taste, building upon unrealized projects that he had long contemplated. Among these was the idea of a Bach ballet, which Benois had suggested to Diaghilev in 1913, but which the latter abandoned when he dismissed Nijinsky. In his memoirs Benois describes the researches that lay behind the unrealized ballet— playing through suites, figures, preludes, and other compositions, first on his own in St. Petersburg, then with Diaghilev, Nijinsky, and Walter Nouvel in Baden-Baden, where they chose the music for the ballet.[12] This approach, which Diaghilev later applied to any number of "time-traveling" scores, now guided Benois' work for Rubinstein, with modern composers enlisted to patch together and orchestrate the music—Darius Milhaud for *La Bien-Aimée*, Arthur Honegger for *Les Noces de Psyché et de l'Amour*, and Stravinsky for *Le Baiser de la Fée* (although, unlike the others, he created a genuinely original work).

By February 1928 Nijinska had signed on as Rubinstein's choreographer. "Esteemed Ida Lvovna," she wrote:

> I was so pleased to receive your letter concerning our agreement about my work for your company and to know that you have approved it.
>
> For my part, I wish to confirm once again that I assume responsibility for creating five ballets for your repertory and for your company. I must complete this work within six months, from the 1st of March to the 1st of June

1928 and from the 15th of August to the 15th of November 1928, for a fee of 10,000 French francs per month.[13]

In fact, Nijinska choreographed six ballets for the Paris season, with a seventh premiering later in Monte Carlo. An eighth, *David*, was staged by Léonide Massine.

In the spring, Nijinska began recruiting and auditioning dancers. Frederick Ashton borrowed five pounds to finance a trip from London and was thrilled when Nijinska accepted him.[14] She signed up dancers who knew her work well—Anatole Vilzak as the company's leading man and his wife, her old friend Ludmilla Schollar, as its *première danseuse*, along with her former Kiev students Anna Vorobieva (who had been dancing in Sofia, Bulgaria, after stints in Poznan and Rome), Eugene Lapitzky, Serge Unger, her husband Nicholas Singaevsky, and one of the English members of Theatre Choréographique, Joyce Berry. She also made the rounds of Paris dance studios. At Nicolas Legat's she recruited Nina Tikanova, at Olga Preobrajenska's Nina Verchinina, at Lubov Egorova's Alexis Dolinoff—all "Russians of Paris," Tikanova's phrase for those who had come to the city as children and received most of their training there. She wrote to a teacher at Warsaw's Wielki Theater School, who sent three young graduates—Roman Jasinski, Yurek Shabelevsky, and Ludovic Matlinsky. There were "old-timers" (again, Tikanova's term) from the Imperial Theaters; "renegades" from the Diaghilev company; "Soviets," meaning recent émigrés; and dancers from countries all over Europe and even a few from the United States.[15]

The troupe of fifty or so dancers that reported for rehearsal on August 1 was thus a precursor of the "international" companies that flourished in the 1930s. It was a group, moreover, that brimmed with talent, youngsters who had already had quite a bit of performing experience and two who would leave a mark as choreographers on the dance world in years to come—Ashton and David Lichine (still dancing under his real name, David Lichtenstein). Rubinstein, reminisced the dancer-turned-designer William Chappell many years later, "had beautiful manners, she knew every single nationality of every person in the company [and] addressed them in their own language."[16] Anna Ludmila, a soloist, was paid 2,000 francs a month for rehearsals, 2,500 francs when performances began, and 3,000 francs on tour.[17] Corps dancers received considerably less—in Ashton's case 1,000 francs as rehearsal pay, then worth about £20, too little, as he discovered, to afford a bath.[18] However, the women received four pairs of pointe shoes a month, for which they routinely overcharged Rubinstein. And everyone had six-month contracts. For Nina Tikanova, "it was heaven, paradise."[19]

Nijinska worked the polyglot company hard. "Nijinska is a wonderful woman more wonderful than I had even imagined, her efficiency is overwhelming & her knowledge & vitality something quite super-human & inspiring," Ashton wrote to Marie Rambert.

> She gives a brilliant class, very difficult & never dull & in doing it one realises over & over again that the best system of dance training is obviously Checcetti (I can't spell his name, disgrace!). Her arms are I should say entirely based on his & her bar is the same except that she introduces various sorts of developees before the petit battement which one afterwards does in the centre & she very seldom makes us do rond de jambes en l'air. Nearly all her steps in the centre are jumping, she demonstrates the whole time & smokes incessantly her own jump is wonderful & gives one some idea of what Nijinski's jump was like in quality. She is a beautiful dancer & a dancer above all her ugliness.

He went on to describe the grueling schedule, which left little time for anything outside the "village" life of the Salle Jouffroy, where the company rehearsed:

> We have two groups for classes and they take place alternate weeks at 9 am & 10 am after them we rehearse till lunch & back at 3 or 4 till dinner & then back at 9 or 10 till 11:30 or 12 pm. Generally one doesn't rehearse more than twice a day sometimes 3 as she takes people in groups till the ballet is finished & then calls full rehearsal. . . . But I have been going 3 times a day as I have been understudying.[20]

There was no marking, no walking, Roman Jasinski remembered. "We worked full-out every rehearsal every day."[21] By late August *The Swan Princess* was done, and the company was working on *La Bien-Aimée*.

Meanwhile, Rubinstein was taking her annual exotic holiday. On August 11 she wrote to Nijinska from Algeciras, on the letterhead of SY *Arpha*, the oceangoing yacht owned by Walter Guinness, Rubinstein's longtime lover:

> I cannot tell you how much I miss our work and how ashamed I am to be on holiday, thinking about how you are now devoting everything to

our undertaking. On Saturday I received a telegram from Mlle. Régnié [Rubinstein's secretary], who tells me that you are pleased and that everything is going well. I so want this creative work to bring you only happiness.

Rubinstein assures Nijinska that she has been doing her exercises "every day", but she isn't jumping because the sea has been rough. "I go through our dances every day from memory, and until now I have forgotten nothing; but, naturally, it is impossible to dance."[22] From the Straits of Gibraltar the *Arpha* headed east across the Mediterranean toward Greece. On August 21, Rubinstein wrote again:

> I was overjoyed to receive your letter yesterday and deeply moved. How I should have liked to have seen *The Swan Princess*, which Mlle. Régnié says is marvelous. And I want so much to work with you again.

She then turns to a few production details:

> I completely agree with you about the gates in the second scene. I have written to Mlle. Régnié, asking her to get [Orest] Allegri to go immediately to the Salle Jouffroy . . . and . . . widen the gates as much as possible. As to the length of the costumes (for the Boyars), I have written to Mlle. Régnié asking her to talk this over with Muelle [the costume house]. As regards the Ryndas [bodyguards of the tsars in the Muscovite period], I certainly think they could hold the icons. So, please do not change anything in your staging. I shall ask Alexander Nikolaievich [Benois] to order the necessary icons when I get back. I think that your choice for the Schubert/Liszt is very good. May I, once again, thank you from the bottom of my heart for your devotion to your work.[23]

Rubinstein may have busied herself with details. But ever the grande dame, she left the nitty-gritty of production to others.

Nothing could be more different from Diaghilev's hands-on management style or Nijinska's perfectionism. However much Rubinstein spent, however professional her collaborators, she herself remained a distant star contemplating what she had set in motion until it came time to step into the theater of her imagination. But that lay months away. For the time being the dancers took class and rehearsed. From Preveza in northwestern Greece, Rubinstein sent Nijinska one of many effusive telegrams; another followed from Spain

Plate 1 Vadim Meller, *Fear*, 1919.

Plate 2 Easter greeting from Nijinska's students, 1919.

Plate 3 Vadim Meller, *Mephisto Waltz*, 1920.

Plate 4 Alexandra Exter, poster design for Theatre Choréographique, 1925.

Plate 5 Alexandra Exter, *Night on Bald Mountain*, 1925.

MADAME IDA RUBINSTEIN

Plate 6 Ida Rubinstein as the Swan Princess, 1929.

Plate 7 Expression of gratitude from the Opéra Russe à Paris dancers, 1930.

Plate 8 Poster, "Bailes Rusos Nijinska," Teatro Nuevo, Barcelona, 1933, with cover art by the dancer Rudolph Andriassoff.

Plate 9 Yury Annenkov, *Les Comédiens Jaloux*, 1932.

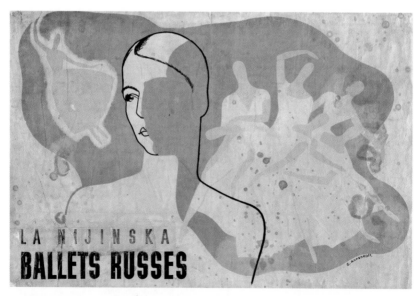

Plate 10 Yury Annenkov, poster for "La Nijinska Ballets Russes."

Plate 11 Polish National Ballet, Teatr Wielki-Opera, 1938.

Plate 12 Teresa Roszkowska, *The Legend of Cracow*, 1937.

Plate 13 Boris Aronson, *Pictures at an Exhibition*, 1944.

on September 12: "Rejoice that I will soon see the beautiful result of your work. Best wishes to all. Affectionately, Ida Rubinstein."[24] She returned to Paris about ten days later.[25]

Nijinska's letters to Rubinstein have disappeared, but a draft of one, probably from early September, survives in her archives. "Dear Ida Lvovna," she writes,

Thank you for your kind letter and telegram. The whole company thanks you for your attention and sends greetings. They want me to tell you that they are all waiting for you.

Our work is progressing. In the mornings from 9 until 11:30 there are two classes. Rehearsals are from 11:30 until 12:30, then from 3 until 5, and in the evenings from 9 until 11:30. Everyone is working well and enjoying their work. All the dances in *The Swan Princess* have been choreographed. *Schubert/Liszt* I shall complete tomorrow or Monday. The peasants came out well and also the "Grisettes" and the students. In *Swan* [Nadejda] Nicolaeva is still rather weak. But she is working, so all that is necessary will probably come later.[26]

On September 3, for Nijinska's name day, the dancers wrote her a greeting that over forty signed, beginning with Ludmilla Schollar and ending with Serge Unger, with Joyce Berry carefully transliterating her name into Russian and Nicolas Goulak d'Artemovsky writing his rather grandly in Latin script.[27] Another signatory was George Sari, who published an article about his Rubinstein experience in *The American Dancer*. He noted that everybody had to wear regulation practice wear: black tunics with "flesh tights" and shoes for the women, black tights and white shirts for the men.[28] Nijinska, he wrote,

differs from most ballet producers in this respect: she takes several bars of music and rehearses the few steps or movements dozens of times, until they are practically perfect. Then she takes another few bars, and keeps adding, bit by bit, until the entire production has reached a degree of perfection. . . . [O]thers (Massine, for example, and Mordkin and Pavlowa) usually rehearse the whole act of a ballet right through, so that by the time the end is reached the beginning has been forgotten. . . . In Nijinska's way it sometimes takes almost two weeks to finish one Ballet, but in the long run it proves to be much quicker, for although the others finish the ballet in a few days, they must then expend weeks and weeks to get it perfect.[29]

The company's most ambitious project lay ahead: *Le Baiser de la Fée*. This was a forty-five-minute ballet conceived from the first as the most important item in the season's repertory. The ballet was inspired by Hans Christian Andersen's "The Ice Maiden," a tale set in the snow fields of Switzerland where Rudy, the hero, is kissed at birth by the terrible Ice Maiden and then stolen from her to grow up among mankind. Now a goatherd, he falls in love with Babette, a rich miller's daughter, and is about to marry her, when the Ice Maiden returns to claim him. Stravinsky purged the story of most of its narrative. What remained was an allegory with echoes of *Apollo* and *La Sylphide*: a boy, separated from his birth mother, is marked by destiny for a higher calling. As a young man, he falls in love, but like James in *La Sylphide* abandons his fiancée on their wedding day, unable to resist the supernatural call of the Fairy, who carries him off to her eternal dwelling place among the glaciers.[30] In mid-August, Stravinsky told Benois that he had changed the title to *Le Baiser de la Fée* in order to emphasize the ballet's allegorical meaning, and that he would write a brief preface to the score "saying that I relate the fairy to Tchaikovsky's Muse . . . for the Muse similarly marked him with her fatal kiss, the mysterious imprint of which one senses on all the works of this great artist."[31] The tension between the allegorical and the representational, the transcendent and the here-and-now was never fully resolved.

Unfortunately, Stravinsky did not begin composing the music until July and only finished the score in October, nearly two months after the September 1 deadline[32] and little more than a month before the November 27 premiere at the Paris Opéra. For whatever reason he was of two minds about sharing it with his collaborators. As he wrote to his publisher, Gavril Païchadze, on October 17:

> I hasten to share with you the joy of finishing the music for the Fée. . . . I am sending the whole end of the piano score to you in a few days for engraving, not for familiarizing Ida with it, or Nijinskaya or Benois. . . . It is necessary for people such as they are—not particularly initiated—that I play the music for them myself. Therefore I ask you not to let anyone look at it before my arrival. Nijinskaya will howl, but do not pay any attention to that.[33]

As always, Stravinsky was not being entirely candid. According to Stravinsky's biographer Stephen Walsh, the composer had been dispatching individual sections of his music to her from Switzerland, where he was spending the summer with his family, and in late August or early September had conferred with her in Paris at the offices of Edition Russe.[34] Stravinsky was in closer touch with Benois, who on September 9 relayed to Nijinska a long list of the composer's directives about the first two scenes. In Scene 1, the Prologue, at rehearsal 8, the first female spirits appear; at rehearsal 11, additional ones; at rehearsal 14, four male spirits; at rehearsal 15, six others; finally, at rehearsal 27, four spirits in silver bring in Rubinstein as the Fairy. When the curtain rises on Scene 2, a Swiss village festival, the stage is full of people dancing. At rehearsal 63, there is a Tyrolean dance for the men; at rehearsal 64–67, a wedding procession; at rehearsal 70, Rudy and five companions appear; at rehearsal 73–74, the Tyrolean "yodelers"; finally, at rehearsal 78, Babette and her friends.[35] By mid-October, Rudy and Babette had become the Young Man and his Fiancée, although some critics, including *Le Temps*' Henry Malherbe, continued to use the characters' original names.[36]

For Nijinska, after the triumph of *Les Noces*, Stravinsky's behavior must have seemed like a slap in the face. And it can only have been a source of enormous frustration to her that the music for Rubinstein's all-important pas de deux with Rudy at the end of Scene 3 and for the Apotheosis arrived so late. Clearly anxious, Rubinstein pleaded with Nijinska to lend her the music for an hour so she could show the choreography to Benois, adding that the pas de deux was "very beautiful."[37] Stravinsky did not share Rubinstein's sanguine view of the choreography, although as he admitted in his autobiography, the ballet's weaknesses were partly his own fault: he had not made time to attend rehearsals.

> I found some of the scenes successful and worthy of Nijinska's talent. But there was, on the other hand, a good deal of which I could not approve, and which, had I been present at the moment of their composition, I should have tried to get altered. But it was now too late for any interference on my part, and I had, whether I liked it or not, to leave things as they were. It is hardly surprising in these circumstances that the choreography of *Le Baiser de la Fée* left me cold.[38]

Unhappily for Nijinska, Stravinsky wasn't the season's only musical laggard. Ravel had accepted what he thought would be an "interesting" commission—orchestrating pieces of *Iberia* by Isaac Albéniz. But then, on holiday in late June with his friend Joaquín Nin, he discovered that the music was already spoken for—the Spanish composer Enrique Fernández Arbós had orchestrated it for a ballet that La Argentina was planning to stage the following year as *Triana*. Ravel was mortified. Weeks passed. Finally, Nin received a short letter in which Ravel announced that he was working on a somewhat unusual work. It had "no form as such, no development, no or almost no key changes, [and] a Padilla-like theme"—José Padilla was the composer of songs like "Valencia" and a regular contributor to the Moulin-Rouge. This was *Bolero*.[39] Ravel had not just saved the day but composed an entirely new work, one that proved a hit with critics and would have a long dance afterlife. However, it wasn't finished until mid-October, around the same time that Stravinsky turned in the score for *Baiser* and Nikolai Tcherepnin finished orchestrating the music for *Nocturne*.[40] With all three ballets premiering in the same week, rehearsals during the last month must have gone on non-stop.

The press seemed happily oblivious. The advance publicity focused on Rubinstein, the fact that the nine or ten ballets that she was planning to give were all totally new, and the impressive list of living composers she had commissioned either to compose or to orchestrate the music. Journalists vied with one another for superlatives. For P.-B. Gheusi in *Le Figaro* she "incarnated the noblest conscience, the prestige of a fervor unequaled in the mystical realization of a calling alien to all mediocrity": this didn't mean much, but it sounded good, especially when accompanied by an exotic photograph or two.[41] Nijinska never got to talk to the press, but there was usually a sentence or two about "her incomparable talent and imagination" and the "wonders" she had worked in Monte Carlo and "on the stage of the Opéra itself," and it must have pleased her that she, not her brother, was now the "celebrated dancer and choreographer."[42] *VU*, the new French pictorial weekly, sent André Kertesz to photograph rehearsals, and although Nijinska is nowhere in sight, one senses her presence in the strong working bodies, uniform practice gear, and stylized hands and épaulement of the intensely focused dancers.[43] Rubinstein is absent as well. Alone or with her partner, Anatole Vilzak, she rehearsed in the privacy of her own mirrored studio at 7 Place des Etats-Unis, a townhouse on the leafy square where the King of Egypt had a palatial home and the Vicomtesse Marie-Laure de Noailles held court among the surrealists.[44] Very occasionally, Rubinstein appeared at the Salle Jouffroy, arriving in her Rolls-Royce and alighting on a red carpet, accompanied by Nijinska, Singaevsky, and Mlle. Régnié. She wore an immense ermine coat and a floor-length dress by Worth, this at a time when skirts barely grazed the knees. The company applauded. She was "thin, very tall, and a bit stooped, with very long feet in flat shoes," Tikanova recalled.

[S]he still retained traces of her past beauty, but a facelift had tightened her skin and left her features frozen. The weary expression of her half-closed eyes did not soften her now angular profile nor did the artificial red color of her hair. . . .

A quarter of an hour later she left just as theatrically, even giving Nijinska a very faint smile. The company applauded again, but remained dumbfounded and even troubled by what it had just seen.[45]

Nijinska may have been a hard taskmaster where the company was concerned, but Rubinstein was another story. She often canceled rehearsals, pleading illness, fatigue, a chill, or other business. "To my distress I cannot rehearse today," she wrote in one undated note. "I will await you on Monday at five o'clock. And we will make up what we have lost."[46] With the season's first performance only days away, Rubinstein pleaded with Nijinska for another private rehearsal. "I am a little fatigued today and think that you will agree that it is better for me not to tire myself," she wrote.

> I telephoned Anatolii Isoifovich [Vilzak] not to go to the Opéra but to come here, to my house, at 1:45 today to rehearse *Boléro*. I will send a servant to the Opéra to wait there for the five men and bring them here. . . . Don't say no, and be at my house at 1:45. I kiss you warmly, I. R.

Of course, Nijinska couldn't say no, but it must have been galling to have all one's hard work—and the talent and hard work of so many others—depend on the whims of a grande dame who wanted only to step into one or another spectacular vision of herself.

Stage rehearsals were off-limits to the press, but *L'Intransigeant* managed to get a photograph of Rubinstein in *Bolero*, surrounded by men and wearing a conventional practice tutu, and another of Nijinska's "well-disciplined" corps of female dancers at rest in their regulation tunics, headbands, and pointe shoes.[47] One enterprising reporter, Jean Lasserre, slipped into the Opéra pretending to visit a singer and from the presidential box observed Nijinska conducting a rehearsal of *La Bien-Aimée*. Rubinstein was nowhere to be seen—"too tired, in a bad mood, who knows?"—but Nijinska made a deep impression:

> Mme Nijinska, indicating a movement, crossed the stage. This dancer, magnificently expressive and intelligent, is in street clothes deprived of grace.

Her legs are too muscled, her breasts too small, and her severe face has no softness. Yet when she dances by what miracle does she become a magnificent animal? Like a greyhound, so beautiful galloping, so awkward and gauche on a leash.

On the piano Mme. Nijinska has placed an enormous file of annotations on loose sheets, sketches, and diagrams. She consults them before giving the least direction to her dancers.[48]

Ashton told his biographer David Vaughan that Nijinska "used to analyse the music in great detail in advance and begin by giving the dancers their counts."[49] Stravinsky's pronouncements to the contrary, she was definitely "initiated."

On opening night the Paris Opéra was "packed from floor to ceiling," noted the *Daily Telegraph*, with a brilliant audience that "recall[ed] the days of pre-war prosperity," an evening that critic Louis Laloy pronounced not only "magnificent" but fully "worthy of the Opéra."[50] P. J. S. Richardson, who came from London to cover the season for the *Dancing Times*, was astonished at the throng at the fourth and final performance. "It appeared to me," he reported,

that every available seat in the huge building was occupied, and during the intervals the crush in the Foyer was very great. It was astonishing the number of stars of the dancing firmament whom I saw exchanging notes on the ballets they were witnessing. M. Diaghileff was there, pleased with "David" but doubtful of the others; M. Svetlov was obviously comparing what he had seen with the "grands ballets" of earlier days.... I saw M. Staats, the old ballet master of the Opera, exchanging notes with M. Aveline, the premier danseur, and M. Jean Borlin, the former leader of the "Ballet Suedoise" [sic] was another interested spectator, whilst M. André Levinson paced up and down.[51]

The reviews were many and mixed, with the music critics coming down especially hard on the season's "assembled" scores. Pierre Lalo in *Comoedia* found the choice of Bach pieces in *Les Noces de Psyché et de l'Amour* "disconcerting," and was surprised that a "celebrated violin solo" had been orchestrated. Milhaud had made a "bad job" of *La Bien-Aimée*. "The orchestration that Mons. Darius Milhaud has inflicted on Schubert's music," Lalo asserted, is ugly, heavy, and vulgar. Schubert is not a great inventor nor a great virtuoso when it comes to the orchestra. . . . But his instrumentation has charming color and poetry, an exquisite sense of the value and expression of tone. Nothing resembles him less than this big, heavy, and confused noise.[52]

The critics went wild over *Bolero*. For Emile Vuillermoz in *Excelsior* it was the "great musical success" of the opening program; for Jane Catulle-Mendès in *La Presse* "a ravishing musical bibelot—almost nothing . . . but perfect."[53] Henry Prunières, who covered the season for the *New York Times*, felt that Ravel had outdone himself. The composer, he wrote,

loves to toy with the hazardous, and difficulties always lure him. The problem he has set himself seems impossible of solution: it is apparently to write a dance composition on a single theme, repeated time and again for nearly twenty minutes without the least variation, and yet to succeed in sustaining interest from start to finish, to arouse the emotions of his hearers and finally to stir them to a high pitch of enthusiasm at the finale. This is what Ravel has done by a miracle of orchestral virtuosity.[54]

Several critics called attention to the decor. André George felt that the sordid tavern scene was the most original of Benois' sumptuous tableaux.[55] Louis Laloy described the setting as "a Spanish-style tavern, but fantastic." There was an

oversize table and lamp, and in the shadowy recesses the silhouettes of muleteers and smugglers, acclaiming the dancer in a black bodice on the table, who, in her sheath of light, without lascivious writhings or provocative gestures indicates the movement of the dance that transports her; she does not seem to see them; without swirling shawls or flashy jewels, she attends only to the call of the music, which is the soul of the dance. The fascinated groups clap their hands, spring to life, and spin around the table always dominated by this tall figure whose inner energy creates the rhythmic twisting that magnetizes the space.[56]

For many, this was Rubinstein's finest performance of the season.[57] In certain respects the ballet was an outgrowth of Nijinska's version of *The Polovtsian Dances*, with its focus on a lone dancing woman encircled by lustful men. However, in *Bolero* the scale is far grander and the erotic charge more potent, magnified by the sheer number of men transfixed by the central figure, beating out rhythms, and wild with desire. The table, so closely associated today with Maurice Béjart's 1960 version, seems to have been Nijinska's invention: in her papers is the postcard of a gypsy woman dancing on a platform in an Andalusian patio.[58] When Nijinska revived *Bolero* in the early 1930s, she claimed the principal role for herself, a sign that it held personal resonance—both as memory and desire.

Unsurprisingly, given Stravinsky's stature, much ink was spilled on *Baiser*. The most influential critics registered disappointment, in part because they disliked Tchaikovsky but also because they were dismayed, as Prunières tactfully put it, "to see such a genius muffle himself . . . in another's mask."[59] The composer must have cringed when he read Pierre Lalo's review in *Comoedia*. "The music of *Le Baiser de la Fée* is one of the most disconcerting things to hear," he began. "It is benign, benign, benign, as Molière says in *The Imaginary Invalid*, and it is sober, sober, sober. No sparkle, no bright color, no stroke of force" recalling the tremendous things of *The Rite* and *Les Noces*.[60]

About Nijinska's contribution there was little dispute. Nearly every critic took note of the strong, disciplined troupe she had created in less than four months, a "magnificent company of dancers," in the words of Emile Vuillermoz, that performed with "amazing fire and ardor."[61] It was a company, moreover, bursting with talent. Along with Anatole Vilzak, a "cavalier who sacrifices himself to his partner" (i.e., Rubinstein) and Ludmilla Schollar, an "exquisite soloist," with elegant turns and *staccato* "beaded from her witty pointes," a number of dancers caught André Levinson's eye, including Alexis Dolinoff, "a carnival devil who pirouettes with passion." However, the "revelation" of the opening performance was the "young Anna Ludmilova"—as the American Anna Ludmila (*née* Jean Marie Kaley) had been further Russified—above all in her duet with Rupert Doone in *Les Noces de Psyché et de l'Amour*, where the sweep and "winged ease" of their jumps seemed to "rush through the . . . listless action" like a refreshing wind.[62] The venerable Russian critic Valerian Svetlov, now writing for an émigré newspaper published in Riga, added Unger and Lapitzky to the list. Svetlov went on to praise Nijinska's "colossal work" both as a choreographer and a teacher, noting the company's excellent discipline and very short rehearsal period.[63] The non-stop rehearsals had paid off.[64]

Still, the reviews make clear that the choreography was "uneven," as Jane Catulle-Mendès wrote in *La Presse*, even if it "revealed passion, spirit, and originality."[65] *Bolero* was certainly a high point. The "popular" scenes of

Baiser were another. In *Le Temps*, Henry Malherbe called them "wonderful in their spirit and liveliness" where Nijinska had "exercised all her mastery and captured our minds."[66] (Nearly twenty years later critics recalled the "triumph" of Nijinska's "peasant dances" when reviewing Balanchine's version of the ballet.[67]) Levinson, who called Scene 2 "a Tyrolean rhapsody," thought it was Nijinska's greatest success in the ballet:

> The heavy and jovial double-time . . . *Schuhplattler*, a jumping dance in flat shoes, prelude to the harmonious swirling of the waltz movement. The costumes of the country people in their Sunday best are thoroughly charming, and the idea of the gossips, sitting on a bench, stamping impatiently as they watch the others dance, is a thoroughly happy one.
>
> I liked the "grand pas" and the pas de deux in the mill scene . . . less. Here the frenetic Nijinska tones down her instrument, by order one would think, so constantly is the refined difficulty and ingenious combination avoided. . . . The grotto of stalactites of the eternal dwelling place . . . makes us dream of *La Maladetta* and . . . Carlotta Zambelli. . . . For this attempted resurrection of a ballet of yesterday . . . fails for lack of a star, a *prima ballerina assoluta*.[68]

As Levinson well knew, Nijinska was stuck with Rubinstein. However, it is quite possible that by the time the music for Scene 4 arrived Nijinska had run out of creative steam. Nevertheless, it is hard to imagine her choreographing a scene along the traditional lines that Levinson seemed to expect. She did not view ballet as a hierarchy with classical style and the ballerina as the summit. Indeed, to the extent that her own body served as the matrix of her most personal choreographic work, this was the antithesis of Levinson's aesthetic idealism. She believed that classical forms had to evolve and that ballet was a living art. She was a creative artist, Levinson a critic haunted by a past she had no interest in resurrecting.

Nevertheless, as even Levinson recognized, she could choreograph in conventional classical style. Reviewing the first program in *Candide*, a literary journal, he was kinder than usual toward Nijinska. Speaking of *Bolero*, he wrote:

> The choreography, simple but intense, is by Mlle Nijinska, as is the choreography for the "rococo" ballet and the "romantic" ballet. The latter two compositions are of a classicism of the highest order, when it is not reduced

to the means, so to speak, of the star. In these circumstances, the opportunities to shine are dispersed parsimoniously among a young, quite skilled,
and very well rehearsed troupe principally composed of Russians. I will
only cite the "faux-Russian" name of Mlle. Ludmilova, an unknown who
made a stunning debut.[69]

Like *Bolero*, *The Swan Princess* allowed Rubinstein to shine. The ballet had
music by Rimsky-Korsakov from his opera *The Tale of Tsar Saltan*, staged
the previous year at the Teatro Colón with dances by Nijinska. Now she
reworked the music into what became one of her favorite ballets. Vuillermoz
called it a "choreographic paraphrase" of the opera, with the adventures of
Prince Guidon summarized in a few scenes. "What remains," he wrote,

> is only the . . . episode of the transformation of the swan into the young
> princess who marries Guidon, now king of a mysterious city risen mirac-
> ulously from the ground. . . . [T]he spectacle is magnificent. Through very
> simple means . . . , Benois has realized effects of astonishing grandeur and
> poetry. . . . And Nijinska's choreography—always freer and more original
> when it comes to a holiday scene—is worthy of its setting.[70]

Raoul Brunel in *L'Oeuvre* described the transformation scene that astonished
Vuillermoz—the revelation, little by little, of a "wondrous" city of palaces,
followed by "magnificent *entrées* of numerous characters," all in preparation
for Rubinstein's arrival in a gown covered with pearls made by the couturière
Jeanne Paquin. With its "dazzling cascade of dances inspired by Russian folklore," the ballet had a huge success.[71]

Henry Malherbe in *Le Temps* was as rhapsodic as his colleagues. "The
spectacle," he wrote, "is of the greatest splendor."

> It delights the eye, captures the soul, and wins over the spirit. Never
> has Mons. Alexandre Benois risen to such sweeping and brilliant
> evocations. . . . Mme. Nijinska has again touched the public with her
> strong-minded, canny, and impassioned intelligence. The choreography of
> *The Swan Princess*, at once precious and direct, remains her masterpiece.
> Through the lines of the human body, she has composed architectural fig-
> ures of a strange and penetrating harmony.[72]

Valerian Svetlov also remarked on the great beauty of the groupings and their patterns in space and noted that Nijinska had taken a big step forward in linking individual groups with the overall idea of the ensemble. Her choreography, he concluded, was a modern response to classical dance.[73]

Another critic lurked in the audience—Diaghilev. He attended all four performances of the Rubinstein season, checking out the competition: just before Christmas the Ballets Russes was to open its first season at the Opéra since 1922. On December 18, after most of the reviews had appeared, the Russian émigré journal *Vozrozhdenie* (Renaissance) published an interview with him about the Rubinstein enterprise. He was not kind: "Apart from [Massine's] *David*, . . . all the other works were a complete shambles, without a single moment of creative imagination or any fresh thought." He was especially cruel to Rubinstein, with her "hunched figure" and "hopelessly bent knees": "the total confusion of her classical spasms made the secondary, but competent ballerina of her troupe appear a heroine of the old, traditional adagios invented half a century ago." Finally, he questioned the entire premise of her classical efforts or "undisguised pastiches" as he calls them. "When the classics are a 'restoration of the past,'" he asserted, "not only must one not safeguard them, but on the contrary, one must further their destruction, since it is a poison that can infect the organism,"[74] an iconoclasm that did not wholly fit the Diaghilev who had resurrected *The Sleeping Princess*. He was far nastier in his letters to Serge Lifar. After the opening performance he wrote:

Let me begin with Ida. The house was full, but there was a good deal of paper about, mostly her friends. Not one of us, though, were given seats, neither myself nor Boris [Kochno], Nouvel, Sert, nor Picasso. . . . The whole thing was astonishingly provincial, boring, and long-drawn-out, even the Ravel, which took fourteen minutes. It's a big company, but totally lacking in experience: they were just making fault after fault and seemed not to have the slightest notion of ensemble. . . . The best dancer turned out to be Rupert Doone, the little Englishman we both know. And then, in the middle of the ballet, something really wonderful happened, for a certain gent in an open pink shirt . . . suddenly appeared borne triumphantly on his colleague's arms, and began dancing *something that vaguely resembled a classical variation*: it was Unger, yes, Unger![75]

A few days later Diaghilev was back at the Opéra for the premiere of *Le Baiser de la Fée*. "Igor's ballet," as Diaghilev called it, inspired another stream of invective.

> It's difficult to say what it was meant to represent—tiresome, lachrymose, ill-chosen Tchaikovsky, supposedly orchestrated by Igor in masterly fashion. I say "supposedly," because it sounded drab, and the whole arrangement lacked vitality. . . . Bronia showed not the least gleam of invention, not one single movement that was decently thought out. As for Benois' décor, it was like the sets at the Monte Carlo Opera House. . . . The whole thing was stillborn.[76]

Diaghilev was more than a little envious of Rubinstein's wealth and the opulence of her productions, at one point referring to her company as "the Jewish ballet." "We've got to prove to this bourgeois crowd how immeasurably superior we are, in spite of the fact that our sets weren't painted yesterday [and] our costumes aren't quite so fresh." Particularly irksome to Diaghilev was the fact that Rubinstein was dancing "to full houses, every seat *bought and paid for*."[77]

After the third performance he wrote another long letter to Lifar. *Nocturne*, which the critics universally dismissed as inconsequential, he somewhat liked, although he found Tcherepnin's arrangement of the music "simply shocking." As for *The Swan Princess*, it was a "bad sort" of *Firebird*, with a set "that must have come straight from the *Casino de Paris* plus a postcard or two."

> The changes aren't bad, but why the Smolny nunnery should rise from the bottom of the sea passes understanding. . . . Ida did more dancing in this than in any of her other ballets. She appeared dressed like a Pavlova swan, specially got up for some Moulin Rouge performance (her bodice one mass of false diamonds, and her wings all covered with spangles). . . . Everyone's cursing and disappointed—except, it appears, Bronia, who keeps on telling Ida she's a genius.[78]

For the dancers the "Ida problem" was demoralizing. Nina Tikanova recalled the first stage rehearsal in which Rubinstein took part:

> We danced uneventfully the first three episodes of *La Bien-Aimée*. In the fourth Ida Rubinstein was supposed to appear to Schubert, interpreted by

Anatole Wilzak. Gathered around the stage, the whole troupe waited. . . . On one of the waltzes, Wilzak rushed passionately toward someone making her entrance with a grand jeté in a romantic tutu. . . . Horrified, we all turned away. The sight of Ida Rubinstein, lifted by Wilzak, dangling like wet linen, with her stooped back and poorly stretched legs, exceeded our most terrible apprehensions. Sweat poured down her forehead and tears from our eyes. . . .

After months of unremitting work in which many of us had put our hearts and all our strength, the dancing of our "boss," reducing our efforts to nothing, was a disappointment hard to endure.[79]

For the company's "young hopes"—Tikanova, Nina Verchinina, and Klavdia (or Claudia) Lotova—the experience was crippling. Rubinstein brooked no competition, so her ballets gave talented youngsters few opportunities to grow. In a sense the dancers themselves hardly mattered. Despite her enormous wealth, Rubinstein never sent them bonbons, had a buffet set up on days when rehearsals ended at midnight, gave a post-performance cast party, or invited them to her home.[80] They existed merely to frame her and give material substance to her fantasies of self-creation.

As Levinson later remarked, "never has munificence . . . been accompanied by such a total absence of artistic disinterest. . . . Mme Rubinstein has consecrated some twenty-five years of her theatrical life solely to the glorification of herself."[81] In *Excelsior*, Emile Vuillermoz took her to task in unusually strong terms:

After discreetly inviting her to make a professional examination of conscience, must the critic then loudly tell Mme. Ida Rubinstein that her obstinacy in reserving for herself the best role in each of her ballets and her impertinent contempt for the elementary technique that she should possess to justify this diabolical perseverance, removes from her ballet season a big part of its artistic significance?

One can accept an error in casting but not a bias of this sort. How can an *animateur* of this stature not understand that her glory and personal success would be far more solidly assured if she had the wisdom of confining herself to roles in keeping with her abilities, such as the one she takes most correctly in Ravel's admirable *Bolero* instead of compromising her prestige and her authority by foolishly trying to pass as an imitator of Zambelli?[82]

The novelist Colette summed up the problem succinctly. "Madame," she wrote in *Candide*, "you are not a dancer."[83]

Once the Paris season was over, the company headed to Brussels and the first leg of a European tour—three performances at the Théâtre de la Monnaie that were an enormous success. Then it was back to Paris where Nijinska met individually with the dancers, renewing their contracts and in some cases promoting them, and also giving classes.[84] Then, after the holidays, an even bigger company set off for Monte Carlo.[85] Here, Nijinska would finish choreographing *La Valse*, which premiered at the Théâtre de Monte-Carlo on January 15, 1929. The Monte Carlo audiences were enthusiastic. But since the reviews were filed before the premiere of *La Valse*, the controversial ballet left no critical traces.[86] Nijinska herself was far from happy. "You cannot imagine what a horror the costumes and decorations are for Ravel's *La Valse*," she wrote to a friend.

> [N]owhere have you seen such meanness and lack of taste. The choreography gets lost in them all, that is, it takes on a completely different meaning—painful to look at. "Ida" has gone to Paris—she is making new costumes. I don't know if it is possible to save them from the awful scenery—I am sick about it—especially as in itself the ballet worked very well. In Monte Carlo our season had a very big success. We will probably be there next year.[87]

Today, she continued, "S. Diag. and his company arrived in MC." Nijinska fled to nearby Menton "to avoid them and not to upset him."

> They say that he "hates" us very much and has vowed to destroy us. I feel sincerely sorry for him, and it is a shame given his obvious sense. He is a big boy, but about rivals he turns into a petty shopkeeper. He reckons as enemies all those who work in art in and for itself. The creation of any theater is unbearable to him.[88]

In Vienna, where the company traveled next, Rubinstein gave several interviews, conducting them in German, French, and Russian, offering her views on a wide range of topics. She told *Der Tag* that she had "special affection" for "classic and mythological materials," adding that she had commissioned a new ballet from Honegger and another from the very young émigré composer Nicolas Nabokov, and was considering still another commission from the German composer Paul Hindemith.[89] "I believe in the modern artist," she asserted in *Neues Wiener Journal*, and strove to give such artists "an opportunity to advance."[90] When Nijinska arrived a day later, she told *Die Stunde* that "Ida Rubinstein is a great artist and a wonderful woman, full of enthusiasm for the cause she serves."[91]

There were only two performances, and Ravel conducted at both—*Bolero* on February 22 and *La Valse* two nights later—receiving tumultuous applause.[92] Nijinska's choreography for *Bolero* was considered "brilliant," testifying both to her taste and to a "fine sensitivity for the aesthetics of order in space." About *La Valse*, critics felt that the choreography did not correspond to the music but that the work was the most artistically interesting of the season. There were no waltzing couples, no Biedermeier setting; apart from Rubinstein's solos, only "floor-covering clusters of rhythmically convulsing bodies" and costumes that glowed fantastically.[93]

Milan's Teatro alla Scala was the next stop. Five performances were scheduled for the two-week season. The dancers were ecstatic: rehearsing in one of the theater's "lounges," dancing on the steeply raked stage, absorbing the "artistic treasures" of Italy—nothing could have been more exciting.[94] The Italians, alas, did not share their enthusiasm. Audiences thinned with every performance, staying to the end only because of *Bolero*.[95] *Le Baiser de la Fée* was given only once, which enraged Stravinsky,[96] and the reviews were almost uniformly negative. About *La Valse*, which also received only one performance, the critics had less to say mainly because Ravel's music wasn't new. *L'Ambrosiano* found some of Nijinska's "choreographic combinations" architecturally interesting while *Il Corriere della Sera* described the stage as a "strange Hellenic palestra where masses of dancers form and dissolve . . . into statuary groups. Dancing alternates with sculpture: a modern rhythm marks the time for synchronous and harmonious movement." Because of the contrast with the music, the critic concluded, this "gymnastic spectacle" could never be fully satisfying.[97]

Three performances followed at the Real Teatro di San Carlo in Naples, where audiences were warmer and critics more receptive. From there the company returned to Paris for another season in May. With three of the season's four dates coinciding with the Ballets Russes season at the Théâtre Sarah-Bernhardt (May 21–June 12), Rubinstein was placing her efforts in direct competition with Diaghilev's.

For Nijinska, Paris would be the crucial test for *La Valse*. This was the major event of Rubinstein's season, the first theatrical performance in

Paris of a work conceived in 1920 for the Ballets Russes, then turned down by Diaghilev with the terrible words: "Ravel, it is a masterpiece . . . but it is not a ballet."[98] Ravel himself described the music as "a sort of apotheosis of the Viennese waltz which I saw combined with an impression of a fantastic whirling motion leading to death. The scene is set in an Imperial palace around 1855."[99] Although *La Valse* had yet to be performed in Paris as a theater piece, the music was already well known as a concert work. Most Paris dance critics were actually music critics, and they had definite ideas about how the ballet should look.

Nijinska had her own ideas. She moved the setting to the present, eliminated Ravel's scenario, and had Benois design knee-length flapper dance dresses—sheer, yellow or blue, with a dropped waist and flaring double-tiered skirt—perfect for dancing at a Paris night spot.[100] In other words, the idea was simply to update the ballet, transforming Ravel's Imperial ball into a modern Paris nightclub, with costumes appropriate to that changed locale. However, by the time the ballet premiered in Monte Carlo, its concept had radically changed. Gone were the cocktail dresses and evening wear, replaced instead by short gold lamé tunics and close-fitting headpieces, costumes that in their uniformity recall Goncharova's for *Les Noces* and Exter's for *Holy Etudes*.

The choreography, Ashton recalled, was "somewhat reminiscent of *Les Noces* in its massive building up of groups."[101] The work was angular and abstract, with complex configurations of dancers ranged both symmetrically and asymmetrically across the stage sometimes on platforms and even the floor. Massed together in groups of three, four, or five, the bodies in each group seem to dramatize selected elements of movement itself: the exact bend of the torso or curve of an arm, the depth of a lunge in parallel or angle of an extended leg—gestures as precise as the movements of a machine. This is not ballet in a conventional sense, even if the women wore pointe shoes. Nor did it have much to do with the waltz—no swirling, interlaced couples, billowing gowns, or circling floor patterns. For one eminent music critic, "Everything that could evoke the waltz has been systematically removed."[102] Nijinska's daughter, Irina, believed that her mother was responding to the tragic quality of Ravel's music.[103] The composer himself alluded to this in a letter to Sonia Korty, who choreographed an earlier production in Antwerp: "No cotillions, no interludes, no story: you have to think of *La valse* as a kind of tragedy."[104] Benois also seemed to pick up on this: the set's black marble columns draped in blue velvet had what André Levinson called a "heavy, tormented splendor."[105] It certainly took courage for Nijinska to take a well-known piece of music by France's greatest living composer, throw out the scenario, and create a totally new work. To be sure, she was only doing what Meyerhold, Tairov, and Les Kurbas had done in post-Revolutionary Russian and Ukrainian theater. However, France of the late 1920s was a very different place.

Expectations ran very high. "Not since 'Petrouchka' has such a magnificent opportunity been presented to the choreographer to compose a ballet," wrote Walter Hanks Shaw in a Paris theater roundup that borrowed liberally from Levinson.

> Filled with anticipation and apprehension, the cream of the Parisian public crammed the Opera for the first performance. Ravel conducted the orchestra himself; Ida Rubinstein starred. . . . But the moment the curtain rose all hope vanished.[106]

Emile Vuillermoz was also dismayed. Much as he admired Nijinska, he told readers of the *Christian Science Monitor*,

> by temperament, she was just as little designed to interpret the music of Ravel as Nijinski [*sic*] was to portray that of Debussy. The great French musicians have decidedly no luck with that family. The angular interpretation of "L'Après-Midi d'un Faune" was an indisputable mistranslation. The plastic reading of the "Valse" is another.[107]

Appalled by what had been done to Ravel's score, Levinson took an even harder line. He thought the dancers looked like acrobats and that Rubinstein's short silver tunic and plumes "bordered on the ridiculous." As for the choreography "imagined by Mme Nijinska's geometric spirit," he hated every bit of it:

> [L]oud and brutal . . . [i]t consists in having the gilt-edged gymnasts mark the musical phrase with all their force and all their weight. . . . [T]he job is divided between the male group and the female group. The first marks the vigorously accented tempos, the men landing with all their might after a *changement de pied* or executing a brusque pirouette turn; the second runs and jumps on the *temps liés*. Everybody uses only the most rudimentary steps of the *danse d'école*. Or they traverse the stage in teams on the

diagonal with big jumping steps. . . . No *couple* emerges from the crush, and yet the interlacing and spinning of two beings incited by the intoxication of the . . . rhythm is the basic fact and symbol of the waltz.[108]

Meanwhile the word was out. As Henry Prunières told readers of the *New York Times*, "according to universal opinion, the stage production of Ravel's 'Valse' was a complete failure."[109]

Nijinska was devastated. In an unusually personal note Rubinstein tried to raise her spirits. "I am writing to you because I fear that you left feeling sad," Rubinstein wrote just before the company's last performance on May 30:

I so wish that your creative work for our common enterprise were a source of satisfaction to you. I am so <u>grateful</u> to you for the genuine feeling that you have brought to our work. I realize that you have devoted yourself entirely to our work, and I believe that everything created by you will be truly beautiful.

   With sincere affection and deep devotion,
   I. Rubinstein[110]

Nijinska kept a rough draft of her reply:

I was very touched by your warm letter—you know that it has always been my dearest wish to do the best I can to fulfill my art with the other founders of your Theater.

   One thing continues to make me sad, that I have caused you worry, especially on the eve of your performance. I so want that the Cause to which we have devoted ourselves continues to give you . . . only joy, now and forever, even if "La Valse" is hard to accept.

   Always, with all my soul devoted to you and your Cause,
   B. Nijinska[111]

According to her daughter, Nijinska suggested to Rubinstein that Benois redesign *La Valse* in order to salvage it, and Rubinstein demurred.[112] However, it is clear that what damned the ballet was its choreography. Benois would indeed redesign *La Valse*, but not for two years, when Nijinska choreographed a completely new version for Rubinstein—one with crinolines, furbelows, and many waltzing couples. For the moment, however, Rubinstein was taking a long furlough from ballet. After the last performance on May 30, the company disbanded, and Nijinska, as usual, began scouting for other projects. Meanwhile, the Ballets Russes was going from strength to strength. Balanchine's *Prodigal Son*, which premiered three days before *La Valse*, received rave reviews. Seemingly determined to efface Nijinska from his repertory, Diaghilev had her old Kiev student Serge Lifar rechoreograph *Le Renard*, one of her early Ballets Russes successes. It was his debut as a choreographer, and the clowning of the mostly male cast won him considerable applause. To Nijinska it must have seemed that Paris had turned against her.

Despite the unhappy ending, Nijinska's fifteen months with Rubinstein opened a new era in her evolution as a choreographer. During those months she staged more than a half-dozen ballets—the most important body of work she had created since her years with Diaghilev. Remarkably varied in style and subject matter, they demonstrated her breadth and continued vitality as a choreographer, her mastery of contemporary forms from "Russian" and "Spanish" to neoclassical, "baroque," and "modern," and her belief in the *danse d'école* as the springboard for contemporary movement invention. Although Rubinstein temporarily disbanded the company, several of its ballets remained in repertory, with Nijinska herself reviving *Bolero*, *Le Baiser de la Fée*, *The Swan Princess*, and *La Bien-Aimée* in the 1930s for the Teatro Colón, Markova-Dolin Ballet, and her own Théâtre de la Danse, and *Bolero* and *La Bien-Aimée* in the 1940s for American companies. Both Ashton and Balanchine choreographed *Le Baiser de la Fée* in the 1930s and *La Valse* in the 1950s. *Bolero*, too, had a long international career, with Serge Lifar staging it for the Paris Opéra Ballet in 1941, Pilar López and her sister Argentinita for Ballet Theatre in 1943, and Maurice Béjart for the Ballet of the Twentieth Century in 1960. Except for *La Bien-Aimée*, all remain living scores in the library of twentieth-century ballet music.

At the same time, Nijinska augmented her core group of dancers, creating an ensemble sympathetic to her approach and willing to put up with her perfectionism and temper. This included Nina Tikanova, Thomas Armour, Anna Ludmila, and Alexis Dolinoff, in addition to dancers such as Lapitzky, Unger, Joyce Berry, Ludmilla Schollar, and Anatole Vilzak group, who had worked with her for nearly a decade. Strong classical dancers with a contemporary sensibility, they followed her from company to company, studied with her, and became the living embodiment of her ballets. In this sense the Rubinstein company enabled Nijinska to create a semi-permanent ensemble bound not to an institution or a company but to Nijinska herself, not unlike the relationship she had enjoyed with the dancers of the School of Movement. Even if she lacked the organizational and financial wherewithal to set up a school in Paris, this pool of skilled dancers enabled her to carry on as a choreographer.

The repertory unveiled at the Paris Opéra in November and December 1928 looked forward to the 1930s rather than back to *les années folles*. Rejecting modernist irony, Rubinstein's ballets exuded a new romanticism. *La Bien-Aimée*, with its Liszt-Schubert music and poet-hero yearning for his departed Muse, set the new tone; it was the "first of the new romantic ballets," as the English critic Arnold Haskell later observed, the first hint of the decade's "romantic revival."[113] Another was *La Baiser de la Fée*, with its cradle-snatching fairy whose "fatal kiss" left the imprint of genius on her victim. Mystery, memory, dream, suggestion, the irrational and unconscious—all were ingredients of Surrealism, even if Russia Abroad steered clear of André Breton and Louis Aragon with their pro-Soviet sympathies and Freudian obsessions. With Benois and Nijinska at its helm, Rubinstein's company became—like the Ballets Russes—the incubator of a distinctly émigré sensibility in ballet that not only melded modernism and neoclassicism but also embodied a hybrid, diasporic idea of Russianness. Indeed, only *The Swan Princess* openly proclaimed a straightforward Russian identity.

***

Like the actresses Sarah Bernhardt or Eleonora Duse, Rubinstein was both the *animateur* and star of her own company. Unlike them, she was also rich enough to bankroll it. A statement of account from the Opéra for the month of December 1928 reveals that she paid more than a half-million francs for music rights, orchestra, chorus, crew, dressers, student dancers, accident insurance, and cleaning expenses as well as Massine's fee (35,000 francs) and Ernst Ansermet's conducting fee (25,000 francs).[114] However, this is only a fraction of what she spent. Everything else was extra: the salaries she paid Nijinska, Benois, the dancers, scene painters, and rehearsal pianists, the hundreds of costumes from M. J. Muelle and Maison Mathieu et Solatgès, the wigs, shoes, and other accessories, the studio space and scene-painting ateliers, in addition to all the travel and shipping expenses for the tour.[115] For the four performances at the Opéra the receipts totaled 436,305 francs, and one imagines that receipts elsewhere barely covered expenses.[116] Money for Rubinstein simply didn't matter. She acted, Nijinska wrote a few years later, "without thought of expense and with purely the instinct of a Maecenas of that far-off era when patrons would spend money on the renown of Russian art and devote all their energy to it."[117] For Nijinska, who was still paying off her debt to Zenon and his mysterious creditor Vassily,[118] Rubinstein was a throwback to the great Russian merchant patrons of Silver Age art, literature, and theater. Still, as Nijinska wrote in 1930 with more than a touch of bitterness, Rubinstein tossed ballets into storage like last year's fashions.[119]

To be sure, Nijinska had to cater to Rubinstein's whims and her particular set of talents. However, this is exactly what Nijinska had to do with Diaghilev. For all the freedom she enjoyed, he was the one who decided what was to be produced and who was to be cast, promoted, and publicized. Indeed, in the late 1920s, the Ballets Russes was more than ever a showcase for male talent, and its repertory had become almost wholly male-centered. "To tell the truth, the men are superior to the women," remarked Henry Prunières in his June 1929 report from Paris for the *New York Times*. "The incomparable Lifar, the supple and sensitive Woizikovsky, the elegant Dolin, were hardly equaled among the ballerinas."[120] Women were necessary, but in the larger scheme of things unimportant. From the beginning, Diaghilev had exalted the male dancer, aligning him with the idea of the modern, while relegating the ballerina to a secondary role and identifying the feminine with the antiquated forms of the nineteenth century. With very few exceptions—Nijinska being the chief one—the company's administrative staff and artistic personnel consisted solely of men.

By contrast, Nijinska's ballets for Rubinstein were dominated by a female sensibility. Anticipating another shift discernible in the 1930s, Rubinstein treated the stage as a largely feminine domain, dominated by a female protagonist (herself, of course), with meaty roles for women, even if her own had to be keyed to her limitations. Although Tikanova chafed at the limited opportunities, Nijinska made sure there were cameo roles for dancers—both male and female—who showed promise and worked hard. With Nijinska as Rubinstein's ballet master (even if she was paid considerably less than Massine for considerably more work) and Hélène Benois as one of the chief scene painters,[121] women occupied important offstage positions in the Rubinstein troupe as well.

As the letters following the disastrous reception of *La Valse* reveal, a current of personal feeling seemed to exist between Rubinstein and Nijinska, a sympathy that transcended their many differences, a bond that Nijinska had never really had with Diaghilev. He, after all, had rejected her, as had her real father, abandoned her as had her brother, leaving her to fend for herself. Now, with Rubinstein, there was a chance to re-create the female world of mothers and daughters, teachers and students that had carried on the daily practice of ballet in the rehearsal halls and studios of Nijinska's childhood. "I am very sorry that your mother is ill and from the bottom of my heart I hope that she will recover soon," Rubinstein wrote to her, probably in May 1928, when Eleonora's leg had to be amputated.[122] Her mother's screams ripped through Nijinska's soul. "I cannot bear the pain," Nijinska wrote in her diary.[123] Ludmilla Schollar offered to take care of the children and find money if she needed it.[124] Eleonora survived, while Nijinska, as always, soldiered on.

Although she practically lived in the studio, the dancers knew only the hard-driving teacher, obsessed with intrigues. "She saw traitors everywhere," recalled Tikanova.[125] Singaevsky fanned her paranoia, using his position to spy on the dancers and report their infractions, meaning that it was the dancers who bore the brunt of her temper. "Her screams were deafening," wrote Tikanova.[126] Roman Jasinski remembered her shrieking at Singaevsky in front of everyone.[127] Driven, taxed, and relentless, Nijinska by now had developed the carapace that masked her emotional turmoil. She may have been productive, but as her journals reveal, she was torn by self-doubt. She lived on black coffee and cigarettes: in Anatole Vilzak's quaint phrase, she "over-indulged in smoking."[128] Her husband must have been a disappointment. Although he worshiped the ground on which she walked, he acted against her best interests, and there is no evidence that along with managerial duties he ever assumed the role of first critic or advisor. Artistically, she was alone, stubbornly so, and while most of the time this may have served her well, there was nobody to avert or mitigate a disaster like La Valse.

Finally, he could never supplant Chaliapin. Although Nijinska had not seen him in the flesh for eight years (and then from afar at a concert), the singer dominates her journal. Eighteen years before he had awakened her sexual passion. Now he remains alive through the spell of her own words— an imaginary friend, a companion in struggle, an ever-present lover. When she stops in Rome on her way back to Paris, she recognizes the city as made in his image, colossal, with a soul of genius, and is overwhelmed with excitement.[129] As the Paris Opéra season approaches, she becomes obsessed with his seeing her work. "Where are you," she wonders on November 11. "Perhaps what tortures me the most is not to know where you are."

I cannot escape this attachment, . . . [an] obsession, a kind of mania, a disease that destroys me. . . . They ask me where I get my strength and tell me that from the outside it is incomprehensible how so many ballets can possibly be made by one person. . . . "Only nerves and tension and de-sire." . . . My art is love and a conversation with him.

On November 18–19:

I read your words as if they were written about me. You think about my art and know that you are leaving your footprint in it—inspiration.

On November 22:

Finally, the first performance. Is it good or bad? I don't know, but you won't be here.

On November 28:

Two performances have taken place. You are not here. My heart can't sur-vive this sorrow. . . . God! How unbearably difficult it is to breathe.

On December 7:

All the performances have passed, without the happiness I begged and waited for. . . . Guests came over, but not the one who should have told me "how beautiful your eyes are today"; "what beautiful things you are making and how wonderfully you compose everything into a true art." The accolades of other people do not reach my heart, and it feels as if a black casket stands in the middle of an empty hall—my love.

Even if it had been years since she had spoken with him, he was the inspi-ration that sustained her and the validation she craved. Her need was im-mense, and nothing or nobody could satisfy it. Not even Chaliapin. Like all the other men who peopled her imaginative life, he left her to carry on alone.

11

A Choreographer for Russia Abroad

With the Rubinstein company on hiatus, Nijinska found herself scrambling for work. Small jobs came her way: rehearsing a new cast in the revival of *Alceste*, choreographing the Venusberg "ballet" in Wagner's *Tannhäuser*— her last commission at the Paris Opéra.[1] She staged divertissements for Anna Pavlova's company,[2] a short ballet for Olga Spessivtzeva at the London Coliseum,[3] and a dance-pantomime for Henriette Pascar.[4]

A bright spot was *Aubade*, a ballet that reunited her with Poulenc. Commissioned by the Vicomte and Vicomtesse de Noailles for their June 1929 "Materials Ball," it exemplified the couple's eclectic taste and avant-garde inclinations. Patrons of the first rank, collectors, honorary surrealists, and godparents of the experimental film *The Andalusian Dog*, they intended their grand *fêtes* to be a meeting ground for artists and the *beau monde*.[5] Nijinska joined the collaboration quite late, and it is likely that Poulenc contacted her after seeing *Le Baiser de la Fée* and *The Swan Princess* at the Paris Opéra. But it was only in late March that the two got together. Still ample time remained before the June 19 performance date. As Poulenc reassured the Noailles, it took only a month to "arrange *Les Biches*, which was much more compli- cated." *Aubade*, by comparison, was child's play.[6]

As Poulenc hunkered down to write, a tide of melancholy washed over the music, a measure of his personal "distress" in discovering that his child- hood sweetheart did not return his love and in embarking upon "what was almost certainly his first passionate homosexual relationship."[7] "The people who heard it," he told the mezzo-soprano Claire Croiza, "were both a little surprised and vexed that 'charming Poulenc' had stirred them this time to tears."[8] Years later in an interview with Claude Rostand, he elaborated:

It's a ballet about the chastity of Diana. At daybreak, surrounded by her companions, Diana revolts against the divine law that condemns her to eternal purity. Her companions console her and restore her sense of di- vinity by giving her her bow. Diana seizes it with sadness, then bounds into the forest, seeking in the hunt an outlet for the torments of love.

Aubade, he concludes, "is a ballet of women, of female solitude."[9]

Nijinska followed Poulenc's directions to the letter. The two had next to nothing in common except mutual respect, but in *Aubade* as in *Les Biches* she sensed something in the music that spoke to her directly: Poulenc was not alone in experiencing the torments of unrequited love and solitude, even if Nijinska hid her distress from friends, buttoning up her feelings except on those rare occasions they could find an outlet in her work. *Aubade* was such an occasion. "The composition of *Aubade* forms sadly, like tears," she wrote in her diary on June 12. "Poulenc says, 'it's good they cry at the end of *Aubade*.'"[10] Nijinska confided the role of Diana to Anna Ludmila, the young American singled out by critics during the Rubinstein season. The goddess's "Followers" (Tikanova, Claudia Lotova, and Nina Verchinina) and "Friends" (Leonida Stal and Irène Lucezarska) came from the Rubinstein company as well. Rehearsals took place at the Noailles' splendid *hôtel particulier* at 11, Place des Etats-Unis, only a few doors from Rubinstein's townhouse at No. 7, although it's unlikely their owners ever met. Poulenc, who had yet to finish the score, had moved in with the Noailles and would drop off sheets of music in his bathrobe as the dancers rehearsed in the grand salon.[11]

Nijinska crafted what seems to have been a small gem. Since this was a private performance, the ballet was not reviewed, and Nijinska for some reason never revived it. Nina Tikanova had only the happiest memories of *Aubade*, where to her "incomparable joy," she danced a "difficult and tiring" solo, her very first, and admired Anna Ludmila's sparkling talent and technique in the role of Diana. A rare photograph of Ludmila holding a bow overhead suggests her bold modern line and stage presence. Her pointe shoes are broken in—ready, one imagines, for the grand-scaled movement of Poulenc's tragic heroine, such as when she bounded across the stage in the Allegro Féroce, abandoning herself to despair. Her dress, with its easy skirt, cowl collar, and merest hint of panniers at the waist, nods to early 1930s fashion as much as to the eighteenth century.[12]

In later articles and interviews Poulenc referred to *Aubade* as an "unlucky" ballet. He was nettled that Balanchine, when he choreographed it in 1930 for the Vera Nemtchinova company, rewrote the scenario, eliminating what might be called its "queer" elements. As Poulenc explained to readers of the English journal *Ballet* in 1946—an article prompted by Serge Lifar's restaging of the work for the Nouveau Ballet de Monte Carlo:

[E]xcept at its first private performance in the garden of the Vicomtesse de Noailles, . . . I have always been let down by [*Aubade*'s] choreographers. At that first performance I collaborated with Nijinska, who realized my idea to perfection; but for the public performance at the Théâtre des Champs-Elysées I was weak enough to let Balanchine modify my libretto by intro- ducing a male part into the ballet which I had composed for women dancers only. . . . At a period of my life when I was feeling very sad I found that dawn was the time when my anguish reached its height. . . . I chose Diana as my symbolic heroine. She, a goddess and a beautiful woman, was doomed to perpetual chastity among women, with no other distraction than the chase. Every day the goddess must reluctantly resume her hunting in the forest, carrying the bow that was as tedious to her as the piano was at that time to me.[13]

In good 1920s fashion, *Aubade* was the climax of a highbrow variety show, which included a drag act, a magic-lantern show with music by Auric, and a rejuvenated court ballet featuring witty costumes by a legion of dressmakers. Then, finally, came *Aubade*. People chattered away, occasionally applauding, but indifferent to the heroine and her plight. The dancers received their fee and discreetly left by the service staircase, with Nijinska presumably in tow.[14] Meanwhile, the artists who really counted—Jean Cocteau, Valentine Hugo, Max Ernst, Salvador Dalí—partied till dawn.

***

On August 19, 1929, as Venice woke to a new day, Serge Diaghilev died on the Lido of complications from untreated diabetes. To Stravinsky the con- ductor Ernest Ansermet wrote that he died alone in a hotel like a vagabond, having quarreled with his closest friends, and taking "a piece of our life" with him.[15] The news ricocheted around the world. Scores of obituaries memori- alized his accomplishments.[16] André Levinson in *Comoedia* sought to cap- ture what he called "the romance of a great existence" in all its contradictions. In Diaghilev a man of action coexisted with a dilettante, a grand seigneur with a touring director, a courtier with a rebel, a dictator with an anarchist; he was a des Esseintes and a Barnum rolled into one, a Russian *barin* become citizen of the world.[17] Diaghilev was buried in Venice, on the island ceme- tery of St. Michele, after a funeral service crowded with well-wishers in the Orthodox church of St. George. As it slid through the city's canals, his black-draped gondola was captured in a photograph that appeared on the cover of *La Russie illustrée* with the headline "The End of a Beautiful Life."[18] In Paris a Panikhida service was held at the Russian church in the rue Daru where Nijinska wept uncontrollably, and a few days later a requiem mass, which she probably also attended.[19]

Some of the dancers and members of Diaghilev's inner circle scrambled to keep the company together; others jumped ship. Lifar and Balanchine headed to the Paris Opéra (where Lifar would spend most of the next three decades); Anton Dolin (accompanied by Anna Ludmila) resumed his career on the revue stage. An effort by Serge Grigoriev to lead a company of thirty collapsed, Boris Kochno wrote, in "difficulties and intrigues."[20] Meanwhile, René Blum, now artistic director of the Théâtre de Monte-Carlo, sought to engage what remained of the company for the winter opera season.[21] Massine, who learned of Diaghilev's death while on vacation in Virginia Beach, wrote to Comte Etienne de Beaumont, asking if he would take over direction of the Ballets Russes. "I would leave everything here in order to help you."[22] Nijinska called them all "predators on Diaghilev's corpse."[23]

Nijinska had long since severed her ties with the Ballets Russes. But Diaghilev was woven into the mesh of her imaginative life and into her store of personal and professional memories. He was the father whose approval she craved, the paternal surrogate who stood behind her greatest triumphs and cruelest rejections. He had criticized her maliciously and impeded her work, she wrote toward the end of her life, but in the early 1930s she was far more generous, confessing a nostalgia that wiped away his faults, leaving only his cultural significance.[24] There were so many reasons for Nijinska to be nostalgic: Diaghilev's kindness to her mother and boundless love for her brother Vaslav, his belief, to which both siblings came to subscribe, that one should live solely for art. When he died, she wept for days. "We lived through so much together in life and in theater," she wrote to a friend, "that it always made us close. No one has ever known me and loved me and appreciated me as much as Diaghilev."[25] She was indebted to him for a place in the choreographic succession that began with Fokine and in the emerging historical narrative of ballet modernism outside Russia. Thanks to him, she was both a transnational artist and an artist of Russia Abroad, and it was here, in the aftermath of Diaghilev's death, that Nijinska chose to make her way, in the ballet studios of the Russian diaspora where émigré teens dreamed of fame and dancers from elsewhere tried their luck, a transnational community bonded by sweat, hunger, and devotion to art.

***

In the winter and spring of 1929, as Nijinska accompanied the Ida Rubinstein company on tour, "another grand enterprise," as Nina Tikanova wrote, "was born in Paris."[26] The Opéra Privé de Paris, also known as the Opéra Russe à Paris, was founded by the singer Maria Kuznetzova and her husband, the banker and industrialist Alfred Massenet, a nephew of the composer Jules Massenet, with Kuznetzova's son, Michel Benois (by her first husband, Nikolai Benois, a nephew of Alexandre Benois), as artistic director. Capitalizing on the "tremendous vogue for Russian opera" in Paris, the Opéra Privé also celebrated the city's deep reservoirs of émigré talent. The repertory consisted of four works—*Prince Igor*, *Tsar Saltan*, *The Snow Maiden*, and Rimsky-Korsakov's *Legend of the Invisible City of Kitezh*—and nothing but the best would do to bring them to life. The conductor Emile Cooper, stage director Nikolai Evreinov, set and costume designers Ivan Bilibin and Konstantin Korovin, choreographers Michel Fokine and Boris Romanov—all of whose artistic origins lay in the Silver Age, the Imperial Theaters, and the Ballets Russes—were enlisted in the new enterprise. "A simple call from Maria Kousnetsoff sufficed to resuscitate, as if by magic . . . the incomparable soul of old Russia," exulted Gustave de Pawlowski. "They all came—singers, dancers, painters, and musicians, without thought of money, with the sole desire of proclaiming . . . the triumphant immortality of Russian art."[27] The day before the first performance, which took place on January 27, 1929, at the Théâtre des Champs-Elysées, the Metropolitan of Paris blessed the enterprise in the foyer, as the chorus sang psalms, and everyone down to the prompters kissed the cross—a moving, "purely Slavic" ceremony, observed one journalist.[28] The reviews were rapturous. When the season ended, the company embarked on a long tour of South America, where it enjoyed great success but ran into financial difficulties. At a crucial moment, Kuznetsova's son absconded with the receipts, forcing everyone to find their own way home.[29]

At that point a new savior appeared: Prince Alexei Tsereteli. Descended from a noble Georgian family, Tsereteli was an impresario and "impenitent enthusiast" of opera (in Nina Tikanova's phrase), founder of private companies in Kharkov and St. Petersburg, former manager of Narodny Dom, and, after a stint in Barcelona, cofounder of the Paris theatrical agency Zerbazon with Vasilii Grigorevich Voskresensky—better known as Colonel Wassily de Basil (of whom much more later)—and Ignaty Zon, who had owned a café chantant in Moscow.[30] Stepping into the breach, Tsereteli announced a new season at the Théâtre des Champs-Elysées, baptizing his enterprise the Opéra Russe à Paris.

The "grand season of Russian opera" that opened on May 17, 1930, at the Théâtre des Champs-Elysées was both the zenith and the swan song of Russian opera in Paris, before it fell victim to the Depression of the 1930s. Tsereteli threw good sense and caution to the wind. There were new productions and new stagings of existing ones. Nijinska was now the company's ballet master and its choreographer. Although her name did not appear in the press until the first days of May, she must have started rehearsing the fifty dancers, including several from the Rubinstein company, well before then.[31] Tikanova was now a soloist, while Nijinska and the former Bolshoi ballerina Alexandra Balashova shared leading roles. The new émigré arts magazine *Mir i iskusstvo* (The World and Art) devoted a chunk of its second issue to the company, including photographs of Nijinska with members of the creative team and rehearsing with the dancers. For the magazine and the community it served, the Opéra Russe was one of the outstanding events of Russia Abroad.[32] Fittingly, on the eve of the company's debut, Anna Pavlova herself came to watch Nijinska rehearsing the dancers, her eagle eyes absorbing every detail as she whispered in Russian with the choreographer.[33]

However familiar *Prince Igor* may have been, the critics were overwhelmed by the Opéra Russe production. "All those who collaborated on this performance," wrote Henry Malherbe in *Le Temps*,

> are united in spirit and ambition. Unceasingly, with study and persever-
> ance, they seek to win acceptance for the intellectual treasure of their na-
> tion, the ideal of their race. . . . They have worked night and day to reach
> their goal, which they consider sacred. A rare and touching example that
> should inspire us as well.[34]

Above all, Malherbe credited Nijinska and director Alexander Sanin for achieving this "elevated quality."

> Mlle. Nijinska had arranged the ballet after Mons. Michel Fokine's rousing
> and vivid choreography. In the course of the divertissement—a magical
> evocation of ancient Tartar splendor—we applauded Mlles. Balachova [sic]
> and Monna Stall, and Mons. Ploucis, at the head of the leaping cortège of
> Polovtsian warriors. There is in this ballet a fury of imagination, exuber-
> ance, and bounds that have a strange fascination over the soul. . . . An apex
> of Russian national inspiration, *Prince Igor* is presented with devotion, like
> an icon, in a cover sparkling with gems.[35]

Glinka's *Ruslan and Ludmila*, the season's second offering, did not go down as well. The music was too uneven, too Italian, despite its national theme (inspired by a poem of Pushkin's) and use of popular music sources (which made it the prototype of a new kind of Russian opera). "The myth of the Slavic hero and his cosmic symbolism escapes us Latins," wrote Charles Tenroc. "Still, the dozen tableaux . . . offer us the enchantment of settings and costumes, scenes of picturesque life by Mons. [Nikolai] Evreinoff, visions, and exciting dances."[36] The costumes and scenery were by Boris Bilinsky, a young, up-and-coming artist best known at the time for his work in film, who would soon join Nijinska's circle of collaborators. *Ruslan* was full of dances: Jesters in Scene 1; Enchantresses in Scene 9; and, finally, in Scene 11, a cascade of Turkish, Arab, and Circassian Dances. Tikanova loved Nijinska's choreography for the Enchantresses, remembering it as "light and classical."[37]

Sadko, the season's third premiere, was another Rimsky-Korsakov opera introduced to Paris by way of the Ballets Russes. The new production finally did the opera justice, thought Henry Malherbe, revealing the composer as a landscape master in sound. "We find ourselves," he wrote, "in the presence of vast sea frescoes that recall, in their musical transposition, the *Water Lilies* of Claude Monet."[38] The designs were by Alexandre Benois, and Malherbe, remembering the artist's work for Diaghilev and Rubinstein, thought that Benois had outdone himself. "His tableaux, fantastic in their pomp, will remain engraved on our memory," he wrote in *Le Temps*. As for Nijinska, he went on,

> she makes her algae-bedecked undines float with movements of the utmost harmony. A dancing garland embellishes each refrain of popular song tracing the particular rhythm of each page folklore so happily animated. Thus, in the hands of a ballet mistress of such high inspiration, the system employed in our fashionable operettas is given new resources and renewed with poetry.[39]

Some of that fantasy is evident in the sea waves and mermaids circling an expression of gratitude to Nijinska and her "unforgettable leadership of the 'Opéra Russe à Paris' ballet" presented to the choreographer at a *fête* after the premiere of *Ruslan and Ludmila* and signed on the back by more than forty dancers.[40]

The six-week season ended with *Sadko* on June 30, 1930. It had been a busy spring for Nijinska, with non-stop rehearsals and performances since at least mid-April. A break in July and August was followed by a season at the fashionable Spanish resort of San Sebastián. Three performances were announced, but the ecstatic reviews and demand for tickets led the Gran Kursaal to schedule four additional performances. *Prince Igor*, which left the critic of *El Día* spellbound by the triumph of "each and every artist," closed the season on September 21.[41] Then, with Singaevsky in tow, Nijinska returned in Paris. In early August she had signed a contract engaging her services as "Maître de Ballet" for the next round of Opéra Russe performances that began on November 15.[42] In the meantime she had another engagement to fulfill, and so the couple headed almost immediately to Vienna.

***

On August 30, 1929, Nijinska had written to Paul Bechert, one of Vienna's leading concert and theatrical managers. Contemplating a future without a reliable salary from Ida Rubinstein, she was looking for work. She noted in her diary a few weeks later that she hadn't worked for three months and that the "immobility" was driving her to despair and a loss of faith in her own artistic powers. "Now," she wrote, as if giving herself a pep talk, "I must overcome all obstacles and get what I need."[43] Bechert quickly responded in French. Yes, an engagement in Vienna or an important theater in Germany was definitely possible. What kind of remuneration did she want? Was she looking for a short-term assignment or work for an entire year?[44]

Things moved forward swiftly. On September 23, Alfred Schlee, one of Bechert's associates and the editor of the journal *Schrifttanz*, brought her up to date. Although the Berlin State Opera (where Rudolf Laban had just become ballet master) had turned her down, Clemens Krauss, the newly appointed director of the Vienna State Opera, was very interested. "Contrary to his predecessor," he wrote,

> director Krauss intends to include the ballet to a great extent in the opera's repertoire. To that end he is planning a fundamental reform of the Viennese Opera Ballet. The ballet master shall not only execute occasional guest productions but also direct a large ballet school and create a new corps de ballet with young blood.

Would Nijinska consider such an engagement in the fall of 1930?

With respect to Nijinska's demands, Schlee did note a number of problems. Her asking salary of 4,000 schillings was too high, although he thought there might be ways of supplementing what the Staatsoper was prepared to pay by allowing her to stage works outside Vienna or during an extended vacation period or by collecting royalties for her works. In closing, Schlee wrote that "it would be a great personal pleasure" if Vienna were to be the center of her "artistic endeavors."[45] Within days Nijinska confirmed her agreement.[46]

With Nijinska's approval in hand, Krauss cabled the German-born Argentine musicologist Johannes Franze, asking him for "detailed information about the ballet master Nijinska."[47] A conductor, Krauss was in his late thirties; he had met Nijinska in Buenos Aires and was determined to shake up the Opera's venerable ballet troupe, on which Diaghilev's revolution in ballet aesthetics had left few traces. Franze quickly responded to Krauss's inquiry, giving Nijinska a ringing endorsement. During her tenure at the Teatro Colón, he wrote, she had transformed its "scruffy" troupe into an "artistic organism." Her production of *Les Noces* was remarkable; she loved "geometric stylization" but used it with "great expressive power." She was at her best doing Russian things, and her *Prince Igor* and *Night on Bald Mountain* were very successful. She was a "progressive dance director," and he felt sure she would perform well under "more mature organizational conditions and with more expressive human material."[48] Krauss invited Nijinska to Vienna.

Nijinska was deeply conflicted about a long-term engagement in Vienna. She hated the thought of abandoning Paris—"my native town," as she called it in her diary—and she was torn about uprooting her family, nomads since leaving Kiev eight years before. But an artist's homeland, she reflected in another diary entry, is where his art can flourish, where he can be most productive, where a choreographer like herself could have a company of her own. "They will give me a theater with eighty artists," she wrote.

> They want me to restore the ballet to its former glory and to reorganize the school. Everything! I have to go, though it is difficult to leave Paris. I must turn everything upside down—my whole family, my house, my children's education. But these are mere details. The main thing is that I will have a Theater.[49]

Nijinska arrived in the Austrian capital on January 21, 1930.[50] With the Rubinstein tour still fresh in people's minds, her arrival was big news, as were her meetings with Krauss and other administrators. She attended several rehearsals and also visited the company's affiliated ballet school: the idea was for her to modernize both institutions and to spend the whole year in Vienna. She talked at length with a reporter from the *Neues Wiener Tagblatt*, who described her as "a medium-sized, slender woman with brown hair pulled back into a simple bun. . . . Her brown silk dress is simple too, . . . and her movements, when she speaks, are almost modest. Only her large grey eyes express her energy and willpower."[51] Growing more animated, she talked about her work, relaying key ideas of the treatise that she would publish a few months later in the progressive dance journal *Schrifttanz*. "It is odd that one must stress this," she explained,

> but it is important to say it to save artists from incorrect forms of expression: The element of dance is movement, not the pose. Dance is an entirely self-sufficient form of art that communicates with the eye, while music communicates with the ear. I could even imagine a dance without any music! The grand, classical basis of ballet was developed by French and Italian masters of the nineteenth century. The task of all art is to move forward in time, and so ballet, too, must develop together with other contemporary art forms in order to exist in the framework of today's culture.[52]

She ended the interview on a high note. "I would be happy . . . to work in a city where the art of Fanny Elssler and Taglioni still lives on in its forms of expression, and I would be delighted to create something new worthy of the grand tradition of the Viennese ballet."[53] When she returned to Paris a few days later, everything pointed to a successful conclusion of the project. "During the next few weeks she will draft a report summarizing her artistic plans for the State Opera Ballet," reported the *Neues Wiener Tagblatt*. "On the basis of this report Mme. Nijinska's definitive appointment will be decided."[54] It was expected that a contract would be signed in three or four weeks.[55]

Nijinska's report—if she ever wrote one—has disappeared. However, in April 1930 the journal *Schrifttanz* published her treatise "On Movement and the School of Movement." Founded in 1928 and edited by Alfred Schlee, *Schrifttanz* quickly became a forum for writing about all aspects of dance.[56] Returning to the theoretical speculation she had put aside when she emigrated, Nijinska sought both to define the essential nature of dance, while also defending the classical school against both the moderns epitomized by Laban, Mary Wigman, and their followers, and conservatives such as Levinson. Echoing her interview with *Neues Wiener Tagblatt*, she begins with a simple statement, "Movement is the principal element in dance."[57] She laments that dance technique exercises often forced the dancer to focus the whole of her attention on positions or poses that provide shape for the body but are lifeless unless animated by movement.[58] Finally, she declares, "The classical school simply is the foundation of dance." The last twenty-five years had brought about a revolution in choreographic art, dividing the dance world into "friends" or "enemies" of the classical school, which the former want to retain "intact" and the latter deny in its entirety. Nijinska, by contrast, argues for reform, the "fundamental reform" that Krauss hoped to achieve by hiring her. "One must totally sweep away useless things, but . . . not . . . the things that constitute the foundation, the basis of the mechanics of the art of dance. This must become the principal duty of dance reformers." Only then, she argues, will it be possible to build a " 'new' artistic life" on the foundation of the old.[59]

On January 23, 1930, Krauss formally requested approval from Franz Schneiderhan, the *Direktorintendant* (or chief executive officer, as we would say today), to hire Nijinska, arguing that in Austria the only suitable ballet master was Carl Godlewski, who at sixty-eight was too old, while the German ballet masters were too "one-sidedly modern." Nijinska, he wrote, is "one of the most important choreographers and ballet masters of the present day"; she had "engaged in pedagogical work for years," and she possessed two qualities that in his view were essential to managing the Vienna company—"energy and patience." On February 21, Schneiderhan's office, in consultation with the State Ministry of Finance, approved her appointment.[60]

Under the terms of her contract, Nijinska was to be hired as ballet master, ballet director (*Ballettregisseurin*), and director of the ballet school, with the additional responsibility of teaching one class in the school from September 1, 1930, to August 31, 1933. Upon request of the management, she was required to perform solo roles. She would receive vacation days during the Staatsoper's off-season and agreed to limit her activities as a ballet master to Vienna. In Paragraph 3 she agreed to choreograph all new ballets and the dances in operas as well as to record their choreography in written form and make them available to the management. This last was a new stipulation on the part of the Staatsoper management, possibly prompted by growing interest in the German-speaking world in Labanotation, but also reflecting practices long in place at the Paris Opéra, which allowed for the restaging of choreography once its creator was gone. Knowledge of German was another contractual obligation.[61] Everything seemed fine, and Nijinska consulted a moving company in Paris about packing up her apartment and transporting its contents to Vienna.[62]

Then the problems began. When Paragraph 3 was amended, she balked at the stipulation that she waive the right to future royalties and all copyright claims to new choreography.[63] Bechert, however, assured her that whatever concerns she had were "entirely unfounded" and begged her to "thoroughly acquaint [her]self with the German language in the meantime since this is the only issue that might create some difficulties."[64] The press, meanwhile, had sensed that Nijinska was getting cold feet. "It seems as if Madame Nijinskaja will hardly produce as much as we had all hoped for," wrote the Vienna correspondent of the *Dancing Times* in May. "So great are the obstacles of the set opera programme and of her residence in distant Paris from where she has not yet definitely moved, that we shall be happy if she can manage two new productions and about a dozen performances in all."[65]

Of course, the real problem was that she now had a job with the Opéra Russe. Still, in mid-July *Die Stunde* reported that she was set to arrive in Vienna at the beginning of September, that she would stage the dances in the opera *Schwanda, der Dudelsackpfeifer* (Schwanda, the Bagpiper), that two "modern ballet evenings" were being planned, one to include *Bolero*, and that she intended to bring in new dancers, some from her Paris school.[66] Then, on August 21, the *Neues Wiener Tagblatt*, citing a notice from Paris, announced that Nijinska wasn't coming after all, and the following day *Die Stunde* elaborated: "As reason for her decision she cites artistic differences with the opera's administration regarding the question of her intellectual property as well as financial ones." By August 23 the *Neues Wiener Tagblatt* had learned from Russian sources in Paris that she had just signed with Prince Tsereteli and would direct the Opéra Russe ballet company for the coming season. A few days later the newspaper reported that the "most serious clash" with Nijinska was because she had not learned German. Nonetheless, on September 5, *Die Stunde* announced that she would be staging *Les Noces* and there was strong interest in *Les Biches*.[67] By then, however, Nijinska had gone to Spain with the Opéra Russe.

Paul Bechert was beside himself when he learned that she was in Spain. Valiantly trying to salvage an engagement that had promised so much, he proposed additional amendments to the contract. Yes, she had the right to dance but was under no obligation to do so and would be paid separately for those performances; no, Krauss had only the best of intentions toward her; the protracted nature of contractual negotiations had to do with the need for all contracts to be ratified by the Ministry; the excellent lawyers he had consulted had assured him that the contract was legal and that she was obligated to come to Vienna; he and Krauss had made "superhuman efforts" to fulfill her wishes. He was obviously shocked by her duplicity.

> Yesterday, on September 7, I learned for the first time that you did, <u>in fact</u>, agree to travel to Spain with . . . the Opéra Russe for 10 to 14 days. . . . You must understand that this was an awkward surprise to me. On Tuesday (September 2) Mr. Singaevsky had assured me over the phone that you had <u>not</u> entered an agreement with the Opéra Russe. Nonetheless, you began rehearsals with the Opéra Russe on Thursday (September 4). It seems very clear that there had been a contractual agreement between you and the Opéra Russe much earlier, that is, long before our conversation on the phone.

In closing, Bechert reminded her again of everything he had done on her behalf to secure a place with "means and possibilities" infinitely greater than those of a "provincial, traveling" Russian opera troupe.[68]

Despite all this, on September 25, four days after the San Sebastián season ended, the new ballet master and her husband finally arrived in Vienna. She met with Krauss and Lothar Wallerstein, the chief stage director, and immediately went to work. She told the press that a sore throat and very high fever had delayed her departure from San Sebastián, and that apart from the dances in *Schwanda*, her future projects were still up in the air. But she knew the company and the fine training of its dancers from her previous visit, and did not envision any difficulty in realizing her intentions. She was working on her German, but language was no barrier to working in the studio. Personal example and demonstrating the "smallest details" were what counted most.[69] A few days later Hedy Pfundmayr, one of the company's leading dancers, told *Die Stunde* that she expected Nijinska to perform wonders—as she had done in Buenos Aires—and bring about a "renaissance" of the Vienna ballet.[70] As for Krauss, he was "absolutely thrilled by her work. With her strong personality, she pushes the ensemble to a new level. She demonstrates exactly what she wants in a very convincing manner. She is currently working on *Schwanda*, but I want to give her the opportunity to show her own work as soon as possible. . . . I would like to show . . . the range of her stylistic capabilities, perhaps by letting her work on Stravinsky, in order to mix Viennese and Russian traditions."[71]

During her early weeks in Vienna, Nijinska wrote two reports for Krauss. The first, dated October 18 and titled in her rough Russian draft a "Plan for the Reform of the Vienna Opera School," was her most complete statement about the education of a twentieth-century ballet artist in a state institution not unlike the Maryinsky. First, she describes the training as it then existed: a class for children aged six to fourteen, conducted by Marie Peterka; a second "mixed" class for dancers of the corps de ballet aged seventeen to twenty-one and for students aged fourteen to eighteen, conducted by Raimund Czadil; and a third class for all the remaining ballet artists, aged twenty-one to sixty, when they were pensioned, conducted by Carl Raimund. Four or five ninety-minute classes a week were given at each level; the training was in classical dance, and the children were used on stage in operas and ballets. The exact same training, Nijinska noted, was offered by many teachers in Vienna. Instead, Nijinska wrote, the Staatsoper school should "provide a complete dance education, train a fully prepared artist, and therefore be an exemplary ballet school."[72]

Her first recommendation was to separate "the task of the ballet school from that of the ballet artists." The Staatsoper should create its own separate dance academy for children aged eight to seventeen or eighteen, when they would be hired by the Staatsoper ballet company. She recommended the creation of two graded levels in each of the student classes, the first for children aged eight to twelve, the second for students aged twelve to eighteen. Levels were absolutely necessary, since "seven-year-olds who have just entered the school cannot possibly work with those who have been attending the school for four or five years." Classes, she insisted, had to be held between three and six o'clock in the afternoon to allow the children to "continue their general education in other schools." She wanted to introduce a number of supplementary subjects immediately. These included "lectures" on art history as well as costume and makeup, in addition to music theory. She herself would give the other supplementary classes, most of which dated back to her curriculum for the School of Movement—Form and Rhythm of Movement, Expression in Movement, Style of Movement, National Dances, and a new addition, Dances of All Eras and Cultures. Such a curriculum, she asserts, would "mark the beginnings of a future grand 'School for Choreography.'"

She then goes on to discuss the needs of the professional dancers. She proposes the creation of two company classes—one for the female soloists and coryphées and all the men, and a second for the "ladies" of the corps de ballet. In terms of her own work, she would teach each company class twice a week, and on the other days she would work with the classes taught by Messrs. Czadil and Raimund. Additionally, she would supervise the other classes, both at the school and for the company. She underscored how important this was both to raise the "quality of the ballet" in general and to perform the new choreographic repertory envisioned by Krauss in particular. Finally, she requested that the dancers be "exempted from all other work in the theater during the hours of instruction (10–11 A.M., or on days with stage rehearsals, 9:30–10:30 A.M.)." This was "vital," she explained, "for any theater in which the ballet must consistently be concerned with the execution of the choreographic repertory." Here, in a nutshell, was the secret of Russian success: graded classes, daily practice, the discipline of the classroom combined with the experience of performance. Sometime that month Nijinska presided over the admission exams for new students at the school.[73]

Her second report to Strauss, dated October 25, was about repertory.[74] She begins by explaining that the list of proposed works grew out of two considerations: the need for works that were "artistic" and the need to "highlight" the "specific characteristics of the Staatsoper troupe." His proposal that she stage two ballets on a single program made this task considerably easier, since one could be "on the basis of character dance," the other on the basis of "contemporary 'classical' dance." She also welcomed his suggestion that one ballet have Russian music and the other Austrian or French. She suggests *Le Baiser de la Fée*, Stravinsky's most recent ballet, produced by the Rubinstein company but not performed in Vienna, and also *Petrouchka*, which she describes as a "pantomime ballet" with many "very good character dances" that had been restaged with great success. She writes a long paragraph about *Les Noces*. This, she says, was received with "great enthusiasm" by the press and the public when it was staged in her choreography by the Diaghilev company. She details its considerable requirements—a large chorus, four soloists, four pianos, and an orchestra of percussion instruments—and explains that because of its huge cost it was the only Diaghilev work unknown to German audiences. She notes that it was given at the Teatro Colón during two seasons "always" with the greatest success. Finally, she adds something about the ballet itself. It is "not a Russian wedding as this is usually presented, full of joy, frolicking, cheerfulness, and drunkenness. It is much more of a ritual, a ceremony, a prayer form of early Christianity as it advanced from Byzantium into what was still pagan Russia." Her interpretation of the text is quite different from the author's, "but Stravinsky accepted my choreography ... entirely."

She proposes two new works. The first was a ballet to Prokofiev's Third Concerto for Piano and Orchestra, with a libretto after Goldoni ("if the composer allows it"). The second was *Pictures at an Exhibition*, in Ravel's orchestration of the Mussorgsky music ("strange music for which I have always been interested in finding a libretto and using it for ballet"). The list continues with works she had already staged: *La Princesse Cygne, Daphnis and Chloë* ("very nice music but an old ballet that might not interest today's audiences very much"), *Les Biches*, her Paris Opéra ballets *Les Rencontres* and *Les Impressions de Music-Hall, La Bien-Aimée, Holy Etudes, Aubade*—together with *Noces, Baiser*, and *Petrouchka* they comprised her artistic capital. The one outlier was *The Nutcracker*. "I almost do not dare list this ballet," she warns Krauss, "since the entire first act is performed by a large group of children and would require a lot of preparation. It would be very desirable in principle, however, to have this ballet in our repertory, and I'm very interested in doing it." She ends by recommending that for the season's first ballet program it would be best to stage a ballet new to the Staatsoper, but that during the second half of the season "it would be desirable to perform several pieces from your ballet repertory."

Meanwhile, Nijinska was busy choreographing the dances for *Schwanda*. Rehearsal photos appeared in the press, showing her in a dark tunic and tights and banged-up pointe shoes huddled among the dancers as though she were part of the choreography. *Schwanda* was a folk ballet, filled with polkas and other dances in 3/4 rhythm, so the dancers wore character shoes (and anklets) rather than ballet slippers. But practice wear was far from uniform. Some women wore prints, and one fellow sported plaid belted trousers tucked into high boots. Nijinska drily commented on the clipping from *Das interessante Blatt*: "This was in the first days—now they are dressed alike—all in black."[75]

A folk opera in two acts and five scenes by the Czech composer Jaromir Weinberger, *Schwanda, the Bagpiper* premiered on October 16, 1930, to enthusiastic applause. The reviews commented favorably and at length on the music, heard for the first time in the Austrian capital, and the notices of Nijinska's choreography were excellent. The music was largely built on Czech folk melodies, which the audience loved, and there were numerous dances that showcased the large corps de ballet led by Herma Berka and Fritzi Fränzl. There seem to have been polkas galore, and, according to Julius Korngold, the prestigious music critic of the *Neue Freie Presse*, even a "polka-fugue for the purposes of the ballet" and a "dance in hell" that Nijinska had turned into "an orgy of movement." The critic for *Die Stunde* also singled out the choreography: "Dances like those of the women at the queen's court and the wild round dance in hell have not been seen on our stage in a long time." Just about everyone agreed that the company, under her direction, was heading to a new and better place. When the curtain came down, Nijinska joined the composer, Krauss, who conducted the performance, and the stage director Lothar Wallerstein for a bow.[76]

Meanwhile, Nijinska was in touch with Ida Rubinstein. On August 27, while cruising off the Kyle of Lochalsh in Scotland, Rubinstein sent her a note on her personal stationery. "I write you a few words to tell you with what pleasure I recall our work and how I regret that the time for it came to an end so quickly. I will return to Paris in very early October and hope from the bottom of my heart that you can give me the necessary time for our work. Despite the nasty weather, I work a little every day."[77] Rubinstein was flummoxed when she returned to Paris and discovered that Nijinska was working in Vienna. The possibility had arisen, Rubinstein wrote, "to take our ballets abroad in early spring." Would it be possible for Nijinska to obtain five months' leave? What she had in mind was a month-long work period beginning either November 1 or 15, during which she and Nijinska would work together every day, revive and rehearse her dances, and assemble the company. This would be followed by a three-month rehearsal and performance period. Finally, she needed a month or two weeks in May or June 1931 for a season in London. She hoped she had explained it clearly ("it seems to me I write Russian so badly"). In closing, she wrote, "I hope that you are pleased with your work and happy, but still—don't forget about us entirely," adding as a postscript, "I am very happy that you have the possibility to take a leave this fall as it will be more convenient for you."[78] Nijinska didn't miss a beat. On October 23, barely a week after the premiere of *Schwanda*, she wired, "All well here. Arranging my leaves."[79] Rubinstein said she would call on Saturday, November 1. Singaevsky replied that in case they were cut off, he wanted her to know that Nijinska was very pleased with her offer and "intends to set off on Tuesday or Wednesday," that is, November 4 or 5. She had one additional request: could Rubinstein wire an immediate advance of 5,000 to their address in Vienna and let her have an additional 5,000 when she arrives in Paris, since she cannot receive her salary before leaving? As soon as she arrived in Paris, they would work out the schedule.[80]

By now, it is fair to say, Nijinska was enmeshed in a triple game. She had an agreement with the Staatsoper. She had a contract with the Opéra Russe starting November 15. And now she was under contract to Rubinstein. With nine months of work lined up in Paris, there was no reason to settle for exile in Vienna. Even if the Staatsoper contract was for three years, even if it was a year into the Great Depression—which might have given others pause—Nijinska wanted out. On Friday, October 31, payday, she requested an advance on her salary. This request, as *Die Stunde* reported, was denied on the grounds that she had started work without a signed contract. What the press didn't know was that this was Nijinska's third request for an advance and the previous two had been honored.

Krauss, as usual, tried to make peace. He called a meeting with the general manager on Monday, November 3, which neither Nijinska (who pleaded illness) nor Singaevsky attended, nor did either of them attend the meeting with Krauss that evening. Krauss wrote to Nijinska, reiterating all the concessions he had made in her contract and assuring her that he would gladly fulfill her justified request for salary disbursements once she signed the attached contract.[81] Nijinska replied that the contract still did not meet her expectations and that the Staatsoper management was trying to force her into signing it.[82] In an interview with *Die Stunde* published on November 5, she claimed that she had been told that "due to a general exhaustion of the budget, it was not quite clear if and to what extent there were even going to be ballets at the Staatsoper this season."[83] Krauss, in an interview with *Neue Freie Presse*, also published on November 5, gave his side of the controversy:

> The difficulties with the wording of the artist's contract began in February, immediately after we had begun negotiations with Mme. Nijinska. At that time, Mme. Nijinska requested only the alteration of one point, regarding royalties. Once this request had been granted she requested in July the addition of five new points to the contract, among them the guarantee of three months' paid vacation, . . . permission to stage her own dance performances in Vienna during her vacation, and . . . permission to work in film. Additionally, she was granted an advance in the amount of two months' wages . . . with the condition that she work at the Staatsoper for at least one year. She wishes, however, that this sum be deducted from the wages of her second year's vacation. . . .
>
> The day before yesterday I urged Mme. Nijinska . . . to sign the new contract before yesterday evening. Today, however, she replied that a document of such importance could not be signed without some deliberation, and the proposed deadline did not allow her enough time to study the contract in

detail. She said she had not received her salary on Friday, . . . and therefore there were no grounds for her to continue her work. . . . It appears as if
Mme. Nijinska has the intention of creating a situation without a contract.[84]

Krauss's efforts to reach Nijinska by telephone were unsuccessful. She had
already left for Paris. However, before she departed, she sent a telegram to the
Staatsoper dancers. "My dear friends," it began,

It is with a heavy heart that I leave you. I urge you to continue to work
with the utmost confidence in the pure quality of truly great ballet. I am
very sad that I can no longer work with you and help . . . to showcase your
talent . . . to the world. I am with you always. With deepest and most affectionate feelings, Nijinska.[85]

Gusti Pichler responded on behalf of the company:

We greatly appreciated your telegram and truly value such high praise from
one of the most important representatives of the art of dance. I must tell
you how much I came to . . . love you during the short period you worked at
the Vienna Opera . . . [and] how much I learned from you during that time,
and how saddened I am that I will not have the opportunity to learn more
of your great art. You were so charming and pleasant in your intercourse
with us that we were completely won over by you. For me you were the ideal
of a ballet mistress, and . . . I admired your great knowledge of human nature. . . . Only one thing remains and that is to thank you profoundly for
your kindness and generosity.[86]

Gunhild Schüller, the Austrian scholar who wrote a monograph about
Nijinska in the 1970s, alleges that the "true reason" for Nijinska's quick departure from Vienna was the attitude of "authoritarian" officials such as the stage
director Lothar Wallerstein toward ballet. In Schwanda, Schüller claims,
Wallerstein had his own ideas about the dance interludes that Nijinska could
not and would not comply with.[87] Although the differences between the two
did not surface in the press, they may explain the aggrieved tone in the long,
rambling letter that Nijinska drafted to an unnamed correspondent when the
pay and contract dispute came to a head. "She was invited as a ballet master,"
she says, but was "forced to be some sort of assistant, and her artistic works
are being unceremoniously ruined . . . and filled with absurd insertions."

She cites as an example a dance that is supposed to take place in eighteenth-century Venice in which the women "clench their fists and stamp their heels in time with the music, as if they were in a German beer hall." "In general," she continues, "everything she is forced to do is artistically revolting to her, [including] this Dalcroze 'style.'" The mention of Dalcroze leads her to recall visiting Hellerau with Diaghilev and Nijinsky when she was nineteen and dismissing the Dalcroze school as a "sanatorium for rhythmic idiots." This in turn prompts a memory of "Mim"—Marie Rambert, who had stolen her place at Nijinsky's side—and her "anti-musical" way of "hammering the accents" when she danced a piece of choreography. Instead, Nijinska concludes, "One must see and hear the musical line and flow into it or cover it with another dance rhythm."[88] Clearly, she had not the slightest interest in Vienna's lively modern dance scene.[89]

It is unclear what provoked this outburst, against whom it was directed, and whether it was about artistic differences or who held the reins of power. It is also unlikely the letter was ever sent. Not that it mattered. On November 6, less than six weeks after her arrival in Vienna, Nijinska had returned to the cocoon of émigré Paris. She told the press that she had come by "special authorization of the Vienna Opera . . . to arrange the choreography of . . . works to be mounted by the Opéra Russe,"[90] another fib, but by now Krauss and his associates were beyond caring. Needless to say, she never returned to Vienna.

The new Opéra Russe season opened on November 15 with *Prince Igor*, a gala performance with Chaliapin in the role of Prince Galitzky and the celebrated Polovtsian dances in Act II performed in Nijinska's version of Fokine's choreography. The dancers knew those dances well. They had performed them all spring (if not before) and several times in San Sebastián, but one imagines Nijinska rushing to the Théâtre des Champs-Elysées to put them through their paces, infusing them with her energy and ambition. Chaliapin had not sung the role in Paris for many years, and his "formidable figure" and "power of expression" propelled the troupe to even greater heights, from the principal singers to the "choristers animated by a living flame and love for their art," the "corps de ballet frenzied, maddened by the rhythm of the choreography," and finally the "admirable Straram orchestra."[91] Backstage with her dancers, at such close quarters with the artist for so long her idol, Nijinska must have shared that awe. The season continued with another familiar work, *Sadko*, and two operas new to the company's repertory, *The Tsar's Bride*, by Rimsky-Korsakov, and *Rusalka*, by Alexander Dargomyzhsky, and like most Russian operas they included dances. *Rusalka*, especially, seems to have inspired Nijinska. In *Le Petit Parisien* Charles Tenroc called her Bohemian dances in Act II "a choreographic marvel"; in *Le Matin* (12–23) Jean Prudhomme noted that they were encored, while in *Comoedia* Pierre Maudru marveled at their "saltatory exaltation attaining a kind of wizardry."[92] To be sure, the opera was dominated by Chaliapin, who gave an unforgettable performance as the Miller. "In the Russian repertory," wrote Maudru,

> he is incomparable. His body is one with the music. . . . The assurance of his gestures, the power and rough suppleness of his voice, the truth of his attitudes, the expression of his face and of his mask, all convey down to the least detail the grandeur of the tragedy.[93]

The ovations were interminable.

The new year witnessed the last and greatest of the season's operatic reprises—*Boris Godunov*. Ever since Diaghilev's 1908 production at the Paris Opéra, *Boris* had become an exotic presence in the international repertory, its brooding atmosphere and dynastic politics a far cry from the works of Puccini or Massenet, with their tragic heroines and romantically charged plots. Now it received probably its best production since Diaghilev's revival at the Théâtre des Champs-Elysées in 1913. In those performances one senses the final glow of *Mir iskusstva*, Savva Mamontov's Private Opera Company, and the old Ballets Russes, Silver Age theatrical culture memorialized and resurrected through art. Week after week, crowds thronged the Théâtre des Champs-Elysées. Finally, on February 23, the season ended with Chaliapin singing his most celebrated role.

A novelty of the winter season was the programming of ballets independent of the opera repertory and even full evenings of dance. Nijinska had fought unsuccessfully for this in her contractual negotiations with Clemens Krauss—the right to restage works created for the Staatsoper on other companies, a key step in building the repertory for a company of her own. In December she staged her first ballet for the Opéra Russe—*Petrouchka*. This was a work she had performed ever since its Ballets Russes premiere in 1911, and she had staged variants and individual scenes in Kiev and Buenos Aires. Now, before an exigent Paris audience, she mounted the first post-Diaghilev production of the ballet. For the most part she adhered closely to the original: she had to, she explained on the eve of the premiere to Marc Semenoff, a Russian-speaking critic who wrote for *Le Courrier musical*, because of "the fixed text of the libretto, which conditions and determines the decors and dances." At the same time, she had to come up not only with "a new mise-en-scène" but also with "an independent choreography." Her *Petrouchka* parted company with Fokine's in a number of ways. She refused to use amateurs as supernumeraries, as Diaghilev had done in the later years of the Ballets Russes. As she told Semenoff, "At the Opéra Russe we have excellent technicians, and each performer owns his role emotionally and intellectually." She eliminated "individual divertissements" in order to "concentrate the entire force of movement on the ensembles of the crowd." More significantly, she viewed the "heroes" of the ballet, not as people who occasionally exhibited puppet-like behavior, as in the Fokine version, but as "*puppets*" who enjoyed what she called "the complexity of human feelings." Yes, she agreed with Semenoff's idea that "we are all a little like *puppets* whom destiny holds by the strings in one hand, while the ironic and the dreadful enact the drama." But she wanted to show the "inconsistencies" in the drama of Petrouchka, the Ballerina, and the Moor—the clashes of temperament. Above all, she wanted to show "our Petrouchka, with his beautiful misunderstood soul, hang[ing] over the barre before an implacable life [and] destiny."[94]

For some critics the changes hardly mattered. The ballet unlocked memories of the golden years of the Ballets Russes and its first generation of stars. Wrote Henri de Curzon in *Le Journal des Débats* about the revival:

> One could wish for nothing more with Monsieur Stravinsky's *Petrouchka*, which returned to the stage to end the evening. It was in the year 1911 that we made its acquaintance in the auditorium of the Châtelet, among Astruc's prestigious "Russian ballets," with Nijinsky and Tamar [sic] Karsavina; one remembers still its pungent, slightly crazy originality.[95]

For Levinson, too, the revival opened the floodgates of memory. *Petrouchka* was a unique spectacle, he told his readers. Under its carnival mask lurked not the "byzantine splendor" of the first tsars or the "gleaming imagery" of epic legends, but the St. Petersburg of Nicholas I, "the most fantastic capital of the world, conciliating the most contradictory elements, mingling Occident and Orient, present and past in a striking mélange of colors." He recalled the three superimposed planes of Fokine's original—the magnificent disorder of its strolling crowd and brouhaha of "realistic" animation; the Russian folklore intensified almost to the point of "burlesque hyperbole"; and finally, the puppet-ballerina of the barker's stall, heartless and mechanical, whose "inner emptiness" Fokine conveyed through a parody of classical dance. Finally, Levinson noted that the revival in post-Revolutionary Petrograd was "true to the spirit of the Parisian version."[96]

When the curtain rose on the Opéra Russe production, Levinson was amazed. "An intense life" had invaded the stage, a "tableau of popular jubilation," produced by a company that was not only young but also smaller and less seasoned than its predecessor. (According to Nina Tikanova, Nijinska put "more life and greater detail" into the fairground scenes than Fokine, who left a lot to improvisation.[97]) However, once the puppets appeared slumped over a barre instead of beating their little feet, Levinson's pleasure vanished.

No longer do we find the jokes, step combinations, grimaces, and gestures staged by Fokine. Not that the accepted version seems to us untouchable! But it remains the best by far. Nothing justifies the tricks of the ballet mistress, who is also the protagonist. . . . [S]he dances well, as befits a former soloist of the Imperial Ballet, but the host of "temps," profusion of *petite batterie*, and wealth of *entrechats* are entirely uncalled for when they render the movement dry and impoverished.[98]

Levinson had several other complaints. Most of Petrouchka's "mute monologue" in Scene 2 was gone, and all of the "amusing" episode of the Moor worshiping a coconut in Scene 3 (easily the ballet's most problematic treatment of race). Levinson's final word about Nijinska was as cutting as its many predecessors: she was too intent on destroying to invent something new. But his overall conclusion was more ambivalent. "The Opéra Russe has done well to revive *Petrouchka*," he wrote. "But it . . . could have done a better job."[99]

Levinson was not alone in criticizing Nijinska's approach to *Petrouchka*. Alexandre Benois, the ballet's librettist and designer, after voicing his discontent in *Poslednie novosti* continued to fume in an interview with Marc Semenoff published in *Le Courrier musical*. "Neither Stravinsky nor Diaghilev . . . nor I conceived of any philosophical substructure for *Petrouchka*," he told Semenoff. "The present Opéra Russe à Paris asked me to 'redo' *Petrouchka*, which as you know has been performed with modifications in Petersburg, Copenhagen, and Milan." Unhappily, time was short, and Benois, to his chagrin, had little contact with Nijinska about the dances. "Allow me to tell you," he added, "something about this sincere and immensely gifted artist. . . . She possesses, alas, a dictatorial spirit—so feminine, I believe—that causes her to live a little too shut up in her own conception and barely listen to the observations, however justified, of any-body else."[100] Her predecessors had not been so stubborn. Fokine, Leonid Leontiev (who had staged the ballet at the former Maryinsky Theater in 1920), and Boris Romanov (who had staged it in Milan) had all followed Benois' conception.[101]

Semenoff ended by musing on what he called "this vast and difficult problem of interpretation." What would Shakespeare, Molière, or Bach think about performances of their works today? Nearly twenty years had passed since *Petrouchka* had seen the light of day, and the work—regardless of what Benois thought—had hardly stayed the same. Serge Lifar, in an attack on the Opéra Russe revival, argued that Diaghilev had left the ballet in tatters, keeping it in repertory only to please the public. True, the production had seen better days, but the ballet—unlike numerous others that Diaghilev had quietly dropped—remained in repertory throughout the life of his com-pany, with Tamara Karsavina invited again and again to reprise her role. For Levinson and Benois, Nijinska's choice to sacrifice Fokine's traditional, "ca-nonical" choreography to her personal way of seeing was indefensible. Yet the primacy of individual artistic vision was the essence of modernism and a key tenet of the modernist approach to revival. Largely confined to the émigré press, the cavils of the émigré cultural elite did little to dampen the enthusiasm of audiences, including Russian ones and émigré celebrities such as Anna Pavlova, who was amazed by Nijinska's performance and by the fact that she had staged the ballet in ten days. In her diary, Nijinska recounts a reassuring conversation with Chaliapin. "Many people are attacking me," she explained, "and I want to know from you . . . is [*Petrouchka*] really that bad?" "He put his hand on my heart. 'Don't trust them, Bronia, when they attack you. It's always like that.'"[102] For a community intent on preserving a culture under siege by an increasingly entrenched Soviet state and the intensifying forces of assimilation, it was easy to see change as a symptom of cultural loss.

As the Opéra Russe's in-house ballet master, Nijinska was constrained by the need to produce identifiably "Russian" works. Hence the presence of *Petrouchka* and *The Polovtsian Dances* on every "gala" program and the ab-sence of "non-Russian" works such as *Daphnis and Chloë* and *Bolero*. The creative team and backstage personnel were overwhelmingly Russian, as were the producers and a majority of the dancers. In *Capriccio Espagnol*, to Rimsky-Korsakov's orchestral suite inspired by Spanish folk melodies, and *Etude*, she briefly stepped out of this creative ghetto. The final version of her "Bach ballet," *Etude* was a milestone, with Levinson alone devoting two long columns to it, the first in *Comoedia* and the second, a few weeks later, in *Candide*. This was Nijinska's fifth encounter with the work (if one includes the Kiev one that was never produced), and its abstraction—more than two years before Massine's first "symphonic" ballets—sparked controversy. She had long opposed the use of libretti, arguing that the author of a dance work was its choreographer (although legally, at the time, it was the librettist). The "word," she told Semenoff in a revealing interview, "is powerless to determine, inspire, and order the movement. . . . It can simply serve as a fortuitous pretext."[103] In *Le Ballet contemporain*, published in 1950, Pierre Michaut explained for a later generation that *Etude* was "free of all descriptive, dramatic, or picturesque intent," an attempt to transpose musical forms into choreographic forms through the interplay of symmetry, contrast, and alternating plastic themes. A phrase of Jules Lemaître appeared as an epigraph in the program: "I would readily admit that a ballet may do without a libretto, express nothing precise or continuous, and be only a succession of figures pleasing to the eye."[104] For Michaut the ballet was "monumental, complex, and rigorous." Under a "night sky full of stars and traversed by concentric circles," he wrote, "tiered, 'constructed' groups animated moving, symmetrical, and 'collective' architectures. *The noble sonorities of Johann Sebastian Bach*, the argument stated, *seem to live their own life and create their own plastic forms; spiritualized beings move in an unreal world*."[105] Vuillermoz was taken with the work as well:

> The serenity and superhuman grandeur of [Bach] has led the painter Boris Bilinsky to situate the work in a sort of zodiacal paradise. . . . There immaterial beings . . . evolve, form groups, gather, and construct strange living architectures. On their foreheads a gold diadem evokes the halo of the blessed. Their naked arms crossed above their heads suggest the joined wings of Seraphim. And the veils attached to their shoulders complete the stylization. . . . When the curtain went up, the effect was dazzling.[106]

For Fernand Divoire, one of the very few Paris critics who followed the work of concert artists outside the ballet field, *Etude* was quite simply one of the most beautiful ballets he had ever seen, ranking with *Les Noces* as Nijinska's masterpiece. "Imagine," he wrote in *La Revue de France*,

> a backdrop with a milky and dark sky peopled with stars, signs, and concentric circles, and in front, a pyramid of clouds with tiers of beings. I say

"beings" because I cannot speak of them as men, angels, souls, or planets. They are the beings of a new harmony . . . dressed in short bluish tunics and short capes . . . which are not wings but constantly make you think of them. . . . When they move, they do so without heaviness, petrification, or architectural rigidity so complex and so carefully structured are their groupings. . . . One comes away with the impression of . . . a whole in which music, color, and dance meld in a kind of perfect spirituality.[107]

Nothing could be further from the reading of the work by Levinson. To him, Nijinska was guilty of many sins. On an "arbitrarily shrunken basis of the *danse d'école*, she [had] built a style unique to herself and split into three elements: *classicism*—but rooted in simplified and frozen patterns— *Germanism* (melding the individual with the team and replacing harmony with orders), and *Sovietism*." Levinson hastens to add that he does not mean Soviet in a political sense but as a "spiritual attitude." Once, he writes, Marius Petipa had reigned over the coryphées, soloists, and stars of the Imperial stage. Now, Nijinska submits that world to a "dictator's absolute . . . authority." Levinson's chief complaint was that her dancers had lost their humanity in her complex architectural arrangements. The dancer in *Etude*, he writes, "is no longer the living, elegantly chiseled traditional opera dancer who circulates in space." Instead of "happy shades" making and unmaking "the airy scaffolds" of the *ballet blanc*, Nijinska's dancers are "caryatids or giants of granite bent under the weight of a massive architrave." "The grandeur is decorative, monumental, and inhuman.[108]

I know that all beauty is tyrannical. . . . But this excess, this abuse of the choreographer's power reducing man to the state of pure plastic element, impersonal and inanimate mechanism, bothered and even revolted me in the realization of Stravinsky's *Les Noces*. . . . Man as object, tool, pawn, log, or stone—this is what struck me as being of *Soviet* origin.[109]

Writing in *Candide* for a literary rather than theatrical audience, Levinson abandoned his elaborate architectural similes, but continued to hammer away at the "Soviet" aspect of *Etude* and Nijinska's style generally.

In Mme. Nijinska's aesthetic, there is something impersonal, inhuman, and tyrannical that comes from collectivist discipline and the Bolshevist galley slave. If I am not mistaken, Mme. Nijinska was in Russia in 1918 or

1919, those terrible years, at the head of a dance theater. She retains the imprint. The exercises that she imposes on her dancers always remind me of forced labor. In *Etude* she seems to insist on the labored character of her style. When the soloists finally detach themselves from their groups and are allowed to gambol freely on the stage, it appears that this freedom is only a delusion, for they must execute all their steps, take all their poses, with their fists crossed as if bound by an invisible chain: moral handcuffs.[110]

Clearly, *Etude* (like *Les Noces*) triggered memories that Levinson could not—would not—forget. He had suffered the fury of the Revolution, seen his Parnassus on the Neva destroyed, while Nijinska had joined forces with the regime. It was an unforgivable sin on her part, and it drew Levinson's implacable wrath.

Although the effects of the Great Depression were initially less devastating in France than in Germany or the United States, they cast a pall over the subsidized theaters, where during the whole of 1930, there were almost no new productions.[111] Levinson alludes to this dearth in his *Candide* article. Only the young troupe of the Opéra Russe gave any signs of life. Made up of recruits, "only yesterday students or amateurs, without experience or tradition, learning their métier while exercising it," these novices had actually succeeded in making something new. First came the revival of *Petrouchka*, in a version that "captivated us with the *élan vital* of the ensemble." Then came the "mischievous Slavic scherzo and . . . the frenetic gypsy tumult of *Russalka*" that was as good as the Polovtsian horde in *Prince Igor*.

> One could never have elicited such fireworks or so extreme an effort from a makeshift corps de ballet, if the dancers had not been electrified by the will, ambition, and determination of a leader. The young girls, still teenagers, are not the salaried members or functionaries of a subsidized stage; they lead the . . . precarious existence of émigrés, torn between study and earning their bread. The enthusiasm . . . and dynamism of these half-formed artists . . . who burn up the stage is a most surprising moral phenomenon. It attests to the gift or, even more, the choreographic calling of the Russian people.[112]

Levinson then turns to Nijinska, finally doing her some justice:

> This leader, this dictator, this magnetic presence is Mme. Nijinska, sister of that spectre of the rose who is, alas, only a specter now, and a collaborator of

Diaghilev. Although there are things that bother and even revolt me in this ballet mistress's way of thinking and making work, she is an astonishing and energetic teacher. In one month, she has created two new or almost new works for an enterprise only secondarily interested in dance—imagined them, staged them, and rehearsed them.[113]

Nina Tikanova conveys something of the dancers' passionate commitment to their work when she describes the first performance of *Etude*. The premiere had been postponed a few days, so it took place on January 23, the day Anna Pavlova died in the Hague. The dancers were on stage waiting for the curtain to go up, when someone in the house read a telegram from Holland announcing that Pavlova was dead. The whole audience stood up, and the curtain rose. There was a long minute of silence.

> Slowly, the conductor's baton brought the Bach overture to life. Under an immense starry sky, we danced *Etude*, grave, pure, and full of grandeur, each of us with the concentration that is a prayer, our *De Profundis* for the greatest artist of dance of all time.[114]

Apart from Levinson, nobody was thinking of handcuffs or Soviet dictators.

***

With the Opéra Russe season at an end, Nijinska concentrated on preparations for Ida Rubinstein's season at Covent Garden. She agreed to rehearse privately with Rubinstein from January 17 to March 17; with Rubinstein and Anatole Vilzak, her partner, from March 17 to April 17; and with the entire company from April 17 to July 18. Ever generous, Rubinstein agreed to pay Nijinska 70,000 francs for six months of rehearsal, and an additional 40,000 francs for a new production of *La Valse* and for the first act of *Orphée*, to the music of Roger-Ducasse. Finally, Nijinska agreed that from March 17 to July 18 she would devote herself entirely to Rubinstein's enterprise and not take on any other assignments, a promise she briefly regretted when she discovered that Chaliapin was singing with the Opéra Russe in London.[115]

As always, working with Rubinstein created havoc for her collaborators. Instead of opening in London on June 3, the season was put off to July, to allow for two gala performances at the Paris Opéra.[116] A steady stream of notes and telegrams from Rubinstein canceled dates, rescheduled rehearsals: she was in bed, she had a cough, she was very anxious to see Nijinska, she needed to see Singaevsky (who was acting as company manager)—always polite, always the lady: "I am so distressed," she wrote in early December, "but I cannot go to the theater tonight; I am in bed. But all my thoughts are with you. My friends saw you on Friday [the premiere of *Petrouchka*] and telephoned me in raptures."[117] Many of the dancers had followed Nijinska from the original Rubinstein company to the Opéra Russe, in addition to working with her on other assignments (such as *Aubade* and *Paysage Enfantin*). Now she strengthened this core group with new dancers, often recruited from Lubov Egorova's studio, where most of the students, from impoverished Russian émigré families, studied for free.[118] Among the newcomers were Kyra Abricossova (later known as Kira Bousloff), who came from a Moscow confectionary manufacturing family and eventually settled in Australia; Lily Krassovska and her fifteen-year-old daughter, Nathalie Krassovska, a star of the 1940s; an American named Joseph Crandall; the English dancer Rollo Gamble, who became an actor and stage director; Vera Lipskaia (Nina's sister), who had studied at the School of Movement, and her future husband, Serge Vladimiroff; and, finally, Nijinska's own daughter, dancing as Irina Istomina. As ballet master, Nijinska's chief task was reviving the ballets she had staged in 1928 and 1929 for Rubinstein—*Nocturne*, *Bolero*, *The Swan Princess*, *Les Noces de Psyché et de l'Amour*, and *La Bien-Aimée*. *Les Enchantements d'Alcine* and *David* were also on the list of works to be revived, but the rehearsals were supervised by Massine, who was also hired to choreograph *Amphion*, a sung, danced, and spoken work to a "poem" by Paul Valéry. According to Alexis Dolinoff, who served as Massine's assistant, the two choreographers did not get along, and there were a number of unpleasant incidents.[119]

Valéry was a major French cultural figure, and *Amphion*, his first work for the theater, was widely (if unenthusiastically) reviewed. By comparison, Nijinska's new version of *La Valse* received short shrift, although Nijinska noted in her diary that it was a "great success."[120] Critics who did write about the ballet, now set in a Viennese ballroom at the time of Napoleon III, liked what they saw. In *Le Ménestrel*, Jean Chantavoine commended the felicitous decision to replace the disconcerting scenario of 1929 with one that fully realized the intentions of the composer.[121] Levinson, too, alluded to that "strange scenario," which moved "teams of swimmers or skaters" around an Italian baroque interior. However, "this time we are given a *Valse* after Ravel," with waltzes, cotillon figures, a mazurka, and sparkling pas de basque steps.

If before, Nijinska had played too freely with the music, now she "bends too docilely to the intentions of the composer and, in her concern for fidelity, resists giving free rein to her imagination."[122]

From Paris the company headed to London. This was the real focus of Rubinstein's efforts, a two-week season at Covent Garden during which she would present not only a repertory of ten ballets but also her two most celebrated dramatic works—*The Martyrdom of Saint Sebastian*, the play by Gabriele d'Annunzio that had made headlines in 1911, and *La Dame aux Camélias*, the Alexandre Dumas play made famous by Sarah Bernhardt that Rubinstein first performed in 1923. It was a huge undertaking, involving dozens of actors, singers, and dancers, as well as several tons of luggage, which arrived by boat train, although Rubinstein herself flew to London on July 4, two days before the first performance.[123] She spoke to reporters in flawless English, and fibbed in an interview with the *Observer* that she had "never found time to visit England before."[124] Unsurprisingly, *Saint Sebastian* did not fare well with London's critics. It was too opulent, the acting too histrionic, the language too mannered and ornate, and it was all in French. "What chiefly remains in one's memory," Richard Capell wrote in the *Daily Mail*, is "Bakst's spectacle of 3rd century Rome interpreted with references to 15th century Florence . . .—and then Mme. Rubinstein's singular impersonation of the saint: a slender, ascetically slender figure, a sexless-looking figure . . . with austere face, seen first in the golden armour of a captain of the archers (like a Donatello St. George) then in the second act a Joan of Arc."[125]

The ballets were far more successful. Still, the numerous changes in program and exceptionally long intervals indicate that all was not well backstage. The troupe had been rehearsing since April, but time apparently ran out, forcing many last-minute changes. *Orphée* was announced, then canceled; Ravel failed to conduct *Bolero* and *La Valse*, and both *Les Noces de Psyché et de l'Amour* and *Les Enchantements de la Fée Alcine* were postponed to the end of the season. "We rehearsed from morning to night and went by taxi from the theater to a studio in the city," Nina Tikanova recalled.[126] *Amphion*, the most ambitious of the ballets, failed to impress, and critics made mincemeat of Henri Sauguet's music for *David* ("shapeless and feeble").[127]

Nijinska's contributions fared considerably better. *The Swan Princess*, *Nocturne*, and *La Bien-Aimée* were generally liked, and *Bolero* and especially *La Valse* sparked genuine excitement. "I could see 'La Valse' half a dozen times and still want to see it again," wrote the editor of the *Dancing Times*.[128] Tikanova loved dancing the new version of *La Valse*. She found it mysterious and unreal, and was thrilled by the "bit" Nijinska had slipped in for her and her partner at the start of the ballet. Benois had designed a mid-nineteenth-century drawing room, and when the curtain rose a scrim seemed to envelope it in mystery. As the melody grew clearer, F. Bonavia told readers of the *New York Times*, "the gauze lifted and the ladies and cavaliers, who had seemed of marble came to life. . . . [T]he eye was charmed by the riot of color provided by the costumes of soldiers, diplomats, various 'gentry' and crinolined women."[129] Cyril W. Beaumont was reminded of a painting by Eugène Lami, "a crimson and gold ballroom lined with enormous mirrors and lit with groups of candelabra. At the far end folding doors thrown back give on to a second ballroom." The dancers formed various figures, he noted, sometimes in small groups and sometimes in massed formations.

At another stage, dancers are seen in the distant room, and a very interesting form of choreographic counterpoint is provided by the dancers in the second room moving quickly in a chain, while those in the foreground slowly revolve to the languorous strains of the waltz; later, the rhythms are reversed.

La Valse, Beaumont concluded, "was a lovely conception and well worth revival."[130] Alas, Rubinstein thought otherwise and in 1934 had Fokine redo the choreography.

The Rubinstein season took place at London's most prestigious theater under the patronage of the French minister of fine arts. Although Rubinstein was wealthy, the very magnitude of the season, to say nothing of its lavishness, suggests that she had financial help: not from the French government but from her longtime lover, the Anglo-Irish politician and brewery owner Walter Guinness. Their twenty-year liaison was no secret, and once, as a joke, one of the dancers put up a sign in the studio with the advertising slogan for Guinness Stout—"Guinness is good for you."[131] Privileged treatment was evident in other ways during the season. On July 16 the second and last performance of *David* was broadcast live from Covent Garden on the BBC National Program, although as "Lis'Ener" wondered in the *Manchester Garden*, why bother, when the Sauguet music was the least important part of the ballet? The broadcast was then retransmitted the following night on the National-Programme in France.[132] And on July 24, well after the season had ended, *Comoedia* reported the "magnificent success" of the season. Thanks to Rubinstein, "poets and musicians of France were the heroes of these beautiful artistic repasts, which England will long remember."[133] By then, however, Rubinstein had disbanded the company and left on a long cruise of the Pacific.

***

When Rubinstein departed, Nijinska had been working steadily for nearly a year and a half. She had created a number of new ballets, restaged and re-created others, and added to the repertory of works that defined her distinctive personality as an artist. She had developed a strong group of dancers, using them in various undertakings to make up for the absence of a permanent company. She had won over critics, even Levinson to some degree, although he certainly admired her more as a ballet master and teacher than as a choreographer. In London she had earned the respect of a new generation of critics, solidifying her Diaghilev reputation and reintroducing herself to British audiences. In *Balletomania*, published in 1933, Arnold Haskell calls her "influence on dancing . . . of first-class importance" and refers to *Les Noces* and *Les Biches* as landmarks. He recalls the "near masterpieces" of the Rubinstein season (marred because of Rubinstein herself), especially *La Valse*, "with its . . . whirling mass of couples in an enfilade of brightly lit and mirrored rooms."[134] Finally, Massine's presence in the Rubinstein company in 1931 introduced—or reintroduced—him to works in Nijinska's repertory that would leave clear traces in his own ballets during the decade to follow. *La Bien-Aimée*, for instance, had a theme very similar to Massine's 1936 *Symphonie Fantastique*, while the "living pyramids" of *Amphion* and a number of later Massine ballets suggest a debt to *Les Noces*, which Massine may well have seen in rehearsal or performance in the late 1920s.[135]

***

On August 23, 1931, word reached Nijinska that Lapitzky had died. "Zhenia has left us," she wrote in her diary with a cross after the date. "My student, my son in art. Everything real and alive is leaving my world."[136] She had brought him out of Russia, and he had remained ever loyal, following her when she left the Ballets Russes and dancing in all her companies, however stillborn or short-lived. He had drowned near Nice, swept away by the current. Seriozha Unger, her other devoted student from Kiev, was bereft. "Yesterday, the 28th, at 4 o'clock, I buried our dear kind Zhenechka," he wrote to Nijinska. "Why didn't I die instead of him? . . . Bronislava Fominichna, is it possible to understand everything? I loved Zhenia. I quarreled with him often, but it was so transitory. . . . And now—the end. He was not a friend to me but a brother. Without him the only one left is you."[137] Nijinska immediately wired money to help pay for the funeral and sent him letters whose kind words kept him going. He wrote to Zhenia's father in Moscow and sent his address to Nijinska and asked her to approve what the priest had drafted for the gravestone.[138] It was a sad way to end the summer.

Meanwhile Nijinska idled, hoping for work. In October she went to see Rubinstein, now back from her travels, doubtless to persuade her to resuscitate her company, but Rubinstein was still recovering from her recent exertions.[139] Later in the month Nijinska received a letter from Pierre Tugal announcing the creation of the Archives Internationales de la Danse, founded by Rolf de Maré in memory of the Ballets Suédois and Jean Borlin, and inviting her to "collaborate" with the new organization, adding that he would send a Russian-speaking staff member to speak to her.[140] Finally, in November, the famed German theater director Max Reinhardt invited her to Germany to "doctor" the ballets in Jacques Offenbach's *Tales of Hoffmann* at Berlin's huge Grosses Schauspielhaus. The opera was based on three short stories by E. T. A. Hoffmann, each centering on a poet's unsuccessful loves—for Olympia, a mechanical doll, Antonia, a singer, and Giulietta, a courtesan. Reinhardt was celebrated for the scale of his productions and for his ability to weld armies of actors, dancers, and singers into scenes of intense emotionality and absolute harmony, achieving a true Wagnerian *Gesamtkunstwerk*. There was little dance per se, but movement was everywhere. It was what tied scenes together, made acting a form of rhythmic pantomime, and transformed stage direction at least partly into choreography. Nijinska doubted that Reinhardt really needed her, but she needed the money, so she went. As it turned out, the dances Anton Dolin had staged were so poor they had to be redone. Dolin devotes several pages to this episode in his memoir *Ballet Go Round*. Yes, the Doll Dance "was awful and had to be done all over again," but he did it all himself.[141] No mention of Nijinska, although the program clearly states that the choreography was by "Nijinskaja und Dolin" in that order. Nijinska also rechoreographed the concluding ballet featuring Nini Theilade. Reinhardt was ecstatic: "You are a great artist," he told Nijinska. "This is just the beginning. We will create great things together."[142]

By now, Nijinska had worked with many stage directors. However, the productions themselves had been relatively conventional. But for Reinhardt,

Offenbach's opera was only the starting point for the creation of a work about E. T. A. Hoffmann. Whole new scenes were added, along with music, dances, comic business that stretched the evening to four hours. For Nijinska there was no doubt: she was in the presence of pure genius. It was a "great gift of fate" to work for even a few days with someone of Reinhardt's caliber, to have the chance to create choreography that melded so perfectly with the production. After returning to Paris, she ruminated about the director in her diary. Reinhardt, she writes on December 2, is like Diaghilev and Chaliapin, "obsessed, possessed by the theater." On December 11 there is an exceptionally long ten-page entry, and all of it is about Reinhardt.

> I have never had a chance to see something similar to what I saw with Reinhardt. . . . From the very first, his conception surrounds, envelops the viewer. . . . There is nowhere for the viewer to turn, to let the focus slip away, and get caught up in external details.
>
> Reinhardt does not use conventional methods used by other directors. . . . There is not a single mass scene in the entire play. . . . The action never stops. . . . There is a feeling of grandeur, an almost complete absence of breaks, a constant acceleration of the action, and a perfect fulfillment of the conception by talented creators, artists, and stage masters—all of it subdues the audience completely!
>
> Unforgettable achievement!
>
> Reinhardt is a true creator of Theater![143]

Nijinska was deeply touched by Reinhardt's respect for her, and one can be sure that she was thinking of Diaghilev, Rouché, and the many directors and innumerable bureaucrats she had encountered when she confided these thoughts to her diary. She had written to Reinhardt before leaving Berlin, and his answer—in French—reached her in Paris. "I was delighted to be able to work with you and by the great success of your marvelous choreographic conception. I hope we can soon repeat the experience of working together."[144] Less than two months later, Nijinska was back in Berlin. But the depth of Reinhardt's esteem only became clear in 1934 when he invited her to Hollywood to choreograph the dances in his pathbreaking film *A Midsummer Night's Dream*.

12

Les Ballets Russes de Bronislava Nijinska

Serge de Diaghileff n'est plus, mais Bronislava Nijinska maintient la tradition.[1]

> (Serge Diaghilev is no more, but Bronislava
> Nijinska carries on the tradition.)

Nijinska spent most of October 1931 in despair. "Mundane chaos has shattered the fairy tale," she wrote in her diary.[2] The Opéra Russe had suspended operations, leaving her without work and without a company. At home in Paris, she took to her bed. But as she must have known, given how quickly news sped around the ballet world, a new company was in the offing. Although it was signing up *her* dancers from the Opéra Russe à Paris and the Ida Rubinstein company, the organizers—Colonel de Basil and René Blum—had passed over her in favor of Balanchine and Boris Kochno. The previous spring, Blum and de Basil had begun discussing the idea for a company based in Monte Carlo. Blum was to provide the theater and financial support; de Basil, the dancers, repertory, scenery, and costumes, while forfeiting the right of the Opéra Russe to produce future ballets. On October 12, the same day Nijinska took to her bed, de Basil hired Serge Grigoriev, Diaghilev's former *régisseur général*, and he in turn started hiring dancers. By November most of the company was in place, with Balanchine as *maître de ballet* and Kochno, Nijinska's old nemesis, as *conseiller artistique*. Idled, with so many cards stacked against her, Nijinska sank into a deep depression.[3]

***

In the late 1920s, Nijinska began titling and copying her diaries. She made at least two "clean" copies of her 1927–30 diary, calling the first *Diaries of Gratuitous Pain*, and the second, *Two Loves*, with *Diaries of Gratuitous Pain* as a subtitle. She titled her 1930–31 diary *Rain on My Parnassus, or Love Madness*, adding an epigraph by the fourteenth-century mystic Jacopone da Todi, "*Oh, this mute love that is afraid of speech and full of mystery.*" And she called the longer version of her 1931–32 diary *Without Consciousness, Only Heart*.[4] None of the "copies" are identical, although they usually start out as attempts to "clean up" a previous version. But sooner or later Nijinska begins to edit them, correcting a word here and there, crossing out a sentence, or in some cases, deleting whole passages, as if to home in on the narrative—and then she simply keeps writing. And what is that narrative? As the titles and epigraphs suggest, it is the grand story of her love, mute, unspoken, hidden from all except her friend Henriette Pascar, for the larger-than-life Fedor Chaliapin, twice married, a charmer of innumerable affairs and irrepressible sexual drive, who once consulted Tolstoy about how to curb his sexual appetites given that he liked almost every woman he met.[5]

Nijinska had met him in the spring of 1911 in Monte Carlo. He singled her out, enchanted by her innocence and adoration, telling Diaghilev that she was very gifted. He took her for drives and under the moonlight gave her a first kiss. Her brother was appalled. Diaghilev, equally appalled, warned the singer off. And so ended her one true romance. She married, had two children, married again, survived revolution, civil war, emigration, and exile, re-created herself as a performer, became a choreographer, and never forgot. "How few were those enchanted days . . . but how much from them has remained with me for life," she concluded in a reminiscence.[6] They were like the Muse's "fatal kiss" in *Le Baiser de la Fée*, marking the dawn of her creative self-awareness, the moment of her birth as an artist and a woman. For Nijinska never doubted—at least in these diaries—that she owed the inspiration for her creative achievement to Chaliapin. In their obsessiveness, in the endless ruminations on love, emptiness, unhappiness, and personal suffering, the diaries maintain this fiction. Writing made him infinitely more present than reality.

Once Nijinska began working for the Rubinstein company, her craving for his physical presence intensified. As opening night approaches, all she can think about is Chaliapin and whether he will be in the audience. He isn't. He misses all of the season's performances, denying her the pleasure of hearing how much he admires her art.[7] Returning from tour, she sees him day and night in her dreams. They are "full of caresses," she writes, and she wakes up happy. It doesn't really matter, she adds, if this "happiness" is real or not: "I was with you."[8]

In the winter of 1930–1931, Nijinska finally found herself at Chaliapin's side in the Opéra Russe. At their first meeting, they embraced and exchanged banalities.[9] In the weeks ahead she reads happiness and despair into the smallest action. His proximity drives her wild, even as she struggles to hide her inner turmoil. Of course, he misses the opening of her *Petrouchka*,[10] has nothing to say about her dances in *Sadko*, and ignores her ballet programs. The following summer, in despair, she makes a pilgrimage to Lourdes, although she had long ceased to be a practicing Catholic. "My art was a marriage to F.," she writes a few days later. "With every movement I communicated something important." But Chaliapin sees and hears nothing.[11]

With their interminable scenes of self-abasement and humiliation, Nijinska's diaries are painful to read. The suffering is so all-consuming and the sense of worthlessness so pervasive that one is hard pressed to find a connection between the love-struck adolescent of the diaries, fixated on a romantic interlude in an ever more distant past, and the driven, successful choreographer. Time often plays havoc with memory. But in Nijinska's case, because the romance of her life remained confined to her imagination, it survived intact, like a wound that never healed. Nijinska's "love," magnified in the aftermath of her encounter with Chaliapin to include her activities as a choreographer, offered her the succor of a powerful artistic figure and blanket approval of her accomplishments, including the sacrifice of her family's well-being to her "destiny." To be sure, that approval was only a figment of her imagination. As her diary attests, Chaliapin had no interest in being either her mentor or her lover. And even if he inspired her art, he also diminished it by withholding his validation.

***

In the fall of 1931, as Blum and de Basil plotted and schemed, Nijinska was making plans for a season at the Opéra-Comique the following spring. Chaliapin was the linchpin: he would sing *Prince Igor*, *Mozart and Salieri* (as yet unknown in France), and the ever-popular *Boris Godunov*, which would alternate with evenings of ballet by a company of her own. On December 27, Nijinska's forty-first birthday by the old Julian calendar, she learned that Chaliapin had signed the contract.[12] De Basil immediately got wind of it and tried buying her off with an exceptionally lucrative contract in return for creating two original works.[13] But de Basil (with Balanchine and Kochno in tow) was no match for the seductive presence of Chaliapin, and on January

22, she signed the contract for her company to appear as part of the "Russian Season" the following spring at the Opéra-Comique. "May God help me," she wrote in her diary.[14]

Nijinska's repertory was ambitious and wide-ranging, intended to display the multiple facets of her choreographic identity. It included two new works: *Les Comédiens Jaloux*, to Alfredo Casella's playful "Scarliattiana" for piano and orchestra, and *Variations*, to Beethoven's "32 Variations on an Original Theme in C minor" for solo piano orchestrated by Vladimir Pohl, a founder and professor at the Russian Conservatory in Paris and her son's music teacher.[15] Nijinska revived two of her Rubinstein ballets, *Bolero* and *The Swan Princess*, the Opéra Russe version of *Etude*, and *Les Biches*, unseen since Diaghilev's death. She also staged the *Polovtsian Dances* and the Polonaise in *Boris Godunov*, as well as a program of divertissements. Of the ballets proper, only *The Swan Princess* had music by a Russian composer, suggesting that Nijinska intended to use this "Russian" season to insist upon her identity as a "European" artist.

Once again Nijinska was under the gun, racing against time, responsible for almost everything, assisted only by Singaevsky, who also served as company manager. In early March she wrote to Poulenc telling him that she was planning to revive *Les Biches*. "What joy to learn that we will see *Les Biches* again," he replied.[16] She commissioned new scenery from the ballet's original designer, Marie Laurencin,[17] and approached Boris Bilinsky to redesign *The Swan Princess*, rejecting Rubinstein's sumptuous pageantry. Years later she explained her decision in a letter to the Soviet ballet historian Nikolai Eliash, who was writing a book about Pushkin and ballet. The sets and costumes by Benois were "far more suitable to a grand opera production than to a ballet." Bilinsky's designs, by contrast, were "closer to the Russian popular *lubok*" and to the spirit of "Pushkin's gay little tale." The choreography for both productions was the same, but at the Opéra-Comique the Rimsky-Korsakov music was performed with chorus.[18]

Nijinska had already worked with Bilinsky on several projects. Marc Chagall, by contrast, was a ballet outsider when she approached him to redesign *Bolero* as well as create the scenery and costumes for *Variations*. In late March, Chagall showed her his sketches; she paid him 1,000 francs as an advance and urged him to finish the costume designs as soon as possible. And then silence. Chagall responded angrily:

> We agreed on the price. I gave you a discount. Nik. Nik. [Singaevsky] promised to me the rest of the advance in 2–3 days. . . . Almost two weeks went

by—with no sign of him. Finally, Nik. Nik. calls and tells me that you have changed your mind. You no longer like painting on stage and your admiration for my work . . . was merely a compliment on your part, and so on and so forth.

I was taken aback. I had worked under pressure . . . and . . . according to him, you don't like painting at all, even though you knew I was a painter. . . .

Even though I am insulted . . . you are free to give the job to someone else.

I hope, however, that my ideas and scenery will not be used on stage.[19]

Although Chagall had reduced his price, money was clearly an issue. However, it was not the only one. Although Nijinska turned to her old friend Natalia Goncharova for the *Bolero* designs, she commissioned Yury Annenkov (or Georges Annenkoff, as he was known in France) to design both *Variations* and *Les Comédiens Jaloux*. A multidisciplinary artist only a year older than Nijinska, Annenkov had spent several years in the Soviet Union before emigrating to France and pursuing a successful career in theater and film. It is unclear when Nijinska met him, but in the 1930s he designed all of her company's new works as well as a poster for "La Nijinska Ballets Russes."[20] Unlike Chagall, Annenkov was not an easel painter but an artist whose innovative stagecraft brought a new dimension to Nijinska's work. Nina Tikanova, for one, regarded his designs for *Variations* as "very avant-garde for the era." In the first tableau, set in the classical world, she remembered a sky brushed with the suggestion of a cloud, a striking touch of green, an ancient column, and a stage bathed in light. In the second, a swing replaced the column, and Russian peasants performed their rounds until a storm drove them from the stage. The third tableau reminded Tikanova of the sculptures of François Rude celebrating the French revolutionary spirit.[21] She was equally impressed by Annenkov's gay and ingenious scenery for *Les Comédiens Jaloux*, consisting of screens that the dancers themselves shifted, changing the scene in the blink of an eye.[22]

Nijinska began rehearsing the dancers in early February 1932.[23] Ten days later, Margaret Severn, a spirited American dancer whose mother was in Budapest working with the Freudian psychoanalyst Sandor Ferenczi, donned heavy black wool tights, a black tunic, white socks, and pink toe shoes, and with a dozen other hopefuls auditioned for the new company. The audition took the form of a short class, which the well-trained Severn (who had studied with Luigi Albertieri and Fokine in New York, and Lubov Egorova, Olga Preobrajenska, and Nikolai Legat in Paris) sailed through, and she was engaged as a soloist.[24] Nijinska was impressed by her technique and appetite for hard work. As Severn explained to her mother,

> The schooling is very stiff; she goes in for a sort of dramatic tension of move-ment which is very effective, but she overdoes it, just as Fokine overdoes his softness. She includes very few pirouettes in her routine (but she clapped her hands with joy one night to see how I could do 'em—THEY can't do 'em, of course, because they don't practice enough). No toe work and nothing of a plastic nature. . . . You gotta hand it to old Albertieri—he had them all beat for a comprehensive routine of steps.[25]

They had class every morning, followed by three hours of rehearsal in the afternoon and three at night. Severn was in heaven; even Nijinska ex-perienced a "surprising" sense of peace.[26] The only rub from the dancers' point of view was money. As was the case of most hard-up Russian compa-nies, rehearsals were unpaid, and the dancers had to buy their pointe shoes. "Well, this is more fun than a picnic," Severn told her mother, "if only I had a way . . . to make my bread and butter, I'd be perfectly happy."[27] (Doubtless her mother came to the rescue.) Others had it much harder. "The financial situation of our family was catastrophic," remembered Nina Tikanova, who knitted for pennies, as did other dancers in the company. "The rent was un-paid, the electricity cut off, and when the grocer's credit dried up, we lived on bread and coffee. In the fifteenth arrondissement, people like us abounded."[28]

Performances began on May 23 with *Prince Igor*. However, weeks be-fore, on April 10, the "Ballet Company of Bronislava Nijinska" (Compagnie des Ballets de Bronislava Nijinska) made its debut at a Salle du Trocadéro benefit performance for needy Russian children in France. Nearly all the "dance divertissements" on the shared program (which included "airs" from *Eugene Onegin* and a gypsy chorus) came from Nijinska's repertory—"The Three Ivans" and the Harlequin and Columbine variations from *The Sleeping Princess*, the Bohemian dances from *Rusalka*, and her old solo *La Poupée*. Anatole Vilzak, the company's *premier danseur*, danced a Harlequin variation that Nijinska had staged for him, while his wife, Ludmilla Schollar, led a cast of women in a new ensemble dance, *Valse-Fantaisie* to Glinka. There were secondary roles for Thadée Slavinsky, a Diaghilev veteran, and for Tatiana Ouchkova, a talented young dancer who was the daughter of a Moscow mil-lionaire, a niece of Chaliapin's wife, and the sister-in-law of the conductor Serge Koussevitzky. As for Margaret Severn, Nijinska not only allowed her to dance two of her own numbers, *Valse Brillante* and *Caprice Viennoise*, but even to keep her own name, rather than Russify it.[29] "Nijinska had a great ovation," she wrote to her mother the day after the performance, "which, of course, had other elements in it than just her performance, it being an audience of Russians. But her performance was splendid—she is a great artist." And Severn was happy to report, her waltz was "a decided success." "Sin," her nickname for Singaevsky, told her "he liked it, Madam liked it, critics liked it and public liked it, 'it' being me."[30]

Nijinska made very few entries in her diary during the weeks of rehearsal. We know from Severn's letters that they finished *Bolero* in mid-March and that around the same time Nijinska choreographed a short but "snappy little dance" for her in *Variations*. "The dance is one of the most brilliant and most difficult concoctions I have ever seen," she wrote to her mother.

> It is jammed full of pirouettes, finishing with very fast fouettés, but not arranged in the usual way; it has nuances which cause it to sparkle the more. It's on toe, 3/4 tempo, and just a trifle like that waltz I once did at the Hippodrome, . . . only more vigorous. It is, in fact, so difficult as to be almost impossible, and I am wondering if I can really execute it all quite perfectly in the stage. . . . One especially difficult part is where, after a small very quick circle of "little turns" on toe, I suddenly stop and do a very slow relevé on one toe, lifting the other high and carrying around from front to back, while I remain on the one toe . . . and then develop it into a very slow fouetté, increasing to a frenzy of speed for the finish. . . . Nij grinned from ear to ear, and when I had done it for the last time (and with remarkable perfection) the whole troupe burst into uproarious applause.[31]

Severn clearly enjoyed the challenge. "I must repeat," she told her mother on March 8, "that her choreography is simply lovely. She uses simple ballet steps to better advantage than anyone else that I know, and her dynamics are very good. . . . Very little Fokine softness and no German writhing. A great deal of virility, passion, and severity in her movements. Also, humor, and in the Russian things, a quaint charm."[32]

Nijinska had worked with about half the dancers before. Among the newcomers, apart from Severn, was Igor Schwezoff, a graduate of the former Maryinsky school and various Soviet companies, and Serge Bousloff, a young Russian dancer, who later settled in Australia. But they did not make up for the dancers who had left her for the Ballets Russes de Monte-Carlo, including those like David Lichtenstein (now known as David Lichine), Nina Verchinina, and Hélène Kirsova, who owed their start in the professional ballet world to her. Despite the presence of such well-known dancers as Vilzak, Schollar, and Slavinsky on the roster, Nijinska was her company's only real star. All the publicity centered on her, and she would have looked askance at youngsters courting the press. As the novelist Louis Céline told Margaret Severn, "You'll never get anywhere in that company. It will always be Nijinska, Nijinska, and Nijinska."[33]

Rumor had it that Nijinska wanted Olga Spessivtzeva for the season. However, the ballerina was dancing in South America, so she approached Alice Nikitina, a Diaghilev star of the late 1920s. Her arrival struck consternation into the ranks of the company's rising soloists, who saw longed-for opportunities suddenly vanish. "It wasn't so bad being in the corps de ballet when there was no première," Margaret Severn complained to her mother on March 12,

> but I feel that it is so rightfully my place that I have hard work to refrain from swatting her one on the nose when I see her. That she is not "working for" Nijinska is evidenced by the simple fact that Nijinska requires everybody to rehearse in black. Nikitina wears pale blue tights, deep blue tunic, red overtights, and a green and white striped sweater—and trails a perfectly marvelous dream of a coat in the dust.[34]

For Nikitina, who hadn't danced in Paris since Diaghilev's death, a lot was riding on the season. She was reprising the role of the Garçonne in *Les Biches* and dancing new roles in *Variations* (Diane), *Etude*, and *The Swan Princess*. Others might have gone the extra mile. But Nikitina preferred to dash off to London and Morocco, and unlike everyone else in the company had the means to do so. Soon she left for good. In her memoirs Nikitina claims that she did so because Nijinska had decided to dance parts that she considered hers.[35] More likely she feared being overshadowed by the company's young talents. By May, Tikanova was learning the role of Diane, which she ultimately danced, and Severn that of the Garçonne. Suddenly, out of nowhere (or, at least, that's how it appeared to Severn), Vera Nemchinova, who had originated the role in 1924, materialized to claim it, becoming the company's de facto star.[36]

***

The Opéra-Comique's "Saison russe" opened with *Prince Igor* on May 23, 1932. Despite high ticket prices, the house was packed, and the Russian community turned out in droves. Critics pulled out all the superlatives they could muster to praise Chaliapin, the Opéra Russe chorus, and the *Polovtsian Dances*, in which Nijinska followed the "grand lines" of Fokine's celebrated choreography.[37] The second program fared less well. Rimsky-Korsakov's opera *Mozart and Salieri* was new to Paris and not much liked, save for the excerpts from Mozart's *Requiem* sung by the "magnificent" Opéra Russe chorus. Bilinsky's designs for *The Swan Princess* were generally praised, and Tatiana Ouchkova, in the role originated by Ida Rubinstein, was loudly applauded, even if some critics regretted Rubinstein's absence.[38] As before, the response to *Etude* was mixed, with some critics overwhelmed by its beauty and symbolic character and others hating it. Critics were also divided over the merits of Nijinska's all-ballet program. Although *Les Biches* was universally acclaimed—its very French charm appealed at a time of mounting nationalism—*Bolero* fared poorly, with much of the criticism directed at Nijinska, who had stepped into Rubinstein's role. Henry Malherbe in *Le Temps* baldly stated what many privately thought, that Nijinska was "as far as possible from the image of a Spanish dancer," while Emile Vuillermoz chided her for placing the critic in the unhappy position of giving her advice, but "an artist of her quality" should know how to avoid such a grievous "error in casting."[39] Still, she had her defenders. Nijinska "was quite simply incredible," wrote one, "a call, brutal and irresistible, to love and sensual pleasure."[40] Capitalizing on her athleticism, Nijinska had infused it with naked sexual power.

For Nijinska, much rode on the season's two new works. *Variations* was the more ambitious, not only stylistically but also intellectually. It had three scenes, each evoking an era and an atmosphere—the Pyrrhic, a radiant vision of antiquity in the style of Jacques-Louis David, with Fauns, Warriors, Bacchantes, and a virtuoso part for Tikanova as Diane, all enticing youth and charm; the Pastoral, an idyll in the Russia of Alexander I with peasant dances led by Tatiana Ouchkova; and, finally, the Pathetic (*Pathétique*), set (as Maurice Brillant wrote) on "the morrow of the [French] Revolution and the eve of the imperial epic." Brillant found the *Pathétique* deeply moving, even if the subject matter was unconducive to dance and there was little conventional dancing. Especially memorable was the "beautiful tableau formed by the Merveilleuses and the Incroyables, all striking in red," although the "orthodox balletomane" would certainly "frown at this invasion of the mimetic."[41] Like Brillant, the theater critic of the *Daily Mail*'s Paris edition came away impressed by the episode's "sinister power" and by Annenkov's "extraordinary" use of color in designing the scenery and costumes—a "symphony in red of all shades."[42]

For Lolli Lvov, writing in the émigré weekly *Rossiia i Slavianstvo*, this concluding episode was about Russia, even if the grim, chaotic scene takes place under the menacing outline of Notre Dame. "The images are deeply tragic," she wrote, "the poses, gestures, and mimicry of the dancers penetrated with howls and cries. . . . For many of us Russians, who still preserve the echoes of catastrophe in our faces, this performance is unforgettable."[43] In Nijinska's rumination on the Russian past, one detects not only a personal note but also a historical impulse similar to that behind Massine's first symphonic ballet, *Les Présages*, which premiered less than a year after *Variations*. Massine's ballet, like Nijinska's, was set to non-programmatic music (in his case, Tchaikovsky's Fifth Symphony), had several episodes but no plot, and an underlying symbolism—man's struggle with destiny.

Nijinska's other new ballet, *Les Comédiens Jaloux*, worked lighter territory. Inspired by the stock characters and routines of the old *Commedia dell'arte*, the ballet was full of movement (some thought too much movement), performed with split-second timing and speeded up like an old silent film.[44] Casella's score, based on themes by Scarlatti, harked back to Diaghilev's "time-travelling" ballets so popular in the postwar years. "With *Les Comédiens jaloux*," explained Henry Malherbe in *Le Temps*,

> Madame Nijinska wanted to give us a real *Commedia dell'arte* show. On a public square actors in the style of Théodore de Banville . . . perform a sort of ballet-bouffe in which we see Pantalon as the butt of all the tricks of the sly valet Pedrollino. Pantalon wants to marry off his daughter, Clarisse, to a rich suitor such as Spavento or Captain Crocodillo, but in the end she marries Flavio whom she loves and who is as graceful as he is poor. . . . Mme. Nijinska plays the travesty role of the starving valet Pedrollino and manages even to look like Charlot [as the French called Charlie Chaplin].[45]

Nijinska's diary for the months leading up to the Opéra-Comique season are sparse, meaning that she was working night and day but otherwise at peace. "My two loves—you and art—have finally met," she wrote on March 12.[46] Her creative euphoria soon ebbed. Chaliapin refused to meet with her, treating her like a stranger, which caused her momentarily to regret going forward with the season.[47] "Constant stress at work, reckless determination to take responsibility for creating my own ballet company—all of it on the single foundation of my desire to be working with F[edor] for a few hours."[48] When the season begins, Chaliapin enthuses over the works that share the stage with his operas but does not attend a single one of her all-ballet programs. "It would have been better not to be alive," she writes after the last performance.[49] She can do nothing to arrest his eye, touch his heart, speak to his mind, commune with his spirit, or spark his erotic interest.

The first performance of Nijinska's all-ballet program took place on June 10, with subsequent performances on June 13, 15, and 17. The Blum–de Basil Ballets Russes de Monte-Carlo opened a day earlier, on June 9, followed by performances on June 11, 14, and 16. Both companies laid claim to the Ballets Russes name; both were led by choreographers who owed their choreographic fame to Diaghilev, and both included a small number of Diaghilev principals. Inevitably, the two were compared, and seldom to the detriment of the Monte Carlo company. "One would like to praise these dancers"— meaning Nijinska's—"for their discipline and their solid technique," Henry Prunières told readers of the New York Times, "yet they do not enchant in the manner of the other troupe, [and] Mme. Nijinska, the protagonist, is no longer young."[50] Dominique Sordet, an acolyte of Levinson who wrote for the right-wing Action Française, commented on looks as well as age in his review. "The ballerinas are less young and less pretty, a decided inconvenience" on the small Opéra-Comique stage, he wrote, ignoring in good sexist fashion the attributes of the company's men.[51]

As for Levinson, he ignored Nijinska's season entirely. He had been at war with her for nearly a decade, and now he had something better to write about—the young teenaged girls whom Balanchine had discovered in the studios of ex-Maryinsky ballerinas like Olga Preobrajenska. With their technical tricks, ballerina airs, and extreme youth—a precocity driven by economic penury, cultural pride, and the absence of institutional constraints—they embodied the triumph of St. Petersburg and its Parnassian dream over the deluge of revolution, as symbolized in ballet. If Balanchine seemed unwilling to create a "ballet of pure classical inspiration," Levinson was nonetheless entranced by the company as a whole, in which "the danse d'école [was] professed as a faith [and] practiced as an enthusiastic discipline," especially by its young ballerinas. "How grateful one must be to the organizers of this truly springlike season for having placed

at the head of the cast these little girl-stars (fillettes-étoiles), a new generation, the flower of this Russian adolescence, hard-working, precocious, and
formed in exile!"[52]

Not all Russian émigré critics shared Levinson's view. Valerian Svetlov
viewed both companies as contributing to the rebirth of Russian ballet. He
also noted features common to both ensembles: a sense of the contemporary,
the desire to explore modern ideas of choreography, and a shift away from
static, grotesque, and mechanical elements. He goes on to note that Nijinska
was initially intrigued by automatism and puppet-like movements. However,
with time, her approach had shifted, and she began, instead, to "derive
her modern compositions from classicism . . . using its values to their fullest extent."[53] Prince Sergei Volkonsky, the onetime director of the Imperial
Theaters and Russian advocate of eurhythmics who now wrote dance and
theater criticism for Poslednie novosti, the most widely read émigré daily, also
noted the shift in Nijinska's aesthetics, although he lamented the intentional
absence of unity between movement and music in many of her works and her
dismissal of what he called the sujet—meaning narrative or plot—although,
as he notes, she was by no means alone in this. Volkonsky welcomed the program as a whole and Les Comédiens Jaloux in particular, "a pantomime in the
best sense of the word and one of the most brilliant performances" that he
had recently seen. It was funny from beginning to end, and, like her Romeo
and Juliet for the Diaghilev company, mixed reality and theatrical performance. He loved the controlled backstage mayhem of somersaults, flying
plates, and "playful haphazardness" and how Nijinska had perfectly synchro-
nized them with Casella's "frames of rhythm." Volkonsky was also very taken
with Annenkov's movable scenery, which "seems to beat the record for con-
ciseness and crispness so loved by Diaghilev."[54]

Even if the dancers were mainly Russian, the flavor of the Monte Carlo
season was French. Two of Balanchine's ballets were designed by Christian
Bérard, a third by André Derain, while the music was by Bizet, Chabrier, and
Georges Auric. Even Les Sylphides had a Gallic makeover, with new scenery
in the style of the French romantic painter Corot. Here, then, were works
with no discernible Russian content but that were only superficially French,
works as stateless and cosmopolitan as their makers, and accepting in every
way of the cultural status quo. "A certain avant-garde atmosphere, a little
snobbish, with a drop of reactionary classicism," wrote Christian Dahl in
the arts journal Diapason, "instantaneously formed around the Monte Carlo

troupe."[55] After praising Balanchine and the company generally, he moved on to the season's other Russian company.

One must not try to compare these ballets with what Nijinska has given at the Opéra-Comique. Here, one should no longer talk of ballets, but of something separate, higher perhaps. Nijinska is such an intriguing personality, restless, tormented, ardent, anti-public, aggressive. She hurls at you strange works that the bourgeois in the circle or the snob in the orchestra does not easily digest. She does this not to please, but to enter the mind and suggest a thousand reflections outside dance and perhaps outside the theater. . . . There was in her performances moments that remain etched in memory in an aureole of beauty. Will we ever see again that moving dance of the Incroyables and Merveilleuses in the Beethoven *Variations*, tragic and lifted by hope? And the cascades of invention in *Les Comédiens jaloux*, that comic folly, that scene of burlesque intoxication, all that chaos of endearments, laughs, veiled tears, and blows! . . . [R]arity is the only word to define that quality so special to Nijinska. Nothing is anticipated, and what happens amazes like the whim of a very aristocratic and always critical being.[56]

Dahl went on to praise Annenkov's contribution to the high scenic quality of the season—his attention to color and light, and the exquisite harmony of the ensembles—commending artist and choreographer alike. Finally, he turned to the press, voicing his "indignation at its spinelessness," and speculating why so many didn't seem to understand what they were seeing. Was it "fear of displeasing those who viewed Nijinska only as an instrument?"—almost certainly an allusion to Levinson, the "Great Critic" he alludes to earlier in the article. The sole consolation, Dahl concludes, "was the welcome of the public, which surrounded Nijinska and her faithful troupe with comforting enthusiasm."[57]

Nijinska was not unaware of what was happening. In mid-June she noted in her diary that her ballets were enjoying great success with the public. Ravel was happy with *Bolero* and "adored" *Les Comédiens Jaloux*, while the composer Florent Schmitt considered *Etude* her best work. She heard praise from other artists as well. "They say that *Les Biches* is better than Sergei Pavlovich's (truly it's not worse!). Costumes, stage sets, all good. My ballets look like 'New Theater.'"[58] She admitted that *Variations* was not intelligible to everyone, but those who managed to follow it considered it the best work on the program.

All this comes, she writes, from authoritative people, thoughtful people. "But in the press there is a real persecution; they even question my right to call my work, 'Ballets Nijinska.' As if I were not the author, had not created the ballets and assumed the entire artistic responsibility, all the brutality of the theater." Her thoughts then turn to recent betrayals. "Ida Rubinstein and de Basil—my . . . clients—Lifar and Nikitina—students of mine who owed their careers to me—all of them 'my creations,' now want to sweep Nijinska away. Rouché also defends his Opéra against Nijinska. And there are other enemies who envy the . . . woman able to create such a production."[59] Although the émigré press covered Nijinska's season, the lion's share of attention went to the Ballets Russes de Monte-Carlo. *Vozrozhdenie*, for instance, devoted no fewer than four articles to the new company, including an interview with Colonel de Basil, headlined "Renaissance of the Russian Ballet."[60]

Chaliapin sang his last *Boris Godunov* on June 29. A week later, Nijinska's company made a rare appearance at a society event, dancing at a soirée given by Prince Charles-Louis de Beauvau-Craon, president of the Union Interalliée.[61] And, then, nothing. Singaevsky did his best to drum up business at summer resorts, but found no takers, in part because Lifar was making a tour of "of all the chic resorts" with baby ballerina Irina Baronova as his partner.[62] Nijinska continued to hope that the Opéra-Comique might provide a home for her company, which had turned out to be a box-office success, but the house was in serious financial difficulty, and in late September, Louis Masson submitted his resignation on the grounds that he was unable to make ends meet. The causes for this disastrous situation, commented the *Manchester Guardian*, "are not far to seek. All theatres have been suffering from the competition of the cinema, wireless is keeping many people at home at night, and the trade depression has restricted expenditure in entertainments. But grand opera is in a particularly difficult position. Its running expenses are infinitely higher than those of other theatres. Moreover, . . . the public which frequented grand opera is disappearing; the young generation takes no interest in it."[63] Instead of a diet of operas by Massenet and Puccini, the Ministry of Fine Arts contemplated a shift in repertory to lighter music, such as operetta. Sensing correctly that the shift did not bode well for her future at the Opéra-Comique, Nijinska wrote to Jacques Rouché begging him to engage her company for performances that autumn or winter. Everything is ready, she told him—repertory, dancers, scenery, and costumes—and, in an unusual concession, she offered to have his own stars perform the leading roles.[64] But the Opéra was now closed to her.

As if all this wasn't enough, Nijinska's beloved mother, Eleonora, died on July 23. She noted it briefly and simply in her diary. "On Saturday, at 20:30, my mother died. She passed away quietly, as if she had fallen asleep. My dear, beloved mother. . . . No longer will she gaze silently at me as if she were directing my life. . . . [T]ender, even at the final farewell."[65] Eleonora had been Nijinska's succor and tower of strength, the caregiver who made it possible for her to pursue a career that entailed long days and months away from home, whose presence allayed at least some of Nijinska's guilt at "dragging my entire family down."[66] Mother and daughter had lived together for almost all of Nijinska's life. Together they had weathered war and revolution and Nijinsky's catastrophic illness. Eleonora breathed confidence into a daughter whose moodiness and barely suppressed anger had to have reminded her that mental illness not only ran in the family but in all likelihood originated in her own genes.

***

During the long dry season that followed the Opéra-Comique season, Nijinska opened her own studio.[67] Eventually, arrangements fell into place for a winter tour, and for a Christmas Eve performance at the Trocadéro under the auspices of the Théâtre National Populaire. For the latter, Nijinska engaged Alex Vlassoff's Russian Chorus, promising him 2,100 francs to accompany the *Polovtsian Dances* and *The Swan Princess* and give a short a cappella concert.[68] However, the performance never took place. The directors—Fermin Gémier and Alfred Fourtier—had learned that the entire stock of her Opéra-Comique scenery and costumes had been seized for debt. Could she guarantee that she would have them by Christmas Eve? She couldn't, and on November 29, the show was canceled.[69]

But Nijinska plowed ahead. Just after Christmas she and three of her dancers—Nina Tikanova, Irène Blotska, and Tania Oboukhova—left the cold damp of Paris for a week of sunshine in Nice, where they were to film the "Oriental" ballet in *La Mille et deuxième nuit* (The 1002nd Night), directed by Alexandre Volkoff and starring Ivan Mosjoukhine. Both were celebrated members of the Russian émigré film community, although "talkies" would bring Mosjoukhine's legendary career to a premature end because of his strong Russian accent. The filming took place at the famous Victorine Studios just outside Nice. It was an all-Russian production, from Joseph Ermolieff, the producer, to most of the cast and crew, with Boris Bilinsky designing the costumes. Singaevsky had stayed in Paris, and Nijinska, for once, was in an excellent mood.[70] After she returned to Paris, she wrote a fulsome letter to Volkoff, thanking him for the "bright days" in Nice and sending heartfelt wishes for Christmas and the New Year.[71]

The impact of Russian émigrés on French cinema of the 1920s was enormous,[72] and although it lessened in the 1930s, except in the area of design, it now provoked a xenophobic backlash. "Once there was a *French* film," wrote an anonymous critic in *Ciné-Déchaîné* as Volkoff's film neared completion:

> Do you want to know the names of the collaborators of this French production? . . . Producer: *M. Joseph Ermolieff*; director, *M. Alexandre Volkoff* . . . Music by Professor *Sobaneieff*; orchestra of 50 musicians conducted by *M. Pomeranzeff*; ballet with 50 dancers arranged by *Mme. Nijinska* . . . Costumes by the painter *Bilinski* . . . Among the interpreters: *M. Ivan Mosjoukine, Mme. Nathalie Lissenko, M. Stück, Mlle. Laura Savitch.* As for the numerous extras, nearly all are Russians. . . . Apart from that, this . . . is a *French* film.[73]

Russians were the "model" minority of postwar France. They didn't get into fights like the politically fractious Italians; they worked hard, looked after their own, were perceived as loyal and adaptable, and enjoyed preferential legal status compared to other groups. Moreover, as the most visible and culturally influential interwar immigrant group, Russians occupied an exceptional position in French popular and high culture. Now they were under attack. On May 6, only days before the Russian season opened at the Opéra-Comique, an émigré named Paul Gorguloff, with the cry "To die for the Fatherland," assassinated French president Paul Dormer. The entire Russian community was "devastated," wrote Tikanova.[74] But to her amazement, the season proceeded without a hitch. Nevertheless, by the early 1930s, historian Katherine Foshko writes, "A growing popular protest against foreign influence became a noticeable element of French politics. . . . Making matters worse, the wide-ranging law of 1932, designed to 'protect the native workforce', 'fixed' the proportion of foreign workers employed in private industrial and commercial enterprises, while placing significant quotas on foreign recruitment in such trades as clothing, food and service and entertainment, where the Russians were heavily represented."[75] At the end of 1931, French musicians began to picket and to interrupt foreign orchestras, and soon afterward foreigners were excluded from the practice of law and medi-cine.[76] Quotas for entertainers lay ahead.

Nijinska seems to have left Nice with the funds to redeem her scenery and costumes. Back in Paris, rehearsals were underway for the coming tour. She had taken on a number of new dancers, including the choreographer Boris Kniaseff, Nadezhda Nicolaeva (Nikolai Legat's second wife), and Dorothie Littlefield (of the well-known Philadelphia ballet clan). The tour began in Lyons, then continued to Marseilles, Toulon, Nice, and Cannes. It was the height of the social season on the Riviera, and although tourism had fallen off, houses were full. Audiences loved the company, and the dancers were in seventh heaven. Then they were off to Spain and a week of performances at Barcelona's Teatro Nuevo.[77]

The critics were in rapture. Again and again the press drew comparisons between Nijinska's Ballets Russes and its Diaghilev forebear. "Great news! Good news! . . . The Ballets Russes is reborn," began a review in Nice's *Eclaireur du Soir*.[78] "Divine Nijinska! She remains the faithful guardian of an art . . . one feared was lost after the dismemberment of Diaghilev's fa-mous Ballets Russes," began another in *Petit Niçois*.[79] In Barcelona where the Diaghilev company had danced on several occasions, the press was even more congratulatory. J. R. de Larios in *La noche* was typical: "In our judg-ment, since the death of Serge Diaghilev, she alone deserves to hold pri-macy in dance. Avoiding comparisons, always odious, the memory of other Russian dance companies does not succeed in effacing the impression of Nijinska's art."[80] When a journalist from *Las noticias* interviewed her, the re-sult was an article titled "Bronislava Nijinska, the Shadow of Diaghileff."[81] Sebastià Gasch, a leading Catalan arts critic, analyzed her ballets as contin-uing the tradition of Fokine. He emphasized her work's strong classical foun-dation (the pas de deux in *The Swan Princess*, he says, was the most perfect he had ever seen) and singled out her brilliance as a performer. He also took on André Levinson, whose writings he clearly knew well, calling him a "bal-letomane *enragé*," rigid and dogmatic, one of those "fanatics of the classical ballet" who view any deviation from its laws as heresy.[82] After the mixed press in Paris, the adulation must have been wonderful. But not even suc-cess could make Nijinska forget what Tikanova called her "old habits." One morning when Tikanova and Tania Ouchkova were having breakfast in a cafe, the director of the Teatro Nuevo stopped to congratulate them. Nijinska saw them and, white with rage, accused the two of scheming. Dancers, she barked, shouldn't talk to directors.[83]

Early on there was talk that the tour would continue to Madrid, Rome, Milan, and Budapest. None of these engagements materialized, and instead the company's soloists traveled to the Italian city of Brescia, where Nijinska choreographed the dances in Alfredo Casella's opera *La favola d'Orfeo* in addition to staging *Petrouchka*, with local dancers supplementing soloists from her own company. Tikanova recounts how stupefied everyone was by her rehearsal outfit of tunic and tights; in Brescia the corps de ballet still wore practice tutus, as in the nineteenth century. Although Nijinska must have had her hands full, for her dancers the ten days in Italy were like a holiday. At the end of February 1933 they all returned to Paris, where another Spanish tour was in the offing. It seemed to Tikanova that at long last the Nijinska company had a future.[84]

***

Then, without telling anyone, Nijinska took off for Buenos Aires. The Spanish contract had not been signed, and the Teatro Colón was offering her a lucrative one. As a friend of the family, Serge Unger was privy to Nijinska's sudden change in plans, and on Easter he finally got up his courage to tell Tikanova. She was devastated. For "us," she wrote, meaning the dancers, "it was terrible—pure moral treason and a financial catastrophe."[85] Singaevsky, as always, accompanied Nijinska, leaving Irina, now nineteen, in charge of fourteen-year-old Levushka, assisted by Unger and friends such as Nina Sirotinine. Unger was also devastated and wrote regularly to Nijinska, begging her to send for him, reporting on the family, and relaying ballet gossip.

Unger's letters during Nijinska's months in Argentina offer rare glimpses of the family absent from her diaries.[86] On April 18 he reports that he is spending almost all his time with Irochka and Levushka, and everything is fine. Irochka has registered Levushka at the lycée and the Russian conservatory. He spends an hour and a half every day practicing the piano and working hard at his finger technique. On May 1, Unger reports that Levushka is enjoying school and Irochka has celebrated her Angel Day. (The name day of the martyr Irina in the Orthodox calendar is April 29.) On June 14 he suggests that Nijinska invite the children to visit her in Buenos Aires. (She didn't.) On July 23 he describes the trip he made with them to Boulogne-sur-Mer, where they swam, sunbathed, and dispatched the costumes she wanted on a ship bound for Argentina. On August 23 he reports that he went with Irina to beg the landlord to postpone payment of the rent for a couple of days; it was due on the 15th, and they are waiting for money. A month later, on September 23, he writes that he and Irochka are dancing with Nadezhda Nicolaeva-Legat.

Scrambling for jobs, the dancers scattered. Tikonova joined a small group organized by her teacher Alice Vronska. Others began working with Alice Alanova, a successful art dancer. Two of the men, Constantin Petrakevitch and Rudolf Andriassov, left for Belgium. Nijinska's old partner, Vladislav Karnetskii, was expelled from Germany, a victim of the ban on foreigners working in German theaters, while Egon Wusty, a German, was hired by the Berlin Wintergarten. On April 27 quotas for foreign artists were established in France—20 percent for classical dancers, 50 percent for music-hall performers, 50 percent of film personnel (reduced to 25 percent within 18 months), 10 percent of extras. "There is no chance of finding work in Paris," Unger lamented.[87]

Unger kept his eye on Balanchine, who expressed interest at one point in taking over Nijinska's studio. He invited Olia (Olga Kopseva) and Ania (Anna Volkova) to join his company, known as Les Ballets 1933, but they demurred, preferring to wait for Nijinska. (A few months later they joined the de Basil company.) At the same time, he turned down Dorothie Littlefield because of her "voluptuousness," in Unger's quaint phrase, then changed his mind. (Within a year she would be teaching at the School of American Ballet in New York.) Tania Ouchkova and Natasha Krassovska were other defectors, but Unger refused Balanchine's invitation, telling him through a third party that he only worked with Bronislava Fominichna. The only good news was that "Niusia" Vorobieva had become ballerina of the Sofia Opera.

Unger also reported on the competition. Lifar's new ballet at the Opéra was a fiasco. De Basil is giving four performances in May, then goes to Barcelona and London. Ida Rubinstein is contemplating a new season and reviving some of Nijinska's ballets—if she can find people to stage them. Balanchine's "American"—a reference to Edward James, who was actually English—was covering the city with posters for Les Ballets 1933. At the dress rehearsal, Unger glimpsed Francis Poulenc, Georges Auric, Marie Laurencin, and Jean Cocteau as well as members of the Chauve-Souris. The Ballets Russes de Monte-Carlo is much stronger than last year and very well rehearsed. In *Les Présages*, the first of Massine's "symphonic" ballets, he felt Nijinska's "colossal influence" throughout.[88] Rubinstein, meanwhile, was moving forward with her spring 1934 season amid jockeying by de Basil to minimize competition between her company and his.[89]

There is no evidence that Nijinska had actively sought the position at the Teatro Colón. The arrangements had been rushed. On April 2 the Colón cabled her; she responded affirmatively the same day, and by May 6 she was in Buenos Aires. Given that she was probably in debt, the money had to be tempting—12,000 pesos for a six-month contract as choreographic director, with an additional 4,000 for dancing principal roles in several ballets. She even squeezed a small salary for Singaevsky.[90] Apart from the dances in a half-dozen operas, Nijinska choreographed nothing new during this stint at the Colón. Instead, she used the six-month engagement to prepare for her next Paris season. She revived *Les Noces* (the first time she had done so since 1927), reworked *Le Baiser de la Fée*, and restaged her entire Opéra-Comique repertory, except for *Les Biches*. She had the sets and costumes for *Variations*, *Les Comédiens Jaloux*, *Bolero*, *Etude*, and *The Swan Princess* shipped from Europe, which enabled her to give a comprehensive account of her recent work, while partly recouping her initial investment. *Les Sylphides*, the *Polovtsian Dances*, *La flor de Irupe* (an Argentine-themed ballet choreographed by Boris Romanov), and divertissements completed the season's ballet repertory.[91] As usual, the season was grinding, and by September she was having trouble with her foot.

Nijinska arrived in Buenos Aires at a time of political turmoil at the Colón. In February 1933 the city's Intendente Municipal appointed the music patron and writer Victoria Ocampo, along with the composer Constantino Gaito and the architect Alberto Prebish, honorary directors of the theater. Unlike the bureaucrats and representatives of conservative musical institutions, all three were well-known intellectuals and modernists. Many welcomed the new "avant-garde" triumvirate. However, there were many naysayers, and some of the criticism directed at Nijinska in the months ahead was intended for those who had brought her to Argentina.[92] Her arrival was greeted with fanfare. At the dock she was met by dancers as well as reporters, and whisked off to the Colón to sign her contract; a few days later she was the guest of honor at a lunch with the company's ballerinas.[93] She quickly got down to work. Juan Carlos Mendoza, an Uruguayan journalist, observed her in the Rotonda, the Colón's large rehearsal hall, teaching class under the watchful eye of Victoria Ocampo. Noting Nijinska's thoroughness and attention to detail, he understood how in a matter of weeks she had restored the company to its "former splendor." *La Prensa* ran a page of rehearsal photos, and *Sintonía* announced that "an idyllic peace reigns in Madame Nijinska's domains," as if "cliques, envy, or jealousy among the ballerinas had never existed."[94] (Blanca

Zirmaya, interviewed a few days later in *Ultima hora*, spoke bitterly of Boris Romanov, on whose account she had left the Colón for Rome, but not before slapping him.[95]) In an interview Nijinska hinted at "partisan gossip," but emphasized her pleasure at

> returning to take the reins of this company to which I had devoted my best efforts in training dancers and teachers such as Leticia de la Vega and others. . . . [M]y acceptance was a gesture of the old romantic who wants to return to the artistic nest. . . . Let everything be for art and for this young country, which I love and respect very much.[96]

Another journalist, interviewing her during a short break, was struck by her broad culture and apparent obsession with her art. "She speaks of this with a fervor inexplicable to a layman but which instills a feeling almost approaching exaltation in those around her."[97]

The dancers spent most of the winter opera season learning and rehearsing the ballet repertory, nearly all of which was new. Moreover, all the ballets had large casts, which entailed numerous rehearsals. Although her opera choreography was favorably reviewed, midway through her contract the press began to attack her. On July 31, *La Razón* published a series of statistics about the Colón season, including subscription revenue, box office receipts, and the cost of the Italian and German "teams." Finally, the author got to the "director of the ballet corps." Singling out Nijinska by name, he spelled out the generous terms of her contract, the fact that her husband was also on the payroll, that she had insisted on the Colón hiring Anatole Vilzak as "bailarín solista," and that she was paid by the Colón for the rental of her own scenery and costumes.[98]

A little over a week later, under intense pressure, Victoria Ocampo and the architect Alberto Prebisch resigned. The press was out for blood. *Crítica*, for instance, denounced the "hundreds of thousands of extravagances" committed by these "aristocrats of name and talent."[99] It was in this atmosphere that Nijinska presented her first ballet program—*Etude*, *Les Comédiens Jaloux*, and *The Swan Princess*—on August 27. The critics were not kind. "A Mediocre Program at the Teatro Colón: The Plastic-Choreographic Versions of Three Musical Outrages," screamed the headline in *La Razón*.

> The program is composed of three "ballets" devised by Madame Nijinska to the music of Bach, Scarlatti, and Rimsky-Korsakoff. For *Etude* . . . an

anonymous arranger has thrown together, without rhyme or reason, diverse pages by the glorious "Cantor" of Leipzig. For *Les Comédiens Jaloux* a new version of some of Scarlatti's compositions was devised with a certain skill by Alfredo Casella, but without benefit to either Casella or Scarlatti. And to "create" the "ballet" *Swan Princess* the score of Rimsky-Korsakov's opera *Tsar Saltan* was pitilessly massacred. . . . This is one of the most extraordinary artistic outrages in the history of the so-called "Ballets Russes."[100]

The author had many other complaints from the cost of renting the musical parts to the lamentable performance of the orchestra. It was a colossal waste of time and money.

Others blasted the imported designs. Bilinsky's scenery for *Swan Princess* was "poor,"[101] Annenkov's for *Variations* could have been done by a four-year-old;[102] only Goncharova's designs for *Bolero* passed muster, probably because she had worked with Diaghilev. What little was said about the choreography was generally negative. *Swan Princess* was a work of "intolerable banality";[103] *Variations* was "impersonal and monotonous" as well as confusing.[104] In *Bolero*, Nijinska was sharply criticized for lacking that "Spanish grace and plasticity" so magnificently exemplified by La Argentina, whose concerts at the Colón had ended only weeks before.[105] One critic went so far as to dig up negative French reviews of *La Valse*, *Variations*, and even *Petrouchka* in order to discredit her.[106]

With the revival of *Les Noces* on October 14 and the premiere less than two weeks later of *Le Baiser de la Fée*, the tone of the reviews changed perceptibly. Both works had scores by Stravinsky, and *Les Noces* was a certified masterwork. Both, moreover, were designed in-house, *Baiser* by the Colón's new scenic director, Héctor Basaldúa, whose sparse set and use of projections could not be more different from the lush realism of Rubinstein's production.[107]

Critics were cooler to *Baiser* than *Noces*, chiefly because of the shift in Stravinsky's musical style. But there was considerable praise for the three principals and, especially, for Nijinska's choreography. The critic of *Bandera Argentina* was among the most enthusiastic:

Faithful to the idea that engendered the music, Bronislava Nijinska has composed a choreography that in intimate communion with Stravinsky's work evokes the glorious tradition and distant splendor of the Imperial

Theaters. The simple story of the child, marked in infancy by the kiss of a beautiful fairy, who abandons bride and happiness on his wedding day to follow her, has elicited from Mme. Nijinska a ballet of extraordinary appeal. Conceived within the purest canons of "classical ballet," *Baiser de la Fée* makes one think again and again of the great ballerinas no longer with us who triumphed in similar creations such as the winged figure of Anna Pavlova in *Snowflakes*. . . . Bronislava Nijinska's new ballet is one of the great choreographic successes of recent years.[108]

The season ended on November 6.

***

Once back in Paris, Nijinska had less than a month to pull her company and season together. They rehearsed, one of the dancers remembered, in a freezing attic wearing coats and gloves, waiting for a payday that never materialized.[109] As before Nijinska was piggy-backing on a series of Chaliapin performances organized by Michel Kachouk, this time at the Théâtre des Champs-Elysées, in whose storied auditorium *The Rite of Spring* had premiered. The season opened on Christmas Eve with Chaliapin singing *The Barber of Seville*, followed on Christmas Day by two performances of Nijinska's Ballets Russes. Opera and ballet alternated during the packed one-week season, which ended for Nijinska on New Year's Eve. Consisting of *Swan Princess*, *Les Biches*, and *Les Noces*, the ballet program offered a mini-retrospective of her finest works. It was the first time since Diaghilev's death that Paris had seen *Les Noces*, and with its huge Russian chorus and cast, it impressed critics as ageless. Galvanized with energy, Nijinska resuscitated her company, enlarging it with new dancers, including Nina Youshkevitch, the daughter of the playwright and novelist Semyon Yushkevich; Mia Čorak, a Croatian dancer who would find fame as the ballerina Mia Slavenska; and Ruth Chanova (née Kahmann), a young dancer from Chicago who became a protegée of the choreographer. The company had three top-tier soloists—Felia Doubrovska, the former Diaghilev principal who took over Nijinska's role as the Hostess in *Les Biches*; Boris Kniaseff, who danced the Groom in *Les Noces* (and other roles); and Anton Dolin, who came over from England to dance the lead in *Les Biches* and turned out to be the season's sensation. Interviewed on Christmas Eve after twelve hours of rehearsal with an obviously delighted Nijinska, he told a reporter: "Madame Nijinska gets everything she wants from me. I was her student; she formed me, and I owe her a great deal."[110]

The reviews were ecstatic. *Les Noces* was overwhelming, and if *Les Biches* was showing its age, this had more to do with Poulenc's score than with Nijinska's choreography or the dancing. In *Le Populaire*, the socialist newspaper, Louis Lévy opened his review: "Serge de Diaghileff is no more, but Bronislava Nijinska maintains the tradition."[111] Similarly, Jean Laurent closed his review in *La Volonté*: "Nijinska remains with Fokine one of the greatest choreographers of the Ballets Russes."[112] Laurent was very taken with Doubrovksa as the Swan Princess, describing her "sharp and angular body giv[ing] her the strange grace of a wounded bird," and with Dolin's combination of "miraculous force and lightness."[113] Her nemesis André Levinson had died only a few weeks earlier, and for the first time since 1922 Nijinska could read a favorable review of her efforts in the pages of *Comoedia* and find herself referred to as a "great artist."[114]

As soon as the season ended, she was off to Monte Carlo. With an American tour in the offing, Colonel de Basil had hired Nijinska to discharge his obligations in Monte Carlo from January to May 1934. Engaged as Ballet Mistress, she was to stage the dances in the season's operas and, subsequently, "mount, refresh, and supervise FOURTEEN ballets for the Ballet season commencing 8 April 1934." The result was a repertory closely approximating the Diaghilev model, a combination of classic Fokine works (*Carnaval*, *Firebird*, *Petrouchka*, the *Polovtsian Dances*, and *Les Sylphides*); an abbreviated version of *Swan Lake* credited to Petipa; Massine's *Scuola di Ballo*; and five of her own creations (*Les Biches*, *Bolero*, *Les Comédiens Jaloux*, *Etude*, and *Variations*). De Basil promised Nijinska a company of twenty-four dancers during the opera season and an extra eight to ten, including stars, for the ballet season, and Nijinska promised to furnish the sets and costumes for her ballets. So, after nearly a decade in Paris she moved her family back to Monte Carlo.[115]

Even apart from the money (60,000 francs), there were many advantages to the arrangement, including the chance to spend five uninterrupted months with her son. She was also thinking of the future. She had an ambitious season of her own lined up in June with a London tour to follow, and naturally wanted her ballets in good repair and her dancers at their best, which continuous paid employment would make possible. However, most of her Opéra-Comique dancers were unavailable, having joined Ida Rubinstein's newly reconstituted company, with the expectation that Nijinska would be joining it as well. So once again she spent the winter teaching and coaching a largely new group of dancers. A few she knew from Diaghilev days, others from the Rubinstein company. But apart from herself there was nobody who knew the full repertory or even most of it. Although Fokine's ballets were relatively well known, Nijinska's had little currency outside the Rubinstein company (where they were being erased) and the Teatro Colón thousands of miles away. Still, she must have been excited to work again with Leon Woizikovsky and Alexandra Danilova, both former Diaghilev stars.

With Danilova, Nijinska forged a close bond. She cast the ballerina in many of her own roles, including the Dancer in *Bolero*, Hostess in *Les Biches*, and "Merveilleuse" in *Variations*, and coached her in others. Danilova learned one of the most valuable lessons of her career from Nijinska. She "taught me how to act with my body. . . . A great actress expresses what she is feeling with her body and her voice, not by making monkey faces, and Nijinska helped me find that expression in dance."[116] At the same time, Danilova, like so many others who crossed paths with Nijinska in the 1930s, did not stint in cataloguing her shortcomings. She was unattractive, even if "she could submerge herself so deeply in the role which she was portraying, that she contrived to assume actual beauty while dancing."[117] She was "demanding." No talking was allowed in her rehearsals, no sewing pointe shoes: everybody had to pay attention. She was also "eccentric." She wore white gloves, which made the dancers feel, as Danilova put it, "as if we all had leprosy."[118]

Tamara Tchinarova, one of the dancers dispatched by de Basil to fill out Nijinska's company, loathed her. She made the "most insulting, humiliating remarks," Tchinarova later wrote, and insisted the new dancers rehearse on pointe (even when her own dancers wore soft shoes).

> She kept us on our toes out of sheer fear. We could not deny that the precision of her work, clear and accurate, the brilliant way she instructed us in class, could only improve our standard, but during many rehearsals tears had to be swallowed and lips bitten hard . . . . Her severity was fierce, but we had no alternative but to get on with the season and try to forget the insults.[119]

Nijinska was certainly demanding and insisted upon imposing her authority. But she must have experienced more than a few pangs of jealousy at the attention showered on de Basil's teenaged stars. Moreover, Nijinska was intent on developing her own ballerina talent. The programs make clear her efforts to promote Ruth Chanova and Nina Youshkevitch. She saw Chanova, who would die prematurely in 1943, as a lyrical dancer and cast her in the Prelude in *Les Sylphides* and the Andante in *Etude*, both soloist roles. Youshkevitch received the plum assignment of the Garçonne in *Les Biches* and the Waltz in *Les Sylphides*. Even the unknown Mia Čorak snared a solo part—the Polovtsian Girl in *Prince Igor*. Not all the dancers complained. Kyra Abricossova, a rising coryphée, worshipped Nijinska. "I thought she was so inspiring," she told an Australian interviewer in 1990, "To me she was the greatest of them all."

> She had the most extraordinary eyes. They were very blue and very light, and slightly cat eyes, raised there at the corner. Ugly woman. Small. She had nothing in her appearance. Very thin hair pulled up in a tight bun in the back. Smoking continuously. But my God, what a teacher, what an inspiring woman.

She demonstrated everything, even the boys' parts. "A few years ago when I could move more freely, because of her inspiration, I used to get down and do the . . . prisiadka, to demonstrate. I used to lift the girl, a light one, to show how to partner a girl, because that's what Nijinska used to do, and she impressed me so strongly. . . . [And] she would go on and show the boys' steps, full speed. Fantastic woman."[120]

Nijinska's relationship with Leon Woizikovsky was more complicated. Like her, he had a long history with Diaghilev. He was a gambler and a ladies' man, a splendid actor and demi-caractère dancer. He also had an excellent memory. For Nijinska he reprised the title role in *Petrouchka* and Harlequin in *Carnaval* and the Polovtsian Chief in *Prince Igor*. He danced in most of her ballets, and Nijinska cast him as Pedrollino in *Les Comédiens Jaloux*, which now became a "straight" male role. There was more than a touch of competition between them. Both were Polish, she by background, he by birth and training, and both were struggling to define their place in the Ballets Russes succession. Nijinska recounts a conversation with him shortly after Diaghilev's death. "All of us," he told her, "the last of the Diaghilev troupe, came to a decision yesterday: only a dancer who was part of the company in the last two years can be considered a member of the Diaghilev ballet." The decision was necessary, he went on to explain, so that "if someone wants to engage the Diaghilev Ballet, we are the only ones with the right to this name." Under the new dispensation, she responded, even Nijinsky would be out.

"Well," Woizikovsky replied, "Nijinsky is ill so it doesn't concern him." The "one and true heirs," she commented, were beginning to claim their rights.[121]

For Nijinska the Monte Carlo season was an unqualified success.[122] De Basil congratulated her for the season's "brilliant opening" and sent her an alligator purse by way of thanks for her "titanic" work. In one of his letters he tells her that he has formed a second company with some "American elements" and sent them on tour; a few weeks later he reports that he has dispatched seventeen dancers who all love and esteem her. As the season winds down, he tells her that he has many things to discuss with her when he returns to Europe in early May and asks that she hold off making a decision until they meet. He hopes she doesn't believe the rumors that are circulating: he will never let her down.[123]

On May 17, Nijinska again signed with Michel Kachouk for a mixed opera and ballet season with Chaliapin, this time at the Théâtre du Châtelet, where she had first danced with the Ballets Russes twenty-five years earlier. The company was to have a minimum of thirty dancers, including at least two stars, and once again she was personally responsible for providing not only the dancers and choreography but also the scenery, costumes, and music. Kachouk was responsible for publicity, the orchestra, and backstage personnel. The two would split the box office, with Nijinska receiving 40 percent of the gross after taxes and Kachouk 60 percent.[124] Raw deal though it was, for Nijinska it was the prelude to a much grander project—a four-week season at the London Coliseum opening on July 9. Barely two weeks before the Paris season opened on June 19, she signed a contract with Sir Oswald Stoll in which she committed to providing a company of forty dancers and a minimum of twelve ballets and to giving eight performances a week, including two matinees—a grueling schedule for a company that had seldom danced more than three or four times a week. Unlike the arrangement with Kachouk, she would be paid £550 at the end of each week, regardless of "take."[125]

Nijinska had never shied from hard work. But this time she set the bar too high. She had just over a month to rehearse the season, and she was also choreographing a new ballet, *Hamlet*. Ida Rubinstein's season had come and gone, and many of Nijinska's most loyal dancers, including Nina Tikanova, Anatole Vilzak, Ludmilla Schollar, Joyce Berry, and Serge Unger, had rejoined her. However, it soon became clear that, apart from Leon Woizikovsky, most of the dancers on loan from de Basil were returning to him, even Alexandra Danilova whom Nijinska had groomed as her ballerina. She needed scenery and costumes for *Hamlet*, which was being designed by Yury Annenkov, and costumes for *Le Baiser de la Fée* commissioned from Léon Zack. *Les Noces* was dropped, as well as *Bolero*, the latter because she couldn't secure the music rights.[126] She was in desperate need of guest stars for London, and with Stoll's approval engaged Camille Boos and Lucienne Darsonval from the Paris Opéra. She authorized him, moreover, to enter into discussions with Olga Spessivtzeva.[127] Finally, Nijinska needed dancers for the corps. Although ballet was growing in popularity, the pool of available dancers in Paris was small. "It is difficult with female dancers right now," Serge Unger told Nijinska in February. "No one is available. 10 girls are going with [Nicholas] Sergeyev to England for 5 weeks, and then [Natalie] Komarova made up a group of 20 girls to go to Nice.... There are no men at all."[128]

Behind the scenes, chaos reigned. Nijinska, absorbed in choreographing *Hamlet*, was stretched to the limit. She fought with everyone. One after another the dancers left, and new ones appeared. Even Vilzak and Schollar walked out, leaving the company without a star classical dancer, until Anton Dolin, three days before the opening, arrived to save the day. Cast in the title role of *The Swan Princess*, which she had never danced and Nijinska never found time to rehearse, Tikanova was in tears the night before the premiere. Singaevsky brought her a glass of champagne from a neighboring café, and thus fortified, she rehearsed the pas de deux with her new partner, Alexis Dolinoff.[129] Dolinoff, who had danced with the Rubinstein company in 1931, acted as something of an assistant to Nijinska. She asked him to teach Dolin the male lead in *Le Baiser de la Fée* and to rehearse the *Polovtsian Dances*, then berated him for staging Fokine's choreography not hers. And she was outraged when he changed the arms in *Baiser* so he could execute the double tours.[130]

The first performance was a mess, more like a working rehearsal than an opening for press and public. A stagehand seemed surprised when the curtain went up, a pipe fell, one of the backdrops failed to materialize, the voice of a dancer coaching another could be heard over the orchestra, the music was badly played, and the ensembles looked improvised. The company had good dancers, it just needed more rehearsal, sympathetic critics said, and went back for a second look.[131] But not everyone was kindly disposed. In *Figaro*, Reynaldo Hahn ended a shopping list of complaints by telling Nijinska to rectify matters if she wanted "to retain the favor she enjoyed because of her merits and uphold the prestige of a name her unforgettable brother had rendered illustrious."[132]

Hamlet, the season's highlight, opened on June 25, a gala performance celebrating her twenty-five years of artistic activity in France. Nijinska never spoke publicly about her choice of subject or her decision to interpret the title role. She must have been aware that Shakespeare was everywhere in Paris that spring—at the Palais Garnier, which programmed Ambroise Thomas's opera *Hamlet* again and again; the Comédie-Française, which presented an entire festival of Shakespeare plays, including *Hamlet*; and the Odéon, which staged *The Merchant of Venice*. But more personal reasons must have drawn Nijinska to the play and its hero. Choreographer and character had much in common: anger, broodiness, truculence, loneliness, unresolved family and sexual issues, a pronounced sense of victimization, guilt, and paranoia. Perhaps for a moment, as Hamlet, she became all those men in her personal and professional life who had humiliated and abandoned her, with Ophelia embodying the emotional female self of Nijinska's own diaries who is their victim. As Hamlet, Nijinska donned the intellectual and creative identity of a visionary artist.

To prepare, Nijinska must have read one of several Russian translations of the play, possibly the one by Grand Duke Konstantin Konstantinovich published in 1899, which included abundant secondary material in addition to the translation side-by-side with the English text. She called her work a "choreographic poem," emphasizing its intimate and meditative character. The action was compressed into eight short, rapid scenes, with only the simplest indications of place and action:

   I. The terrace at Elsinor Castle. The Ghost appears.
   II. Ophelia and Hamlet.
   III. At Elsinor Hamlet again encounters the Ghost.
   IV. The great hall of the castle. The king, queen, and court. The players perform an old tragedy that represents the scene of the murder.
   V. At Elsinor. Hamlet and Ophelia. The death of Polonius.
   VI. The madness and death of Ophelia.
   VII. The scene in the cemetery.
VIII. Hamlet's revenge.[133]

For Fernand Divoire, a longtime admirer of Nijinska's work, the ballet was the "whole history of Hamlet with his romanticism, the whole psychological history of Hamlet without the metaphysics of the words."[134]

Liszt's "Hamlet" is dark and atmospheric, full of rumblings and brass crescendos, storms of sound and lyrical interludes. Nijinska must have spent months studying the music and working with someone (although no one was credited) to incorporate excerpts from other Liszt tone poems into the ballet score. (In her archives there is a great deal of Liszt music but not the score used in performance.[135]) Although she had run into trouble with Bach and Beethoven, music critics found the Liszt "quite skillfully adapted," suggesting that she had grown defter at creating scores for her choreography.[136] As in *Variations*, Annenkov relied on screens and lighting for *Hamlet*'s scenic effects. Maurice Brillant, a poet, Hellenist, art critic, and dance writer, described the setting as integrating light, transparency, and movement, and resonating with poetic images. Nijinska herself described it as "transparent black tulles with painting and drawing on them . . . not exactly what I wanted, but still extraordinarily beautiful."[137] "The scenery is strange," wrote Brillant.

On an "upstage" of translucent curtains with blurry lines, gauze curtains bear certain painted elements, duly stylized (thus at the start: the terrace at Elsinor—a sketch of the donjon and scattered greenery), and the actors play either in front of or behind the gauze (like the Ghost), which, aided by the play of color in the lights, gives the whole a mysterious poetry. The most developed episode, although still rapid in movement, is the Players' scene in a high hall bathed in reddish light; it is an image, mise-en-scène, and decor that I will long remember. The death of Ophelia offers an ingenious detail; behind the gauze, two low-bearing ones with wavy lines simulate the river; Ophelia commits herself to this frail passageway, leaving only her upper body visible; then her arms harmoniously sketch the gestures of a swimmer, and soon she disappears, engulfed by the invisible current. This Ophelia is the character who dances most in the ballet, and the poetic lightness of her name and her legend demand that she only walk, aerially, on her pointes; in the second tableau, her companions, surrounding her, form melodious groups that likewise undulate on their pointes; these fragile steps form only a modest dance; there is more dance and some jumps and even some *temps battus* in the scene, very agitated, of the players. But it is true that dance strictly speaking has scarcely a place in *Hamlet*.[138]

The term "pantomime" was much bandied about in reviews of the ballet, and not favorably, given the widespread acceptance of Levinson's notion of ballet as "pure" dance. Brillant sought to refute this prejudice by placing *Hamlet* within the context of eighteenth-century theory of the *ballet d'action*. This, Brillant explains, is "a drama or comedy in silence, a ballet that tells its story without words and in which, by necessity, gesture and pantomime have a part and sometimes a very big part," which for those who believe that ballet first and foremost is dance is "heresy."[139] In *Hamlet*, Brillant argued, Nijinska was following the tradition of Jean-Georges Noverre and being attacked, as he had been, for dispensing with "technique." "*Entrechats*," Brillant declared, "have no part in the tragic adventures of the Danish prince."[140]

Some critics found themselves unexpectedly drawn into the mysterious heart of the work. "A poignant emotion reigns" throughout the final tableau, Albert Lestray wrote in *La Liberté*, "and one follows with passion the evolutions of the dancers who, by their precise gestures, render the most complex and beautiful feelings."[141] Henry Malherbe singled out Nijinska's "arresting image" as Hamlet and Ruth Chanova's "penetrating charm" as Ophelia.[142] Max Frantel, a writer and man of letters who reviewed the ballet for *Comoedia*, was enchanted by Annenkov's "stylizations . . . on transparent hangings" and the ballet's "expressive atmosphere above all for the death of Ophelia."[143] As for Brillant, he left two snapshots of Nijinska. In one she is handsome and melancholy, in the other pale, feverish, and tragic: in both she is dressed all in black and seemingly beyond gender categories.[144]

A few days later in *Figaro*, Reynaldo Hahn savaged not only *Hamlet* but Nijinska's undertaking in general.

Dance *Hamlet*? Why not? Does any subject exist with a chance of escaping the choreographic mania of Russians and their imitators? . . . You will see that little by little . . . they will adapt, orchestrate, choreograph, decorate, costume, dance, and mime Pascal's *Pensées*, Czerny's exercises, . . . Palestrina's Masses, Cicero's speeches, . . . Molière's *Misanthrope*, and the railroad timetable—this at least could give rise to picturesque evocations. But all these efforts would not be equally happy, and this is the case of *Hamlet*. Reduced to a slender plastic scheme, the "Tragic History of Hamlet, Prince of Denmark," has no mystery, grandeur, or any meaning. Decors that at first delight the eye . . . soon tire it by a preference for smokiness . . . ; a pantomime so vague, so "stylized" that a spectator ignorant of what is going on can understand nothing; a musical accompaniment . . . played, so to speak, without having been rehearsed—this is the "novelty" intended as a treat for the Parisian public by the *Ballets Russes* at the Châtelet.[145]

Disaster had occurred, however, long before any reviews appeared. Nina Tikanova recalls the chaos at the dress rehearsal when Stoll's representative appeared in the hall and watched as she and Dolin improvised their parts in *Les Comédiens Jaloux*, which Tikanova had never rehearsed and Dolin had never seen.[146] Representations soon followed about the quality of the orchestra, lighting, stagehands, and dancers. On or about June 25, that is, the day before *Hamlet* premiered, the Coliseum recommended that Nijinska "cancel the contract as if by her own wish." Nijinska replied that she was ready to execute the contract. Two days later, Stoll himself arrived in Paris. At this point the Russian-born orchestral conductor Albert Coates, who had instigated the negotiations with Stoll, spoke privately to Nijinska—even Singaevsky had to leave the room. Coates told her that "there existed some obscure causes . . . which compelled the Management of the Coliseum not to hold the Nijinska ballet season." He then proposed that she refuse the existing contract and "sign a new one in order to arrange her ballets for the Basil Company of Ballets Russes for the season at the Coliseum which will have to be given instead of her engagement." Unsurprisingly, Nijinska refused to do this, and as a result received a letter from Stoll, "announcing the fact of the breaking of the contract on account of the material impossibility of Mme Nijinska to execute her contract according to the instructions of Sir Oswald Stoll."[147] Nijinska replied by telegram that she was ready to execute the contract, and that on July 2, as agreed by contract, he was to deposit £275 in her account. However, it turned out that Nijinska could only dispose of this sum by opening a joint account with Stoll. Since Stoll had "willingly and knowingly broken" the contract, Nijinska requested damages of £3,000. Eventually, Stoll paid her the advance, and on July 5 the press announced that "because of artistic difficulties over which the management has no control," the four-week season at the Coliseum that was to have started the following Monday was canceled.[148]

***

A second disaster followed. Michel Kachouk owed money to the Châtelet, and since he lacked the wherewithal or inclination to pay, the theater seized all of Nijinska's sets and costumes, assuming they were his property rather than hers. She was frantic. Although the Coliseum engagement had fallen through, she still had dates in Vichy and Touquet Paris Plage. Singaevsky wrote to René Blum, director of the Monte Carlo Theatre, but Maurice Lehmann, the Châtelet's longtime director, was adamant: he was holding her material until Kachouk paid up.[149] "Two catastrophes in one day is too

much," she wrote to her friend Anna Teplicka. Describing the season to another friend, she wrote that no matter what her "enemies" did to her—and
she had been sorely tested—she at least had her Hamlet.[150]

So ended Les Ballets Russes de Bronislava Nijinska. Reading the press of
the 1934 season, one is astonished that not a single critic wondered where the
money came from, who was paying the dancers, designers, studio rentals,
and music rights, to present a handful of performances of a handful of ballets, no more than two of *Hamlet*, on which she had worked so hard and with
such passion. An allusion to creditors being somewhat pacified in her letter
to Anna Teplicka suggests that Nijinska had again borrowed, and the double
blow that fate had just dealt her was financially devastating. Nina Tikanova
wrote that the season "ruined" Nijinska.[151]

Among her papers are two notebooks in which Nijinska recorded her
ideas about *Hamlet*. The larger is rougher, the smaller more polished and
consciously literary, with passages from the play and a preamble with her
thoughts about its hero.[152] Not only did she identify with Shakespeare's protagonist, but she also endowed the poetic narrative of his inner life with the
contradictions of her own character. She writes:

Hamlet is passionate and hot-headed, but struggles with inner doubts
and vacillations. He commits revenge only under the pressure of
circumstances (4).

Shakespeare . . . built his play upon the peculiarities of Hamlet's nature,
his world view, way of thinking, and temperament. He emphasized the pes-
simistic elements, disillusionment, melancholy, and skepticism (5).

For the Romantics, Hamlet is merely a "thinking hero": reflection is the reason for his sluggishness in taking revenge. Contrary to
Goethe . . . Figner . . . sees Hamlet not as a . . . dreamer . . . but . . . as a passionate nature, uncontrollable and even cruel. The key to his lethargy is the
fact that, despite all his passion, he gets trapped in a net of destruction, in an
enchanted circle of reflections (9).

Nijinska might have been commenting on her own obsession with
Chaliapin, and her own compulsive writing about it, as though she, too, like
Figner's Hamlet, were caught in an "enchanted circle of reflections."

Once the season was over and the subsequent performances canceled,
time must have hung heavy on Nijinska's hands. During the long months of
professional idleness, one can imagine her re-creating the ballet in a notebook

destined for posterity, writing out the mimetic actions and choreographic gestures, polishing, refining, and even re-copying them, but leaving the whole unfinished. Whether she was conscious of this or not, re-creating *Hamlet* through writing was a healing act, closing wounds and nursing her bruised psyche back to health by resurrecting what others had conspired to destroy. Hamlet was Nijinska's last role, and the Châtelet her last engagement as a dancer and her last season with Chaliapin. Recording the ballet was thus also an act of mourning—for the loss of her company, her career as a performer, her dancer's body, and perhaps even her identity as a woman. She describes quietly erotic moments in Scene 2 where Ophelia gently caresses Hamlet's face or where he takes her hand and kisses it.

In 1934, Nijinska stood at the helm of a company that represented an alternative to the Diaghilev tradition represented by de Basil. Two years later, striking a triumphalist note, de Basil told a French reporter that his ballets were "a direct continuation of those of the late Serge Diaghilev, a spiritual as well as a temporal heritage, since I possess his decors, costumes, and music."[153] Although Nijinska continued to create dances until 1960, Les Ballets Russes de Bronislava Nijinska was the last time she created a visionary, intensely personal work of theater.

13

On the Road

Although the Great Depression still lingered, ballet in the mid-1930s was thriving. In England, across North America, and as far away as Australia, Colonel de Basil's Ballet Russe was enjoying a huge success, introducing a vast new public to the work of Fokine, Massine, and Petipa. Ballet movies and ballet books were on the rise, and there was even ballet on British television. In this expanded world of Russia Abroad, Nijinska would create major new works in the years before World War II. Always a traveler, she was more than ever on the road, even as the dream of a company of her own became ever more elusive.

In November 1934, accompanied as always by Singaevsky, Nijinska boarded the French Line's SS *Champlain* sailing from Le Havre to New York. It was her first trip to the United States, and she took advantage of the crossing's eight days of pampered freedom to read her sister-in-law's biography of Nijinsky. Ghost-written by Lincoln Kirstein, edited by Arnold Haskell, published in London in 1933 and New York the following year, and immediately translated into French, the book fast became a *succès de scandale*. Kirstein had spent months talking to Romola. But nothing was fact-checked, and Romola had an often tenuous grasp of truth. She knew next to nothing about her husband's early life or the genesis of his most celebrated ballets and all but wrote Nijinska out of the narrative. Even if Kirstein's lucid analysis of *L'Après-midi d'un Faune* gave the book a certain intellectual heft,[1] its portrayal of Diaghilev as a homosexual Svengali with Nijinsky as his accommodating Trilby shocked those who knew them. "I am unable to describe the fury I experienced reading this disgusting farce," Nijinska wrote in an unpublished note.[2]

Others shared her outrage, including Sergei Grigoriev, who invited her in 1934 to join a group of Diaghilev's friends to counter Romola's book. A new book was on its way, he told her, a biography of Diaghilev written by Arnold Haskell in collaboration with Diaghilev's old friend Walter Nouvel that would correct the "biased and evil assertions, and distorted 'portraits' and biographical 'facts' about Diaghilev, his group, and Nijinsky's friends and family." But when *Diaghileff: His Artistic and Private Life* was published in 1935, Nijinska found to her dismay that Haskell's book, far from correcting the historical record, made use of the same "false and even dirty information" as Romola's.[3] At the heart of the problem was the relationship between the two men, still illegal in the Anglophone world and characterized in Haskell's book as well as Romola's as "degenerate," "abnormal," and a "thoroughly unpleasant subject."[4] It is unclear what disturbed the reticent Nijinska more: the public disclosure of her brother's non-conforming gender identity, his affair with Diaghilev, the gay male circles they inhabited, or her own silent acknowledgment of their relationship.

By the time Nijinska landed in New York, she was beside herself. When dockside reporters asked what she thought of Romola's biography, she answered that it was full of inaccuracies and "just a fairy tale." She also announced that she was writing her own book about her brother in which she hoped to emphasize Nijinsky's art more than "personal matters."[5] In fact, even before Nijinska sailed for New York, she had drafted the outline for a volume of memoirs. Only the last third survives, an account of her own life, beginning with the Palace Theatre season in 1914 and ending with *Hamlet* and "the enemies of art": she was still smarting from the seizure of her scenery and costumes and the cancellation of her London season.[6] Her off-the-cuff remark notwithstanding, the book she intended to write at that point was about herself.

Two days after arriving in New York, Nijinska boarded a train for Los Angeles, the first of many transcontinental journeys in the next twenty years. She went to Hollywood at the invitation of Max Reinhardt, who had fled Germany when the Nazis came to power in 1933. He had asked her to choreograph the dances in a star-studded screen version of *A Midsummer Night's Dream*, the first big-budget movie produced by Warner Brothers since the advent of the Great Depression. With Anita Louise as Titania, Olivia de Havilland as Hermia, James Cagney as Bottom, and Mickey Rooney as Puck, *Midsummer* had a stellar cast.

Within a week of arriving at Union Station, Nijinska, Reinhardt, and his German codirector William Dieterle were auditioning hundreds of dancers to find the 150 "coryphees" who would transform Shakespeare's Athenian woodland into a space of dreams. Hollywood reporter Douglas W. Churchill described the process in the *New York Times*:

> Dr. Reinhardt and his ballet mistress, Mme. Bronislava Nijinska, herded the girls, fifteen at a time, into formation. Then, to a spiritless dirge of a

piano, they went through a routine movement. Assistant directors, holding charts showing the position of each dancer, conferred with the bent heads of Dr. Reinhardt, Mme. Nijinska and Mr. Dieterle. The conversation was always in Russian. Never more than three of the fifteen girls were selected. Elated, they rushed into an adjoining room, while the luckless ones dragged their feet to the side of the stage, where they pulled their coats over their bathing suits or rehearsal costumes and departed.[7]

On the set, Nijinska was "spritely, agile and eager," as lively as the "youthful ballerinas" who surrounded her. She demonstrated everything herself, carrying a long cigarette holder, and worked miracles even with the tiny children, some as young as two-and-a-half, who picked up her movement "in a twinkling."[8] After more than a decade working with dancers who spoke a half-dozen languages, Nijinska had mastered the art of speaking with her body rather than words.

Nijinska choreographed several dance episodes for *Midsummer*. She called them ballets, which is how they are credited, but they don't look like ballet. None of the dancers wears shoes, and, except for Nini Theilade, the première danseuse of several Reinhardt productions who now played the role of Titania's fairy, they seldom perform an identifiable step. Instead, they walk and run, luminous in net leotards woven with strips of shredded cellophane. The fairies appear about a half-hour into the film, gliding upward along a spiral (actually a "process-blue" ramp), shimmering in the moonlight. Everything seems caught in movement. Water flows, leaves rustle, while Titania's transparent train dances joyously in the dark. Meanwhile, Oberon prowls about on horseback, attended by men in bat-wings who sweep up Titania, scatter her attendants, and seize Theilade, who flees undulating her arms in exquisite protest like Pavlova in *The Dying Swan*. Here is the silent world of ballet-pantomime—dramatic, expressive, and permeated with music.[9]

Whatever misgivings Nijinska may have had before coming to Hollywood, and however "primitive" film people's understanding of ballet (as she wrote in her diary),[10] once *Midsummer* was over, she wanted to stay. Hollywood salaries were generous. Between mid-November 1935 and early January, Nijinska sent home nearly 17,000 francs. They paid the rent, moving expenses to a one-bedroom apartment, gas and electric bills, food, Christmas tips, and medical expenses. They also helped her climb out of debt, enabling her to pay Joyce Berry, Nina Youshkevitch, Nina Tikanova, and other dancers who had worked for little or nothing during the Châtelet season. She repaid the costume makers Karinska and Maison Sollatgès; Crait, a venerable maker of dance shoes; the clippings service Argus de la Presse, the scenic artists Allegri and Cioccari.[11] And there was money for a ring and leather jacket for Léo and other presents.[12]

With the rise of fascism, Los Angeles attracted a growing number of European refugees. *Midsummer*'s production team exemplified this new cosmopolitanism: Reinhardt was Austrian, as was composer Erich Korngold, director William (Wilhelm) Dieterle German, Nijinska Russian, and set designer Anton Grot Polish.[13] Many former Ballets Russes dancers had settled in the Southland, creating a pool of well-trained dance talent. When journalist Isabel Morse Jones took her to visit the Hollywood Bowl, Nijinska confided that she could easily imagine choreographing a ballet for the amphitheater nestled in the Hollywood hills. One by Bach, "with a splendid orchestra playing . . . a certain Brandenburg concerto and a piano concerto and a flute sonata, combined and orchestrated to make a part of a magnificent ballet."[14] By then, with most of her *Midsummer* work behind her, Nijinska was thick in negotiations with MGM to supervise the dances in an upcoming picture; there was even talk of the contract becoming a "long-termer."[15] But nothing came of it, and by late January she was back in New York. She now hammered out a contract with Hurok Attractions Inc. for an eight-week American tour of her company, now called the Nijinska Ballet, during the 1935–1936 season.[16] Chaliapin, a long-time Hurok artist, was probably the intermediary.

He was certainly on her mind that winter. When she ran into him at a performance in New York, she was struck by how ill he looked. She combed newspapers for word of him. Was he dying? Was he better? She prayed for him, bargaining with God that if he survived, she'd never see him again. (He lived, and she kept her vow.) In her diary she writes that she was down to her last dollar and had even sold her collection of ballet etchings for twenty-five dollars, most of which she sent to Irina and Léo in Paris, when she was saved by an unexpected friend. Yet she continued living at the Sevillia on West 58th Street, a Victorian apartment hotel complete with restaurant that maintained its status throughout the 1930s and must have cost a small fortune. How did she afford it? She had no discernible income, nor did Singaevsky. But she hung on, week after week, sleepless with worry about Levushka, imagining he was ill. "My heart never ached for [my children] as it did in America," she later wrote.[17] Why didn't she go home?[18]

To be sure, Nijinska was taken with New York. In March she caught performances of the American Ballet's first New York season, which included several new Balanchine works, including his now-classic *Serenade*.[19] One may be sure she attended Chaliapin's recital at Carnegie Hall on March 3 and very possibly the tea at the Plaza where artwork by the singer's son, Boris Chaliapin, whom she knew, was exhibited in a small ballroom.[20] Later in the month she must have seen the Ballet Russe de Monte Carlo, which limped into town after a grueling tour of ninety cities but gave a spirited performance of *Aurora's Wedding*.[21] She sat for an interview with *The American Dancer*'s Ruth Eleanor Howard, where she explained with "elfin charm" and a "quick smile" that what American dancers needed was the "practical, actual experience of the theatre" and that the recent performances of the American Ballet were "an excellent start."[22]

Finally, she met several times with Lincoln Kirstein. In early April he recorded in his diary that he went to see her with Roger Pryor Dodge, to show her "all the pictures we have of Vaslav," many of which Kirstein later published in *Nijinsky Dancing*. "[S]he told us many interesting things and was wholly charming," he continued.

> Said that everyone observed only his superficial mannerisms. The technical contributions he made like a new kind of jump . . . all that had been ignored. . . . She showed me a series of action pictures of "Les Noces" taken in Buenos Aires. Very good. How Diaghilev tried to get her to change her name and would never allow Vaslav and her to be photographed together. . . . Showed me photos of her son with a strong resemblance to Vaslav, also pictures of her parents I'd never seen before.[23]

Ten days later they met again. This time Nijinska turned the conversation to herself. "She wants me to work on her memoirs," Kirstein wrote in his diary.

> Showed me pictures of her ballets but would not let me have slides made of them. She wants $1500 in advance from a publisher which she'll have a hard time getting. She showed me little sketch ideas she'd made of Vaslav at school, his ballets; even Tyl which she'd never seen. In 1921 in Kiev she was doing a Mephisto Valse, . . . never knowing he's done it.[24]

Kirstein was in a quandary. His own book, *Dance: A Short History of Classic Theatrical Dancing*, was due out later in the year, and he wasn't sure he had the time. But he was tempted, promising to do what he could with Putnam's.[25] A few days later Kirstein reported that his contact needed to have a prospectus. She told him that she already had one in Russian, as if this were American publishing's lingua franca. Then, she returned to her stories, seducing Kirstein with their magic. Even more than Romola, Nijinska was a link to ballet's great tradition, a source of firsthand, living knowledge, and she wanted him to do for her what he had done for her brother. A week later Putnam's turned down Nijinska's book. By then, Kirstein's own interest in the project had flagged,[26] and decades would pass before any of Nijinska's auto-biographical writings saw the light of day. Like so many others, Kirstein was content to write Shakespeare's sister out of the picture.

***

A Midsummer Night's Dream gave Nijinska's career a tremendous boost. It enabled her to climb out of debt, reclaim her scenery and costumes, cho-reograph new dances, work with highly regarded collaborators, bask in the international limelight, and, during the nearly six months she spent in New York, reassess her relationship with the de Basil company. She had seen how popular it was, observed the dancers it attracted (including many who had performed in companies she had choreographed for), and come to ap-preciate Hurok's mastery as a presenter. How could she compete? Was it even worthwhile trying? She had salvaged de Basil's 1934 season in Monte Carlo by combining the dancers from her company with a small group from his. But none of her works had entered his repertory, and she had created nothing new. Now, the possibility of an independent Nijinska company with the backing of Hurok seems to have spurred de Basil to action. In short order, he commissioned a major new ballet from her, with additional works promised for the 1935–1936 American tour.[27] Swallowing her pride, Nijinska returned to what she called de Basil's "theatrical emporium," hoping that even in an at-mosphere where business mattered more than ballet she could preserve her "sincerity" and "create a little piece of true art."[28]

Nijinska's *Les Cent Baisers* (or *The Hundred Kisses*, as it was also known) exacerbated tensions that in 1937 led to Massine's acrimonious separation from the Ballet Russe. Since its first season he had been the company's domi-nant artistic force through his restagings of Diaghilev-era works, charismatic performances as a dancer, light-hearted crowd pleasers, and ballets set, con-troversially, to symphonies by Tchaikovsky and Brahms. In 1932 de Basil had dismissed Boris Kochno as well as Balanchine to give Massine a free hand. Now he invited Kochno to return to the fold. According to Arnold Haskell, *Les Cent Baisers* "started with a musical score by Frederick d'Erlanger written to a very definite programme carefully mapped out in its timing and detail by Boris Kochno."[29] Only when the score was completed and Jean Hugo had agreed to design the ballet was the project turned over to Nijinska.

Inspired by Hans Christian Andersen's fairy tale "The Swineherd," *Les Cent Baisers* had a complicated libretto and long program note.[30] A "fey and capricious" princess rejects the modest gifts of a nightingale and a rose from a prince who seeks her hand. Disguised as a swineherd, the prince returns with a magic crock, whose music enchants the princess and the courtiers. She begs the swineherd for the instrument, which he agrees to give her in exchange for a hundred kisses. When the King sees his daughter kissing a swineherd, he banishes her from court, while the Prince, revealing himself, abandons her. The libretto ended with a moral: *"Which only shows that some things that do not glitter are gold."*

The score was described by critics as "elegant," "charming," and "adequate for ballet purposes,"[31] a far cry from the modernist or Romantic music that Nijinska favored. D'Erlanger, a banker as well as a composer, financed the production, and he wanted Irina Baronova as his princess. In early June, de Basil invited Nijinska to a meeting with Kochno, Baronova, and "Uncle Freddie," the sixteen-year-old ballerina's pet name for the composer. "Nijinska was small and broad," Baronova wrote in her memoirs, "sort of four by four. She wore a severe black suit over a white shirt, her mousy hair flat over her ears and secured in a tiny bun at the back of her head. She had a broad face, slightly slanty eyes and full lips. . . . Her blank expression as I was introduced to her was very off-putting."[32] The French-born Erlanger was all charm, expressing his delight that Madame would choreograph his ballet for Mlle. Baronova, at which point Nijinska snapped, "I don't want Baronova. I want Danilova!"

> In the ghastly silence that followed, Nijinska's husband—a tall, lean, charming man—tried to murmur something into Madame's ear. She brushed him away. . . . Colonel de Basil wiped his specs . . . , Kochno gazed pensively at the floor, Uncle Freddie . . . left the room, saying quietly, "I'm going back to London."[33]

Alone with Nijinska, who nonchalantly inserted a cigarette into a cigarette holder, Baronova took the bull by the horns.

I approached her chair, sat on my haunches and put my hands on her lap while she stared at me with a mixture of incredulity and astonishment. "Bronislava Faminishna [*sic*] . . . I know you have worked with Danilova before, and I understand your reluctance to work with me but you do not know me. Please, please try me. I have looked forward so much to working with you. . . . Please give me this chance!" Nijinska half turned towards her husband. . . . "Nicolai Nicolaevich, what did she say?" Oh, *dear*, I thought, *she must be hard of hearing*, and so I repeated my little speech in a loud voice. When I finished, Nijinska snapped . . . , "Don't shout, I'm not deaf!" But a shadow of a smile crossed her face and she added, "I heard you the first time. All right. I will try to work with you."[34]

With peace restored, Nijinska listened to the music, settled on a date to go to London, then drove off with Singaevsky in their car.

The ten-week London season, which coincided with George V's Silver Jubilee, opened at the Royal Opera House, Covent Garden, on June 11. With twenty-five ballets, the repertory was huge and dominated by the works of Massine, with Fokine a strong second, but only token representation of Nijinska and Balanchine. *Cent Baisers* was scheduled to premiere on July 18, and by June Nijinska was in London rehearsing every afternoon with the corps, which included the young Japanese American dancer Sono Osato, one of twelve Maids of Honor. "I wasn't prepared for the kind of movement Nijinska demanded," she recalled in her memoirs:

> Her torso and arms writhed like sinuous snakes, their movement phrases often ending in a sudden snap of the wrists. Simultaneously her iron-strong legs whizzed through glissades, brisés volés, and innumerable entrechats six. Though plump, Nijinska was incredibly light and fast on her feet. Her unorthodox combinations were assertive, syncopated, and wriggly in the torso, while sharply classical in the legs. . . .
>
> We never waited with Nijinska. Every step was clearly organized in her mind. As soon as one detailed phrase had been danced to her satisfaction, she would move on to the next sequence. Irina [Baronova] could be very mischievous during rehearsals and often burlesqued her dramatic roles. But during those days she rehearsed on pointe, full out, and completely serious. She quickly captured the Nijinska style, with all its strange subtleties, without losing her own fluidity of movement.[35]

During the first week of July "a small group of experts" were invited to observe the ballet's "first preliminary rehearsal" in one of the company's studios.
"The performers were only three," wrote playwright Hubert Griffith in the
Observer, "Nijinska herself, in a dark sailor suit, with a long cigarette holder
in her mouth and . . . the two young dancers . . . [who] will dance . . . the principal part, [Tatiana] Riabouchinska and Baronova, in black practice-dresses."
Griffith was fascinated:

> The process by which the movements of a dance (complete already in the
> head of the choreographer) are communicated to the pupil are beyond the
> understanding of an outsider. Nijinska gave her instructions in a low voice,
> or else indicated personally. The two girls followed her like shadows. The
> music was taken bar by bar sometimes being repeated a score of times. At
> the end of a long morning's work perhaps twenty bars had been rehearsed
> in this way.[36]

Even before this "preliminary rehearsal," Baronova had started working
with Nijinska at the Drill Hall in Chenies Street. Donning white gloves and
lighting the first of numerous cigarettes, the choreographer got down to work.
For her first entrance she had Baronova "whirl through the large gates of the
castle, starting with *chaînés* . . . and finishing with *pirouettes*," spinning non-
stop to the other side of the stage. It was very effective to look at, Baronova
thought, but technically very difficult, although technical challenges were
something she relished. Like Osato, Baronova observed that from the waist
down the choreography "was purely classical but from the waist up it was
stylised—the posture, the angle of the shoulders, the turn of the head, the
arms slightly bent at the elbows with the hands bent back from the wrists."
This posture, Baronova felt, "conveyed the haughty, capricious personality of
the Princess." She found it an inspiration to watch the choreographer demonstrate, and the two "worked in a friendly, happy atmosphere. . . . All aloofness
gone, [Nijinska] emerged as a lovely human being—eccentric, yes, but wonderful to work with."[37]

Although the costumes were made by Karinska and the commission bro-
kered by Kochno, Hugo's designs left much to be desired. At the eleventh hour,
recalled Osato, the dancers discovered that many of the nuances they had
rehearsed so carefully were lost under voluminous tutus, leg-of-mutton sleeves,
and the fussy excess of wigs, feathered hats, gloves, and bows.[38] According to
Hugo, Nijinska would have preferred a more modern approach.[39]

The *Dancing Times* declared the new ballet "an event of first-class importance." Once again, wrote editor P. J. S. Richardson, explicitly comparing *Les Cent Baisers* to *Les Noces* and *Les Biches*, Nijinska had proved that "through the medium of classical ballet it is possible to express any emotion."[40] Caryl Brahms called classicism the "spine" of Nijinska's choreography, J. H. M. in the *Manchester Guardian* the ballet's "most noticeable quality," while Edwin Evans noted that the "reversion to classical virtuosity" was accompanied by "the resourcefulness gained in modern experience."[41] "There can be very little in the choreography of *Les Cent Baisers* that is not to be found in the centre-practice of every serious ballet school," Brahms explained.

> It is [Nijinska's] selection and placing of the *pas* and in the classical purity of her line that the charm of a Nijinska *enchaînement* is to be found. Her scoring for the male dancers in the work is strong, economical and academic. Her treatment for the ballerina is classical, interesting and full of character. Her grouping treats the dancers individually as well as plastically, and states, in a Degas-like manner, the beauties of instep, thigh, and *tu-tu* in a dancer at rest and *sur la scène*.[42]

The gala premiere on July 18 was a night Baronova would long remember. Before the curtain went up, Nijinska made the sign of the cross over the young ballerina's chest, then took her place in the wings. The applause was tumultuous, with more than twenty-five minutes of curtain calls, bouquets for all the female dancers and laurel wreaths for the men, and, for Nijinska, a basket of flowers from "Uncle Freddie." There was a supper party at Boulestin, the smart French restaurant in St. James, where the guests ate *Truite à la Princesse Abandonnée* and *Selle d'Agneau Nijinska*.[43] Another gala supper followed the July 24 Grand Jubilee Performance in aid of the Russian Red Cross and a Benevolent Fund for the company's artists. The program (*Les Cent Baisers*, *Le Tricorne*, and *La Boutique Fantasque*) was chosen by the Duchess of York, mother of the future queen, and the supper was held on the Royal Opera House stage after the performance.[44] It had been years since Nijinska had found herself fêted in such illustrious company.

***

Still, old enemies lurked. Chief among them was the company's all-powerful régisseur Sergei Grigoriev, in whose capable but partisan hands lay the institutional memory of both the Diaghilev company and its self-anointed successor. With Fokine, Nijinsky, and Balanchine out of the picture and Massine focused on his own choreography, Nijinska was one of the very few with the authority to challenge Grigoriev's tending of that memory, the authenticity of his restagings, and his arbitrary definition of what constituted the Ballets Russes legacy. A few days after the premiere of *Les Cent Baisers*, Nijinska showed Baronova her own version of the "Finger" variation in *The Sleeping Beauty*. They worked together in the dim light of the pilot lamp on stage. "We had no pianist," Baronova later wrote,

> so Nijinska hummed, sang, roared and mimicked the music of the variation. The steps were the same, but the execution of them was totally different. The seemingly ordinary variation became an extraordinary and devilishly difficult one. It had life, style, and *brio*.[45]

Grigoriev and his wife, Lubov Tchernicheva (who taught company class and for whom *Thamar* and *Schéhérazade* were revived), had taught their version of the "Finger" variation to Baronova. When she told "Papa Grigoriev" that she had learned Nijinska's version, the régisseur, with barely contained fury, forbade her from dancing it—which, of course, the high-spirited ballerina proceeded to do with great success, whereupon he sighed, "You are a bad, naughty girl."[46]

Few Ballet Russe dancers measured up to Baronova's high standard. Touring exacted a heavy toll, and success made it easy for dancers to rest on their laurels. When the Ballet Russe limped into New York in March 1935, critic John Martin thought the company looked so bad it should have skipped the city and sailed for Europe.[47] In London, critics complained about the fall-off in technical standards and sloppy ensemble work. "Surely," wrote one exasperated reviewer, "the elementary virtues inculcated by the drill sergeant are not beyond the capacity of this *corps de ballet*?"[48] On tour the hard-working dancers slept on trains, learned roles on the fly, and warmed up where they could. Night after night the show went on, with company class a luxury reserved for long seasons. It was the antithesis of how Nijinska worked, and it didn't allow for perfectionism. "Nijinska is considered difficult by some people," wrote Haskell at the end of the London season.

> I can well say in what that difficulty lies. She will make no artistic compromises of any kind. She will be right or wrong, but according to her conception which she will follow through to the end.[49]

Les Cent Baisers ushered Nijinska back into the ballet mainstream. In the decade since leaving the Diaghilev company, she had lost touch with developments in London. She spoke no English and thus lacked access both to the growing ballet literature in that language and to the authors, editors, and critics who produced it. Of these none was as prolific as Arnold Haskell. An ardent balletomane infatuated with everything Russian, he wrote two of the most influential ballet books of the 1930s. The first, *Balletomania*, came out in 1934 and stayed in print for decades. Haskell doesn't actually ignore Nijinska; in fact, he calls *Les Noces* a "landmark," *Les Biches* the "most perfect of all the 'decadent' ballets," and several of the works she choreographed for Ida Rubinstein "near masterpieces."[50] Yet despite the "great admiration" he expressed privately,[51] she is missing from his chapter on Diaghilev's choreographers, and the one paragraph he devotes to her elsewhere damns even as it praises. "The only successful woman choreographer in history," he wrote, she was also "the only ugly dancer to find fame,"[52] a sideswipe long reiterated by British dance writers.

Haskell takes a similar tack in his equally influential biography of Diaghilev, published within days of the premiere of *Les Cent Baisers*. He tells us that Diaghilev's admiration of Nijinska was so great that he said, "If I had a daughter, I would like one with such gifts."[53] But there is no real discussion of those gifts or of Nijinska's aesthetics generally; for Haskell, even her best ballets belong to the era of Diaghilev's quest for "lost youth," an era associated by the author with decadence and *snobbisme*.[54] This idea, coupled with the notion that the "outlook" of her Diaghilev-era ballets "denied them permanence," consigned her to the sidelines of history.[55] Adrian Stokes, a painter and influential art critic, did the same in *Russian Ballets*, making barely a mention of her in a book published during the 1935 season and dedicated fulsomely to Diaghilev, "the man who worked a miracle (in recalling the ballet to a new life)."[56] Haskell's influence is equally evident in Caryl Brahms's *Footnotes to the Ballet*, published in 1936, especially in her attitude toward Diaghilev's works of the 1920s, when "an emaciated cerebration was to disseminate a schlerosis [*sic*] of the *chic* in the spine of its thematic material."[57] Yet Brahms, writing in the wake of *Les Cent Baisers*, sensed how Nijinska had played with style, using it to give an ironic edge to the ballet's classical movement and mundane plot.

> She took her theme and established it straightway in the realm of Once-Upon-A-Time (admittedly in a stylish province of the State). . . . And

being given a spoilt Princess, a stylish court with *chic* ladies-in-waiting, and a frosty, inimical King, she animated them with the *pas* and pose that proved her to be in direct succession to the Maryinsky choreographers. Her Princess was an ill-tempered first cousin to the beautiful Tsarevna of [*Firebird*] . . . spoilt and wilful . . . [with] a feminine sophistication where the Russian Princess had only a trustful simplicity.[58]

Irony and artifice allowed Nijinska to reclaim the ballet from collaborators who controlled every element but the choreography. John Martin, who reviewed the work in New York in October 1935, called it an "arch travesty." She had been "merciless in her demands on the dancers," he wrote, but the result was worth it, for she had "achieved a somewhat frantic staccato quite unrelated to the music that makes for an extremely amusing style." He liked the "fantastic solo by Lichine, in which the movement [was] totally at variance with the sadness of his meditation; two gently absurd dances of presentation by [Roman] Jasinsky and [Yura] Lazovsky and a nice piece of buffoonery in a delicate vein by [Vania] Psota." Unlike London's balletomane writers, Martin dismissed the ballet's "pointless" story and "hopelessly commonplace music." Stylistically speaking, he asserted, "practically everybody was out of step but Nijinska."[59]

Nijinska, the prodigal daughter of the Diaghilev family, had come home. As the London season wound down, announcements in the *New York Times* alerted American readers that when the Ballet Russe returned to the United States in October it "would add to its répertoire a number of ballets by Bronislava Nijinska."[60] Massine, however, in an interview with the *Observer*, told Hubert Griffith something quite different, mentioning plans for numerous productions, all by him.[61] But whatever disagreements lay behind the scenes, Nijinska left London with high hopes for the future.

***

Returning to France with her husband, Nijinska looked forward to a family holiday with the children. But on September 4, 1935, tragedy struck. In Normandy, near the medieval town of Evreux, the couple's car skidded and crashed into a tree on the main road from Deauville to Paris. Léo was killed instantly and Irina gravely injured. Both had been sitting in the "dickey" or rumble seat of the American two-seater and received the full force of the impact. Singaevsky, who was driving, and Nijinska, seated next to him in front, escaped with bruises. Irina was rushed to Evreux Hospital with a fractured arm and severe cuts to the head. After visiting her, Nijinska returned to Tournedos to arrange for the removal of Léo's body to Paris for the funeral. Reports of the accident appeared in British, French, and American newspapers as well as in the émigré press. De Basil issued a widely quoted statement: "Bronislava Nijinska's loss touches me more than I can say, since not only is she a popular and talented member of my company but Leon was a youth who had shown great promise. I am afraid that Nijinska herself received an injury to the chest, but she is so stricken that she has refused to pay attention to it."[62] The funeral service was held on September 7 at Saint Ferdinand des Ternes, a Catholic church in the seventeenth arrondissement, and among those who came to pay their respects were Mathilde Kschessinska, Olga Preobrajenska, Vera Trefilova, Prince Tsereteli, and Boris Kniaseff.[63] Léo's head was surrounded by white flowers, and his music teacher, Vladimir Pohl, penned a reminiscence that was published in *Vozrozhdenie*.[64] The onset of mental illness in his last tragic months remained a family secret.

Nijinska spoke to no one. She never wrote about Léo's death or alluded to it publicly. It was a private grief, endured in silence. Léo, who had turned sixteen the previous January, was the apple of his mother's eye, a musician and aspiring composer. According to his French identity certificate, he had blond hair and grey eyes, and was five-foot-ten or so, and as the photo attests, he resembled his uncle Vaslav, whose name he bore as his own middle name.[65] Singaevsky had long acted as the father of Nijinska's children. But it was Nijinska who led them on the harrowing journey into emigration, settled them in middle-class neighborhoods, found schools for them to attend and clothes for them to wear, and put food on the family table. Cushioning the shock of emigration, she created a Russian-speaking world around them. Although Nijinska herself was Roman Catholic, the family kept Orthodox Easter with pashka and kulich, socialized almost exclusively with Russian émigrés, and pursued careers dependent on Russia Abroad.

Nijinska doted on her son. She kept his report cards and his letters and even some of his music. In one letter, written from Russian summer camp in the early 1930s, he describes how they marked the anniversary of the last Tsarevich by parading in front of the flag, laying a wreath in front of his portrait, and listening to a "magnificent speech" about his short life that left many comrades in tears. Twice a week, he told his mother, Monsieur Guardène gave them a Russian history lesson. He "brought to the camp many photographs and books that are striking documents of the famine and poverty in Russia today" and of "lying Bolshevik propaganda."[66] After Eleonora's death, Irina became Léo's surrogate parent. Barely out of her teens, she took her responsibilities seriously. The long months Nijinska spent in the United States were hard on both siblings, but especially Léo. "Irina and I are very sad not to receive a letter from you in two weeks," Léo wrote on March 1, adding that they still didn't know when she was returning.[67]

Léo was getting older, caught up in adolescent angst in an émigré world that was rapidly fracturing and a French one gripped by rising nationalism and economic distress. "Tomorrow," he wrote to his mother early in 1935, "I will start working on my identity card with Irina."[68] More than three months later he was still working on the paperwork. "The French," he wrote on March 19, "are becoming more and more unpleasant above all when you go to the Prefecture. [You should hear] how they speak to foreigners."[69] It was not until June that a new document was issued, one that allowed him to cross borders but would become void if he entered the Soviet Union. To the French, Léo was a foreigner, with an unpronounceable surname. He had lived in France since 1922, gone to French schools, and only wrote in French. But he was far from assimilated. Culturally and to some extent linguistically he belonged to a Russian world, but one increasingly irrelevant to the French, who had just signed a treaty of mutual assistance with the Soviets.[70]

A teen in search of an identity, Léo was also in search of a future. He seems to have been a budding composer—Nijinska, for one, had great confidence in his career[71]—but his letters to her during the American trip, unlike earlier ones, make no mention of music or his studies with Pohl. Although his "Mamusia" showered him with presents, money was always short. In late March he tells her that he wants to go to a camp for four days for Easter but fears it will cost too much. He finds it hard to work alone at home and more than anything wants to study dance; he is practicing every day on his own but would prefer to practice elsewhere, with Preobrajenska, for example, who has a beginner's class from three to four in the afternoon that several of his friends are taking. If that is too expensive, he could study with Lydia Nesterovska, who would charge much less because she was a family friend. What does she think of this idea? "I am already 16," Léo explains,

> and I need to think about what to do in life, for in a few years I have to be the family breadwinner, and for that I must now work hard. I think about it all day, and it gives me headaches. I am nervous and don't sleep at night, for it is very unpleasant not to work. I am very worried about my fate.

He ends by saying how much he wants to see her, either in France or elsewhere.[72]

When Nijinska returned to Paris in May 1935, she was shocked by the change in Léo. He seemed terribly thin, she wrote in her diary, and was complaining about his heart and seizures and "spasms" in his head. Irina had already taken him to six doctors; Nijinska now took him to a seventh, but all they would say was that "organically" he was fine. On long walks together, she was touched when he took her by the arm and stood tall, introducing her to classmates in the Bois de Boulogne. He told her that he was not afraid of dying and that he thought he should give up music. "The way I want to play," he told her, "I will never get there. . . . And, most importantly, *Maman*, nobody today needs art. That is why it is senseless to create art; no one will understand it."[73]

When Nijinska left for London in June, she wanted to take the children with her. But they chose to holiday on their own in Savoy, despite her misgivings and at considerable expense.[74] The bottom was falling out of Léo's life. One afternoon, while Irina was out for a drive, he began a long letter to his "*chère Maman*" in a small notebook.[75] Like Nijinska's own notebooks, Léo's focused on his state of mind, an inner life seldom revealed to others. On the cover he wrote: "Return to Madame Nijinska herself, if possible, this notebook in which her son has written the last lines of his life." Worse was to come. He tells her that he is crazy and wants to go to a sanatorium somewhere in the mountains. Above all, he adds, "<u>I do not want Irina to be with me</u>, for her life should always be very beautiful . . . not like mine, which was fine until I turned 16 and has been a terrible nightmare for more than 6 months and gets worse every day." "I never knew a man could suffer as I suffer," he wrote. "I feel . . . the blood pounding in my head more and more every day. . . . I am very unhappy, *Maman*, that I will never see you again with a sane mind, talk to you again, and hug you as before." He tells her he wants to die and even thinks of killing himself, except that suicide is a mortal sin and would make things worse for them. "I feel like someone who has been sentenced to death and sees the hour of his end, which is like a nightmare." And then, he drew three circles, each representing a hug—one for his mother, one for Irina, and one for Kolia.

After Léo's death Nijinska abandoned her diary for nearly two years. When she resumed it, she explained: "A long time has passed. I lacked the strength to . . . write about the horrible accident. . . . Everything collapsed. My life became . . . useless."[76] She buried her son in Paris, near his grandmother, and tended Irina, who slowly recovered. Her heart was broken.

Nijinska spent the fall of 1935 grieving. In December she surfaced for
the gala French premiere of *A Midsummer Night's Dream* at the Cinéma
Marbouf.[77] But it was not until spring that she rejoined the Ballet Russe in
New York, with Irina, not Singaevsky, accompanying her. Alone, he tended
the country house or *dacha* they had just bought in rural Louveciennes, a
town popular with artists about an hour from Paris. Anaïs Nin lived for a
time just down the road, and there was a small Russian community. With
seven rooms, Nijinska's house was ample.[78] But it needed a lot of work,
and Singaevsky spent much of the spring fixing, painting, and planting. "I
dream of you . . . sitting quietly in your little room to read, think, or work,
or even better, to rest," he wrote in one of many long letters to her.[79] He went
to church, Orthodox as well as Catholic ones, and often visited Léo's grave,
leaving flowers for him and "grandma," as he called Eleonora. For Singaevsky,
it was a time for healing, and also, one senses, for repairing his relationship
with Nijinska.

Arriving in New York on March 25, Nijinska rejoined the Ballet Russe on
the last leg of a six-month tour and immediately began rehearsing *Les Noces*,
which was scheduled to premiere at the Metropolitan Opera House on April
20. How the company found the time and the dancers the energy for this huge
project is anyone's guess. The Met season, which opened on Easter Sunday,
April 12, crammed nineteen ballets and twenty performances, including five
matinees, into the next two weeks, leaving the overworked dancers without
a day off. For the Ballet Russe dancers the project was daunting. According
to Sono Osato, they only learned about it when they reported for rehearsal in
the Met's vast, top-floor studio. "In next ten days, we do Nijinska *Les Noces*,"
de Basil announced. The dancers looked at each other in disbelief.[80] "With
only ten days to complete the mounting of the ballet," Osato wrote,

> Nijinska worked with extra determination. She never changed a movement.
> Again and again, she took our damp arms in her gloved hands, pressing
> them down with the command, "Down, more down!" Impatient with our
> failure to grasp things immediately, she'd yell, "Poot feet in ground, *more!*"
> Then grunting, she would crouch her small plump body, rounding it over
> her knees, and inch forward like some animal in search of food. At night
> in my dreams, I heard the counts and Nijinska's voice shouting repeatedly,
> "*Zemla! Zemla!* Earth! Earth!"
>
> Without any time to have the ancient Russian peasant rituals explained
> to us, we had to let the pulsating music and bizarre choreography teach us

what we had to know. Dancing in a haze of exhaustion, we were mesmerized by the peculiar sounds and throbbing energy of the score. We drove ourselves relentlessly, almost fanatically. The ten days passed in one huge effort, sustained by a curious sense of exaltation.[81]

The dancers had rehearsed with counts and a single rehearsal piano, but until the first orchestra rehearsal, they had never heard the music. Now, it overwhelmed them—the chorus of Russian voices, the wail of the soprano, the tympani, the four pianos.[82] In despair they moved from tableau to tableau, counting and swearing in confusion, while de Basil kept rushing onstage to placate Nijinska in her mounting distress. Backstage the Russians were crossing themselves. Nijinska, wearing an evening gown and impassive as always, stationed herself in the first wing. Wrote Osato:

> The curtain went up, the ballet began, and as we struggled through it, she became more and more agitated, hissing the counts so loudly that the audience might have heard her. She had worked herself up to such a pitch that by the last movement, it wouldn't have been surprising if she had plunged onto the stage and led us through it herself.

When the curtain fell the dancers were spent. They heard nothing.

> Then the applause began, slowly at first, but then growing and swelling into a low roar, punctuated by shouts of "Bravo!" Our fear and fatigue turned into pure joy.[83]

Nijinska herself was called repeatedly before the curtain and received some of the "most roundly earned bravos of the season."[84]

The next day in the *New York Times*, John Martin pronounced *Les Noces* "one of the great works of our time."

> Here is in essence a peasant ceremony, though there is only the merest hint of actual peasant material in it. It is overcast with profound mysticism, almost with a kind of terror for the solemnity of the occasion, yet there is no overt statement of any such attitude. The full vigor of the emotional undercurrent which dominates the action is revealed not through any emotionalizing on the part of the dancers, but through the sheer eloquence of the choreography projected as simply as possible. The faces are masklike;

there is nothing fairly to be called miming; there is only that kind of creative movement which comes out of an inspired composer when he is carried away by his material.[85]

Edwin Denby, in his first dance review for *Modern Music*, declared the ballet "one of the finest things one can see anywhere." He noted that Nijinska had used few movement "motives," but that they all "accentuat[ed] the direction into the floor." He noted, as Martin had, the "special significance and hardness" of the pointework, which he likened to "tapping," and wrote that the "general downward direction [gave] the heaped bodies a sense beyond decoration and . . . the conventional pyramid at the end the effect of a heroic extreme, of a real difficulty." Finally, he commended "the stillness of the . . . company at the end after all their frenzy," calling it a "climax of genius." For the dancers he had only praise. "The way they are overworked," he wrote, "by the management is inhuman, . . . that they can still offer so much is a miracle."[86]

Martin was sufficiently fascinated by the ballet to devote a long Sunday essay to it. He praised the Ballet Russe for producing one of the season's "most distinguished events," especially because it was inconceivable that the ballet would ever prove popular at the box office. "It has nothing for 'Lovers of Beauty'—. . . no personal display, not a moment of coyness; it is exclusively for those who can take their dancing without syrup and do not object to be disturbed by it."[87] The ballet's modernism must have appealed to the city's vibrant modern dance community. As Marcia Siegel points out, *With My Red Fires*, which Doris Humphrey began choreographing in the aftermath of the Ballet Russe season, covers some of the same conceptual ground as *Les Noces*.[88] And surely there are echoes of *Les Noces* in the rhythmic dynamism and relentless masses of Martha Graham's *Chronicle*, which premiered at year's end.

No sooner had the curtain fallen on *Les Noces* than Nijinska left for Buenos Aires to supervise the staging of *Petrouchka*, *Firebird*, and *Le Baiser de la Fée* for a three-week festival of Stravinsky's works at the Teatro Colón. It was the composer's first visit to Buenos Aires, and the festival offered something of a retrospective, with early "Russian" works such as *The Rite of Spring* programmed with later "international" ones, including *Apollon Musagète* and *Symphony of Psalms*. Among the premieres was *Perséphone*, performed as a concert piece, with Victoria Ocampo speaking the text originally performed by Ida Rubinstein.[89]

Getting to Buenos Aires from New York was no easy matter in 1936. The festival's first ballet performance was scheduled for May 7, which meant that sailing was out of the question. So Nijinska and Irina flew, first to Miami, then Puerto Rico, where they set off southward and eastward over Trinidad, the Guianas, and the vast expanses of northern Brazil, until arriving in Rio de Janeiro aboard Pan Am's "Trinidad Clipper" on April 27.[90] They spent the day in Rio, visiting the "Escola de Dansa" at the city's Theatro Municipal with Maria Olenewa, Brazil's leading classical teacher, who persuaded Nijinska to stage *Petrouchka* on her return from Buenos Aires. Then on April 28 she and Irina left for Argentina. The first ballet performance on May 7 featured two ballets from the Colón's "Russian" repertory that Nijinska did not choreograph—Boris Romanov's *Petruschka* (1928) and Fokine's *Firebird* (1931). The program was repeated two days later at popular prices, and on May 14 Nijinska added *Le Baiser de la Fée* to the third and last of the festival's ballet programs. On May 20 she was back in Rio, where the *Petrouchka* project fell through: the Theatro Municipal lacked the means to produce it. Then she and Irina sailed for Europe. The journey had exhausted Irina even more than her mother, who was used to working at high intensity.[91]

***

The assumption was that Nijinska would join the Ballet Russe in London. As the advance press made clear, *Les Noces* was to be a highlight of the season. In the *Dancing Times*, the "Sitter-Out" devoted several pages to the ballet and even reproduced H. G. Wells's letter attacking the "conspiracy of wilful stupidity" that led British critics to trounce the London premiere. *Les Biches* was also announced, as well as a revival of Nijinsky's *L'Après-midi d'un Faune*.[92] Hubert Griffith, in an advance piece for the *Observer*, also mentioned the addition of *Les Noces* and *Les Biches* to the repertory, and in a later article Nijinsky's *Faune* and *The Rite of Spring*.[93] But the Colonel kept putting off a conversation with Nijinska. In April she wrote that he "hadn't said anything about business," but that she understood that she was with them at least until London if not longer.[94] There was still no news in mid-May, when the company was in Paris for a few performances. Singaevsky stopped by the office. But de Basil said nothing about business, or the rumored "second" company that Nijinska may have hoped to direct, and Singaevsky didn't bring them up either. But the Colonel, he told Nijinska, was "very pleasant."[95]

The Ballet Russe season opened at Covent Garden on June 15, 1936, and Nijinska probably joined the company just before this. Not for the first time, London was in the grip of Russian ballet fever. In September, barely a month after the Ballet Russe had left the British capital, a company led by Leon Woizikovsky played a nine-week season at the London Coliseum, overlapping with shorter seasons by Marie Rambert's Ballet Club and the Sadler's Wells Ballet, followed in winter by a ten-week run of a new company organized by two of Diaghilev's leading British alumni, Alicia Markova and Anton Dolin. Then, on May 15, the Ballets de Monte-Carlo, led by de Basil's erstwhile partner, René Blum, with Fokine as maître de ballet/chore-ographer, opened a two-month engagement at the Alhambra Theatre. The de Basil season was even longer, a full ten weeks until it ended on August 29. Competition accelerated the rush of people to the box office. "The cult of the ballet now occupies two of London's largest theatres," wrote a *Times* corre-spondent in early July. "It has a vast and adulating public, and a host of special apologists whose superlatives of praise know no restraint."[96] For Constant Lambert the "renaissance of ballet surpasses in popularity the palmiest days of Diaghileff." He also noted that the "vast new ballet audience" was "less snobbish . . . but also less exacting" than the old Diaghilev public.[97] The season also witnessed the publication of an unprecedented number of books about ballet—Caryl Brahms's edited volume, *Footnotes to the Ballet*; Prince Peter Lieven's *The Birth of Ballets-Russes*; Rayner Heppenstall's *Apology for Dancing*; and two new books by the indefatigable Arnold Haskell, *Prelude to Ballet* and *The Balletomane's Scrapbook*.[98]

For Nijinska, however, the season was a bitter disappointment. Inexplicably, on June 19, Massine's first ballet, *Midnight Sun*, and *L'Après-midi d'un Faune* replaced *Les Noces*, which was "deferred" until later in the season and eventually scratched.[99] *Les Biches* was also canceled, as was Nijinsky's *Rite of Spring*. Even *Les Cent Baisers* was kept under wraps until midsummer and then buried in August. By July, as the drumbeat of pub-licity for Massine's new *Symphonie Fantastique* grew ever louder, Nijinska must have understood that de Basil had lured her to London under false pretenses. By 1936, as Massine's biographer, Vicente García-Márquez, notes, the relationship between de Basil and Massine had "seriously deteri-orated."[100] Massine had many reasons to distrust the sly and manipulative Colonel, beginning with the latter's refusal to appoint him artistic director. "He objected to not being consulted about the hiring of Nijinska" and was angry that de Basil refused to authorize a revival of his *Rite of Spring*.[101]

The production of *Les Noces* in New York must have galled him, along with the groundswell of British interest in the ballet. *Symphonie Fantastique*, to the first of Berlioz's four symphonies, was a huge work, calling on the entire company. Rehearsals began in Barcelona and continued in London, with daylong weekend calls that left the dancers exhausted.[102] Although the ballet was scheduled to premiere in late July, Massine made sure there wasn't a free hour for Nijinska to rehearse. He wasn't the only culprit. Despite the success of *Les Noces* in New York, de Basil seems to have gotten cold feet. *Les Noces* was unabashedly highbrow, and in the Colonel's book this meant bad for box office. Unwilling to antagonize his vast new audience with Stravinsky's bewildering "cacophonies,"[103] he chose to sacrifice both Nijinska and *Les Noces*. De Basil had all but jettisoned Diaghilev's modernist legacy.

In 1934, de Basil had begged Nijinska to head a second Ballet Russe company so he could fulfill his obligations vis-à-vis Monte Carlo, while the main company raked in dollars on a Hurok-managed American tour. Now, in the summer of 1936, rumors circulated about the likelihood of de Basil forming a second company that would tour Australia, while the main company danced in Germany and the United States. Thomas Armour, an American from Miami who had danced with Nijinska at the Châtelet, then joined the Leon Woizikovsky company, wrote to a friend on April 22, "I have been told de Basil really plans this year to have two companies and that Nijinska will be in charge of the second."[104] However, nothing was decided. Meanwhile, both Nijinska and Woizikovsky found themselves in London, the latter dancing with René Blum's Ballets de Monte-Carlo. On July 10, even before the Blum season ended, Armour reported, "rumor had it that [Woizikovsky] ha[d] signed with de Basil using us as the nucleus for a second company." Another rumor, Armour added, was "that Nijinska is to head a company of her own financed by a very wealthy woman." By July 20 the Australian tour, with Woizikovsky as director, was a done deal, and Armour, as he put it, "signed on the dotted line."[105] Jan Hoyer, once a student of Nijinska's in Kiev, was the company *régisseur*. Even Blum, who not only admired Nijinska's work but also regarded the 1934 Monte Carlo season as the genesis of his own company, managed to avoid programming a single one of her ballets, even *Bolero*, which he apparently considered a masterpiece, and *Aubade*, which he did produce, but in Balanchine's version, not hers.[106] How a season that augured so much ended so badly is difficult to fathom. Betrayed on every side, she saw her finest creations erased from memory and displaced from the canon of twentieth-century masterworks. It is hard to resist the conclusion that in the world of Blum, de Basil, and Woizikovsky being a woman made all the difference.

***

Ever since Nijinska had taken him under her wing, Anton Dolin had stood by her. Now, after the disastrous summer of 1936, he invited her to join the young company he had founded with ballerina Alicia Markova. The engagement involved teaching company class, rehearsing and coaching the classics, and staging three of her ballets—*Les Biches, Hamlet*, and *Variations*. She was to start on January 18, 1937 and work with the company for six months, first on tour and then in London for the Coronation Season (in celebration of the Coronation of King George VI and Queen Elizabeth). Philip J. S. Richardson heard the news from Dolin and quickly shared it with readers of his "Sitter-Out" column in the *Dancing Times*.[107]

A touring company, the Markova-Dolin Ballet spent much of its time on the road, performing throughout England, Scotland, and Wales. The distances were minuscule compared to the long coast-to-coast tours of the Ballet Russe in North America, allowing time for classes, rehearsals, and out-of-town tryouts, without the dancers being run ragged. With thirty-five dancers and a changing slate of ballets, the Markova-Dolin company offered a range of "classics, revivals, and novelties" that gave "a distinctive flavour" to its repertory.[108] Like the Ballet Russe, the company performed Fokine's *Les Sylphides* and *Carnaval*. Its nineteenth-century repertory included *Giselle*, Act II of *The Nutcracker*, and *Swan Lake*, and both the Blue Bird pas de deux and Rose Adagio from *The Sleeping Beauty*, all staged by Nicholas Sergeyev.[109] Works by British choreographers, including a number of women, completed the repertory.[110]

Nijinska's work attracted considerable interest in British dance circles and led to the publication of one of her most important essays, "Reflections about the Production of *Les Biches* and *Hamlet* in Markova-Dolin Ballets." Commissioned by the *Dancing Times* and translated by Lydia Lopokova, the essay recounts Nijinska's shock at Diaghilev's decision to produce *The Sleeping Princess* and his stubborn attachment to the ballet libretto, even as Nijinska herself was exploring works that negated it in favor of what she called "a pure dance form." She insisted that all her works were "raised on the basis of the classical dance," enriched by choreographic discoveries in design, bodily forms, and new dancing rhythms.[111] Far more strongly than in her 1930 *Schrifttanz* essay, she insisted that

> [t]he classical dance must always be the foundation of a true choregraphic [sic] school, with no need for another school to take its place, nor for strivings towards a rhythmical or plastic school of dancing. No matter how far removed from the classical dance the choreography may seem to be, every true choreographer [sic] creates on the foundations of the classical school. You can develop this school, you can enlarge it, but never be at pains to break it or re-create it. For a school is created for a long period of time through the continuing life of the art as a whole by continuous accretions given and deposited with it by master geniuses.[112]

An arduous six-week rehearsal period began in London in mid-January, with the first performances at the King's Theatre, Hammersmith, in early March. Never in her wildest dreams, Nijinska told Dolin, had she expected to find "such a fine company of dancers, so easy to work with, so disciplined." She staged *Les Biches* in two weeks, "arranged" a Petipa pas de deux for the two stars to dance in a pantomime, and rehearsed the company's *Swan Lake*, *Nutcracker*, and *Les Sylphides*.[113] Dolin found her drilling of the corps in *Les Sylphides* thrilling to watch, as she instilled "into these English dancers something of that mysterious quality that the Russians, and those who have had the opportunity to work with them, seem to be the only ones to really possess."[114] Not everyone remembered the drilling so fondly, including Liverpool-born Frederic Franklin, who made his debut at the Casino de Paris and danced in vaudeville, supper clubs, and West End musicals before joining the Markova-Dolin ballet. "I was in a ballet company that was run by Alicia Markova and Anton Dolin," he recounted in the 1980s,

> and we heard that this very famous lady, La Nijinska, if you please, was coming to see us and maybe do a ballet. . . . She came in the door, and she was wearing a white smock and navy blue trousers and white kid gloves. . . . The next thing, we were doing *Les Biches*. First it was, would all the boys go on one side and all the ladies go on the other side. Then she said, of course through the husband, "I don't want any newspapers in this room, and I don't want any knitting. If I'm not interesting enough to watch while I'm doing my ballets, go out." Well, of course, nobody dared

move. . . . She had [also] come to help with some of the . . . repertory. We were doing the last act of *The Nutcracker*, and I was doing the trepak . . . as a solo. . . . [W]e started, and one hour and two pairs of boots later, we finished. I don't know how.[115]

Critics were quick to note the marked improvement in the company's "general standard of performance." In *Swan Lake*, Nijinska freshened up the choreography for the celebrated lakeside scene, altered some of the groupings, and interpolated a variation from Act IV for Dolin. But it was Markova she transformed. "It was a rare pleasure to watch classical dancing of such standard," wrote the anonymous critic of the *Times*.

> Miss Markova's Odette has always been technically flawless, but she brings to the part now a softness and grace which was less evident before. Her *developpé* is more languorous, the carriage of her head and arms more supple; and for the *coda* she has all the right brilliance.[116]

Markova, for her part, "adored" working with the choreographer. "She'd be in the front row during rehearsals and really helped me perfect the classics," she told a radio interviewer in 1981.[117] Nijinska coached Markova in what became one of her most acclaimed roles—Giselle. "Mme Nijinska really started me thinking about the role at the time of the Markova-Dolin Ballet," she told critic Richard Buckle. "She said: 'You've got to have all that strength technically, but that isn't Giselle's character.'"[118]

From Hammersmith the company headed to Southsea, a resort on the Channel coast, where *Les Biches* and *The Beloved One* (as *La Bien-Aimée* was now called) premiered. Both were local events, with "masses of flowers" and "a stirring reception" for Nijinska and the principals. In Manchester, the *Guardian*'s J. M. commended Nijinska's impact on the company, visible in the "increasing rhythm, exactness, and fluency" of the corps. He found *The Beloved One* "strange and beautiful and moving," with the inventiveness of the dance putting the triteness of the subject matter to flight." "What will stand out in the recollection," he concluded, "are the peasant dances, the polished, slightly inhuman virtuosity of Markova, who darted once like a shooting star across the stage, and the very human, rhythmic crescendo of the carnival dance."[119]

Technically, *The Beloved One* was a revival. The music (by Schubert and Liszt) was the same, as was the Benois scenario. However, the scenery and costumes were by George Kirsta, a Russian émigré artist who had met Nijinska in Kiev, renewed acquaintance with her in Vienna, and corresponded with her until his death in London in 1955. At her behest he came up with a new set of designs in what proved to be "a happy and brilliantly successful" collaboration. She also made substantial changes in the choreography, creating two new pas de deux for the Poet and the Beloved that Dolin considered "some of the loveliest work" that she had ever done.[120] But the greatest difference between the two productions was the role of the Beloved, which Nijinska completely rechoreographed, transforming it from a largely gestural role to one tailored to Markova's virtuosic technique and ethereal presence. "To Nijinska must go the credit of having discovered and transformed Markova," wrote Arnold Haskell after seeing *The Beloved One* for the first time. "Here at last is a great role for a dancer who has never been seen to full advantage since she danced 'The Cat' as a child prodigy. For the first time, also, she acts with her entire body."[121]

Nijinska was supposed to stage three ballets for the company—*Les Biches*, *Variations*, and *Hamlet*. The replacement of *Variations* with *The Beloved One* certainly made sense, given how well the title role suited Markova. As to dropping *Hamlet*, "Nijinska was not easy nor cheap to engage," wrote Dolin. "Her tastes in ballet were extravagant. Everything had to be of the best."[122] Laura Henderson, who managed the business side of the company, found the money for Nijinska, Kirsta, and Karinska; she paid for a six-week rehearsal period. Trouble began when Nijinska and Henderson sat down to discuss the third ballet. Dolin personally hoped that Nijinska would produce *Hamlet*, which he had seen in Paris and had a wonderful role for Markova as Ophelia. However, Nijinska refused to do so "unless the scenery and costumes were bought from her and brought over from Paris. On this point she was emphatic. Equally adamant was [Henderson's partner] Vivian Van Damm not to buy them." Nijinska refused to allow anyone else to design the ballet, all but dooming it to oblivion.[123]

During Nijinska's five-month stay in England she had acquired an influential champion in Arnold Haskell, who, after lauding her recent achievements with the Markova-Dolin Ballet, now proposed that she become its artistic director.[124] More significantly, he published a long interview with her analogous to the interviews he had conducted with Diaghilev's other choreographers for his now classic *Balletomania*.[125] He explains that "La Nijinska," as she was usually referred to in England, was the last of the choreographers whose views he was "transcribing," because he had had more conversations with her than with the others, and "ha[d] always been too interested to stop and take a record."

I am not going to make the mistake of saying that she is the greatest, for there is no greatest, and one cannot grade such different talents, but I do believe that in her aims she is the most completely artistic of all, certainly the most materially disinterested. A long experience has shown me that she is neither interested in money nor in the commonest failing of all—advertisement. She is one of those rare natures that whether I praise or rail to understand her work she not only behaves the same towards me, but I know that she feels exactly the same, respecting and sympathizing with my point of view. . . . Had she understood more of theatrical politics her work to-day would be more universally known. . . . I firmly believe that now she will play an increasingly important role in the ballet.[126]

To Haskell's question about her "methods of composition," she explained that she had "no fixed methods":

Sometimes I have an idea and must find the music, sometimes the music suggests the idea. . . . It is very difficult to put the whole process into words. Movement must not illustrate music. There is a link between the two and once I have found that link, the essential structure, then everything comes naturally. Till I have found it, it is a long and painful process.[127]

Haskell also questioned her about the influence of particular dancers in a company on her treatment of a composition. In practice, of course, when the dancers cannot perform certain works, she would "abandon but never modify a project." But, she added,

it is an essential part of my work to discover and develop the dancer. In each one I try to draw out something that is not obvious on the surface. Nemchinova appeared superficially to be a straightforward . . . technical classical dancer. I felt differently . . . and developed her in that direction. Just as I developed Dolin for *Le Train Bleu*, Lichine, Verchinina, and other dancers such as Nina Youchkevitch [*sic*], Ruth Chanova. I like to create the artist for the work. Talent in an artist is not enough. It is only the necessary beginning. One must first develop talent and then combine it with other talent. That is the chemistry of choreography.[128]

Nijinska had finally met a critic who understood her.

Almost as soon as she arrived in England, Nijinska was deep in negotiations about her next project. Since the early 1920s, Polish ballet lovers had dreamed of creating a national company to display the richness of Polish culture, traditional music, dance, and the other arts. To be sure, a ballet troupe, with an affiliated school, existed at Warsaw's Wielki Theater, where Nijinska's parents and many Ballets Russes dancers had trained. However, since the end of World War I, the troupe had languished under the uninspired direction of Piotr Zajlich. Independent companies had come and gone, but all fell short of the ideal of cultural nationalism to which the organizers of Nijinska's new project aspired.[129] This was the creation of a national company to appear at the International Exposition of Art and Technology, a major attraction of the 1937 summer tourist season in Paris, and subsequently to perform at Covent Garden, in more than a score of German cities, and throughout Poland. The repertory would be new and exclusively national in character, with music, choreography, scenery, and costume design by contemporary Polish artists and an ensemble made up of Polish dancers.

The undertaking was the brainchild of Jan Lechoń, a celebrated poet and the cultural attaché at the Polish Embassy in Paris, who enlisted Arnold Szyfman, the founder, director, and manager of Warsaw's highly regarded Teatr Polski, who became the new company's director general, and Leon Schiller, a well-known theater director who was charged with creating the repertory with the assistance of prominent writers and composers. Szyfman, with no experience of ballet, was to collect the dancers (in this he was assisted by former Pavlova dancer Mieczysław Pianowski), locate a home for the new company, and find a choreographer.[130] According to Polish dance historian Janina Pudełek, there were only two names on the list—Nijinska and Leon Woizikovsky, who was leading the "second" de Basil company on its long tour of Australia. Szyfman, in the late 1950s, explained that Nijinska was chosen "because of her appeal as the sister of Vaslav Nijinski, her Polish lineage, and her reputation in Europe and America, which the ballet's founders hoped would attract outstanding Polish dancers, many of whom were then dancing abroad."[131]

For Nijinska, the idea was certainly appealing. However, she also envisaged any number of problems. How committed was the Polish government to the project and to paying for it? On March 11, Nadine Bouchonnet, whose agency, Office Théâtral Européen, was working with the Polish Embassy, assured Nijinska that the "Polish Ballet is definitely formed in the sense that money has been found and the Government has approved all the plans." Could she meet with the Ballet's director the following week in Paris?[132] With the Markova-Dolin tour in full swing, Nijinska couldn't get away, so negotiations moved forward by letter. On April 10, Bouchonnet confirmed that she had relayed Singaevsky's request to the Polish Embassy for 30,000 francs and a month of rehearsals for each production.[133] Ten days later she announced that the Direction of the Polish Ballet was prepared to pay Nijinska 30,000 francs per month, but for two or three ballets, not one, and preferred that royalties be paid separately through the Société des Auteurs, an arrangement that Bouchonnet thought would be more advantageous to Nijinska, given that the Direction wanted to commission a total of five or six ballets.[134] Szyfman turned up in the British capital for three days of the "most difficult" negotiations he had ever conducted, before the two sides reached an agreement.[135] Finally, on June 18, Nijinska signed a three-year contract at the Polish Embassy in Paris.[136] She then packed her bags and left with Singaevsky for Poland. Irina, who was undergoing treatment for a stomach problem, followed.[137]

In Warsaw, Nijinska was dismayed to learn that she was expected to share artistic responsibility with Schiller, who held the title of artistic director, while she occupied the subordinate position of ballet mistress and resident choreographer. She erupted in fury. "Nijinska was standing at the window moodily smoking a cigarette," Szyfman recalled.

Schiller was sitting in a dark corner of the room with a downright somber face. When Nijinska saw me she demanded a private discussion that very minute. In the administrative office, she declared to me huffily in a gibberish of Polish, Russian, and French that she wouldn't collaborate with Schiller because he belonged neither to ballet nor music, and she didn't care about his dramatic productions and his renown in the theatre—and this was her last word on the matter. . . . My arguments did nothing to help, nor did the interventions of the Ministry of Foreign Affairs or Lechoń's phone calls from Paris, or even his arrival at my behest.[138]

However, a ballet master and choreographer with Nijinska's credentials simply did not exist in Poland, and Schiller was fired. Woizikovsky, apparently at Szyfman's invitation, then presented himself as a candidate. Nijinska sent him packing as well.[139]

By then, Nijinska had put in two months of hard work with the forty-odd dancers. Headed by the Wielki ballerina Olga Sławka, they were an ill-matched bunch, mostly young and stronger in character than in classical work. The future Ballet Russe de Monte Carlo star Nina Novak (then known as Janina Nowakowna) was still a student at the Wielki school when Nijinska tapped her for the new company.[140] Although it was intended to showcase Polish talent, Nijinska insisted on hiring Nina Youshkevitch, who had spent the previous year on tour with the Ballet Russe, as well as two teenaged Preobrajenska students: Vladimir Dokoudovsky, a Russian émigré, and the Finnish boy who was living with his family, Kari Karnakoski.[141]

The company rehearsed in the eighteenth-century Orangerie in Łazienki Park, a gem of a building that housed the baroque Royal Theater, with a ceiling depicting Apollo surrounded by his muses.[142] It was her usual tough regime—class in the morning, followed by long hours of rehearsal as the repertory for the rapidly approaching Paris season took shape. In good weather, they took breaks outside, where a magazine photographer caught them doing handstands and wearing what by now had become standard practice clothes for Nijinska's dancers—dark tunics for the women and dark shorts and white shirts for the men.[143] The "Terms of Employment" required dancers to attend all rehearsals, performances, and classes, which were compulsory. Dancers had to arrive at the theater at least one hour before curtain, wear the costume and makeup assigned to them, handle costumes, wigs, and props with maximum care, and keep their shoes clean. They had to perform every role to the best of their ability and with maximum effort, and to understudy and share roles as requested by the directors. In an unusually punitive set of provisions, they were forbidden to criticize management decisions or the overall management system imposed by the Terms of Employment or other decrees or notices; discuss ballet rehearsals or preparatory work for performances with a third party; give interviews to the press or anyone else without special permission from the management; or organize any kind of promotion in print or photographic form. Both in and outside the theater, the "Artist" had to be "modest, cultured, generous, and polite," especially toward colleagues; wear "tidy, orderly and clean attire," and display "exquisite tact and comportment."[144]

Szyfman, who worked closely with Nijinska, developed enormous respect for her professionalism. "She was actually on good terms with the ensemble," he wrote.

> There were very few misunderstandings despite the severe discipline she imposed. . . . She held two rehearsals a day and worked marvelously with

a deep knowledge of the art and technique of dancing, with an absolute musical ear, phenomenal musical memory and a bottomless, fantastic imagination in spatial design.[145]

Not everyone in the company shared Syzfman's good opinion. According to Dokoudovsky, the men hated her, albeit respecting her because she was a great artist.[146] She made life miserable for Nina Novak, firing her at one point, then taking her back.[147] And she rode herd on Irina, whom Dokudovsky remembered as a little plump, but not a bad dancer and "really . . . sweet," despite all the complaints about her mother's harsh discipline.[148] The fact that she was Russian by culture if not descent added to the tensions. Resented by the other male dancers, Dokoudovsky became Dokudowski. Kari Karnakoski became Karnakowski, while Irina abandoned both her real (Kochetovsky) and assumed (Istomina) surnames in favor of Nizynska. When the English dancer Bessie Forbes-Jones later joined the company, she became Hélène Wolska.[149] (Taking her adopted identity seriously, Wolska joined the Anglo-Polish Ballet during World War II and in 1952 published a book about Polish dances.)

As always, Nijinska was hardest on dancers with promise. Dokoudovsky spent six hours repeating the opening steps and bow for his entrance in *The Recall*. "'No! That's not what I showed! This is the way I want it. No! You look too feminine. No! . . . You look like a butcher, not a "petit marquis."' . . . And the finger had to be this way; the head had to be this way. And it went <u>on</u> and <u>on</u>. . . . I think her idea was to make it very hard at the beginning. . . . Then when you got it, . . . she left you alone." By way of thanks, Nijinska choreographed a special variation for him, full of jumps and turns that always brought down the house. "It was the <u>most</u> difficult dance I ever danced in my life," he later said.[150]

Five ballets made up the repertory—*Chopin Concerto* (a plotless work to Poland's national composer), *The Legend of Cracow* (a Polish version of the Faust theme set in sixteenth-century Krakow), *The Song of the Earth* (based on traditional Polish folk rites and dances), *The Eternal Apollo* (showing him from ancient god to modern bather), and *The Recall* (in which a young Polish expatriate, nostalgic for his native soil, abandons the pleasures of Vienna to return home). All the works had scenery and costumes by contemporary Polish artists and, except for *Chopin Concerto*, music by contemporary Polish composers, and both *Legend* and *Apollo* had "arguments" by Polish writers.[151] Except for *Chopin Concerto*, the repertory was chosen by the company's organizers, with Nijinska reshaping the individual pieces as much as possible, talking (and sometimes fighting) with the costume and set designers, and working closely with the conductor, Mieczysław Mierzejewski. She insisted that Teresa Roszkowska do a second set of costume designs for *The Legend of Cracow*: the first, commissioned by Schiller, had been done without consulting her. "She was right!" the Kiev-born artist told an interviewer many years later. "She wanted [the ballet] to be Polish, not international. And Schiller had done something international. Schiller designed it in the spirit of the Renaissance. And after all, this is Krakow, is it not? No, she was entirely right!"[152]

In September 1937, Nijinska made the first entry in her diary in more than two years. After Léo's death, she wrote, her life became "empty, useless." Now, she felt life slowly returning. "I am on my native soil. . . . Working here, I feel my heart take fire again—*The Legend of Cracow*, now *Chopin Concerto*—my soul is fully invested in them."[153] Not long after arriving in Warsaw, she tried to explain to her old friend "Ania" Teplicka what happened when she began working on a new piece.

> Today I worked from 10 a.m. to 9:30 p.m.—officially, and then at home until 2. It is now 2:45 as I write you this letter. Tomorrow will be even harder— the final casting of dancers, discussions with Szyf[man], another musical theme for the new ballet—I have to listen to it, work with the dancers, and then at night—work at home. . . .
>
> Here, my dear Ania, is the reason why I am the way I am. . . . Right now, I am possessed by visions; they torture me with their lack of clarity. Perhaps, as it always happens, when I see them, I will fall passionately in love with them, and when the "marriage" happens, i.e., when the ballet comes to life, my sorrowful existence . . . will [end].
>
> It is so great that I need to make 5–7 ballets; it is the light of my life.[154]

Of the five works that Nijinska ended up choreographing, *Chopin Concerto* was the one she kept in repertory. It was an abstract ballet, "a manifestation of pure dancing," as the program note read, that looked back to Fokine's *Les Sylphides* and to works by her contemporaries. Like Massine's symphonic ballets, *Chopin Concerto* was staged to a defining form of nineteenth-century musical culture, not to the polonaises, waltzes, and mazurkas that inspired so many of the composer's works. Like Balanchine's *Serenade*, the ballet was both neoclassical and intensely romantic, with the stylized geometries and reiterated curves of Art Deco: the designer, Wacław Borowski, was closely associated with the aesthetics of the New Classicism.[155] There were two ballerinas, the blond Olga Sławska and the brunette Nina Youshkevitch, and fourteen women, all wearing long pleated tunics that followed the movements of the body, and a male ensemble of ten, led by Czesław Konarski. Critics singled out the two principals, commenting on their exquisite grace and harmony, while at least one critic noted that Nijinska's use of groups to underscore the music recalled Massine's symphonic ballets.[156]

Soon all eyes turned to Paris. A generously illustrated forty-page souvenir program was designed by Tadeusz Gronowski. Nijinska went over every sentence of the text before Gronowski left for Paris to have it printed. On November 15, 1937, the Polish Ballet, with Nijinska at its head, arrived at the Gare du Nord, where they were greeted by representatives of the Polish Embassy and members of the press.[157] Three days later, journalists and friends were invited to a rehearsal at the Théâtre Mogador, where Nijinska in a black pyjama outfit stood smoking in the fourth row of the orchestra, until springing up to speak to the conductor or join the dancers on stage. At the reception that followed, she told M.-A. Dabadie of *L'Epoque*, "I am very moved and profoundly happy. I owe so much to my country, which has enabled me to form a company of dancers who are all very young."[158] The following night was the *répétition générale*, and on Saturday, November 20, the gala opening. After the performance, a grand ball at the Polish Embassy, attended by numerous members of the diplomatic corps, high Paris society, the city's Polish colony, and personalities from the artistic world, sealed the company's success.[159]

The brilliant opening was the last artistic event of the International Exposition of Art and Technology in Modern Life, Europe's last world's fair before the outbreak of World War II in 1939. From late May until late November the Exposition proved a magnet for ballet companies, national dance groups, and modern-dance recitalists, bringing to Paris, in the words of the *Dancing Times*, "a sample of choreography [sic] from every corner of the world, and a fresh aesthetic experience."[160] The Exposition added two new buildings to the Paris cityscape—the Palais de Chaillot and the Palais de Tokyo, examples of the era's stripped-down classicism but endowed with French harmony and grace. But it was the placement of the German and Soviet Pavilions opposite one another near the Eiffel Tower that spoke directly to Europe's growing political divisions and fears of war. Spain was already a battleground, with Picasso's *Guernica*, protesting the destruction of the Basque town by German bombs, exhibited for the first time in the Spanish pavilion, which also hosted performances by regional folk dance groups enlisted in the anti-fascist cause.[161] Poland, squeezed between an expanding German Reich and a muscle-flexing Soviet Union, viewed the strengthening of the Polish-French alliance as key to its political and military security. For Juliusz Łukasiewicz, Poland's ambassador to France, the Polish Ballet was part of a larger diplomatic effort to cement that relationship.[162]

Orchestrated with intelligence and taste, the season generated reams of French press. There were advance pieces, including one in *Figaro* by Serge Lifar, now "maître de ballets" at the Paris Opéra, and many reviews, all for the most part positive, even when noting the company's weaknesses.[163] "This young troupe," began composer Henri Sauguet's review in *Le Jour*,

> has all the good qualities and all the faults of youth. First, the good qualities: fire, enthusiasm, energy, [and] freshness . . . joy and love. Now for the faults: an obvious lack of technique, a certain rhythmic confusion in the ensembles, . . . and a regrettable absence of soloists of the highest order. But the promise is great, and we would not be surprised to soon learn that some of these dancers have become stars.[164]

Excelsior's longtime music critic Emile Vuillermoz was also complimentary. Indeed, like many of the critics, he bent over backward to excuse the company's technical and artistic shortcomings.

> To end its participation in the 1937 Exposition, Poland has just sent us the most graceful of embassies in the form of a ballet company. . . . [I]t is an ensemble of volunteers and isolated talents, assembled for the occasion by Mme Nijinska and composed especially for these performances. . . . These dancers immediately won us over by their youth, fervor, and enthusiasm: only time will give them the balance and cohesiveness still missing from their work as an ensemble.[165]

Another longtime critic, *Figaro*'s Reynaldo Hahn, began his review with an unexpectedly warm appreciation of Nijinska, given his harsh words for her 1934 season:

> The name of Mlle Bronislava Nijinska compels attention: the creations of this interesting artist and the ideal they espouse inspire respect. Nothing

she does can leave one indifferent, even when she errs, and her new effort, whose results Parisians have just seen, lends extra interest and importance to the fact that it marks a revival of ballet in Poland. Mlle Nijinska is endowed with a fertile and bold imagination; she possesses a profound knowledge of her art; she is in her prime and, consequently, has many years ahead of her; she has dancers full of ardor. . . . One can therefore predict a long and glorious career for the Polish ballet.[166]

Hahn shared the enthusiasm of most critics for the two Polish-themed works on the first program, especially *The Legend of Cracow*. A kind of Carpathian *Faust*, it was full of action and color, especially in the market scene, while the second scene, set in hell, seems to have inspired some of Nijinska's most sophisticated group choreography. L. Franc Scheuer, who covered Paris for the *Dancing Times*, went back again and again to see the ballet, realizing by the second performance that it "was as perfect and as flawless an example of character ballet as he had seen in a long time."

In fact, the oftener he [the critic] saw it—the more this impression grew, being confirmed at each performance by freshly discovered details, by a concealed gesture, a spot too subtle for immediate perception or one hidden beneath the richness of the choregraphical [sic] design. . . . And never before—not even in *Les Noces*—has Nijinska created mass movement of a more convincing significance.[167]

To be sure, *Chopin Concerto* prompted criticism about Nijinska's choice of music and the absence of a "program." Still, there were those, like René Baron in *La Revue musicale*, who pronounced the ballet "a complete success," revealing through its "two peerless artists, Mlle Juszkiewicz . . . and Mlle Slawska," the essence of dance itself and "the purest image of its eternal beauty."[168] Others noted the harmony of lines, the fleeting constructions of volumes and curves, and the "utter reciprocity between the flight in space of the body . . . and the musical movement propping it up."[169]

The season lasted little more than a week. Houses were packed, and there were many standing ovations. In December the Exhibition jury awarded Nijinska the Grand Prix, its highest honor, in recognition of her outstanding achievement. Meanwhile, invitations poured in, for the Polish Ballet to perform in London, New York, Brussels, and Germany. On November 29, the day after the last performance, Wacław Jędrzejewicz, minister of public education and director of the Polish Ballet's umbrella organization, wrote to express his gratitude and recognition of her exceptional artistry, which accounted not only for the high artistic level of the performances but also for their success.[170] In early December, Szyfman returned to Warsaw, and Nijinska and the company left for England.

The critical and popular reception in Paris justified the investment of time and money in the Polish Ballet as a diplomatic strategy. In London, where the company was to perform for three or four weeks at Covent Garden, however, the season was a critical and financial failure. Compared to the elaborate arrangements for the Paris season, there was next to no advance publicity. "I understand that the Polish National Ballet may be expected in London this month," was all the *Dancing Times* could say in its December issue.[171] About a week later the company of forty-five emerged from Victoria Station in the "dripping darkness of one of London's worst December nights."[172] At some point journalists and "prominent personalities in the ballet and musical world," including Osbert Sitwell and Val Gielgud, the BBC drama director, were invited to the Polish Embassy to meet the company.[173] As in Paris, its debut was both a social and a diplomatic occasion, with "God Save the King" sung before the performance and titled dowagers in the Royal Box.[174]

Then the first-night notices began to appear, and they weren't kind. Not because critics didn't like the costumes or the music, or the idea of a Polish national company, but because the dancing fell short of what they had come to regard as a professional standard. Typical is the review by J. H. M. in the *Manchester Guardian*:

> The Polish Ballet recently won the Grand Prix for ballet at the Paris Exhibition, but it must be admitted that the standard which this achievement implied was scarcely revealed to-night when the company opened its season at Covent Garden.... This was not a company which ... had achieved a precocious maturity; it was one which was manifestly in its childhood, though it had in Nijinska a guiding force capable of making something important of it in time.[175]

The *Times* was kinder, with warm praise for *The Legend of Cracow*, with its "splendidly vigorous" dancing in the market scene and the ensembles of devils and other inhabitants of Hell in the second. *Chopin Concerto* made clear, however, that the company "seems more at home in long boots than in ballet-shoes and on points."[176] Horace Horsnell in the *Observer* largely ignored *Chopin Concerto*, preferring to write about *The Legend of Cracow*, which "showed how well the company works together and defies both gravity and fatigue." Like several other critics, he noted Nijinska's "inventive use of massed figures," with the pyramid being a "recurrent inspiration."[177]

Nijinska was at the height of her fame. Critics hailed her as a great choreographer, intensely creative, a maker of dancers, a daughter of Diaghilev. But there were many complaints, and they demonstrated to what extent a nationalist and increasingly narrow consensus had taken root in London during the 1930s. "The programme was as unfamiliar to English audiences as the names of the dancers," wrote the London critic of the *Birmingham Post* after the first performance, "and one had not the advantage of seeing the company even in the classical 'Les Sylphides' that is such a useful yardstick for gauging the quality of a fresh team."[178] There was no "ballerina of the starry order,"[179] and the Polish names were jawbreakers. A letter to the *Ipswich Evening Star* begged Mr. Bernard Shaw and his colleagues on the "B. B. C. Committee" to help with the pronunciation of "such surnames as Pokrzynsinska, Roszkowska, Sniezynski, Grochowska and Rutkowska."[180] Apart from Chopin, critics carped that the music was too "modern," too "anthropological," too "insignificantly melodious," and even "beneath consideration" (the latter courtesy of Ernest Newman in the *Sunday Times*).[181] Privately, Ninette de Valois wrote that the company was "<u>awful</u>" and that Nijinska didn't seem to have "very much more to say," adding ambiguously: "But then I don't think any woman choreographer can sustain the entire production work of a company."[182]

Initially, the company planned to remain in London until after the new year. But audiences thinned, in part because of the reviews but also because it was Christmas, when theaters staged traditional pantomimes and other holiday fare.[183] Specially reduced prices were introduced, but the bills continued to pile up, and on Saturday evening, January 1, a week earlier than anticipated, the company danced its last London performance.[184] However, they remained to dance selections from their repertory on a live television broadcast on January 4.[185] Then the dancers returned to Warsaw and Nijinska to Paris to prepare for the coming German tour.

Did Nijinska appreciate the gravity of what Szyfman called "the material catastrophe in London"? "I have had several sleepless nights over this," he wrote to her on January 10, "and despite the fact that I was not in London, I was with you and the company this whole time, for, in reality, most of my time goes to the ballet and its affairs."[186] He tells her not to "lose spirit," for

Fig. 37 *Illiustrirovannaia Rossiia* (*La Russie Illustrée*), with Ida Rubinstein on the cover, 1928.

Le ballet de l' " OPÉRA RUSSE A PARIS ",
avec Mme Nijinska, Prince Zereteli, M. de Basil, Michel Steiman, Nicolas Evreinoff.

Répétition des ballets sous la direction de Mme Nijinska.   *Photos Markovitch.*

Fig. 38 Nijinska with the dancers and artistic staff of the Opéra Russe à Paris, 1930.

Fig. 39 Natalia Goncharova, portrait of Nijinska, [1932].

Fig. 40 Boris Chaliapin, portrait of his father Fedor, 1932.

Fig. 41 Nijinska's *Le Baiser de la Fée*, with scenery by Héctor Basaldúa, Teatro Colón, 1933.

Fig. 42 Rehearsing *A Midsummer Night's Dream*, Hollywood, 1934.

"Ballet Russe" in Process of Rehearsal

Director General De Basil and Bronislava Nijinski at work on the new ballet, "The Nuptials," by Stravinsky. At the right is Tomara Grigorieva, the bride

Fig. 44 Alex Gard, " 'Ballet Russe' in Process of Rehearsal," New York, 1936.

Fig. 44 Nijinska (second from left) seated between Diaghilev's cousin Pavel Koribut-Kubitovitch (with the beard) and René Blum, with members of Colonel de Basil's Ballets Russes, Monte Carlo, April 1934.

Fig. 45 Nijinska (in hat and tie), with her husband Nicolas Singaevsky, son Léo, daughter Irina, and Irina's friend Nina Youshkevitch on a family outing, 1934. The car is the one in the accident that killed Léo.

Fig. 46 Gordon Anthony, portrait of Nijinska, mid-1930s.

Fig. 47 Nijinska (second from right) rehearsing the Polish Ballet in Łazienki Park, Warsaw, 1937.

Fig. 48 Olga Sławka (right) and Nina Juszkiewicz (Youshkevitch) in *Chopin Concerto*, 1937.

Fig. 49 Rehearsing for the Hollywood Bowl, 1940: Cyd Charisse and William Hightower (left) in *Etude*, Maria (right) and Marjorie Tallchief in *Bolero*.

Fig. 50 Irina Baronova as Lise in *La Fille Mal Gardée*, Ballet Theatre, 1941.

Fig. 51 Nijinska rehearsing *Pictures at an Exhibition*, Ballet International, 1944.

THE
DANCING TIMES
A REVIEW OF DANCING IN ITS MANY PHASES
With which are incorporated "THE AMATEUR DANCER"
and "DANCING & THE BALLROOM"

New Series   DECEMBER, 1947   Monthly
No. 447   One Shilling

Photo by]   [Duncan Melvin
Bronislava Nijinska and Yvette Chauviré
An informal snapshot taken in the gardens of the
Vichy Casino.

Fig. 52 Nijinska and ballerina Yvette Chauviré in Vichy, 1947.

Fig. 53 Nijinska and Rosella Hightower, late 1940s.

Fig. 54 André Eglevsky and ensemble in *Brahms Variations*, late 1940s.

Fig. 55 Marquis de Cuevas with his "Sylphides."

Fig. 56 Nereids in *The Sleeping Beauty*, 1960.

Fig. 57 Rosella Hightower as Aurora in *The Sleeping Beauty*, 1960.

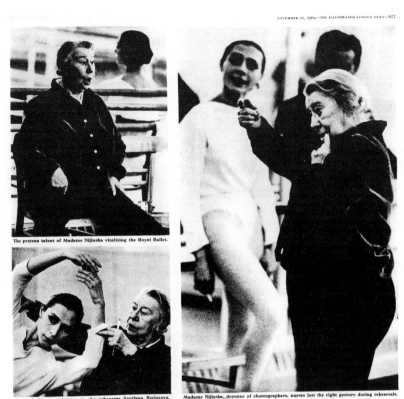

The protean talent of Madame Nijinska vitalising the Royal Ballet.

Care, precision, tenderness as she rehearses Svetlana Beriosova.

Madame Nijinska,.doyenne of choreographers, nurses just the right gesture during rehearsals.

Sir Frederick Ashton and Georgina Parkinson listen to the authentic voice of the legendary Russian Ballet.

NIJINSKA REHEARSES

A WHITE-HAIRED 73-year-old lady has been putting the Royal Ballet through their paces during the last few weeks. She is Madame Bronislava Nijinska, who has returned to London after 25 years' absence to produce her own *Les Biches*, due to open at Covent Garden on December 2. Principal roles at the first performance will be danced by Svetlana Beriosova, Annette Page and David Blair. The sets and costumes will be based on the original designs of Marie Laurencin seen at the world première in 1924, when the Diaghilev Company (including Dame Ninette de Valois and Mme. Nijinska herself) presented the ballet in Monte Carlo. Madame Nijinska has become a legend in her own time. As the creator of over 70 ballets, she is one of the great choreographers; as a dancer, she rivalled her famous brother Nijinski. She still retains a phenomenal energy. She rehearses for hours, throwing herself into each role in turn, shouting and gesticulating, pulling her young dancers into the precise composition she needs. Her vitality, indeed, echoes the pace of *Les Biches* itself, described by one commentator as "so frenzied that it reaches exhaustion point." But Madame Nijinska stays magnificently composed. *Photographed for The Illustrated London News by Erich Auerbach.*

Fig. 58 Nijinska rehearsing *Les Biches*, Royal Ballet, 1964.

Fig. 59 Nijinska and Frederick Ashton at the dress rehearsal of *Les Noces*, Royal Ballet, 1966.

Fig. 60 Nijinska and Kathleen Crofton with Central Ballet of Buffalo dancers before the Jacob's Pillow season, 1969.

Fig. 61 Central Ballet of Buffalo in *Les Biches*, Jacob's Pillow, 1969.

Fig. 62 Niagara Fontier Ballet, with Jeanne Armin and Tatsuo Sakai, in *Chopin Concerto*, 1970.

Fig. 63 Galina Ulanova in the backyard of Nijinska's home in Pacific Palisades, 1962.

Fig. 64 Nijinska with Svetlana Beriosova at the dress rehearsal for *Les Noces*, Royal Ballet, 1966.

Fig. 65 Nijinska and Anna-Marie Holmes, Buffalo, 1969.

as long as he remains director, he "will do everything within the realm of possibility to steer us back to safer waters."[187] He deferred all conversations about London and the future until they met in Berlin. The "machinations" and "intrigues" that Nijinska mentions in her diary probably had to do with her continued position in the company.[188]

Szyfman then turns to more immediate concerns. In light of "German stipulations," by which he means the Reich's anti-Jewish regulations, Arnold Haskell's article about her had to be dropped from the souvenir program. Jan Lechoń's introduction also had to be scrapped because he was a councilor of the Polish Embassy in Paris. Szyfman himself would remain in Poland for most of the tour, probably because he was Jewish. The German tour, he explained to Nijinska, "has a rather official character." It was taking place under the patronage of Joseph Goebbels, the German minister of propaganda, and Józef Lipski, the Polish ambassador to Germany, with the Ministry of Propaganda overseeing the tour itself. It opened with a gala performance at the Deutsches Opernhaus on January 27 attended by Goebbels, the German foreign minister Baron Constantine von Neurath, the German ambassador to Poland Ulrich Rauscher, and many other high-ranking officials. Adolf Hitler himself had promised to come, but declined at the last minute, expressing the hope to see the company in another city. (He didn't.) A reception at the embassy followed, attended by many German dignitaries as well as the "whole corps de ballet."[189]

Given the conservative taste of the first-night audience, Szyfman had recommended programming *The Eternal Apollo*, *Chopin Concerto*, and *Song of the Earth*; they were the "safest works," he told Nijinska, proposing that they save *The Legend of Cracow* and *The Recall* for the second performance. (However, even this "safe" program proved too much for Goebbels, the power behind the Degenerate Art Exhibition six months before, who dismissed the music as "real screeching" and faulted the ballets for failing to uplift.[190]) Szyfman was adamant that the company present itself "in the best possible light." That included everything from the company's "internal behavior" to how the sets were hung and the lighting organized, "so that we do not shame ourselves in the Germans' eyes." They needed a second conductor to travel ahead and rehearse the local orchestras, someone who spoke good German, knew the repertory, and wasn't Jewish. Finally, Szyfman wants to know if Nijinska has thought about the libretto for Roman Palester's new ballet. Would she be using the composer's or her own? If the latter, how would she prefer to be paid? However, it appears from her diary that she was only rehearsing repertory, not working on anything new.[191] The summer's euphoria had given way to creative apathy.

The German tour was grueling. The company performed in thirty cities, and most were one-night stands.[192] From Warsaw, Szyfman followed the tour closely. On February 24, 1938, he wrote to tell her how "incredibly happy" he was with the news from Germany and the reviews that were coming in. "I am so very happy with your success and the success of the entire company, for this is the only fitting reward for all the efforts involved in these several weeks of work."[193] He then relays the company's future plans: performances in Warsaw from April 2 to April 10, a week of vacation followed by a two-week tour of Poland, and finally, two weeks off for the remainder of the contract, which has been extended to mid-May. There are offers of future work, but nothing firm. He ends by wishing her a "restful break" between Freiburg and Munich.

From Munich the company headed north to the great industrial cities of the Ruhr Valley, with its coal mines, steel mills, and weapons factories that fed the juggernaut of German power. On March 12, the company was in the Ruhr city of Hagen when German forces marched into Austria and annexed it, an act known as *Anschluss*. The news did not bode well for Poland, under pressure to surrender Gdansk and the so-called Polish Corridor to an increasingly aggressive Reich. Even if Nijinska did not speak German, her husband and the Polish administrative staff certainly did, and the news must have quickly spread through the company. One can imagine the dancers counting the days until March 23, when the tour ended and they could go home.

On April 6, 1938, after nearly five months on the road, the Polish Ballet finally made its debut at Warsaw's Wielki Theater. The opening performance was a gala benefit for the "Gift of Easter" charity, followed by performances from April 7 to April 10.[194] Then the company set off on a tour of Polish cities, dancing in Katowice and other Silesian towns, Kraków, Łódź, Poznań, and cities like Lwow (Lviv) and Wilno (Vilnius), where Nijinska's Aunt Stepha had lived, that are no longer part of Poland.[195] In Warsaw the critics were waiting to pounce. Although Nijinska had immersed herself in the study of Polish folk dances, attending a national folk festival with dancers from all over Poland in Vilnius during the summer of 1937, and collecting images of traditional Polish costumes by the artist Zofja Stryjeńska, she was accused of committing the unpardonable sin of russifying the Polish national dances and some of the Polish costumes.[196] The sparkle and dynamism of Nijinska's Russo-Polish polkas, kujawiaks, mazurs, and krakowiaks may have enchanted Paris, but they were offensive in Poland, where "after only twenty years of freedom the hatred against the Russians and everything that even smelled of Russia was still very strong. The critics' reaction to Polish dances executed in Russian style and Polish girls in something like Russian sarafans simply could not have been other than hostile."[197] This wave of criticism, Janina Pudełek speculates, presented the Ministry of Foreign Affairs with a "major problem. How could the company under Nijinska's leadership successfully serve as a means of popularizing national culture abroad?"[198]

The controversy, like so much else, is absent from Nijinska's diary. On April 11 she records that the day before an old acquaintance from the Kiev Opera turned up at the theater during intermission. He was now a stage director at the Wielki, and together they reminisced about Chaliapin. Although Nijinska doesn't give his name, her visitor was probably Adolf Popławski, for several years the Wielki's chief *régisseur*.[199] The following day, she wrote an entry from Belovezh. Straddling the border with Belarus, it was the site of a Romanov hunting lodge and one of Europe's few remaining areas of virgin forest, a place that opened a floodgate of ancestral memories. "Russian soil, a Russian village, ancient Russian forest," Nijinska exulted. "Historically, Belovezh was part of Poland, and still is today. But everything here reminds me of Russia. How great my heart feels here! Russian soil calls up the past, and the forest is gigantic."[200] That same day Chaliapin died in Paris. Nijinska made no comment about his death until April 19, when the company was on its way to Lwów. True to her vow, she hadn't seen him since New York; now he was gone. "Dead, dead. . . . Fedor, my Fedor."[201]

Nijinska left Warsaw on June 10. Anna Teplicka had come from Łódź to spend time with her friend before she returned to Paris. An exchange of impassioned letters followed Nijinska's departure, although only Teplicka's to her "beloved" Bronichka have survived. "Ania," who was involved in a messy divorce, was almost certainly the "Anichka Vol'f (Volkova)" mentioned in Nijinska's notes about the School of Movement, a student who danced in her first choreographic works and then left for Poland.[202] She immerses herself in recollections of Nijinska's physical presence—her blue eyes, her dancing fingers, the expression of her arms and voice. "I want to remember everything, every moment of our joint existence, because everything in me longs for you!"[203] In several letters she urges Nijinska to see a doctor about her nerves or her heart and expresses serious concern about the state of her health: how much of this is related to overwork, depression at Chaliapin's death, or uncertainty about the future is unclear.

In July, Nijinska learned that her services as artistic director of the Polish Ballet were terminated. The news arrived in a telegram from Wacław Jędrzejewicz, minister of public education and director of the Polish Ballet's umbrella organization, with a personal letter from Szyfman following on July 6. "As you anticipated some months ago," he wrote,

on July 1 I resigned from the Ballet as director for good. I could no longer reconcile my work in the theater with my work on the ballet without harming one or the other.

Unfortunately, to this day, no replacement has been named, and this is presumably only the beginning of the disasters to come. The desire to continue the ballet still exists, and there are certain funds available that would allow the ballet to continue on a more modest budget . . . until April of 1939.

Personally, I think this project has not yet run its course, and if we find a good replacement, . . . we could revive it in an instant. It would be to my great dismay if our work were to be for naught, particularly since I believe in the ballet's future, and I see excellent directions for the Polish Ballet, which currently has the opportunity to pick up excellent Polish dancers previously signed to the de Basil Ballet.[204]

At the top of the list was Leon Woizikovsky.

The Polish Ballet archives disappeared during World War II, so it is impossible to piece together the full story. On August 6, Irina drafted a letter in French on behalf of her mother to Jan Lechoń. By then it had been more than a month since Nijinska had been fired, and her requests for payment of royalties and damages for breach of contract had gone unheeded:

You know very well that the termination of work was unanticipated by me and the payment of my salary was cut with one day's notice. . . . I was left without money and I cannot even rest and go to? a spa, which in the opinion of the doctors I need to do for my health and which is only natural after my very hard work for the Polish Ballet. It is quite strange that the Direction, after refusing me permission to mount ballets on other companies during the months of July and August, should be so cavalier in its obligations to me.[205]

She ended by expressing the hope that everything could be settled without going to court. The legal threat produced a response from Aleksandr Guttry, who explained that everyone, except himself, was away from Warsaw on vacation, so no decision could be made.[206] By September 1 the Board members were back from vacation, but there was still no money.[207]

Finally, on September 16 the dilatory behavior of the Direction was explained. Thanks to intense efforts on its part, the Polish Ballet was continuing its work, albeit on a somewhat more limited scale because of the severe deficit from the previous season. To direct the company they had engaged Leon Wójcikowski, whom they expected to provide the company with the required technical skills and the choreographers with attentive supervision over the execution of their artistic conceptions. They were now turning to Nijinska, as artistic director during the company's first tour, to continue her artistic partnership. Specifically, they wanted to engage her to choreograph two or three ballets for the company's international tour. Could she begin work at the beginning of October? Finally, they got around to the money they owed her. Although they were doing all they could to arrange it, the "easiest recourse" would be to settle all financial matters in person upon her arrival in Warsaw.[208] It seems clear that the whole point of the summer charade of suspending the company was to remove Nijinska as artistic director and appoint Woizikovsky in her place, while retaining her services as a choreographer and rehearsal director of her own repertory. The duplicity, coupled with the unwillingness to pay either royalties or damages until six months had passed, was breathtaking.[209]

Directing the Polish Ballet had exhausted her, and its aftermath left her profoundly depressed. She buried herself in the countryside, saw no one, and wrote to no one.[210] In January 1939 she made a very brief entry in her diary: "I am mortally ill and have no strength to fight for life. . . . I long for death."[211] A long entry follows on June 5. It starts as the draft of a letter, probably to Teplicka, who had visited Louveciennes in spring:

My dear, do you remember Belovezh? Belovezh—there I felt good, like in spring when I was young or in Russia. But recollections are tainted with sadness and torture me these days. Belovezh . . . back when I didn't yet know my fate.[212]

She then talks about her state of mind:

It happens sometimes that you fall asleep in great sadness; the heart . . . is restless, and the unconscious clouds reality. And then they wake you up and ask: "So how did the misery affect you?" And, then, for the first time, you take a look at yourself and have nothing to say . . . because . . . you don't recognize yourself any more and no longer know what parts of you are still alive. . . . You know, I really have the feeling that I've been gone for an entire year. And now I wake up and suffer, and the most terrible thing is I realize that I will no longer create anything in my art.[213]

Because of her commitments to the Polish Ballet, Nijinska had turned down other work, including an offer from La Scala to stage *The Nutcracker* with designs by Alexandre Benois.[214] In March 1939 she was approached by René Blum on behalf of Ida Rubinstein, who wanted Nijinska to revive *Les Noces de Psyché et de l'Amour* so long as her terms were "modest." (They weren't, and the project collapsed.[215]) Around the same time, Nijinska was in touch with Nadine Bouchonnet of Office Théâtral Européen, this time acting on behalf of the "English director" of the Covent Garden Russian Ballet (as the de Basil company, minus de Basil, was now known), with a proposal to revive *Les Biches*, *Le Train Bleu*, and possibly other ballets for the company's season at Covent Garden in June and July.[216] Nothing came of that idea, but in early July Nijinska signed a contract with the company's new director (and ballerina Irina Baronova's husband), German Sevastianov, to work with the company during the second half of its London season, which ended on July 30.[217] Tatiana Leskova, a newcomer from Paris, recalled rehearsing both *L'Après-midi d'un Faune* and *Les Cent Baisers* with Nijinska, and the *New York Times* reported that both *Les Biches* and *Le Train Bleu* were being revived.[218] Nijinska also reached an agreement with Ealing Studios to assemble a company and choreograph the ballets for the "cinematograph film" *A Bullet in the Ballet*, based on the comic mystery by Caryl Brahms and her collaborator S. J. Simon. The engagement was to start on August 15 and last for no more than six weeks; she would be paid a total of £700.[219] Meanwhile, behind the scenes a tempest was brewing. As reported in the *Observer*, Sevastianov had announced his resignation, Baronova was leaving with him, and Fokine was terminating his association with the company. The latest news was that Sevastianov and Baronova "intend to found a small ballet company on their own, with the famous M. Alexandre Benois as an artistic director, and Madame Nijinska as choreographer."[220] The *Manchester Guardian* added a few other details: Nijinska was to "refurbish" *Hamlet* and *Etude* (now described as a "Bach Chorale"), both new to London, as well as *Les Biches*.[221] With so much work in London, Nijinska, with Singaevsky and Irina, settled into lodgings at Museum Chambers, Bury Place, a few steps from the British Museum.[222]

On September 1, German troops crossed into Poland. Great Britain and France quickly declared war. By the end of the month, Poland was occupied by Germans, its eastern territories secretly ceded to the Soviets. In September, Nijinska returned to France, signing over the scenery, costumes, and other properties in storage in Paris to Irina.[223] She closed up her house in Louveciennes and packed more economically than ever before. "Everything I could not imagine living without," she later wrote, "I had to leave home this time. Even Levushka's last letter."[224] She asked a friend, Maria Prianishnikova, to look after everything and then returned to London. Here, along with hundreds of others, she booked passage for herself, Singaevsky, and Irina on the *American Trader*, a ship leaving for New York on October 8. They received transit visas in London only four days before they sailed, a wait that must have been nerve-wracking.[225] Finally, on a rainy Sunday, sick with anxiety about German submarines prowling the North Atlantic, they began the ten-day trip to their second exile.

14

In Wartime America

When the *American Trader* docked in New York on October 18, 1939, Nijinska joined a wave of refugees, including many dancers, fleeing Europe for the neutral shores of the United States.[1] Stranded in Paris, Massine's Ballet Russe de Monte Carlo scrambled to find transport, with half the company arriving only hours before their twice-postponed opening at the Metropolitan Opera House. The De Basil–Covent Garden–Educational Ballets continued to fracture, with most of the company heading to Australia while a smaller band, including Irina Baronova, decamped for New York and Massine's enterprise.[2] Meanwhile, a new company was forming, and as Ann Barzel breezily remarked, "almost everyone in the country who had any reputation was signed up."[3]

The new company was Ballet Theatre. Its goal, explained journalist Lucius Beebe in a program essay, was "to present the greatest possible variety of choreographic repertory . . . the best that is traditional, the best that is contemporary, and the best that is controversial."[4] The foremost names in the ballet world had rallied to the enterprise, he rhapsodized. "Out of virtual retirement came Fokine, greatest of living choreographers; from California flew Bolm; from England came . . . Antony Tudor and Andrée Howard; . . . from Poland . . . the fabulous Nijinska; in New York was Mordkin." For all its international gloss, however, Ballet Theatre was conceived as a uniquely American endeavor. As Beebe noted: "In these productions American artists . . . can display their talents—not in musical comedy, revue, stage presentations or the films, but in their own field which is ballet."[5] Although small American ballet companies had emerged in the 1930s, the scale and sheer ambition of Ballet Theatre—"21 Ballets, 6 World Premieres, 5 American Premieres, 85 Dancers"—dwarfed and largely subsumed them.[6]

On November 5, a month after Ballet Theatre rehearsals began, Nijinska signed a "memorandum of agreement" to stage *La Fille Mal Gardée*.[7] John Martin called her "the ideal choice," for "besides being one of the greatest choreographers of our time she is a master of style, and an old work of this sort loses much of its value if the flavor of its period is not restored along with it."[8] Nijinska's staging was based on the Maryinsky production she had known and danced in her youth. With music by Peter Ludwig Hertel (which had replaced the older Ferdinand Hérold score) and choreography chiefly by Lev Ivanov, the ballet was closely associated with the ballerina Mathilde Kschessinska, who chose it for her farewell performance, an unforgettable evening in which Nijinska took part and that she recalled decades later in her memoirs.[9] Nijinska went over the score with Lucia Chase and Dimitri Romanoff, who had danced the leads in Mordkin's 1937 production, and reviewed the pantomime scenes with them. She also eliminated the music by Delibes, Minkus, Pugni, and others that had crept into the Hertel score.[10] Finally, she transformed Alain from a pantomime to a dancing role and his character from that of a simpleton to an "immature young man whose heart was set on catching butterflies" rather than marrying Lise.[11] At the Sevillia (where she had stayed in 1935), Nijinska used hotel stationery to sketch ensemble groupings, movement patterns, and spatial configurations, leaving the steps for when she entered the studio.[12]

A perfectionist, Nijinska had always worked slowly. But time was in short supply in the weeks before Ballet Theatre made its debut in January 1940. With a score of ballets to mount, dancers and studios were at a premium. "Tempers flew," Orest Sergievsky recalled.[13] Although *Fille* was a two-act ballet with a large cast, Nijinska wasn't given enough rehearsal time, one of many slights she endured as a "Russian" in a company that declared itself "strictly American."[14] Sergievsky himself had a good personal relationship with Nijinska, probably because he spoke Russian and as a child had taken his first ballet classes with her in Kiev. But even he acknowledged that she wasn't popular. Her rehearsals were "exhausting"; she couldn't speak English very well, and "she would put us through crazy rehearsal schedules."[15] Annabelle Lyon, who had studied with Fokine and danced in Balanchine's American Ballet, was one of Lise's four friends, a role the season's first-cast Giselle must have regarded as a comedown. Lyon couldn't understand what Nijinska wanted, despite Singaevsky's solicitous efforts to translate, and even when Nijinska demonstrated, her girth and the way she moved made it difficult to "see clearly."[16]

Patricia Bowman, a Fokine student and star of the popular stage who danced the role of Lisette (as Lise was now called), had other complaints. She had come to Ballet Theatre from the Mordkin Ballet where she had danced all the major classical roles, and regarded Ballet Theatre's "no star system" as a personal put-down. "[T]hey would be rehearsing three ballerinas for Giselle, and four ballerinas for Swan Lake, [a]nd . . . three ballerinas for La Fille, and you didn't know who was going to . . . dance," she told John Gruen in the 1970s. The company wanted the three Lisettes to alternate, until Nijinska put her foot down and said she wanted Bowman.[17]

Despite the chaos, the season that opened on January 11, 1940, and ran through February 3 offered an embarrassment of riches for audiences and critics alike. John Martin of the *New York Times* and Walter Terry of the *New York Herald Tribune* spent nearly every night at the sold-out Center Theatre. They wrote advance pieces, Sunday pieces, and follow-up pieces. And, with mounting excitement, they covered every premiere and revival, from Fokine's *Les Sylphides* to Eugene Loring's *The Great American Goof*, Tudor's *Lilac Garden*, and Agnes de Mille's *Black Ritual: Obeah* for the company's "Negro" unit. And, early in the second week of the season, they attended the premiere of Nijinska's romantic pastoral *La Fille Mal Gardée*.

Nijinska could not have wished for more enthusiastic reviews or warmer audiences. Anatole Chujoy, who had probably seen the ballet in Petrograd during World War I, was delighted with Nijinska's version, calling it "one of the finest ballets given this season," with a "naive simplicity" that "cannot help but captivate the most sophisticated audience."[18] Walter Terry was equally delighted. " 'La Fille Mal Gardée,' " he wrote,

> may be in its second century, but last night's audience at the Center Theater found it still fresh and sparkling. This beloved work has been given a superb production by the Ballet Theater, and Bronislava Nijinska's direction has made it the merriest ballet to be seen. . . . The action is quick and amusing . . . interspersed with colorful ensemble dances that have little or no bearing on the plot, but which are completely delightful. Patricia Bowman gave a flawless performance as the girl, dancing with brilliance and vivacity. As the yokel lover Shabelevsky had his first big role of the season. It was a treat to see him project the gauche and ardent qualities of his character and dance with skill and vigor.[19]

John Martin, who called Bowman a "born Lisette," also singled out Alexis Kosloff's "marvelous" performance as the "butterfly-chasing Alain." He praised the "final scene of dancing," with its "amusing comedy threesome, a brilliant pas de deux, and a gay ensemble." All in all, he concluded, *Fille* was "a most distinguished revival of an antique that is worth all the care one chooses to expend upon it."[20]

When Ballet Theatre gave its final performance on February 3, there was talk of a spring season followed by a summer tour and another New York season in the autumn. However, the company was hopelessly in debt. Neither ticket sales nor Lucia Chase's private fortune sufficed to pay the bills for so many productions, including union-scale salaries that began at $45 a week. (By contrast, the non-union Ballet Russe de Monte Carlo paid only $22.50.[21]) Behind the scenes, Richard Pleasant worked feverishly. In February and early March, he contacted Nijinska about one or two new works for the spring season. Did she have Poulenc's music for *Les Biches*? Could she stage *Le Train Bleu* or *Hamlet*? Finally, he told her, "Now is the right time to compose a Mexican ballet. Listen to Aaron Copland's *El Salón México*."[22] Nijinska wired back two days later:

> Absolutely advise *Biches* should have great interest and success. Music rental Edition Musicale Heugel Paris. . . . As second ballet suggest *Bach Etude* also sure of great success. I have the music. I could begin rehearsing [while] awaiting decision [about] music for *Biches*. Stop. If not Ravel's *Valse* or *Bolero*, *Hamlet* or Stravinsky's *Baiser de la Fée* one can get the music. Stop. Would very much like *Hamlet* but it needs many rehearsals. Stop. I will listen to the music [of the] Mexican ballet. Stop. As soon you are sure of season, please inform me immediately so I can make arrangements.[23]

But by then, as the magazine *Dance* reported, Ballet Theatre had "temporarily suspended operations, with "options on principals' contracts relinquished [and] corps de ballet laid off."[24] Nijinska, meanwhile, had left New York for Hollywood where she was teaching "classic ballet," character, and "plastique" at the Nico Charisse School.[25]

Within weeks of arriving in California, Nijinska spoke to the *Los Angeles Times* journalist Isabel Morse Jones. She described the move to the West Coast as an "extended sojourn" and spoke at length about the positive change in American attitudes toward ballet since her last visit to Los Angeles.[26] The family settled in Hollywood in a large apartment building at 6350 Franklin Avenue, where a census taker in April 1940 recorded both her occupation and Singaevsky's as "manager" and their line of work as "theater business."[27] By then, reported Dorathi Bock Pierre in *American Dancer*, Nijinska was "working with young dancers, whom she hopes to use as a nucleus for a company such as the Ida Rubinstein Company."[28] Seeking to broaden her professional outlets, she wrote to Max Reinhardt, but by 1940 the director was no longer doing film work. "My dear Mme. Nijinska," he replied in English. "Your friendly letter . . . made me only distressed that I have no production in preparation that could involve your artistry and choreography."[29]

Classes went only so far in training artists, Nijinska believed. The dancer's education was completed on stage, in "the practical, actual experience of the theatre."[30] As if to demonstrate the validity of her credo, after little more than two months of intensive rehearsal she presented a company of young California dancers—all from her classes—at the prestigious Hollywood Bowl. Dancing three of her ballets—*Bolero*, *Etude*, and *Chopin Concerto*—to music by the Los Angeles Philharmonic, they shared the week with the soprano Lily Pons and the celebrated conductor Bruno Walter. The company was more than forty strong, the nucleus of the permanent organization she hoped to form in Southern California. For Nijinska much rode on this single Bowl performance, and the photographs that appeared in local papers reveal the intensity she brought to the final rehearsals. The dancers did their best, but to Isabel Morse Jones's critical eye, not all of them had the "long and sufficient training" to sustain a full-evening program. Still, Jones was impressed by *Chopin Concerto* and mentioned several of the dancers by name.[31]

Albertina Vitak, who covered the performance for *American Dancer*, was taken with *Chopin Concerto* as well. She also devoted quite a bit of space to *Bolero*, claiming that for many it was "the most interesting" work on the program because it "achieved for the first time the complete integration" of Ravel's music and dance. "The insistence of the repetition of the music," she wrote in an unusually perceptive description of the choreography,

> was repeated in the movement of the leading dancer, . . . representing the single unchanging theme of the music, and very well supported by the crescendo represented by . . . two men. . . . There were other dancers forming a semi-circle in deep shadow who moved and clapped . . . but always the feeling was not of dancers performing some strange exotic *tour de force*, but simply people forced to movement by the music to become . . . so integral a part of that rhythm that they cease to exist as entities and become themselves simply the visualization of the sound.[32]

Remarkably, three future stars danced for Nijinska at the Hollywood Bowl. The first was Cyd (or Sid, as it was then spelled) Charisse, an eighteen-year-old Texan with long legs and sculptured feet who had danced with the Original Ballet Russe (as Maria Istomina and Felia Sidorova), married her teacher Nico Charisse, and went on to Hollywood fame in *Singin' in the Rain* (1952), *Silk Stockings* (1957), and many other movies. When MGM was about to launch her career in a big way, Charisse told the Hollywood gossip columnist Louella Parsons that she was busy studying ballet with "Madame Nijinska, a sister of the famous dancer. . . . Madame Nijinska was her brother's partner and just as good as he. She is a great teacher."[33]

Nijinska's second future star was Betty Marie Tallchief, later the prima ballerina of the New York City Ballet. In 1942, fresh out of high school, she signed with the Ballet Russe de Monte Carlo and changed her name to Maria. She was only fifteen when she began to study with Nijinska. Walking into the studio, the teenager sensed she was in the presence of greatness. "Everyone in the school was in awe of her," she later wrote. "When we would come into class, it was like going to church."[34] Dancing *Chopin Concerto* at the Hollywood Bowl "so entranced her that thereafter she concentrated on ballet," giving up her piano studies.[35] Although Tallchief always spoke of Nijinska as her principal teacher in California, Nijinska was often away. "My dear Madame," Tallchief wrote in June 1942. "My sister and I miss you so very much, and are very sorry that you will not be here for the summer months. . . . I am now very anxious to get in one of the ballet companies. . . . I wish you were here so I could have a lesson every day with you this summer and then go in one of the Ballets this fall."[36] Betty Marie got her wish. Traveling to New York with the choreographer David Lichine and his wife, the ballerina Tatiana Riabouchinska, who were joining Ballet Theatre, she was hired by the Ballet Russe de Monte Carlo.[37]

Nijinska's third Bowl star was Tallchief's sister Marjorie. Younger by two years, she joined not the Ballet Russe de Monte Carlo (where Nijinska feared the sisters would "get in each other's way"), but Ballet Theatre, followed by a stint with the Original Ballet Russe. Subsequently, she joined the Grand Ballet du Marquis de Cuevas, a French-based company with which Nijinska would be affiliated during the late 1940s and 1950s. A celebrity in Europe, Marjorie became première danseuse étoile of the Paris Opéra in 1957, the first American dancer so honored.[38]

Nijinska's Hollywood Ballet School, which she opened at 855 South La Brea, attracted a number of celebrity students, many associated with the film industry. When the Ballet Russe companies came to town in the early 1940s, Maria Tallchief was thrilled to observe their dancers taking class and Alexandra Danilova, the "biggest star of all," presenting roses to Nijinska as she sank into a *révérence*. Class lists from the late 1940s and early 1950s record other visitors—ballerina Tatiana Riabouchinska, dancers from the San Francisco Ballet, Oleg Tupine and his wife Natalie Clare from Ballet Russe, Ruth Anne Koesun and Melissa Hayden from Ballet Theatre, Joseph Rickard, who founded the First Negro Classic Ballet, and most famously Cyd Charisse.[39] But as notices in regional papers testify, Nijinska's influence as a teacher spread far beyond Southern California and its celebrities. From Walla Walla, Washington, to San Antonio, Texas, her name appears in tandem with local dancers, teachers, and choreographers.[40]

Maria Tallchief left an unforgettable picture of Nijinska in her Hollywood studio:

Because her English was practically nonexistent Madame Nijinska rarely spoke. She didn't have to. She had incredible personal magnetism and she radiated authority. Most of the time she demonstrated. It was hard to imagine her as a ballerina, but how she moved! Her footwork was phenomenal. She jumped and flashed around the studio. I was under her spell. . . .

In her pointe class, we'd have to repeat steps over and over, learning how to balance and how to hold a position so that our entire backs were being utilized. . . .

She was insistent on port de bras, and she told us the reason her brother could jump so high and hover in the air so long was because of the control he had over his abdominals. It was from Madame Nijinska that I first understood that the dancer's soul is in the middle of the body and that proper breathing is essential.[41]

Allegra Kent was eleven when she began attending classes at the Hollywood Ballet School in 1948. After studying with Irina for a year, Kent graduated to classes with "Madame." Nijinska taught a set barre,

which meant that the same exercises were done every day to the same music. One piece by Burgmüller was played for grand battement, and when I hear the piece today I think of Mme. Nijinska, the woman who told us "arms cannot be like spaghetti." One day in class, she asked me to try to push her arms around. I exerted great effort, but they wouldn't budge. She wanted me to see her underlying strength and power, which ballet requires in order to project its airy look. . . . Madame herself was on the heavy side, but, in a demonstration of how to hold the body, the men who lifted her were amazed at how easy she was to raise from the floor. This was the dichotomy—the achievement of fragility and delicacy meant a core of strength. Butterflies are not weak.[42]

From Nijinska, Kent learned not to fear competing with men.

> Toward the end of class one day, Madame took my hand. The men had just done a big jumping step across the floor and covered an enormous amount of space. Now the two of us, an old woman and a child, were going to do the same. I looked in Madame's face. She was gloriously ready. She signaled for the pianist to start. We would not be outdone by the male dancers—or anyone, for that matter. . . . And so we were off and flying. We did it. "Very good," Madame said in Russian, smiling wildly.[43]

One of the school's many GIs was Robert Barnett, who grew up tap dancing in Washington State, took part in GI musicals in occupied Japan, and in 1946, after being demobilized, gravitated to Nijinska's school in Hollywood. Not only were there classes for older students but there was a whole program under the GI Bill. "I took twelve classes a week: tap, ballet, and character class," he told Joel Loebenthal.

> We had music theory. We had French classes. It was like a little academy. Our classes started from ten to twelve noon. Then we'd have a break and we'd go from 2:00 to 3:30. After another break we'd start at 6:00 and go to 8:00.
>
> Nijinska taught you musicality as well as steps. You had certain things you did on certain days, like Cecchetti. But you always did, say, four petit allegro things that were linked musically. She would take one piece of music and you would do something front and back and on a diagonal, you would do it crossways, and then you'd do something turning. All on the same piece of music. Then, at the end of class, you would put that all together like a variation. And the boys would always do a manège, jumps diagonally, grand pirouette, and double tours.[44]

Richard Thomas was eighteen when he came from Seattle to study with Nijinska. She turned pale when she met him. Thomas bore a strong resemblance to Léo, looked like Vaslav, and his surname was the same as Nijinska's father. She spoke to him in Russian and ran her hands all over his face, something he found "very dear and very sweet." Nijinska arranged for him to live with a widow in her seventies, and he earned his keep by working in the garden. Nijinska's classes were way over his head. He was expected to stay in the back of the room, do everything twice with every group, and keep out of the way.

> The class was wonderful. She basically taught the Imperial school, not deleting the Cecchetti from the training because the barre . . . was only sixteen minutes. It started with grand plié and then tendu, grand batte-ment . . . exactly like the Cecchetti school. . . . Then we left the barre, and we did the Cecchetti exercises in the center. . . . So her basic principles of teaching were of the St. Petersburg school and then, of course, she had her own sense of style and movement, like Balanchine, like any choreographer.
>
> The first part of the class was built right up through that. And then she would begin to choreograph. . . . [T]he class would go on and she would choreograph these long passages of movement. On diagonals and circles and up and down and around, and I had trouble because if you got in the way you could be run over.[45]

Hundreds of dancers may have "come" from Nijinska, but not everybody got to study with her. Joseph Rickard, a star-struck Midwesterner from Ann Arbor, moved to Los Angeles in the late 1930s to get into movies. He had never studied ballet, but was a gifted athlete and swimmer, assets that stood him in good stead when he found his way to Nijinska. One day in 1946 he saw a young African American girl being turned away from Nijinska's school. In response, Rickard founded his own school in an abandoned ballroom at the corner of Jefferson and Normandie in the heart of the African American community in Los Angeles. In 1947 the country's first "Negro ballet group" made its debut at the Danish Auditorium on a program of concert music and dance works, all choreographed by Rickard.[46]

Nijinska gave up her diary in 1939, and few personal letters survive from her early years in the United States. However, she remained an active corre-spondent, as indicated by the drafts of personal letters dispersed among the business correspondence in her notebooks.[47] Like Nijinska, her old friend Nina Sirotinine had managed to secure a US visa. But she was living on Manhattan's Upper West Side, separated by a continent from her friend.[48] "Forgive me," Nijinska wrote on Easter 1940,

> for still not having answered your letter which made me so happy—I thought we would see each other soon—I was sure that I would come to

New York to choreograph two ballets—the same company that invited me before and was negotiating for me to come, but it turns out that their spring season will not happen.[49]

In Hollywood, she teaches every day except Saturdays. There were few students at first, but now there are many more. "[W]e live modestly.... We pay our rent, food, even a car, ... but there is nothing left for anything else. Hopefully, God will bring some kind of work, but for now I am happy I am not in debt."[50]

In late June she wrote to Nina about preparations for her performance at the Hollywood Bowl:

Right now I am rehearsing . . . the Bach "Etude," "Chopin Concerto," and Ravel's "Bolero." A lot of things to do: assemble a group, create the costumes, etc. . . . So much work and all for just one performance, but to put it on well is very important for all my future work, especially financially. The performance will be July 30th. At the same time my contract with the school ends. I so want to open my own school, but right now, I don't have the resources— it's too bad as right now I have quite a few students.[51]

Nijinska invested heavily in her Hollywood Bowl evening. With costumes for all ten of her company's ballets inaccessible in Paris, she ordered new ones from Jacks of Hollywood and had others made in-house. They cost her, she later wrote, $100 each.[52] These costumes represented her first major investment in re-creating her capital and made it possible to revive those works during the war years. They made it easier for companies to hire her, even as her family tethered her to Southern California, forcing her to turn down work although she was the breadwinner. "I'm very sad that you and your family don't live here right now," Nijinska wrote at one point.

I can't explain how good and beautiful it is here. I am being offered a job, also in a school, in New York, but neither Ira nor Nik. Nik. want to even hear about leaving California.[53]

On December 27, when Nina wired greetings for her fiftieth birthday, Nijinska lamented the loss of her house outside Paris.

I have been very homesick for our Louv[eciennes]. . . . Irina really likes America and does not want to leave here whereas my heart tears to go back home more and more. Seems I will not be able to root myself to this land and live peacefully with everybody here. I know that from the practical side, this is ridiculous as I live in a heavenly environment . . . [and] although it's not easy, I make enough money for our family to live and am in need of nothing. I have students who love me and work hard, but I still desperately want to go home.[54]

Everything has gone—Louveciennes, her books, her friends—and she can't send money to Paris for "Levushka's grave."[55]

***

Nijinska spent the winter and spring of 1941 in Los Angeles, teaching and waiting for jobs to materialize. In September there was a flurry of interest from Ballet Theatre. But after Richard Pleasant's initial telegram no follow-up letter materialized, and neither the November–December season at the Chicago Civic Opera House nor the February 1941 season at New York's Majestic Theatre had anything by Nijinska, not even *La Fille Mal Gardée*.[56] Meanwhile, de Basil had resurrected himself, although his company, now called the Original Ballet Russe, was in disarray because of the loss of nearly all his ballerinas, a demoralizing strike by the dancers demanding fair wages, and Sol Hurok's decision to back the rival Ballet Russe de Monte Carlo. To stabilize the "Original," new dancers were hired, and by June Nijinska was set to join the company in Washington.[57] It turned out, however, that David Lichine was performing the "duties and functions" for which Nijinska was engaged. She protested, de Basil ignored her, so she hired a lawyer from the left-wing New York firm of Boudin, Cohn and Glickstein to demand payment at her contract rate from August 19, when she arrived in New York, to the "present date" of October 7, and that "immediate arrangements be made . . . either to carry out the balance of [her] contract . . . or to compensate her adequately for the breach of contract, including reimbursement for . . . transporting costumes and scenery from California to New York at Col. de Basil's request."[58]

As before, the Colonel was content to throw Nijinska overboard. However, Nijinska's business dealings were never straightforward. Only days after she agreed to join de Basil, she signed a formal contract with German Sevastianov, Ballet Theatre's new managing director, to stage *La Bien Aimée* (as *The Beloved*) and rehearse *La Fille Mal Gardée*. Rehearsals were to begin on or about August 11, and she was to be paid $500 for the rights to *La Bien Aimée*, $200 per week for the staging and rehearsing of the two ballets, with a guaranteed minimum of six weeks. She had the right to choose the original cast and agreed to rehearse understudies for each role. The choice of scenic designer and costume designer would be subject to her approval.[59]

Ballet Theatre rehearsals began at Jacob's Pillow, where a nucleus of the company's dancers turned the rustic setting into a hive of activity. In the Old Barn, Antony Tudor was choreographing *Pillar of Fire* and Anton Dolin "restoring" the Rose Adagio from *The Sleeping Beauty*, while in a studio on a "far hilltop" Nijinska revived both *Fille* and *La Bien Aimée*. Margaret Lloyd of the *Christian Science Monitor* watched as Nijinska demonstrated and conversed with Dolin in "agitated Russian, calling the ballet terms in their native French."[60] The advent of Hurok management began what was later known as the "Russianization" of Ballet Theatre. New principal dancers arrived, including Irina Baronova and Alicia Markova, and it was for Nijinska's favorite ballerinas that *Fille* was returning to repertory and *La Bien Aimée* revived. New designs were commissioned from Nicolas de Molas, a Russian-born artist who had already designed a half-dozen Ballet Theatre productions.

The Beloved opened in Mexico City at the Palacio de Bellas Artes on October 24, 1941. Don Cayetano, writing in *Novedades*, had nothing but praise for the ballet. "Its general mood, which is that of 'Les Nuits' by Alfred de Musset," he wrote,

> is beautifully caught and reflected. It is commonplace to talk of the haunting beauty of Alicia Markova, of the unearthly loveliness of her dancing, but I know of no other words to express that particular sensation she conveys unless it be to say that she seems to possess a kind of inner quietude which communicates itself to the public. . . . Dolin most impressively mimed and danced the fortunate musician who has Markova as his muse.[61]

In New York, where the newly reorganized Ballet Theatre opened in November, the critical response could not have been more different. Walter Terry was especially harsh. " 'Beloved' is about the most uninventive ballet that I have seen in a long time," he wrote,

> for Nijinska's choreography seems to consist of endless waltz steps and half-hearted posturing. It concerns itself, as far as I could make out, with

a poet, his muse and his musings, and it has all the sparkle of a long-opened bottle of dying vichy water. The Schubert-Liszt score was about on a par with the choreography, so you can see that all was not gay with "Beloved."[62]

John Martin took a more tempered view. He noted that *Beloved* had a long history, having been created originally for Ida Rubinstein in 1928, then reworked for the Markova-Dolin company in 1937. Given that it shared thematic material with Massine's *Symphonie Fantastique*, it "must inevitably seem to those of us ... who are seeing it after the Massine work, like a rather attenuated echo." Nijinska, however, had managed "to achieve a sustained line of sentiment" that held the episodes together. Even if the only excuse for the ballet's revival was the role it provided for "the incredible Alicia Markova," for Martin that was enough.[63]

Two days later Irina Baronova stepped into the role of Lise in *La Fille Mal Gardée*, now called *The Wayward Daughter*.[64] The role fit her like a glove, showing off her brilliant technique and sparkling personality. The curtain fell to "bravos and yells," and in Terry's mind, the reason was Baronova. Even if the ballet represented "good craftsmanship," its length, insignificant music, and "large doses of old-fashioned miming did not entirely match the twentieth-century pace."

But Baronova herself gave zip to the work, for her characterization of the mischievous, romantic maiden was the work of a first-rate dancing actress. In her hands the old miming became as articulate as current speech, and the wayward daughter emerged as a lovable and sparkling character. In the pure dance sequences the Russian ballerina outdid herself and practically everyone else.[65]

Long after the premiere Baronova recalled Nijinska appearing on the empty stage as she was warming up.

She said she had come early to see that all was well with me. . . . She spoke softly, tenderly caressed my cheek and made the sign of the cross over my chest. I was deeply moved and wished that those who had been the victims of her sarcasm and bad temper could see her now and believe that she was not one hundred per cent dragon! Underneath the often-displayed horrid bad temper, there lurked a tender heart.[66]

One person who did not see that tender heart was Jerome Robbins. Rosella Hightower remembered that Nijinska would "go into a rage" when he entered the studio.

> She couldn't stand him. If he . . . walk[ed] across the room, she would stop . . . the rehearsal and . . . talk about how impolite and how ill-mannered it was to walk across the floor when someone was in the act of creating.[67]

Of course, this was the kind of behavior that Robbins himself couldn't stand when he became a choreographer.

Nijinska remained on the East Coast long after she had fulfilled her commitments to Ballet Theatre. In mid-November 1941 she began teaching at Ballet Arts, which had studios at Carnegie Hall, giving daily two-hour morning classes and three late-afternoon classes for a period of nine months.[68] She lived nearby at the Hotel Woodward on Broadway and 55th Street, a huge Art Deco apartment hotel that had seen better days, later moving to the plainer Hotel Van Dorn a few blocks away on 58th Street. She visited Singaevsky's sister, who had married a Russian-born building contractor and settled in Newtown, Connecticut, and talked to a reporter from the *Bridgeport Sunday Post*. Here, for the first time, she mentioned the short memoir she had written, which she called *Diary of a Young Dancer*.[69]

Unlike California, where Nijinska was intellectually and artistically isolated, in New York she had friends. Through Henriette Pascar, whose son, Alexander Liberman, would soon become art director of *Vogue*, Nijinska met J. P. Didier, who arranged for the manuscript to be translated and then became her literary agent, submitting contents and sample pages of text to various publishers. However, like most of her other writings, *Diary of a Young Dancer* remained unpublished, possibly because the tone left editors puzzled about its intended audience.[70] (Many years later, excerpts, now identified as notes or entries from a long-lost diary, were incorporated into *Early Memoirs*.) *Diary of a Young Dancer* is a story of artistic and personal awakening. Here Bronia, Nijinska's younger self, learns what it means to grapple with a piece of choreography and make it her own, infusing it with her own subjectivity. She falls in love with Chaliapin and is separated from him, experiencing desire for the first time and a sense of herself as a creative being. She offers the first behind-the-scenes account of the genesis of her brother's choreography for *Faune*, describing his search for a new form of physical expression through her own bodily experience of it and placing herself at the very center of his modernist quest. Unlike the grand narratives of the early Diaghilev seasons, Nijinska's is an intimate account, set in the studio and in the dancer's day-to-day life, with its hard work and friendships, aspirations and confidences. And for the first time she reveals the narrative voice that would become the stylistic signature of *Early Memoirs*, a combination of plain, truth-telling speech and absence of artifice.

As always, writing took a backseat to work in the studio. In 1942 she spent the summer at Jacob's Pillow, where Ted Shawn was organizing an ambitious summer dance festival devoted to "a survey of the whole field of the American dance, including the various foreign influences which have had definite bearing on it."[71] With more than forty performances, the festival offered programs of American folk dance, Spanish and Latin American dances, American ballroom dancing, dances of the "Orient," American concert dance, and "European Classic Ballet," performed by a remarkable array of artists. Nijinska was on the resident faculty, teaching for eight weeks alongside Shawn, the German modern dancer Steffi Nossen, and Joseph Pilates ("stretching, limbering, conditioning, correctives"), and restaging two of her Hollywood Bowl works—*Etude* and *Chopin Concerto*.[72]

With so many personalities, the summer was full of drama for Shawn, and Nijinska, who arrived with Singaevsky on July 5, contributed to the mayhem. Shawn's letters to Barton Mumaw give an often hilarious account of day-to-day life at the Pillow.[73] Fern Helscher, who ran interference for Shawn, was the Pillow's business manager.

July 7: "My god, what a day it's been. . . . [F]irst came word that Nijinska refused to teach her afternoon class on the hill . . . then she decided she would. Then a wire that her star male dancer was arriving for the whole summer . . . and as we had never heard of this, there is literally not a bed on the place. So I run smack into Nijinska and Singaevsky, and have a session with them, all gracious on both sides, but adamant on theirs that we have to take care of the male dancer 8 weeks . . . plus paying them for performances!"

July 25: "The petty irritations go on constantly—one Leila Volkova, forced on us by Nijinska as a scholarship student, . . . is leaving today because she won't walk from the Hill down here for her meals and back."

Aug. 13: "Prof. Aron has quit—says Mme. Nijinska is completely unbearable."

Aug. 15: "Fern [Helscher] . . . had a terrible session with Singaevsky and Mme. over the pianist problem. . . . Fern went all to pieces and cried, and Mme. took Fern on her lap and comforted her! It was all so Russian."

Aug. 23: "Yesterday was as mad a day as I have ever lived through.... Fern had been hiding from Singaevsky all morning. . . . [Later] I . . . ran smack into Singaevsky and Nikita [Talin] and they jumped me. I held fast, and reiterated what we would do and what we wouldn't. Then Mme. came and she wanted to start it all over again—but I kissed her hand and ran for the house . . . they followed to the foot of the stage and started to yell for Fern, and she had to come down. Then it raged, and I got fed up with it, and swooped down on them and outyelled the Russians—boy, it was a scene."

The day before the premiere on September 3, Nijinska invited Shawn to watch rehearsal. He couldn't believe his eyes. He wrote to Mumaw that he

was simply amazed at what she has accomplished—with beginners, mixed ages, sizes, backgrounds—she has achieved two ballets of completely professional finish, stunning ballets, and it looks like an organization that has worked together for some time.

Despite bad weather, opening night netted $100 and "was a very smooth performance." "The Bach is done in costumes all alike," he wrote to Mumaw on September 4,

boys, girls, corps de ballet, and stars all the same—a blue-grey tunic, banded in gold, a mantle of lacquer-red from shoulders to knees, and a grey-blue skull cap surmounted by a halo of gold. . . . They were very effective, and the music was grand, and the ballet danced without one visible flaw, and it is very finely conceived—impersonal, geometric, noble—perfectly in the mood of Bach....

The second ballet to the Chopin concerto was in long white tutus, the eight boys in dark blue velvet jackets, white satin shirts and grey tights. . . . At the end, flowers for all the stars . . . Then after many curtains the audience called for Nijinska, and when she came out, in tailored dark blue, no make-up, it was a great ovation. . . . It was a great and memorable occasion—a genuine tribute to a truly great artist.

Life at Jacob's Pillow was spartan. Nina Youshkevitch, who had recently arrived from Europe as a refugee, remembered the dancers and students sleeping on folding cots in an open barn. The diet was mostly celery and carrot sticks, so once a week Nijinska took her out for a steak and glass of red wine to keep up her strength.[74] In the morning everyone sat on the grass, listening as Shawn told them they were pioneers and that one day the Pillow would be famous. Nijinska gave "very hard classes," Youshkevitch recalled, "because she needed to get the students in shape."[75] One of those students was Ann Hutchinson Guest, who went on to become a professional dancer and an authority on dance notation. At the time she was "still in the throes of mastering ballet," and although she found the classes valuable, she felt that if Nijinska had been easier to understand she would have gotten a great deal more from the experience. Still Nijinska singled her out and even invited the young Anglo-American modern dancer for tea at her cabin.[76] Irina Sirotinine, Nina's daughter and Nijinska's goddaughter, was another familiar face and also a Russian speaker.[77]

For Nijinska the summer offered a golden opportunity to "preview" the ballets that she would stage in the 1942–1943 season for the Ballet Russe de Monte Carlo. However, the initial announcements mentioned neither *Etude* nor *Chopin Concerto*, but two other ballets, *The Snow Maiden* and a revival of *Legend of Cracow*, which the Polish Ballet had danced at the New York World's Fair in 1939. With funds short, Denham scratched *Legend of Cracow*, thereby saving money on scenery and costumes, and replaced it with *Chopin Concerto*. The ballet's thirty costumes were at hand, and Nijinska now sold them to Denham with the musical material and the choreographic rights for $1,800.[78]

Nijinska had exactly five weeks to stage *Chopin Concerto* and finish choreographing *The Snow Maiden* between the time she left Jacob's Pillow on September 6 and opening night at the Metropolitan Opera House. She had choreographed most of *The Snow Maiden* between June 22 and July 5, before leaving for the Pillow, where she wrote Denham, "it's been a while since I worked so well and with such inspiration."[79] But the ending remained undone, and she was too busy at the Pillow to finish it.[80] Even apart from Nijinska, Denham had his hands full. In late September, when the Ballet Russe left for Canada, the immigration authorities refused to grant re-entry permits to many of the dancers, so twelve foreign members of the corps de ballet had to remain in the United States.[81] Somehow, amid all this chaos, Nijinska completed her two ballets, and by opening night, October 12, the troupe, as Robert Lawrence wrote in the *Herald Tribune*, "rose from its own ashes . . . like the bird of legend."[82]

John Martin expressed admiration for *Chopin Concerto* in several reviews. He found it the more impressive of Nijinska's offerings, abstract and compositionally sophisticated, a work that told no story but conveyed emotion through mood and atmosphere, with a personal voice and style. "Set to the E minor concerto of Chopin," he told readers of the *New York Times*,

> it is an abstract composition couched in purely academic vocabulary with a minimum of stage setting and the simplest of costumes. . . . As a dance work it is a thoroughly beautiful one, formally little short of perfection, serene in mood and with a crystalline clarity.
>
> Two solo figures (Alexandra Danilova and Nathalie Krassovska) occupy the foreground of the design while the ensemble is treated as a series of small and unified groups, occasionally breaking into individual figures but always reassembling so that their collective and contrapuntal quality is maintained. Within this large pattern there is [a] wealth of choreographic imagination, easy and effortless in its creation and supremely transparent. After the turbidity of the novelties which this season has previously boasted, its classic spirit, albeit with the Nijinska tang, comes as pure balm.[83]

In a review of the second performance, Martin spoke about Nijinska's approach to music and her use of stillness. He felt that she had projected the concerto's "underlying romanticism with fine musicianship, as well as with a magnificent sense of the visual theatre."

> Even the pianistic quality of the solo instrument is imaged in a kind of resonant percussiveness in the style of movement, though the essential spirit of the academic ballet is never violated. The two free-flowing solo roles are placed against a background of small groups, which alternate phrases of movement with what might almost be called phrases of stillness, so admirably built are the passages of complete motionlessness.[84]

Edwin Denby, still writing a dance column for *Modern Music*, called *Chopin Concerto* the season's "one novelty . . . in the big-time tradition and with a fresh approach." It was "a kind of *Sylphides* thirty years after," although it didn't "feel at all like" the Fokine ballet. "There is no psychology," he wrote, no nostalgia, there is only limpid and constantly interesting change. There is a real subject, the weight and the lightness of the body seen in motion. . . . And from a slow awkward beginning it takes flight toward the end in several more and more extended solo variations, a continuous flutter of little steps and low rapid leaps, astonishingly unforced in conception and fantastically brilliant in execution.[85]

With Wacław Borowski's original backdrop for *Chopin Concerto* unavailable, the Ballet Russe commissioned new designs from Alexander Ignatieff, an artist who lived in Los Angeles and worked at Universal Studios. Instead of a painted backdrop, all but ubiquitous in post-Diaghilev ballet, Ignatieff created a decor whose simplicity of means recalled Nijinska's collaborations with Yury Annenkov in the 1930s. There were grey velvet curtains, which Claudia Cassidy in the *Chicago Daily Tribune* described as turning "honey beige, moonstruck silver, or neutral grey under the magic of lighting." Ignatieff's stage, wrote John Martin, was "totally without decoration," but "change[d] its entire feeling" with each lighting cue.[86]

The Snow Maiden opened on the same program as *Chopin Concerto*. The idea was Denham's and by far the more popular of the two ballets, a Russian fairy tale about a girl made of snow (Nathalie Krassovska) who loves the village shepherd (Igor Youskevitch) but is lost to him when she melts at the coming of spring (Alexandra Danilova). The ballet, to Alexander Glazunov's "Seasons," climaxed in the "Autumn Bacchanale," now a cascade of Russian dances but once a blazing duet for Anna Pavlova and Mikhail Mordkin.[87] Praising the combination of delicacy and naïveté, and the "affectionate understatement" of Nijinska's handling of the narrative, Martin considered the work an admirable addition to the Ballet Russe repertory. Again, he wrote, "the ensemble is handled exquisitely and the solo roles of the snow maiden who melts with the warmth of human love, of the mother, Spring, and of the young shepherd, are charmingly devised."[88] In a Sunday piece, he emphasized, as he had with *Chopin Concerto*, that *Snow Maiden* was a "work of great delicacy and tenderness of imagination" that needed to be danced by artists unworried about its "technical surface" who "can devote themselves wholly to the projection of its inner feeling."[89] Margaret Lloyd, writing in the *Christian Science Monitor*, was the only critic to discern in Nijinska's "treatment of the ancient folk tale rooted deep in the Russian earth" the "directing hand of the great choreographer of 'Les Noces,'" as well as the yearning for Russian soil, so eloquently expressed in Nijinska's account of her visit to Belovezh.[90]

Although Ballet Russe finances were very tight, Denham commissioned sets and costumes from Boris Aronson. Born in Kiev, the son of a rabbi and a student of Alexandra Exter, he arrived in New York in the 1920s, worked for the Yiddish Art Theatre, and by the 1930s had begun to design for Broadway. Aronson's costumes were simple—Russian shirts and pinafores for the peasants, unitards for the trees, a long gown for the Snow Maiden, who was all in white. With its clumps of greenery and overhanging limbs, the scenery was plain yet, as Claudia Cassidy wrote, "subtly exact" in projecting the ballet's "shifting moods."

> The curtain rises on a bleak winter scene with the wan Arctic sun casting the palest light over silver birches. . . . The color palette runs from white to black thru a range of grays. . . . Then spring enters, a glowing figure in . . . floating arabesques. The villagers begin the jubilant rites of spring and the snow maiden falls in love with the piping shepherd. . . . [T]he trees shed their bleakness for sprouts of green, and suddenly the snow maiden is gone.[91]

In Aronson's archives are notes that Nijinska must have given the artist to assist him in designing *The Snow Maiden*. But the visual prompts are minimal. Her main interest lay in the drama of the Snow Maiden, her transformation from a creature of ice to a woman who experiences for the first time "the warmth of awakened feelings [and] the ability to love." Mother-Spring (as Nijinska refers to Spring in her notes) cautions her that the sun is getting hot, but the Snow Maiden, bent on "merrymaking and . . . love," ignores her, only to melt in Lehl's arms after their pas de deux.[92] One can easily imagine Nijinska infusing the ballet with her own romantic longings.

At the end of the New York season it seemed to John Martin that the Ballet Russe de Monte Carlo stood "on the verge of a new period in its career."

> Two new choreographers have produced three new works, all of which are good and one of which is a box office smash. . . . There is a strengthening of morale . . . and toward the end of the recent engagement . . . some admirable performances, with a fine spirit and a newly awakened feeling for ensemble dancing.[93]

Two of the works were Nijinska's. The "smash," however, was Agnes de Mille's *Rodeo*, to the celebrated Copland score, which remains in repertory today.

The three had been rehearsed together, and throughout the New York season and subsequent national tour, they were often programmed together.

Martin was sufficiently impressed by the presence of two women on the choreographic roster of a ballet company to comment on it not once but several times. As he noted in an advance piece, the three novelties were of "especial interest" because they were all by women, and furthermore women who had not previously contributed to the Ballet Russe repertory. De Mille, moreover, was the "first American woman choreographer to break into the ranks of any Ballet Russe and the second American of either sex."[94] Martin may have been quick to applaud the "feminine invasion" of the Ballet Russe de Monte Carlo's "choreographic ranks,"[95] but de Mille took no notice. In her entertaining account of *Rodeo* in *Dance to the Piper*, one of the most popular dance memoirs of the 1940s, she alludes to works by Fokine and Massine, lists the celebrities who attended *Rodeo*'s premiere (Martha Graham, Richard Rodgers, Oscar Hammerstein II, even her mother), but omits all mention of Nijinska, simply writing her out of the 1942 season.[96]

By late November 1942, Nijinska was back in Southern California, where she was planning to spend the winter.[97] Already there was talk that she would stage two new ballets for the 1943–1944 Ballet Russe season in addition to taking charge of the company's "entire classical repertoire, restoring 'Swan Lake,' 'Giselle,' and other ballets." De Mille was also to create two new ballets, while George Balanchine was to work in "close association with the troupe as choreographer," a plan, one may be sure, that Nijinska would never agree to.[98] (As Frederic Franklin put it, "Nijinska hated Balanchine and Balanchine hated her, and Balanchine hated Massine, and Massine hated them both.")[99] In any event, in 1943, Balanchine went to work for Ballet Theatre, while de Mille left to choreograph *Oklahoma!*

Meanwhile, Nijinska was in touch with Ted Shawn and Fern Helscher about returning to Jacob's Pillow in the summer of 1943 to take charge of the ballet program. Shawn wanted her, and Nijinska, with warm memories of "her so . . . artisticly [sic] satisfactory and so friendly collaboration with Mr. Shawn," as Singaevsky replied on her behalf, was anxious to "renew her work at Jacob's Pillow for this summer."[100] It would be an excellent way to refamiliarize herself with *Variations*, which had not been performed for nearly a decade. However, money proved a sticking point. As Singaevsky pointed out in his letter to Helscher, an additional $150 had to be added to the agreement for travel expenses. Moreover, gas rationing had gone into effect, and Nijinska would need a cabin or other lodging near the school. With money very short, Shawn was in a quandary. In late March, he told Helscher to write to Nijinska and explain

> what a struggle it is to keep going at all this summer . . . and ask if she will play ball with us. We will give her $560 cash for the summer's teaching plus room and board for the two of them. Then if we have more than 20 full course pupils, plus 16 scholarship—half pay students—we will also pay her transportation, stating a definite amount for that. Ask for an immediate answer so we can announce names in next magazine. Say that we want her more than anybody—but will have to take a cheaper priced ballet teacher . . . if she feels she cannot accept our offer.[101]

However, the real obstacle was the cost of travel from Los Angeles to New York and back. Shawn just couldn't afford the additional $200 (Singaevsky would pay his own way). Although Nijinska expressed the hope that she could return the following summer, this ended her relationship with Jacob's Pillow.[102]

By June, Nijinska was pressing Denham for a decision about her assignments for the 1943–1944 season. For months they corresponded about *Etude* and *Variations*, but it was only in May, as the company's New York season drew to a close, that he finally wrote to her, proposing an outright purchase of *Etude* ($1,800 for the choreographic rights, musical material, and costumes) and an exclusive contract for *Variations*, for which he would pay her $500. "Please do not think that I am stingy," he wrote, which is exactly what she did think: "500 is simply impossible. . . . It is a long ballet, one of my best, in three scenes, and 40 minutes long. It demands a lot of work. I can offer you a friendly deal and stage it for $1,200." And she definitely could not grant him "exclusivity," since the two ballets were part of her repertory in Paris. "I could stage those ballets for you and give you the right to perform them, and, if you wish, 'exclusivity' for one year in America," indicating that she continued to think of Paris as her permanent future home.[103] She eventually settled for "exclusivity" in the Americas, which is what the more practical Denham was really concerned about.

Denham then decided that instead of *Variations* he would have Nijinska produce another cut-rate ballet, *Ancient Russia*, using the scenery and costumes that Natalia Goncharova had designed for Massine's *Bogatyri*, which had disappeared from the Ballet Russe repertory not long after its premiere in 1938. *Etude* was still on the production schedule, and at some point, after bumping into Salvador Dalí, Denham wondered if Nijinska would consider having the celebrity painter create a front curtain for the ballet. "I am certain," he wrote, "that a collaboration with you would produce a magnificent effect."[104]

In one of his ruminations about *Chopin Concerto*, John Martin observed that "abstractions are frequently not popular with the public, but if this one proves not to be, the public will be missing a notable ballet."[105] *Chopin Concerto* managed to hold its own, but his remark could well apply to the reception of *Etude*. This was Nijinska's oldest extant piece of choreography, and although much had changed over the years, it represented a link with her past. The ballet, which was set to the first and sixth of Bach's Brandenburg Concertos and his Third Suite, opened in Cleveland on October 9. Reviewing it for the *Chicago Daily Tribune*, Claudia Cassidy found the ballet striking—a "plastic abstraction" she called it—"simply staged in a smoke blue grotto with dancers like young Greek warriors in tunic and helmet, gray and gold, vermillion caped"—another work in which Nijinska had envisioned the stage as a luminous space.[106]

Ann Barzel, who covered the Chicago season for *Dance News*, wrote that when the curtain rose on *Etude*, Ballet Russe fans "groaned." "Here was one of those abstractions, a stale breath from the 20s complete with dancers posed on various stair levels."

> But after the first few minutes one knows that Etude is not that. It is a beautiful ballet with a great deal of beautiful dancing set to some of Bach's Brandenburg Concerti, and danced in functionally short tunics designed by Boris Bilinsky. . . . Etude is a pointe ballet in Nijinska's most stylized manner. The several variations are very demanding technically, but the piece is not an exercise in dance [*sic*] d'école, because the groupings and the individual position of the body and particularly of the arms are stylized to give the religious atmosphere the choreographer has made the keynote of the ballet.[107]

After months on tour, the Ballet Russe arrived in New York in April 1944 for a three-week season at City Center, "the people's theater" inaugurated the year before by Mayor Fiorello La Guardia, while Ballet Theatre opened for a month at the Metropolitan Opera House. The April ballet war brought huge audiences to both theaters. Never before, as Jack Anderson has remarked, had New York been so "ballet-conscious."[108]

As on the road, critics divided over *Etude*, its costumes, extreme stylization, religious spirit, and use of the Bach music. Edwin Denby, now writing
for the *New York Herald Tribune*, was intrigued by the ballet.

> The movement is formalized in a sort of Byzantine manner, and has a
> solemn rapture in the expression. The palms facing forward, wrists crossed
> above the head, suggest wing-tips of icon angels; and the legs extended in
> arabesque, sometimes hint at the line of the wing below. Because the move-
> ment is wilfully stylized, it is difficult to give it sweep and vitality. . . . As a
> result one did not have the impression that these angels were controlling an
> immense power in their reserve, as I think had been the choreographer's in-
> tention. . . . Miss Tallchief, in some steel-hard pirouettes, seemed to indicate
> better than anyone else what the whole ballet should have looked like.[109]

John Martin, on the other hand, thought the Bach music "highly unsuited to choreographic purposes."[110] He found the ballet "dated and old-
fashioned," especially the long opening adagio, with its "pseudo-religious
mood," minimal movement, and "commonplace figurations." He disliked
the short pleated tunics and capes of the ballet's uniform, unisex costumes
and headpieces, which made it "quite impossible even to tell the women from
the men except by examining their bare knees." However, in the "stunningly
composed solos stunningly danced" of the middle section, he found something of the "characteristic Nijinska flavorsome invention, and some admirable dancing by Nathalie Krassovska and Anna Istomina [the Canadian
Audree Thomas] particularly, and also Dorothy Etheridge and Maria
Tallchief."[111] Mary Ellen Moylan, another young American entrusted with
a solo, found working on *Etude* a "fascinating" experience. Nijinska "had
very much a feeling of soul about her," Moylan recalled in the late 1970s. She
wanted the eyes in "Byzantium style," so the seventeen-year-old dancer went
to museums and tried to imitate the Italian masters to get the makeup right
and capture Nijinska's "feeling." Moylan danced in a pas de quatre that was
all beats and jumps, and she also did a solo to a polonaise. "[Nijinska's] polonaise, I felt that it breathed. . . . There was an intake of air incorporated into
the choreography. It was an elevated kind of thing."[112]

Ancient Russia, by contrast, pleased no one. Set, incongruously, to
Tchaikovsky's Piano Concerto No. 1, the ballet was old hat—the rescue of
captive Russian maidens from a Tatar camp, a victory celebration, and the
betrothal of the Russian hero to the princess he has saved. It was certainly

a hodge-podge, with Tchaikovsky's "ear-filling score" at loggerheads with Goncharova's "eye-filling" designs.[113] Ann Barzel was particularly upset by scenes with "twenty ballet boys bravely brandishing wooden swords" at a time when "audiences . . . read daily of bombs and blood, tanks and destroyers."[114]

By now, Denham seems to have had a change of heart about Nijinska. As 1943 slipped into 1944, he made one excuse after another for not paying her, dodging her requests for new projects, while at the same time, expressing his gratitude to Nijinska for her work and moral support. He also expressed the hope that Nijinska would not leave him for the competition. By March 1944, when the last installment for *Ancient Russia* arrived and Denham had unceremoniously dumped her, she was planning to do just that.[115]

Small companies, with eager young dancers willing to work hard and on whose devotion she could count, always held a strong appeal to Nijinska. August 1943 found her in Chicago, at the behest, apparently, of former students, and with the financial backing of Carla Bradley, who had engaged Nijinska as artistic director of Ballet Repertory Company, a new group of about twenty-five dancers.[116] Nijinska was to create two ballets, *Vision*, to Brahms Piano Sonata No. 1, and *Hitch Your Wagon to a Star*, to Tchaikovsky's Capriccio Italien and the final movement of Suite No. 3 (which Balanchine used four years later in *Theme and Variations*). The musical choices added to her growing repertory of nineteenth-century music; all were "dancey," with contrasting moods and rhythms and a strong underlying pulse: in *Hitch*, where a poor violinist captures the love of a ballerina with his music, there was even a story.[117] Given the prohibitive cost of commissioning new music, choreographers had little choice but to use music that was out of copyright.

Claudia Cassidy, who observed one of Nijinska's rehearsals in Chicago, left a vivid picture of her during an early rehearsal of *Vision*. "A deceptively chubby little figure," she wrote,

> all muscle and no fat, dressed in well cut slacks and a trim blouse, her pale hair in haphazard variation on the ballerina's bun—flopped in utter relaxation against the mirrored wall, snatching a rest as she pondered what came next. Her exquisite little hands, tipped with long, unpainted oval nails, made curlicues in the air with a cigaret [sic] she forgot to smoke, and her tiny ballet slippered feet traced tentative patterns on the bare floor. Suddenly she leaped into the air like a rubber ball shot from an uncoiling spring, clapped her hands decisively, made a curious sound to the clairvoyant pianist, and set her little group of enchanted dancers in motion.

The heat was excruciating in that pre–air conditioning era, but the dancers slaved devotedly. "Nijinska took this devotion for granted," Cassidy commented,

> and why not? It has been her lot from the day she started teaching, because dancers always tell you, "She never asks for anything she can't do herself." Furthermore, she does it. "Why talk about dancing?" she demands in that strange mixture of Russian and Polish laced with French and tangled with just enough English to throw you off the track, "I don't tell them. I *show* them."... In less than 10 days' time, Nijinska had worked a minor miracle.[118]

On November 29, when Ballet Repertory Company made its debut at the Eighth Street Theater, the results were "so diverse," as Cassidy wrote, that "they refuse to be captured in a flat statement of success or failure." There were moments "worth saving and encouraging," even in *Vision*, a "not particularly distinguished ballet danced to an execrable orchestration of Brahms' First Sonata." (It was the work of Michał Kondracki, the composer of *Legend of Cracow*, who was now living in New York.) Stanislaw Mitruk, a Chicagoan trained at the Art Institute who earned his living as foreman of a furniture factory, designed both *Vision* and Nijinska's second ballet, *Hitch Your Wagon to a Star*, achieving "a hint of the empyrean effect that can set a ballet stage blazing."[119] (He later said, "She hired me, totally without experience, on a whim—because I could talk Polish with her."[120]) Nijinska, who had come for the opening, was covered with flowers. But *Vision* was dropped from the repertory when Massine, accompanied by a half-dozen well-known dancers, produced a second round of performances the following June. Once the season was over, Claudia Cassidy spent an entire column arguing for the merits of inviting the company that Massine seemed to be forming to settle in Chicago. She explained that Massine "is the most important of living choreographers," and since Fokine, nobody "can touch him in background or accomplishment." As for Nijinska, she added, "it has been a long time since [she] turned out a really distinguished work." Cassidy was not the only critic registering disappointment at the recent trajectory of Nijinska's career. A few months earlier, Margaret Lloyd in a review of *Ancient Russia* had declared that "these slight ballets of hers, using concert music as a background for theater dancing, could well be swapped for one good production of her *Les Noces*."[121]

***

By spring 1944, big changes were shaking up the New York ballet world. George Balanchine, who had spent much of the late 1930s and early 1940s working on Broadway and in Hollywood, was easing himself back into ballet. In spring 1943 he revived both *Apollo* and *Errante* for Ballet Theatre and later in the year talked to *Dance News* about a "pet, long-nursed project" for a New York resident ballet company, with dancers from Broadway shows, performing on Sunday nights.[122] This was American Concert Ballet, which offered the first public performance in New York of Balanchine's *Concerto Barocco* before collapsing. However, within months Balanchine had come to an arrangement with Denham. In April 1944, *Serenade* rejoined the Ballet Russe repertory, and by June the entire Ballet Russe, including its stars, was appearing in *Song of Norway*, an operetta to the music of Grieg with choreography by Balanchine that toured throughout the summer. In September, when the Ballet Russe opened in New York, he had become its resident choreographer. Nijinska must have gotten wind of this early on and understood that it wasn't only money and indecision that was making Denham so cagey, but that he no longer needed or wanted her.[123]

Meanwhile a new player had appeared, and unlike the competition he commanded seemingly unlimited resources. Born Jorge Cuevas Bartholín in Chile in 1885, he had many names, a title, "Marquis," that was probably bogus, and a wife, Margaret Rockefeller Strong, willing to fund his ambitions, which included a ballet company. In 1943 he began signing up dancers, commissioning composers, renovating an old theater on Columbus Circle, and approaching choreographers. Agnes de Mille turned him down: not only was he dressed in the color of Mussolini's Black Shirts, but he was also a self-proclaimed autocrat and promised to tell her what to do.[124] De Cuevas also tried his luck with Massine and Balanchine, and when they rejected his offer, he sent a message via Ludmilla Schollar to Nijinska, who promptly wrote to the Odessa-born, former Ballet Russe administrator David Libidins, who was now her manager. On March 21 he wrote back in his Russian-flavored English. "Few months ago I was urgently requested by telephone to go and see Mr. Cuevas. I went there and from all crazy people I ever saw in my life I definitely saw the best sample in Marquis de Cuevas."

> He called me at the moment he received from Massine a draft of a contract Massine wanted for himself.... Mr. Massine wanted to be the one and exclusive director with all rights and profits, with tremendous salary, leaving to Cuevas the only part of polishing his shoes and paying all bills. Cuevas was

[so] excited . . . he broke all furniture in his apartment. . . . Cuevas . . . told me that he is ready to put in this business $24,000. I started to laugh and I advised Cuevas to forget the whole business.

De Cuevas then approached Balanchine, who "monkey[ed] around for a couple of weeks with de Cuevas," but finally "sent [him] to hell and told him he was crazy."

Now, my dear Bronislava-Fominichna . . . No manager in the country will permit to the artist to jump in such an adventure without 100% protection, and you will certainly not expect me to advise you to contact Cuevas direct because he will bring you in such a mess that you will spoil your health and nerves, in six weeks time or less.

Libidins agrees that de Cuevas has been a "good friend" to many artists, sending flowers, arranging parties, even giving a little money. "But to make a new ballet company it means more than $500 or $1000."[125] For Nijinska, however, the Chilean-born millionaire was a godsend, and she quickly signed on (without consulting Libidins). The new company was called Ballet International.

Salvador Dalí's Mad Tristan, inspired by the legend of Tristan and Isolde to the celebrated Wagner music, was to be one of the first season's many highlights. Dalí had already collaborated with Massine on several ballets and expressed the desire to work with Nijinska, "who has a great choreographic talent."[126] Now, with Nijinska as Ballet International's senior choreographer, it was her turn to work with an artist whose unbridled imagination nearly always dominated the stage. "Every night," de Cuevas wrote to the artist in May, "we talk for an hour by telephone with Nijinska. That woman is a genius. So we will end up with the wonderful collaboration of a Spanish genius and a Russian genius, with Wagner's sublime music."[127] Dalí, who was wintering in California with his Russian-born wife Gala, drove to Los Angeles to confer with Nijinska about the project.[128]

By June 1, Nijinska was back in New York where the corps de ballet started rehearsing. Many of the dancers were her former students or had studied with Edward Caton and Vera Nemchinova, although a few came from Balanchine's American Concert Ballet. Dalí, however, remained in California. Meanwhile, "Jorge," as de Cuevas signed his letters to Dalí, was working eighteen-hour days in New York. "I am sick, depressed, and exhausted," he wrote on July 5.

The titanic struggle against all the elements. Only Nijinska remains
faithful. She is tempered steel: loyal, brave, and disinterested. We have con-
quered: Libidins, Denham, Hurok, and a thousand more of the criminal
mediocrity that keeps this country in diapers without allowing it to ac-
quire the indispensable knowledge to develop good taste. . . . [But] Nijinska
doesn't want to work on Tristan without you: she needs you at her side.[129]

Nijinska was definitely getting cold feet. A contract drawn up on July 15
omits all mention of *Mad Tristan*, committing her to restage *Bolero* and to
choreograph two new ballets, *Brahms' Variations* (to the composer's Handel
and Paganini Variations) and *Pictures at an Exhibition* (to Mussorgsky's
music of the same name) for a grand total of $7,500.[130] De Cuevas, fearing
the collapse of the Dalí project, wrote to the artist a few days later, with a rare
comment about the dynamics of Nijinska's relationship with Singaevsky:

The Ballet is driving me as crazy as Tristan, only Tristan went crazy because
of Isolde, and in the Ballet there are thirty Isoldes and 24 Tristans. Madame
Nijinska is working furiously and has unfurled the immortal wings of her
tiger temperament. She asks for seven days a week, eight hours every day,
to rehearse her choreographies, and the other choreographers are crazy too.
Tonight I have invited her to supper to talk to her about Mad Tristan. She
is obstinate, and I see with terror that her husband influences her, reducing
her to his limited, bourgeois spirit. Unfortunately, he is the only person she
listens to and the only one she understands, because the only language she
possesses in depth is Russian.[131]

Signing himself the Knight of the Woeful Countenance, one of Don
Quixote's epithets, de Cuevas unburdened himself with his usual hyperbole:

I have lost my health, spirit, will, and even my gait with the complications of
the Ballet, which is an instrument of Chinese torture invented by the devil
to revenge idealists who have no place in this mechanized American world,
vulgar, practical, and without elevation of any kind. . . . I am so sick that
tomorrow I am leaving for New Hampshire, and I don't know when I will
return.[132]

The press was having a field day. The news seemed to change daily, along
with the repertory and the leading dancers. Vera Nemchinova was the

ranking ballerina; Virgil Thomson and Nicolas Nabokov were composing new ballets; Balanchine was staging *Orpheus* and *Prodigal Son*, Nijinska *Les Biches*, *Hamlet*, and *Hitch Your Wagon to a Star*, Massine *Symphonie Fantastique* and *Choreartium*, and Alexander Iolas *Oedipus the King*. None of this was true.[133]

Backstage, it was chaos. Patricia Wilde, a sixteen-year-old member of the corps who later joined the New York City Ballet, remembered rehearsing three different versions of *Giselle*, including one by Boris Romanov, with extra music and an additional dance for the Wilis. None of these versions was actually performed in New York, although Nijinska's was taken into the repertory when the company moved to Europe.[134] Although Nijinska had staged *Bolero* several times during the 1930s and as recently as 1940 at the Hollywood Bowl, she "seemed to get stuck" when she rehearsed it with the Cuevas dancers. "More heavy," Wilde remembers her saying, "hammering Ravel's rhythm on the dancers' necks."[135] But she didn't waste a second with *Brahms Variations* and *Pictures at an Exhibition*, full company works that she was choreographing from scratch. Decades later Francisco Monción, another corps dancer who became a New York City Ballet principal, remembered how she "practically brought the roof down" after seeing a rehearsal of William Dollar's *Constantia*, which he had choreographed for the American Ballet in 1936 and was now reviving for Ballet International. "She said that was her ballet. . . . Those were her steps. She had done the same music somewhere else and, to her, all of a sudden there it was— plagiarism."[136] To be sure, Dollar had used Chopin's Piano Concerto No. 2 in F minor, whereas Nijinska, in *Chopin Concerto*, had used the Piano Concerto No. 1 in E minor. But there were many musical echoes between the two pieces, and as de Cuevas must have known, Nijinska's ballet had just been danced in New York by the Denham company. "The greatest tragedy of Ballet International," Lucile Marsh pointed out in *Dance Magazine*, "was the lack of a strong, experienced and imaginative leadership . . . that could envision the repertoire as a whole."[137]

By late summer, several ballets were in rehearsal simultaneously. The dancers worked at Anatole Vilzak's studio (he was the company's official ballet master), Ballet Arts, Studio 839 at Carnegie Hall, and the Nola Studios on West 54th Street. On Tuesday, October 24, less than a week before opening night, Nijinska rehearsed *Brahms Variations* from 12:30 to 2:30; *Pictures at an Exhibition* from 2:30 to 4; and *Bolero* from 5 to 6. There were night rehearsals and even Sunday rehearsals, although the dancers were entitled by contract to one free day a week.[138] Monción remembered Nijinska bouncing around the studio like a ball. "She could spring—suddenly she'd be all over the place and showing things. . . . [S]he'd give you the rhythm by dancing it on your body. . . . 'Listen melodia with rhythm,' and she'd dance it, da-da-da-da-da-da, on your chest."[139] It was a grueling pace, and Nijinska was demanding, but for Wilde and the company's other American dancers, including its ballerina Viola Essen, Nijinska was hardly the slave-driver of émigré horror stories. As underdogs, American dancers expected they would have to work harder than their Russian counterparts, and hard work, no matter what the dancer's nationality, always commanded Nijinska's respect. Finally, as opening night approached, photographers snapped pictures of the dancers rehearsing and Nijinska in conversation with Dalí.[140]

***

When the Ballet International season opened on October 30, the gala crowd gazed in astonishment at the splendidly renovated theater, a Stanford White gem refurbished by the architect Joseph Urban with a gleaming dome and "an immense chandelier composed of 27,000 separate pieces of crystal." Patrons wore formal dress, and there was "a heavy sprinkling of gold-braided uniforms," high-society figures, and members of the Russian colony. Outside a double line of late ticket-seekers stretched around Columbus Circle.[141] The "over-all effect of the evening was brilliant," observed a correspondent for the *Christian Science Monitor*.[142] There were heaps of flowers, and after the performance, a party at the Hotel Pierre.[143] The Marquis was in his element.

There were many things to admire about the new undertaking. De Cuevas had tapped a young generation of composers, including Paul Bowles and, most important, Gian-Carlo Menotti, whose *Sebastian* was his first ballet score. He commissioned a number of young American designers, such as Horace Armstead, Oliver Smith, and Raoul Pène du Bois, and gave Edward Caton, André Eglevsky, and Antonia Cobos a chance to choreograph. Finally, he persuaded Dalí to design not one but two ballets, *Sentimental Colloquy*, a pas de deux to music by Paul Bowles, as well as *Mad Tristan*, which Massine ultimately staged. Not all the choices were inspired. John Martin found the powder-pink tulle in the scenery of Marcel Vertès for *Brahms Variations* "far more suggestive of expensive lingerie than of the 'rugged' Brahms."[144] Equally unsuccessful was Enrico Donati's surrealist-flavored scenery for *Bolero*, which seemed to have nothing to do with either its theme or Spanish setting. The *Bolero* costumes, the last of Nijinska's stash from the Hollywood Bowl, were now sold to Ballet International.

Of the three ballets Nijinska contributed to the repertory, *Bolero* was the one that fared the worst. Not only was the music by now well known, but by 1944 thousands had seen Fokine's version at New York's Lewisohn Stadium and numerous versions elsewhere.[145] Still, audiences applauded, and John Martin found the work "highly theatrical and compositionally intriguing with its use of stylized slow motion and counterpoint."[146] However, at sixteen, Nijinska's *Bolero* was showing its age, and many probably agreed with Lucile Marsh's assessment that the work should not have been revived without being rethought.[147] As for Edwin Denby, he savaged the ballet, which he called "Radio City corn of incredible lugubriousness." Nijinska's "Paris version of 'Bolero' . . . was bad," he declared,

> but I did not remember that one as nearly so bad as this. This one begins with a chorus doing the "Volga Boatmen" and then whips them into doing spirituals in the style of Mr. [Rouben] Mamoulian. Miss [Viola] Essen squirms around on a big table in the center, with a smile of autoerotic delight that Hollywood might consider enticing. There is nothing remotely Spanish anywhere around, despite mantillas, knives, flounces and so forth.[148]

Far more was riding on Nijinska's two new ballets, each of which explored a different aspect of her mature artistry. *Brahms Variations*, as the title suggests, was a symphonic work in two scenes, semi-abstract, "taking its form from . . . the musical variations" from which she had crafted the score— the composer's Handel Variations and Paganini Variations, orchestrated by the Russian-born conductor and composer Ivan Boutnikoff. Part 1, she wrote in the program notes, was set on Olympus, where "Apollo, the god of the arts, creates the sublime harmony of poetry, and inspires those about him," Part 2 on Earth, where "the Artist strives to reach and obtain this divinity, and through the modicum of technique, virtuosity, and sensitivity creates the Art."[149] The ballet was a celebration of André Eglevsky, a Paris-trained émigré now in his prime whose virtuosity was renowned and who had just left Ballet Theatre. Nijinska cast him as both Apollo and the Artist, with Viola Essen, his partner, as Diana and (in Scene 2) A Melody. Unsurprisingly, the critics were divided about the work, which clocked in at about forty-five minutes, far longer than the usual one-act ballet. Harriet Johnson, who had recently begun writing music criticism for the *New York Post*, thought the work was one of Nijinska's best, but "much too long and overweighted" and the tempos "badly distorted to fit the needs of the dancers."[150] The *New York Sun*'s music critic Arthur V. Berger agreed about the ballet's length, while criticizing its "episodic, additive variation form" that made him yearn for "some long sustained passage." But he also emphasized the prodigious role that Nijinska had created for her male star. "It was virtually a vehicle for the display of his superb ballet form."[151]

John Martin had nothing good to say about anything. "If apparently unlimited funds and a deep-rooted desire to start a ballet company were all that was necessary, the venture would be an overwhelming success, but what the good Marquis seems to have overlooked is that the minimum requirements of such an enterprise are dancers and a repertoire. Both were sorely lacking." As for Nijinska's new work, with its "unbelievable number of variations" it was both "fragmentary and diffuse, . . . constantly stopping and starting, held together by no visible thematic material or treatment."[152]

Peevishness aside, Martin wasn't alone in feeling that *Brahms Variations* didn't go anywhere. As Anatole Chujoy wrote, "The ballet lasts nearly three-quarters of an hour and nothing much happens. Viola Essen dances well and looks beautiful and André Eglevsky does enough turns and beats to last him a month of performances. But that is all there is to it; it does not get any place."[153] Denby diagnosed the problem in a half-dozen words: "The Brahms . . . is endless, highly ingenious and pointless."[154] A Diaghilev might have persuaded Nijinska to condense the ballet, to use only the Handel Variations, which had a musical arc of their own, but the Marquis, for all his enthusiasm and taste, was no Diaghilev. And Nijinska could be very stubborn.

***

Although she choreographed many different kinds of works, Nijinska's most important ballets of the 1930s and 1940s rejected the demi-caractère orientation of the late Diaghilev company and its Ballet Russe successors. This was evident in reviews of *Les Cent Baisers*, where critics, especially in London, insisted on the classicism of her choreography, and in the many ballets that explored not only classical vocabulary but also virtuosity. For the most part, the music critics who reviewed *Brahms Variations* in New York accepted this: virtuosity was inherent in the very form of a musical work built on theme and variations. But American ballet audiences and at least some American dance critics were uneasy with academicism. "'Brahms Variations' is academic and without future," was how Lucile Marsh dismissed the ballet, as though academicism were an affront to the populism of so much wartime ballet.[155] Works like Agnes de Mille's *Rodeo* or Jerome Robbins's *Fancy Free* (which premiered only six months before *Brahms Variations*), Russian-themed ballets such as Fokine's *Russian Warrior*, Igor Schwezoff's *Red Poppy*, or even Nijinska's *Snow Maiden*, with their generous emotions, familiar characters, and uncomplicated music, appealed to audiences happy to take their classicism in one-act doses (*Aurora's Wedding*, Act II of *Swan Lake*) or at most in two-act works like *Giselle* and *La Fille Mal Gardée*, which were never performed on their own. In other words, *Brahms Variations* anticipated ballets like *Raymonda*, a work rich in variations that Balanchine and Alexandra Danilova would stage in 1946 for the Ballet Russe de Monte Carlo, and *Theme and Variations*, which Balanchine would stage the following year for Ballet Theatre, ballets that embraced both older and newer forms of academicism. An artistic sea change was underway that partly involved a rejection of wartime populism, and this made some people uneasy.

Nijinska's second original ballet for de Cuevas in 1944 was *Pictures at an Exhibition*. It was set to Mussorgsky's well-known music, orchestrated again by Ivan Boutnikoff. Unlike most of the music that Nijinska was using at this time, *Pictures* was programmatic. With ten episodes, each the remembrance of a painting by the composer's friend Viktor Hartmann, it imagined a spectator strolling through an art gallery and contemplating his works: hence, the named sections and their distinctive coloring, and the musical "promenade" that separates them. However, Nijinska threw out the exhibition conceit, imagining the work as a series of reenactments. "Gathering together a group of Russian peasants in a bare barn-like place," wrote John Martin in the *New York Times*,

> she has had them reproduce Mussorgsky's pictures naïvely, with ladders and benches as properties and with a total abandonment of literalism. She has managed to capture a beautiful spirit of play . . . and at times she has taken it to heights of brilliant imagination. The picture of the "Catacombs," for example, is stunning, and the "Great Gate at Kiev" with the "Ringing of Bells" is also extraordinarily fine.[156]

Martin praised what linked *Pictures* to *Les Noces*, which he had seen in 1936—"the most complete economy of means and exhibiting the same mastery of the architectonics of ensemble composition." And he noted the influence of Meyerhold's constructivism and biomechanics, of which, he said, she made "admirable use."[157] Nijinska's "pseudo-Soviet ballet," however, won few plaudits from Denby. He called it

> an orderly group composition in stylized Soviet-Russian clothes, a sort of mechanized Russian farm-celebration, without much dancing or very interesting ideas. Its manner is the "automatism" in movement which was modern in the twenties. . . . The choreography is a stylization of Russian folk steps and village games with a good many chain-gang huddles and a number of rows standing face upward, looking fervently glad; bell-pulling is also imitated. Instead of looking like a monument, the piece looks like a poster.[158]

Again and again, Denby decries the "stage technique" of *Pictures* as old-fashioned, leftovers of the Soviet 1920s. Denby had come to believe that politics had no place in dance, even criticizing Pearl Primus for choreographing protest dances when audiences were "quite amenable" to her ideas.[159] He devoted an entire column to an article by Yuri Slonimsky in which the Soviet ballet historian argued for "a classic Russian ballet" based not on "naive allegories," "folk-motivated steps," "parod[ies] of everyday life," or "industrial spectacle," but "on [the] same spiritual traditions which inspired the collaboration of Tchaikovsky and Ivanov in 'Swan Lake.'" The new stylistic direction, Denby claims, is "not unlike that new classicism which here in America George Balanchine's choreography exemplifies."[160] He wrote over-the-top reviews of Balanchine's *Waltz Academy* and *Danses Concertantes*, which premiered only weeks before *Pictures*, and even turned his review of Balanchine's *Le Bourgeois Gentilhomme* into an attack on modernism, which he equates with "the deformed, the stylized, [and] the bizarre," showing off the choreographer rather than the dancer.[161] Easing Balanchine back into the New York ballet world, Denby's writing left a deep impression on ballet criticism while providing a useful rhetoric for later Cold Warriors.

The critical onslaught must have shocked Nijinska. It seemed as though nearly everyone had joined a cabal against her. Although Denby softened his stance in later reviews, the damage was done. Reviewing the second week of the season, *Cue's* possibly pseudonymous critic Elizabeth Savage lived up to her name:

> Heralded as the big success of the Ballet International's season *Pictures at an Exhibition* . . . was, for us, a major disappointment. All that wonderful music, and a superbly apt set by Boris Aronson gone to waste. Madame Nijinska has been acclaimed as the towering artist of the choreographic field, but we were bored to death by both this ballet and her *Brahms Variations*. Both ballets suffer from an air of "interpretative dancing," which we thought had gone out with the Lost Generation and Isadora Duncan. Whatever Madame Nijinska has to say in this art form is most certainly limited. An ability to move groups of dancers around the stage is surely not the "be all and end all" of the art. There is never one oxygen-breathing, blood-coursing emotion coming across the footlights in anything she does.[162]

Meanwhile, Lucile Marsh opened her *Dance Magazine* review by referring to the "colossal blunder of [Ballet International] putting its worst foot forward at its debut."[163] By then, Nijinska had returned to California to lick her wounds.

***

In the next few years Nijinska flitted from job to job. In 1945, for Ballet Theatre, she choreographed *Harvest Time*, which starred Tamara Toumanova, a guest artist that season, to music by the Polish composer Henryk Wieniawski, and *Rendezvous*, a "character" pas de deux for Lucia Chase and Dimitri Romanoff to Rachmaninoff's "Polka de W. R." Martin described *Harvest Time* as a "long divertissement, a grand pas de deux with ensemble interludes," a format later made familiar by Balanchine. "It might . . . be the big scene in one of the romantic peasant ballets of the late nineteenth century," Martin continued. The dances alternated between "adapted" Polish material and "straight" academic ballet, and all eleven wore "longish" full tutus. "There is no story and no scenery," wrote Martin. "But there is plenty of dancing, and much of it brilliantly conceived and executed accordingly. Though the choreographer has made use of the standard vocabulary, she has phrased it in her highly individual way, especially in the dances she has designed for the ballerina."[164] Speaking of Toumanova, Martin continued:

We have become accustomed to her bravura style, but here, particularly in the earlier variation and adagio, she . . . reveals a side of her talent that is . . . rarely exhibited. Small, precise bourrées, extensions kept down to a becoming height, a softness in the arms and upper body, are all more than welcome in a dancer who is customarily dancing to the limit of her enormous technical resources. The brilliance, when it comes, seems all the more brilliant.[165]

For Toumanova, *Harvest Time* marked the start of a long relationship with Nijinska.

After dismissing *Harvest Time* as an embarrassment to Ballet Theatre,[166] Denby directed his venom at *Rendezvous:*

> One would like to pass over the disgraceful little novelty Ballet Theatre perpetrated at the Metropolitan last night in polite silence, which is almost what the audience did. . . . But coming in the same season as the vapid "Harvest Time" and the clammy "Moonlight Sonata" [by Massine] it made one wonder what is happening to Ballet Theatre. It seemed rather like one of those breaches of manners one's friends are liable to in senility. . . . It is difficult to believe Ballet Theatre could put such a piece on its program.[167]

On May 8, 1945, three days after the premiere of *Harvest Time*, the war in Europe finally came to an end. In New York, "thousands filled Times Square in spontaneous celebration." Still, the *New York Times* reported, the rejoicing was "tempered by the realization that a grim and bitter struggle lay ahead in the Pacific and the fact that the nation was still in mourning for its fallen President and Commander in Chief."[168] (Franklin D. Roosevelt had died on April 12, and two days later Ballet Theatre canceled its matinee as a sign of respect.[169]) Like many Russian émigrés, Nijinska had quickly made out the "first papers" leading to American citizenship. Even before VE-Day she began making inquiries about her house in Louveciennes, only to discover that Nina Sirotinine's sister and brother in-law were squatting there.[170] She also learned that her scenery and costumes had been confiscated in 1943 by the German authorities and placed an advertisement in the Paris émigré newspaper *Russkie novosti*, seeking information about their whereabouts.[171] She sent care packages to her niece Kyra Nijinsky, who was living in Florence with her son, Vaslav Markevitch, and to George Kirsta, who had seen the war through in London.[172] From her French attorney, Alexandre Cremer, she learned that Jacques Rouché had been called to testify about his activities during the Occupation as director of the Paris Opéra, and that Serge Lifar had escaped this indignity only because he was a foreigner.[173] And she learned that like so many Jews living in Poland, Anna Teplicka had disappeared.

**

With Ballet Theatre and the Ballet Russe de Monte Carlo closed to her, Nijinska put out feelers for another engagement at the Teatro Colón. Among the dancers she tried to interest in accompanying her was Sergei Ismailoff, who had danced with her own company in 1932, de Basil's for nearly a decade, and then Denham's and Ballet International. In a letter pressing him to accept the offer Singaevsky outlined its advantages: an eight-month contract (April 1–November 1, 1946), 1,200 pesos a month (equivalent to $300 in US currency), and round-trip transportation by boat. "A room with full service . . . costs about 100 a month," Singaevsky wrote. "We lived there (the two of us) on about 500 pesos a month, which included taxis, entertainment, and minor expenses. One can enjoy a very good life and still save about $200 a month."[174] Ismailoff was unconvinced. Nijinska, however, accepted the Colón's proposal, and on March 20, the couple flew from Los Angeles to Chile, and from there to Buenos Aires, where on April 4 she received a three-month tourist visa.[175]

As always, the season opened with opera. In quick succession she staged the dances in *Boris Godunov*, *Marouf*, *Mignon*, *Carmen*, and *Un Ballo in Maschera*. Her name, with the title of "Directora coreógrafa" (choreographic or dance director), headed the list of the Colón's ballet personnel, followed by Michel Borovsky, the Polish-born Régisseur de Ballet, a position he shared with ballerina María Ruanova, one of the troupe's four "Primeras Bailarinas." Nijinska had taught and worked with many of the company's dancers, and much of the repertory had a familiar ring, even if the choreography of several works was by Margarita Wallmann, a former director of the Vienna State Opera Ballet who had danced with Mary Wigman in addition to studying ballet.[176] The program for the gala opening of the official season announced the five new works that Nijinska had committed to producing: *Les Biches*, which she had been anxious to revive since its last performance by the Markova-Dolin company; *Pictures at an Exhibition*; *Capriccio Italien* (a version of the work she had choreographed for Cora Bradley's Ballet Repertory Company in Chicago); and two ballets by Argentine composers and librettists: *La ciudad de las puertas de oro* (The City of Golden Doors), a "choreographic poem" set on the island of Atlantis; and *El Pillán*, a Mapuche-inspired legend. However, neither these nor any of the other new productions announced by the Colón for 1946 were produced.[177] Her last premiere, the dances in *Un Ballo de Mascara*, took place on July 21, and the last time she is listed as "Directora coreográfica" was August 1. By August 8 she was on a Pan Am flight from Montevideo to New York.[178]

Why she walked out mid-season remains a mystery. In all likelihood it had to do with Wallmann, a savvy competitor who had learned Spanish and how to cozy up to power, a talent that stood her in good stead. Nijinska had a proprietary attitude toward music she had choreographed, and Wallmann had created her own version of *La Valse*, as well as knockoffs of Ballets Russes classics such as Massine's *Le Tricorne* and *La Boutique Fantasque*, and even Ashton's *Les Patineurs*. In this she was following the practice of many opera houses, where repertory decisions for ballet were driven chiefly by musical choices, above all when it came to the modern repertory. Nijinska, moreover, had no use for modern dance, and this was certainly one of Wallmann's selling points. Finally, in 1946 Nijinska did not enjoy unfettered access to the dancers as she had twenty years earlier. The Colón was now an institution, which meant that someone else was teaching them (probably Michel Borovsky, the "Régisseur de Baile"), and others, including Wallmann, were rehearsing them. In other words, Nijinska had to share them, and sharing was something she never liked to do. It is also possible that the populism associated with the newly elected president Juan Perón and his wife, Eva Duarte de Perón, had an adverse effect on working conditions at the Colón.[179] There may have been criticism of the new ballets she was choreographing. Or something better may have appeared on the horizon.

Returning home via New York, Nijinska spent the next few months teaching and surveying the changing ballet landscape. The big news was the return of Colonel de Basil's Original Ballet Russe from South America, where it had spent several years. Before long, he had forged an agreement with Sol Hurok (who would soon be divorced from Ballet Theatre) for a New York season and a US tour beginning in the fall of 1946. However, the company had slipped technically and artistically in the intervening years. Enlisting the financial backing of the Marquis de Cuevas, Hurok agreed to revive two works originally produced by Ballet International with the Marquis' own dancers appearing in their original roles. At the same time, Hurok hired a roster of "stars," including Alicia Markova, Anton Dolin, André Eglevsky, and Rosella

Hightower, who were under contract to him and well known in the United States.[180] The refurbished troupe made its debut at the Metropolitan Opera on September 29, 1946. With Ballet Theatre opening the following night at the Broadway Theatre, "the great ballet battle of 1946," as John Martin referred to the overlapping seasons, was underway.[181]

Nijinska must have used her time in New York lobbying de Cuevas to revive one of her own Ballet International works. On February 9, two days after the "Original" opened a two-week engagement at Philharmonic Auditorium in downtown Los Angeles, she notified the Colonel that at the Marquis' request she had agreed to restage *Pictures at an Exhibition* in time for the company's March season at the Metropolitan. She was to receive $2,000, a royalty of $10 per performance, and two return trips from Los Angeles. Rehearsals began in Hollywood, and one may be sure that among the newcomers were dancers from her studio auditioned by Hurok at the start of the season.[182]

Nijinska was on hand to acknowledge the applause when *Pictures* opened in New York. As before, John Martin found it "interesting and beautiful . . . thoroughly Russian in . . . feeling, although it rarely utilizes any literal Russian dance movements." Nobody, he continued,

> can handle an ensemble with more authority and invention than Mme. Nijinska, and when she uses her groups of dancers as she does here as abstract architectural units, so to speak, she is at the top of her form.[183]

The ballet's one weakness, Martin commented, was the absence of what he called a "clear overall approach to lead the spectator at once to the choreographer's intention." Is the ballet to be taken literally as "a kind of village charade" or is it meant to be "a semi-abstract suite of dances"? At least two viewings were required for the "shape and purpose of the composition" to emerge, although, he hastened to add, the ballet was eminently worth seeing twice.[184]

Meanwhile, with Hurok's backing, Alicia Markova and Anton Dolin had formed a small touring ensemble and asked Nijinska to choreograph a new work for them. The result was *Fantasia*, another of her delvings into the nineteenth-century Romantic musical repertory, in this case the Schubert-Liszt "Wanderer Fantasy."[185] In contrast to *Pictures at an Exhibition*, *Fantasia*, thought Terry, was

> a lively and stylish arrangement of pure dance patterns, straightforward in its choreographic purpose, . . . shrewdly rather than imaginatively

made. . . . The few emotional overtones are on the "yearning" side, but the ballet is on safe ground when . . . traditional feats of virtuosity are brought in to give accent or climax to an episode of dance.[186]

That summer, in one of his Sunday columns, John Martin remarked that "the great ballet boom seems to be over."[187] He was referring to Hurok's retirement from the ballet field, and the "new alignments and re-alignments" that were taking place. But this is also a useful way to bookend Nijinska's American career, which reached its zenith during World War II and now virtually ended. She had worked for all the major ballet companies of the period, but formed a permanent tie with none. Rushing from assignment to assignment, she sank few roots, even compared to other itinerant choreographers of the time. She had an acute sense of grievance. She was expensive. She refused to speak English. She lived in Los Angeles rather than New York. She let fly in rehearsals. She was hired, but seldom rehired. "It is hard to be alive," she wrote after the war to artist George Kirsta. "It is all speculation, commerce, syndicates, journals, and one still has to work. . . . It is so sad that the things we dreamed of are impossible to accomplish."[188] She was only in her mid-fifties, but she looked old and haggard. America had taken its toll.

With Europe now at peace, ballet people were eager to visit or, in many cases, return to the war-torn continent. In 1946, Ballet Theatre danced at London's Royal Opera House. The following year the Original Ballet Russe performed at the storied house, the site of so many of its erstwhile triumphs, while Balanchine took a six-month engagement at the equally storied Paris Opéra. That year, too, the Marquis de Cuevas established the second iteration of his Ballet International. The company was called the Grand Ballet de Monte-Carlo, and Nijinska, after nearly eight years in the United States, joined it in Vichy.

15

The Final Act

The company now headed by the Marquis de Cuevas had already gone through a number of iterations. Founded in 1942 as the Nouveau Ballet de Monte-Carlo, a haven for dancers fleeing the Germans, it was re-formed in 1946 by the impresario Eugène Grünberg, with Serge Lifar (temporarily purged from the Opéra as a collaborator) as artistic director. Now, with the Marquis as its chief financial backer, the company became the Grand Ballet de Monte-Carlo. Grünberg was forced out; Lifar, back in the government's good graces, returned to the Paris Opéra along with most of the French dancers, and the Marquis began stocking the troupe with American dancers and repertory. In May 1947, Nijinska reached an agreement with the Marquis to stage *Les Biches* and *Brahms Variations* for his new company, and by early summer, she was back in France, in time for its debut on July 12 at the Vichy Opera House.[1]

The Grand Ballet du Marquis de Cuevas (as the company became in 1950) is nearly forgotten today, overlooked among the great national companies— Britain's Royal Ballet, the New York City Ballet, the Bolshoi Ballet—that dominated the post–World War II ballet landscape and continue to dominate histories of the period. But at the time it carved out a niche for itself, especially in Europe. Like its Diaghilev ancestor, the Grand Ballet was a contemporary company, with a repertory of original ballets by living choreographers complemented by a handful of Fokine favorites and abbreviated nineteenth-century "classics." It was also an international company, home to the last generation of White Russian émigrés and assorted Europeans, with a sizable contingent of Americans at every rank, including two of its greatest stars, Rosella Hightower and Marjorie Tallchief. Finally, like other companies modeled on the Ballets Russes, it was a touring company, performing all over Europe and the Americas. For a European-based company the Grand Ballet was decidedly odd. Headed by a Chilean-born self-invented seigneur, it was registered in New York State, and most of its capital, artistic as well as financial, came from the United States. The company presented works unseen in Europe such as Balanchine's *Concerto Barocco* (1941), introduced American choreographers to European audiences, and nurtured younger American dancemakers such as John Taras, Ana Ricarda (Anne Simpson), and Antonia Cobos (Phyllis Nahl). For many dancers, Nijinska's California studio was a gateway to a job with this Russo-Franco-American entity.

Nijinska's association with the Marquis' variously titled companies lasted until 1960. Five years her senior, he was the grand patron she had yearned for, loyal, devoted, enamored of art, and untainted by commerce. She was his "Madame chérie," "Douchka chérie," "Douchka Madame," and "Darling," he the "true and loyal friend" who sent her love. He scrawled letters in green ink, begging her repeatedly to join him: "I need you," "the life of the company depends on you," "without you I feel lost."[2] And, again and again, she returned. But it was more than love of art that drew her. De Cuevas was a generous man. He paid well, never quibbled, and indulged her taste for luxury.[3] With the Marquis as her patron, there were first-class accommodations on ocean liners like the *America* and *Queen Elizabeth*, and on Air France's "Golden Parisian," the new de luxe service between New York and Paris, complete with "Private Sky-rooms," magnificent cuisine, and only thirty-two passengers.[4] There were good hotels in Paris, Cannes, Deauville, and elsewhere. And it was all for two, because Singaevsky accompanied her everywhere. With no income, the man who gave his name as Nicolas Singaevsky Nijinska when he became a US citizen in 1949 simply lived off his wife.[5]

"Nijinska set a tremendous number of ballets for us," Rosella Hightower recalled in the 1990s.[6] These included Nijinska's last original ballets—*In Memoriam* (1949), to Chopin's Fantasy in F Minor, marking the centenary of the composer's death, and *Rondo Capriccioso* (1952), to Saint-Saëns' virtuoso piece for violin and orchestra. She also restaged many of her older ballets— *Brahms Variations*, *Les Biches*, and *Pictures at an Exhibition* for the first Paris season in 1947; *Aurora's Wedding* (as *Princess Aurora*) in 1953; *Chopin Concerto* and *Bolero* in 1954. She reset and coached the company's Ballets Russes works: Fokine's *Les Sylphides* (1949), *Petrouchka* (1952), *Le Spectre de la Rose* (1952), and *Polovtsian Dances* (1949), and her brother's *L'Après-midi d'un Faune* (1950). And she restaged most of the company's nineteenth-century repertory—*Coppélia* (1949), *La Fille Mal Gardée* (1949), *Swan Lake* (1950), and *Arlequinade* (1954)—culminating in an ill-fated *Sleeping Beauty* (1960) that finally drove a wedge between the Marquis and his "Douchka" and had to be finished by somebody else. Nijinska also served intermittently as ballet master. The company's publicist Irène Lidova described her visits as a course of treatment intended both to stimulate and discipline a troupe that neither the Marquis nor his longtime ballet master John Taras ever quite managed to bring to heel. In 1953 and 1954, with Taras off the scene, she became both the company's ballet master and its "Artistic Advisor," and in 1960, after he had returned to New York, its "Choreographic Director."[7]

Although the company's French dancers were new to her, Nijinska had worked with most of the Americans, including the stars of the group, André Eglevsky, her former student Marjorie Tallchief, and George Skibine (who would soon marry Tallchief). Nijinska formed an extremely close relationship with Rosella Hightower, the Oklahoma-born half-Choctaw ballerina who had danced with the Ballet Russe de Monte Carlo, Ballet Theatre, and the Markova-Dolin company before joining de Cuevas.[8] The two began to work together in Vichy, and Hightower quickly joined Alicia Markova and Irina Baronova in the pantheon of Nijinska's muses and ideal collaborators. "She was a true genius and all-around artist," Hightower later said, and "she was a great musician. . . . She went further musically and realized . . . that much of technique and virtuosity is rhythm."[9]

The choreographer was now in her late fifties, "dumpy," "a little fat," Hightower told Elizabeth Kendall in the 1970s, and she smoked all the time. She had "beautiful eyes, piercing eyes, grey hair that never stayed in place," and she was "always intense." She was also "very suspicious," the reason, Hightower believes, that Nijinska pretended not to understand French or English, although "she understood both languages perfectly well." She would do this to protect herself, Hightower felt, because she was afraid of people's reactions or needed time to make up her mind.[10] "She would whisper things and . . . do things with her hand, and . . . [gesture] and you had to put all this together and know what she was thinking. . . . And if you couldn't do it, . . . [s]he would go into a rage." She demanded "complete concentration, intense concentration. Well, you can get it from one artist, from a solo artist, or from the danseurs étoiles, but from 50 corps de ballet, it's rather difficult. And so this was . . . always the drama of Nijinska."[11]

[W]hen she would say, . . . "I want you to do this and this and this," [most people would respond] it's impossible. . . . But it was never impossible. . . . And she could tell you exactly how. . . . [But] only . . . if you [did] exactly what she wanted musically. The whole key to her extraordinary technical . . . virtuosity was the musicality of the thing. And if you could understand . . . the phrasing . . . and the [musical] accents that she wanted, . . . then you could do technically what she wanted.[12]

Their collaboration began with rehearsals for *Les Biches* and *Brahms Variations*, which premiered in Paris in November 1947. But Hightower understood that Nijinska's approach could apply equally to the classical repertory. "[I]t gave you the possibility of . . . suspension [and] balance in movement," instead of producing a succession of static poses—something Nijinska had insisted on years before in her treatises on movement. "[T]hat's why, for me," Hightower asserted, "she was absolutely the door that opened my whole future afterwards to the way I was going to dance."[13] In teaching the role of the Garçonne, Nijinska emphasized that posture was the key to the role's stylization and the means of doing multiple turns without preparation. "It's the difference [between] working with the outer layer of muscles and working with the muscles that are next to the skeleton."[14] Hightower sensed, however, that the role spoke to the virility in Nijinska's own character. "She was very, very masculine, really. She had a tremendous force." In *Biches*, Nijinska "did not want a lesbian sort of thing. She wanted a force, . . . a womanly force. [I]n order to do this, you had to always be strong but strong on the inside. And so . . . you kept pulling up . . . your back, . . . pulling up in a straight line in the back. . . . And because of that, I developed such muscles." Hightower recounts how Nijinska would put her fist in the middle of her back, until she automatically pulled up, something like the elongation that Martha Graham wanted in a contraction. "There is a tremendous force that comes from this lift in the central part of your body. Because it's a lift that must come through an elongation on balance, because if it comes from tension, then you can't move. You can't even breathe."[15]

When Nijinska revived ballets, she also revised them. With Hightower as her lead, *Brahms Variations* became what the ballerina described as "sheer madness." "The music used to send her," Hightower reminisced. "She was in ecstasy." The resulting feats of virtuosity held critics and audiences spellbound. Nijinska loved turns, Hightower says, but she always wanted something extra going into or coming out of the spiral. This led her to invent "incredible things" for the ballerina—like "fouetté, fouetté, fouetté, double pirouette, . . . with rond de jambes as you did your third pirouette. Incredible things! . . . [S]he'd play the music and . . . sit me down and then move her fingers on my shoulder. She would do the steps. . . . She would beat out exactly what she wanted me to do. . . . She'd dance it on my shoulders." You had to "efface yourself completely and just follow her. . . . And, then, when you get up and put yourself into action, . . . suddenly you understand that it . . . wasn't just mental fantasy or imagination . . . [but] a whole system."[16]

It wasn't all work that first summer in Vichy. Nijinska met the great French ballerina Yvette Chauviré, an encounter memorialized in a snapshot of the two in the gardens of the Vichy Casino.[17] In the Russian church Marjorie Tallchief married George Skibine. Her sister Maria came down from Paris with George Balanchine, now ballet master of the Paris Opéra, whom she had married the year before. Nijinska was there of course, and she decided to give Balanchine a piece of her mind. (According to Skibine, the two choreographers had not spoken since Diaghilev's death.) From a long history of slights, she latched on to his revival of Le Baiser de la Fée in 1946 for the Ballet Russe de Monte Carlo with his wife as the Fairy. Baiser was Nijinska's ballet; she had choreographed it for Ida Rubinstein, revived it for her own company and for the Teatro Colón. Now, with Nijinska out of the picture, Denham presented Balanchine's version, using Alice Halicka's scenery and costumes from the American Ballet production, and Nijinska's own protegée as the ballet's muse. So, festering with grievance, she confronted Balanchine. "Not only you took my music, but you took Maria, my star pupil, who showed you the steps that I did for her! . . . I thought you were a gentleman!" Taken aback, all Balanchine could say, and he said it over and over, was "But I *am* a gentleman!" Finally, things all quieted down. "In fact," Skibine remembered, "after the reception they walked out together holding arms and talking, reminiscing about Diaghilev."[18]

After Vichy the company went to Paris. No theaters were available, so the Marquis rented a music hall, the Alhambra, off the Place de la République. The house was packed for the opening performance on November 7, and by the time Brahms Variations was underway the audience was "delirious," "galvanized" by Rosella Hightower's "rare virtuosity."[19] To be sure, arguments broke out over Les Biches, the way Nijinska had "hardened" the classical dance, turned harmonious curves into angular movements, and added stiff shoulder turns, arguments that recalled Levinson: in fact, a number of critics active in the 1920s and 1930s were still writing. Maurice Brillant wondered about the ballet's effect on new audiences. For those with long stage memories, a category in which he included himself, Les Biches "recalls a beautiful and precious time. But it is true that one can never fully resurrect—except by a stroke of genius—a ballet mounted by that 'prodigious magician,' Diaghilev."[20] According to Irène Lidova, who later became the company's French publicist, the real sensation of this first Paris season was caused by the "American étoiles: Rosella Hightower, whose 'Black Swan' electrified the theater, and willowy Marjorie Tallchief, with her strange Indian face."[21] Their astonishing virtuosity "brought the message of a new world, an unknown physical audacity, a thrilling force" attained through "relentless work and continuous sacrifice."[22]

Hard though it had been for Nijinska to settle down in Los Angeles, this first trip abroad made clear that California had become her home. In 1946, Irina—now known as "Irene K. Nijinska"—married Gibbs Raetz, a Nebraska-born aerospace engineer who had settled in California during World War II. The following year she gave birth to a son, George, and in 1950, to a daughter, Natalie Iola, making Nijinska a grandmother twice over.[23] Nijinska adored little George and was ecstatic when Denham agreed to be the baby's godfather, even though he couldn't join them for the actual christening but sent a cross instead. "We feel your presence here with us," she wrote to him. "And I feel so happy that my grandson will wear your blessing."[24] In fact, with their professional relationship in abeyance, Nijinska's letters to Denham attest to a genuine friendship between the two. She tells him about nursing her "lemon grove" in San Fernando back to health after a frost "burn."[25] She thanks him for visiting her school and arranging for "Shura"—Alexandra Danilova—to teach when she is away.[26] She recommends dancers to him. And she tells him about Louveciennes, which she visited for the first time after the war in 1947. "I found my house very dirty and ruined on the inside," she wrote. Although pretty much everything had survived, "apart from a few items stolen by 'nobody-knows-who,'" the house was in dire need of repair. And then remarkably, "I am really looking forward to returning home, though France is still beautiful."[27]

In 1948, Nijinska was back in Europe, rehearsing the de Cuevas company for its second Paris season, this one at the storied Théâtre des Champs-Elysées. In *Revue de la Danse*, one of several new dance publications launched after the war, the poet Victor-Michel Sager wrote a glowing review of *Brahms Variations*, which was danced on opening night. Unlike his American counterparts, Sager both admired the work and understood its relationship to the émigré canon. "Madame Nijinska's ballet," he wrote, "is a masterpiece. It incorporates and develops the entire history of the Ballet Russe, from Fokine to Lifar, in an original and living whole, with an extraordinary sense of the stage space."

The theme is commonplace, traditional even: the drama of artistic creation under its twin guises, divine and human. But the simplicity allows for great richness of expression and a dramatic elucidation of all the nuances of Brahms' admirable music....

Madame Nijinska's ... groupings are never static but in continual movement, breaking up and then reforming in accordance with the musical and
dramatic flow. ... [In the first tableau] the ensemble choreography is based
on classical steps and on the two-dimensional movements that Fokine in
Daphnis and Chloé and Lifar in his version of *L'Après-midi d'un Faune* used
to animate the expressive archaism of Greek vases. ... Madame Nijinska
achieves this [synthesis] with a great sense of the plastic and dynamic qualities of the body, without falling into the exaggerated pathos that sometimes
spoils the choreography of Lifar and his students.[28]

The long months abroad in 1948 weren't easy for Nijinska. She was
working from morning to night and was sick much of the time, she told
Denham. However, when she returned to California, she had almost all her
books with her.[29] Six months later she was off again, sailing in February 1949
on the *Queen Mary*. In Monte Carlo, where the Grand Ballet had its headquarters, she restaged *La Fille Mal Gardée*, choreographed *In Memoriam*,
and drilled the company's repertory works. In June, when the Grand Ballet
opened in London, the results of her hard work were evident. As Martin
Cooper wrote in the *Spectator*, "The corps de ballet, severely criticised during
the company's previous appearance in London, had obviously taken a great
deal of trouble with Swan Lake Act 2 on the opening night, and, though there
were one or two very ragged passages in *Les Sylphides*, the performance was a
noticeable improvement on last year's."[30] Nijinska remained in Louveciennes
for the Covent Garden season. She longed to be back in the United States, but
as she wrote Denham in July, "I can't just leave things here the way they are—
they will torture me and bankrupt me again." She had finally "liberated" the
house from "the 'thieves.'"[31] Now she returned to the United States and for
the next couple of years put her relationship with the Marquis and his Grand
Ballet on hold.

***

Although most of Nijinska's personal property survived the war, her
costumes and scenery were gone, confiscated by the Services de Réquisitions
Allemands in 1943. She may not have been Jewish, but there had been no
one to vouch for her "Aryan origin" to the satisfaction of the Commissariat-
General for Jewish Affairs; moreover, she was living in the United States, an
enemy country. "The only practical solution," recommended her attorney, a

Russian émigré named Alexandre Crémer, in July 1945, "was to have the competent Authorities conduct a search for the missing objects in Germany."[32] Thus began a fruitless, decade-long plod through the slow-moving French bureaucracy as she sought the restitution of her property or compensation for its loss.

Nijinska never saw her scenery and costumes again, and she never recovered a penny for them, even after spending a fortune on legal fees, filling out innumerable forms, providing lists and descriptions of the lost items, receipts for their value in 1939, affidavits, insurance policies, notarized copies of identity, and citizenship documents. Something was always wrong, and something was always missing. In 1949 the Ministry of Reconstruction and Urbanism temporarily lost her file, and when it reappeared, Nijinska was told they needed "proof" that the missing property was "essential to the exercise of her profession."[33] Then, there was the problem of nationality. According to the Ministry, the "restoration of a ballet that is not French . . . is of no interest to the French State," unless the sets and costumes "were made in France."[34] As Crémer explained to Singaevsky: "According to the law what matters is the nationality at the time of the disaster. . . . [I]f I secure damages, it is solely thanks to sympathy for the Ballets Russes, and especially for Mme. Nijinska, who is a great Russian artist. An American . . . will receive nothing. Americans are too rich to receive funds in France for their ballets."[35]

None of Nijinska's missing property was ever found, and the case now moved into its second phase—compensation. In 1951, Singaevsky alerted the Chase Bank in Paris that he expected to receive a substantial sum from the French government in war damages. But the government fell, and business at the Ministry ground to a halt.[36] Two years later, Singaevsky was still waiting. At that point—it was now 1953—the Ministry demanded a new round of documents, most of which had been submitted years before.[37] But in June 1955, fully ten years from the start of her quest and more than twenty since the collapse of the company for which the missing property was created, the Ministry asked her to document the company's business practices and contractual relationships, down to the royalties and taxes she had paid and the accident insurance she had taken out.[38] Suddenly, her debt-ridden Ballets Russes, with its intermittent performances and underpaid dancers, in a Depression-era economy rife with quotas and growing nationalism, was being held to the standard of a thriving, profit-making enterprise like the Folies-Bergère. In December 1956, Nijinska's claim was finally rejected. As Crémer informed Singaevsky, her company was "completely" illegal. It had never been registered as a commercial enterprise, never paid taxes, and it would be nothing short of a "miracle" if they received any kind of remuneration.[39] And on that sorry note ended the saga of the plundered remains of Nijinska's Ballets Russes. Apart from the odd costume or two, the properties remain unaccounted for, lost like so much else in the detritus of World War II.

***

On April 8, 1950, two days before Natalie's birth, Vaslav Nijinsky died in a London hospital after a brief illness caused by nephritis. He was sixty years old, and mental illness had consumed more than half his life. Nijinska had last seen him in 1938, and she only learned of his death, she told the *Los Angeles Times*, from a "newscaster."[40] Neither Nijinska nor Kyra, Nijinsky's elder daughter who was now teaching in Italy, attended the funeral, which was held with great fanfare in London. Five hundred people crowded the requiem mass at St. James' Roman Catholic Church, and the six pallbearers were Serge Lifar, Anton Dolin, Frederick Ashton, Michael Somes, Cyril W. Beaumont, and Richard Buckle, who would one day write a biography of Nijinsky. It was an all-star event orchestrated by Romola Nijinsky, the grieving widow, accompanied by a cousin, Count Paul Bohus, and the dancer's celebrated partner, Tamara Karsavina. The burial took place on April 14 at Marylebone Cemetery in East Finchley.[41] Nijinska had written to Anton Dolin, and at her request, he had "very beautiful flowers laid beside Vaslav's body." He told her that Vaslav looked "peaceful and quiet" and that the funeral service was "sincere and most impressive." "I know how sad you must be, but I was proud to feel that I was there as your always loving and devoted pupil, to whom I owe so much."[42]

Four months after Nijinsky's death, Romola tried to enlist Adolph Bolm and his wife Beate, who were now living in Los Angeles, to help her make peace with Nijinska. "I do not know if you see Bronia," Romola wrote. "If yes please tell her to write to me. I will bring her a lot of things of Vaslav, and also of his written works and choreographic compositions, which he has written down and I [have] kept carefully."

> I wish you would explain to Bronia, that she ought to see a sister, a friend in me. I know she always disliked me and her husband speaks very badly about me and he stirs her up against me. In spite of all this I love Bronia and admire her as an artist more than she knows.[43]

It would take a great deal more than an apology for Nijinska to forgive the woman she always blamed for her brother's illness.

***

In January 1951, as Denham began making plans for his 1951–1952 season, he wrote to Nijinska about "restor[ing] to our repertoire some of your ballets, such as CHOPIN CONCERTO and possibly SNOW MAIDEN." However, after dithering for months and often not even responding to his letters, Nijinska said no, wiring that she considered it "impossible [to] restage Concerto in so short and busy [a] time," thereby passing up the chance to put her work once again before thousands of Angelenos at the Hollywood Bowl.[44] Nijinska now renewed her relationship with Ballet Theatre. By August 24 she was in New York, with contracts to choreograph a new ballet (to Schumann's Piano Concerto in A minor), revive *Princess Aurora* (another title for *Aurora's Wedding*), and direct the Ballet Theatre School.[45] Among the teachers she enlisted was her old friend Ludmilla Schollar, who was in charge of the children's classes. Schollar, who heard the news from Lucia Chase, was "happy and proud" to be part of Nijinska's new project. "Believe me when I say," she wrote to Nijinska, "that all Russian dancers are sincerely happy for you and consider this to be a victory for Russian art."[46] Edged out were Cecchetti disciples such as Margaret Craske, who had been teaching at Ballet Theatre since 1946.[47]

Schumann Concerto was Nijinska's last choreographic work for a major American company. Like most of its predecessors, it was set to a lush Romantic score, in this case by the composer of *Carnaval*, the ballet in which she had danced her first important role more than forty years before. The concerto was out of copyright, and its royalty-free status, mentioned in her contract, was only one of its attractions. Chopin, Schumann, Liszt, Tchaikovsky, Brahms, Glazunov: like Ariadne's thread, their music drew her into a maze of form and sound, image and emotion. Nijinska's late works did not endear her to critics. The ballets seemed to be about nothing, but as Martin and a few other critics sensed, they were pervaded by melancholy, a sense of loss, nostalgia even. "The prince who woke me up once upon a time, for whom I always wanted to be beautiful in my art, has passed away," she wrote around this time. "Now I am dead."[48] There was nothing left to say, nothing she wanted to say. There was only music.

Neither John Martin nor Walter Terry appreciated *Schumann* on first viewing. "This is not the Nijinska of 'Les Noces' and 'Les Biches' and 'Pictures at an Exhibition,'" Martin wrote, "but rather of 'Chopin Concerto' and 'Brahms Variations' and 'Etude,' which is decidedly the lesser Nijinska." The new ballet was a throwback to the 1930s, "nostalgic in . . . mood and form," like an early symphonic ballet, with little in the way of integration or dramatic build-up. While he admitted that there was "a certain style to the movement," he thought it was too "slender [a] thread . . . on which to hang so much music." It was "all pointless in the extreme."[49]

Walter Terry was more sympathetic. Nijinska's "pretty-pretty ballet," he wrote, seeks to "[reflect] in dance action something of the formal structure and something of the emotional content of the music."

> Mme. Nijinska's new piece is wholly classical in technique and romantic in style yet there is remarkable freshness to be found in several of its passages. Her many tableaux . . . frequently fall into fresh designs or, perhaps, she will enliven a static group of figures with one or two moving bodies. Although she has dragged out the whole bag of virtuosic tricks, she has assembled them . . . in fresh combinations. Fouettes have been paired with other kinds of turns, sequences of beats are fitted out in new arrangements, accents have been shifted or rhythms altered to bring newness to traditional steps.[50]

Nijinska cast Alicia Alonso and Igor Youskevitch, Ballet Theatre's star couple, as her principals, and they brought the house down. "Miss Alonso," wrote Terry, "accomplished some miraculous dancing—everything from the most delicate adagio to the speediest of multiple spins. . . . Youskevitch was right on a par in his performing of the showoff patterns created for him. Both should be grateful to Mme. Nijinska for providing them material which projects their special skills so handsomely."[51] Nijinska also worked with Alonso on the revival of *Princess Aurora*, which she crafted into a celebration of Ballet Theatre's "bright and shining star." Martin was amazed by Alonso, "her entrance, her variation, the phenomenal 'Rose Adagio'"—all restored by Nijinska from Act I of *The Sleeping Beauty*—"and the grand pas de deux constituted the real body of the piece. . . . Here was truly the dancing of a ballerina."[52]

Nijinska must have been dismayed by the brevity of her tenure directing the newly organized Ballet Theatre School. (In 1951 she purchased a vacant lot in Riverdale, a leafy community along the Hudson just north of Manhattan where Toscanini and other wealthy people had estates, probably with the idea of settling at least part-time in the New York metropolitan area.[53]) According to Richard Holden, a penniless ballet student paying for his classes at the Metropolitan Opera Ballet School by appearing as a "super" in operas, "there came an announcement that Bronislava Nijinska was to be the director of the new B[allet] T[heatre] school. . . . I was very excited about it because even from age 14 I knew all about the Nijinsky saga from Romola's book. I managed to go to her class [which] I think may have been . . . her first class there."[54] Awed by her presence, Holden only later realized what a wonderful class she had given. "Her combinations were intricate and challenging, and fun to do," he recalled, and she gave him one or two corrections. But he couldn't afford the tuition. In high school, with the help of a Russian-English dictionary, Holden had taught himself rudimentary Russian. So, after class, he summoned the courage to ask her for a scholarship. She said, "Of course, boy [*malchik*], come here to class."[55]

But Nijinska didn't last long as director. According to Holden, after only a month or so, a rumor went around that there had been some kind of conflict with William Dollar, one of the teachers. Whatever it was about, Nijinska was let go. She was paid a total of $708.88, representing two weeks' salary, a small commission, and her round-trip air fare, minus withholding tax. "Believe me, Mme. Nijinska," wrote John Onysko, treasurer of the Ballet Theatre Foundation, on November 30, "I am sorry that our association has not worked out satisfactorily. If there is anything we can do for you at any time, please contact us and we shall be happy to accommodate you."[56] On this sorry note ended another episode begun so auspiciously. Check in hand, Nijinska flew back to California and closed the door on Ballet Theatre and New York.

***

In August 1952 a letter arrived from the Marquis de Cuevas begging his "Madame chérie" to "help him restage Petrouchka"—a favorite of his wife's—for the opening of the Paris season on October 23.[57] It was an offer she could not refuse. "I was so happy to receive your letter," he responded. "The Marquise is always asking about you, and she is enchanted—as I am and Rosella is—that you will soon be joining us."[58] Thus opened a new chapter in Nijinska's relationship with the Grand Ballet. As always, the Marquis was generous to his "Douchka." In addition to first-class transportation, he paid her a salary of $300 per week, an additional $500 for each new ballet or revival, a $10 royalty per performance, and a $750 advance.[59]

Arriving in Europe in early autumn, Nijinska set to work grooming Serge Golovine to dance the title roles in *Petrouchka* and a second Fokine ballet closely associated with her brother, *Le Spectre de la Rose*. Both were in active repertory during the 1940s and 1950s, although few productions had the imprimatur of authority that Nijinska lent them.[60] She had danced in the very first performance of *Petrouchka* in Paris in 1911 and for more than twenty years had staged, restaged, and supervised rehearsals of the ballet. And in London in 1914 she had danced the Girl in *Spectre* with her brother. Born in France of a Russian father and Breton mother, Golovine was the nephew of the Russian painter and theater designer Alexander Golovin (who designed the original *Firebird*). He received his early training in Nice with the former Maryinsky soloist Julie Sedova, studied at the Paris Opéra School, then languished in the Opéra's corps de ballet until rescued by the Marquis (who also hired his siblings Georges and Solange). When Golovine died in 1998, Mary Clarke, the longtime editor of the *Dancing Times*, called him "the supreme French male classical dancer of his generation, revered worldwide ... and idolised in Paris."[61]

Already hailed for his grace and breathtaking technique, Golovine would be transformed by Nijinska's coaching, just as his frequent partner, Rosella Hightower, had been. "Madame," wrote Jean Coquelle, a critic for the magazine *Toute la Danse*, to Nijinska after seeing the premiere of *Spectre*: "Never have I felt in so powerful a fashion the beneficent influence that a master of your class can have on an artist. In my opinion, you have given a soul to Serge Golovine who until now has only been a technician of unequaled perfection ... but cold."[62] Another critic wrote:

> In *Spectre* the scenery and costumes are poor and Golovine's partner [Andrea Karlsen] weak, but there was Serge Golovine and the miracle took place. Led down the deceptive path of virtuosity, he abruptly changed course, when fate dispatched Nijinska to him, and prince charming awakened. The "old" Bronislava Nijinska had gone. Softened, humanized one could say, this famously inflexible personality looked after the lost young man with almost maternal care, which has given the most splendid results. As for Petrouchka ... Golovine's ... mime ... is perfection. Sober, natural, and profound, his acting, inward yet transparent, grows in intensity until it becomes heart-breaking. His agony is shattering.[63]

Olivier Merlin, the critic of *Le Monde*, also underscored the importance of Nijinska's revival of *Petrouchka*, comparing it favorably to the Serge Lifar–Nicolas Zverev version at the Paris Opéra:

The Empire stage is certainly less suitable than the Garnier stage, but the dancers make up for their inferior numbers with a more authentic Slavic ardor: a majority bear names that would not spoil the novels of Pushkin, and no one is better appointed than they to revive the bustling atmosphere of Carnival in Petersburg at the time of Nicholas I. The crowd movements, the fairground parades, the magic tricks, the boot dances, here is the true Russian stew turned white under a Christmas snow.[64]

Among the most enthusiastic of the ballet's critics was Marie A. Levinson, daughter of Nijinska's one-time nemesis, André Levinson. "After *Spectre*," she wrote in *Pour la Danse*,

Nijinska has devotedly applied herself to rendering all its folkloric vigor, all the primitive flavor dulled at the Palais Garnier by an extremely Frenchified interpretation. The proverbial "Slavic soul," reduced to a synonym for excess in the eyes of many, finds at last in Nijinska's *Petrouchka* its inner sense, its profound and symbolic meaning—a complete restoration. . . . I shall not soon forget the pale, dramatic face, the hobbled gestures, the figure at once limp and rigid of the unhappy puppet incarnated by Golovine. He has surpassed himself. . . . Here is a young lad who is quietly and unaffectedly reaching mastery. May God and Terpsichore will that the Nijinska-Golovine collaboration continues for the greater joy of those who persist in believing after Valéry that "the soul and the dance" are one.[65]

A month later, Levinson spoke of Nijinska's "second miracle." This was *Rondo Capriccioso*, a "choreographic sketch" to music of Saint-Saëns that brilliantly displayed Rosella Hightower's easy virtuosity and magnificent presence. "Insatiable Nijinska! Not content with the 'Golovine miracle,' she is now performing the 'Hightower miracle,'" exulted Levinson.

Her *Rondo Capriccioso* . . . is a masterpiece of refinement, a small but scintillating diamond, blazing with fire. . . . Dressed or, rather, undressed ravishingly by Jean Robier, no longer a woman but a magical birdlike creature, half-angel, half-beast, Rosella Hightower demonstrates, like Golovine, that when she allows herself to forget the letter for the spirit, she is the equal of the greatest ballerinas of yesteryear.[66]

The Marquis adored his dancers, especially his "Goddess," Rosella Hightower. She, in turn, was deeply grateful to him. "The Marquis belonged to a world that I didn't know. . . . He liked me; he admired me, and he put a company at my disposition. . . . And . . . he taught me to live."[67] Eglevsky was never personally close to the Marquis, but he, too, found him open-handed and generous. "You have to understand," he told an interviewer in the mid-1970s, when Mikhail Baryshnikov and other stars were commanding huge fees for a single performance, "that in those days a dancer did not receive the sums the dancers receive today. . . . If you received $100, $125, $150, $200 a week, you were very, very lucky." But for de Cuevas, "price was irrelevant. If he liked you he gave you what he wanted."[68]

Nijinska did not return to California after the season, but stayed on, signing a contract for 1953.[69] She spent several months in Cannes, the company's winter home, and probably traveled to Bordeaux where the company opened the city's annual festival in May. And she participated in the most spectacular of the Marquis' extravaganzas, a ball held on September 1, 1953, at the Chiberta Country Club near Biarritz in the Basque country.[70] It was a *Fête Champêtre*, and the 2,000 (or so) guests were invited to come in eighteenth-century costumes. De Cuevas, who opened the ball as the "King of Nature," fussed for months over his gold-threaded tonnelet and wig of golden grapes designed by Pierre Balmain. Two hundred fifty policemen dressed as lackeys in knee breeches kept order among the rich and titled, especially after the champagne began flowing. Merle Oberon was Titania; Elsa Maxwell Sancho Panza; Sylvia Ashley ("Madame Clark Gable") Flora. There were hunters, harlequins, and pashas galore, heralds with torches, a court magician who was really a bullfighter, dozens of *entrées* on an outdoor stage arranged by Nijinska (who demanded two rehearsals of the parading guests), and in a category of her own Renée (Zizi) Jeanmaire, who arrived on a camel wearing next to nothing. The high point came when Rosella Hightower, costumed as Odette, appeared with a dozen enchanted swan-maidens on a floating stage in Lake Chiberta to the overture of *Swan Lake*. The effect must have been dazzling, worthy of the summer entertainments at Peterhof in the days of the Tsars. Rumored to have cost nearly $200,000, the event generated reams of press and attacks by both the Vatican and local communists appalled by the wanton display of wealth in a France not yet recovered from the war.[71]

Once the Chiberta extravaganza was behind her, Nijinska turned to another revival, this time of her own ballet *Aurora's Wedding*. The work, which she had first staged in 1922, stitched together dances from *The Sleeping Beauty* with others such as "The Three Ivans" choreographed from scratch. *Aurora's Wedding* quickly became a repertory staple of the "international companies," a direct link with the classical traditions of the Maryinsky, albeit transformed along modernist lines into a one-act ballet with minimal narrative. Nijinska's name gradually disappeared from the credits, except for "The Three Ivans." Like the second act of *Swan Lake*, *Aurora's Wedding* existed in copyright limbo: it belonged to everyone and no one. While familiar outside France, inside the country it was relatively unknown. Now, in 1953, Nijinska restaged the ballet, which she called *Princess Aurora*.

The ballet premiered at the Empire on October 29. It was the gala opening of another three-month season, an "ultra-brilliant" evening crowded with celebrities from Cécile Sorel (in white ostrich plumes), Leslie Caron, and Kirk Douglas to the painter Leonor Fini. This time the Marquis made his entrance to drum rolls by members of the Republican Guard, costumed like grenadiers from Napoleon's day. The novelty of the program, *L'Ange Gris*, was sandwiched between *Swan Lake* and *Rondo Capriccioso*, with *Princess Aurora* closing the performance in triumph.[72]

Olivier Merlin was one of several critics to note the classical turn the company seemed to be taking under Nijinska. It was a turn Merlin welcomed. For *Princess Aurora*, he explained to readers of *Le Monde*, "Nijinska has been inspired by the version she presented in London in Diaghilev's time, with the greatest names of the day, . . . beginning with Maestro Cecchetti . . . as Carabosse, Trefilova, Egorova, Nemchinova, Zvereff, and . . . Nijinska herself. The present version, a little like the *Divertissement* staged by Lifar and Zvereff at the Opéra in 1948, mixes the sparkling divertissements from the ballet's wedding act with the charming Rose Adagio from Act 2 and interludes from *The Nutcracker*." Merlin ends with a burst of enthusiasm for the "mine of exquisite melodies" in the "great Tchaikovsky's score."[73]

Most critics agreed that the Nijinska effect went beyond the principals of the company. *Combat's* Dinah Maggie, for instance, was struck by the "new spirit animating the troupe," especially evident in the corps de ballet. "The mechanical gestures, indifference, indolence even, have given way to a clearer appreciation of the role, a more active participation in the development of the ballet, a more refined sensibility. The corps de ballet has started to dance—at last!"[74] Other critics remarked on dramatic improvements in the orchestra, changes they ascribed to Nijinska's "happy" influence. To be sure, discordant notes could be heard in the chorus of praise. Why program so few new works? There were allusions to her temper, a few calls for her dismissal, and one or two homophobic accusations about the effeminacy of Golovine's dancing in *Spectre* for which she alone was held responsible.[75] A few critics mentioned the absence of John Taras, whose dismissal she almost certainly engineered.

Nijinska disliked Taras intensely. A member of Ballet Theatre in the 1940s, he had studied at the School of American Ballet, and when he began to choreograph Balanchine's influence was evident. Taras joined the Grand Ballet in 1948 both as a choreographer and ballet master, and immediately clashed with Nijinska. With so many former students in the company, Nijinska followed Taras from afar. Most wrote to her in French, telling her about their travels, the full houses they were enjoying, who was dancing what ballet, and how much it rained. They also told her how much they missed her classes and disliked those taught by Taras, which company members had to take. "Taras gives class every morning," wrote Paul Maure in 1951, "and believe me never in my life have I seen classes as bad as his. But . . . one has to do what he wants even if everybody detests him."[76] Ten days later Nancy Clement wrote: "The class of Mr. Taras is the most awful thing in the world. But everyone must take it or pay a fine. So I work by myself after the class and remember all the things Madame says. . . . I wish Madame was here to give a class and to direct the company."[77] Maure also related Taras's efforts to revive *Les Biches.* "Next week we start Madame's ballet (Les Biches), but I think it will be a lot of work since Taras does not know the ballet very well, and all the dancers . . . are new."[78] Marie Levinson described him as a "conscientious ballet master . . . but only a very mediocre choreographer," speculating that it was to "counterbalance Taras's failures that the Marquis had just engaged Nijinska."[79] Taras, who spent the next several years choreographing in Europe, described her years later as ungrateful and "jealous." "She criticized everything," he told the former Cuevas dancer Taina Elg.[80]

By 1953, Marie Levinson had become a fierce Nijinska partisan, arguing that "the passing of the years instead of hardening her had exalted her." Citing her father's frequent criticism of "the rigidity of [Nijinska's] formulas and the dryness of her manner," Marie declares that André Levinson would have welcomed "her new way of being." She went on to address the issue of Nijinska's exigent personality.

> Nowadays . . . the force of a personality and the authority it confers too often collide with the passivity or the incomprehension of young people calling immediately for rescue from dictatorship. Petipa or Cecchetti, were they

resurrected, would be confronted in all likelihood with a world resistant to their mark. Who can say if their genius, colliding with innumerable *vetos*, would develop and mature in harmony?

Bronislava Nijinska has, as one says colloquially, her work cut out for her. She must efface the Taras influence, which extends from choreography to teaching, alas! She must restore a repertory distorted by negligence and obliviousness; she must, in a word, re-gild the shield of a company that begins to run out of steam. . . . Let us leave her to carry out this time-consuming work.[81]

But, she adds, "it is physically impossible for Nijinska to choreograph, rehearse, supervise, and teach simultaneously."[82]

In 1952, not long after Nijinska rejoined the company, the Marquis sent her a note in his favorite green ink, acknowledging that his company was "full of intrigues" and that most of the dancers were "mediocre."[83] With the renewal of Nijinska's contract, the two began cleaning house. Dancers were let go and new ones hired, and the company slightly enlarged. The departures rankled friends and fans, and explain some of the swipes at Nijinska in the press. But her singling out of Golovine as the reincarnation of her brother not only in the casting but also in the press roused the green-eyed monster. George Zoritch, rescued by Nijinska from a lackluster career in Hollywood, was livid. Years later he was still smarting from the humiliation. During rehearsals of *Le Spectre de la Rose* she all but ignored him and his partner.[84]

For Zoritch, a dancer frequently singled out for his beauty, Nijinska was grotesque. Her hair, he wrote in his memoirs, was colorless and grey, dyed some kind of red and "looked like patches of withered grass after flying saucers chose her head for an earthly landing site." He described her looks as "feverish," her eyes "bulging [and] glistening wet," her complexion jaundiced and unhealthy.[85] Such animosity was at least partly payback for her behavior in class. As Brazilian dancer Beatriz Consuelo recalled, even though Nijinska corrected and paid attention to everyone, she was harder on the men, always comparing them unfavorably to her brother.[86] However, Zoritch also baited her. The Mexican dancer Felipe Segura remembered him arriving late to class and without so much as a word of apology beginning his warm-up exercises in the middle of the studio. Nijinska stopped the class; he calmly went on. She exploded at him in Russian, English, and French.[87]

However much the Marquis adored his dancers and his galas, the backbiting and jockeying for roles and position reveal endemic problems of discipline and authority that plagued the company. Who had the final say? Who kept order in the ranks? Who made sure that performances were consistently up to standard, above all on the company's long tours? In 1953, Nijinska was approached by Michel Katcharoff, who had worked for Ida Rubinstein in 1931 followed by more than twenty years with the major Ballet Russe companies, first as a dancer and since the mid-1940s as a régisseur or rehearsal master for Denham. Could she use him? Yes, she could, and within weeks he had signed a contract with the Marquis. By the time he arrived in December, Nijinska was back in California, and it was Katcharoff who conducted rehearsals, while another newcomer, Felia Doubrovska, gave company class. In March the Grand Ballet began its travels: three weeks in Egypt, a week in Paris, then Belgium, Bordeaux, and South America. Katcharoff wrote that he and Yura—George Skibine—were coping with rehearsals and performances, but discipline could be better.[88] On June 30, Katcharoff wrote to her from Rio, where they were in the middle of a three-week season. He tells her how hard it has been for him to work. "The dancers don't want to do anything, and there is nobody to discipline them. . . . Total chaos." The principal dancers—Hightower, Skibine, etc.—rehearse several ballets, but he is not allowed to work with them. At the same time, none of them wants to rehearse *Petrouchka*, and when they do rehearse, they behave horribly, with Michel Resnikoff, one of the company's principals, being "especially rude."[89] Katcharoff managed to hang on until 1955.

Nijinska deserved at least some of the blame. She wanted to rule the roost but refused to put in the time, and regarded pretty much everyone as usurping her place unless she had proof in advance of their loyalty. The Marquis, of course, wanted Nijinska at his side full-time or at least nine months of every year. When she left Paris in December 1953, he was desperate. "Douchka chérie," he cabled on December 22. "Situation very serious. Come back soon. Sorry to ask this sacrifice, but life of the company depends on you."[90] On February 2 he sent her another cable, begging her to go with the company to Argentina: "Forgive me for insisting, but I need you, and if you can endure fatigue of the Argentine trip, would keep you the whole year."[91] A letter soon followed: "Without you I feel lost. I would like most vehemently to have you back with the Company. In London they were a discredit to me. I understand that you get tired with all the difficulties but we should arrive at an arrangement whereby you should be with me for nine months of every year as long as you like, and that during the three months you have a rest in the States."[92] In the end she agreed to a five-month contract beginning on August 1,[93] an acknowledgment perhaps that she wasn't really cut out to be an artistic director, however much she wanted things her own way. George Skibine, who knew her well, suggested as much in an interview in the 1980s:

[S]he was never an artistic director. What she was was a very innovative choreographer. I think she influenced many people. Ashton . . . wrote that she influenced him very much. Now Balanchine, he says not, but I'm sure he was very influenced by Nijinska. And the younger choreographers, even myself, we were more influenced by her than by Massine. . . . She was musical [and] . . . [h]er choreography had logic. . . . She didn't leave many ballets. In a way she was running a continuous workshop. Even when she redid those ballets, she never did the same choreography—she was always changing and improving, always looking for something else. Also, she had so much integrity, and I think that besides Balanchine she had the most integrity. . . . Once we got into a fight—or let's say a big discussion—and afterward, I think, she felt that her argument had been wrong and she came to me and she said, "Forgive me . . . but for me ballet is a religion—and I am a fanatic!" And it's true, she was.[94]

Perhaps because they had studied with her and owed their jobs to her, the American dancers got on better with Nijinska. So, too, did Vladimir Oukhtomsky, in part because he had experience in dealing with "deaf people." "She was greatly respected," he told Michael Meylac in 2005. But she was also "rather deaf."

The dancers were forewarned . . . to speak to her loudly and clearly or she would get very angry. And nobody understood what she was saying either—like all deaf people she was afraid of raising her voice. She whispered or, when she wanted to correct something, she tapped lightly on the shoulder. But I had an easier time than most. The thing is, . . . [m]y Ossetian grandmother had very bad hearing, so I knew how to converse with Nijinska. I shouted, "Forward," "Back," "Yes" and "Good," and so on. Everyone was terrified, but she was delighted and gave me roles—even more difficult ones than I might have wished for.[95]

In addition to hearing problems complicated by language ones, Nijinska's treatment of her husband alienated men in the company. Carlos Carvajal, a dancer from San Francisco who met Nijinska in 1960, felt that she tended "to emasculate men," especially Singaevsky, who followed her about like a "big puppy," always with an ashtray, since she smoked non-stop.[96] When one of the French dancers lit up a cigarette, Skibine recalled, "she charged up to him and said, 'You shouldn't smoke!' . . . 'But madame, what about you—you're smoking.' Then Nijinska . . . turned around to her husband, who was . . . walking behind her carrying an ashtray . . . and flicked her cigarette at him and said, '. . . yes, but *I* have an ashtray!' "—a statement unlikely to endear her to anyone.[97]

Although the de Cuevas company spent months on the road during the early 1950s, Paris was its home. Here Nijinska became something of a celebrity, interviewed, invited to book signings, cocktail parties, and the magnificent suppers hosted by the Marquis after premieres. The Association of Dance Writers and Critics organized a reception in her honor.[98] In June 1953, when Serge Lifar had Nijinsky's remains dug up in London and reburied in Paris at Montmartre Cemetery, Nijinska was there, along with the "Tout-Paris of Dance, Letters, and Journalism," as the magazine *Pour la Danse* reported. Lifar, overcome with emotion, "exalted the unforgettable artist and saluted the day . . . as a victory," while a government official declared, "At last [Nijinsky] returns to France, which he loved, served, and whose National Ballet continues his great dream."[99] As Françoise Reiss, one of the younger French dance journalists, confided to Nijinska, the sole reason Nijinsky's body was disinterred was "publicity for S. L."—Serge Lifar.[100]

By then the two women had developed a rapport and even something of a friendship. In January 1953, as the Empire season wound down, Reiss conducted a long interview with Nijinska that she would publish in the 1952–1953 edition of her "dance annual," *Sur la Pointe des pieds.* Wearing a black suit, smoking numerous cigarettes, and speaking French, Nijinska roamed freely over her past, clearly enjoying the attention and the experience of sharing her ideas with a knowledgeable, intelligent listener. Reiss was one of the few journalists Nijinska ever talked to about the School of Movement in Kiev, describing its curriculum and calling it a "laboratory of dance." Here, she asserted, she became a choreographer by creating the "demonstrations" that were intended to prepare her students to dance her brother's choreography. But she doesn't mention the repertory of solos she created, or her first plotless dances, or her published and unpublished theoretical texts. Everything, in her telling, was for Vaslav—the school, its artists, and herself, the willing handmaid of his genius. For Nijinska at this point Vaslav could do no wrong. "He was the God of the Dance and . . . the most honest artist I have ever known," she told Reiss. "There was nothing small-minded about him. He worked . . . to enrich his soul. . . . Vaslav was great because of the soul he had to express."[101]

Nijinska did mention the book she was writing about Vaslav and their family. "One part of this book," she told Reiss,

> remained in Paris. The other was begun in America. It is a continuation of the diary that I have been writing since I was eighteen. Numerous pages are devoted to my brother [and] . . . how he danced in different ballets. The need to earn my living has kept me from finishing a task that I consider a duty because there are certain truths to rehabilitate.[102]

It's unclear whether the part she says she left in Paris was a memoir (as outlined in the mid-1930s) or a book focused on her brother. The second part, written in the United States, was *Diary of a Young Dancer*. Suddenly, the book she had wanted to write for over twenty years, ever since the publication of Romola's biography of Nijinsky, seemed important again. Paris joined Nijinska's past to her present, emphasizing her historical link with the Imperial Theaters, the Diaghilev company, and the here-and-now. She had staged authoritative versions of *Spectre*, *Petrouchka*, and *Princess Aurora*, stood at her brother's grave, met people familiar with the long arc of her career: all this confirmed the sense of artistic worth that living in California and working in the United States had undermined. And she could communicate directly with critics and others in French as she couldn't in English. Energized, Nijinska decided to spend the first half of 1954 in California working on her book.

In May 1953, Gallimard, one of the most prestigious French publishers, brought out the French version of Nijinsky's diary, translated from the English volume published by Romola in 1937. Françoise Reiss, who read the diary as soon as it was published, immediately wrote to Nijinska about adding a "chapter" about it to her "Annual." "The book has shaken me, making present . . . a great soul whom I have not had the privilege of knowing in the flesh. . . . Can you meet me tomorrow?"[103] As Reiss later explained, her idea was to write a "study of the subject comparing the points of view of the psychiatrist, philosopher, and theologian." However, this proved too ambitious for the "Annual," and Reiss was advised by the publishers to incorporate her idea into a more biographical work. Reiss then wrote to Nijinska (who had returned to California) about her change of plan, but the address was wrong, and the letter was returned; Reiss wrote her a second letter, to which Nijinska responded in fury. She was deeply offended and accused Reiss of interviewing her under false pretenses in January 1953 and of stealing her idea for a book about Nijinsky. Reiss assured her that at the time of that interview, "I didn't dream of writing a book about your brother. I came to see you, you, as you very well understood." She also addressed Nijinska's doubts (since vindicated) about the authenticity of the diary, which she had never seen as Romola kept the Russian original under wraps.[104] Finally, she assures Nijinska that it was never her intention to "compete" with her book about her brother. "As I explained to you in the first letter which you are only receiving today, I am persuaded that the more books an artist inspires, the greater is the proof of his genius. And if the works by parents and other close witnesses are indispensable and precious documents, it does not exclude works written from a different angle for [later] generations."[105] The disagreement ended her relationship with Reiss, who received a doctorate in aesthetics from the Sorbonne in 1956 with a thesis that she subsequently published as *Nijinsky, ou La grâce*.[106]

Nijinska made no further mention of her book when she returned to Europe in early August 1954. This time, in addition to restaging *Prince Igor* and *Swan Lake*, she was reviving two of her own ballets. Both had premiered in Paris—*Chopin Concerto* in 1937 by the Polish Ballet and *Bolero* in 1928 by the Ida Rubinstein company—and they would be Nijinska's swan song to the de Cuevas company until 1960. In fact, 1954 marked the end of Nijinska's close relationship with the Grand Ballet, which was running out of money. "You do know that I cannot go on without you," de Cuevas wrote in his French-flavored English in February 1954.

> Only I have to be frank. My possibilities are very limited. I have been obliged to transfer the property of my ballet company to the Ballet Institute. You will wonder . . . what this has to do with you. It is only to explain to you, darling, that we have no free capital left. We have expended all of the funds that we had free out of the Trust. The income of the Trust, of course, is taxed at 92% by the [US] Government, so when we receive $100,000 we have to pay to the government $92,000, leaving only $8,000 for us.

As usual, Cuevas exaggerated: high earners often paid less. Still, the handwriting was on the wall. As he explained to Nijinska, he had to cut back, reduce the number of dancers, and limit expenses.

> [Y]ou are my Guardian Angel, the inspiration of my ballet. I cannot maintain the level of the Company without you and, at the same time, I cannot

go over the amount that I am allowed. Then do you think we can agree with two round-trips yearly for you and Nikolas [*sic*] and $275.00 per week for twenty weeks, plus $150.00 per month additional for five months to take care of Mr. Carlin having deprived you of choreographing in the past, making a total of $6250.00?

Please, Dushka, let me know if this is agreeable to you, as I have the best will and tenderness for you.[107]

Nijinska responded to her "Cher Marquis" in similar high-flown language. "It is not me, but you who are the Guardian Angel of Ballet, its prosperity and life. We must all make concessions so that it can exist." Nijinska accepted his terms.[108]

As always, the opening of the Paris season, which took place this year on October 5 at the Théâtre Sarah-Bernhardt, was a grand affair. All the stars of the Sadler's Wells Ballet had come (the company was dancing at the Paris Opéra), and dahlias, mimosas, and lilies scented the theater. A glamorous supper party followed at the Tour d'Argent—who would believe the Marquis was out of money? It was the company's tenth anniversary, but Nicole Hirsch, the dance critic for *France-Soir*, was impressed both by the "youth and vitality of the troupe" and by the "creative power of its principal choreographer, Madame Nijinska." The "most important" of the evening's creations, she wrote, was "without doubt" her *Chopin Concerto*.

We are in the presence here of a work in which the dance aims only to express and illustrate the music. In arranging the groups, in fixing the steps of the dancers, Mme. Nijinska has thought first and foremost of rendering the delicate poetry and sensibility of Chopin's work.

She has succeeded too in lightly stripping the choreography. One thinks at times of Fokine and at other times of Balanchine. Marjorie Tallchief, even more touching and precise than usual, was an ideal interpreter. The adagio she danced with George Skibine remains one of the high points of the evening and also of *Chopin Concerto*, one of the most important creations of the year.[109]

To be sure, there were critics who found the ballet too classical, too abstract, too busy, and too old-fashioned. However, Emile Vuillermoz, still reviewing music and dance in his mid-seventies, called Nijinska's "translation" of

Chopin the work of an "authentic musician,"[110] which, given their past history, must have gratified her immensely.

A month later, on November 12, came the first performance of *Bolero*. Unlike *Chopin Concerto*, *Bolero* arrived with a pedigree. The music was by Ravel, the first production by Ida Rubinstein, and the original choreography by Nijinska. Now, with Natalia Goncharova, who had designed Nijinska's version of the ballet at the Opéra-Comique, she set about restoring the original. As in New York, there were critics who objected to Nijinska's faux Spanish choreography. Marie Brillant rose to her defense: "Mme. Nijinska did not choose to create an authentically Spanish choreography (in the folkloric sense of the term), but to render the hot Iberian atmosphere with flexibility and refinement (just like the author of *Carmen*, who never crossed the Pyrenees)."[111] Another critic wrote, "all praise to the Marquis de Cuevas for enabling us balletomanes of 1954 to see the *Bolero* that Nijinska staged twenty-six years ago! Of course, she has made changes. In twenty-six years what hasn't changed. . . . *Bolero*, with *Les Noces*, is Nijinska's best and most theatrical ballet."[112] Most critics expressed admiration for Marjorie Tallchief, but felt that she was miscast as the Dancer, with Dinah Maggie, for one, writing that she would have preferred seeing a "real gypsy" such as Rosita Durán in the role. (Durán had recently appeared at the Théâtre des Champs-Elysées with Vicente Escudero and Carmencita García.[113])

In the debate about *Bolero*, one voice is conspicuously absent—Maurice Béjart. After several years of dancing abroad, he had returned to Paris, where he created some of his earliest ballets for a company he had recently founded, Ballet de l'Etoile. In 1960 he moved to Brussels, and the following year, for his Ballet of the Twentieth Century, he choreographed his own celebrated *Bolero*. As in Nijinska's version of the work, the focus in Béjart's was a lone woman dancing for a crowd of lusting men. Nijinska had muted the suggestion of gender violence by placing women in the tavern crowd (although they had no functional purpose) and emphasizing the exotic Spanish setting. Just as he did in his staging of *The Rite of Spring* (which premiered in 1959), Béjart stripped the stage of scenery and dressed the dancers in the equivalent of practice clothes, universalizing the action by divorcing it from time and place. Béjart also eliminated the women from what now became an all-male group, a move that heightened the sexual tension between the single unattainable woman and the men around her. But he kept Nijinska's table, probably the most important link between the two productions. Although it apparently never occurred to her, Béjart's reinvention of her ballet length-ened its life by several decades.

Although Nijinska's contract had stipulated that she was to remain in Europe until December 31, she seems to have left before then.[114] No doubt she wanted to spend Christmas in California with her family. But one senses that changes were underway that Nijinska probably felt did not bode well for her continued association with the Grand Ballet. Rosella Hightower had left the company, depriving Nijinska of a beloved muse and the Grand Ballet of its greatest star. Although immersed in her own work, Nijinska cannot have been unaware of events that portended changes in the future direction of twentieth-century ballet. One was the gala season of Soviet ballet scheduled at the Paris Opéra in May 1954 by stars of the Bolshoi and Kirov compa-nies (the Kirov was the Soviet name for the Maryinsky starting in the 1930s) led by Galina Ulanova and Natalia Dudinskaya, the first ballet tour to take place in the wake of Stalin's death. But with the humiliating French defeat at Dien Bien Phu by the Soviet-backed Viet Minh a few days before opening night, the season was canceled by a government anxious to avoid hostile demonstrations. Although it came to naught, the season was a forerunner of the great Cold War ballet tours that began in 1956 when the Bolshoi Ballet visited London.

In August 1954, shortly after Nijinska arrived in Deauville, an exhibi-tion marking the twenty-fifth anniversary of Diaghilev's death opened in Edinburgh. Curated by the critic and editor Richard Buckle, the exhibi-tion coincided with the city's celebrated performing arts festival and drew so many people that it was transferred to London, where an expanded version opened at Forbes House in November. Buckle was indefatigable. He wrote to anyone who was anyone in his quest for the hundreds of designs, costumes, portraits, photographs, music, and memorabilia that documented the Diaghilev company's twenty-year history. He scheduled near-daily concerts, lectures, and discussions, and even had Diaghilev's fa-vorite Mitsuko perfume sprayed in the galleries. By the time the exhibi-tion closed in January 1955, more than 100,000 people had visited Forbes House (in addition to the 25,000 who saw the exhibition in Edinburgh).[115] A critical and popular success, the show revived interest in virtually every aspect of the Diaghilev company. Yet while it spoke directly to Nijinska's past as a dancer and a choreographer, she herself was all but absent from the exhibition and its publications. She lent nothing and was the only one of Diaghilev's major choreographers whose name did not appear on Buckle's

Committee of Honour. Although she appeared in two group photographs, there were no portraits of her, and her choreographic contributions to *The Sleeping Princess* and *Aurora's Wedding* are missing from Buckle's chronology of Diaghilev productions. There is no evidence that she was invited to the opening at Forbes House. For whatever reason she was effectively erased from Buckle's history of the company to which she had contributed so much. It is hard to resist the conclusion that being a woman had something to do with this.

Although a loving telegram or two followed Nijinska's return to the United States, it was only in March 1955 that the Marquis invited her to spend August and September "working her magic" before the opening of the all-important Paris season.[116] Anxious to know the lay of the land, Nijinska wrote to Prince André Wolkonsky, one of the company's administrators. He responded almost immediately. The company had enjoyed great success in North Africa, and as always the season in Cannes had gone well. In mid-April the Marquis intended to give the company three or four weeks off, but he had yet to finalize contracts for the remainder of the year, although Wolkonsky thought that the Paris season would take place at the Théâtre des Champs-Elysées. John Taras, after a number of freelance commissions, had been engaged as ballet master for the Egyptian tour only.[117] By August the Marquis' plans were still up in the air. Taras was now ballet master, but as Wolkonsky wrote, "this is absolutely not permanent." However, the Marquis had changed his mind about Nijinska. Instead of having her rehearse the company in Deauville, he was inviting Alicia Markova to work with the dancers before they opened in Paris.[118] And so, without even a line, the Marquis abandoned his "Douchka Chérie."

***

In May 1954, Nijinska and Singaevsky applied for a $12,500 mortgage from the Glendale Federal Savings and Loan Association to buy a new one-story house at 15207 Friends Street in Pacific Palisades, where they would spend the rest of their lives. The small backyard overlooked Potrero Canyon Park to the south and the Pacific Ocean to the west: a spectacular view for an unpretentious house, although it was packed with one of the finest ballet collections in Southern California. "I often wonder how she managed to get along," Skibine mused in an interview. "She just barely made a living. . . . Oh, she was well paid when she worked, but she never stayed long enough."[119] After returning from Europe in December 1954, Nijinska didn't immediately go back to teaching, as she usually did—at least not according to her income tax statement, although she may have done some teaching off the books. Instead, in 1955, the couple sold the vacant lot in Riverdale they had bought in 1951, the year they sold the lemon grove in San Fernando. Then, in 1957, they sold another property, this one in North Salem, a town of rolling hills an hour north of New York City, which they had purchased in December 1944. Each of these properties represented roads not taken, dreams of lives that failed to materialize. Because they were US properties, they appear on the couple's income tax returns, unlike the house in Louveciennes, which must have been sold by the early 1950s, when references to it in Nijinska's correspondence cease. The mortgage application lists other assets—a 1941 car purchased in 1947 and worth $1,550; furnishings for a complete house worth $5,000; over $4,300 in bank accounts, and a 2,000-volume library of art and theater books worth $20,000.[120] Cheating on taxes is a national pastime, and Singaevsky, who looked after the family finances, had learned how to use deductions to minimize the couple's net taxable income, which seldom exceeded $5,000 and sometimes dipped to below $1,000. Travel expenses, books, magazines, laundry, luggage, dry cleaning, records, work costumes and shoes, car depreciation, hearing aid adjustments, and evening dresses, along with hotels, meals, and tips for the time she spent abroad or in New York—everything was deducted, whether the expenses were personal or paid by employers such as the Grand Ballet and Ballet Theatre.

Among those who now worked privately with Nijinska was Tamara Toumanova, who settled in Los Angeles shortly after World War II. By then she had embarked on a freelance career, with prestigious engagements at the Paris Opéra, La Scala, London Festival Ballet, and the Marquis de Cuevas company. She made several feature films, including *Tonight We Sing* (1953) in which she played her idol, the ballerina Anna Pavlova, and had a starring role in *Invitation to the Dance* (1955), directed by Gene Kelly. In the mid-1950s, Toumanova began an international concert career with Wladimir Oukhtomsky, who had also settled in Los Angeles, as her regular partner. They toured extensively in Latin America and made frequent appearances in Southern California, with a repertory of warhorses such as the *Don Quixote* pas de deux and *The Dying Swan* in addition to new pieces. With no other commissions on the horizon, Nijinska created several short works for the ballerina and Oukhtomsky—*Italian Suite, Phaethon, Le Berger, The Three Dreams*—all of which were performed on tour and none of which, as Toumanova complained to the publisher of *Early Memoirs*, was even mentioned in the book's chronology of works.[121] There were probably others.

Another dancer who worked privately with Nijinska in the 1950s was Nina Novak. A teenager when Nijinska cast her in the Polish Ballet, Novak spent the early years of World War II studying in the ruins of German-occupied Warsaw with Leon Woizikovsky. Her family wasn't Jewish, but her father died in Dachau, a brother, Józef, in Auschwitz, and in 1944 she was arrested and sent with a sister to a labor camp near Buchenwald. Novak was one of the fortunate ones. Not only did she survive, but she managed to get to New York, where she began the arduous task of regaining her technique. In 1948 she joined the Ballet Russe de Monte Carlo, and two years later appeared in *The Polovtsian Dances*, rehearsing Nijinska's old part with the choreographer herself.[122] In 1955 she spent her summer vacation in California working with Nijinska on the role of Giselle, which she had never danced.[123] She didn't get the chance until 1958, and though a few critics found her interpretation bold and refreshing, most thought she was miscast.[124]

By then, Nijinska was finished with Denham. She was livid to discover that in October 1957 at the University of Puerto Rico, Denham had produced Novak's first ballet, *Variations Classiques*, which not only borrowed heavily from Nijinska's *Brahms Variations* but also used the same music, Ivan Boutnikoff's orchestration of Brahms's Handel Variations. "The use of this ballet," she wrote to Denham, "is a breach of copyright laws and ethics, and harms me morally and financially." Numerous students of hers had learned the ballet in her classes, including Novak; hence, it was only right that he remove the work from the company's repertory.[125] Denham would have none of it. He was besotted with Novak and had just hired her brother and sister-in-law. "The Brahms music belongs to the world," he replied. He had always wanted to use it for a ballet but being "reluctant to repeat ballets done by other companies," he decided to make a new one. "I certainly know that the choreography differs from yours as heaven from earth." He tells her that the company has new studios and regrets that she is so far way and does not "take a more active part in our balletic life."[126] So ended another very long relationship.

In 1959, after living quietly for several years in California, Nijinska was summoned one last time by the Marquis de Cuevas. His health was failing, and he had run out of money. But he would not leave without a farewell gift that would seal his legacy as a patron *extraordinaire*—a full-length production of *The Sleeping Beauty*, something no French company had ever done. For this glorious project the Rockefeller purse strings were loosened, and the Marquis invited his "très chère" Madame Nijinska to stage the production, along with a revival of *Rondo Capriccioso* for Hightower, for what he delicately referred to as the "same terms"—a salary of $250 a week commencing February 1, 1960, when she was to join the company in Cannes, and round-trip first-class travel for two. The three-month contract was extended for a second three-month period, and then on August 1 for another three months.[127]

As company ballet master and choreographer, Nijinska took charge of rehearsals as soon as she arrived in Cannes. De Cuevas was away, and in a letter she tells him that during intermission she visits his portrait in the foyer and imagines him thinking about all his ballets. "Discipline in the company is very good," she reports, "and the atmosphere . . . is very friendly and welcoming." Finally, she shares a few thoughts about *The Sleeping Beauty*. "Ever since my youth," she writes, the ballet's

> scenic realization always seemed too heavy, too cluttered, lacking . . . the naive quality of a fairy tale. . . . Already I see it differently from what other companies have done, but I can't and don't want to reach any decision until I see you and hear from your own lips your conception and suggestions.[128]

By late March, the company had left for Italy. Nijinska, however, was on her way to Paris for a meeting with Raymundo Larraín, a young nephew of the Marquis who was designing the production. She rejoined the dancers in South America. By April 23, when the company began a three-week season at the Teatro Colón, she had staged the Rose Adagio for Rosella Hightower, who performed it on opening night. The tour was Nijinska's sixth visit to Buenos Aires, and she returned as something of a celebrity. She was interviewed by Ofelia Britos de Dobranich for the magazine *Vea y lea*, and as was often the case when she was interviewed by women journalists, she replied to questions thoughtfully, sharing things that she normally kept under wraps. Nijinsky, she told Britos, did not leave a formal school, because he never gave classes. "I was the one who transformed his practice into theory. I realized intellectually what Vaslav did artistically"—perhaps the clearest statement of what she brought to their relationship. She believes that a classical foundation is essential in ballet, and in principle would eliminate scenery. Finally, she asserts that while the Bolshoi eloquently demonstrates the continued relevance of

Russian ballet, the company itself was stuck. "It remains magnificent, but it hasn't changed. There is no reflection, for example, of the change in Russia wrought by the Revolution. It is an art of 40 years ago, in which one remarks only an excess of the acrobatic. In a country of such sweeping development, dance continues looking to the past."[129]

After performances in the Argentine cities of Rosario and Mendoza, the company flew over the Andes to Santiago de Chile. Here they were greeted by dancers from the Ballet de Arte Moderno, a new classical repertory company. There were five performances at the Teatro Municipal, and although the stars were commended, at least one critic found the corps wanting in technical precision and professionalism.[130] On May 21 an earthquake struck Chile's southern region, destroying most of the city of Concepción; a musicians' strike had miraculously kept the company in Santiago, although the set for Giselle's house (which had been shipped in advance) became temporary shelter for the homeless. There were tremors in Santiago, and with Marie Fredericksz as their intrepid leader, the terrified dancers fled north to Lima, where a new round of tremors sent them back to Buenos Aires. From here they moved up the Atlantic coast, performing in Montevideo, São Paulo, Rio de Janeiro, Cali, Medellín, Bogotá (where bottles of oxygen enabled the exhausted dancers to perform despite the altitude), Caracas, and finally Mexico City.[131] Despite everything, company discipline was maintained, and this was noted by critics. As Renzo Massarani observed in Rio, "Nijinska's improvements have brought the Company to an apogee. The ensemble moves in perfect harmony, and nothing . . .—a step, a gesture—is ever out of place: a Company that during three hours was perfect."[132]

Gradually, *The Sleeping Beauty* took shape. Like Diaghilev's production, it was never intended to be an exact copy of the Maryinsky original or a revival that laid claim to "authenticity." George Skibine, who did not take part in the ballet, told Peter Anastos that he didn't think Nijinska remembered any of Petipa's choreography although she certainly "understood the style of the classics." He also claimed that the reason she "gave up" the production (of which more later) was that she didn't have "a good memory for other people's ballets. She knew some of the variations, but for the whole staging she was at a loss."[133] Jack Anderson, who interviewed Nijinska for *Dance Magazine* in 1963, described her approach to the "standard classics" as "preserv[ing] the original choreography when possible, creat[ing] new dances in the proper period style when the old choreography is lost. And, if she deems it necessary, she adjusts parts of the ballet to contemporary taste, without destroying period feeling"—the reason she created additional dances for Prince Florimund.[134] Rosella Hightower was the first-cast Aurora, and as always she was Nijinska's inspiration. "The first act was traditional," Hightower explained in the 1970s. "The usual pas d'action. . . . The Rose Adagio was traditional. The variation in the first act was traditional. And the last act. . . . She didn't want to change the last [act]. . . . But the Vision Scene . . . when Nijinska did it, she really did her [own] ideas."[135] According to Hightower, Nijinska rechoreographed the whole Vision scene, including Aurora's variation. "It was . . . special in the same way that *Brahms [Variations]* and *Rondo Capriccioso* [were] special . . . so technical and so flowing and so *lyrique* and so brilliant and just so many things."[136]

A fragment of Nijinska's variation performed by Hightower can be seen today on YouTube. It looks totally different from Russian-derived versions with their repeated leg foldings, "nailed" balances, and limited repertory of turns. Instead, there are turns in arabesque and *à la seconde* that seem to float of their own accord from position to position, their mechanics hidden and at times so slow as to seem almost suspended in space. When the tempo picks up, Hightower launches into a series of quick fouetté turns, with the working leg just above the ankle, followed by quick, tight chaînés. Hightower's Aurora is anything but a girl-child in search of first love. She is an extraordinary woman dancing alone.[137]

By August, Nijinska was back in France, where the company was performing in the spa town of Aix-les-Bains in the Alps. Here she received a letter from Horacio Guerrico expressing his gratitude for the "understanding" she had shown with respect to problems (not spelled out) posed by *The Sleeping Beauty* and looking forward to seeing her during the company's Deauville season.[138] By now seriously ill, the Marquis was living in Cannes at his villa "Les Délices," cut off from Nijinska and largely incommunicado. On September 15 she wrote to Guerrico, returning her contract with suggested changes and raising the issue of "order and discipline." It had become impossible to continue working with the French-trained ballet master Daniel Seillier, and she reminds Guerrico that he had given her his "word as a gentleman" that the situation would change once they got to Paris. She then tells him that "the power and all the responsibilities of the company's 'Ballet Director' should be solely and completely in my hands—this is how I was engaged, and I have a contract with the Marquis from when I began my work on 'Sleeping Beauty' that excludes absolutely the presence of another Ballet Master during the 'Sleeping Beauty' season. I await your final decision on this matter so that I can continue my work."[139] At this point Act III remained unfinished.

Less than two weeks later, Nijinska was fired. The letter dismissing her, shakily signed by the Marquis, was blunt. "You were engaged by the Company for three months beginning 1 February 1960. Your contract was extended for a new three-month period. Since more rehearsals were needed, it was necessary to consider extending your contract for a second time. We did not agree on the terms for this extension. Consequently, you are no longer a member of our Company, since your contract has not been extended. . . . Your first-class return ticket to Los Angeles will be at your disposal as soon as you let us know the date of your return to the United States."[140] Nijinska tried to reason with the Marquis but to no avail. In desperation, Nijinska removed the piano score of the ballet, then sheepishly returned it.[141] By then, barely a week remained before the premiere.

What provoked the crisis? According to Irène Lidova, the company's publicist, when Nijinska saw the costumes designed by Raymundo Larraín, she flatly refused to use them. There was a huge blow-up, and "to the great despair of the Marquis," she decided to withdraw without finishing the work. The Marquise was called to help. She arrived from New York, but despite the hundred roses that she sent her, Nijinska remained intractable.[142] This supports Nijinska's contention in a 1963 *Dance Magazine* interview with Jack Anderson that the costumes and scenery were "a betrayal" of Petipa and Tchaikovsky, and in some cases so bulky that the dancers could barely move.[143]

De Cuevas had always had a fatal attraction to the opulent, to the feathers and frou-frou of theatrical fantasy. But Larraín's costumes for *The Sleeping Beauty* were over the top, even for the Marquis. Nothing was left untouched, no surface plain or unadorned. Here was the age of Marie Antoinette rendered as an extravagant, outré masquerade—towering headpieces, some more than two feet high; plumed and jeweled crowns; feather-covered tutus, claws, cobwebs, spindles, fronds, baubles and gewgaws of every kind, huge faux gemstones, and drop-dead makeup. Literally nothing recalled the storybook innocence of Nijinska's vision of the ballet or of any other production, however sumptuous.

Rosella Hightower paints a more complicated picture. Nijinska, she recalled, "suffered terribly" with Larraín's "huge, complicated, expensive, and emotionally unsettling undertaking" and was appalled when her demand that the most cumbersome costumes be modified was rejected. Hightower saw what was happening but could do nothing to stop it. "Suddenly, Robert Helpmann arrived and Nijinska immediately walked out."

> It was a very difficult time. Helpmann came to me for help, and I did what I could. He was very upset and rightfully so, because he had no idea Nijinska was still involved until he arrived. . . . [I]t was a horrible experience.[144]

Helpmann, who was credited with the production's *mise en scène* but not its choreography, was a leading member of the Sadler's Wells Ballet during the 1930s and 1940s as well as an experienced choreographer. According to Hightower, he finished Act III and "re-worked certain things," presumably bringing them in line with the Sadler's Wells *Beauty*, a ballet he knew well. But Hightower was adamant that everything she danced was choreographed by Nijinska.[145] Meanwhile, to counter rumors that she had resigned, Nijinska contacted critics and editors of Paris newspapers, declaring that "contrary to what is being said I did not give my resignation to the Marquis de Cuevas." Rather, it was "the company's management that suspended my work for a reason that . . . I prefer not to elucidate." She also wanted to make clear that her "mission was not to reconstruct the old choreography of Marius Petipa" but "to create a new choreographic version, which I have done."[146]

The Sleeping Beauty opened on October 27 at the Théâtre des Champs-Elysées, where *The Rite of Spring* had premiered in 1913, an irony not lost on more historically minded critics.[147] With eighty dancers, including seven *étoiles*, seventy musicians, and 200 costumes, the production cost somewhere between 100 and 150 million francs, well over a million dollars today. To finance it, Cuevas had sold the grand apartment on the Quai Voltaire, then, with his usual flair for publicity, announced to the press that *Beauty* was his last ballet, that he had given it everything—his money, his health, and his passion, and that the company would dissolve at the end of the Champs-Elysées season.[148] There were bulletins from Cannes about his health, rumors that he had died, finally, news of a rally that meant he could travel to Paris for the premiere. This time, there was no Republican Guard to welcome the gala audience. Instead, there was the Marquis himself, flown from Nice, driven by ambulance to the Plaza Athenée Hotel, and now sitting in a wheelchair in the "Loge d'Honneur" as statesmen, ambassadors, movie stars, well-known writers, painters, composers, and a considerable delegation of European aristocracy paid homage to the man who had spent his entire fortune on ballet and offered his final spectacle in Paris. It was long after midnight when *Beauty* ended under a shower of rose petals. But hundreds of spectators remained in the theater as Rosella Hightower embraced the Marquis in his box. It was pure theater.[149]

Olivier Merlin, who reviewed the production for *Le Monde*, was not altogether convinced by the choreography. He begins by asking whether *Beauty* could be reconceived along modern lines as Roland Petit had done with *Carmen*. He also muses about updating the ballet's look. "One could have had recourse to a modern like Dalí, [Antoni] Clavé, or [Jean] Carzou, or a frankly abstract painter," he writes. "Instead, Mr. Raymond Larraín, who is the Marquis' nephew, has given us sets and costumes of enchanting richness and color that reach back to the plumed style of a [Jean] Berain via the surrealists of 1925." But he wonders how "the fifty unhappy dancers, who already have a hard time keeping their heads on their shoulders and not treading on other people's toes, could dance under the tons of plumes and fabrics?"[150] In *Arts* music and dance critic Jacques Bourgeois reproached Larraín for the "assemblage of candy-box colors in the first scene and the tortured orientalism of the last." But he also praised the scenery for the Enchanted Forest and costumes like Carabosse's, along with details such as the precious stones that covered Aurora's hair and part of her face in the wedding scene and the rose-plumed court mantles for the royal couple in the apotheosis.[151] It was a feast for the eye even if, as a cynic in the audience remarked, all the talk was about feathers: how many, how much they cost, and whether there were more at the Casino do Paris.[152]

Although many came for the spectacle, others went back again and again for the dancers. One was Monique Paravicini, a ballet enthusiast from Monte Carlo and something of a company insider, who sent Nijinska photographs of Hightower as Aurora just after the New Year. Once in Paris, Paravicini went to see Nijinska's "beautiful ballet" numerous times, "all the time thinking of you," as she wrote, "and [your] tremendous work."

> I am sure you already know all about its triumph, which is your triumph and Rosella's as, of course, you felt from the beginning. She is the only real "Beauty," the only one who is able to look as marvellous as a dream. She is more and more extraordinary every day.
>
> From my feeling and I think everyone's, the greatest part is the "Vision" of Act II. I didn't miss one of her performances; we could see this "variation" again and again forever.[153]

The Marquis also returned again and again to the Champs-Elysées. He sobbed to reporters, "If I must die, I will die backstage."[154] The producer Eugène Grünberg described these nightly performances as ensuring a long run for the production whose success was by no means guaranteed. "The Marquis . . . is an actor of genius," Grünberg wrote to Nijinska.

> Yes, he is ill, . . . but he is not dying, as gossip has it. Of course, his appearance at the theater was sensational. . . . The dying man loves theater so much he comes to his own theater to die. . . . But he didn't die, and the public started coming day after day to see the spectacle. You will say I'm spiteful, but I assure you, my dear, that I am right.[155]

Nijinska, meanwhile, was still waiting to be paid. Her pleas fell on deaf ears, and borrowing money to pay her bills, she flew home on November 19. Back in California, she waited until early December to approach the Marquise de Cuevas, imploring her to "resolve my relationship with the Administration of the Ballet."

> I assume that you are aware that my work was forcibly stopped on September 28, in the most unexpected and most undeserved way for me—as everything I had done and intended to do was, as always, only for the good and the success of the Company—and only what my artistic conscience and theatrical experience directed me to do. In addition to this serious moral pain, the Administration has not even bothered to settle my account.

Would the Marquise kindly request the Ballet's New York office to pay her?[156]

Eugène Grünberg was shocked by how shabbily she had been treated. Not that he was surprised—he was an old-timer in the theater business—but he didn't think they would treat "La Grande Nijinskaia" as badly as they had treated him. The people around Cuevas, Grünberg explained, are a "horde of gangsters trying to prove they are protecting his interests."[157] It was not until April 1961 that the New York attorneys for the Ballet Institute, which had a fiduciary relationship with the Grand Ballet, settled her claim, although she was still owed a considerable sum in royalty payments. Nijinska then sued the company for breach of contract. According to her tax statements, she was awarded $5,250 in damages in 1961 and received royalty payments of $2,060 and $2,000 in 1962 and 1963, respectively. With this her relationship with the Grand Ballet du Marquis de Cuevas came to an end.[158]

By then, the Marquis was dead, and his company no more. Nijinska learned of his passing in February 1961 from a Russian newspaper, probably *Russkoe slovo*, and immediately wrote to Rosella Hightower. "Although we knew for a long time that the Marquis' passing was imminent, I know . . . that for you it was a great sorrow. You worked so long with the Marquis, and he appreciated you so highly as a great and unique dancer, and was always so proud of you. . . . I sympathize deeply with your loss and recall with all my heart all the good we have received from him, and I share with all the Marquis' artists our common grief. . . . I think a lot about you and your future in ballet. I am sure you will bring great joy to the world of theater and ballet for a long time."[159]

The Grand Ballet du Marquis de Cuevas was liquidated on June 30, 1962. But before it limped to an end—the same year, ironically, as Sergei Denham's Ballet Russe de Monte Carlo expired—it had one last flash of glory. On June 23, 1961, Rudolf Nureyev, who had just defected from Leningrad's Kirov Ballet, danced the role of Prince Florimund with Nina Vyroubova as Aurora in the Grand Ballet's *Sleeping Beauty*.[160] A new era in the history of ballet was dawning, and Nijinska would be part of it.

16

Resurrection

Battered and humiliated, Nijinska returned to California. On December 27 (Old Style), 1960, she turned seventy. One imagines that Irina and her family came to celebrate and that Nijinska was happy to see her grand-children, George, who had just turned thirteen, and ten-year-old Natalie. Otherwise there was little to celebrate. It's likely that she experienced an episode of depression, as she had in 1931 and 1938, when periods of in-tense effort had ended in the crippling loss of her work. She later wrote that for three years after *The Sleeping Beauty* she had no desire to work in ballet.[1]

By the early 1960s, however, Los Angeles was a hive of homegrown ballet activity, as many of Nijinska's former students returned to California, where they opened studios and formed ensembles that performed throughout the Southland. In 1964 a new player appeared—George Balanchine, whose New York City Ballet had been making frequent tours of Los Angeles. People began to clamor for something more than the city's usual "scrappy" performances, and who better to come up with a solution than Balanchine, who had just received the lion's share of a Ford Foundation grant earmarked for ballet companies and moved his New York City Ballet with great fan-fare to Lincoln Center?[2] Now, with assistance from Ford and under the aegis of James A. Doolittle, general director of the Greek Theater Association, Balanchine was brought to Los Angeles to audition local dancers and set up a school and a new company. He shared his breathtakingly naive—not to say patronizing—plans with Albert Goldberg, the *Los Angeles Times* music critic:

"I will bring my people—the teachers, choreographers and technicians— to get things started here. At the beginning we will probably have to send soloists too, for everything must be first class. . . . We will try to teach the local teachers how to teach and will send them money for scholarships. The best students will get to come to New York to study, with their living expenses and lessons paid for."[3]

In Pacific Palisades, Nijinska was irate. With her husband as a less than capable amanuensis, she wrote a long letter to the newspaper's editor-in-chief protesting this and two other interviews with Balanchine published in the previous two months. She called them "offensive to the existing Ballet Arts in Los Angeles and detrimental to their professional status, and in the same way touching me personally."

> Mr Balanchine . . . allows himself to criticize insultingly the standing of the Ballet Schools of Los Angeles and their leaders; speaking of them as being lost . . . and he being the only one who can bring them forth into the light of civilization. . . .
>
> Speaking of his project to create a "Los Angeles Ballet," Mr. Balanchine promises to bring from his New York Ballet and School the following: Teachers for Ballet Schools, Teachers to instruct the teachers how to teach; all of this flavored by his own interpretation of Dance Art, promising to send us all his own ballerinas, soloists, choreography of Balanchine, Costumes and Scenery, all other technical personnel (this is the Film Capitol [sic] of the World) and naturally all this under his own direction.
>
> His interview also sounds like a monopolistic dictatorship. . . . This is very detrimental to the development of this Art; making a closed door to the development of this Art; making a closed door to all other Ballet Artists and any new and different from his ways in Ballet progress.

Nijinska went on to list the city's many outstanding teachers and their leading students. "Los Angeles," she declared, "does not need the leadership of Mr. Balanchine, who hasn't anything in common with the Ballet Life of Los Angeles."[4] The *Times* declined to publish her letter, probably because of its length and grammatical shortcomings (although both could have been remedied by editing) but also because what she was saying challenged what the city's muscle-flexing cultural elite (and the *Times*) had decided to champion. As for Balanchine's Ballet of Los Angeles, by 1967 it had collapsed.[5]

On September 22, 1964, a week after she dispatched her letter, a telegram arrived inviting Nijinska to mount *Les Biches* for the Royal Ballet at Covent Garden in December. It came from Frederick Ashton, who had recently succeeded Ninette de Valois as the company's artistic director.[6] She wired back the following day. Yes, she would be "very happy to revive Biches for magnificent Royal Ballet" and could start on October 15.[7] The invitation was part of a broad strategy by the new director to expand the company's offerings, especially of twentieth-century works little known in mid-century Britain. Thanks to Ashton, Balanchine's *Serenade* and *Apollo* and Antony Tudor's *Lilac Garden* entered the company's repertory, along with the Shades scene from *La Bayadère*, mounted by Rudolf Nureyev in its first modern staging outside Russia. Most important of all, according to Ashton's biographer David Vaughan, "Bronislava Nijinska's masterpieces *Les Biches* and *Les Noces* were brought back to the stage after years of neglect."[8] Ashton explained why *Les Biches* was so high on his list:

> It has always been one of my favourite ballets and I look forward with extreme pleasure to seeing it again, and to having you among us. . . . To my way of thinking it is essential that the Royal Ballet should have a masterpiece in its repertoire from one of the greatest choreographers of our time.

He signed himself, "Your ancient pupil, Freddie."[9]

***

Nijinska's reputation in Britain was at a low ebb after World War II. Memories of her work for the Markova-Dolin Ballet, Colonel de Basil Ballet Russe, and Polish Ballet had faded. Critics wrote her off. Fernau Hall in *An Anatomy of Ballet*, published in 1953, got stuck again and again on Nijinska's "peculiar" looks, while decrying her choreography as exemplifying "post-expressionist pseudo-classicism," a style he abhorred. All her works, he claimed, "have the same cerebral quality: the steps are fitted to the music with characteristically expressionist mechanical precision, giving an effect of depressing pedantry to the choreography."[10] Peggy van Praagh and Peter Brinson, in *The Choreographic Art*, published ten years later, reiterated the connection between neoclassicism and expressionism in her work, even though they also acknowledged that her choreography "extended the range of classical movement through a neo-classical style which seemed sometimes to continue what her brother never completed."[11] Meanwhile, Arnold Haskell's *Balletomania* and biography, *Diaghilev,* continued to circulate, relegating her to a marginal position in the Diaghilev legacy, his warm words of the mid-1930s forgotten. And Richard Buckle wrote her out of his Diaghilev exhibition.[12]

Anton Dolin, who remained in touch with Nijinska, later claimed credit for planting the seed that led to the Royal's decision to revive not only *Les*

Biches but also *Les Noces*. As he recounted, he was visiting Nijinska in Pacific Palisades, when she told him of "her earnest desire" to "re-create" them for the Royal Ballet. "Anton," Singaevsky begged him, "please talk to Ninette and Fred. You know Madam is no longer young and before she dies it is her great desire and longing to come again to London." Returning to London, Dolin passed on Nijinska's request to "Sir Fred." "Good God," Ashton responded. "Does she, can she remember them? Amazing!" Dolin assured him that her memory was "one hundred per cent."[13]

And so on October 17, 1964, less than a month after Ashton's initial telegram, Nijinska left California, flying via New York with her "secretary-husband," as she called Singaevsky. It was the first time Nijinska had been in London since 1939, and she must have been astonished at the explosion in style, fashion, and popular music that had transformed the city into an epicenter of the youth revolution. Instead of Bloomsbury, she was staying at the Rembrandt Hotel across from the Victoria and Albert Museum in fashionable Kensington. And so began the resurrection of her finest Diaghilev-era ballets, her rediscovery by a young generation of dancers and audiences, and the renewal of friendships that reached far into her past. The experience left her emotionally, intellectually, and artistically reinvigorated.

When rehearsals began on October 20, Nijinska finally met the splendid company that Ninette de Valois had built over the past thirty-eight years with vision, tenacity, and enlightened despotism. According to Ashton's biographer Julie Kavanagh, the dancers were initially a "little wary of the old woman with her crackling hearing-aid, who could communicate only in French."[14] But as the rehearsals went on, James Monahan wrote in the *Dancing Times*, the ballet became "a love-match between Nijinska and Sir Frederick's dancers."[15] Ashton sat in on rehearsals and went with her to costume fittings, reminding her that long ago in Paris she had told him, "*Tu es mon fils*."[16] Nijinska was now seventy-three, but her energy was phenomenal. "She rehearses for hours," a journalist commented, "throwing herself into each role in turn, shouting and gesticulating, pulling her young dancers into the precise composition she needs. . . . But Madame Nijinska stays magnificently composed."[17] She had left the studio autocrat at home and was "charm itself" to a reporter from the *Sunday Times*. "She says the Royal Ballet is so brilliant and well disciplined that she doesn't have to be so strict," he wrote.[18]

Still, what journalists saw and cameras recorded was not the whole story. Geraldine Morris, a very young, new member of the corps in the second cast of "pink ladies," remembered Nijinska eliminating people she didn't like or didn't think were working hard enough or paying attention to her.[19] In 1964 things were "still pretty unpleasant in the ballet world," Morris explains, but Nijinska "was much more frightening." She worked non-stop, repeating everything over and over until the style was right, all afternoon, without even a fifteen-minute break; the dancers were afraid of leaving the studio even for a glass of water. Morris has vivid memories of Nijinska demonstrating épaulement and using ballet "hand language" for the footwork. She was very insistent on detail in the shoulder and in the under-pull of the chassé. She wanted deep bends and a sense of weight, even in the way the dancers walked. Finally, Nijinska wanted speed. "*Les Biches* was fast," much faster than it is today.[20]

The casting was done by company people, although Nijinska had the final say.[21] Georgina Parkinson was not a contender in the company's mind for the Girl in Blue, but Nijinska had glimpsed her rehearsing Myrtha in *Giselle* during the lunch break and decided that this was the dancer she wanted. From the first rehearsal, Parkinson remembered,

> it was just as if I really couldn't do anything wrong. . . . [S]he loved everything. . . . By any standards, [I] was just not good enough. . . . I understood stylistically what she wanted because I could look at her, and immediately I could see what it was. But I couldn't execute it. . . . It was her unflinching faith in me. . . . She just always looked at me . . . as if she knew it would be all right. And it was, finally. But I have never had anybody believe so completely in me over so long a period of time. She never doubted me for one moment.[22]

Much of what Nijinska wanted challenged company practice. As Parkinson explains,

> The light invisible preparation. She wanted you to jump up to the sky, but she didn't want to see you preparing. Right then, we were in the middle of our Nureyev period—pliés down to the floor. One's preparations took *hours*. She didn't want to see that.[23]

Like many dancers, Parkinson's technique was transformed by Nijinska. ·

> We all thought we had used our bodies before Bronislava arrived, but we had not started, in terms of body movement. It was . . . only when Bronislava

came and taught us *Les Biches* that we realized what breathing was and what actual body movement was.[24]

The cast was splendid. Apart from Parkinson as the Girl in Blue, it included David Blair, Keith Rosson, and Robert Mead as the muscle-flexing Athletes (or "beefcake boys," as Peter Williams called them),[25] Merle Park and Maryon Lane as the "inseparable" Girls in Grey, and Svetlana Beriosova in Nijinska's own role as the Hostess. (Fluent in French, Russian, and English, Beriosova was Nijinska's unofficial translator.[26]) Marie Laurencin's scenery and costumes had been reproduced with "infinite care," and in the program was a "historical note" by Ivor Guest.[27] It was the grand premiere that Nijinska had never had. Waiting at Covent Garden were telegrams from Arnold Haskell; Ana Ricarda, who was now teaching Spanish dance at the Royal Ballet School; and Nijinska's "Blue Girl," Georgina Parkinson, thanking the choreographer for the "greatest role of my career" and expressing the hope that she will be able "to do you justice."[28] She needn't have worried; most critics agreed that she walked away with the evening's honors. And what an evening it was. As Richard Buckle observed, few new ballets or revivals had been so "enthusiastically received at Covent Garden in recent years as the production of 'Les Biches.' "[29] When the curtain fell, Nijinska received a thunderous ovation, and floral tributes, including one from Ninette de Valois, that turned the stage into a "garden of abundance," a "tribute," James Kennedy wrote in the *Guardian*, "to this stalwart survivor from the famous Diaghilev days, who has had the energy and detailed skill to teach to a new company a ballet which she first presented 40 years ago."[30]

The reviews were glowing, especially for the principals. Several critics commented on the change in mores that had lessened the shock value of the original "perfumed fable" (Coton), and wondered if the ballet, with its "old-fashioned choreography" and "day-before-yesterday chic" was "strong enough to live again" (Kennedy). Most remarked that *Les Biches* was the starting point for neoclassicism, noted the originality and "strong personal flavor" of the choreographic invention, and referred to the erotically ambiguous atmosphere, invoking the names of Proust and Ronald Firbank.[31] "The *special* thing about [the ballet] is its ambiguity," explained Richard Buckle.

Is the older woman with the Chanel pearls a hostess or a madam? Is the female dancer in the blue *gilet* with white gloves, who gets off with the leading man, meant to be a page-boy? Are the two blue-grey girls having an affaire? When the two athletes slump on the sofa are they exhausted with sex or female nattering? In fact, is everybody making love or conversation? It is so delightful not to know.[32]

Buckle was aware, as were a number of critics, that Nijinska had made changes in the Royal version, which she regarded as definitive. What, Buckle wondered, did old-timers have to say about them? Diana Gould (Menuhin), who had danced the role of the Hostess in the 1937 Markova-Dolin revival, acknowledged changes in "some of the details." But "the wonderful *épaulements* are the same and that essential Diaghilev quality which was Russian passion filtered through French taste."[33] Buckle also spoke to another former Hostess, Lydia Sokolova, who had taken over the role when Nijinska left the Ballets Russes. Given her mixed feelings about Nijinska generally, she was understandably huffy about the revival. She told Buckle, who had ghostwritten her memoir *Dancing for Diaghilev*, that "the once marvelous entrance and the pattern of the Hostess's dance were quite altered, and not for the better." The opening number with the pink girls now dragged, and the finale seemed meaningless.[34] For the critics, however, the choreography, as Clive Barnes declared, was "as solid as a sonnet."[35]

During the nearly two months that Nijinska spent in London, she renewed old friendships and reconnected with vital parts of her past. She was the honoree at a dinner at the Gautier Club attended by Haskell, Nigel Gosling, Mary Clarke, G. B. L. Wilson, and other dance writers.[36] She was invited to speak at the Oxford Ballet Club.[37] Joyce Berry, her devoted English student, who had danced in so many of her companies beginning with Theatre Choréographique, came up from Sussex to see her. "I was so happy to see you again—quite overjoyed," she wrote after Nijinska had returned to California, signing herself in Russian, "Always yours, Joyce."[38] Nijinska found time to visit Sergei Grigoriev in the hospital. She spent time with "Lubochka," his wife Lubov Tchernicheva, but was sad it couldn't have been longer.[39] Nijinska also renewed her friendship with Marie Rambert, and, as with Tchernicheva, this contact blossomed into a correspondence. In November, Rambert attended a rehearsal of *Les Biches* and was thrilled. "When I asked to come to the rehearsal, it was ... to see you demonstrate," she wrote in Russian. "Everything in the way you move is so interconnected, wide, and deep. I haven't seen this in anyone, except Vaslav. I doubt it exists nowadays. Today, everybody knows how to do everything, but there is no richness in the movement. In your voice one can hear all the harmonies—you know, like the notes that resonate when the main one has ended. . . . I am so excited about the premiere and will applaud till I go crazy."[40]

On April 21, 1965, the Royal Ballet opened a four-week season at New York's Metropolitan Opera House, the company's last in the "old Met" before it moved to Lincoln Center. Ballet was booming, and the Margot Fonteyn–Rudolf Nureyev partnership was at the dizzying height of its celebrity. The Met was packed to the rafters with notables from every walk of life, including Vice President Hubert Humphrey, to see the glamorous super-couple in the American premiere of Kenneth MacMillan's *Romeo and Juliet*. Altogether there were nine performances of the new ballet, plus five *Giselles* and six *Swan Lakes*, more than double the number of mixed bills, which included repertory favorites, a vehicle for Nureyev and Fonteyn, and the US premieres of Ashton's *The Dream* and the Shades scene from *La Bayadère*. In such company, *Les Biches*, inevitably, was overshadowed. There were only three performances, and although the principals were singled out, Allen Hughes of the *New York Times* was underwhelmed, in part because of John Lanchbery's "sluggish" tempos, which cast a pall over the ballet's bright and witty doings.[41]

A national tour followed. In late June the company opened at the Shrine Auditorium in Los Angeles, headed north for a week in July at the San Francisco Opera House, then returned south for three performances at the Hollywood Bowl. *Les Biches* was performed twice in both cities. Unsurprisingly, Los Angeles all but ignored the ballet, and one would never know either from the advance publicity or from the dismissive two paragraphs in Albert Goldberg's review in the *Los Angeles Times* that Nijinska had been living there for twenty-five years. "The dances were amusing, the music of Francis Poulenc is mordantly witty, and it all did not have quite enough substance for its length."[42]

In San Francisco, however, the ballet struck a receptive chord with the young dance critic Renee Renouf. "Dear Mme. Nijinska," she wrote on July 8, a few days after performances in the Bay Area had ended:

> Will you permit me to tell you how moved I was to have the chance to see Les Biches when the Royal Ballet performed it in San Francisco? It is a link with an era of which we younger balletomanes have little understanding and how alive your ballet made it, not only for myself but several other ballet devotees, dancers and teachers in this area. . . . I now feel I have had a

reliable insight and peek into the era of the Twenties which speaks to me a bit more clearly than F. Scott Fitzgerald.[43]

Thanks to a Ford Foundation fellowship, Renouf was about to embark on a whirlwind tour to observe professional and educational dance in Europe, the United States, and Asia. Before leaving, however, she wanted to stop in Los Angeles to talk to Nijinska about choreography. Nijinska, touched by Renouf's letter, agreed.[44] Accompanied by a friend, she visited the choreographer in September and a few days later described the visit to her nephew. "She lives in Pacific Palisades at the end of a street which overlooks the ocean with her second husband, with a great many memories and some beautiful books on ballet, [and] many, many pictures and posters of the ballets she choreographed. . . . She showed us all her pictures and books, and . . . after . . . inspecting Noverre's letter, she got very emotional and kissed it."[45] Jack Anderson, who interviewed Nijinska for *Dance Magazine* in 1963, adds other details to the domestic scene—walls covered with scenery and costume sketches, an extensive library and collection of dance memorabilia, drawings by Rodin and Raphael.[46]

***

As 1965 slipped by, Nijinska prepared for the revival of her greatest Diaghilev-era work—*Les Noces*—for the Royal Ballet in spring 1966. In the decade after she left Diaghilev, she had struggled to keep the ballet in repertory, restaging it several times at the Teatro Colón, for her own company in Paris in 1933, and for the de Basil company in New York three years later. Thirty years had elapsed since the ballet's last performance anywhere, and nearly forty since it had appeared in London. During those intervening decades *Les Noces* had entered the limbo where unperformed ballets languish until all hope of resurrecting them is gone. Thanks to Ashton's inspired leadership, *Les Noces* was spared, awakened like Aurora from a long sleep.

Nijinska's two great ballets bridged the eras of Massine and Balanchine, and their presence in active repertory reconfigured Ballets Russes history of the 1920s. Together, they insisted on her place in ballet's "apostolic succession" and the canonical status of her major Diaghilev-era works, placing them in conversation with those of her contemporaries. Reviewing a later performance of *Les Biches*, for instance, Alexander Bland noted the ballet's influence on Balanchine, singling out "the sudden, touching moment when the

Athlete lays his cheek in the hand of his beloved" that Balanchine repurposed in *Apollo*.[47] The revivals challenged received ideas about neoclassicism, plotlessness, and gender in ballet, and resuscitated Nijinska's reputation as a choreographic thinker. As Geraldine Morris observes in her book about Ashton, they "return[ed] Nijinska's work to mainstream dance theatre," while also "reviv[ing] interest in her choreography as a whole."[48]

Nijinska arrived in London on February 4, settled in at the Rembrandt Hotel, and spent the next six weeks rehearsing at the Royal Ballet studios in Barons Court. The rehearsals, which generally began at noon and ended at five, were grueling for both Nijinska and the cast. Nijinska herself never seemed to flag; even at seventy-five she still summoned the energy to demonstrate, displaying the "incomparable endurance" she had enjoyed in Diaghilev's day.[49] As Monica Mason told John Gruen, it didn't matter if she could barely speak English, "because she could show it. And it was the same quality that this old woman projected that gave us such insight" into the work.[50]

Nijinska cast Svetlana Beriosova in the all-important role of the Bride, which called for little dancing but a luminous presence, and Georgina Parkinson as the lead female Friend. Robert Mead was the Bridegroom, and over Nijinska's initial objections Anthony Dowell stepped into the role of the lead male Friend after her first choice was injured. She cared very much about the height of the women in the first tableau—they all had to be tall—and she spent a long, long time, according to Morris, braiding the heads in the pyramid at the end of the ballet. "She placed those heads over and over again, and we were hanging around. She didn't care. She went on and on."[51] Morris was hardly the only dancer who found the experience of reviving Nijinska's masterpiece less than gratifying. When Ian Woodward of *London Life* asked cast members for their views of the ballet, one well-known dancer told him that she "found it all rather 'stupid, senseless and eccentric.'" Another complained, "'What's bugging me about the whole thing is that we've not had a proper daily class for over a week.'" Only one of Woodward's respondents found the ballet "stimulating to do," "a rare experience" although "very 'un-Royal Ballet.'"[52]

As with *Les Biches*, the Royal stinted on nothing. Natalia Goncharova's designs were faithfully reproduced by the Covent Garden Production Department, as were the costumes, also made in-house. Taking a page from Diaghilev's playbook, the company enlisted four British composers—Richard Rodney Bennett, John Gardner, Edmund Rubbra, and Malcolm

Williamson—as pianists. The solo and chorus singers were from the Covent Garden Opera Company, and John Lanchbery conducted the Stravinsky music.[53] There was a long program note by Ivor Guest and an excerpt from *Expositions and Developments*, one of Stravinsky's "conversation books" with Robert Craft.[54] Nijinska herself wrote an article about the creation of *Les Noces* for Covent Garden's magazine *About the House* that for some reason wasn't published.[55]

The reviews were stupendous, a vindication for Nijinska after a lifetime of slights, rebuffs, and misunderstandings:

"It is Nijinska's choreography that comes as the evening's great shock. . . . Such surface simplicity inflected with such subtlety, such powerfully sculptured groupings, such a transformation of Russian folk dance into something new and beautiful. Even this choreographer's . . . *Les Biches* . . . had not prepared us for such strength and invention." (*Times*)[56]

"Nijinska plaits her dancers together, kneads them into knotted mounds, tugs them backwards and forwards like lengths of thick hemp. . . . The idiom is turned-in, crouching, crab-like, rhythmic, twisted as a Scythian brooch . . . and fiendishly difficult to dance, with point-work, jumps and runs in fantastic distorted poses. . . . How could the same mind create this solid sacrament . . . and also 'Les Biches'? . . . To see them together in this same programme—the foundation-stone of neo-classicism and a fountainhead of Modern Dance—was to set Nijinska securely in a top choreographic niche." (Alexander Bland, *The Observer*)[57]

"With 'Les Noces' . . . time has dealt kindly. . . . In fact the combination of Stravinsky's percussive score, . . . the small choir and the stamping, fierce energy of the choreography amounts to an enduringly successful attempt to express the roughness and simplicity of a Russian peasant wedding in theatrical terms. It is a ballet without stars . . . but its choral movements have a magnificent strength, at once simple and highly theatrical, and many of its groupings have a truly sculptural effectiveness." (James Kennedy, *Guardian*)[58]

"['Les Noces'] must now be classed among the handful of great ballets that can sustain comparison with the finest achievements in any medium. At the end I realised, as I have never done in 'Parsifal,' why some people feel applause is out of place. With potential tears gathering in my eyes I sat slowly returning to everyday things while waves of applause and enthusiasm surged around me. Only when Nijinska finally came on stage, a living embodiment of ballet's glorious past, . . . did I find myself applauding like a schoolboy." (Nicholas Dromgoole, *Sunday Telegraph*)[59]

When the curtain fell, Nijinska, surrounded by her dancers and masses of flowers, bowed again and again. A day or two later she received a French fan letter from Anthony Asquith, the noted British film director and son of Diaghilev's longtime patron Margot Asquith. "I must write to you, my dear Bronia, although I know that I will never find the words to express what I felt yesterday evening and what will always remain with me—humble admiration before a masterpiece. . . . When they threw flowers at you, I wept. . . . Ever your devoted Anthony."[60] A few days later Nijinska returned to California. A letter from Ashton, addressed to his "dearest Bronia," followed: "All the performances of 'Les Noces,'" he wrote,

> have had great impact and have given a great deal of pleasure. I, myself, find it a work of great genius, and I am very proud to have it in the company. It was, as always, a delight to have you with us, and I wish to thank you for leaving a great work in our careful possession. Please keep in touch from time to time as my devotion and gratitude to you know no bounds and I want you always to be a part of my life. All my love, Freddie.[61]

In 1967 the Royal Ballet included *Les Noces* in the repertory of its six-week season at the "new" Metropolitan Opera House in Lincoln Center. Unlike London, the work did not fare well in New York, where two years earlier critics and audiences alike had acclaimed the version of *Les Noces* brilliantly produced by Jerome Robbins for American Ballet Theatre's twenty-fifth anniversary season. Clive Barnes, now the influential dance critic of the *New York Times*, made plain his dislike of the Nijinska work, arguing again and again that the Robbins ballet was superior. One reason was that it complied with Stravinsky's wishes in placing the musicians and singers on stage. Another was because Robbins was "the finer choreographer." "His new version has a poetry and passion beside which the old original tends to pale."[62] Three days later, Barnes devoted an entire column to the Nijinska work, which he now called "fascinating and disappointing in equal measure."

> Seeing, for the first time, this Nijinska version . . . , I can at last apprehend its fantastic and joyous quality. Yet, for all its marvelous values, Stravinsky

really was right. Mr. Robbins, by following Stravinsky's message (and, let's be fair, following with genius), has produced a superior work.[63]

Barnes admitted that Nijinska's ballet had its "charms," but grudgingly. Although he could not put *Les Noces* on the same level as *Les Biches*, "it still retain[ed] the salty taste of originality and the special rhythmic pulse of true genius." He admired "its sumptuous and surprising architectural groupings, its fiercely rhythmic peasant accents," and "most of all . . . the dancing of the ensemble." But—and this is how Barnes ends his review—"choreographically, Mr. Robbins's version . . . is artistically superior."[64] Two weeks later Barnes returned to the subject. With the Robbins version being danced at the New York State Theater, just across the plaza from the Met, where the Royal was still in season, Barnes homed in on what the two productions shared, while pigeonholing Nijinska's ballet as "a child of its time."

> This is the great expressionist ballet—the groupings, almost gothically architectural, with hand laid on hand and head laid on head, and the automatically mechanized rhythmic punch represents the twenties with the certitude of a canvas by Léger. The Royal Ballet has preserved this feeling, not in dead amber but totally alive, so that its modernity lives.[65]

Barnes expressed the hope, as did a number of other critics, that both versions would remain in repertory. Los Angeles, however, never got to see Nijinska's ballet. The Royal did not perform it there (by one account, because of Sol Hurok's "conservatism").[66] Robbins himself, however, was overwhelmed by the Nijinska work. "It is a work of majestic inspiration," he wrote after seeing it.[67] Years later he told Irina Nijinska that if he had seen her mother's production, "he would never have created his own ballet to the same Stravinsky score."[68]

***

The resurrection of *Les Noces* and *Les Biches* at Covent Garden led to invitations to stage those ballets around Europe. The most promising came from Sonia Gaskell, artistic director of the Dutch National Ballet. Like Nijinska, Gaskell hailed from the borderlands of the Russian Empire, spoke Russian, and had a love of dance history; she was feisty, forward-looking, and independent-minded. Now, for a June 1967 premiere in Amsterdam, she invited Nijinska to choreograph Claudio Monteverdi's early Baroque opera *Orfeo*, and when Nijinska agreed, asked whether she could also mount *Les Biches* and *Les Noces*.[69] A contract for *Orfeo* followed on February 27.[70] It was Nijinska's first encounter with the Monteverdi score and her first project in decades that called for close collaboration (in this case with Raymond Rouleau, whom Gaskell described as "a very well-known and capable director").[71] By March 1, Gaskell had found a double room with bath at a "very good hotel near the theater for eighteen dollars a day," which Nijinska could easily afford with her fee of $2,500.[72]

Three weeks later Nijinska collapsed. "Madame Nijinska is very ill," Singaevsky cabled Gaskell. "Absolutely unable to come stage Orphee is terribly sorry . . . but forced . . . to cancel engagement.[73] In April, Nijinska wrote confirming her husband's telegram, explaining that she was now back home after two weeks in the hospital, but that the doctor had ordered two or three months of complete rest.[74] Gaskell was devastated. She then floated another proposition. Perhaps, when Nijinska recovered, she could stage *Les Noces*, *Les Biches*, and *The Sleeping Beauty*, "since, to tell the truth, the only good part of Cuevas's *Sleeping Beauty* was yours."[75] But for months afterward Nijinska lacked the energy to travel, and nothing came of Gaskell's proposition.[76]

In 1968, Aurelio Milloss, the Hungarian-born choreographer and dance director who had settled in Italy in the late 1930s, invited Nijinska to stage *Les Biches* at Rome's Teatro dell'Opera the following June. Over the years Milloss had created his own versions of numerous Diaghilev-era works, but never any of Nijinska's. Now, in the wake of the Royal Ballet's triumphant productions of *Les Noces* and *Les Biches*, he sought to remedy that. In 1966, two months after *Les Noces* returned to Covent Garden, he premiered his own version of the ballet at the Vienna Staatsoper, and two years after that, he revived it at the Rome Opera while Nijinska herself was there staging *Les Biches*.[77] The trip was Nijinska's first visit to Italy since the 1930s, when she had staged *Petrouchka* and the dances in Alfredo Casella's *La favola d'Orfeo* in Brescia, and her first time in Rome since 1929, while on tour with the Rubinstein company. The negotiations took place quickly, with the Italians accepting her $3,000 fee and $25 per performance royalty without quibble. She told Milloss that she needed "2 prima ballerinas, 2 solo danseuses, 3 danseurs with a strong classical technique, and 12 danseuses for the corps de ballet."[78] Her Girl in Blue was the young La Scala–trained ballerina Elisabetta Terabust, a dancer who recalled the young Margot Fonteyn and would reprise the role in Florence when the ballet was programmed with Balanchine's *Apollo* and Milloss's *La Giara* at the prestigious Maggio Fiorentino festival.

***

In 1969, Nijinska devoted most of her creative energies to a new company directed by Kathleen Crofton in Buffalo, New York State's second largest city. Crofton had danced with Anna Pavlova and in several companies in which Nijinska played a part. After World War II, Crofton opened a studio in London, taught occasionally at the Royal Ballet School, and wrote criticism for the *Christian Science Monitor*. In 1966, three years after she became director of the Metropolitan Opera Ballet, her friend Alicia Markova brought Crofton over from London to teach company classes.

Today, Buffalo may be a symbol of rust-belt America, but in the 1960s it was flush with dollars from New York State, now governed by arts patron Nelson Rockefeller. The city had a number of fine ballet teachers, including Stella Applebaum, who directed a studio called Dance Arts and sent a steady stream of students to the School of American Ballet, the Joffrey Ballet School, and Canada's National Ballet School for advanced training. Why not create a professional academy in Buffalo that would offer ballet training, academic schooling at a local private high school, and a residence for students from out of town, coupled with an exceptionally generous scholarship program? And why couldn't this school become the foundation for a professional ballet company? Applebaum's friend Lenore Glauber, a visual arts maven who shared her vision, set herself the task of persuading Franz T. Stone to fund the innovative project. The millionaire chairman of the Columbia McKinnon Corporation, Stone promoted the arts throughout western New York.[79] Not only did he agree to support the ballet project, he also became its exclusive benefactor. When Applebaum had to leave the Buffalo area, the Metropolitan Buffalo Association for the Dance, of which Stone was president, invited Kathleen Crofton to direct the new enterprise.[80]

The Ballet Center of Buffalo opened in a refurbished church at 111 Elmwood Avenue on September 11, 1967.[81] The scholarship students came from around the Northeast; they were between thirteen and seventeen years old, and all were chosen by Crofton at auditions in New York City and Buffalo.[82] In addition to "classical ballet," pointe, pas de deux, character dance, and "classical repertoire," the curriculum included mime, musical training, dance notation, history of ballet and costume, and makeup and general stagecraft—subjects seldom offered in American ballet schools.[83] Later, modern dance, taught by Cristyne Lawson, a Juilliard graduate and former member of the Martha Graham company, would be added. In other words, the curriculum was intended to give the pre-professional student a full ballet education. By its second year, noted *Dance Magazine*, the school had one hundred students and "the beginnings of a professional company."[84]

From the start, Crofton wanted Nijinska to be part of her new American project. "Dearest Madame," she wrote to Nijinska on March 17, 1968. "More than anything else in the world I want to see your wonderful work again, and this is giving me the courage to write to you now."[85] She explained that a strong effort was being made "to promote the arts here in Buffalo," including a plan to have "a first-rate ballet company . . . formed mainly from dancers trained in the Ballet Center of Buffalo."[86] Crofton then made her pitch. "Dearest madame, will you do us the great honour of mounting one or two of your marvelous ballets for our opening? This would be the most wonderful thing that could happen to us! Your work would be loved and cherished, and everything humanly possible would be done to present it properly."[87] Crofton specifically mentioned *Brahms Variations*, which Nijinska had choreographed for Ballet International and revived for the Marquis de Cuevas company. Given its technical demands, the ballet was an odd choice for a well-trained but inexperienced company and guest artists who could hardly be expected to match the combination of bravura and mature artistry of André Eglevsky, Rosella Hightower, and Marjorie Tallchief. Still, Nijinska was intrigued. In September 1968 she made a quick trip to see the dancers Crofton had been training for the past year, telling a local reporter, "I came to Buffalo because I always like to help new beginnings. I like to give my experience to young companies."[88]

In 1969, Nijinska spent nearly six months in Buffalo, traveling there on three occasions, with a fourth visit in the summer of 1970. During that time she staged *Les Biches*, *Brahms Variations*, *Aurora's Wedding*, *Chopin Concerto*, and two "suites," one from *Petrouchka*, the other from the second act of *Swan Lake*. She even hinted to a reporter in 1970 that she had something new in the works. ("I have an idea, but I don't want to talk about it."[89]) In other words, Nijinska's creative juices were still flowing. However, she was chiefly concerned about her legacy. Apart from *Les Biches*, all the works she staged in Buffalo were out of repertory, and she trusted Crofton to keep them alive and in good repair. Crofton's company was far from the Royal Ballet. However, it was a serious enterprise with admirably trained young dancers. "Last year,"

Nijinska told a reporter in 1970, "I mounted 'Les Biches' in Rome, and this year in Florence, both with professional companies, . . . and this company compared very favorably, from the point of view both of technique and artistry."[90] Nijinska had good reason to think that the Niagara Frontier Ballet, as the company was renamed in 1970, would survive and, along with it, her ballets.

Nijinska staged *Les Biches* and *Brahms Variations* for the company's 1969 debut season at Jacob's Pillow. Arriving in Buffalo in the dead of winter, she spent six weeks setting *Les Biches* before returning to California for Easter. After catching her breath in Los Angeles, she flew to Rome around May 1 to set the ballet at the Teatro dell'Opera. Then she returned to Buffalo for a second round of rehearsals, during which she staged *Brahms Variations* and readied the company for the Pillow season in August. Everything was first class. Costumes were commissioned from Grace Costumes, Inc., a New York City house whose founder, Grace Miceli, was a protegée of Karinska. The concert pianists Jean Hamilin, Margaret Wincenc, and Sumiko Kohno provided the music. Jack Mitchell came up to Buffalo for a photo shoot before the company left by bus for the Pillow.

Today, the dancers still have fond memories of those months with Nijinska. They remember her as a little barrel of a woman, with an aura of greatness when she entered the studio. "Everything about her was impressive, beginning with her storied past."[91] She wore her usual loose trousers but with a huge man's shirt (that didn't quite hide the battery for her hearing aid) and sock-slippers with pompoms (because her feet were often swollen). She shuffled. She smoked (although she wasn't supposed to) through a long cigarette holder. She had huge expressive hands, which she used to mark the steps. When she rehearsed, she made a "funny, whispery sound" (which several can still imitate), demonstrating with her upper body, showing a head or an arm, and tapping the musicality of a phrase on the dancers' shoulders as though hammering the rhythm directly into their bodies. Mary Barres remembers "the whooshing sounds she would make in your ear as she demonstrated steps with her hands; her soft wrinkled skin; . . . getting into an exact fifth position to demonstrate certain chassés," and yelling to her from across the room, "No Mary! Not Madonna!" when she turned her palms upward like a statue of the Virgin Mary.[92] Like so many teachers of her generation, Nijinska spoke a goulash of English, Russian, and French that generations of American students learned along with ballet technique in the country's émigré studios.

Nijinska occasionally taught class, coming up with fiendishly difficult combinations (like rond de jambe en l'air on demi-pointe en tournant, which Deborah Hess remembers) that everyone tried their hardest to do, even if they came up short: their effort, coupled with the fearlessness instilled in them by Crofton, delighted their teacher.[93] By all accounts, Nijinska had mellowed. Not that there weren't tears, as Nijinska herself told a reporter. Before leaving for Jacob's Pillow, "I told them I was criticizing not because they were doing badly, but because art is always difficult."[94]

One doesn't normally think of Nijinska as particularly motherly. Nor at this point in her life does one associate her with Poland, despite her family background. Yet Michelle Lankowski, a Polish American student, found in Nijinska both a "woman and mother who was trying to mentor me in making a life-changing decision to accept a three-year scholarship from the Kosciusko Foundation to study in Warsaw . . . or . . . in the USA."

I am a second generation Pole and spoke some Polish. Bronislava would ask that I sit next to her during Les Biches rehearsals, and I could only speak Polish, no English. She was not pushing for me to go to Poland, . . . but thought I had a better chance of survival if I could speak fluently, if I should go. She asked to speak directly with my father; I was 14, and she was very concerned that my chances of coming back to the USA or home for a holiday would be difficult at best. . . . Together they decided my fate, and I did not go to Poland. Bronislava delivered the news, and I was sent home for several days to be with my family.[95]

In August 1969, after nearly thirty years, Nijinska returned to Jacob's Pillow. Here after a six-hour bus ride from Buffalo, the company opened on August 5.[96] It was thirty-strong, including a half-dozen guest artists, although Nijinska cast sixteen-year-old Mary Barres as the Hostess in Les Biches. Among the guests only Anna-Marie and David Holmes had more than the briefest exposure to Nijinska's style and methods.[97] Freelance Canadian dancers who had studied in Leningrad and performed with the Kirov Ballet, Anna-Marie danced the Girl in Blue and David the lead Athlete, and they also had the lead roles in Brahms Variations. When Crofton phoned to invite them to join her fledgling company, saying they would have a chance to work with Nijinska, they jumped at the opportunity. The couple spent most of 1969 in Buffalo, taking class and rehearsing with her. Nijinska "absolutely adored me," says Anna-Marie.[98] Unusually strong, she never had to worry about technique. In *Les Biches* she nailed the double pirouettes ending on pointe every time, much to the admiration of Crofton's teens. In *Brahms*, she recalls, Nijinska "threw a lot of steps at me," including complicated pirouette sequences.[99]

Nijinska and Anna-Marie were close. Unlike Crofton or any of the company's other dancers, Anna-Marie spoke Russian; she was older and a mid-career professional, who had danced internationally. Anna-Marie remembers Nijinska talking about how hard she had worked, and how people today didn't. There are snapshots of the two drinking tea together in the apartment where Nijinska was living; in one she has a little white dog on her lap. Although Crofton's dancers speak only of how kind Nijinska was, Anna-Marie says she could be "brutal," and she softened Nijinska's Russian remarks rather than translate them faithfully. (Nijinska, who understood a lot more English than she let on, would then tell her in Russian "that's not what I said.") Even after Crofton dropped the Holmes couple from her roster of guests, Anna-Marie kept in touch; their last conversation took place the day before Nijinska's death.

With two of her ballets making up the entire program, Nijinska was Crofton's calling card, her name mentioned in all the advance publicity. Since the 1940s the Pillow, still under Ted Shawn's direction, had developed into an influential institution, acting both as a showcase and a professional stepping-stone, its weekly programs viewed by knowledgeable audiences of dance-goers and reviewed by critics from around the Northeast. A few days before the company's first performance, Clive Barnes devoted an entire Sunday piece in the *New York Times* to the "re-emergence of La Nijinska." Emphasizing the importance of *Les Biches* and *Les Noces*, he called her ballet *Etude* a "precursor" of Massine's symphonic works and even suggested that while she had no direct influence on Balanchine, "her works and her interest in dance as dance may have helped create the artistic climate in which such a ballet as 'Apollo' could flourish"—heresy at a time when Balanchine was widely regarded as a lone genius.[100] Thus, a great deal was riding on the Pillow season for Nijinska, nothing less than her reputation as a major twentieth-century choreographer. And that validation rested on the shoulders of Crofton's very young dancers.

To be sure, the season meant a lot for Crofton too. As Richard V. Happel wrote in the *Berkshire Eagle* after the first performance, "There's something engagingly brash about a company as young as the Center Ballet of Buffalo starting out in the dance world by making an appearance at Jacob's Pillow," and to "carry the entire program for a week." But the company turned out to be "a happy and exuberant lot, appearing to dance for the very love of it, despite the certainty that all had toiled and struggled through many an hour of training and rehearsal."[101] Margo Miller in the *Boston Globe* felt the dancing showed "great promise; it was quite clean, clear and already shows the ability of the company to do expressive and actorly things with their faces and heads. All of which is essential for the ballets of Nijinska."[102] Anna Kisselgoff, just starting out her career as a critic at the *New York Times*, thought the company had "obviously benefitted greatly from the choreographer's personal guidance." But she felt that only Mary Barres, as the Hostess, and Deborah Hess and Francesca Rochberg as the Girls in Grey had caught the style of *Les Biches*.[103]

Although most of the season's critics knew something about *Les Biches*, *Brahms Variations* was new to almost everyone. Happel in the *Berkshire Eagle* thought it "showed off the company in splendid fashion," that David Holmes, as the Poet in the ballet's second scene, "electrified the audience," and that the company members "excelled in the many variations."[104] He was not alone in finding the ballet a good fit for what Kathleen Cannell in the *Christian Science Monitor* called "the budding style of the Buffalo group." She described the first scene, to the composer's Variations & Fugue on a Theme by Handel, as being "in pure 18th-century Greek balletic style. The gods gather on Mount Olympus, suggested by broken spears and columns, as Apollo (Mr. Uthoff) creates celestial music among the stars and clouds, figured by the corps."[105] The diminutive Pillow stage did not serve Nijinska well, as Margo Miller pointed out; it obscured the "counterpointed textures" and "subtle cross-currents" of her ensemble choreography and made *Brahms Variations* "[look] messier than it is."[106]

Nijinska watched the first-night performance from the house, then came out on stage for a curtain call that turned into a standing ovation.[107] She was surrounded by friends and admirers, and the parents of many of the dancers.[108] Arlene Croce was not among the well-wishers. In an obituary published in *Ballet Review*, the doyen of American critics later described Nijinska's aging body as if she were a female eyesore. "I met Nijinska once three years ago when she was 78," Croce begins,

> a woman no more than four feet ten inches tall who looked like a troll or an elephant carved in ivory. She had perfectly square feet like an elephant's and wore ankle-strap shoes. Her earlobes were distended by dangle earrings.

The face slit by Mongoloid eyes and the third slit of a mouth with its toothy smile were all I recognized from photographs. This was at Jacob's Pillow.[109]

Although few critics were overwhelmed by the Nijinska program, only Walter Terry, the most prestigious critic to review the company, skewered it. Writing in the *Saturday Review*, where he had a regular column, he condemned everything about the Buffalo project, beginning with Nijinska, whose works, except for *La Fille Mal Gardée*, he had never liked. There were swipes at British critics, chest-thumping allusions to effeminacy (one of Terry's longtime bugaboos), and some good old-fashioned flag-waving. In other words, he had several axes to grind, and the youngsters from Buffalo paid the price. "There is, patently, a Nijinska cult, and it is probably the most difficult ballet cult to explain," he began.

It is centered, mainly, in Britain, but it has American expressions too. Try as I might, over the years, to discover for myself whatever it is that makes so many people, the Britishers especially, view Bronislava Nijinska as a major choreographer, I cannot. . . . British-trained critics bow to Mme. Nijinska, but even they are inclined to the opinion that she is best represented by two ballets, *Les Noces* and *Les Biches*. I don't think either is very good. . . .

All of this brings me to the Center Ballet of Buffalo (directed by Kathleen Crofton, a Britisher), which appeared here in the Jacob's Pillow Dance Festival in two ballets by Nijinska, *Les Biches* and *Brahms Variations* (themes of Paganini and Handel), staged under the supervision of the choreographer herself, sister of the great Vaslav Nijinsky. The result? Sheer disaster. . . .

As for *Brahms Variations*, now twenty-five years old, "embarrassing" is the only word to describe it. It is one of those idiot pieces in which a Poet . . . moons about looking for an inspiration, and in which very mortal dancers, including some very bad ones, attempt to portray the gods and goddesses of Olympus. . . . But why go on? It is a dreadful ballet with nauseating poses and posturings, awkward *enchainements*, and no sense of continuity whatsoever.[110]

Whatever Terry had to say, in late October 1969 Nijinska was back in Buffalo to rehearse for the company's "Holiday Special" at Kleinhans Music Hall, a handsome International Style building designed by Eliel and Eero Saarinen. In addition to *Les Biches* and Scene 2 of *Brahms Variations*, the program included *Aurora's Wedding*, staged—as noted in the program—in a version that incorporated many innovations of the Diaghilev production. These included the seven Fairy variations from the Prologue of *The Sleeping Princess*, with the Sugar Plum variation from *The Nutcracker* being danced by the Lilac Fairy; the Chinese Dance, another borrowing from *The Nutcracker*; and "The Three Ivans." In addition, Nijinska staged the "Awakening" scene from *The Sleeping Beauty*, possibly indicating Crofton's intention of one day presenting the entire ballet.[111]

For Crofton's dancers this was a happy time. They performed all the solo roles, and Nijinska rehearsed privately with many of them. She taught Lynn Glauber the "Canary" variation, now called the Fairy of the Songbirds; when Nijinska demonstrated, Glauber remembers, her fingers never stopped fluttering.[112] Mary Barres, cast as the Lilac Fairy, performed the Sugar Plum Fairy variation, and recalls Nijinska giving her special hand exercises to increase the suppleness and fluidity of her little hand rolls while gesturing toward her foot.[113] Deborah Zdobinsky, who was tall and lyrical, danced the traditional Lilac Fairy variation as the Fairy of the Sunlit Glades. When Nijinska coached Anna-Marie Holmes as Aurora, she came to their rehearsals with notes about Spessivtzeva's interpretation in *The Sleeping Princess*.[114]

Nijinska cast Ruth Pérez in her own role as the Fairy of the Hummingbirds. The variation involved a "lot of quick, clean, sharp movements of the arms and hands with the index fingers pointing and stabbing the air, darting quickly in different directions like the darting of the tiny bird itself and accentuated by the feet on pointe," Pérez explains.

> Time and time again, Madame would get up from her chair and shuffle over to me, taking my hands by the wrists to emphasize how to rotate them to get the maximum effect, or how to accentuate the head from the upper back. . . . The arms, hands, legs, and feet were to be sharp, but the head, neck, and shoulders were to be quick with clean movements but not "snapped." . . . We repeated and repeated and repeated. . . . [In] the grands jetés . . . I had to jump farther and cover more space, but the preparation for them was to be hidden—. . . they were to be sudden small explosions coming from seemingly nowhere. . . . I worked like a maniac.[115]

After staging *Les Biches* at the Maggio Fiorentino in April–May 1970, Nijinska returned to Buffalo in July to teach *Chopin Concerto*. The rehearsals were slow-going, so slow the dancers thought the ballet was being choreographed from scratch. In a sense it almost was: the last time Nijinska had staged the ballet was in 1954 for the Marquis de Cuevas company. In Buffalo she had only her memories and notes to guide her, aides-mémoire in a project that she probably conceived as the definitive staging of one of her major works—the reason perhaps that she allowed Elizabeth Cunliffe, who taught at the school, to notate the ballet.[116] The women wore long, lightly pleated Grecian gowns, inspired by Wacław Borowski's original designs, and hair like Anna Pavlova's, parted in the middle and pulled back over the ears— vestal virgins in the service of music. The corps never left the stage; grace- fully posed, they were part of the ambience, a backdrop for the soloists. Pérez remembers Nijinska flying off the handle during one of the rehearsals and spewing something in French that made a Canadian dancer in the company gasp, "She just said something so vulgar a French sailor would blush!"[117]

Nijinska left Buffalo in August, around the time the dancers began a short tour. Jeanne Battey Lewis saw the company in Washington, DC, as part of the city's Shakespeare Summer Festival and found it "markedly" improved since Jacob's Pillow, although the men were "disastrously weak"; she also disliked the ballet's "sculptural tableaux," which gave it the air of a "period piece."[118] Veteran critic Ann Barzel, who caught a performance at Buffalo's Upton Hall Theater, was far more impressed. She too noted the strides the company had made since the previous winter and thought the revival was "at its best in the second movement . . . dominated by a lovely (and fiendishly difficult) pas de deux, danced beautifully by Jeanne Armin and Tatsuo Sakai."[119]

By now, Crofton was rapidly expanding the repertory. David Lichine set *Graduation Ball*, Anna-Marie and David Holmes the second act of *Swan Lake* and the divertissements from *The Nutcracker*, Alicia Markova *Carnaval*—all staples of the post-Diaghilev "international" companies—while Hans Brenaa set August Bournonville's *La Sylphide*. By June 1971, Crofton's dancers were in Europe for an ambitious six-week tour to fourteen cities headed by Rudolf Nureyev—the star who probably made the tour possible—and the ballerinas Eva Evdokimova and La Scala's Liliana Cosi. Nijinska had hoped to spend time with the company in London. She had never met, let alone rehearsed, Crofton's new group of soloists, and she worried that the performances would damage her reputation as a choreographer.[120] Critic John Percival saw a performance in Dusseldorf, and although he devoted much of his review to Nureyev's inspired performance of James in *La Sylphide*, he was clearly impressed with the company's disciplined style and rewarding repertory. In *Les Biches* he singled out Mary Barres in the Rag Mazurka and praised the male trio for "an athletic prowess which has eluded the Royal Ballet's production." He found the "*corps de ballet* girls rightly giggly and exuberant" and their lyrical style in *Chopin Concerto* admirable.[121] Backstage, however, it was chaos. The company manager walked out in Madrid without paying the dancers, and "one or two agitators" (in Crofton's words) urged them to strike until money arrived. Miraculously, the company got through the tour, but for Crofton the experience was a nightmare.[122]

Nijinska had given the last of her declining energy to Crofton's company. It was her swan song as a choreographer, a last-ditch effort to shape her legacy, to salvage works other than *Les Noces* and *Les Biches*. At great personal cost, Nijinska had gone to Buffalo because she believed in Crofton's vision and because she believed that Crofton honored hers and would care for her works as no other company in the United States was prepared to do. But within months of returning to the United States, Crofton's enterprise was abandoned by its patron, Franz T. Stone. It limped along for another year, when a fire destroyed its archives, scenery, and costumes. In 1973 the company disbanded.[123] Crofton soon re-emerged as director of the Maryland Ballet, where she replicated her success in developing an exciting young ensemble but again ran afoul of her financial backers. She never again produced a ballet of Nijinska's.

***

In November 1970, Nijinska traveled to Venice to stage *Les Noces* at the venerable Teatro La Fenice with a company put together by her old friend Irène Lidova. For years she had dreamed of visiting this magical city again, so full of memories of Diaghilev and the site of his grave.[124] However, staging the ballet would prove no easy task. As Lidova explained, there were "serious problems with the Italians, who according to the unions must be as numerous as foreigners." Unfortunately "good Italians" were few, and she asked Nijinska to reduce the size of the corps to twelve men and twelve women to ensure a "good group." On the other hand, she had engaged a "ravishing Bride"—the Paris Opéra's Ghislaine Thesmar—and for the Groom a young Russian, Aliosha Gorki, with a "truly ideal face."[125]

Although Nijinska had calculated the number of hours she needed for rehearsal, she hadn't taken account of Italian labor law, which limited rehearsals to three hours a day, with three required fifteen-minute breaks. Nijinska found the restrictions "absurd" but had to abide by them. At night she couldn't sleep, fearing she wouldn't be able to finish. (Eventually, Robert Mead came from the Royal Ballet to help.) "I still see her," wrote Lidova in *Ma Vie avec la danse*, "sitting upright in her . . . chair, dressed in long black trousers and a loose blouse, her thin grey hair rolled into a bun . . . her feet . . . in thick felt slippers. She taught the ballet indicating the choreography by movements of the fingers and hands, but the dancers understood her, although they were unaccustomed to such precise and detailed work. Some wrote the counts on little cards that they pinned to their leotards and consulted constantly."[126] Not everyone grasped the ballet's style, even Ghislaine Thesmar, whose acting as the Bride led Nijinska to exclaim, "No cream, Mademoiselle, above all no cream."[127] And when Nijinska showed one of the more complicated configurations, work immediately stopped for a break. "It pained me," wrote Lidova, "to see this great artist, who had struggled her whole life for her art, to resign herself at the end of her life to concessions because of too little time and because of the inattention of certain dancers."[128] Still, when the ballet premiered on January 15, 1971, it was a resounding success, and Nijinska, elegant in a black silk dress, took a curtain call with the principals.[129]

Despite all the problems, Nijinska was gratified to be in Venice. She stayed at the Hotel de La Fenice et des Artistes across from the theater, a marvelous old place filled with divas and celebrated tenors. At the local pizzeria she and Irina had a corner table, where Lidova often joined them for lunch. She celebrated New Year's Eve there as well, ordering champagne and wearing a paper hat. A few days before Christmas, accompanied by Serge Lifar (who was staging *Daphnis and Chloë* on the same program), she paid her last visit to Diaghilev's grave at the island cemetery of San Michele.[130] When she left Venice, Lidova accompanied her to the boat station. Nijinska suddenly seemed very old. With great sadness she said, "*I will never see Venice again.*"[131]

Unlike many of her fellow émigrés, Nijinska never abjured the Soviet Union. In 1934, when she arrived in New York on her way to Hollywood, she told a reporter that she did not consider herself an exile and sometimes even dreamed of going back.[132] And she experienced intense emotion in 1938 when she visited Belovezh, setting foot on what had once been Russian soil. Although the Bolshoi Ballet had taken London by storm in 1956, it wasn't until 1959 that Nijinska saw the company at the Shrine Auditorium in Los Angeles. "The company's visit was such a great event," she wrote to the Russian literary scholar Elisabeth Stenbock-Fermor. "What a wonderful troupe! . . . What awe-inspiring discipline lies behind their dance. Every dancer is perfectly 'polished.' . . . The quality amazes me." As to the choreography, "I could talk for a long time." Yury Grigorovich was the great hope of Soviet ballet in those years, a protegé of Fedor Lopukhov who had scrapped the Stalin-era *drambalet* for narratives with a modern, classical flavor. In *The Stone Flower* she found his Russian dances "wonderful" from beginning to end but was dismayed by the "cheap, trite modernism" of his classical choreography. As for *Les Sylphides* (or *Chopiniana*, as it was still called in Russia), the steps were almost right, but the magic had gone, and Nikolai Fadeyechev as the Poet was all wrong.[133] "The high quality of the Soviet ballet is undeniable," she wrote to "Seriozha" Lifar in 1967. "But why for fifty years have they been so stagnant?" After decades of estrangement, Nijinska and her former student had reconciled, but she could not accept his uncritical embrace of Soviet ballet, above all with respect to the man who had meant so much to them both. "[A]ll that is great in Diaghilev's ideas is rejected," she wrote. "For them, he is a criminal, an emigré, a nobleman, and everything he created is un-Russian."[134]

However cut off Soviet and Western ballet had been since the 1930s, the Thaw that followed Stalin's death in 1953 opened the door to communication between long-severed families and connections. Nijinska had no close relatives in Russia (apart from her half-sister Marina Nizhinskaia, whom she had long refused to acknowledge), but she belonged to a generation fractured between East and West, with only the most fragmentary communication between them. In 1962, when the Bolshoi returned to Los Angeles, she invited the company's recently retired ballerina Galina Ulanova and her husband, the Bolshoi's chief designer, Vadim Rindin, to her home in Pacific Palisades, a visit memorialized by snapshots of the two in Nijinska's backyard.[135]

Ulanova's visit was followed by a growing number of contacts between Nijinska and the Soviets. In 1963 she donated Franz Winterhalter's portrait of Avdotia Istomina to the Pushkin Museum in Leningrad, signing herself "Bronislava Nizhinskaia, Ballet Artist of the former Maryinsky Theater, and Choreographer."[136] In 1965 she sent the Russian ballet historian and critic Nikolai Eliash a detailed response describing her ballet *The Swan Princess* and the differences between Ida Rubinstein's production and the one she mounted for her own company; excerpts appeared in his book *Pushkin and the Ballet*.[137] The following year, when the Bolshoi Ballet was in Los Angeles, she gave them a Paris Opéra poster with a portrait of Chaliapin, who is really "esteemed in Russia," as she told an old Russian friend.[138] In 1967, when the critic, historian, and *Dancing Times* correspondent Natalia Roslavleva invited her to contribute to a volume on Marius Petipa, Nijinska sent her an excerpt from "Diary of a Young Dancer." She was recovering from a serious illness, she explained, and didn't have time to write something new.

Undeterred, Roslavleva pieced something together that answered at least some of the questions she had sent to the book's prospective contributors.[139] The essay starts by recalling a rehearsal of Petipa's last ballet, *The Magic Mirror*, where the venerable choreographer placed his hand on her head and said "bien," and the many other ballets in which she took part as a child. She describes her growing disenchantment with Petipa's choreography and the Maryinsky ballet in particular—the dramatic and stylistic incongruities, extensive use of mime and acrobatics, and, after Petipa's death, the absence of creative leadership. "During a performance of 'Raymonda' in 1911," she writes, "I realized that the Imperial ballet was foreign to me. And my heart grew cold toward the house of my childhood and youth." Nijinska also discussed her contributions to Diaghilev's production of *The Sleeping Princess*, and confesses that because Petipa's ballets were so "overburdened with non-dance elements," their "texture . . . is not dear to me." And yet, she adds, "his dances glow with genius." In the end, it was Petipa's "concern for the school of classical dance [that] . . . left more of an impression on my creative work than his ballets."[140]

With the critic and historian Vera Krasovskaya, who had attended the Leningrad Choreographic School and danced for nearly a decade with the Kirov Ballet, Nijinska developed a close epistolary friendship that lasted until her death. Here, at last, was a woman who shared her keen intellectual passion for ballet, who knew it from the inside but also as a body of knowledge with a literature and a history. In October 1967, Krasovskaya wrote to Nijinska, explaining that she was working on the third volume of her history of Russian ballet and that this volume, covering the years 1900 to 1917, would have a long section on Nijinsky both as a dancer and a choreographer. She is particularly interested in *The Rite of Spring* and questions some of the things she has read in Lydia Sokolova's *Dancing for Diaghilev*. She would be deeply grateful for Nijinska's help. Nijinska, already familiar with Krasovskaya's writings, was more than willing. In December she wrote a long, long letter to "Vera Mikhailovna," not only supplying family information, but also rebutting Sokolova's accusation of "vagueness" in Nijinsky's choreography. Just the opposite was true: in staging the ballet, he precisely defined every movement, down to the position of every finger.

With respect to her Chosen Maiden solo, Nijinska begins by describing her rehearsals with Vaslav, noting how quickly the work progressed and how exciting and original she found the choreography. "Vaslav didn't narrate anything in words," she wrote, "he only said that the solo was the Maiden's ritual, sacrificial dance. . . . [T]he maiden was dancing in a frenzy, her harsh, forceful, elemental movements seemed to engage the heavens in battle, to defend the earth against a threatening sky; she falls down in a trance, and at the end, in her frenzy, must kill herself by dancing."[141] Nijinska then attempts to describe the movements of the dance, cautioning that "with the passage of more than fifty years, it is difficult . . . to reconstruct the choreography . . . , especially since it was very complex not only in terms of dance, but also musically. I can remember only a few separate movements. . . . But I can't vouch for [their] precise sequence . . . and so ask you to see them only as my perception of . . . this choreography. . . . Of course, the whole essence of these movements lies in their musical rhythms, accents, and pauses." Without the cautionary note, Krasovskaya quoted Nijinska in her book chapter; subsequently, Millicent Hodson used those excerpts in her reconstruction of *The Rite of Spring*.[142]

Within hours of receiving this extraordinary letter, Krasovskaya sent Nijinska her chapter on Vaslav, along with "huge thanks for this precious gift . . . for the history of Russian ballet, in particular, and for all of Russian art, in general," an expression of gratitude that must have warmed the choreographer's heart.[143] Nijinska devoured the chapter as soon as it arrived. "I read your essay from morning to night," she wrote to Krasovskaya on New Year's Day 1968. "[I]t is so wonderful, interesting, and rich. Most importantly, it introduces Nijinsky as an innovative choreographer. . . . It is so precious to me that this kind of writing is appearing in Russia, and it is your accomplishment: you are the first person in the Soviet Union to write about Nijinsky. . . . I do not have any comments or objections, but am filled with admiration for your work." She ends by sending regards to "everyone who studied with me in the Theatre Academy, and remembers me as I remember all of them."[144] Two weeks later, on January 14, "the first day of the new year, old style," Krasovskaya asks Nijinska for a signed portrait to hang over her desk. At the same time she sends her a copy of her latest book.[145] In return Nijinska sends "Vera," as Krasovskaya was now signing herself, a photo of herself as the Fairy of the Humming-Birds in *The Sleeping Princess* and a Cocteau drawing, presumably the one from his book on *Les Biches*.[146]

As time goes on, the letters grow more personal. Both women scrupulously avoid the subject of politics, but when the Soviet post office returns the new version of Krasovskaya's chapter on Nijinsky on the grounds that "it wasn't allowed to send manuscripts," we understand, as Nijinska must have, that this was intended to keep dissidents from smuggling manuscripts abroad for publication in the West.[147] Although Krasovskaya's letters were apparently uncensored, she—like most Soviet citizens—was seldom allowed to travel abroad. "I really want to see you," Nijinska wrote at one point. Perhaps Krasovskaya could visit the United States with one of the Soviet companies, or perhaps, she, Nijinska, could realize her dream of visiting Leningrad and Moscow. (They did manage to meet, probably in Paris, in 1969 or 1970.[148]) But it wasn't only people who were kept separate; the repertory of Russia Abroad, except for Fokine's *Les Sylphides*, did not exist in the Soviet world. The Thaw began to remedy this, with the first Soviet productions of *The Rite of Spring* and *La Valse*, and the first revival since the 1920s of *Petrouchka*. Another effort along these lines was Maris Liepa's staging of Fokine's *Le Spectre de la Rose*, which Nijinska saw in Los Angeles on a "Stars of the Bolshoi Ballet" program. She described it to Krasovskaya as a valiant effort on Liepa's part, although it naturally fell short of the original, in which Nijinsky and Karsavina were "inimitable." She then asks Krasovskaya about a twenty-year-old Kirov dancer whom Anton Dolin was raving about but whom nobody in the West had seen—Mikhail Baryshnikov. "Is he really such a unique talent?"[149] In the remarkable correspondence between these two exceptional women, one senses both a shared love and knowledge of ballet and the continuing presence of the Cold War.

When Krasovskaya decided to turn her chapter on Nijinsky into a book, she had no hesitation about pumping Nijinska for information. However, it wasn't until 1971 that she realized that Nijinska was also writing a book about him. "This is wonderful," Krasovskaya wrote, "since no one can write about him as well as you." She promised to stop "bothering" Nijinska for information and includes a fillip, a copy of Nijinska's two-sentence letter to the directorate resigning from the Imperial Theaters in 1911 (which doesn't appear in *Early Memoirs*), as well as responses to her resignation that Krasovskaya had found in the archives and press. But rather callously she continues to use Nijinska as a sounding board. "I dropped everything to focus on the book," she confides. "I cannot delay it; it is ripe within me. Maybe that is why it is going so fast, perhaps too fast. I always worry when it is too easy to write. But I tell myself it's because I have carried this book inside myself for a long time."[150] By the end of the letter she is again pelting Nijinska with questions about her brother. And in her last surviving letter, written in June 1971, Krasovskaya spends nearly three pages laying out her theories about *Jeux*, especially the idea that "Nijinsky's sportsman . . . appeared to the public as a 'harbinger of generations that would live through not one but two world wars.'" Only at the very end does she allude to Nijinska's book, insisting "It must, must be finished!"[151] Krasovskaya's impassioned commitment to her project may well have undermined Nijinska's faith in her own powers as a writer and in the story she had to tell.

In 1968 the composer Vernon Duke, who lived in Santa Monica and wrote poetry and music criticism for émigré periodicals under his birth name, Vladimir Dukelsky, contacted a number of people on Nijinska's behalf about the book she was now calling "My Brother Vaslav Nijinsky." Over the years it had gone through numerous transformations, with chapters written and rewritten, copied and corrected in notebooks from the many countries where she had lived and worked. The first person Duke contacted was his New York literary agent, Bertha Klausner, who told Nijinska that she couldn't wait to see the manuscript. But after years of living with the book, Nijinska was loath to part with it. She replied that the manuscript still needed to be edited and translated, and that Duke had advised her to publish it first in Russian, to which Klausner rejoined that Duke thought their mutual friend, Anatole Daroff, a novelist and freelance journalist for *Novoe russkoe slovo*, would make a good translator.[152] In November 1968, Daroff agreed to edit the Russian manuscript. Despite Nijinska's tinkering over the years, it was still in poor shape; it also needed an ending. But it would be more than a year before Daroff returned the manuscript, and even then it wasn't finished; in July 1971, Nijinska wrote that she was still working on the last chapter and would send him the new material to edit.[153]

By then it had been over a year since she began feeding the edited chapters to Nathalie Wollard to translate. However, Wollard, a former lyric soprano and sister of Nijinska's former dancer Nina Youshkevitch, had managed to complete less than a third of the manuscript's 450 pages.[154] Meanwhile, with 1972, the centenary of Diaghilev's birth, rapidly approaching, Nijinska had received several offers to publish her book. She had been asked to submit the manuscript "as is," being assured there was no problem finding a good, experienced translator. However, Nijinska rejected the offers, preferring to keep the manuscript close at hand. The upshot was that she spent her last four years dithering over the editing and translation of a manuscript that could have been published to acclaim in her lifetime rather than nearly a decade after her death. When she died in 1972, her book remained unborn.

***

On April 26, 1968, Nijinska's husband of forty-three years passed away. His health was failing, and the doctor had sent him to the hospital. In two days he was gone. "I was not prepared for this great loss," Nijinska wrote to Kathleen Crofton. "We were all hoping that he [would] recover soon, but his heart failed. Now my daughter Irina is near me all the time."[155] All marriages have their ups and downs, and Nijinska's was no exception. But it had endured. She had depended on Kolia and probably loved him; he certainly adored her, taking her name, carrying her bags, filing her tax returns, and attending to her correspondence, a combination of butler and secretary. He also indulged her, allowing her to behave in ways that were unprofessional if not unethical, and against her own best interests. But she had indulged him as well, agreeing to settle in California and allowing him to become wholly dependent on her financially. The day before he died she wrote him a note, explaining that she didn't visit him because the abscess under her toenail was still hurting but he shouldn't worry; Irina "watches over me as if I were a child, as you would, and cleans the whole house." "May God be with you!"[156]

She shared her anguish with Krasovskaya, who sent love and kisses to her newly widowed friend.[157] Nijinska wrote back: "I felt your gentle compassion for me in my grief. . . . I embrace and kiss you from the bottom of my heart." Two weeks later, Nijinska wrote her a second, unusually personal letter, describing Irina's heroic efforts to take care of her:

> God has given me the greatest gift—my daughter. I cannot explain to you how this precious child of mine cares about me, torn between her house and mine. I live in the house where I lived with Kolia, who reminds me of his presence everywhere. I cannot move in with Ira, since there are four of them and they don't have a spare room for me to live and work—write. Everyday my daughter sleeps over at my place, then leaves to see her husband and children between breakfast and lunch.[158]

She ends: "Write to me, Verochka. I am always happy to receive your letters."

***

Krasovskaya was not the only Soviet with whom Nijinska engaged in extended correspondence in these final years. Throughout the decades she had lived in emigration, Nijinska had crossed paths with people she had met in Kiev. Many were professional colleagues, but others, such as Nina Sirotinine and Anna Teplicka, became close personal friends. Both were former students of hers, members of that distant utopia that Nijinska had spent her life in emigration trying to recapture. Anna was long dead; Nina, too, had died, although Nijinska didn't learn of her passing until 1970, three years after it occurred.[159] Another former student with whom Nijinska reconnected and later became a friend was Bella Shutaia (Schuty) Tietz. Bella, who was Jewish, had married in Germany and settled in London with her family in the 1930s. By the 1960s she was working as an interpreter, accompanying the growing number of Soviet artists touring abroad on cultural exchange programs.[160] In 1966, when Nijinska was staging Les Noces, Tietz performed a number of small services for her, and they often talked by phone.[161] The following September she writes that she has planted the seed for a Soviet production of Les Noces. Meeting the Bolshoi's chief musical director Gennady Nikolaevich Rozhdestvensky that summer in London, Tietz suggested that it would be very interesting for Russian audiences to see the ballet staged at the Bolshoi. He agreed and asked for Nijinska's contact information. "I started this conversation," Tietz wrote, "only because you told me how much you'd like to go to Russia, work there, do something there to be remembered for."[162] That fall, Tietz spent a week in Moscow, where she talked with Rozhdestvensky about Les Noces. He told her that he had already taken "some steps," and that both Ulanova and Yury Grigorovich, the Bolshoi's new artistic director, also think it could be very interesting. "Grigorovich is filled with admiration for you!"[163] Grigorovich, meanwhile, had been trying to reach Nijinska by phone, but had lost the number that Tamara Toumanova had given him. He congratulates her on the success of Les Noces in London, signing himself "a great admirer of your wonderful talent."[164] Two years later, when Vera Krasovskaya attended a rehearsal of Grigorovich's new ballet, Spartacus, in Moscow, he told her about meeting Nijinska, how interesting it was, and asked Krasovskaya to send her his "warmest regards."[165] By now, with the Thaw rapidly coming to an end, there was no more talk of staging Les Noces.

Ever since learning about Mikhail Baryshnikov, Nijinska had yearned to stage L'Après-midi d'un Faune at the Kirov Ballet with the young Russian dancer in her brother's role. In August 1970, instead of attending the Washington premiere of Chopin Concerto by the Buffalo dancers, Nijinska flew to London, where the Kirov was performing and where she was to begin rehearsals for *Faune*. "Mikhail Baryshnikov is the dancer wonder of the age," wrote Clive Barnes of the future star's Western debut, "almost certainly the finest product of the St. Petersburg School since Nijinsky, and it is interesting that Nijinsky's sister, Bronislava Nijinska, and his wife, Romola Nijinska [*sic*], were in the audience Thursday to applaud his triumph in 'Vestris.'"[166] A few days later, Irina wrote to a friend in Los Angeles: "My mother is teaching the members of the Kirov Ballet Vaslav Nijinsky's *L'Après-midi d'un Faune*. From Sept. 6–Sept. 13 we will be in Amsterdam, Holland, with the Kirov and my mother will be rehearsing there also every day."[167] Nijinska's letter to Krasovskaya hasn't survived, but Krasovskaya's reply conveys Nijinska's excitement about working with the Kirov, which she praised for keeping the great traditions and purity of the Russian "school" alive. "I am especially pleased by your high praise of Misha Baryshnikov. He is a really great dancer with a big future. When you say he reminds you of Vaslav Fomich, there can be no better praise. It would be amazing if they revived 'Faune,' so long as they don't depart too much from the original. . . . Of course, the best thing would be for you to work with [the dancers] up to the premiere. How wonderful it would be if you came here."[168] Nijinska never did go home, nor was her brother's ballet ever performed in Russia during the Soviet period. When the company left for Holland, ballerina Natalia Makarova stayed in London. Her decision to defect had numerous repercussions, including the dismissal of the Kirov's longtime artistic director, Konstantin Sergeyev. *Faune* was collateral damage.

***

Moscow harbored a group of Nijinska's former students, and in 1968, thanks to Serge Lifar, who sent them her address, they contacted her. The first to write was Lena (Elena) Krivinskaia, who introduced herself as the "girl with two braids" who used to dance *The Mask* and *Chopin's Mazurka No. 17*. "Forty-six years separate us from the dramatic farewell when you were leaving Kiev." What followed was the kind of testimonial a life in emigration had denied her.

> Through all these long years I see clearly the importance of my meeting with you; it left such a deep mark on my life and my choice of profession. . . . When you left, we lost a unique teacher with her own didactic system, who wonderfully combined classic dance with experiments in new

choreographic forms and possibilities. We lost the joy of being around a wonderfully talented ballet master of rare individuality and mastery. Every lesson, every rehearsal . . . what a celebration for us. Nothing is forgotten, and I want to let you know what a deep trace you left here and how the memory of you is cherished in the Motherland.[169]

Krivinskaia was now a visual artist, designing for the stage, while "Pati" (Kleopatra) Batueva-Shakhovsky and "Zhenia" (Evgenia) Strelkova were painters. When word spread in January that Serge Lifar was speaking at Moscow's Dom Khudozhnika—House of Artists—everyone who knew Nijinska rushed there—Pati, Zhenia, Lena, her sister Lisa (also an artist), and Yuly Flor. In "good Russian," Lifar spoke about Nijinska, himself, his encounters with other artists. "It was interesting and sad to be there, to see the marks of time on his face."[170] Nijinska wrote back immediately. "Everything about your letter impressed me deeply," responded Lena,

> that you answered on the same day, that my letter made you happy, that you appreciated and remembered our endless gratitude. I am impressed that you remember us all. I couldn't imagine it was possible. By writing to you, I only wanted you to know that we remember the wonderful days of our youth. . . .
>
> It is sad that you did not find a theater company that matched your aspirations and plans. . . . What a great loss it must have been for you. . . . I don't know how your career would have worked out in the Soviet Union, but one thing is sure: you would have had your own theater and troupe, with no financial worries. Our government is constantly trying to improve the ballet and spends money on it. Even in wartime, ballet was kept alive.[171]

After learning that Singaevsky had died, Lena evoked him as he had been a half-century before. "I remember him very well," she wrote.

> Fine features, wonderful bright eyes, an elegant, tall figure, kind smile, friendliness. We knew that you had married, but then someone said that you had separated, which is why I didn't dare ask you about him. . . . It is good that you and Irochka are close, also geographically. And most importantly that you have a great thing to accomplish, the book about your brother. . . . And then, I suppose, comes a book about yourself, your long

artistic path, experiments, discoveries, and "system," everything that you have done for ballet. No one can write it better than you.[172]

By now, Nijinska was in touch with other members of the group. They tell her about their families, their trips, their projects (Zhenia was working on a portrait of Maya Plisetskaya), and their plans. They exchange photos, magazine articles; one sent her the picture of Irochka that Nijinska gave her before she left.[173] "It's all in the past but alive in my memory," writes Sonia Volkova, who never became a "real artist," but an applied one, designing accessories for women. "I see you, with your stick, at our morning class, and little Irochka, who would sometimes run into our room. Our evening rehearsals, to which artists and musicians would come, and our frequent visitor Professor [Felix] Blumenfeld." After expressing her condolences for Singaevsky's death, she wonders what became of his mother and sisters.[174]

Of all the women, it was "Lenochka" who became a friend, a confidante even, to whom Nijinska wrote with candor as well as feeling. She was thrilled by the pictures of Kiev that Lena sent her.

Your pictures of Kiev gave me such joy. You have barely changed! I would have recognized you even today. You are still as beautiful as you were in your youth. . . . [And] to see you, even in a photo, . . . in my dear Kiev, which even now is fresh in my mind, on the shore of the Dnieper, with its Andreevskaia [Saint Andrew's] Church. One of the most beautiful cities on earth, along with my favorite Petersburg–Leningrad.[175]

Then she turns to the unanswerable question she had probably asked herself for years. What if she had stayed in the Soviet Union? "You talk about the privileges I would have enjoyed," she wrote.

I don't doubt it. . . . When I was leaving Kiev, I had a similar proposal for my entire studio to go to Moscow. But at the same time I received a letter from Vaslav's wife that I should . . . go to Vienna with my mother. The doctors . . . thought our arrival and meeting might shock Vaslav and aid his recovery, since he was very attached to me and my mother. Of course, that was my main reason for leaving and no material temptations could make me decide otherwise. Being in Kiev, surviving on so little, I did not feel that I was deprived of anything. Here . . . you see luxury and excess everywhere, and at home there is no food for the family. That is what kept me here: taking care of my family, my mother's health, my children. Moreover, ballet work excited and sucked me in more and more. I convinced myself that I was working for World Ballet, in which my native Russian, Soviet ballet was also participating. . . .

Moreover, to be closer to the Motherland would also have been more productive for me, in the sense that more of my creations would have stayed alive. There are only two ballets, *Les Biches* and *Les Noces*, which are still performed . . . in London. And maybe a few things in Buenos Aires. Small ballet groups that appear here and there do not live long, and with them everything I create disappears. I still hope that I will come to the Motherland in my old age and see you all.[176]

Krivinskaia assured her that nobody ever thought that Nijinska was abandoning the "motherland" in pursuit of material pleasures. But it is devastating that her experiments and innovations, to say nothing of her pedagogical work, never brought her financial stability and that her "ballet labor" was never filmed. "It is hard to read your words about feeding your family without bitterness. We all live very modestly; our incomes are far from high, but we do not worry about tomorrow. And we have our regime to thank for that."[177] Just as Nijinska toyed with the idea of returning to Russia, Krivinskaia was cherishing what she called her "rose dream" of seeing Nijinska abroad. "We live in two different worlds, and without a personal meeting it is difficult for you to understand our daily lives and conditions and everything that our beloved Motherland has lived through this whole time."[178]

Meanwhile, the group was searching for Nijinska's old friend Nina Moiseevna, Levushka's godmother, who was still living in Kiev. Years before, Nijinska had left an album of Japanese etchings with Nina for safekeeping. Miraculously, the album had survived, and now Nijinska wanted it sent to her in California. So friends were marshaled to collect and send the album together with Nina's photographs of Kiev to Moscow. From here Zhenia Strelkova's brother-in-law was to deliver them to Nijinska in Pacific Palisades. His mission accomplished, he then returned to Moscow with presents for everyone, including a rose petal, its color and scent intact, for Krivinskaia.[179]

Among the ballet goings-on in Moscow that Krivinskaia reported to Nijinska was a lecture by Nikolai Eliash at the Bakhrushin Museum in a room hung with photographs of Nijinsky and Nijinska. "He started more or less like this," Lenochka wrote:

I haven't randomly put these two names together, because both of them represent a major point of interest in the development of twentieth-century ballet. Both introduced the world to our Russian ballet art. With regard to Bronislava Nijinska, our scholars unjustly excluded her from the list of the most important names promoting Russian ballet on the international scene. I hope this will be fixed. I myself am guilty. I got to know her, her theory of dance, her career and artistic method only recently.

He spoke about your creative path (without forgetting about Kiev), ballets you had staged, roles you had danced; he said that even now you are full of energy and creative plans. He spoke about your family, your mother Eleonora, and, of course, Vaslav . . . about books written about [him] and said that the best book has yet to be written, . . . and that it will be a book by Bronislava Nijinska about her brother. He did not know this from me.[180]

For some time Nijinska's health had been failing. Needless to say, this was a topic of concern to her Moscow correspondents. The group included two ex-smokers, Pati and Zhenia, who were rabid on the subject of Nijinska's smoking. "For such a strong, willful person as you," Krivinskaia chided her, "smoking is unforgivable. As far as I understand, you have a thrombosis on your leg that will not heal if you don't quit. We all beg you: please stop!"[181] Thrombosis is the formation of a blood clot within a blood vessel. It prevents blood from flowing normally and can lead to a heart attack and stroke. Age, obesity, immobility, and smoking are risk factors, and Nijinska experienced all of them. But she plowed forward. Within less than a year of Singaevsky's death, she was back at work, with engagements in Buffalo and Rome in 1969, and Florence (where she fell and hurt her leg), Buffalo, and Venice in 1970. By 1971 she was writing fewer letters, and in Moscow they were asking if she was all right. But she seems to have been conserving her strength. After Thanksgiving that year she wrote to Maria Prianishnikova, thanking her once again for bringing flowers to the graves of her "beloveds," and announcing that she would be staging *Les Biches* in Dusseldorf the following year. "[I]n early September 1972 I will be in Europe, if God gives me health. And I will see you. I want to see you often; I want to be with you and talk." After living in the United States for over thirty years, Nijinska continued to feel like an outsider, culturally and linguistically isolated, and increasingly lonely. "I really don't get this American way of life," she wrote. "Irina has really good friends, whom she sees often. I have nobody here. The only Russian lady from

Kiev died when we were in Venice."[182] Around the same time she dreamed of Chaliapin, telling Irina he was coming to take her.[183]

***

On February 21, 1972, Nijinska died of a heart attack at her home in Pacific Palisades. The day before, when Anna-Marie Holmes called, she sounded fine.[184] Soon the obituaries appeared, long adulatory articles in the *New York Times* and the British newspapers.[185] Unsurprisingly, the *Los Angeles Times* ran only an unsigned death notice full of factual errors; even her daughter's name was wrong.[186] A few days later, Wladimir Oukhtomsky, a member of the Marquis de Cuevas company who had settled in the Southland, sent a long letter to the editor of the newspaper. Now co-chair of the Ballet Department at Indiana University, he had just learned of Nijinska's death and wanted to say a few words about her "on behalf of the many Californian dancers trained, groomed and inspired by her." With minor editing, Oukhtomsky's words appeared as an article a month later.[187] Focusing more on her teaching than her choreography, it was unique among the appreciations that followed her death, evoking her not only as an internationally acclaimed artist and brilliant teacher, but also as a Californian. In her "small home on the cliffs of Pacific Palisades," he wrote, she "rested and meditated, . . . mornings in the sea shadows, evenings in the blazing Pacific sunset," thinking, one imagines, of bodies in movement, as life ebbed away and her soul took flight to join her "beloveds."

List of Works

The following list does not include sketches, divertissements, or other occasional dances.

Original Ballets

Russia/Ukraine (including the School of Movement)
La Poupée (1915)
Autumn Song (1915)
Twelfth Rhapsody (1920)
Mephisto (1920)
Demons (1920)
Marche Funèbre (completed, but not publicly performed, 1921)

Diaghilev's Ballets Russes
The Sleeping Princess (selected dances, 1921)
Aurora's Wedding (1922)
Le Renard (1922)
Les Noces (1923)
La Fête Merveilleuse (1923)
Les Tentations de la Bergère (1924)
Les Biches (1924)
Les Fâcheux (1924)
Night on Bald Mountain (1924)
Le Train Bleu (1924)
Romeo and Juliet (1926)

Théâtre National de l'Opéra
Les Rencontres (1925)
Les Impressions de Music-Hall (1927)

Theatre Choréographique Nijinska
Holy Etudes (later called *Etude*, 1925)
Touring (1925)
Jazz (1925)
On the Road (1925)
Le Guignol (1925)

Henriette Pascar
Recital of *danses mimées* (1926)
Nini (or How a Shopgirl Became a Star) (1930)

Teatro Colón
El carillón mágico (1926)
Cuadro campestre (1926)
A orillas del mar (new version of *Le Train Bleu*) (1926)
Las amazonas (1926)
La Giara (1927)
Ala y Lolly (1927)
Pomona (1927)
Le Baiser de la Fée (new version, 1933)

Ballets Ida Rubinstein
Les Noces de Psyché et de l'Amour (1928)
Le Baiser de la Fée (1928)
Bolero (1928)
La Bien-Aimée (1928)
La Princesse Cygne (*The Swan Princess*, 1928)
Nocturne (1928)
La Valse (1929)
La Valse (new version, 1931)

Vicomte Charles de Noailles
Aubade (1929)

Olga Spessivtseva Ballet
Paysage Enfantin (1930)

Opéra Russe à Paris
Petrouchka (new version, 1930)
Capriccio Espagnol (1931)
Etude (definitive version, 1931)

Les Ballets Russes de Bronislava Nijinska/Théâtre de la Danse Nijinska
Valse-Fantaisie (1932)
Les Comédiens Jaloux (1932)
Variations (1932)
Bolero (new version, 1932)
The Swan Princess (new version, 1932)
Hamlet (1934)

Col. Wassily de Basil's Ballets Russes de Monte Carlo
Les Cent Baisers (1935)
Gypsy Dances (*Danses Slaves et Tsiganes*, 1936)

Markova-Dolin Ballet
The Beloved One (new version of *La Bien-Aimée*, 1937)
Fantasia (1947)

Polish Ballet
Chopin Concerto (1937)
La Légende de Cracovie (1937)
Le Chant de la Terre (1937)
Le Rappel (1937)
Apollon et la Belle (1937)

Ballet Theatre
La Fille Mal Gardée (1940)
Harvest Time (1945)
Rendezvous (1945)
Schumann Concerto (1951)

Ballet Russe de Monte Carlo (S. J. Denham)
Snow Maiden (1942)
Ancient Russia (1943)

Ballet Repertory Company
Hitch Your Wagon to a Star (1943)
Vision (1943)

Ballet International
Brahms Variations (1944)
Pictures at an Exhibition (1944)

Grand Ballet de Monte-Carlo/Grand Ballet du Marquis de Cuevas
In Memoriam (1949)
Rondo Capriccioso (1952)
The Sleeping Beauty (1960)

Tamara Toumanova Concert Programs with Wladimir Oukhtomsky
(performance dates at the Palacio de Bellas Artes in Mexico City)
Suite italiana (1956)
Phaeton (1957)
Le Berger (1961)
Los tres sueños (1962)

Dances and Ballets in Operas

Ballets Russes (1922): *Mavra* (Stravinsky)
Ballets Russes (1924): *Le Médecin malgré lui* (Gounod)
Monte Carlo Opera (1924): *Tales of Hoffmann* (Offenbach), *Sorochinsky Fair* (Mussorgsky), *Manon* (Massenet), *Roméo et Juliette* (Gounod), *Samson et Delila* (Saint-Saëns), *Prince*

Igor (Borodin), *Faust* (Gounod), *La Damnation de Faust* (Berlioz), *Mefistofele* (Boito), *Aida* (Verdi), *Faust* (Schumann)

Théâtre National de l'Opéra (1925): *La Naissance de la Lyre* (Roussel)

Théâtre National de l'Opéra (1926): *Alceste* (Gluck)

Teatro Colón (1926): *Carmen* (Bizet), *Hamlet* (Thomas), *La Gioconda* (Ponchielli), *Rigoletto* (Verdi), *Ollantay* (Gaito), *Tannhäuser* (Wagner), *Aida* (Verdi), *La Traviata* (Verdi)

Théâtre National de l'Opéra (1927): *Naila* (Gaubert)

Teatro Colón (1927): *Rigoletto* (Verdi), *Le Rossignol* (Stravinsky), *La Wally* (Catalani), *The Tale of Tsar Saltan* (Rimsky-Korsakov), *Manon* (Massenet), *Thaïs* (Massenet), *La Traviata* (Verdi), *Faust* (Gounod)

Théâtre National de l'Opéra (1930): *Tannhäuser* (Wagner)

Opéra Russe à Paris (1930): *Prince Igor* (Borodin), *Ruslan and Ludmila* (Glinka), *Sadko* (Rimsky-Korsakov), *The Tsar's Bride* (Rimsky-Korsakov), *Rusalka* (Dargomyzhsky)

Vienna State Opera (1930): *Schwanda, der Dudelsackpfeifer* (Weinberger)

Opéra Russe à Paris (1931): *Boris Godunov* (Mussorgsky)

Grosses Schauspielhaus, Berlin (Max Reinhardt) (1931): *Tales of Hoffmann* (Offenbach)

Ballets Russes de Bronislava Nijinska (1932): *Prince Igor* (Borodin), *Boris Godunov* (Mussorgsky)

Teatro Grande di Brescia (1933): *La favola d'Orfeo* (Casella)

Teatro Colón (1933): *Die Königskinder* (Humperdinck), *Andrea Chénier* (Giordano), *Rigoletto* (Verdi), *Khovanshchina* (Mussorgsky), *L'amico Fritz* (Mascagni), *La Forza del Destino* (Verdi), *La Vida Breve* (Falla)

Teatro Colón (1946): *Boris Godunov* (Mussorgsky), *Marouf* (Henri Rabaud), *Mignon* (Thomas), *Carmen* (Bizet), *Un Ballo in Maschera* (Verdi)

Films

La Mille et Deuxième Nuit (1933) (directed by Alexandre Volkoff)
A Midsummer Night's Dream (1935) (directed by Max Reinhardt)

Revivals

The titles of Nijinska's works varied. To avoid confusion, only the original or most commonly used titles are given below.

Les Rencontres (1926)
Etude (1926, 1931, 1940, 1943)
Les Noces (1926, 1933, 1936, 1966, 1971)
Night on Bald Mountain (1926, 1933)
Le Train Bleu (1926)
Les Impressions de Music-Hall (1927)
Les Biches (1932, 1934, 1937, 1947, 1964, 1969, 1970)
The Swan Princess (1933, 1934)
Bolero (1933, 1934, 1940, 1944, 1954)
Le Baiser de la Fée (1933, 1934, 1936)
Variations (1933, 1934)
Les Comédiens Jaloux (1933, 1934)
La Bien-Aimée (1937, 1942)

Chopin Concerto (1940, 1942, 1954, 1970)
Pictures at an Exhibition (1947)
Brahms Variations (1947, 1969)
Autumn Song (1949)
La Fille Mal Gardée (1949)
Aurora's Wedding (1951 [as *Princess Aurora*], 1953, 1969)

Revivals of Works by Other Choreographers

Petrouchka (Fokine, 1920, 1927, 1930, 1933, 1934, 1952, 1969)**
The Sleeping Beauty (Petipa, 1921, with Nikolai Sergeyev; 1960)*
L'Après-midi d'un Faune (Nijinsky, 1922, 1926, 1927, 1933, 1950?)
The Polovtsian Dances (Fokine, 1923, 1926, 1930, 1932, 1933, 1949)**
Daphnis and Chloë (Fokine, 1924, 1927)
Blue Bird Pas de Deux (1926)
Les Sylphides (Fokine, 1927, 1933, 1934, 1949,1959)
Carnaval (Fokine, 1934)
Firebird (Fokine, 1934)
Swan Lake (Act II) (Petipa-Ivanov, 1934, 1950, 1969)
Coppélia (Saint-Léon, 1949)
Le Spectre de la Rose (Fokine, 1952)

*Although Nijinska's 1960 staging of *The Sleeping Beauty* for the Grand Ballet du Marquis de Cuevas was technically a revival of the Petipa original, the Vision Scene was extensively rechoreographed by Nijinska.

**Most of Nijinska's stagings of *Petrouchka* and *The Polovtsian Dances* were "after" Fokine rather than faithful revivals of his choreography.

Illustrations and Credits

Frontispiece Bronislava Nijinska, 1953.
Photo by Serge Lido, inscribed to "dear, charming Mariusha Fredericksz," 1953.
Collection of Marie Nugent- Head.

Plate 1 Vadim Meller, *Fear*, 1919.
Bronislava Nijinska Collection, Library of Congress / https://www.loc.gov/item/ihas.200196684/.

Plate 2 Easter greeting from Nijinska's students, 1919.
Bronislava Nijinska Collection, Library of Congress / https://www.loc.gov/item/ihas.200154623/.

Plate 3 Vadim Meller, *Mephisto Waltz*, 1920.
Bronislava Nijinska Collection, Library of Congress / https://www.loc.gov/item/ihas.200196685/.

Plate 4 Alexandra Exter, poster design for Theatre Choréographique, 1925.
Bronislava Nijinska Collection, Library of Congress / https://www.loc.gov/item/ihas.200154598/. Alexandra Exter Archives and Estate, Paris, France.

Plate 5 Alexandra Exter, *Night on Bald Mountain*, 1925.
Bronislava Nijinska Collection, Library of Congress / https://www.loc.gov/item/ihas.200154624/. Alexandra Exter Archives and Estate, Paris, France.

Plate 6 Ida Rubinstein as the Swan Princess, 1929.
"Les Ballets de Madame Ida Rubinstein" souvenir program, Académie Nationale de Musique et de Danse, May 1929. Courtesy of Toronto Public Library.

Plate 7 Expression of gratitude from the Opéra Russe à Paris dancers, 1930.
Bronislava Nijinska Collection, Library of Congress.

Plate 8 Poster, "Bailes Rusos Nijinska," Teatro Nuevo, Barcelona, 1933, with cover art by the dancer Rudolph Andriassoff.
Bronislava Nijinska Collection, Library of Congress / https://www.loc.gov/item/ihas.200154608/.

Plate 9 Yury Annenkov, *Les Comédiens Jaloux*, 1932.
Théâtre de la Danse/La Nijinska Ballets Russes souvenir program, 1934. Carina Ari
  Library.

Plate 10 Yury Annenkov, poster for "La Nijinska Ballets Russes."
Digital image © The Museum of Modern Art/Licensed by SCALA / Art Resource, NY.

Plate 11 Polish National Ballet, Teatr Wielki-Opera, 1938.
Bronislava Nijinska Collection, Library of Congress / https://www.loc.gov/item/
  ihas.200154610/.

Plate 12 Teresa Roszkowska, *The Legend of Cracow*, 1937.
Bronislava Nijinska Collection, Library of Congress / https://www.loc.gov/item/
  ihas.200154578/.

Plate 13 Boris Aronson, *Pictures at an Exhibition*, 1944.
Boris Aronson Papers and Designs, Billy Rose Theatre Collection, New York Public
  Library for the Performing Arts. Courtesy Aronson-Budhos Collection.

Fig. 1 Nijinska at the Imperial Ballet School, 1908.
Photo by Karl Fischer. St. Petersburg State Museum of Theatre and Music.

Fig. 2 Nijinska in *Chopiniana*, Maryinsky Theater, 1908.
Photo by Karl Fischer. St. Petersburg State Museum of Theatre and Music.

Fig. 3 Nijinska in her graduation finery, 1908.
Photo by Karl Fischer. St. Petersburg State Museum of Theatre and Music.

Fig. 4 Nijinska at the time of her graduation, 1908.
Photo by Karl Fischer. St. Petersburg State Museum of Theatre and Music.

Fig. 5 Nijinska (third from left), with Adolph Bolm (left), Ludmilla Schollar, Valerian
  Svetlov, and others in Monte Carlo, spring 1911.
St. Petersburg State Museum of Theatre and Music.

Fig. 6 Nijinska as the Street Dancer in *Petrouchka*, 1911.
Album/Alamy Stock Photos.

Fig. 7 Nijinska with her daughter, Irina, St. Petersburg, 1914.
Bronislava Nijinska Collection, Library of Congress.

Fig. 8 Nijinska and her brother in *L'Après-midi d'un Faune*, 1912.
Photo by Baron de Meyer. Eakins Press Foundation.

Fig. 9 Maurice Ravel (left), with Nijinsky and Nijinska in Paris, 1914.
Heritage Image Partnership Ltd./Alamy Stock Photo.

Fig. 10 Alexandra Exter, 1910s.
Alamy Stock Photo.

Fig. 11 Nina Moiseevna (left), Alexander Kochetovsky, Pavel Gorkin, and Anton
Muravin outside the Kiev City Theater, 1916.
Bronislava Nijinska Collection, Library of Congress.

Fig. 12 Nijinska's handwritten announcement of the School of Movement, 1919.
Bronislava Nijinska Collection, Library of Congress.

Fig. 13 *Demons*, as sketched by Nijinska, 1920.
Bronislava Nijinska Collection, Library of Congress / https://www.loc.gov/item/
ihas.200154646/.

Fig. 14 "La Nijinska" as the Fairy of the Humming-Birds in *The Sleeping Princess*,
1921.
Ballets Russes souvenir program, Paris Opéra, May–June 1922. Private collection.

Fig. 15 Nijinska in Larionov's makeup for the role of Kikimora in *Contes Russes*, 1922.
Ballets Russes souvenir program, Théâtre de la Gaité-Lyrique, 1923. Private collection.

Fig. 16 Nijinska (standing left) in the Prologue of *The Sleeping Princess*, 1921.
Stiftung John Neumeier, Hamburg.

Fig. 17 Mikhail Larionov, Nijinska rehearsing her brother's role in *L'Après-midi d'un
Faune*, 1922.
© The State Tretyakov Gallery, Moscow.

Fig. 18 Nijinska as the Polovtsian Girl, London, 1924.
Performance photograph published in the *Daily Mail*. Private collection.

Fig. 19 Eleonora Bereda Nijinsky, Vienna, 1922.
Photo by Willinger. Bronislava Nijinska Collection, Library of Congress.

Fig. 20 Nijinska and her son Léon, spring 1924.
Bronislava Nijinska Collection, Library of Congress.

Fig. 21 Eugene Lapitzky, mid-1920s.
Bronislava Nijinska Collection, Library of Congress.

Fig. 22 Serge Unger, mid-1920s.
Bronislava Nijinska Collection, Library of Congress.

Fig. 23 Natalia Goncharova, female choreographic group, *Les Noces*, 1923.
© N. Goncharova / UPRAVIS 2021, ARS, NY. Victoria and Albert Museum, London.

Fig. 24 Natalia Goncharova, male choreographic group, *Les Noces*, 1923.
© N. Goncharova / UPRAVIS 2021, ARS, NY. Victoria and Albert Museum, London.

Fig. 25 Felia Doubrovska as the Bride in *Les Noces*.
W. A. Propert, *The Russian Ballet, 1921–1929* (London: John Lane, The Bodley Head, 1931), Plate 7.

Fig. 26 Felia Doubrovska and members of the Diaghilev company rehearsing *Les Noces*, London, 1926.
Collection of Robert Greskovic.

Fig. 27 Portrait-postcard inscribed by Francis Poulenc to Nijinska with "deep affection," 1923.
Bronislava Nijinska Collection, Library of Congress / https://www.loc.gov/item/ihas.200156306/.

Fig. 28 Nijinska as the Hostess in *Les Biches*, 1924.
Bridgeman Images.

Fig. 29 *Le Train Bleu*, London, 1924.
Bronislava Nijinska Collection, Library of Congress / https://www.loc.gov/item/ihas.200156354/.

Fig. 30 *Les Noces* and *Romeo and Juliet*, London, 1926.
The Sphere, 3 July 1926, 24a.

Fig. 31 Nijinska in a grotesque role, possibly for Theatre Choréographique.
Bronislava Nijinska Collection, Library of Congress.

Fig. 32 Nijinska (lower right) and members of Theatre Choréographique in *Touring*, 1925.
Bronislava Nijinska Collection, Library of Congress.

Fig. 33 Nijinska as the Ballerina in *Petrouchka*, Opéra Russe à Paris, 1930.
Photo by Boris Lipnitzky. Roger-Viollet via Getty Images.

Fig. 34 Nijinska (front) and members of Theatre Choréographique in Alexandra Exter's costumes for *Holy Etudes*, 1925.
Photo by Claude Harris. Kenji Usui Ballet Collection, Hyogo Performing Arts Center, Japan.

Fig. 35 Nijinska, Nicholas Singaevsky (to her right), and members of Theatre Choréographique outside "Caleb Foxwell Breeches Maker" on tour in England, 1925.
Bronislava Nijinska Collection, Library of Congress.

Fig. 36 Nijinska (center) surrounded by dancers of the Teatro Colón, 1926–1927.
Historia General de la Danza en la Argentina (Buenos Aires: Fondo Nacional de las Artes, 2008).

Fig. 37 Illiustrirovannaia Rossiia (*La Russie Illustrée*), with Ida Rubinstein on the cover, 1928.
Columbia University Libraries.

Fig. 38 Nijinska with the dancers and artistic staff of the Opéra Russe à Paris, 1930.
"Opéra Russe à Paris" souvenir program, Théâtre des Champs-Elysées, Spring 1930. Private collection.

Fig. 39 Natalia Goncharova, portrait of Nijinska, [1932].
Collection A. Parton and J. C. Wailes, UK. © N. Goncharova / UPRAVIS 2021, ARS, NY.

Fig. 40 Boris Chaliapin, portrait of his father, Fedor, 1932.
Fedor Chaliapin, *Man and Mask: Forty Years in the Life of a Singer*, trans. Phyllis Megroz (London: Gollancz, 1932), frontispiece.

Fig. 41 Nijinska's *Le Baiser de la Fée*, with scenery by Héctor Basaldúa, Teatro Colón, 1933.
Roberto Caamaño, *La historia del Teatro Colón 1908–1968* (Buenos Aires: Editorial Cinetea, 1969), II, n.p.

Fig. 42 Rehearsing *A Midsummer Night's Dream*, Hollywood, 1934.
Bronislava Nijinska Collection, Library of Congress.

Fig. 43 Alex Gard, " 'Ballet Russe' in Process of Rehearsal," New York, 1936.
New York Herald Tribune, 19 April 1936, sec. 5, p. 2.

Fig. 44 Nijinska (second from left) seated between Diaghilev's cousin Pavel Koribut-Kubitovitch (with the beard) and René Blum, with members of De Basil's Ballets Russes, Monte Carlo, April 1934.
Collection of Nina Youshkevitch. Courtesy of Robert Johnson.

Fig. 45 Nijinska (in hat and tie), with her husband Nicholas Singaevsky, son Léo, daughter Irina, and Irina's friend Nina Youshkevitch on a family outing, 1934. The car is the one in the accident that killed Léo.
Collection of Nina Youshkevitch. Courtesy of Robert Johnson.

Fig. 46 Gordon Anthony, portrait of Nijinska, mid-1930s.
© Gordon Anthony / Victoria and Albert Museum, London.

Fig. 47 Nijinska (second from right) rehearsing the Polish Ballet in Łazienki Park, Warsaw, 1937.
National Digital Archives, Warsaw.

Fig. 48 Olga Sławska (right) and Nina Juszkiewicz (Youshkevitch) in *Chopin Concerto*, 1937.
National Digital Archives, Warsaw.

Fig. 49 Rehearsing for the Hollywood Bowl, 1940: Cyd Charisse and William Hightower (left) in *Etude*, Maria (right) and Marjorie Tallchief in *Bolero*.
Bronislava Nijinska Collection, Library of Congress.

Fig. 50 Irina Baronova as Lise in *La Fille Mal Gardée*, Ballet Theatre, 1941.
Photo by Maurice Seymour. Jerome Robbins Dance Division, The New York Public Library for the Performing Arts.

Fig. 51 Nijinska rehearsing *Pictures at an Exhibition*, Ballet International, 1944.
Photo by Philippe Halsman © Halsman Archive.

Fig. 52 Nijinska and ballerina Yvette Chauviré in Vichy, 1947.
Courtesy of *Dancing Times*.

Fig. 53 Nijinska and Rosella Hightower, late 1940s.
Private Collection, The Stapleton Collection/Bridgeman Images.

Fig. 54 André Eglevsky and ensemble in *Brahms Variations*, late 1940s.
Marquis de Cuevas Collection, Henry Ransom Center, The University of Texas at Austin.

Fig. 55 Marquis de Cuevas with his "Sylphides."
1951 Season Souvenir Program, Grand Ballet de Marquis de Cuevas. Bronislava
   Nijinska Collection, Library of Congress.

Fig. 56 Nereids in *The Sleeping Beauty*, 1960.
Photo by Serge Lido. *Ballet Panorama: Photographies de Serge Lido* (Paris: Société
   Française du Livre, 1961).

Fig. 57 Rosella Hightower as Aurora in *The Sleeping Beauty*, 1960.
Photo by Serge Lido. *Ballet Panorama: Photographies de Serge Lido* (Paris: Société
   Française du Livre, 1961).

Fig. 58 Nijinska rehearsing *Les Biches*, Royal Ballet, 1964.
Photos by Erich Auerbach. *Illustrated London News*, 21 November. 1964, 827.

Fig. 59 Nijinska and Frederick Ashton at the dress rehearsal of *Les Noces*, Royal
   Ballet, 1966.
Photo by Houston Rogers. © Houston Rogers / Victoria and Albert Museum,
   London.

Fig. 60 Nijinska and Kathleen Crofton with Center Ballet of Buffalo dancers before
   the Jacob's Pillow season, 1969.
Photo by Jack Mitchell/Getty Images.

Fig. 61 Center Ballet of Buffalo in *Les Biches*, Jacob's Pillow, 1969.
Photo by John van Lund. Jacob's Pillow Archives.

Fig. 62 Niagara Frontier Ballet, with Jeanne Armin and Tatsuo Sakai, in *Chopin
   Concerto*, 1970.
Courtesy of Sandra Applebaum.

Fig. 63 Galina Ulanova in the backyard of Nijinska's home in Pacific Palisades, 1962.
© A. A. Bakhrushin State Central Theatre Museum, Moscow.

Fig. 64 Nijinska with Svetlana Beriosova at the dress rehearsal for *Les Noces*, Royal
   Ballet, 1966.
G. B. L. Wilson / Royal Academy of Dance / ArenaPAL.

Fig. 65 Nijinska and Anna-Marie Holmes, Buffalo, 1969.
Courtesy of Anna-Marie Holmes.

Archives, Collections, and Other Sources

Abbreviations

BN	Bronislava Nijinska
EM	*Early Memoirs*
IED	*International Encyclopedia of Dance*
IN	Irina Nijinska
NS	Nicholas Singaevsky
RN	Romola Nijinsky
SD	Serge Diaghilev

Archives

AN	Archives Nationales, Paris
BM-Opéra	Bibliothèque-Musée de l'Opéra, Paris
BNC	Bronislava Nijinska Collection, Music Division, Library of Congress
CAL	Carina Ari Library, Stockholm
HRC	Harry Ransom Center, University of Texas
HTC	Harvard Theatre Collection, Houghton Library, Harvard University
JPA	Jacob's Pillow Archives
NYPL	Jerome Robbins Dance Division, The New York Public Library for the Performing Arts
OHHSTA	Osterreichisches Haus-Hof und Staats-archiv
V&A	Theatre and Performance Collections, Victoria and Albert Museum

Collections

ABT Records	American Ballet Theatre Records, NYPL
Ancestry Library	Online database of census data, vital records, immigration, travel, citizenship, and other documents
Aronson Papers	Boris Aronson Papers and Designs, Billy Rose Theatre Collection, NYPL
Astruc Papers	Gabriel Astruc Papers, Jerome Robbins Dance Division, NYPL
Bolm Papers	Adolph Bolm Papers, Special Collections Research Center, Syracuse University Libraries

Denham Records	Sergei Denham Records of the Ballet Russe de Monte Carlo, NYPL
Ekstrom Collection	Ekstrom Collection: Diaghilev and Stravinsky Foundation, Theatre and Performance Collections, V&A
Fonds Kochno	Bibliothèque-Musée de l'Opéra, Paris
Gallo Papers	Fortune Gallo Ballet Russe Business Letters, NYPL
Grigoriev Papers	S. L. Grigoriev Papers, Harvard Theatre Collection, Houghton Library, Harvard University
Helscher Papers	Fern Helscher Papers, NYPL
Ismailoff Papers	Sergei Ismailoff Papers, NYPL
Jacob's Pillow	Jacob's Pillow Dance Festival Archives, Becket, MA
Kirstein Papers	Lincoln Kirstein Papers, c. 1913–1994, NYPL
Koch Collection	Frederick R. Koch Collection, Beinecke Rare Book and Manuscript Library, Yale University
Lewis Lloyd Papers	Yale Collection of American Literature, Beinecke Rare Book and Manuscript Library, Yale University
Nijinska Archives	Materials consulted at Nijinska's California home in the 1990s but not found at the Library of Congress
Reinhardt Archives	Max Reinhardt Archives, Binghamton University Libraries
Rickard Papers	Joseph Rickard Papers, Huntington Library, San Marino, CA
Vrangel Collection	Vrangel Collection, Hoover Institution, Stanford University

Newspapers

CDT	*Chicago Daily Tribune*
CSM	*Christian Science Monitor*
LAT	*Los Angeles Times*
MG	*Manchester Guardian*
NYHT	*New York Herald Tribune*
NYT	*New York Times*
WP	*Washington Post*

Journals and Magazines

BR	*Ballet Review*
DM	*Dance Magazine*
DR	*Dance Research*
DRJ	*Dance Research Journal*
DT	*Dancing Times*
JAMS	*Journal of the American Musicological Society*
NRF	*Nouvelle Revue française*
TLS	*Times Literary Supplement*

Notes

Preface

1. Bronislava Nijinska, *Early Memoirs*, trans. and ed. Irina Nijinska and Jean Rawlinson, introd. Anna Kisselgoff (New York: Holt, Rinehart and Winston, 1981). For how this differed from Nijinska's Russian manuscript, see Lynn Garafola, "Crafted by Many Hands: Re-Reading Bronislava Nijinska's *Early Memoirs*," *DR* 29, no. 1 (Summer 2011), 1–18.
2. *Modernism in Kyiv: Jubilant Experimentation*, ed. Irena R. Makaryk and Virlana Tkacz (Toronto: University of Toronto Press, 2010).
3. Nicholas Dromgoole, "Still Brand New," *Sunday Telegraph*, 27 Mar. 1966, Covent Garden Production File, Mar. 1966, V&A.
4. The term "Ballets Russes" is used for the company directed by Diaghilev and for the earliest manifestation of the company directed by Colonel de Basil. However, in the United States, the de Basil company usually dropped the final "s" from its name as did the company known as the Ballet Russe de Monte Carlo, which was founded in the late 1930s and directed by S. J. Denham. "Monte-Carlo" (with a hyphen) was typically used in France and Monte Carlo; without a hyphen in the United States and sometimes England. Inconsistency is evident in press materials, reviews, and memoirs.
5. Ted Shawn to Barton Mumaw, 4 Sept. 1942, JPA.
6. Jean Cocteau, "Deux Ballets actuels," *Revue de Paris*, 15 June 1924, 910; Arnold L. Haskell, *Balletomania: The Story of an Obsession* (London: Gollancz, 1934), 86.
7. "Diary (1932–1938)," entry for 12 Apr. 1938, 59/13, BNC.

Chapter 1

1. Qtd. in V[era] Krasovskaia, *Russkii baletnyi teatr nachala XX veka* (Leningrad: Iskusstvo, 1971), 404.
2. V. A. Teliakovskii, *Dnevniki direktora imperatorskikh teatrov, 1906–1909*, entry for 6 Apr. 1908, ed. M. G. Svetaeva (Moscow: Artist, Rezhisser, Teatr, 2011), 426.
3. *EM*, 247.
4. For Hebe, see the 1909 edition of the Yearbooks of the Imperial Theaters (Vol. 3).
5. *EM*, 309. On September 1, 1909 her annual salary rose from 600 to 700 rubles; the following September 1 to 800 rubles, and a month later to 900 rubles. These salary increases as well as her promotion to coryphée were announced in the *Zhurnal rasporiazhenii po Imperatorskim S.-Peterburgskim Teatram*, 2–5 July 1909 (No. 56), 29 Apr.–2 May 1910 (No. 36), 2–4 Aug. 1910 (No. 63), 30 Sept.–3 Oct. 1910 (No. 81).

6. For Nijinska's performances see the Yearbooks of the Imperial Theaters for 1909–1910 (Vol. 6) and 1910–11 (Vol. 6).

7. *EM*, 246–47. Nijinska speaks of the "oppressive and stifling" atmosphere on page 311.

8. Ibid., 311.

9. BN, draft-letter to Krasovskaya, 1 Jan. 1968, 48/12, BNC.

10. *EM*, 180.

11. Teliakovskii, *Dnevniki*, 170. Twelve was the highest grade, one the lowest.

12. *EM*, 179–80.

13. BN, personal dossier, Fond 497, Opis' 5, e.khr. 2222, Russian State Historical Archive (RGIA).

14. Carolyn G. Heilbrun, *Writing a Woman's Life* (New York: Norton, 1988), 13.

15. *EM*, 185.

16. Ibid., 219.

17. Ibid., 244. For Nijinska's room, see 243.

18. *EM*, 217. A clean Russian typescript of Nijinska's chapter, "Prince Lvov: Friend of Our Family," is in 32/1, BNC.

19. Lvov's relationship with the family is pieced together from *EM*, 197–200, 212–19, 230–35, 237–40.

20. Keith Money, *Anna Pavlova, Her Life and Art* (New York: Knopf, 1982), 13; Vera Krasovskaya, *Vaganova: A Dance Journey from Petersburg to Leningrad*, trans. Vera M. Siegel, introd. Lynn Garafola (Gainesville: University Press of Florida, 2005), 51–52.

21. Sjeng Scheijen, *Diaghilev: A Life*, trans. Jane Hedley-Prôle and S. J. Leinbach (London: Profile Books, 2009), 144.

22. Simon Karlinsky, "Russia's Gay History and Literature from the Eleventh to the Twentieth Centuries," in *Gay Roots: Twenty Years of Gay Sunshine, An Anthology of Gay History, Sex, Politics, and Culture*, ed. Winston Leyland (San Francisco: Gay Sunshine Press, 1991), 92.

23. Simon Karlinsky, "Russia's Gay Literature and Culture: The Impact of the October Revolution," in *Hidden from History: Reclaiming the Gay and Lesbian Past*, ed. Martin Bauml Duberman, Martha Vicinus, and George Chauncey Jr. (New York: New American Library, 1989), 351.

24. Teliakovskii, *Dnevniki*, 456. The Benckendorffs were a large, aristocratic family close to the throne. Teliakovsky may have been referring to Count Dmitrii (Mita) Aleksandrovich Benckendorff, who was an amateur painter and patron of Bakst.

25. *EM*, 229–31.

26. Scheijen, *Diaghilev*, 162. Scheijen's account of the dancer's pursuit of Diaghilev (161–63) substantially follows an unpublished account by Walter Nouvel, a longtime colleague and confidant, who was also gay. For Lvov's contribution to the 1909 season, see *EM*, 262.

27. *EM*, 259–60.

28. For Nijinska's account of the season, see *EM*, chap. 30.

29. Ibid., 285–86.

30. Ibid., 169–70.

31. V. A. Teliakovskii, *Dnevniki direktora imperatorskikh teatrov, 1909–1913,* ed. M. G. Svetaeva, M. B. L'vova, Mariia Khalizeva (Moscow: Artist, Rezhisser, Teatr, 2016), 426 (entry for 24 Jan. 1911). See also Scheijen, *Diaghilev,* 215–19, and *EM* (317–24).

32. "Balet: Pervyi vykhod g. Nizhinskago," *Rech',* 25 Jan. 1911.

33. "Teatr i muzyka: K uvol'neniu V. F. Nizhinskogo," *Rech',* 29 Jan. 1911.

34. "Bronislava Nijinska, Artist," to the St. Petersburg Office of the Imperial Theaters, 15 Feb. 1911, Fond 497, Opis' 5, e.kh. 2222, l.21, RGIA. Her resignation was formally accepted on 22 Feb. 1911 (A. Krupenskii, for the Director of the Imperial Theaters, Fond 497, Opis' 5, e.kh. 2222, l.22). I am grateful to Elizabeth Souritz for copies of these documents.

35. Teliakovsky, qtd. in Krasovskaia, *Russkii baletnyi teatr,* 404.

36. *EM,* 325–26.

37. Ibid., 260.

38. Ibid., 251.

39. This list of roles has been chiefly compiled from playbills at CAL.

40. Adolphe Julien, "Revue Musicale," *Journal des Débats,* 9 June 1912, 1; Robert Brussel, "Les Théâtres. — Grande saison de Paris: *Ballets russes,*" *Figaro,* 8 June 1911, 5; Robert Brussel, "Les Théâtres. — Au Châtelet: Grande Saison de Paris," *Figaro,* 14 May 1912, 5; J. Douduzier, "Lettre de Londres: Saison d'hiver," *Figaro,* 4 Mar. 1913, 5; "Tout-Paris," "Bloc-Notes Parisien: Au Théâtre des Champs-Elysées; Ballets et Opéras russes," *Gaulois,* 6 May 1913, 1.

41. Julien, "Revue Musicale"; Brussel, "Les Théâtres," 14 May 1912; "Le Masque de Fer," "A Travers Paris," *Figaro,* 22 May 1912, 1.

42. "Conférences et Auditions," *Figaro,* 1 June 1912, 6; "Le Masque de Fer," "A Travers Paris," *Figaro,* 17 June 1913, 1.

43. R. C., "Music Notes. End of the Opera Season. Covent Garden Reflections," *Daily Mail,* 31 July 1911, 8; "Russian Ballet. Exquisite Spectacle of Joy and Grace," *Daily Mail,* 26 June 1911, 3; and "New Russian Ballet. M. Nijinsky as Narcissus," *Daily Mail,* 19 July 1912, 5.

44. Qtd. in Robert Craft, *Igor and Vera Stravinsky: A Photograph Album 1921 to 1971* (London: Thames and Hudson, 1982), 12. The interview with Stravinsky was published in the *Petersburg Gazette,* 10 Oct. 1912.

45. *EM,* 292.

46. Ibid., 335.

47. Ibid., 343.

48. Ibid., 354.

49. Ibid., 283.

50. BN, "Iz dnevnika molodoi tantsovshchitsy, 1910–1912" (From the Diary of a Young Dancer, 1910–1912), unpublished, unpaginated manuscript dated New York 1942, chap. 1 ("Zamechatel'nye novosti" [Wonderful News]). I have translated directly from the Russian to give the flavor of Nijinska's spare and direct prose. For one of multiple versions of this manuscript, see 32/6 (Russian) and 2/8 (English translation), BNC.

51. *EM,* 174.

52. For this and the following quotations, see "From the Diary of a Young Dancer," chap. 3 ("Vaslav and Afternoon of a Faun").
53. Dorothy Bock Pierre, "Bronislava Nijinska," *American Dancer*, Apr. 1940, 13.
54. *EM*, 427.
55. BN, draft letter to Vera Krasovskaya, 11–12 Dec. 1967, 34/22, BNC.
56. Ibid.
57. *EM*, 450.
58. For her relationship with Nijinsky and work with the Ballets Russes, see Marie Rambert, *Quicksilver* (London: Macmillan, 1972), chaps. 4–5.
59. *EM*, 458.
60. RN, *Nijinsky*, 107.
61. Ibid., 188.
62. Marriage certificate, No. 170, Alexander Wladimirovich Kotschetovsky and Bronislava Nijinska, 2 July 1912, Registration District of St. Giles, London; *EM*, 438–39; Richard Buckle, *Diaghilev* (London: Weidenfeld and Nicolson, 1979), 234.
63. I have relied on Nijinska's account in her letter to Krasovskaya and in *EM*, 462–63.
64. The Monte Carlo playbills are from CAL; the Paris ones from BM-Opéra and HTC; and the London ones from the V&A.
65. Marc Semenoff, "Un entretien avec Bronislawa Nijinska," *Journal des Débats*, 6 June 1932, 4. This is one of very few interviews in which Nijinska acknowledges her choreographic ambitions.
66. With Vaslav now living outside Russia, Eleonora moved to a smaller apartment in the fall of 1911. BN, draft letter to RN, 27 Jan. 1966, 63/3, BNC.
67. See "Names and Descriptions of Alien Passengers Embarked at the Port of Southampton," SS *Avon*, 15 Aug. 1913, Ancestry Library. I am grateful to the Argentine researcher Lucía Chilibroste, who first drew this to my attention and sent me copies of the passenger list she discovered in the Buenos Aires maritime archives.
68. *EM*, 472–44.
69. Ibid., 478.
70. Ibid., 489.
71. Ibid., 490.
72. Ibid., 491.
73. Nijinsky to Stravinsky, 9 Dec. 1913, qtd. in Igor Stravinsky and Robert Craft, *Memories and Commentaries* (Berkeley: University of California Press, 1959), 38–40.
74. "The Theatres. Some New Productions," *Times*, 7 Feb. 1914, 10; "Dramatis Personae," *Observer*, 8 Feb. 1914, 8; *EM*, 494–95.
75. "M. Nijinsky's Return. Season at the Palace," *Times*, 25 Feb. 1914, 11.
76. *EM*, 495.
77. Ibid.
78. Saison Nijinsky window card, Box 169, BNC; EM, 495–97. Apart from Nijinsky, Nijinska, and Kochetovsky, the members of the company, as listed, were "Mdlle [Valentina] Viltzak, Bonni, Poeltzivich, Krasnitska, Iwanowa [Johnson], Tarassowa, Larionowa, Darinska [Doris], Ptitzenko, Jakowlewa [Jacobson]; and [Monsieurs]

Kojuhoff, Abramovitch, Morozoff, and Kaweki." The repertory was listed as *Les Sylphides, Le Spectre de la Rose, Carnaval, L'Oiseau et Prince* [sic], "and divertissements which will be constantly changed." For the dancers hired at the Nelidova studio, see Nijinska's autobiographical notes in 66/5, BNC.

79. "Nijinsky and Genée. Notable Week at the Palace and the Coliseum," *Observer*, 1 Mar. 1914, 13.

80. "N. Nijinsky's Illness. How the Famous Dancer's Health Broke Down under Ceaseless Work," *Evening News*, 17 Mar. 1914, 5.

81. *EM*, 498–99, 503. In 1992, Irina Nijinska told an interviewer that *Faune* could not be staged "because the paint on the newly designed sets for it were ruined" (Andrea Grodsky Huber, "A Conversation with Irina Nijinska," *BR* 20, no. 1 [Spring 1992], 47).

82. "Nijinsky's Art. Three Ballets in His Programme," *Standard*, 27 Feb. 1914, 5.

83. Autobiographical notes, 66/5, BNC. Since Nijinska repeats much the same thing in several notes, I have combined the relevant sentences.

84. G. H. M., "Nijinsky at the London Palace," *MG*, 3 Mar. 1914, 18.

85. Ibid.

86. "M. Nijinsky at the Palace. 'Les Sylphides' and 'Le Spectre de la Rose,'" *Times*, 3 Mar. 1914, 8; "Two Great Dancers," *Observer*, 8 Mar. 1914, 9; "Palace Theatre. Nijinsky's Appearance," *Daily Telegraph*, 3 Mar. 1914, 12.

87. Autobiographical notes, 66/5, BNC.

88. *Carnaval* was to be a highlight of the "entirely new programme" scheduled to begin on Monday, 14 Mar. However, when Nijinsky became ill, it was canceled. The cast, which included Mlle. Boni in Nijinska's Papillon role, was published in the *Standard*, 14 Mar. 1914, 4.

89. "M. Nijinsky at the Palace. 'Les Sylphides' and 'Le Spectre de la Rose.'"

90. G. H. M. "Nijinsky at the London Palace"; "Nijinsky's Return. His Leap into Favour at the Palace Theatre," *Standard*, 3 Mar. 1914, 5; "Two Great Dancers," *Observer*, 8 Mar. 1914, 9; "Nijinsky's Return. A Clamorous Welcome at the Palace," *Evening News*, 3 Mar. 1914, 6.

91. *EM*, 503–4.

92. R. C., "Nijinsky's New Dances. A Chopin Waltz and a Tartar Ballet," *Daily Mail*, 13 Mar. 1914, 8.

93. BN, miscellaneous note, 65/5, Notebook 1, BNC. Romola Nijinsky claims that Nijinska's "violent energy almost frightened her mother" (*Nijinsky*, foreword Paul Claudel [New York: Simon & Schuster, 1934], 119).

94. *EM*, 500–2.

95. Ibid., 505. Romola Nijinsky says that after one such incident Kochetovsky followed her husband to his dressing room, "insulted him, and spat, like a Russian *moujik*, at the floor before him" (*Nijinsky*, 266).

96. "Illness of Nijinsky," *Times*, 17 Mar. 1914, 8; "New Picture House," *Scotsman*, 17 Mar. 1914, 10; "Variety Gossip," *Era*, 18 Mar. 1914, 18; "Nijinsky and the Palace Theatre. An Extraordinary Situation," *MG*, 21 Mar. 1914, 10.

97. "M. Nijinsky's Illness"; "Nijinsky and the Palace Theatre"; "Dancer Nijinsky Ill. Condition So Grave That He May Never Be Able to Perform Again," *NYT*, 17 Mar. 1914, 4.
98. RN, *Nijinsky*, 265.
99. *EM*, 498, 507.

Chapter 2

1. *EM*, 509-12; for Nijinska's address, *Ves' Peterburg* (1912), 633.
2. Autobiographical notes, 66/5, BNC. Scribbled on little pieces of paper, these unnumbered, undated, and otherwise unidentified autobiographical notes were probably written in the mid-1930s, when Nijinska began planning a memoir based on her life. Her outline for an autobiographical volume covering events from 1914–1934 (hereafter "Autobiographical outline") is in 34/15, BNC. For the 1914–1915 Narodny Dom season, see the daily advertisements in *Novoe vremia*.
3. *Teatr i iskusstvo*, 11 May 1915, 382, and 14 June 1915, 422.
4. "Autobiographical outline," 18.
5. The program for the "Grand Evening of Vocal Music and Ballet" is in Box 163, nos. 4 and 5, BNC.
6. Autobiographical notes.
7. Contract between Mikhail Fedorovich Bagrov, director of the Kiev City Theater (Kievskii Gorodskoi Teatr), and Aleksandr Kochetovskii, 2 July 1915, 46/4, BNC. Unfortunately, Nijinska's contract has yet to come to light. For the items left in storage, see Petrograd Private Pawnshop, Gromozdskoe Branch, letter to B. Kochetovskaia-Nizhinskaia, 8 July 1919, 78/30, BNC.
8. Michael F. Hamm, "'Special and Bewildering': A Portrait of Late-Imperial and Early Soviet Kyiv," in *Modernism in Kyiv: Jubilant Experimentation*, ed. Irena R. Makaryk and Virlana Tkacz (Toronto: University of Toronto Press, 2010), 79.
9. Ibid., 88.
10. Contract, 2 July 1915, 46/4, BNC.
11. "Gorodskoi teatr," *Poslednie novosti*, 28 Sept. 1915, 4; qtd. in Marina Kurinnaia, "Kievskie gody Bronislavy Nizhinskoi," *Balet*, Mar.–Apr. 2011, 42.
12. Ibid.
13. Qtd. in Iurii Stanishevskyi, *Natsional'nyi akademichnyi teatr opery ta baletu Ukraïny imeni Tarasa Shevchenka: istoriia i suchasnist'* (Kyiv: Muzychna Ukraina, 2002), 115.
14. Autobiographical notes.
15. Iurii Stanishevskyi, *Baletnyi Teatr Ukrainy: 225 Rokiv Istorii* (Kyiv: Muzychna Ukraina, 2003), 30–31.
16. Autobiographical notes. Susanna Vitalevna Puare (as Poiré, Poiret, and Puare) danced for the Ballets Russes in 1912–1914. Trained in Evgeniia Sokolova's Petersburg studio, she was the niece of the celebrated actress Maria Puare and the Russian-born French cartoonist Emmanuel Puare, better known as Caran d'Ache.

17. Stanishevskyi does not mention *The Polovtsian Dances*, but Nijinska includes the ballet in "World War I and Revolution in Russia: 1914–1921," where she says that it ended the program (66-2). Nijinska intended this chapter (cited hereafter as "World War I and Revolution in Russia") to conclude *Early Memoirs*, but it was held back by the editors. The English-language typescript with revisions by Irina Nijinska is in 40/7, BNC.

18. Stanishevskyi, *Baletnyi Teatr Ukrainy*, 31.

19. BN to Alexandra Fedorova, 23 Feb. 1916, sold at Bidspirit Auction, Moscow, 17 Feb. 2018.

20. Stanishevskyi, *Baletnyi Teatr Ukrainy*, 31–32; "World War I and Revolution in Russia," 66-3; "M. M. Fokin i Vera Fokina," announcement, *Teatr i iskusstvo*, 27 Nov. 1916, n.p.

21. See Mayhill C. Flower in "'A Theatrical Mecca': The Stages of Kyiv in 1907," in *Modernism in Kyiv*, 34.

22. Autobiographical notes. Nijinska writes: "Goleizovsky, who danced Ivanushka the Fool came with her [Karsavina]. It must be said that Kochetovsky was unsurpassable as Ivanushka the Fool. And the audience had been already enraptured with my performances of the Tsar Maiden. . . . Karsavina and Goleizovsky had full audiences but [were received] without enthusiasm."

23. "Po provintsii," *Teatr i iskusstvo*, no. 22, 29 May 1916, 450.

24. The following quotations are from Nijinska's autobiographical notes.

25. "Benefis Bronislavy Nizhinskoi," *Polednie novosti*, 31 Jan. 1917, 4; qtd. in Kurinnaia, "Kievskie gody," 42.

26. Stanishevskyi, *Natsional'nii Akademichnii Teatr*, 118. For Nijinska's teaching of expressive movement to drama and opera students, see Kurinnaia, "Kievskie gody," 42.

27. "Autobiographical outline," 19.

28. Nijinsky to BN, 11 Aug. 1917, 79/1, BNC. Qtd. in English translation in "World War I and Revolution in Russia," 66-5, and in Nijinska's Russian typescript, 47/10, BNC.

29. For Malinovskaia, see Sheila Fitzpatrick, *The Commissariat of Enlightenment: Soviet Organization of Education and the Arts under Lunacharsky, October 1917–1921* (Cambridge, UK: Cambridge University Press, 1970), 112.

30. BN to Kochetovsky, undated, 78/33, BNC. The accompanying envelope is stamped 3 Jan. 1918.

31. "World War I and Revolution in Russia," 66-12. It is hard to know exactly when they danced at the Yar. From November 1915 to April 1916 the former restaurant became a field hospital. It was briefly resurrected, then closed again until February 23, 1918, when it became the site of the Theater of the Butyrskii Sovdep (1918–1919). See "Iar," *Estrada Rossii XX veka: Entsiklopediia* (Moscow: "Olma Press," 2004), 789. Sovdep is the acronym for Soviet of [Workers' and Soldiers'] Deputies.

32. "World War I and Revolution in Russia," 66-7-11.

33. "Svidetel'stvo" [Certificate] issued by the Third Station of the Meshchanskaia District to the "citizen Aleksandr Vladimirovich Kochetovskii residing in this district on 1st Meshchanskaia Street, No. 66/68, to be presented upon request to affirm that he is indeed the person named above, and that he permanently resides in Moscow together with his wife, Bronislava Fominichna Kochetovskaia," 8/13 May 1918, 46/4, BNC.

34. "Autobiographical outline," 19–20.

35. BN, "The School and Theater of Movement 1918," 97, 55/5, BNC.

36. "World War I and Revolution in Russia," 66-12/13.

37. BN, "On Movement and the School of Movement," *Schrifttanz* 3, no. 1 (Apr. 1930), English translation in *Schrifttanz: A View of German Dance in the Weimar Republic*, ed. Valerie Preston-Dunlop and Susanne Lahusen (London: Dance Books, 1990), 55–60; "On Movement and the School of Movement," trans. Anya Lem and Thelwall Proctor, ed. Joan Ross Acocella and Lynn Garafola, in Nancy Van Norman Baer, *Bronislava Nijinska: A Dancer's Legacy*, exhibition catalogue, Fine Arts Museums of San Francisco, 1986, 85–88. For three of the Russian versions, see 55/3, 7–8, BNC.

38. "The School and Theater of Movement 1918," 55/5; "Nijinska 1918," 58/14.

39. "The School and Theater of Movement 1918," 59. Hereafter, pages are given in the text.

40. I am grateful to the Dalcroze scholar Selma Landen Odom for sharing her unpublished paper, "Retrieving Sergei Volkonsky's Work on Rhythm and Expression," and for her many suggestions.

41. Dmitrii Sarabianov, "Kazimir Malevich and His Art, 1900–1915," in *Kazimir Malevich, 1878–1935* (Los Angeles: Armand Hammer Museum of Art, 1990), 166.

42. For the influence of esoteric thought, including theosophy and the fourth dimension, see Rose-Carol Washton Long, *Kandinsky: The Development of an Abstract Style* (Oxford: Clarendon Press, 1980), chap. 2; Linda Dalrymple Henderson, "The Image and Imagination of the Fourth Dimension in Twentieth-Century Art and Culture," *Configurations* 17, no. 1 (Winter 2009), 131–60; and John Milner, *Kazimir Malevich and the Art of Geometry* (New Haven: Yale University Press, 1996).

43. I am grateful to the Slavic scholar Nicole Svobodny for pointing this out.

44. For Exter's designs for the Kamerny Theater, see Jean Chauvelin and Nadia Filatoff, *Alexandra Exter* (Chevilly-Larue: Max Milo Editions, 2003), 96–115; and Georgy Kovalenko, *Alexandra Exter*, trans. Brian Droitcour (Moscow: Moscow Museum of Modern Art/Maier Publishing, 2010), I, 218–37.

45. Alexandra Exter, "The Artist in the Theater," in *Amazons of the Avant-Garde: Alexandra Exter, Natalia Goncharova, Liubov Popova, Olga Rozanova, Varvara Stepanova, and Nadezhda Udaltsova*, ed. John E. Bowlt and Matthew Drutt (New York: Guggenheim Museum/Abrams, 2000), 303.

46. Alexander Tairov, *Notes of a Director*, trans. and introd. William Kuhlke (Coral Gables, FL: University of Miami Press, 1969). Pages are noted in the text.

47. "On Movement and the School of Movement," in Baer, *Bronislava Nijinska*, 85.

48. Ivan Bunin, *Cursed Days: A Diary of Revolution*, ed., trans., and introd. Thomas Gaiton Marullo (Chicago: Ivan R. Dee, 1998). These impressions come from the section entitled "Moscow 1918" (27–74). For the daily bread ration, see W. Bruce Lincoln, *Red Victory: A History of the Russian Civil War* (New York: Simon & Schuster, 1989), 59.

49. Nina Berberova, *Moura: The Dangerous Life of the Baroness Budberg*, trans. Marian Schwartz and Richard D. Sylvester (New York: New York Review of Books, 2005), 36.

50. "World War I and Revolution in Russia," 66-13.

51. Ibid. Nijinska says the family returned to Kiev at the end of August 1918. However, the Kiev newspaper *Poslednie novosti* (Latest News) reported on October 15, 1918, that she had just returned.

52. For the very complicated political, social, and ethnic background, see Michael F. Hamm, "'Special and Bewildering': A Portrait of Late-Imperial and Early Soviet Kyiv," in *Modernism in Kyiv*, 52–96; and Myroslav Shjkandrij, *Jews in Ukrainian Literature: Representation and Identity* (New Haven: Yale University Press, 2009), chap. 3.

53. For the "Bat" Theater, see "Teatr i muzyka: Spektakli 'Letuchei myshi,'" *Kievskaia mysl'*, 31/18 Oct. 1918, 3; for Evreinov and the Mordkin studio and company, see in the same paper the announcements on 6 Nov./24 Oct. 1918, 1; 11 Oct./28 Sept. 1918, 1, and "Gorodskii teatr," 9 Oct./26 Sept. 1918, 2, respectively.

54. Qtd. in Heorhii [Georgii] Kovalenko, "Kyiv, 1918: Alexandra Exter and Her Studio," in *Ukrainian Modernism: 1910–1930* (Kyiv: National Art Museum of the Ukraine, 2006), 116.

55. I borrow the phrase from the title of Makaryk and Tkacz's book *Modernism in Kyiv: Jubilant Experimentation*.

56. Kovalenko, *Alexandra Exter*, II, 14–15.

57. Ibid., 47.

58. BN, draft-letter to Andrei B[orisovich] Nakov, [1971], 65/2, BNC. For Nakov's catalogue essay, see Andrei B. Nakov, *Alexandra Exter* (Paris: Galerie Jean Chauvelin, 1972).

59. Exter to BN, n.d., 72/32, BNC. The letter is published in Russian and in a somewhat different English translation in Kovalenko, *Alexandra Exter*, II, 308–9.

60. Exter to BN, 28 Mar. 1924, 72/32, BNC. See also Kovalenko, *Alexandra Exter*, II, 308–9.

61. For the addresses of Nijinska's studios, see the miscellaneous note in 66/5, BNC. In "World War I and Revolution in Russia" (66-14), Nijinska says that "she rented a studio at the private residence of Prince Troubetsky and the Vichnevsky's on Funduklievskaya Street." For the address of Exter's studio, see Chauvelin and Filatoff, *Alexandra Exter*, 10. According to Nijinska, the studio was bombed during one of the many changes in government, and classes resumed at her apartment. However, a photograph in the Serge Lifar room at the Museum of Cultural Heritage, Kyiv, shows the location of the studio off Khreshchatyk Street, the city's main thoroughfare. Given that his discovery of dance came in late 1920 or early 1921, this was probably a later studio.

62. For his birthdate, see his baptismal certificate from St. Alexander's Roman Catholic Church in Kiev, 14 July 1919, in Russian and Latin, with accompanying French translation, dated 15 Mar. 1935, 46/5, BNC.

63. A document issued by the Bronislava Nijinska School of Movement on May 26, 1919, certified that Sofia Nikolaevna Dybovskaia "has been a student at my school in which lessons take place from 4 to 7 o'clock and entail physical work." Former collection of Sofia Nikolaevna Volkova (née Dybovskaia) sold at Bidspirit Auction, Moscow, 28 Nov. 2019.

64. Gunhild Schüller, "Nijinska's 'Studio' and the Beginning of Choreographic Activity," 55/1, BNC. Schüller, an Austrian dance scholar, wrote her doctoral thesis on Nijinska, and these notes, which she probably made for Nancy Van Norman Baer, drew on interviews with dancers who had studied with Nijinska in Kiev. In her autobiographical notes Nijinska also mentions movement classes and her work with singers.

65. Schüller gives a somewhat different list of subjects—classic dance, character dance (following Nijinska's own system), expression in movement, make-up, costume studies, ensemble, art history, painting, art of the theater, and theory of music. She describes the "expression in movement" classes as designed to improve the student's creative faculties and musicality.

66. Although Serge Lifar went on to a professional career, he only studied briefly with Nijinska in Kiev.

67. BN, draft letter to Nijinsky, undated [Mar. 1919], 79/1, BNC. See also Emilia de Pardány Markus to BN, 12 Oct. 1918, 75/23, BNC.

68. Kurinnaia, "Kievskie gody," 43. The reference to SARABIS (the acronym for Soiuz rabot[nikov] iskusstva) is in 66/5, BNC.

69. Hanna Veselovska, "Kyiv's Multicultural Theatrical Life, 1917–1926," in *Modernism in Kyiv*, 257.

70. Qtd. in Irena R. Makaryk, "Modernism in Kyiv: Jubilant Experimentation," in *Modernism in Kyiv*, 16.

71. I refer to *Amazons of the Avant-Garde*, the 1999 exhibition documenting the contributions of Exter, Natalia Goncharova, Liubov Popova, Olga Rozanova, Varvara Stepanova, and Nadezchda Udaltsova to the Russo-Soviet visual arts and theater (see note 45).

72. "Kotchy's Escape from Revolutionary Russia," chapter from an unpublished biography, 4, 46/4, BNC. The author is unidentified.

73. Kochetovsky to BN, 25 July 1919, 78/33, BNC.

74. BN to Nina (Sirotinine), undated [1919], 76B/2, BNC.

75. For a sense of the confusing events of this period, see "Denikin's Forces in Ukraine Capital," *NYT*, 5 Sept. 1919, 13; "Occupation of Kiev Announced," *CSM*, 6 Sept. 1919, 1; "Anti-Red Forces near Petrograd," *NYT*, 21 Oct. 1919, 19; Harold Williams, "Denikin's Advance Strongly Resisted," *NYT*, 5 Nov. 1919, 17; "Denikin to Quit Kiev," *The Sun*, 16 Nov. 1919, 2; "Big Battle Rages in South Russia," *NYT*, 10 Dec. 1919, 16; "Denikin's Flanks Advance Again," *NYT*, 23 Dec. 1919, 15.

76. The four untitled name lists are in 66/5, BNC. The reference to Shifrin designing *Petrouchka* is in the 29 Dec. 1919 (Old Style) entry, "Diary 1919–22." Although the secondary literature is silent on Shifrin's collaboration with Nijinska, the brief biography in *Tradition and Revolution: The Jewish Renaissance in Russian Avant-Garde Art 1912–1928*, ed. Ruth Apter-Gabriel (Jerusalem: Israel Museum 1987), mentions that in 1920 he "did the stage designs for plays by Molière and Cervantes, performed by the Russian Drama Theatre, and for Stravinsky's ballet, *Petrushka*" (244).

77. "Class at the Jewish Studio," she noted in her diary on 27 Dec. 1919 (Old Style), "Diary 1919–22."

78. Shifrin, qtd. in *Khudozhniki teatra o svoem tvorchestve* [Artists of the Theater on Their Creative Work], ed. F. Ia. Syrkina (Moscow: Sovetskii Khudozhnik, 1973), 333. See also Kurinnaia, "Kievskie gody," 44. Nijinska's reaction to *Petrouchka* and rehearsing *Egyptian Nights* are in her diary entries for 2 Jan. and 18 Feb. 1920 ("Diary 1919–22").

79. Françoise Reiss, *Sur la Pointe des pieds: Annales chorégraphiques* (Paris: Editions Lieutier, 1953), 63.

80. Entry for 27 Dec. 1919 (Old Style), "Diary 1919–22." Hereafter, the dates will be given after a quotation in the text.

81. Georgii Kovalenko to the author, 19 June 2011.

82. The very full program, which also included *The Doll*, *The Buffoon* (probably the Buffoons' Dance from *Le Pavillon d'Armide*), *White Cat* and *Puss in Boots* (from *The Sleeping Beauty*), and a Spanish-style solo to Tchaikovsky, is transcribed in Georgii Kovalenko, "Bronislava Nizhinskaia i Aleksandra Ekster," *Voprosy teatr/ ROSCAENIUM* 16, nos. 3–4 (2014), 302–3.

83. "Vecher Bronislavy Nizhinskoi," *Kievskii den'*, 8 June 1920, 2.

84. Kurinnaia, "Kievskie gody," 43.

85. I am grateful to Elizabeth Souritz for the information about the relationship between Meller, Shifrin, and their wives.

86. BN, draft letter to SD, 1921, 72/4, BNC. In her "Autobiographical outline" (22), she reiterates this telegraphically: "I do not want to be an étoile—I am simply Nizhinskaia!"

87. "School and Theater of Movement 1918," 16.

88. "God, how much I want to see you on stage," her friend Nina Moiseevna Godkina-Stefanovich wrote to her on 15 Sept. 1922. "Your performances in Kiev will never be forgotten!" (76/51, BNC).

89. Schüller, "Nijinska's 'Studio' "; see also Kovalenko, "Bronislava Nizhinskaia i Aleksandra Ekster" (302–3), for a redaction of the program for the 4 June 1920 "Evening of Bronislava Nijinska's Choreographic Sketches" at the Kiev City Theater.

90. Fernand Divoire, *Découvertes sur la Danse* (Paris: Editions G. Crès, 1924), 66.

91. "Diary 1919–22," entries for 27(?) and 29 Jan. 1920; "Vecher Bronislavy Nizhinskoi," *Kievskii den'*, 8 June 1920, 2.

92. Qtd. in Schüller, "Nijinska's 'Studio.' "

93. Divoire, *Découvertes sur la Dance*, 66.

94. 66/1, BNC. This fragment appears in a notebook dated 1925.

95. Qtd. in Kovalenko, "Bronislava Nizhinskaia i Aleksandra Ekster," 303.

96. "Diary 1919–22," entries for 26 Sept. 1920 (*Mephisto*) and 19 Feb. 1921 (*Marche Funèbre*). Anna Vorobieva, who danced for Nijinska in Kiev, recalled these works as aspiring to a unity of music and movement (Schüller, "Nijinska's 'Studio' ").

97. "World War I and Revolution in Russia," 66-14.

98. Qtd. in James Loeffler, *"The Most Musical Nation": Jews and Culture in the Late Russian Empire* (New Haven: Yale University Press, 2006), 189.

99. Autobiographical notes. A pood was thirty-six pounds, an arshin about twenty-eight inches.

100. "World War I and Revolution in Russia," 66-10.

101. In a letter to Nijinska after she left Kiev, Nina Moiseevna wrote: "I remember how overworking made you ill in Russia, and seeing how much you are [now] doing makes me worry" (10 Sept. 1922, 76/51, BNC).

102. *The White Guard* was published in 1927 by émigré presses in Paris and Riga.

103. Qtd. in Horbachov, "In the Epicentre of Abstraction," in *Modernism in Kyiv*, 170.

104. Autobiographical notes.

105. Lillian Faderman, *Surpassing the Love of Men: Romantic Friendship and Love between Women from the Renaissance to the Present* (New York: William Morrow, 1981), 135.

106. The information about Kurbas and the Young Theater is from Virlana Tkacz, "Towards a New Vision of Theatre: Les Kurbas's Work at the Young Theatre in Kyiv," in *Modernism in Kyiv*, 278–81, and from the "Production List" beginning on page 570.

107. Surits, *Mordkin*, 112. According to an announcement in *Kievskii mysl'* (11 Oct./28 Sept. 1918, 1), Mordkin opened a studio at the City Theater in the fall of 1918 that offered children's and adult classes in ballet, gymnastics, and social dances as well as classes in expressive movement ("plastique") for opera and dramatic artists.

108. Valentina Chistiakova, "Glavny iz vospominanii," *Teatr*, Apr. 1992, 73.

109. Virlana Tkacz, "Les Kurbas's Work at the Young Theatre in Kyiv," in *Modernism in Kyiv*, 298.

110. Chistiakova, "Glavny iz vospominanii," 79. *Oedipus Rex* premiered on 16 Nov. 1918, just weeks after Nijinska returned to Kiev. The rehearsal must have been for a later performance.

111. Les Kurbas, *S'ohodni Ukraïns'koho teatru i Berezil'* (Kharkov: Biblioteka VAPLITE, 1927), 28.

112. BN, "On Movement and the School of Movement," in *Schrifttanz*, 56.

113. Jean Rollot, "Les merveilleux ballets russes de Mme Nijinska," *Paris-Soir*, 5 June 1932, 6.

114. BN, "On Movement and the School of Movement," in Baer, *Bronislava Nijinska*, 85. She refers to it in her diary on February 18, 1920 and January 8, 1921 ("Diary 1919–22").

115. Qtd. in Virlana Tkacz, "Les Kurbas's Early Work at the Berezil: From Bodies in Motion to Performing the Invisible," in *Modernism in Kyiv*, 362.

116. Kurinnaia, "Kievskie gody," 45.

117. "Postanovlenie Narodnogo Komissariata Obprazovaniia" [Resolution of the People's Commissariat of Education], published in the Ukrainian-language Kiev newspaper *Visti* [News] on 1 Mar. 1921.

118. See also Hanna Veselovska, "Kyiv's Multicultural Theatrical Life, 1917–1926," in *Modernism in Kyiv*, 261–64.

119. James von Geldern, *Bolshevik Festivals 1917–1920* (Berkeley: University of California Press, 1993), 28.

120. Ibid., 28.

121. Serge Lifar, *Du Temps que j'avais faim* (Paris: Stock, 1935), 157.

122. Ibid., 161.

123. For the documentation of this relationship, see Patrizia Veroli, "Serge Lifar as a Dance Historian and the Myth of Russian Dance in 'Zarubezhnaia Rossiia' (Russia Abroad) 1930–1940," *Dance Research* 32, no. 2 (Winter 2014), 105–43.

124. Lifar, *Du Temps que j'avais faim*, 162.

125. Vladimir Zlobin, *A Difficult Soul: Zinaida Gippius*, ed. and introd. Simon Karlinsky (Berkeley: University of California Press, 1980), 172, 177.

126. Marko Tereshchenko, *Kirz' let chasu* (Kiev: Mystetstvo, 1974), 19; qtd. in Kurinnaia, *Kievskie gody*, 45.

127. A draft of her letter dated 27 Feb. 1921 is in 71A/10, BNC.

128. A bound volume with these writings—but not Tereshchenko's treatise—is in the collection of the Harvard University Libraries. See *Teatralny poradnyk* (Kiev: Vyd-vo Dniprosoiuzu, 1920–1923).

129. BN, "Theory of Movement," 48/8, BNC.

130. Susan Manning, *Ecstasy and the Demon: The Dances of Mary Wigman* (Minneapolis: University of Minnesota Press, 2006), 29.

131. Vera Maletic, "Laban Principles of Movement Analysis," *IED*.

132. Ibid.

133. Valerie Preston-Dunlop, "Laban, Rudolf," *IED*.

134. Autobiographical notes.

135. RN to BN, 31 Mar. 1920, 78/46, BNC.

136. "World War I and Revolution in Russia," "On the Way to Vaslav," and "Re-Union with Vaslav," 40/7, BNC.

137. "World War I and Revolution in Russia," 66/18-20.

138. "Autobiographical outline," 21.

139. Autobiographical notes.

140. George Leggett, *The Cheka: Lenin's Political Police* (Oxford: Clarendon Press, 1981), 198. See also Christopher Andrew and Vasili Mitrokhin, *The Sword and the Shield: The Mitrokhin Archive and the Secret History of the KGB* (New York: Basic Books, 1999).

141. BN, unpublished note about "Levitskii, Commissar, NAROBRAZ." This note, which appears in an alphabetical list of Nijinska's Kiev students and colleagues, was found by Virlana Tkacz and Irena Madaryk in the Nijinska archives when they were still located at the choreographer's home in California. The typescript is a "clean" and fuller version of the rough draft material in 66/5, BNC.

142. BN, "On the Way to Vaslav." For Nijinska's Polish papers, see her Registration Card No. 3045, issued in Tarnopol, 10 May 1921, 46/1, and her Polish passport, issued in Warsaw, 19 May 1921, 46/11, BNC.

143. BN to SD, n.d. [late June 1921], Pièce 65, Fonds Kochno.

Chapter 3

1. BN, "Sergei Diaghilev," trans. Nathalie Wollard, unpublished typescript, 47/2, BNC, 8. The opening anecdote was absorbed into Chapter 29 ("Sergei Pavlovitch Diaghilev") of *Early Memoirs*, but otherwise the essay and the chapter are quite different. Other versions, including Russian typescripts, are in 34/3 and 34/4, BNC.

2. BN to SD, 17 May 1921, Pièce 65, Fonds Kochno. A draft is in 72/4, BNC.

3. Drobecki to Grigoriev, with a postscript by BN to Lubov Tchernicheva, 25 May 1921, HTC.

4. Peter Ostwald, *Vaslav Nijinsky: A Leap into Madness* (New York: Carol Publishing Group, 1991), 263. Irina Nijinska was Ostwald's source for this.

5. BN, telegram to SD, 25 June 1921, Pièce 65, Fonds Kochno.

6. BN to SD, undated [late June 1921], Pièce 65, Fonds Kochno.

7. BN to SD, 3 July 1921, Pièce 65, Fonds Kochno.

8. For the Residenz-Atelier photograph, see Baer, *Bronislava Nijinska*, 21. For information about Nijinska's engagement, see the Viennese newspaper *Neues 8 Uhr Blatt*, where her name appeared in the Moulin-Rouge's advertisements from August 3–September 16, 1921.

9. The photos, printed on card stock, are in 154/27, BNC.

10. "Autobiographical outline," 34/15, BNC, 22.

11. For an overview of modern dance in Vienna, see *Alles tanzt: Kosmos Wiener Tanzmoderne*, exhibition catalogue, Kunst Historisches Museum, Vienna, 2019.

12. The program for this Russische Konzert-Akademie concert, which took place on 10 Sept. 1921, is in 163/3, BNC.

13. André Levinson, "The Sleeping Princess," in *The Designs of Léon Bakst for "The Sleeping Princess"* (London: Benn Brothers, 1923), 11–12.

14. BN, "Reflections about the Production of *Les Biches* and *Hamlet* in Markova-Dolin Ballets," trans. Lydia Lopokova, *DT*, Feb. 1937, 617.

15. SD, Letter to the Editor, *Peterburgskaia gazeta*, 1 Jan. 1904, in *A Century of Russian Ballet: Documents and Eyewitness Accounts, 1810–1910*, ed. and trans. Roland John Wiley (Oxford: Clarendon Press, 1990), 421.

16. Serge de Diaghilew, "The Imperial Russian Ballet," *Times*, 10 Mar. 1911, 10.

17. Richard Buckle, *Diaghilev* (London: Weidenfeld and Nicolson, 1979), 379.

18. Igor Stravinsky, "The Diaghilev I Knew," trans. Mercedes de Acosta, *Atlantic Monthly*, Nov. 1953, 35.

19. S. L. Grigoriev, *The Diaghilev Ballet 1909–1929*, trans. Vera Bowen (London: Constable, 1953), 167–68. *Chu Chin Chow* was in its fifth, not third, year.

20. René Dumesnil, "La danse à l'Opéra de Paris depuis 1900," in *L'Art du Ballet des origines à nos jours* (Paris: Editions du Tambourinaire, 1952), 142.

21. Contract between SD and Jacques Rouché, 8 Oct. 1921, AJ13/1292, AN. For Kschessinska, see Sitter Out, *Dancing Times*, Oct. 1921, 2, and H.S.H. The Princess Romanovsky-Krassinsky, *Dancing in Petersburg: The Memoirs of Kschessinska*, trans. Arnold Haskell (London: Gollancz, 1960), 205.

22. "Les Théâtres," *Gaulois*, 25 Sept. 1921, 5.

23. For Petipa's brother Lucien, see the scattered references in Ivor Guest, *Le Ballet de l'Opéra de Paris: trois siècles d'histoire et de tradition*, trans. Paul Alexandre (Paris: Opéra de Paris/Flammarion, 1976); for Vsevolozhsky, see Helena Hammond, "Cecchetti, Carabosse and *The Sleeping Beauty*," in *Selected Papers from "An International Celebration of Enrico Cecchetti*," University of Chichester, 31 July 2005, 12–22.

24. D. Merejkowsky [*sic*], "Molière et la Russie," *Comoedia*, 25 Jan. 1922, 1.

25. Marc Raeff, *Russia Abroad: A Cultural History of the Russian Emigration, 1919–1939* (New York: Oxford University Press, 1990). One million is a fairly conservative estimate. Raeff gives the various estimates on page 24.

26. In addition to Raeff's *Russia Abroad*, see Robert H. Johnston, *"New Mecca, New Babylon": Paris and the Russian Exiles, 1920–1945* (Kingston and Montreal: McGill-Queen's University Press, 1988); Leonid Livak, *How It Was Done in Paris: Russian Emigré Literature and French Modernism* (Madison: University of Wisconsin Press, 2003), and Marina Gorboff, *La Russie fantôme: L'émigration russe de 1920 à 1950* (Lausanne: Editions L'Age d'Homme, 1995). For a study of the Russian dance emigration in Paris, see Elisabeth Hennebert, "'Coureurs de cachet': Histoire des danseurs russes de Paris (1917–1944)," 3 vols., Thèse de Doctorat (Histoire), Université de Paris I, 2002; for the relationship with the French fashion world, Alexandre Vassiliev, *Beauty in Exile: The Artists, Models, and Nobility Who Fled the Russian Revolution and Influenced the World of Fashion*, trans. Antonina W. Bouis and Anya Kucharev (New York: Abrams, 2000). For posters, flyers, and tickets designed by Natalia Goncharova and other Russian artists for the Union des Artistes Russes à Paris, see the collection of "Bals des artistes" materials [*MGZP Uni A 1–16], NYPL.

27. Scheijen, *Diaghilev*, 347–50, 417.

28. Johnston, "New Mecca," 67.

29. "A Letter from Igor Stravinsky," dated Paris, 10 Oct. 1921, in Ballets Russes Souvenir Program: *The Sleeping Princess* (London: Alhambra Theatre, 1921), n.p. The draft (in French) that Stravinsky sent to Diaghilev is in Pièce 96, Fonds Kochno.

30. Ernest Newman, "The World of Music: The Russian Ballet," *Sunday Times*, 27 Nov. 1921, 4.

31. On 9 Sept. 1921 Diaghilev wired Nijinska to come directly to Paris. "French consul will receive instructions [about] visa. Telegraph when you get [to] Paris," 72/4, BNC.

32. Nouvel to SD, 20 Aug. 1921, Pièce 69, Fonds Kochno. The "sketches by Kiev cubists" are almost certainly Meller's *Fear* and *Mephisto Valse*, now at the Library of Congress.

33. Ibid.

34. Ibid.

35. Contract between Sergei Pavlovich Diaghilev ("nobleman [and] director of the Russian ballet") and Bronislava Fominichna Nizhinskaia ("artist of the ballet troupe"), 30 Aug. 1921, MS Thr 465, Series II, B, Folder 68, Grigoriev Papers, HTC.

36. SD, telegram to BN, 9 Sept. 1921, 72/4, BNC.

37. The *Ezhegodnik Imperatorskikh Teatrov* gives the starting date of his tenure as régisseur as 6 Oct. 1903. V[era] Krasovskaia in *Russkii baletnyi teatr nachala XX veka* ([Leningrad: Iskusstvo, 1971], vol. 2, 445), gives the end date of his tenure as 1918.

38. Diaghilev's contract with Nikolai Grigorevich Sergeev was signed on 11 Aug. 1921 and covered the six-week period from Sept. 5 to Oct. 17. The contract, which is at the Harvard Theatre Collection, is reproduced in Russian and in an English translation in Maureen Anne Gupta, "Diaghilev's *Sleeping Princess* (1921)," Ph.D. diss., Princeton University, 2011, 304–5.

39. BN, "The Triumph of Petipa," in *Marius Petipa: Materialy, Vospominania, Stat'i*, ed. A. (Leningrad: Iskusstvo, 1971), 317. See also *EM*, 246.

40. Roslavleva, *Era of the Russian Ballet*, 170. This is echoed by Souritz in *Soviet Choreographers in the 1920s*, 39.

41. Ninette de Valois, *Come Dance with Me: A Memoir, 1898–1956* (Cleveland: World Publishing Company, 1957), 127–28.

42. André Levinson, "La Danse: Complainte d' 'Igor,'" *Candide*, 18 July 1929, 23/1, BNC.

43. Gupta, "Diaghilev's *Sleeping Princess*," 20–21.

44. The ten-year-old prodigy eventually became the ballerina Alicia Markova. According to Markova, Diaghilev "spoke to Nijinska, and they thought of putting me in *The Sleeping Princess* and giving me a special variation as the Fairy Dewdrop." Qtd. in John Gruen, *The Private World of Ballet* (New York: Viking, 1975), 46.

45. Gupta, "Diaghilev's *Sleeping Princess*," 21.

46. For a list of Diaghilev's changes in the score and libretto, see Gupta, "Diaghilev's *Sleeping Princess*," 72–74, 80–82. For the opening night cast, see Cyril W. Beaumont, *Bookseller at the Ballet: Memoirs 1899–1929* (London: C. W. Beaumont, 1975), 274.

47. Lincoln Kirstein, *Ballet Alphabet: A Primer for Laymen* (New York: Kamin Publishers, 1939), 19.

48. BN, "The Triumph of Petipa," 317–18.

49. For *The Sleeping Princess* cast list, see the Alhambra Theatre playbill, Box 122 (Scrapbook), no. 5, BNC. The cast list for the 1890 *Sleeping Beauty* is reproduced in M. Konstantinova, *"Spiashchaia krasavitsa"* [The Sleeping Beauty] (Moscow: Iskusstvo, 1990), 61, and an English translation appears in Wiley, *A Century of Russian Ballet* (1990), 361–62. However, neither source lists the children appearing in the "Valse villageoise." The 1999 reconstruction by the Maryinsky Ballet used twenty-four children.

50. André Levinson, "Une dernière étape des 'Ballets Russes': *La Belle au bois dormant*," in *Le Ballet au XIXe siècle*, special issue of *Le Revue musicale*, 1 Dec. 1921, 134/230.

51. "Sergei Pavlovich, apparently, is satisfied with what I'm doing. Out of habit he gives no praise, so the dancer doesn't become full of himself. But I'm of a different nature; I work better when I'm praised" ("Diary 1919–22," 19 Oct. 1921).

52. Beaumont, *Bookseller*, 271.

53. Ibid.

54. Ibid., 272.

55. Qtd. in Boris Kochno, with Maria Luz, *Le Ballet* (Paris: Hachette, 1964), 246.

56. BN, "Sergei Pavlovitch Diaghilev," 6.

57. Scheijen, *Diaghilev*, 399.

58. Qtd. in Gordon Watts, "15 to One," *DT*, Sept. 2013, 36.

59. See, for example, H. G., "The New Russian Ballet: Splendour and Disappointment, 'The Sleeping Princess,'" *Observer*, 6 Nov. 1921, 9, and "Sitter Out," *DT*, Jan. 1922, 332.

60. "Sitter Out," *DT*, Dec. 1921, 181–82.

61. Qtd. in Macdonald, *Diaghilev Observed*, 278.

62. See the photographs of her in *DT*, Dec. 1921, 183, 185.

63. Nina Moiseevna Gorkina-Stefanovich to BN, 29 Apr. 1922, 76/51, BNC.

64. BN, "In the Russian Ballet, London, 1921," Russian-language typescript, n.p., BNC.

65. See Petipa's scenario in Roland John Wiley, *Tchaikovsky's Ballets: Swan Lake, Sleeping Beauty, Nutcracker* (Oxford: Clarendon Press, 1985), Appendix D, 354 (English translation) and 360 (French).

66. Giannandrea Poesio, "The Awakened Beauty," *DT*, Oct. 1993, 38.

67. Vera M. Krasovskaya, "The Sleeping Beauty," *IED*, 608.

68. BN, "In the Russian Ballet, London, 1921," BNC.

69. Ninette de Valois, *Step by Step: The Formation of an Establishment* (London: W. H. Allen, 1977), 22.

70. Ibid., 124–25.

71. Irina Baronova, *Irina: Ballet, Life and Love* (Gainesville: University Press of Florida, 2005), 171.

72. For Nijinsky's Blue Bird, see *EM*, 272; for Papillon, 285–88.

73. "'The Sleeping Princess,' Russian Ballet at the Alhambra, Tchaikovsky's Magic," *Times*, 3 Nov. 1921, 8.

74. Stravinsky, "The Diaghilev I Knew," 35.

75. Ernest Newman, "The Week's Music: 'The Sleeping Princess,'" *Sunday Times*, 6 Nov. 1921, 7; Raymond Mortimer, "London Letter, February 1922," *Dial*, Mar. 1922, 295–96; H. G., "The New Russian Ballet: Splendour and Disappointment," *Observer*, 6 Nov. 1921, 9; W. J. Turner, "The Sleeping Princess," *New Statesman*, 22 Nov. 1921, 169; Turner-, "Drama," *London Mercury* 5, no. 26 (Dec. 1921), 201.

76. SD, card to BN, 2 Nov. 1921, 72/4, BNC.

77. BN, draft letter to SD, 1921, 72/4, BNC. Is it possible that she was angling for a shot at the role of Aurora?

78. Payroll sheet, 1–15 Dec. 1921, former collection of the Stravinsky-Diaghilev Foundation. The highest paid dancers, earning 2,750 francs for the two-week period, were Lubov Tchernicheva (Grigoriev's wife) and Leon Woizikovsky. Lubov Egorova, one of Diaghilev's four Auroras, received 1,500 francs, as did Pierre Vladimirov, the first-cast Prince Charming.

79. SD to Francis Poulenc, London, 15 Nov. 1921, in *Francis Poulenc: Selected Correspondence 1915–1963*, trans. and ed. Sidney Buckland (London: Gollancz, 1991), 43.

80. Kochetovsky's girlfriend was the twenty-one-year-old Bulgarian "artiste" Dorothea (Dora) Rakovsky, who traveled with the Chauve-Souris to New York on the SS *Lapland* arriving on 30 Jan. 1922. New York, Passenger Lists, 1820–1957, Ancestry Library.

81. "Mr. Hornblow Goes to the Play," *Theatre Magazine*, Sept. 1922, 151.

82. Michel Mok, "Lady in White Gloves," *New York Post*, 4 Jan. 1940, Sec. 2, Box 160 (Scrapbook), no. 2, BNC.

83. This note, which appears in an alphabetical list of Nijinska's students and colleagues from Kiev, was found by Virlana Tkacz and Irena Madaryk in the Nijinska archives when they were still located at the choreographer's home in California. The typescript is a "clean" and fuller version of the rough draft found in 66/5, BNC.

84. The others were Leon Woizikovsky and Thadée Slavinsky.

85. Lappa is quoted in the entry on *The White Guard* in the Russian-language version of Wikipedia (https://ru.wikipedia.org/wiki/Белая_гвардия_(роман)).

86. Both photos are in 156/22, BNC.

87. For the Ballets Russes, see "Liste des Artistes 1919," bMSThr 465 (15), and "Thêátre Municipal de la Gaîté," MS Thr 465 (17), Grigoriev Papers, HTC; for the season in Poznan, "Certificate," 16 Sept. 1920, 77/10, BNC; for his arrival in Monte Carlo on April 15, "Permis de Séjour," Principality of Monaco, 29 Apr. 1921, 46/4, BNC.

88. Herman Klein, "The Art of Chaliapin," *Musical Times*, 1 Nov. 1921; qtd. in Victor Borovsky, *Chaliapin: A Critical Biography* (New York: Knopf, 1988), 522.

89. Feodor Chaliapin, *Man and Mask: Forty Years in the Life of a Singer*, trans. Phyllis Mégroz (London: Gollancz, 1932), 348, 355–56.

90. This is the earliest item in Nijinska's Chaliapin scrapbook, Box 128, BNC.

Chapter 4

1. Richard Buckle, *Diaghilev* (New York: Atheneum, 1979), 400.

2. Qtd. in Arnold Haskell, in collaboration with Walter Nouvel, *Diaghilev: His Artistic and Private Life* (London: Gollancz, 1935), 87.

3. Lydia Sokolova, *Dancing for Diaghilev*, ed. Richard Buckle (London: John Murray, 1960), 198–200. Diaghilev wanted Spessivtzeva to dance with the company in Paris, but the French refused to grant her a visa, because "it was whispered, she had connections in certain dubious Russian circles" ("La danseuse . . . indésirable?" *Petit Journal*, 19 May 1922, 4). Weeks earlier, she had wired Bakst, "If Diaghilev sends me my London money I go to Paris" (qtd. in Buckle, *Diaghilev*, 402).

4. S. L. Grigoriev, *The Diaghilev Ballet 1909–1929* (London: Constable, 1953), 176. For Grigoriev's 1922 company lists, see bMS Thr465(6), Grigoriev Papers.

5. The Ballets Russes gave an average of four performances a week during the Opéra season, with operas (such as *Lohengrin*, *Hérodiade*, *Faust*, and *Thaïs*) being scheduled on days when the company wasn't dancing. When the company moved to the Thêátre Mogador, by contrast, it danced six performances a week. A complete run of the programs and playbills mentioned in this chapter are at CAL.

6. Rouché to SD, 26 Apr. 1922, Pièce 86, Fonds Kochno. Excerpts from this letter are translated in Boris Kochno, *Diaghilev and the Ballets Russes*, trans. Adrienne Foulke (New York: Harper and Row, 1970), 180–81.

7. "Diary 1919–1922," 23 Mar. 1921. Dates are given in the text.

8. André Levinson, "Les Ballets Russes à l'Opéra," *Comoedia*, 20 May 1922, 2.

9. Louis Laloy, "Les Ballets Russes à l'Opéra," *Comoedia*, 20 May 1922, 2.

10. Adolphe Jullien, "Revue musicale," *Journal des Débats*, 11 June 1922, 4. Because the Bakst production was impounded, Diaghilev repurposed Benois' scenery and costumes from *Le Pavillon d'Armide*, supplementing them with new costumes by Natalia Goncharova.

11. André Messager, "Les Premières," *Figaro*, 21 May 1922, 5.

12. Jean Poueigh, ""La Musique: Ballets russes," *Carnet de la Semaine*, 28 May 1922, 13.

13. The ballet, which premiered at the Opéra on April 28, 1922, had designs and a libretto by Bakst, a new score by the French composer Paul Paray, and choreography by Nicolà Guerra. See Henry Bidou, "La Musique: Ballets russes et autres," *Opinion*, 3 June 1922, 602.

14. This credit line appeared on playbills throughout the Paris Opéra and Théâtre Mogador seasons in 1922.

15. Levinson, "Les Ballets Russes à l'Opéra."

16. Laloy, "Les Ballets Russes à l'Opéra."

17. This is based on playbills for 1922, 1926 (Lyceum Theatre, London), and 1928 (His Majesty's Theatre, London) in the Carina Ari Library.

18. Ballets Russes playbill, Paris Opéra, 18 May 1922.

19. Igor Stravinsky, *Renard: histoire burlesque chantée et jouée faite pour la scène d'après des contes populaires russes*, trans. C.-F. Ramuz, reduction for piano and voice by the author (London: J. & W. Chester, 1917), "Remarque générale."

20. For reproductions of Larionov's set design and two of his costume designs for the Goat and Fox, see the Ballets Russes souvenir program, Paris Opéra, May–June 1922, n.p. See also Richard Buckle, *In Search of Diaghilev* (New York: Thomas Nelson & Sons, 1956), 66–67; Alexander Schouvaloff, *The Art of Ballets Russes: The Serge Lifar Collection of Theater Designs, Costumes, and Paintings at the Wadsworth Atheneum, Hartford, Connecticut* (New Haven: Yale University Press/Wadsworth Atheneum, 1998), 235–38; Kochno, *Diaghilev and the Ballets Russes*, 178; and for designs in HTC's Howard T. Rothschild and George Chaffée collections, https://library.harvard.edu/sites/default/files/static/onlineexhibits/diaghilev/composers_in_focus/38_1.html

21. Roland-Manuel, "Letter from Paris. A Russian Ballet—'Sleeping Beauty' and 'Renard,'" *Musical News and Herald*, 3 July 1922, in "Nijinska–Ballets 1922–1924," 13; André Messager, "Figaro-Théâtre. Les Premières. Théâtre National de l'Opéra," *Figaro*, 21 May 1922, 5; Adolphe Jullien, "Revue musicale," *Journal des Débats*, 11 June 1922, 4.

22. Gérard d'Houville, "Mes Spectacles," *Gaulois*, 27 May 1922, 4.

23. Laloy, "Les Ballets Russes à l'Opéra."

24. Roland-Manuel, "Letter from Paris."

25. Kochno, *Diaghilev and the Ballets Russes*, 179.

26. Igor Stravinsky, *An Autobiography* (New York: Simon & Schuster, 1936), 161.

27. Ibid., 160.

28. For the original cast and "Argument" of the ballet, see the Ballets Russes souvenir program, Gaîté-Lyrique, May 1921, n.p.

29. Ballets Russes playbill, Théâtre Mogador, 20 June 1922; "Les Ballets Russes au Théâtre Mogador," *Figaro*, 20 June 1922, 4.

30. Florence Gilliam, "Parade," *Gargoyle* 3, no. 1 (July 1922), n.p. For Gilliam, see Morrill Cody, with Hugh Ford, *The Women of Montparnasse* (New York: Cornwall Books, 1984), 166–74; for her connection with the Ballets Russes, see Florence Gilliam, "My Years with Moss—Article II," *Lost Generation Journal* 3, no. 1 (Winter 1975), 40.

31. *Early Memoirs*, 450.

32. "Autobiographical outline," 34/15, BNC, 24. The relevant text reads as follows: "The 'old timers' organize against Nijinska. Why Vaslav's choreography for *The Rite of Spring* is lost. Nijinsky's compositions hinder the 'innovators.' The criticism of [André] Levinson and his latest public attacks on Nijinska and Nijinsky." In an interview published after her death, Irina Nijinska categorically denied that her mother had ever danced in Massine's version of the ballet (Andrea Grodsky Huber, "A Conversation with Irina Nijinska," *BR* 20, no. 1 [Spring 1992], 39).

33. Florence Gilliam, "The Russian Ballet of 1923," *Theatre Arts Monthly*, Mar. 1924, 192.

34. André Levinson, "Propos sur la Danse: Les Deux Sacres," *Comoedia*, 5 June 1922, 4.

35. Ibid.

36. André Levinson, "Les Ballets Russes à l'Opéra. Pétrouchka, L'Après-midi d'un Faune, Soleil de Nuit," *Comoedia*, 29 May 1922, 1.

37. André Levinson, "Les Ballets Russes à l'Opéra. La Chorégraphie, l'Interprétation," *Comoedia*, 20 May 1922, 2.

38. Halberstam briefly talks about this in terms of heterosexual women in *Female Masculinities* (Durham, NC: Duke University Press, 1998), 268–69.

39. Gilliam, "Parade," n.p.

40. Gilliam, "The Russian Ballet of 1923," 193. In *Dancing for Diaghilev* Sokolova claims that when Diaghilev revived *The Rite of Spring* in Brussels in 1928, he cast "Bronia Nijinska in my role of the Chosen Virgin. . . . Bronia, of course, had the strength and the understanding for this role, but her individual type of movement was so different from Massine's, that the dance she did was almost unrecognisable and had little in common with the rest of the ballet. . . . She only danced it once" (265). According to the playbills, it was Alexandra Danilova who performed the role—not once but twice—in Brussels. Nijinska, by contrast, danced the role several times in 1922.

41. Baer, *Bronislava Nijinska*, 30; Huber, "A Conversation with Irina Nijinska," 41.

42. See, for example, André Nède, "'La Belle au bois dormant' à l'Opéra," *Figaro*, 7 May 1922, 1; Paul Roche, "Les Ballets russes à l'Opéra," *Gaulois*, 14 May 1922, 5.

43. Levinson, "Les Ballets Russes à l'Opéra. Pétrouchka, L'Après-midi d'un Faune, Soleil de Nuit."

44. Gilliam, "Parade," n.p.

45. The sketch, "'Bronia' dans le Faune," is in Box 171, BNC. A fuller, more finished version is in the Larionov Collection at Moscow's Tretiakov Gallery. See *Istoriia 'Russkogo Baleta' real'naia i fantasticheskaia i fotografiiakh iz arkhiva Mikhaila Larionova* (Moscow: Izdatel'skaia programma "Interrosa," 2009), 86–87.

46. Woizikovsky danced the role for the first time on 8 Jan. 1924 in Monte Carlo.

47. Haskell, *Diaghileff*, 69.

48. BN, "Sergei Pavlovitch Diaghilev," 6.

49. Igor Stravinsky and Robert Craft, *Memories and Commentaries* (Garden City, NY: Doubleday, 1960), 40–41.

50. Grigoriev, *The Diaghilev Ballet*, 178. For Sakharoff and his wife, Clothilde von Derp, see *Die Sacharoffs: Two Dancers within the "Blaue Reiter" Circle*, ed. Frank-Manuel Peter and Rainer Stamm (Cologne: Wienand Verlag, 2002).

51. Although Nijinska was occasionally referred to as the company's "ballet mistress" in the press, the first time she seems to have been formally billed as such was at the Théâtre Municipal de Bayonne, where the Ballets Russes performed on 15 Sept. 1922.

52. For the supper party given by Sydney Schiff at the ultra-*luxe* Hôtel Majestic, see Clive Bell, *Old Friends, Personal Recollections* (London: Chatto & Windus, 1956), 179; Richard Ellmann, *James Joyce*, rev. ed. (New York: Oxford University Press, 1982), 523–24; Richard Davenport-Hines, *Proust at the Majestic: The Last Days of the Author Whose Book Changed Paris* (New York/London: Bloomsbury, 2006), especially chap. 1.

53. The program for this *soirée musicale*, which took place on May 29, 1922, is at the Carina Ari Library.

54. "Le Monde et la Ville" *Figaro*, 23 June 1922, 2. Additional clippings about the Fête de l'Eté are in "Nijinska–Ballets 1922–1924," 19–22.

55. Jean Bernier, "Danses de Mme Balachova," *Crapouillot*, 1 May 1922, 20. For Bernier's short article introducing *Chout* and *Cuadro Flamenco*, see "Ballets Russes— Quatorzième Saison," Ballets Russes souvenir program, Gaîté-Lyrique, May 1921, n.p.

56. BN, "Sergei Pavlovitch Diaghilev," 3.

57. Grigoriev, *The Diaghilev Ballet*, 178.

58. "Pati" was the nickname of Kleopatra Grigor'evna Zhakhovskaia-Chukhmanenko. In the late 1960s, she was known as Kleopatra Batueva-Shakhovsky.

59. Nina Moiseevna's letters to BN are in 76/51, BNC.

60. This is explained in an unsigned, undated letter, probably written by Nina's husband, Mikhail Stefanovich, in the late 1960s, 76/51, BNC. Nina refers to her efforts to get these to Nijinska and to the fate of the album in her letters of 15 Oct. 1923 and 17 Jan. 1970, respectively, 76/51, BNC. Nijinska describes the book in a miscellaneous note in 66/5.

61. This was another note tucked into Nina Moiseevna's letters, 76/51.

62. Moiseevna to BN, 15 Oct. 1922, 76/51, BNC.

63. Group letter to BN, 12 Mar. 1922, 74/5, BNC.

64. See, for instance, Romola's letters of 11 Apr. 1922 and 25 Apr. 1922, and her telegrams of 14 Apr. 1922 and 26 Apr. 1922, 78/46, BNC.

65. Autobiographical notes.

66. Muravin to BN, 10 Sept. and 12 Oct. 1922, 74/67, BNC.

67. Lapitsky to BN, [7 Aug. 1922], 74/5, BNC.

68. Both telegrams are in 76/10, BNC.

69. NS to BN, 30 Aug. 1922, 78/16, BNC. Singaevsky's contract, which began on August 3, 1921 and ended on August 1, 1922, provided for a monthly salary of 1,000 francs, with two months' rehearsal pay at 400 francs. See 7/3/56, Ekstrom Collection.

70. For these negotiations, see Grigoriev, *The Diaghilev Ballet*, 178–80. For a chronology of the company's performances, see Jane Pritchard, "Serge Diaghilev's Ballets Russes—An Itinerary. Part II (1922–9)," *DR* 27, no. 2 (2009), 255–357.

71. According to Tamara Nijinsky, Romola moved Nijinsky and her two daughters to Paris "some time in 1922 or early 1923." Tamara Nijinsky, *Nijinsky and Romola* (London: Bachman & Turner, 1991), 214.

72. For Diaghilev's "coldness" and the increasing number of "plots" against her, see "Autobiographical outline," 34/15, BNC, 23.

73. NS to BN, 21 Aug. 1922, 78/16, BNC.

74. Grigoriev, *The Diaghilev Ballet*, 180–81.

75. Unger to BN, 19 Sept. 1922, 77A/25, BNC.

76. Unger to BN, 20 Oct. 1922, 77A/25, BNC.

77. Unger to BN, 9 Dec. 1922, 77A/25, BNC.

78. Hoyer, telegram to SD, 9 Dec. 1922, THM 7-2-1-1, Ekstrom Collection.

79. Lifar to BN, 19 Dec. 1922, 74/22, BNC.

80. BN to Nouvel, 28 Dec. 1922, Pièce 65, Fonds Kochno; SD, telegram to BN, 17 Dec. 1922; Drobecki, telegrams to SD, 27 and 28 Dec. 1922; Hoyer, Unger, Lapiski [*sic*], Lifar, telegram to SD, 29 Dec. 1922; Drobecki, telegram to SD, 2 Jan. 1923; Unger to BN, 3 Jan. 1923; Hoyer, telegram to SD, 5 Jan. 1923; Drobecki, telegrams to SD, 5 and 12 Jan. 1923, THM 7-2-1-1, Ekstrom Collection. Serge Lifar in *Du Temps que j'avais faim* (Paris: Stock, 1935) dramatizes the hardships of his journey, but virtually ignores the assistance he received from traveling companions, especially Serge Unger, and his gratitude to Nijinska (210-32). In 1922 Rovno was on the Polish side of the Ukrainian-Polish border.

81. Grigoriev, *The Diaghilev Ballet*, 182.

82. Autobiographical notes.

83. NS to BN, 16 Mar. 1922, 78/16, BNC.

84. Ibid.

85. Ibid.

86. NS to BN, 28 Aug. 1922, 78/16, BNC.

87. NS, to BN, 17 Aug. 1922, 78/16, BNC.

Chapter 5

1. For a list of tour performances and repertory, see Pritchard, "Serge Diaghilev's Ballets Russes—An Itinerary."

2. Grigoriev, *The Diaghilev Ballet*, 179.

3. Ibid., 179–80.

4. See Manfred Kelkel, *La Musique de Ballet en France de la Belle Epoque aux Années Folles* (Paris: Librairie Philosophique J. Vrin, 1992); Stéphane Wolff, *L'Opéra au Palais Garnier (1875–1962)*, introd. Alain Gueullette (Paris: Slatkine, 1962; rpt. Geneva-Paris: Slatkine, 1983); Pompeo Cambiasi, *La Scala 1778–1906: Note Storiche*

et Statistiche (Milan: Ricordi, 1906); Cyril W. Beaumont, *Complete Book of Ballets* (London: Putnam, 1937); Sarah Gutsche-Miller, "Pantomime-Ballet on the Music-Hall Stage: The Popularisation of Classical Ballet in Fin-de-Siècle Paris," Ph.D., McGill University, 2010; and Monte Carlo playbills from the Carina Ari Library. Belloni left for more congenial surroundings once his contract ended.

5. BN to Nouvel, 28 Dec. [1922], Pièce 65, Fonds Kochno.

6. BN, "Creation of 'Les Noces,'" trans. and introd. by Jean M. Serafetinides and Irina Nijinska, *DM*, Dec. 1974, 60. Nijinska's original Russian version is in 19/16, BNC. In 1971 the article was published in French as "Création des 'Noces,'" in *Gontcharova et Larionov: cinquante ans à Saint Germain-des-près*, ed. Tatiana Loguine (Paris: Klincksieck, 1971), 117–22.

7. "Creation of Les Noces," 60.

8. "Diary 1919–22," 20 Sept. 1921.

9. For Goncharova's explanation of the evolution of her designs, see her article (originally published in *Russkiy Arkhiv* [Belgrade] in 1932), "The Metamorphoses of the Ballet 'Les Noces,'" trans. Mary Chamot, *Leonardo* 12, no. 2 (Spring 1979), 137–43. According to Goncharova, Diaghilev told her that the idea for all the costumes being one color originated with Larionov (141). See also Nathalie Gontcharova, "The Creation of 'Les Noces'" *Ballet* 5, no. 4 (Apr. 1948), 23–26.

10. Françoise Reiss, *Sur la Pointe des pieds: Annales chorégraphiques* (Paris: Editions Lieutier, 1953), 69–70.

11. Qtd. in John Martin, "The Dance: Revival of Nijinska's 'Les Noces,'" *NYT*, 3 May 1936, X7.

12. Qtd. in Stephen Walsh, *Stravinsky: A Creative Spring: Russia and France 1882–1934* (New York: Knopf, 1999), 344.

13. Serigny, "Le Monde et la Ville," *Figaro*, 22 Nov. 1922, 2. Proust received military honors as a Chevalier of the Legion of Honor.

14. André Levinson, "Ce que veut être le 'Théâtre Kamerny' de Moscou," *Comoedia*, 26 Feb. 1923, 1.

15. Qtd. in BN, "Sergei Pavlovitch Diaghilev," 4.

16. It is possible that rehearsals began before this date. However, the gap between 1 Nov. and 27 Mar. in Nicolas Kremnev's rehearsal and performance logs makes this impossible to ascertain. Kremnev's logs are in the Serge Lifar Collection at the Archives de la Ville in Lausanne, Switzerland. A detailed list for the period beginning 5 Aug. 1922 and ending 30 Dec. 1923 appears in Appendix 1 of Drue Fergison's dissertation, "'Les Noces': A Microhistory of the 1923 Paris Production," Ph.D., Duke University, 1995, 316–44. Performance information is based on the playbills at CAL.

17. Stravinsky to BN, 27 Mar. 1923, 76B/27, BNC.

18. *Nikitina by Herself*, trans. Baroness Budberg (London: Allan Wingate, 1959), 35. According to Nikitina, the company's other women had to wear black tunics.

19. By contrast, for Paris Opéra dancers there was a morning class, except on Sunday and Thursday, followed by afternoon and evening rehearsals, except when there was a performance. See the 1919 blank printed contract and accompanying "Réglement" in AJ/

13/1702, AN. Additionally, the Réglement specifies that the company had to have no fewer than forty soloists and sixty dancers in the corps. Thus, the Opéra troupe was about three times larger than the Diaghilev company, which meant that individual dancers took part in far fewer performances than their Ballets Russes counterparts.

20. Robert Craft, *Igor and Vera Stravinsky: A Photograph Album, 1921 to 1971* (London: Thames and Hudson, 1982), 56.

21. Nijinska, "Creation of 'Les Noces,'" 60.

22. In an undated letter, Nijinska invited an unnamed critic to observe company class, which she taught every morning from 9–10:15 in the foyer of the amphitheater at the Gaîté-Lyrique. I am grateful to Gordon Hollis of Golden Legend Rare Books and Fine Prints for sharing the contents of this letter with me.

23. Sokolova, *Dancing for Diaghilev*, 206.

24. Grigoriev, *The Diaghilev Ballet*, 185.

25. Paul Baudry, *Ernest Ansermet: Une vie en images* (Neuchâtel/Paris: Editions Delachaux et Niestlé, 1965), 38.

26. Louis Laloy, "Les Ballets Russes à la Gaîté-Lyrique," *Comoedia*, 4 June 1923, 1.

27. Edouard Beaudu, "Ballets russes: répétitions," *Intransigeant*, 10 June 1923, 4.

28. Grigoriev, *The Diaghilev Ballet*, 185.

29. Jacques Brindejont-Offenbach, "Chez la Princesse Edmonde de Polignac: une répétition des 'Noces' de Stravinsky," *Gaulois*, 12 June 1923, 1.

30. Grigoriev, *The Diaghilev Ballet*, 185; Walsh, *Stravinsky: A Creative Spring*, 634/note 56. The pianists for the Paris performances were the composers Georges Auric and Edouard Flament (replacing the composer Francis Poulenc), Hélène Léon, and Marcelle Meyer. Both Léon and Meyer were well-known concert performers. The solo singers were Marie Davidova, Hélène Smirnova, Michel D'Arial (a tenor), and Georges Lanskoy. All four were Russian although Lanskoy seems to have settled in the West before World War I.

31. Margarita Mazo, "Stravinsky's 'Les Noces' and Russian Village Wedding Ritual," *JAMS* 43, no. 1 (Spring 1990), 104–5.

32. Josep Farran i Mayoral, in *La Veu de Catalunya*, 25 Mar. 1928, qtd. in Craft, *Igor and Vera Stravinsky*, 17.

33. Mazo, "'Les Noces,'" 118. For a list of the most common ritual episodes, see 117–18.

34. Igor Stravinsky and Robert Craft, *Expositions and Developments* (Garden City, NY: Doubleday, 1962), 131.

35. Ibid.

36. 14 Mar. 1921, Diary, 1919–22.

37. Waldemar George, "Propos de Danse: les idées de Mademoiselle Nijinska," *Crapouillot*, 1 Sept. 1922, 9. George was a Polish-born critic who supported the Russian Revolution and wrote extensively about modern art.

38. BN, "Reflections about the Production of *Les Biches* and *Hamlet* in Markova-Dolin Ballets," trans. Lydia Lopokova, *DT*, Feb. 1937, 617–18.

39. I have followed the nomenclature in Stephanie Jordan's *Stravinsky Dances: Re-Visions across a Century* (Alton, Hampshire: Dance Books, 2007), 339.

40. See Eric Walter White, *Stravinsky: The Composer and His Works*, 2nd ed. (Berkeley: University of California Press, 1984), 258. For the score, see Igor Stravinsky, *Les Noces in Full Score* (Mineola, NY: Dover Publications, 1998), "an unabridged republication of the work originally published by Chester in London in 1922" [*sic*], which includes the original Russian text, the French translation by C. F. Ramuz, supervised by Stravinsky, and an English translation of Ramuz's French by Stanley Applebaum. The Chester Stravinsky Edition of the vocal score, edited, revised, and corrected by Margarita Mazo, with the Russian text, a transliteration of that text, and the Ramuz translation, was published in 1996. The quotations that follow in the text will be from Applebaum's translation in *Les Noces in Full Score*. Jordan warns that the original (and "official") Chester translation often muffles the ribaldry and eroticism of the original Russian text. For a translation from the Russian (without identifying voices), see Roberta Reeder and Arthur Camegno, "Stravinsky's *Les Noces*," *DR* 18, no. 2 (Winter 1986–1987), 30–61.

41. For Nijinska's occasional acknowledgment of Stravinsky's verbal fragments, see Jordan, *Stravinsky Dances*, 341–42.

42. BN, "Creation of 'Les Noces,'" 59.

43. My remarks are based on the version performed by The Royal Ballet in the 1978 BBC-Television documentary *Stravinsky and the Dance: Les Noces*, produced by John Selwyn Gilbert, presented by John Drummond, directed by Robert Lockyer, and conducted by Leonard Bernstein. For the "braid" image in the menuetto of *Mozartiana*, see *Les Ballets 1933*, catalogue of an exhibition at The Royal Pavilion, Art Gallery & Museums, Brighton, 1987, 40; the Studio Iris photo is reproduced in Jane Pritchard, "Les Ballets 1933," *BR* 16, no. 3 (Fall 1988), 17.

44. Qtd. in André Schaeffner, "Les Chanteurs dans la 'fosse': Une nouvelle forme dramatique," *Revue musicale*, 1 Nov. 1924, 20.

45. Jordan, *Stravinsky Dances*, 337.

46. George, "Propos de Danse," 9.

47. "Les Mondainités: le Gala de la Gaîté," *Gaulois*, 14 June 1923, 2; J. R. F., "La Grande Saison de Paris," *Vogue*, 1 Aug. 1923, 56.

48. Gérard d'Houville, "Mes Spectacles. Les Ballets Russes de Serge de Diaghilew," *Gaulois*, 23 June 1923, 4.

49. E[douard] B[eaudu], "Courrier des Théâtres," *Petit Journal*, 20 June 1923, 5.

50. J. L., "Les Noces de Stravinsky ont remporté un formidable succès," *Vogue*, 1 Aug. 1923, 16.

51. Grigoriev, *The Diaghilev Ballet*, 185–86.

52. Paul Souday, "Hier à la Gaîté. Les Ballets Russes," unidentified newspaper, 15 June 1923, in Fergison, "Les Noces," 383–84; Gustave Bret, "Spectacles. La Musique. Ballets Russes: *Noces*, de Stravinsky," *Intransigeant*, 16 June 1923, 2; Pierre Veber, "Les Ballets Russes," *Petit Journal*, 19 June 1923, 2; G[ustave] de Pawlowski, "Les Ballets russes à la Gaîté. 'Noces,'" *Journal*, 18 June 1923, 4; Adolphe Aderer, "Courrier des Théâtres," *Petit Parisien*, 15 June 1923, 4.

53. See, for example, Raoul Brunel, "Les Ballets russes. 'Noces,'" *Oeuvre*, 17 June 1923, 7; Emile Vuillermoz, "Noces.—Igor Strawinski," *Revue musicale*, 1 Aug. 1923, 71.

54. Georges Auric, "Gaîté-Lyrique. Ballets Russes. *Noces*," *Nouvelles littéraires*, 16 June 1923, 5.

55. Louis Schneider, "La Musique. Gaîté-Lyrique. Ballets russes: *Noces*," *Gaulois*, 17 June 1923, 4; "Music in Paris," *New York Herald*, 17 June 1923, in "Nijinska—Ballets Russes 1922–1924 (black marble binding; grey marble—#24)," 37, http://www.loc.gov/item/ ihas.200181901.

56. Paul Dukas, "'Noces' d'Igor Stravinsky," in *Les Ecrits de Paul Dukas sur la musique*, introd. G. Samazeuilh (Paris: Société des Editions Françaises et Internationales, 1948), 653–54. This review was originally published in June 1923 in *Le Quotidien*.

57. Boris de Schloezer, "La Musique. La Saison musicale," *NRF*, 1 Aug. 1923, 246.

58. Ibid., 247. Three years later Schoezer returned to the independence of music and choreography in *Les Noces*. "How then can the unity of a musical drama be sustained? In another domain, in ballet, this principal is admirably realized with Nijinska's choreography for Stravinsky's *Les Noces*, in which the dances develop in counterpoint, so to speak, with the music, the choreographer having completely rethought and re-created in gestures and poses the musical work of the composer. With this transposition fully realized, the plastic scheme retains its absolute independence" (B[oris] de Schloezer, "Musique d'action scènique," *Revue Pleyel*, July 1926, 9). Throughout her chapter on *Les Noces*, Jordan insists on Nijinska's independent dance voice, analyzing the strategies she developed to achieve this (*Stravinsky Dances*, 344–79).

59. Emile Vuillermoz, "Premières. Ballets Russes: 'Noces', d'Igor Strawinsky," *L'Excelsior*, 18 June 1923, 5. Vuillermoz wrote along similar lines in his review published in the August issue of *La Revue musicale*.

60. Roland-Manuel, "La Quinzaine Musicale. Les Ballets Russes à la Gaîté-Lyrique—Les 'Noces', d'Igor Stravinsky," *Eclair*, 26 June 1923, in Fergison, 439.

61. Raymond Charpentier, "Les Ballets Russes à la Gaîté-Lyrique. 'Noces'. Ballet de M. Igor Stravinsky," *Comoedia*, 16 June 1923, 1.

62. Ibid., 2.

63. André Levinson, "Le décor, la chorégraphie," *Comoedia*, 16 June 1923, 2.

64. Andrei Levinson, "Russkii balet v Parizhe. 'Vesna Sviashchennaia'. 'Igry,'" *Rech'*, 3/16 June 1913; Levinson, "Nijinsky's Ballets: *Le Sacre du Printemps, Jeux*,'" in *Ballet Old and New*, trans. Susan Cook Summer (New York: Dance Horizons, 1982), 55.

65. Andrei [Levinson], "Russkii balet. 'Svadebka,'" *Poslednie novosti*, 27 June 1923, 2; adapted from the translation in Ferguson, 455.

66. André Levinson, "La Danse. Où en sont les 'Ballets russes'?" *Comoedia*, 18 June 1923, 4.

67. Ibid.

68. Levinson, "Le décor, la chorégraphie"; "Russkii balet. 'Svadebka'"; "Où en sont les 'Ballets russes'?"

69. Voirol to BN, 18 June 1923, Box 134, BNC.

70. Boris de Schloezer, "On the Occasion of *Les Noces*: A New Form of Synthetic Art," *Zveno*, no. 24; trans. in Fergison, 452.

71. André Levinson, "Stravinsky and the Dance," in *André Levinson on Dance: Writings from Paris in the Twenties*, ed. Joan Acocella and Lynn Garafola (Hanover, NH: UPNE/ Wesleyan University Press, 1991), 41. This essay appeared in the Nov. 1924 issue of *Theatre Arts Monthly*. The original French version appeared in *La Revue musicale* in Dec. 1923, a special issue devoted to Stravinsky for which Boris de Schloezer wrote the lead article. Nijinska pasted a copy of the French version into one of her scrapbooks.

72. André Levinson, *La Danse d'Aujourd'hui: Etudes, Notes, Portraits* (Paris: Editions Duchartre et Vam Buggenhoudt, 1929), 13–14.

73. Ibid., 84–85.

74. André Levinson, "Etude sur l'Etude: Variations de danse sur des thèmes de Bach," *Comoedia*, 30 Jan. 1931, 1.

75. Henry Malherbe, "Chronique musicale," *Temps*, 27 June 1923, 3.

76. Maurice Brillant, "Les Oeuvres et les Hommes," *Correspondant*, 25 Aug. 1923, 757.

77. Florence Gilliam, "The Russian Ballet of 1923," *Theatre Arts Monthly*, Mar. 1924, 191.

78. Fernand Divoire, "Les Commentaires de la quinzaine. La Danse," *Revue de France*, Sept.–Oct. 1923, 183–84. With minor differences this article was incorporated into Divoire's chapter on the Ballets Russes in *Découvertes sur la danse* (Paris: Editions G. Crès, 1924), 64–66.

79. Divoire, "La Danse," 183–84. Nijinska reiterated many of these ideas in her essay "Creation of 'Les Noces.'"

80. BN, "Sergei Pavlovitch Diaghilev," 3–4.

81. Gilbert Charles, "Les Fêtes de Versailles. Un entretien avec M. Georges Bertrand," *Figaro*, 31 May 1923, 1–2; "La 'Fête Merveilleuse' de Versailles," *Figaro*, 20 June 1923, 1. For additional press, see "La Saison de Versailles," *Comoedia*, 30 May 1923, 3; "La 'Fête Merveilleuse' du château de Versailles," *Figaro*, 22 June 1923, 1; "La 'Fête Merveilleuse' du château de Versailles," *Figaro*, 23 June 1923, 2; "La 'Fête Merveilleuse' du château de Versailles," *Figaro*, 27 June 1923, 2; "La 'Féerique Soirée' du château de Versailles," *Figaro*, 30 June 1923, 1.

82. Sokolova, *Dancing for Diaghilev*, 206; Grigoriev, *The Diaghilev Ballet*, 186.

83. André Levinson, "La Fête Merveilleuse au Palais de Versailles. Le Spectacle," *Comoedia*, 2 July 1923, 1. See also "La Saison de Versailles," Ballets Russes souvenir program, 30 June 1923, *MGZB-Res. 99-1123 no. 2, NYPL; Pierre-Plessis, "Une Nuit triomphale chez le Roi Soleil," *Gaulois*, 2 July 1923, 1; Selysette, "La fête chez le Roy," *Figaro*, 2 July 1923, 1–2; Hubert Morand, "Au Jour le Jour. A la fête de Versailles," *Journal des Débats*, 2 July 1923, 1, and "'La Fête Merveilleuse' de Versailles," *Nouvelles littéraires*, 7 July 1923, 4; "Le Gala de Versailles," *Femina*, Aug. 1923, 34–35.

84. Pierre-Plessis," Une Nuit triomphale." For the American lady and the evening's "take," see "Le Monde et la Ville. La Fête de Versailles," *Figaro*, 2 July 1923, 2, and "Les Mondanités. Petit Carnet," *Gaulois*, 2 July 1923, 2.

85. Morand, "Au Jour le Jour."

Chapter 6

1. Richard Taruskin, *Stravinsky and the Russian Traditions: A Biography of the Works through "Mavra,"* vol. 2 (Berkeley: University of California Press, 1996), 1506.

2. Antoine Banès, "Trianon-Lyrique: *Philémon et Baucis,"* *Figaro,* 12 Feb. 1921, 3; "Courrier des Théâtres," *Figaro,* 6 Feb. 1923, 5; 12 Mar. 1923, 4.

3. Serge Lifar, *Serge Diaghilev: His Life, His Work, His Legend: An Intimate Biography* (New York: 1940; rpt. New York: Da Capo, 1976), 230–31.

4. BN, draft-letter to SD, undated [July 1923], 72/4, BNC.

5. Ibid.

6. SD to BN, 22 July 1923, 72/4, BNC.

7. Grigoriev, *The Diaghilev Ballet,* 188.

8. Daniel-Henry Kahnweiler, *Juan Gris: His Life and Work,* rev. ed., trans. Douglas Cooper (New York: Abrams, 1969), 50.

9. Qtd. in Kahnweiler, *Juan Gris,* 50–51. The decors for *La Colombe* and *Les Tentations de la Bergère* were executed by the veteran scene painters Vladimir Polunin and his wife Elizabeth Polunin.

10. Ibid., 52.

11. Ibid., 38; Francis Steegmuller, *Jean Cocteau: A Biography* (Boston: Little, Brown, 1970), 69.

12. Kahnweiler, *Juan Gris,* 52.

13. Jean Cocteau, *Le Coq et l'Arlequin: Notes autour de la musique* (Paris: Éditions de la Sirène, 1918). An English translation, by Rollo H. Myers, was published in London by the Egoist Press in 1921.

14. Darius Milhaud, *Notes without Music: An Autobiography* (New York: Knopf, 1953), 108–9.

15. Kochno, *Diaghilev and the Ballets Russes,* 200. According to a letter that does not appear in Myriam Chimènes edition of Poulenc's collected correspondence (*Correspondance 1910–1963* [Paris: Fayard, 1994]), Diaghilev was already considering the young composer for a ballet with Massine. See Poulenc to SD, 28 Apr. 1919, 48/976, Koch Collection.

16. SD to Poulenc, 15 Nov. 1921, in *Correspondance 1910–1963,* ed. Myriam Chimènes (Paris: Fayard, 1994), 138–39.

17. For *Mavra,* see Poulenc to Milhaud, [June 1922] in *Correspondance,* 153; for the Karsavina Gala and *Chout,* his letter to Milhaud, 22 [June 1922], 155–56.

18. Francis Poulenc, *Entretiens avec Claude Rostand* (Paris: René Julliard, 1954), 50. For an English version of this interview, see *Francis Poulenc: Articles and Interviews: Notes from the Heart,* ed. and introd. Nicolas Southon, trans. Roger Nichols (Burlington, VT/Farnham, Surrey: Ashgate, 2014), 203–8. The quotation is from page 203.

19. Poulenc to Milhaud, [7 July 1922], in *Correspondance,* 160.

20. Poulenc, *Entretiens avec Claude Rostand,* 51. A copy of the "Programme Officiel" is in the collection of the Carina Ari Library, Stockholm.

21. Poulenc to SD, 24 Sept. 1922, in *Francis Poulenc "Echo and Source": Selected Correspondence 1915–1963*, trans. and ed. Sidney Buckland (London: Gollancz, 1991), 54.

22. Poulenc to Paul Collaer, [7 July 1922], and Stravinsky, [9 July 1922], in *Correspondance*, 162–63.

23. Poulenc to Milhaud, [Aug. 1922], in *Correspondance*, 174.

24. Poulenc to Koechlin, [early Sept. 1922], in *Correspondance*, 175.

25. Poulenc to SD, 24 Sept. 1922, in *Correspondance*, 178. The translation here is from Kochno, *Diaghilev and the Ballets Russes*, 205.

26. Poulenc to Milhaud, [Jan. 1923], in *Correspondance*, 185.

27. Poulenc to Collaer, 12 [June 1923], in *Correspondance*, 196.

28. Poulenc to Milhaud, [29 July 1923], in *Correspondance*, 198–99. The costume was eventually discarded.

29. Poulenc to SD, [Aug. 1923], in *Correspondance*, 202.

30. Poulenc to Ansermet, [Oct. 1923], in *Correspondance*, 210.

31. Francis Poulenc, *Les Biches. Ballet avec Chant en 1 Acte*, manuscript score, with notations by Poulenc and BN, 182/1524, Koch Collection.

32. SD to Kochno, [Nov. 1923], in Kochno, *Diaghilev and the Ballets Russes*, 106.

33. Poulenc to Milhaud, [Nov. 1923], in *Correspondance*, 213.

34. Poulenc to Sauguet, [Nov. 1923], in *Correspondance*, 213.

35. Poulenc to SD, [Dec. 1923], in *Correspondance*, 218–19. Translation from Kochno, *Diaghilev and the Ballets Russes*, 206–7. Babette was the Texas-born high-wire performer and trapeze artist Vander Clyde, who performed in drag.

36. Sokolova, *Dancing for Diaghilev*, 216.

37. Poulenc to Collaer, [8] Jan. 1924, in *Correspondance*, 220–21.

38. Poulenc to Kochno, [Nov.–Dec. 1923], in Kochno, *Diaghilev and the Ballets Russes*, 106.

39. SD to Kochno, [Nov.-Dec. 1923], in Kochno, *Diaghilev and the Ballets Russes*, 106.

40. Christopher Moore, "Camp in Francis Poulenc's Early Ballets," *Musical Quarterly*, Summer–Fall 2012, 301.

41. Ibid., 307.

42. Poulenc, *Entretiens avec Claude Rostand*, 53; Robert Brussel, "Théâtre des Champs-Elysées: Ballets russes de Serge de Diaghilew," *Figaro*, 30 May 1924, 4.

43. SD to Kochno, [Nov.–Dec. 1923], in Kochno, *Diaghilev and the Ballets Russes*, 106.

44. July Méry, "Les Biches; Les Tentations de la Bergère," *Petit Monégasque*, 3 Jan. 1924, in Francis Poulenc, *J'écris ce qui me chante: écrits et entretiens*, ed. Nicolas Southon (Paris: Fayard, 2011), 531. V[ictor] Margueritte's *La Garçonne* was published in 1922 by Flammarion. The following year the novel was published in English as *The Bachelor Girl*. Diaghilev's public would have been familiar with the story of the sexually and socially emancipatory explorations of a young Paris flapper.

45. Moore, "Camp," 308.

46. Louis Schneider, "La Musique. La première soirée des Ballets russes," *Gaulois*, 28 May 1924, 4.

47. Nadine Meisner, "Georgina Parkinson: Ballerina Best Known for Her Performance as La Garconne in Nijinska's 'Les Biches,'" *Independent*, 15 Feb. 2010, 34. Parkinson was cast by Nijinska in the 1964 revival of *Les Biches* for the Royal Ballet.

48. The full quotation reads: "A true spirit of perversity . . . seems to inspire the ballet mistress. She dissects the classical steps with the will of a torturer. She makes beauty grimace and logic ramble. She obliges Mlle. Nemchinova to raise her elbows and to place her gloved hands on her thighs. But when required by the ineluctable necessities of the movement, as in pirouettes, . . . she frees herself from all this decorative jumble . . . and appears very beautiful" (André Levinson, "Théâtre des Champs-Elysées. 'Les Tentations de la Bergères' [*sic*], 'Les Biches,'" *Comoedia*, 18 May 1924, 2).

49. See, for example, G[ustave] de Pawlowski, "Première au théâtre des Champs Elysées. Les Ballets russes," *Journal*, 28 May 1924, 4; Fernand Gregh, "Chronique dramatique," *Nouvelles littéraires*, 31 May 1924, 7.

50. De Valois, *Step by Step*, 22.

51. Sokolova, *Dancing for Diaghilev*, 216.

52. Moore, "Camp," 316.

53. Since rehearsal divisions are not always marked and the pages are unnumbered, it is not possible to identify exactly where the gestures and movements appear. However, in the pages that follow rehearsal 44, there are quite a number of them.

54. Poulenc, *Entretiens*, 52–53.

55. Ibid., 54.

56. Sokolova, *Dancing for Diaghilev*, 217.

57. Poulenc, *Entretiens*, 54; "Francis Poulenc on His Ballets," *Ballet* 2, no. 4 (Sept. 1946), 57.

58. Anton Dolin, *Divertissement* (London: Sampson Low, Marston, [1931]), 49–50, 53–54; *Last Words: A Final Autobiography*, ed. Kay Hunter (London: Century Publishing, 1985), 31–33.

59. BN, "Sergei Pavlovitch Diaghilev," 6.

60. Poulenc to Collaer, [8 Jan. 1924], in *Correspondance*, 220.

61. Grigoriev, *The Diaghilev Ballet*, 189; Dolin, *Last Words*, 43–45; Sokolova, *Dancing for Diaghilev*, 213; John Drummond, *Speaking of Diaghilev*, 240. For a survey of the ballet's history, see Deborah Mawer, *The Ballets of Maurice Ravel: Creation and Interpretation* (Aldershot Hants/Burlington, VT: Ashgate, 2006), chap. 3. For the revival of *Daphnis*, see Garafola, *Diaghilev's Ballets Russes* (New York: Oxford University Press, 1989), 199–200; Auclair and Poidevin, "Les Ballets russes et l'Opéra de Paris," 200, 202.

62. Nijinska was not the first to tinker with Diaghilev's production of *The Polovtsian Dances*. In 1921, Massine created new choreography for the Polovtsian Girls (for which he was duly credited). For Massine's changes to the *Polovtsian Dances*, see playbills for the Teatro Costanzi, Rome (1 Jan. 1921) and Grand Théâtre de Lyon (15 Feb. 1921), and *Argumentos de los Bailes rusos de Sergio de Diaghilew* (Madrid: Imprenta Ducazal, 1921). The full *Prince Igor* was staged in Monte Carlo on March 15, 1924.

63. "The Russian Ballet. Polovtsi Dances from 'Prince Igor,'" *Times*, 11 Dec. 1924, 12. The program credit, which was also published in the daily *Times* theater listings read: "Choreography of the first two dances by Nijinska. Choreography of the final grand ensemble by Michael Fokin [*sic*]" (8 Dec. 1924, 12).

64. BN, draft letter to Fokine, undated [Dec. 1924], 72/44, BNC; final letter, undated [Dec. 1924], Stiftung John Neumeier, Hamburg, #23993. A Christmas pantomime, *A Midsummer Night's Dream* opened on Boxing Day, 26 Dec. 1924.

65. Fokine to BN, 27 Feb. 1925, 72/44, BNC.

66. Ninette de Valois, *Invitation to the Ballet* (London: John Lane, 1937), 43.

67. Grigoriev, *The Diaghilev Ballet*, 193.

68. Qtd. in "Russian Ballet Again: M. Diaghilev and His Plans," *Observer*, 23 Nov. 1924, 13.

69. Playbill, [Serge Diaghileff Season of Russian Ballet], 29 June 1926, His Majesty's Theatre file, V&A. For a review of the Nijinska version, see "The Russian Ballet. New Dances at the Coliseum," *Times*, 25 Nov. 1924, 12.

70. "Les Théâtres," *Gaulois*, 4 Apr. 1921, 4. The Odéon production, which opened on April 7, included all the play's "divertissements and ballets." For Auric, in general, see Colin Roust, *Georges Auric: A Life in Music and Politics* (New York: Oxford University Press, 2020); for his contribution to *Les Fâcheux*, see Michael Edward Lee, "Georges Auric and the Danced Theater, 1919–1924," Ph.D. diss., University of Southern California, 1993, chap. 4.

71. Louis Laloy, "Théâtre de Monte-Carlo: *Les Fâcheux*," *Figaro*, 23 Jan. 1924, 6.

72. Louis Laloy, untitled essay about Georges Auric, in *Théâtre Serge de Diaghilew: Les Fâcheux* (Paris: Editions des Quatre Chemins, 1924), I, n.p.

73. Boris de Schloezer, "Le Festival Français de Monte-Carlo," *Revue musicale*, 1 Feb. 1924, 166.

74. Henry Malherbe, "Chronique musicale," *Temps*, 11 June 1924, 3.

75. For Kochno's background and introduction to Diaghilev, see Buckle, *Diaghilev*, 375–77.

76. For the plot, see "Argument," *Les Fâcheux*, Ballets Russes playbill, 19 Jan. 1924, CAL.

77. Grigoriev, *The Diaghilev Ballet*, 193.

78. Ibid., 194.

79. Dolin, *Divertissement*, 80.

80. Gilson MacCormack, "The Russian Ballet in Paris. Les Soirées de Paris," *DT*, July 1924, 999.

81. Jane Catulle-Mendès, ""Les Fâcheux," *Presse*, 8 June 1924, 2; Fernand Gregh, "Chronique dramatique," *Nouvelles littéraires*, 14 June 1924, 7.

82. Kochno, *Diaghilev and the Ballets Russes*, 213.

83. Laloy, "Théâtre de Monte-Carlo."

84. Louis Schneider, "Les Premières. Les Ballets russes," *Gaulois*, 6 June 1924, 4.

85. De Schloezer, "Le Festival Français."

86. André Levinson, "Au Théâtre des Champs-Elysées. Les Ballets russes: 'Les Fâcheux. Le Spectacle,'" *Comoedia*, 6 June 1924, 1.

87. Ibid., 1–2.

88. According to David Cox, Casadesus was "involved, with his brothers Francis and Marius, in bringing out unknown pieces purportedly by 18th-century composers, but it has long been clear from stylistic evidence that these are entirely the work of the Casadesus brothers, and that has never been denied by the family" (David Cox, "Henri (Gustave) Casadesus," *Grove Music on Line*).

89. André Levinson, "A Monte-Carlo. 'La Tentation de la Bergère'. Autres echos du temps jadis," *Comoedia*, 25 Jan. 1924, 2.

90. Levinson, "'La Tentation de la Bergère.'" For Levinson's review of the ballet's Paris premiere, see "Les Ballets russes de Monte-Carlo. 'Les Tentations de la Bergère', 'Les Biches,'" *Comoedia*, 28 May 1924, 1–2.

91. Grigoriev, *The Diaghilev Ballet*, 188.

92. Ibid., 192.

93. Schneider, "La Musique. La première soirée des Ballets russes."

94. Sokolova, *Dancing for Diaghilev*, 214.

95. "Les Danseurs de Lully: Notes sur le ballet au XVIIe siècle," *Revue musicale*, 1 Jan. 1925, 44–55. This appeared in a special issue on Lully and French opera.

96. Grigoriev, *The Diaghilev Ballet*, 195.

97. Although her name does not appear on the playbill, she must have also choreographed the long ballet in Offenbach's *Tales of Hoffmann*.

98. Sokolova, *Dancing for Diaghilev*, 218–19. The opera was performed on February 9 and 12, 1924. *Night on Bald Mountain* was given twice in April 1924 and subsequently dropped by Diaghilev, although Nijinska herself revived it for other companies. The scenery and costumes were by Natalia Goncharova.

99. De Valois, *Invitation to the Ballet*, 69.

100. De Valois, *Step by Step*, 21.

101. Dolin, *Last Words*, 42.

102. This was inscribed on a photo of herself taken by Gordon Anthony in London in 1937 when she was working with the Markova-Dolin Ballet. Dated Pacific Palisades, 5 July 1966, the photo is in 44/120, Lewis Lloyd Papers.

103. Dolin, *Last Words*, 43. Dolin worked with her intensively again during the summer of 1924 in Monte Carlo (*Divertissement*, 86–87).

104. Ibid., 58.

105. Ibid., 81.

106. Ibid., 80, 56.

107. De Valois, *Step by Step*, 22.

108. "Autobiographical outline," 34/15, BNC, 24.

Chapter 7

1. Jean Cocteau, "Les Biches—Les Fâcheux: Notes de Monte-Carlo," *NRF*, 1 Mar. 1924, 275–78; "Deux Ballets actuels," *Revue de Paris*, 18 June 1924, 908–16. See also *Théâtre Serge de Diaghilew. Les Fâcheux* (Paris: Editions des Quatre Chemins, 1924),

and *Théâtre Serge de Diaghilew: Les Biches* (Paris: Editions des Quatre Chemins, 1924). The article in *La Revue de Paris* reproduced the book essays with only very minor changes.

2. See, for example, Maurice Martin du Gard, "Opinions et portraits: Principauté," *Nouvelles littéraires*, 12 Jan. 1924, 1; L[ouis] L[aloy], "Les Festivals Français de Monte-Carlo," *Figaro*, 7 Jan. 1924, 4; "Sur la Côte d'Azur. 'Les Biches,'" *Comoedia*, 11 Jan. 1924, 3; "Théâtre de Monte-Carlo: 'Les Fâcheux,'" 23 Jan. 1924, 3; André Levinson, "A Monte-Carlo. 'Le Crépuscule sur l'archipel.' 'Le miroir du diable,'" *Comoedia*, 21 Jan. 1924, 1–2; "A Monte-Carlo. 'La Tentation de la Bergère.' Autres échos du temps jadis," *Comoedia*, 25 Jan. 1924, 2.

3. Dolin, *Last Words*, 47.

4. Darius Milhaud to Henri Hoppentot, 10 Feb. [1924], in *Conversation: Correspondance 1918-1974*, 82. The other ballet was *Salade*, commissioned by Comte Etienne de Beaumont for his Soirées de Paris.

5. Qtd. in Frank W. D. Ries, *The Dance Theatre of Jean Cocteau* (Ann Arbor, MI: UMI Research Press, 1986), 92.

6. Dolin, *Last Words*, 61.

7. See, for instance, "La flanelle et la serge blanches reparaissent sur la plage et dans les costumes de sport, avec des paletots de nuance vive," *Femina*, June 1922, 15; "La Coupe Femina sur les links de la Boulié," *Femina*, 1 July 1922, 4–5; "Au volant," *Femina*, Jan. 1924, 3; "Une Séance de gymnastique en plein air" (spotlighting the daily acrobatic workout of music-hall star Fanny Heldy), *Femina*, June 1924, 4–5; "C'est la mode nouvelle," *Femina*, July 1923, 7. The August 1924 cover depicted a cigarette-and-lipstick break during a game of mixed doubles.

8. Kochno, *Diaghilev and the Ballets Russes*, 216.

9. Two identical typescripts of the libretto are in 21/12, BNC. The published libretto is reproduced in Erik Aschengreen, *Jean Cocteau and the Dance*, trans. Patricia McAndrew and Per Avsum ([Copenhagen]: Gyldendah, 1986), 270–73. Another version, translated into English, appears in Ries, *The Dance Theatre of Jean Cocteau*, 192–94. Nijinska wrote on the cover page of her copy that the translation was begun by Kochno, then continued by Alexandra Troussevitch, a company dancer who did secretarial work for Diaghilev. The quotations are from this copy.

10. Kochno, *Diaghilev and the Ballets Russes*, 216. Among the writers who have echoed Kochno are Aschengreen (*Jean Cocteau and the Dance*, 125–35); Ries, *The Dance Theatre of Jean Cocteau*, 92–95; and Edmonde Charles-Roux, *Chanel: Her Life, Her World—and the Woman behind the Legend She Herself Created*, trans. Nancy Amphoux (New York: Knopf, 1975), 229–34.

11. Qtd. in Richard D. E. Burton, *Francis Poulenc* (Bath: Absolute Press, 2002), 76.

12. Jean Jacques Kihm, Elizabeth Sprigge, and Henri C. Béhar, *Jean Cocteau: L'homme et les miroirs* (Paris: La Table Ronde, 1968), 158.

13. In his memoir *Notes without Music* (159), Milhaud mentions Cocteau, Diaghilev, André Messager (who conducted the premiere), Henri Laurens (who designed the scenery), and Chanel. Milhaud's diaries, which Ries consulted, appear to remain in private hands.

14. Qtd. in Kochno, *Diaghilev and the Ballets Russes*, 216.
15. Dolin, *Divertissement*, 67.
16. Qtd. in Kochno, *Diaghilev and the Ballet Russes*, 216, 219.
17. Grigoriev, *The Diaghilev Ballet*, 196; de Valois, *Invitation to the Ballet*, 47.
18. Jacques Brindejont-Offenbach, "Pour la VIIIe Olympiade. Les Ballets Russes à Paris," *Gaulois*, 17 May 1924, 1. See also de Valois, *Invitation to the Ballet*, 46.
19. J[oseph] Kessel, "Une répétition chez Diaghilew," *Gaulois*, 25 May 1924, 1. A journalist and novelist born in Argentina and partly raised in Russia, Kessel was the author of *La Steppe rouge* (1922) and the novel *Belle du Jour* (1928), which inspired the film by Luis Buñuel.
20. Ibid.
21. Pierre-Plessis, "'Les Dieux et les Biches' devant les Princes de Monaco," *Comoedia*, 25 May 1924, 1.
22. Kochno, *Diaghilev and the Ballets Russes*, 219.
23. Dolin, *Divertissement*, 83, and Last *Words*, 62; Kochno, *Diaghilev and the Ballets Russes*, 219; Sokolova, *Dancing for Diaghilev*, 222.
24. Kochno, *Diaghilev and the Ballets Russes*, 219. The others were for *Parade* (1917) and *Le Tricorne* (1919).
25. "Ballets Russes de Serge de Diaghilew, Grande Saison d'Art de la VIIIe Olympiade, Théâtre des Champs-Elysées, Mai–Juin 1924," NYPL.
26. Jacques Brindejont-Offenbach, "Petite Feuille: Le 'Train Bleu' arrive à Paris," *Gaulois*, 20 June 1924, 1.
27. Dolin, *Last Words*, 63.
28. R[obert] B[russel], "Les Théâtres," *Figaro*, 24 June 1924, 4. Brussel's first article was about the concert of Russian music organized by Diaghilev in tandem with his exhibition of Russian art at the Grand Palais ("Concert de l'Exposition de l'Art Russe," *Figaro*, 7 Nov. 1906, 3).
29. See, for example, Jacques Brindejont-Offenbach, "Les Théâtres," *Gaulois*, 10 Apr. 1924, 6; Fernand Le Borne, "Théâtre des Champs-Elysées. Les ballets russes," *Le Petit Parisien*, 28 May 1924, 4; Paul Collaer, "La Saison de Paris," *Arts et Lettres d'Aujourd'hui*, 15 June 1924, 545.
30. Fernand Gregh, "Chronique dramatique," *Nouvelles littéraires*, 31 May 1924, 7.
31. Pierre Drieu La Rochelle, "Chronique des Spectacles," *NRF*, 1 Dec. 1923, 729. The artists he refers to are Milhaud, who was Jewish; the poet Blaise de Cendrars, who was Swiss; and the painter Fernand Léger. Cole Porter did the music and Gerald Murphy the sets for *Within the Quota*. Both works were produced by the Ballets Suédois in 1923 and choreographed by Jean Borlin.
32. "Les Théâtres. On raconte que ...," *Gaulois*, 24 June 1924, 4.
33. See "La Croix Rouge et la 'Nuit de Mai,'" *Gaulois*, 18 May 1924, 1; "Les Echos," *Gaulois*, 21 May 1924, 1; Advertisement, "Courrier des Théâtres," *Matin*, 23 May 1924, 4; "Carnet de la Charité," *Gaulois*, 26 May 1924, 2; "Le Gala de la Croix-Rouge," *Gaulois*, 30 May 1924, 2; "Paris en fête," *Femina*, July 1924, 8; Ninette de Valois, *Come Dance with Me: A Memoir 1898–1956* (Cleveland/New York: World Publishing, 1957), 85–86.

34. Paul Dambly, "Les Concerts. Le bilan des Ballets Russes. Dernières auditions du Festival Mozart," *Petit Journal*, 3 July 1924, 4.

35. Le Borne, "Théâtre des Champs-Elysées"; Louis Vuillemin, "La Semaine Musicale," *Rappel*, 3 June 1924, 3; Adolphe Boschot, "La Musique. Ballets Russes 'Les Fâcheux,'" *Echo de Paris*, 6 June 1924, 5; Louis Schneider, "Les Premières. Les Ballets russes,'" *Gaulois*, 6 June 1924, 4.

36. Louis Vuillemin, "La Semaine Musicale," *Rappel*, 10 June 1924, 3. He says almost exactly the same thing in "La Semaine Musicale," *Lanterne*, 10 June 1924, 3.

37. Henry Prunières, "Le Train Bleu (aux Ballets Russes)," *Revue musicale*, 1 Aug. 1924, 153; R[obert] B[russel], "Les Théâtres. Théâtre des Champs-Elysées," *Figaro*, 24 June 1924, 4; Louis Schneider, "Les Premières. Ballets russes," *Gaulois*, 24 June 1924, 4; Adolphe Boschot, "La Musique. 'Le Train Bleu,'" *Echo de Paris*, 24 June 1924, 5.

38. André Levinson, "Au Théâtre des Champs-Elysées. 'Le Train Bleu.' Le Spectacle," *Comoedia*, 24 June 1924, 2.

39. *Ecrits sur la musique de Georges Auric/Writings on Music by George Auric*, ed. Carl B. Schmidt, foreword Colin Roust, 4 vols. (Lewiston, Queenston, Lampeter: Edwin Mellen Press, 2009).

40. Adolphe Boschot, "La Musique. Ballets russes 'Les Fâcheux,'" *Echo de Paris*, 6 June 1924, 5; Gustave Bret, "La Musique: Soirée d'inauguration des Ballets Russes," *Intransigeant*, 28 May 1924, 2.

41. Jean Cocteau, "Les Biches. Les Fâcheux. 6 et 9 janvier 1924. Notes de Monte-Carlo," *NRF*, 1 Mar. 1924, 275.

42. Jean Cocteau, "Deux Ballets actuels," *Revue de Paris*, 15 June 1924, 909. This essay, which was republished in Cocteau's *Le Rappel à l'Ordre* (Paris: Stock, 1926) is virtually identical to the texts that appeared in the books on *Les Biches* and *Les Fâcheux*. Since the latter are unpaginated and rare, I have quoted from the *Revue de Paris* version, which is available online through Gallica Periodicals.

43. Ibid., 910.

44. Ibid., 910–11.

45. Ibid., 915–16.

46. Qtd. in Kihm et al., *Jean Cocteau: L'homme et les miroirs*, 159. Gautier-Vignal's letter is undated.

47. Boris de Schloezer, "Chronique musicale," *NRF*, 1 July 1924, 118.

48. Fernand Gregh, "Chronique dramatique," *Nouvelles littéraires*, 31 May 1924, 7; Robert Brussel, *Figaro*, 30 May 1924, 4.

49. Jane Catulle-Mendès, "Les Fâcheux," *Presse*, 8 June 1924, 2.

50. Gregh, "Chronique dramatique"; Jane Catulle-Mendès, "Les Ballets russes," *Presse*, 31 May 1924, 2.

51. Louis Schneider, "Les Premières. Ballets russes," *Gaulois*, 24 June 1924, 4; R[obert] B[russel], "Les Théâtres. Théâtre des Champs-Elysées," *Figaro*, 24 June 1924, 4.

52. Fernand Divoire, "La Danse," *Revue de France*, 1 Aug. 1924, 646.

53. J[acques] B[rindejont]-O[ffenbach], "Les Théâtres. On raconte que . . . ," *Gaulois*, 3 July 1924, 3.

54. Dolin, *Divertissement*, 82. A better way of transliterating this would be: *Ia ne mogu. Eto tak strashno*. In *Invitation to the Ballet*, Ninette de Valois also describes Nijinsky's visit, although she remembered it a little differently. In her telling, "the rehearsal continued, but gradually this patient, vacant, staring figure had its effect, and many of the older members of the company, who had worked with him and witnessed his triumphs, ended by breaking down. Only the figure itself remained aloof and unmoved" (50-51).

55. BN, draft letter to RN, undated, 6/1, BNC.

56. Ibid.

57. BN, draft letter to Elena Krivinskaia, undated [1968], 73/36, BNC.

58. BN, "Sergei Pavlovitch Diaghilev," 7.

59. Qtd. in Buckle, *Diaghilev*, 444.

60. Auric to SD, 7 Apr. 1924, Pièce 3, Fonds Kochno; Georges Auric, *Les Matelots* (Paris: Heugel, 1925).

61. Vernon Duke, *Passport to Paris* (Boston: Little, Brown, 1955), 115.

62. Kochno quotes some of these letters in *Diaghilev and the Ballets Russes*, 224-26.

63. On July 10, 1925, Auric wrote to Diaghilev outraged by Kochno's demand for 500 francs as the "publishing price" of ballets for which he had written the libretti. "The royalties of *Les Matelots* are divided three ways and distributed among Massine, myself, and Boris. I consider that if two people should receive more in this division, it should be Massine and myself, whose work and effort are not at all comparable . . . to that of Boris. If anyone *sacrifices* anything, it is me for accepting this distribution (which I readily accept). . . . Moreover, it is *without precedent* that a music publisher pays for a *ballet* scenario. Ask Edition Russe, Durand, and Heugel . . . or someone like Jean Cocteau, who has never received and moreover has never dreamed of receiving anything from the publishers of *Parade* or *Le Train Bleu*" (Pièce 3, Fonds Kochno). For a broader discussion of this, see Lynn Garafola, *Diaghilev's Ballets Russes* (New York: Oxford University Press, 1989), 256-57.

64. Kovalenko, *Alexandra Exter*, II, 101. For the exhibition catalogue, see Edoardo Pansini, *L'Arte alla XIV Biennale internazionale veneziana MCMXXIV* (Naples: Edizione della rivista di belle arti Cimento, 1926). For a gallery view of the exhibition, including the Trotsky portrait, see http://thecharnelhouse.org/2013/03/15/trotskiana/gallery-view-of-the-russian-exhibition-at-the-venice-biennale-1924/#main.

65. Ibid., 105. *Venice* is reproduced on pages 102-3 and a related gouache on page 101.

66. SD to Kochno, 19 July 1924, qtd. in Kochno, *Diaghilev and the Ballets Russes*, 223. The Pansini volume cited above does not mention Diaghilev.

67. Exter to BN, 28 July 1924, 72/32, BNC. This letter and the one cited in the next note are published in Russian and a slightly different translation in Kovalenko, *Alexandra Exter*, II, 308-11.

68. Exter to BN, 15 Aug. 1924, 72/32, BNC.

69. For Diaghilev's movements during the summer of 1924, see Buckle, *Diaghilev*, 434-41.

70. Exter to BN, 15 Aug. 1924, 72/32, BNC.

71. Kovalenko, *Alexandra Exter*, II, 111.

72. BN, Diary, 3 Sept. 1924–3 Apr. 1925, 64/3, BNC. Nijinska dates this entry "the eve of September 7."

73. "Certificate of Divorce," No. 623, issued by the Diocesan Administration of Russian Orthodox Churches in Western Europe on the grounds of the "husband's violation of conjugal fidelity," 22 Apr. 1924; French translation certified by the Russian Consulate in Nice, 28 Aug. 1924, 46/4. For the wedding, see Dolin, *Divertissement*, 92. The Ballets Russes performed at the Grosse Volksoper in Berlin from October 9–26. For the marriage date, see Bronislava Nijinska Singaevsky, Petition for Naturalization, No. 141524, 11 Oct. 1949, Ancestry Library.

74. BN, Diary, 3 Sept. 1924–3 Apr. 1925, entry for Sept. 7.

75. Sir Oswald Stoll to Serge Diaghileff Esq., 23 Sept. 1924, in Macdonald, *Diaghilev Observed*, 293; "Russian Ballet Again," *Daily Mail*, 22 Sept. 1924, 7; "The Sitter Out," *DT*, Oct. 1924, 6.

76. Dolin, *Divertissement*, 96.

77. After the first performance of *Midnight Sun*, this Massine ballet was given with several numbers from *Aurora's Wedding*. Dolin danced the Blue Bird at all of the additional performances, although his partners changed.

78. Richard Capell, "Russian Ballet Memories," *Daily Mail*, 21 Nov. 1924, 8; "Russian Ballet Again. M. Diaghilev and His Plans," *Observer*, 23 Nov. 1924, 13; Theater Directory, *Times*, 26 Nov. 1924, 12.

79. "Ballet of the Bathing Beach," *Daily Sketch*, 26 Nov. 1924, in "Ballet Russe de Serge de Diaghilew [Scrapbook]–1921–1922–1923–1924," 198 (hereafter "Ballet Russe Scrapbook"), https://www.loc.gov/resource/ihas.200181897.0/?sp=1&st=gallery. At this time the *Daily Sketch* was affiliated with the tabloid empire of Lord Rothermere, owner of the *Daily Mail*. For the twenty-one curtain calls, see the theater listings, *Times*, 26 Nov. 1924, 12.

80. Marcato, "The Dance of the Tennis Racket," *Evening News*, [25] Nov. 1924, in Ballet Russe Scrapbook, 187.

81. E. B., " 'Le Train Bleu,' " *MG*, 25 Nov. 1924, 14.

82. "The Russian Ballet. New Dances at the Coliseum," *Times*, 25 Nov. 1924, 12; R[ichard] C[apell], "Bathing Beach Ballet," *Daily Mail*, 25 Nov. 1924, 7.

83. "Keeping Fit," *Evening News*, 29 Nov. 1924, in Ballet Russe Scrapbook, 188.

84. "How the Russian Ballet Dancers Keep Fit," *Daily Mirror*, 5 Dec. 1924, in Ballet Russe Scrapbook, 188.

85. "Sports Expressed in Terms of Dancing: Tennis, Golf, and Swimming Mimed by the Russian Ballet," *Illustrated London News*, 6 Dec. 1924, 1092–93.

86. *Tatler*, 10 Dec. 1924, 501.

87. Haselden, "Twentieth Century Ballet for Everyday Use," *Daily Mirror*, 28 Nov. 1924, in Ballet Russe Scrapbook, 186.

88. "Russian Ballet at the Coliseum. 'The Faithful Shepherdess,'" *Times*, 2 Dec. 1924, 12. For "enchanting" and "classical," see Hubert Fitchew, "The Week's Music," *Sunday Times*, 7 Dec. 1924, 7.

89. Edwin Evans, "Diaghileff, Once More," *DT*, Dec. 1924, 241.

90. See, for example, "An Admirer of the Ballet," "The Russian Ballet and the Coliseum," *Observer*, 30 Nov. 1924, 17.

91. Lopokova to Keynes, 11 Dec. 1924, in *Lydia and Maynard: Letters between Lydia Lopokova and John Maynard Keynes*, ed. Polly Hill and Richard Keynes (London: Andre Deutsch, 1989), 271.

92. "The Empire Theatre," *Times*, 9 Oct. 1924, 12. See also "New London Theatre," *Daily Mail*, 2 Oct. 1924, 6; "Military Tattoo at Empire Theatre," *Scotsman*, 14 Oct. 1924, 6; H[oward] H[annay], "The Week's Theatres. Variety. The Alhambra, Empire, and Coliseum," *Observer*, 19 Oct. 1924, 11; "The Sitter Out," *DT*, Nov. 1924, 116; Cyril W. Beaumont, *Bookseller at the Ballet: Memoirs 1891–1929* (London: C. W. Beaumont, 1975), 314. For the lodgings in Bloomsbury, see Richard Buckle, with John Taras, *George Balanchine, Ballet Master* (New York: Random House, 1988), 28.

93. Lopokova to Keynes, 12 Oct. 1924, in *Lydia and Maynard*, 234. The New Economic Policy (NEP)—in Russian, новая экономическая политика (НЭП)—was a market-oriented policy introduced by Lenin in 1921 to revive the economy after the devastation of the Civil War. While restoring production to near prewar levels, the NEP was accompanied by the "re-emergence of a 'capitalist' class . . . , [rising] unemployment . . . , and anxieties . . . about bourgeois degeneracy" (Lewis Siegelbaum, "The New Economic Policy," *Seventeen Moments in Soviet History* [http://soviethistory.msu.edu/1921-2/the-new-economic-policy/]). With the triumph of Stalin over his rivals and the launching of the First Five-Year Plan in the late 1920s, the NEP officially came to an end. See also "New Economic Policy," *Wikipedia* (https://en.wikipedia.org/wiki/New_Economic_Policy).

94. Buckle, *George Balanchine*, 29. See also Tamara Geva, *Split Seconds: A Remembrance* (New York: Harper & Row, 1972), 331; Alexandra Danilova, *Choura: The Memoirs of Alexandra Danilova* (New York: Knopf, 1986), 66.

95. Buckle, *George Balanchine*, 29–30.

96. Lopokova to Keynes, 30 Nov. 1924, in *Lydia and Maynard*, 265.

97. Cast changes were published in the *Times*'s daily theater columns.

98. Buckle, *George Balanchine*, 31.

99. Buckle, *Diaghilev*, 446. Lifar in *Ma Vie from Kiev to Kiev: An Autobiography* (trans. James Holman Mason [London: Hutchinson, 1970], 46), gives a quite different account, claiming that he did not want to sacrifice the time he needed to become a dancer to choreographing the ballet, and that he therefore asked Diaghilev to relieve him of the responsibility and to "turn over the work to Massine."

100. Grigoriev, *The Diaghilev Ballet*, 200.

101. De Valois, *Come Dance with Me*, 83–84.

102. Danilova, *Choura*, 67.

103. Vicente García-Márquez, *Massine: A Biography* (New York: Knopf, 1995), 185.

104. "Massine and Cecchetti to Rejoin Diaghileff," *DT*, Jan. 1925, 451.

105. Dolin claims that Diaghilev was "saddened and shocked by her departure" (*Last Words*, 67).

106. Grigoriev, *The Diaghilev Ballet*, 202.

107. De Valois, *Invitation to the Ballet*, 170–71.

108. "The Russian Ballet. Return Visit in May," *Times*, 12 Jan. 1925, 10.
109. "Russian Ballet's Farewell. 'Auld Lang Syne' with the Lights Out," *MG*, 12 Jan. 1925, 3.
110. "Autobiographical outline," 34/15, BNC.
111. The ribbon on the bouquet, dedicated to our "dear and respected ballet master and teacher Bronislava Nijinska," is in the Stravinsky-Diaghilev Collection, Series X (Objects), Box 318, HTC. A second ribbon, dated 9 Jan. 1925, Coliseum, London, was signed in Latin characters by "Anton Dolin, Doubrovska, Leon Wojcikowski [*sic*], Lydia Sokolova, N. Zvereff, Vera Nemtchinova, Anatol Wiltzak, Lubov Tchernicheva, [and] Ludmila Chollar."

Chapter 8

1. *DT*, Jan. 1925, 495.
2. Unidentified clipping, *Paris Telegram*, 15 Feb. 1925, 23/1, BNC.
3. For background on Joyce Berry and Doris Sonne, see Laurie Kaden, "Nijinska's Theatre Choréographique Nijinska: The 1925 Tour of English Resort Towns," M.A. thesis, University of California, Riverside, 1988, 61–62. Berry was devoted to Nijinska, whose letters to her (Joyce Berry Papers, Box 2, University of California, Riverside) are full of the maternal concern that Nijinska's Kiev students remembered so well. For a memoir of Sonne by her sister-in-law, the dancer, choreographer, and film director Wendy Toye, see "Doris Sonne," *DT*, July 2000, 897.
4. Draft sketch of announcement for Nijinska's "First Conservatory of Theater Dance, 1924" 65/5, BNC.
5. BN to Stravinsky, 17 Jan. 1925, Stravinsky Collection, Reel 38/0454, Paul Sacher Foundation, Basel.
6. BN to Gest, 20 Jan. 1925, Morris Gest Collection, Box 4, HRC.
7. G[abrielle] M. Picabia, to BN, 23 Jan. 1925, 75/32, BNC. For background on Gabrielle (Buffet) Picabia, see William A. Camfield, *Francis Picabia: His Art, Life, and Times* (Princeton: Princeton University Press, 1979).
8. G. M. Picabia, undated note to BN, 75/32, BNC.
9. RN to BN, 18 Feb. 1925, 78/46, BNC.
10. Astruc to RN, 13 May [1925], GA106-5, Astruc Papers. See also Astruc to RN, 9 May [1925], GA106-3.
11. BN to Eleonora Bereda Nijinsky, 16 Mar. 1925, 78/34, BNC.
12. RN to Rouché, 6 Mar. 1925, L.A.S. Nijinsky, Romola, 8, BM-Opéra. Notwithstanding Romola's assertion, Nijinsky never completed *Mephisto Valse*.
13. RN to Rouché, 3 Apr. 1925, AJ/13/1213, item 1097, AN.
14. For the department and its fate, see Lynn Garafola, "Forgotten Interlude: Eurhythmic Dancers at the Paris Opéra," in *Legacies of Twentieth-Century Dance* (Middletown, CT: Wesleyan University Press, 2005), 85–106.
15. Léandre Vaillat, *Ballets de l'Opéra de Paris (Ballets dans les opéras et nouveaux ballets)* (Paris: Compagnie française des arts graphiques, 1947), 104.

16. Rouché, carbon copy of a letter to "Monsieur Jacques DALCROZE" [*sic*], 30 June 1925, Fonds Rouché, Registre, 6 Apr. 1925–6 Dec. 1925, 162, BM-Opéra. For material related to the closing of the "Section de Danse Rythmique," including carbon copies of letters of dismissal sent to the dancers, see AJ/13/1703, AN. Carbon copies of Rouché's dismissal letters are in Fonds Rouché, Registre, 6 Apr. 1925–6 Dec. 1925, 182 and 212, BM-Opéra.

17. André Levinson, *La Danse d'Aujourd'hui: Etudes, Notes, Portraits* (Paris: Duchartre et Van Buggenhoudt, 1929), 201. For Levinson's "death notice," see "La Danse. Epitaphe," *Comoedia*, 21 Sept. 1925, 3.

18. RN to Rouché, 3 Apr. 1925.

19. RN to Rouché, 17 Apr. 1925, AJ/13/1213, item 1098, AN.

20. Ibert to Rouché, 18 July 1925, L.A.S. Ibert, Jacques, 5, BM-Opéra.

21. Henry Malherbe, "Chronique musicale," *Temps*, 8 July 1925, 3.

22. André Levinson, "'La Naissance de la Lyre' à l'Opéra. Les danses," *Comoedia*, 2 July 1925, 2.

23. "Sitter Out," *DT*, Dec. 1925, 260, 263.

24. Albert Roussel and Théodore Reinach, letter to Jacques Rouché, [1 July 1925], in "Courrier des Théâtres," *Figaro*, 5 July 1925, 4.

25. The spelling of "chorégraphique" is incorrect in French, but was obviously an attempt to capitalize in England on the company's foreign associations. A translation of the company's name might be Nijinska's Dance Theater.

26. The following discussion is indebted to Kaden's "Nijinska's Theatre Choréographique." Kaden did extensive newspaper research in the towns where the group performed. See also Kaden's article, "Nijinska's Theatre Choréographique Nijinska: The 1925 Tour of English Resort Towns," in *Proceedings of the Society of Dance History Scholars*, University of California-Riverside, 14–15 Feb. 1992, 145–58.

27. "The Pavilion," *Bexhill-on-Sea Observer*, 5 Sept. 1925, 5; cited in Kaden, "Nijinska's Theatre Choréographique," 159.

28. For Lucas, see the entry by Ronald Crichton in *Grove Music Online*, and Philip L. Scowcroft, "A Musical All-Rounder: Leighton Lucas (1903–1982)," *The Robert Farnon Society Website* (http://www.rfsoc.org.uk/llucas.shtml). The piano manuscript of "Japonisme," the title of Lucas's music for *On the Road*, is in 20/2, BNC.

29. Kaden, "Nijinska's Theatre Choréographique," 106.

30. "The Pavilion," *Bexhill Chronicle*, 5 Sept. 1925, 7; cited in Kaden, "Nijinska's Theatre Choréographique," 159.

31. *EM*, 503. Joyce Berry described him to Kaden as an "older Jewish man who spoke English" ("Nijinska's Theatre Choréographique," 73). Although he usually signed his name as "F. Zenon," his full name appears on the Memorandum of Agreement, signed by Nijinska and Donald Arthur of Star Attractions on June 26, 1925, 46/10, BNC.

32. Cyril W. Beaumont, *Bookseller at the Ballet* (London: C. W. Beaumont, 1975), 199–200. Beaumont hints at secret money dealings vis-à-vis Diaghilev, but does not spell them out.

33. *EM*, 507–8. Nijinska specifically states that Zenon told her that "all the Nijinsky theatrical properties had been sold because of nonpayment of the warehouse fees during

the war" (508). However, it appears that Zenon had access to some of these sets and costumes and that Nijinska planned to use them.

34. Zenon to BN, 28 May 1925, 77B/18, BNC.

35. Zenon to BN, 19 June 1925, 77B/18, BNC.

36. Memorandum of Agreement, 26 June 1925.

37. Zenon to BN, 3 July 1925, 77B/18, BNC.

38. Zenon to BN, 14 July 1925, 77B/18, BNC. See also his letter of July 7.

39. For Gambs, see "London Friend of Continental Refugees," *Barrier Miner*, 7 Aug. 1935, 2 (http://trove.nla.gov.au/ndp/del/article/46701294); "Russian Who Cannot Be Deported," *Times*, 26 Apr. 1934, 4; "Alien's Daily Report to Police. Claim to Be a Russian Prince," *Times*, 19 Dec. 1934, 11. Antonova was married to Leon Woizikovsky, although they had separated when he and Lydia Sokolova began an affair. Stanislaw Zmarzlik was a young Polish dancer who performed in 1924 with the Soirées de Paris.

40. Zenon to BN, 22 July 1925, 77B/18, BNC.

41. Kaden, "Nijinska's Theatre Choréographique," 109–13. For the Aliens Order, an amendment to the Aliens' Restriction Act of 1919, see "Making Britain," *The Open University* (http://www.open.ac.uk/researchprojects/makingbritain/content/1920-aliens-order).

42. "Ballet Dispute," *Morning Post*, 12 Aug. 1925, 12, qtd. in Kaden, "Nijinska's Theatre Choréographique," 109–10; "Dancers Expelled. Home Secretary & a Russian Troupe," *Daily Mail*, 12 Aug. 1925, 9; "Ban on Ballet Dancers. Enforcement of Aliens Act," *Times of India*, 8 Sept. 1925, 12.

43. "Autobiographical outline," 34/15, BNC, 25. For Diaghilev's whereabouts in late July and August, see Buckle, *Diaghilev*, 457–59.

44. Kaden, "Nijinska's Theatre Choréographique," 113–14.

45. "Random Notes—The Banned Ballet," *Weston-super-Mare Gazette*, 15 Aug. 1925, 6; qtd. in Kaden, "Nijinska's Theatre Choréographique," 117.

46. Qtd. in Kaden, "Nijinska's Theatre Choréographique," 122–23. For the seating capacity of performance venues, see Kadin, Appendix E, 201.

47. Kovalenko, *Alexandra Exter*, II, 129.

48. "Alexandra Exter (1882–1949)," http://www.alexandra-exter.net/en/biographie.php.

49. For a selection of photographs and Exter's designs, see Baer, *Bronislava Nijinska*, 49–57. Exter's costume designs are in Boxes 169 and 170, BNC; the ones for *Jazz* in 169/15–16. Photographs can be found in 107/3. Additional costume designs as well as costume elements, acquired in 2016, are at the V&A. For descriptions of and responses to the costumes, see Baer and Kaden, "Nijinska's Theatre Choréographique," chap. 4; for photographs of *Holy Etudes*, see 107/3, BNC.

50. Baer, *Bronislava Nijinska*, 50.

51. BN, handwritten note concerning *Etude*, 59/4, BNC. Other jottings include "Still not 'Etude'—Bach / 1920—Kiev," suggesting that the ballet originated as one of the many solos Nijinska choreographed for herself in Kiev.

52. Exter's design is in the Word and Image Department, V&A, Accession No. E792-1963 (pressmark LVLE/CC/6). It is reproduced in Kovalenko, *Alexandra Exter*, II, 191.

53. Kaden, "Nijinska's Theatre Choréographique," Appendix A (Tour Chronology), 194.

54. BN to Diaghilev, 6 Oct. 1925, Pièce 65, Nijinska 11, Fonds Kochno.

55. Gala souvenir program, "La Danse à Travers les Ages," Paris Opéra, 3 Dec. 1925, Carton 2238, BM-Opéra. In the second performance, Lazar Galpern (Halperine), an actor-dancer trained by Goleizovsky at the Habima Theater, replaced the Hoyer brothers, and Yvonne Franck of the Opéra's dismantled eurhythmic unit replaced Doris Sonne.

56. RN to BN, 4 Sept. 1925, 78/46, BNC.

57. Mathias Auclair and Aurélien Poidevin, "Les Ballets russes et l'Opéra de Paris (1909–1929)," in Les Ballets russes, ed. Mathias Auclair and Pierre Vidal (Paris: Editions Gourcuff Gradenigo, 2009), 211.

58. Rouché to RN, undated, 76/7, BNC. The return address was the Château de St. Privat, a splendid property near Remoulins in the eastern Languedoc.

59. RN to Rouché, 8 Sept. 1925, L.A.S. Nijinsky, Romola, 10, BM-Opéra.

60. Ibid.

61. RN to BN, 8 Sept. 1925, 78/46, BNC.

62. Rouché, draft letter to RN, 28 Sept. 1925, L. A. S. Nijinsky, Romola, 12bis; RN to Rouché, 22 Sept. 1925, L.A.S. Nijinska, Romola, 12, BM-Opéra.

63. RN to Rouché, 29 Sept. 1925, L.A.S. Nijinsky, Romola, 14, BM-Opéra.

64. "Classes de Danses," with the illegible signature of the "Régisseur de la Danse" and stamp of the "Régie de la Danse," undated [1925], 76/7, BNC.

65. BN to Rouché, 11 Dec. 1925, L.A.S. Nijinska, Bronislava, 1, BM-Opéra.

66. BN, "On Movement and the School of Movement," in Schrifttanz, 58.

67. Group letter to Rouché, 21 Dec. 1925, AJ/13/1703, AN.

68. In an entry dated December 1926 she wrote: "Paris has grown darker—December, fog, and nationalism (in art)—which crawled out from who knows where. In this homeland of artists, on soil fertilized by geniuses of all nations" ("Diary 1926–27," 64/7, BNC).

69. "Avant-première. A l'Opéra: Spectacle coupé: Brocéliande.—L'Ile désenchantée.—Rencontres," Ménéstrel, 13 Nov. 1925, 465–66; Paul Nivoix, 'Trois Créations à l'Opéra. 'Brocéliande'—'L'Ile désenchantée'—'Les Rencontres,'" Comoedia, 18 Nov. 1925, 1.

70. Roland-Manuel, "Les Premières á l'Opéra—au Théâtre Marigny," unidentified magazine, [Nov. 1925], 11; 163/item 23, BNC.

71. Adolphe Jullien, "Revue Musicale," Journal des Débats, 6 Dec. 1925, 4.

72. See, for example, Albert Montel, "Les Spectacles. A l'Opéra," Lanterne, 24 Nov. 1925, 3.

73. Jacques Ibert, letter to Jacques Rouché, 24 Nov. 1925, L.A.S. Ibert, Jacques, 7, BM-Opéra. The répétition générale took place on November 19 ("Avant-premières. Le nouveau spectacle de l'Opéra," Figaro, 19 Nov. 1925, 4).

74. André Levinson, "Les Grands Premières. Trois poèmes à l'Opéra. La chorégraphie," Comoedia, 21 Nov. 1925, 1–2.

75. Jullien, "Revue Musicale."

76. Georges Auric, "La Musique," Nouvelles littéraires, 28 Nov. 1925, 7.

77. Henry Malherbe, "Chronique Musicale," Temps, 25 Nov. 1925, 3.

78. "Courrier des Théâtres. La Reprise d'*Alceste* à l'Opéra," *Figaro*, 6 Feb. 1926, 4.

79. André Messager, "Les Premières. Théâtre National de l'Opéra: *Alceste*, tragédie-opéra de Gluck," *Figaro*, 10 Feb. 1926, 4.

80. For Maudru's review, see "A l'Opéra. 'Alceste,'" *Comoedia*, 10 Feb. 1926, 1.

81. Rouché to BN, 13 Feb. 1926, 76/7, BNC.

82. "Autobiographical outline," 34/15, BNC, 25.

83. Grigoriev, *The Diaghilev Ballet*, 216.

84. Schouvaloff, *The Art of Ballets Russes*, 197. For the fullest account of the Christopher Wood debacle, see Stephen Lloyd, *Constant Lambert: Beyond the Rio Grande* (Woodbridge, UK: Boydell Press, 2014), 55–61. For a discussion of Miró's set and costume designs, see Idoia Murga Castro, *Pintura en danza. Los artistas españoles y el ballet (1916–1962)* (Madrid: CSIC/Historia de Arte, 2012), 68–70. Miró's set design (Fig. 15) is reproduced on page 68.

85. Grigoriev, *The Diaghilev Ballet*, 216.

86. Draft contract, 5 Mar. 1926, Pièce 65, Nijinska 4, Fonds Kochno.

87. Jane Catulle-Mendès, "Théâtre Sarah-Bernhardt. Ballets Russes. *Romeo and Juliet*," *Presse*, 21 May 1926, 2.

88. Pirandello's "comedy in 3 acts" opened in Paris at the Théâtre Edouard VII on July 6, 1925.

89. Playbill, 20 May 1926, CAL.

90. Beaumont, *Bookseller at the Ballet*, 345.

91. Kochno, *Diaghilev and the Ballets Russes*, 236.

92. Grigoriev, *The Diaghilev Ballet*, 220.

93. *Nikitina by Herself*, trans. Baroness Budberg (London: Allan Wingate, 1959), 58.

94. Constant Lambert, "Music and Action," in Caryl Brahms, *Footnotes to the Ballet: A Book for Balletomanes* (London: Lovat Dickson, 1936), 173.

95. Tamara Karsavina, "Serge Lifar and the Last Diaghilev Seasons," *DT*, Mar. 1967, 302–3.

96. André Coeuroy, "'Roméo and Juliet' aux Ballets Russes," *Revue musicale*, 1 June 1926, 284.

97. Fernand Divoire, "La Danse," *Revue de France*, 1 July 1926, 191–92.

98. F. T., "Karsavina's Art," *Morning Post*, 23 June 1926, in "Ballet Russe de Serge de Diaghilew—Paris, London 1926 Romeo and Juliet; Noces" (hereafter Romeo and Juliet Scrapbook), 61, BNC, http://lcweb2.loc.gov/diglib/ihas/loc.natlib.ihas.200181898/enlarge.html?page=61.

99. André Levinson, "Au Théâtre Sarah-Bernhardt. La rentrée des 'Ballets Russes.' 'Romeo and Juliet,'" *Comoedia*, 20 May 1926, 1–2.

100. Pierre-Plessis, "La Vie qui passe. Le retour des Ballets Russes," *Gaulois*, 13 May 1926, 1.

101. Louis Aragon and André Breton, "Protestation," private collection. A translation is in Kochno, *Diaghilev and the Ballets Russes*, 257. For a firsthand account of the "scandal," see the entry for 18 May 1926 in *Sergey Prokofiev Diaries 1924–1933*, trans. and annotated Anthony Phillips (Ithaca, NY: Cornell University Press, 2012), 312–14.

102. "Englishman's Ballet at Last. Diaghileff's Idea Realised," *Weekly Dispatch*, 27 June 1926, in "Romeo and Juliet Scrapbook," 57.

103. Lambert to BN, 5 May 1926, 74/2, BNC.

104. Lambert to Amy Lambert, 24 May 1926, qtd. in Shead, *Constant Lambert*, 56-57. This is also quoted by Lloyd, who notes that the whereabouts of Lambert's letters to his mother is unknown.

105. Buckle, *Diaghilev*, 467.

106. Karsavina, "Serge Lifar," 303.

107. Lambert to Amy Lambert, 24 May 1926, qtd. in Shead, 59.

108. Lambert to BN, 20 May [1926], 74/2, BNC.

109. Lambert to BN, 22 June [1926], 74/2, BNC. What bothered Nijinska most about Diaghilev's meddling, she wrote a year later, was his decision to eliminate the "marvelous ending of the first act" ("Diary 1926-27, Paris-Buenos Aires," 41, 64/7, BNC).

110. Zenon to BN, 26 Nov. 1928, 77B/18, BNC.

111. "Diary 1926-27, Paris-Buenos Aires," 43.

Chapter 9

1. For the history of the Colón, see Roberto Caamaño, *La historia del Teatro Colón 1908-1968*, I (Buenos Aires: Editorial Cinetea, 1969).

2. "Cuadro comparativo entre El Teatro Colón y algunos teatros del mundo," in Ernesto de la Guardia and Roberto Herrera, *El Arte lírico en el Teatro Colón (1908-1933)* (Buenos Aires: Zea y Tejero, 1933), n.p.

3. Caamaño, *La historia del teatro Colón*, I, 110-11. *Excelsior* was staged by Raffaele Grassi, *Brahma* by Cesare Merzagora.

4. Ibid. Caamaño's second volume includes year-by-year listings of repertory and major personnel.

5. Caamaño, *La historia del Teatro Colón*, II, 177.

6. For an interview with Bolm and two reviews of the production, see "A Metropolitan 'Petrushka,'" *NYT*, 2 Feb 1919, 43; James Gibbons Huneker, "Opera: 'Traviata' and 'Petrushka,'" *NYT*, 7 Feb. 1919, 15; "Ballet 'Petrushka' at Metropolitan," *CSM*, 8 Feb. 1919, 14.

7. Her 1926 contract—in Spanish and French—stipulated that she was to serve as "teacher and choreographer" of the Colón's "permanent corps de ballet" from May 1 to November 30. Contract between Bronislava Nijinska and the Intendencia Municipal de la Ciudad de Buenos Aires, 15 May 1926, 46/10, BNC. She signed a second contract on July 15, 1926, hiring her as a "first dancer" for the ballet season following the completion of the opera season. Intendencia Municipal de la Ciudad de Buenos Aires, letter-contract with Bronislava Nijinska, 15 July 1926, 46/10, BNC. She received 1,500 pesos a month (or a total of 10,500 pesos) under the terms of the first contract, and a total of 3,000 under the second.

8. Enrique Honorio Destaville, "Nijinska and Her Work at the Ballet del Teatro Colón," trans. Ana Abad-Carlés, *DT*, Oct. 2008, 45.

9. Ibid.

10. Enrique Honorio Destaville, "Mirada sobre el siglo XIX y el siglo XX en sus primeros años," in *Historia general de la danza en la Argentina* (Buenos Aires: Fondo Nacional de las artes, 2008), 38. According to her May 15 contract, Nijinska agreed to "organize the permanent corps de ballet, . . . subjecting the elements approved by the Jury . . . to a strict daily discipline, in accordance with the usages and customs of the world's great theaters. To this end, she will give a special daily class that will last one consecutive hour that all members of the corps de ballet, without exception, shall be obliged to attend."

11. "Manifesto de 'Martín Fierro,'" *Martín Fierro* 1, no. 4 (15 May 1924), 1.

12. The list of works has been compiled from the daily theater columns of the Buenos Aires newspapers *La Nación* and *La Prensa*.

13. For the announcement of the 1927 spring season, see "Programa de hoy," *La Nación*, 10 July 1927, 13.

14. Ballet performances were given on August 29, 31; September 4, 21, 25; October 12, 19, 22, 24, 30, and 31, for a total of eleven performances. In 1927 performances took place on September 9, 11, 28; October 11, 16, 23, 28, 30; and November 15, 21, 27. *La Giara*, which was performed twice during the 1927 winter opera season, was paired with *Le Rossignol* (*El Ruiseñor*) and *The Barber of Seville*.

15. "Movimiento teatral. El espectáculo de bailes ofrecido ayer en el Colón fué muy bien recibido," *La Nación*, 30 Aug. 1926, 6. Unless indicated otherwise, all reviews come from the Robillant Collection.

16. Ibid.

17. "Iniciación de los espectáculos coreográficos," *La Prensa*, 30 Aug. 1926, 11.

18. Ibid.

19. Marta Giovannini and Amelia Foglio de Ruíz, *Ballet argentino en el Teatro Colón* (Buenos Aires: Editorial Plus Ultra, 1973), 108.

20. Playbill, "Espectáculo de baile," Teatro Colón, 21 Sept. 1926, 51/20, BNC.

21. "Teatro y música. Colón," *La Prensa*, 22 Sept. 1926, 14.

22. "Movimiento teatral. EfectuBse el segundo espectáculo de bailes en el Colón," *La Nación*, 22 Sept. 1926, 10.

23. Both in 1926 and 1927 the pianists were Lina Spena, Mafalda Napolitano, Aldo Romaniello, and Raúl Spivak.

24. "Teatro y música. Colón. 'Bodas' de Igor Stravinsky," *La Prensa*, 20 Oct. 1926, 16.

25. "Movimiento teatral. Se estrenó 'Bodas' de Igor Strawinski en el Teatro Colón," *La Nación*, 20 Oct. 1926, 10.

26. "Teatro y música," *La Prensa*, 20 Oct. 1926.

27. "Diary (1926–27)," undated entry, 64/7, BNC.

28. Alberto J. Melavear, letter-contract with BN, 15 Nov. 1926, 74/35, BNC. However, her formal appointment as the Colón's "Choreographic Director" was signed only on May 4, 1927, after her arrival in Buenos Aires, 46/1, BNC.

29. *Naïla* was designed by René Piot, *Impressions de Music-Hall* by Maxime Dethomas, both of whom worked regularly at the Opéra in the 1920s. For reviews of the program, see Pierre Lalo, "A l'Opéra: 'Naïla' and 'Impressions de Music-Hall,'" *Comoedia*, 8 Apr. 1927, 1; André Levinson, "A l'Opéra. Chorégraphie," *Comoedia*, 8 Apr. 1927, 1–2; Gustave Bret, "La Musique," *Intransigeant*, 8 Apr. 1927, 5; Louis Schneider, "La Musique," *Gaulois*, 8 Apr. 1927, 3; Jane Catulle-Mendès, "Les Générales à l'Opéra," *Presse*, 8 Apr. 1927, 2; R. Cardinne-Petit, "Courrier des Théâtres. Les Premières," *Figaro*, 9 Apr. 1927, 5; Jean Prudhomme, "Les Premières," *Matin*, 9 Apr. 1927, 4; G. de Pawlowski, "Premières à l'Opéra," *Journal*, 9 Apr. 1927, 5; Adolphe Jullien, "Revue musicale," *Journal des Débats*, 25 Apr. 1927, 3; André George, "*Naïla* et *Impressions de Music-Hall* à l'Opéra," *Nouvelles littéraires*, 30 Apr. 1927, 9. The description of Zambelli's skirt comes from Adolphe Boschot, "La Musique. A l'Opéra," *Echo de Paris*, 9 Apr. 1927, 4.
30. Pierné to Rouché, 3 Mar. 1926, L. A. S. Pierné, Gabriel, 80, BM-Opéra. For Staats's career at the Roxy, see George Dorris, "Léo Staats at the Roxy, 1926–1928," *DR* 13, no. 1 (Summer 1995), 84–99.
31. Georges Masson, "Pierné, Gabriel," *Grove Music Online*.
32. Pierné's undated scenario is in 75/35, BNC.
33. Pierné to BN, 29 Mar. 1927, 75/35, BNC.
34. Pierné to BN, 11 Apr. 1927, 75/35, BNC. For announcements of the répétition générale, see E. B., "Théâtre. Courrier," *Intransigeant*, 6 Apr. 1927, 5, and 7 Apr. 1927, 5.
35. Pawlowski, "Premières à l'Opéra," *Journal*. He went on to describe Pierné's music as "clownish hiccups of the orchestra and vague evocations of jazz."
36. Lalo, "A l'Opéra," *Comoedia*.
37. Levinson, "A l'Opéra," *Comoedia*.
38. Catulle-Mendès, "Les Générales," *Presse*.
39. Edition Russe de Musique to BN, 7 Apr. 1927, 75/20, BNC. The signature is illegible.
40. BN to Bereda, 29 July 1927, 78/34, BNC.
41. *Orphée* was choreographed by Léo Staats in 1926, *La Tragédie de Salomé* by Nicola Guerra in 1919. The latter was first produced at the Théâtre des Arts in 1907 with Loie Fuller in the title role, rechoreographed in 1912 by Ivan Clustine for Natalia Trouhanova, and restaged in 1913 by Boris Romanov for the Ballets Russes with Tamara Karsavina as Salomé.
42. "Diary (1926–27)," 64/7, BNC.
43. For the entries that follow, see "Diary (1927–29)," 59/2, BNC. A copy, with additions, revisions, and corrections, is in 59/1.
44. "Shipping," *Times*, 25 Mar. 1927, 2.
45. BN to Bereda, 27 and 19 Apr. 1927, 78/34, BNC. Unless otherwise noted, Nijinska's letters to her mother are from this folder. Lists of dancers for the 1926 and 1927 seasons are in 51/22, BNC.
46. BN to Bereda, 20 May 1927. Although Nijinska does not refer to them by name, Kniaseff and Kirsanova are mentioned in an early announcement of the season

("Llegaron anoche varios artistas que actuarán en el Teatro Colón," *La Nación*, 16 May 1927, 10).

47. BN to Bereda, 23 June 1927.

48. Ibid.

49. BN to Bereda, 17 Aug. 1927.

50. BN to Bereda, 26 Aug. 1927.

51. Lloyd, *Constant Lambert*, 95. For the scenario, as this appeared in the published score, see 92–93. A copy of the score published by Oxford University Press in 1928 and dedicated by the composer to BN is in 191/5, BNC. The dedication reads: "A Madame Bronislava Nijinska / avec l'hommage affectueux de / Constant Lambert."

52. Lambert to BN, 20 May [1927], 74/2, BNC.

53. Lambert to BN, 5 July [1927], 74/2, BNC.

54. BN to Bereda, 29 July 1927.

55. "El Colón inauguró la temporada de bailes: grata sorpresa con 'Petrouchka'; progresa el cuerpo de baile," *El Diario de Buenos Aires*, 10 Sept. 1927, 10, 23/1, BNC. Lambert considered Nijinska's changes to the libretto "quite in order," since "the choreographer has the final say on what is theatrically and plastically effective" (qtd. in Lloyd, *Constant Lambert*, 94).

56. "Colón: el concierto de anoche," *La Prensa*, 10 Sept. 1927, 18.

57. "Con muy buen éxito se iniciaron los espectáculos de baile en el Colón," *La Nación*, 10 Sept. 1927, 10. After four performances *Pomona* vanished from the Colón. But in London, where Frederick Ashton staged it for the Camargo Society in 1930, the ballet had a long and successful afterlife. For the London premiere and Ashton's scenario, see David Vaughan, *Frederick Ashton and His Ballets* (New York: Knopf, 1977), 45–47, 411–12.

58. "Colón: el concierto de anoche." See also "El Colón inauguró la temporada de bailes" and "Con muy buen éxito se iniciaron los espectáculos de anoche."

59. BN to Bereda, 10 Sept. 1927.

60. BN to Bereda, 12 Sept. 1927.

61. BN to Bereda, 20 Oct. 1927. Nijinska's daughter, Irina, told Nancy Baer in 1984 that her mother's "stage directions often were ignored by the crew, whose members balked at taking orders from a woman" (Baer, *Bronislava Nijinska*, 58). Although there is no evidence of this in Nijinska's letters home, it is entirely possible that sexism heightened the stresses backstage.

62. BN to Bereda, 1 Oct. 1927.

63. "Colón: espectáculos coreográficos," *La Prensa*, 12 Oct. 1927, 16; "Se estrenaron dos bailes anoche en el Colón," *La Nación*, 12 Oct. 1927, 10. A playbill for the program's second performance is in 163/29, BNC.

64. The typewritten scenario is attached to a letter to Nijinska from Edition Russe de Musique, 7 Apr. 1927, 75/20, BNC. For the mix-up see *Prokofiev Diaries 1924–1933*, 628.

65. "Se estrenaron dos bailes anoche en el Colón."

66. "Colón: espectáculos coreográficos."

67. BN to Bereda, 10 and 14 Oct. 1927.

68. BN to Bereda, 20 Oct. 1927.
69. Qtd. in Manso, "Cuatro décadas del cuerpo de baile del Teatro Colón," 56. Manso covers much the same ground in his biography *Maria Ruanova (La verdad de la danza)* (Buenos Aires: Ediciones tres tiempos, 1987).
70. "Colón," *La Prensa*, 29 Oct. 1927, 17.
71. "Se estrenó anoche en el Colón el ballet 'Daphnis et Chloé', de Maurice Ravel," *La Nación*, 29 Oct. 1927, 10.
72. See, for example, "Se reprisó anoche el ballet 'Bodas', de Igor Strawinsky, en el Colón," *La Nación*, 16 Nov. 1927, 10; "'Bodas', en el Colón reeditó un gran éxito; la extraordinaria obra de Strawinsky volvió a ser una de las notas de arte más sobresalientes," unidentified clipping, 16 Nov. 1927, 23/1, BNC.
73. Robert Johnson, the son of Irina Nijinska's close friend Nina Youshkevitch, wrote in his obituary of Irina that Eleonora was a diabetic who required insulin shots and a strict diet. Robert Johnson, "Irina Nijinska (1913–1991)," *BR* 20, no. 1 (Spring 1992), 29.
74. Zenon to BN, 26 May 1927, 77B/18, BNC.
75. Zenon to BN, 2 July 1927, 77B/18, BNC. According to "Measuring Worth" (www.measuringworth.com), the relative value of £20 in 1927 was £1,066 in 2014.
76. BN to Bereda, 30 July 1927. It is possible that "Nina" is Nina Sirotinine, her former Kiev student who had settled in Paris in the 1920s.
77. BN to Bereda, 10 Oct. 1927.
78. Qtd. in Manso, "Cuatro décadas del cuerpo de baile del Teatro Colón," 56.
79. Ibid.
80. Blanca and Leticia de la Vega to BN, 12 Jan. 1929, 77A/34, BNC. Much to the chagrin of the de la Vega sisters, Boris Romanov returned to the Colón in 1929 and 1930.
81. "Diary (1926–27)," undated entry, 64/7, BNC.
82. BN to Ira and Lev Kochetovsky, undated (postmarked 14 Nov. 1927), 78/36, BNC. On December 3, 1927, she cabled Eleonora that they were leaving (77B/27, BNC).
83. "Diary (1927–29)," Dec. 19 and 25, 59/1, BNC.
84. BN to Bereda, 12 and 19 Sept. 1927.

Chapter 10

1. See entries for 25 Dec. 1927 and Mar. 1928, "Diary 1927–29," 59/1, BNC.
2. According to the birth records of the Kharkov rabbinate, Rubinstein was born on September 21, 1883 (Old Style). I am grateful to Natalia Lazarevna Dunaeva for a photocopy of Rubinstein's Hebrew-Russian birth record.
3. Marguerite Long, "Ida Rubinstein," *Au piano avec Maurice Ravel*, introd. Pierre Laumonier (Paris: Julliard, 1971), 40–41.
4. Jean Cocteau, "Autour de Diaghilev," *Encyclopédie du Théâtre contemporain*, ed. Gilles Quéant with Frédéric Towarnicki (Paris: Collection de France, 1957), I, 154.

5. William A. Ewing, *Dance and Photography* (New York: Holt, 1987), pl. 91; "L'Heure de la Danse," *Femina*, Mar. 1925, 31; and "Moment Musicale," *Dance*, May 1926, 30.

6. For a photograph of Rubinstein in *Artemis Troublée*, see "Ida Rubinstein in a New Bakst Ballet: The Legend of Actaeon Serves as a Basis for 'Artemis Troublée' Recently Presented at the Paris Opera," *Vanity Fair*, Aug. 1922, 54. Rubinstein's first performance in *The Dying Swan* took place on April 21, 1923, at the Théâtre Edouard VII; the second on June 14, 1923, at the Théâtre des Champs-Elysées; both were in aid of Russian refugees in France.

7. Nina Tikanova, *La Jeune Fille en bleu: Pétersbourg-Berlin-Paris* (Lausanne: Editions L'Age d'Homme, 1991), 86.

8. Ibid., 87.

9. Benois mentions these musical evenings in his entries for May 17, 22, 25, June 10, 26, and July 4, 6, 1927. I am grateful to Dimitri Vicheney for transcribing these and other excerpts for me in the 1990s. They were subsequently published in Pascale Melani's article "Indit: extrais des carnets d'Alexandre Benois, Archives Dimitry Vicheney, Paris," *Slavica Occitania* 23 (2006), 131–57.

10. Benois to Stravinsky, 12 Dec. 1927, qtd. in *Stravinsky: Selected Correspondence*, ed. Robert Craft, vol. 1 (New York: Knopf, 1982), 172, n.134.

11. Richard Taruskin, *Stravinsky and the Russian Traditions: A Biography of the Works through "Mavra,"* vol. 2 (Berkeley: University of California Press, 1996), 1611.

12. Alexandre Benois, *Reminiscences of the Russian Ballet*, trans. Mary Britnieva (London: Putnam, 1941), 350–51.

13. BN, draft letter to Rubinstein, n.d., Nijinska Archives.

14. David Vaughan, *Frederick Ashton and His Ballets* (New York: Knopf, 1977), 26. Ashton concluded his letter to Nijinska asking for an audition, "si vous décidez de m'appeler à votre service, je travaillerai de tout coeur" (70/7, BNC).

15. Tikanova, *La Jeune Fille en bleu*, 88. For Vorobieva, see her letters to BN of 29 Sept. 1927 and 18 Feb. 1928, 77A/44, BNC. For the three Polish dancers, see Cheryl Forrest and Georgia Snoke, *Roman Jasinski: A Gypsy Prince from the Ballet Russe* (Tulsa: Tulsa Ballet, 2008), 30–32. Jasinski was still using his first name, Czeslaw. The following list of the company's dancers in 1928–1929 is culled from programs of Rubinstein's performances in Paris and on tour in addition to Tikanova and Elisabeth Hennebert's "Coureurs de cachet," vols. 2–3. The twenty-seven women were: Maria Alexeeva, J. Allan, Suzanne Andreeva, Lena (Hélène) Antonova, Zina Arenska(ia), Joyce Berry, Olga Chmatkova, Tatiana Firsovska(ia), Godounova, Willy (Willie) Gueneva, Vera Lipska(ia), Klavdia Lotova, Irina (Irène) Lucezarska, Anna Ludmila (Ludmilova), Rachel Matveeva, Genia Melikova, B. (Beate?) Moissi, Nadejda Nikolaeva, E. O. Oulianovska, Ludmilla Schollar, Staczkievicz (Stachkevitch), Léonida Stal, Nina Tikhonova (Tikanova), Ruth Vavpotič (Vavpovich), Nina Verchinina, Vladimorova, and Anna Vorobieva. There were twenty-two men: Nicolas Gouluk d'Artemovsky, Frederick Ashton, Birger Bartholin, William Chappell, S. Cywinsky, Alexis Dolinoff, Rupert Doone, Mikhail Fedoroff, S. Florine, Roman Jasinski, Eugene Lapitzky, David Lichtenstein (Lichine), Arthur Mahoney, Ludovic Matlinsky, Georges Milenoff,

Harry Plucis, Serge Renoff, George Sari, Yurek Shabelevsky, Nicholas Singaevsky, Serge Unger, and Anatole Vilzak.

16. *Omnibus: Sir Fred—A Celebration*, BBC-TV, 1988. I am grateful to Julie Kavanagh for a transcript of Chappell's remarks.

17. Patty Haselbarth, "Anna Ludmila: The Forgotten Ballerina," Ph.D. diss., Texas Woman's University, 1999, 142-43.

18. Vaughan, *Frederick Ashton*, 26.

19. Nina Tikanova, interview with the author, Paris, 14 Mar. 1993.

20. Ashton to Rambert, [Aug.–Sept. 1928], qtd. in Jane Pritchard, "Two Letters," in *Following Sir Fred's Steps—Ashton's Legacy*, ed. Stephanie Jordan and Andrée Grau (London: Dance Books, 1996), 107-8.

21. Forrest and Snoke, *Roman Jasinski*, 35.

22. Rubinstein to BN, 13 Aug. [1928], 76B/10, BNC.

23. Rubinstein to BN, 21 Aug. [1928], 76B/10, BNC. The envelope was postmarked August 30, 1928, and Rubinstein gave as her return address, c/o Thomas Cook and Sons, Athens.

24. Rubinstein to BN, 26 Aug. and 12 Sept. 1928, 76B/10, BNC.

25. "I returned yesterday," Rubinstein telegraphed Stravinsky on September 24, "and last night heard Le Baiser de la fée. How can I express my rapture and my gratitude" (qtd. in Jacques Depaulis, *Ida Rubinstein: Une inconnue jadis célèbre* [Paris: Librairie Honoré Champion, 1995], 369).

26. BN, draft letter to Rubinstein, undated [early Sept. 1928], Nijinska Archives. Nicolaeva was Nicolas Legat's second wife.

27. Name-day greeting from "all your artists," 3 Sept. 1928, 76à/22, BNC.

28. George Sari, "Impressions of Nijinska," *American Dancer*, Dec. 1928, 9. Sari was a California dancer-actor-teacher who had studied with Benjamin Zemach, danced with Pavlova and Mordkin, and was "a disciple of the Cecchetti method" ("Dance Symposium to Be Presented," *LAT*, 5 Mar. 1933, A2).

29. Sari, "Impressions of Nijinska," 25.

30. For the original story, see Hans Christian Andersen, "The Ice Maiden," *Fairy Tales and Stories*, trans. H. P. Paull, http://hca.gilead.org.il/ice_maid.html; for Stravinsky's rethinking of the action, see *Le Baiser de la Fée*, piano reduction, mss., signed and dated Nice, 16 Oct. 1928, Igor Stravinsky Collection, Reel 108, Paul Sacher Stiftung.

31. Qtd. in Vera Stravinsky and Robert Craft, *Stravinsky in Pictures and Documents* (London: Hutchinson, 1980), 284.

32. Stephen Walsh, *Stravinsky: A Creative Spring: Russia and France 1882-1934* (New York: Knopf, 1999), 474; Stravinsky to Ernest Ansermet, 11 Aug. 1928, in *Stravinsky: Selected Correspondence*, ed. Robert Craft, Vol. 1 (New York: Knopf, 1982), 192.

33. Qtd. in Stravinsky and Craft, *Stravinsky in Pictures and Documents*, 285.

34. Walsh, *Stravinsky: A Creative Spring*, 475. Presumably these were the sections that Rubinstein heard after returning from holiday.

35. Benois to BN, 9 Sept. 1928, 15/7, BNC.

36. Igor Stravinsky, *Le Baiser de la Fée*, piano reduction, mss., signed and dated Nice, 16 Oct. 1928, Igor Stravinsky Collection, Reel 108, Paul Sacher Stiftung; Henry Malherbe, "Chronique musicale," *Temps*, 5 Dec. 1928, 3.

37. Rubinstein to NS, "Sunday," 76B/10, BNC.

38. Igor Stravinsky, *An Autobiography* (New York: Norton, 1936), 148.

39. Joaquín Nin, "Comment est né 'Boléro' de Ravel," *Revue musicale*, Dec. 1938, 212–13. Nin, a Cuban pianist and conductor, was the father of the writer Anaïs Nin.

40. Ravel's manuscript of *Bolero*'s full orchestral score, on deposit at the Morgan Library & Museum in the Robert Owen Lehman Collection, is dated July–October 1928 and dedicated to Rubinstein.

41. P.-B. Gheusi, "La Musique au Théâtre," *Figaro*, 24 Nov. 1928, 2. For photographs of her on holiday, see "La vie du théâtre: Au service de la Danse," *Intransigeant*, 18 Nov. 1928, 6.

42. See, for instance, "Notes et Informations: Les ballets de Mme Ida Rubinstein," *Figaro*, 31 Oct. 1928, 6; "Les Ballets de Mme Ida Rubinstein," *Matin*, 2 Nov. 1928, 5; "Les Ballets de Mme Ida Rubinstein," *Excelsior*, 2 Nov. 1928, 4.

43. Michel Georges-Michel, "Ida Rubinstein! Elle avait déjà sa légende savant qu'on vit son oeuvre . . . ," *VU*, 28 Nov. 1928, 820–21.

44. For the Vicomtesse de Noailles, see Francine du Plessix Gray, "The Surrealists' Muse," *The New Yorker*, 24 Sept. 2007, 136–46.

45. Tikanova, *La Jeune Fille en bleu*, 97. For one of Rubinstein's magnificent coats, see Boris Lipnitzki's photo on the cover of *Illiustrirovannaia Rossiia* (*La Russie illustrée*), 1 Dec. 1928.

46. This and the other undated notes quoted below are in 76B/10, BNC.

47. "Sur le plateau de l'Opéra," *Intransigeant*, 25 Nov. 1928, 6.

48. Jean Lasserre, "Mme Ida Rubinstein répète dans le désert," *Ami du peuple*, 23 Nov. 1928, Box 24, BNC.

49. Vaughan, *Frederick Ashton*, 28.

50. "Ballet at Paris Opera. Three New Works," *Daily Telegraph*, 24 Nov. 1928; "Ballet Season Opens in Paris," *Paris-Times*, 24 Nov. 1928, 3; Louis Laloy, "Un beau spectacle d'Opéra. Les ballets de Mme Ida Rubinstein," *Ere nouvelle*, 25 Nov. 1928, 1.

51. "Sitter Out," "In Paris. Some Notes on Stage and Spectacular Dancing in the Gay City," *DT*, Jan. 1929, 511.

52. Pierre Lalo, "Les Ballets de Mme Ida Rubinstein," *Comoedia*, 25 Nov. 1928, 1.

53. Emile Vuillermoz, "La Musique: la semaine des mécènes," *Excelsior*, 26 Nov. 1928, 2; Jane Catulle-Mandès, "Les Ballets de Mme Ida Rubinstein," *Presse*, 5 Dec. 1928, 2.

54. Henry Prunières, "Paris Sees Ballet Novelties," *NYT*, 23 Dec. 1928, VIII, 8.

55. André George, "Les Ballets de Mme Rubinstein," *Nouvelles littéraires*, 8 Dec. 1928, 11.

56. Laloy, "Un beau spectacle d'Opéra."

57. See, for instance, George, "Les Ballets de Mme Rubinstein."

58. "Juerga gitana," postcard from the series *Costumbres andaluzas*, by M. Bertuchi [1920s], 49/17, BNC. For a period reproduction of *Bolero*'s set design, see "Les Trouvailles décoratives d'Alexandre Benois," *Femina*, July 1929, 22.

59. Prunières, "Paris Sees Ballet Novelties."

60. Pierre Lalo, "Les Ballets de Mme Ida Rubinstein. 'Le Baiser de la Fee,'" *Comoedia*, 1 Dec. 1928, 1.

61. Vuillermoz, "La Musique," 2.

62. André Levinson, "Les Ballets de Mme Ida Rubinstein," *Comoedia*, 25 Nov. 1928, 1. Levinson's remarks about Schollar are in "Les Ballets de Mme Ida Rubinstein," *Comoedia*, 1 Dec. 1928, 2. Jane Catulle-Mendès described Ludmila as "full of natural grace" ("Les Ballets de Mme Ida Rubinstein," *Presse*, 5 Dec. 1928, 2).

63. Valerian Svetlov, "Balety Idy Rubinshtein," *Segodnia vecherom* (Tonight), 3 Dec. 1928, 6.

64. "We were a very young company," Ashton explained decades later, "and we were all terribly inexperienced and she just had to whip us into some kind of shape. You were at it all the time. . . . As a result, the standard of performance was extremely good" (Zoë Dominic and John Gilbert, *Frederick Ashton: A Choreographer and His Ballets* [Chicago, H. Regnery Co., 1971], 31).

65. Catulle-Mendès, "Les Ballets de Mme Ida Rubinstein."

66. Henry Malherbe, "Chronique musicale," *Temps*, 5 Dec. 1928, 3.

67. Maurice Brillant, "Quelques trouvailles ne font pas un chef d'oeuvre de la chorégraphie nouvelle du 'Baiser de la Fée," *Epoque*, 6/7 July 1947, Reel 48/481708–9; "Le Baiser de la Fée à l'Opéra," *Opéra*, 9 July 1947, Reel 48/481713; "Intérim," "La Danse à l'Opéra. Le Baiser de la Fée," *Spectateur*, 8 July 1947, Reel 48/481714, Igor Stravinsky Collection, Paul Sacher Stiftung.

68. André Levinson, "Les Ballets de Mme Ida Rubinstein: 'Le Baiser de la Fée,'" *Comoedia*, 1 Dec. 1928, 2. *La Maladetta*, a ballet set in the Pyrenees that premiered at the Paris Opéra in 1893, was closely associated with Zambelli.

69. André Levinson, "La Danse," *Candide*, 29 Nov. 1928, 15.

70. Émile Vuillermoz, "Les ballets de Mme Ida Rubinstein," *Excelsior*, 3 Dec. 1928, 2.

71. Raoul Brunel, "Ballets de Mme Ida Rubinstein," *Oeuvre*, 4 Dec. 1928, 6. An image by the photographer Dora Kalmus, known professionally as Madame d'Ora, shows Rubinstein wearing ropes of pearls, pearl cuffs and earrings, and a pearl-covered fantasy of a traditional Russian headpiece known as a kokoshnik. This image was reproduced in a number of souvenir programs. The phrase "dazzling cascade of dances inspired by Russian folklore" is from Tikanova, *La Jeune Fille en bleu*, 93.

72. Henry Malherbe, "Chronique musicale," *Temps*, 5 Dec. 1928, 3.

73. Valerian Svetlov, "Novye balety Idy Rubinshtein," *Segodnia* (Today), 14 Dec. 1928, Box 124, BNC.

74. Qtd. in L. D. Liubimov, "O klassike," *Vozrozhdenie*, 18 Dec. 1928, in *Sergei Diagilev i russkoe iskusstvo*, ed. I. S. Zil'bershtein and V. A. Samkov, vol. 1 (Moscow: Izobrazitel'noe iskusstvo, 1982), 251.

75. Qtd. in Lifar, *Serge Diaghilev*, 337. In *A History of Russian Ballet* (trans. Arnold Haskell [London: Hutchinson, 1954], 269–71). Lifar quotes a quite different version of this letter. Unfortunately, the original has never surfaced into public view.

76. Lifar, *Serge Diaghilev*, 338–39.

77. Ibid., 339–40.

78. Ibid., 341.

79. Tikanova, *La Jeune Fille en bleu*, 98–99.

80. Tikanova, interview.

81. André Levinson, *Les Visages de la danse* (Paris: Grasset, 1933), 99–100.

82. Emile Vuillermoz, "Les ballets de Mme Ida Rubinstein."

83. Colette, "Sur Madame Ida Rubinstein," *Candide*, 13 Dec. 1928, 13.

84. Reviews of the Brussels season are in Box 124, BNC; for her other activities, see Tikanova, *La Jeune Fille en bleu*, 100, and Haselbarth, "Anna Ludmila," 159–60.

85. "Théatre de Monte-Carlo: Les Ballets de Mme Ida Rubinstein," *Eclaireur* (Nice), 10 Jan. 1929, Box 124, BNC.

86. Tikanova, *La Jeune Fille en bleu*, 100. Reviews from *L'Eclaireur* (Nice), *Le Petit Niçois*, *Gazette de Monaco et de Monte-Carlo*, *Journal de Monaco*, and *France* (Nice) are in Box 124, BNC.

87. BN, draft letter to an unnamed correspondent, undated [mid-Jan. 1929], Nijinska Archives.

88. Ibid. The Ballets Russes performed at the Casino Municipal in Pau on January 14, then traveled to Monte Carlo.

89. "Das modernisierte klassische Ballett. Gespräch mit Ida Rubinstein," *Der Tag*, 21 Feb. 1929, 7. The Nabokov and Hindemith projects never came to fruition. For the Nabokov project, see Vincent Giroud's *Nicolas Nabokov: A Life in Freedom and Music* (New York: Oxford University Press, 2015), 82.

90. "Gespräch mit Ida Rubinstein," *Neues Wiener Journal*, 21 Feb. 1929, Box 124, BNC.

91. "Bronislava Nijinskaja, die Schwester Nijinskis, in Wien," *Die Stunde*, 22 Feb. 1929, Box 124, BNC.

92. "Aus dem Kunstleben. Staatsoper. Ballett Ida Rubinstein," *Deutschoesterreichische Tages-Zeitung*, 24 Feb. 1929, Box 124, BNC.

93. "Ballettgastspiel Ida Rubinstein," *Neues Wiener Tageblatt*, 24 Feb. 1929; J. C. W., "Ida Rubinstein tanzt: Den erste Abend ihres Gastspieles in der Oper," *Die Stunde*, 23 Feb. 1929; F[elix] Cl[eve], "Der erste Gastspiel des Rubinstein-Balletts im Operntheater," *Neue Freie Presse*, 23 Feb. 1929; Felix Cleve, "Das Rubinstein Gastspiel in der Oper," *Neue Freie Presse*, 25 Feb. 1929, Box 124, BNC.

94. Vaughan, *Frederick Ashton*, 30; Tikanova, *La Jeune Fille en bleu*, 101.

95. See, for example, "I Balletti Rubinstein alla Scala," *L'Ambrosiano*, 14 Mar. 1929; "Teatri. Scala," *Il Sole*, 15 Mar. 1929; and, for *Bolero*, "I Balli Rubinstein alla Scala," *L'Ambrosiano*, 7 Mar. 1929, Box 124, BNC.

96. See Stravinsky's letter to Hindemith, 16 Apr. 1932, qtd. in Depaulis, *Ida Rubinstein*, 372.

97. "Nuovi balli di Ida Rubinstein alla Scala," *Il Corriere della Sera*, 15 Mar. 1929, Box 124, BNC.

98. Francis Poulenc, *Moi et mes amis: confidences recueillies par Stéphane Audel* (Paris: La Palatine, 1963), 179.

99. Qtd. in Roger Nichols, *Ravel* (London: J. M. Dent, 1977), 107.

100. For Benois' costume design, see *MGZA Ben A Val 1, NYPL; for his set design, showing a woman in a short dress and a man in something akin to evening clothes, see Sotheby's, "Dance, Theatre, Opera and Music Hall," New York, 23 Apr. 1986, lot

130. Another costume design for the original version—a blue tiered cocktail dress for a woman—is in a private New York collection.

101. Vaughan, *Frederick Ashton*, 288. For a stage photo, see Baer, *Bronislava Nijinska*, 61.

102. Emile Vuillermoz, "La 'Valse' de Maurice Ravel," *Excelsior*, 27 May 1929, 5.

103. Baer, *Bronislava Nijinska*, 61.

104. Qtd. in Erik Baeck and Hedwige Baeck-Schilders, "La création mondiale du ballet 'La Valse' de Maurice Ravel à Anvers," *Revue de Musicologie* 89, no. 2 (2003), 369.

105. André Levinson, "Les Ballets de Mme Ida Rubinstein," *Comoedia*, 25 May 1929, 1.

106. Walter Hanks Shaw, "What Americans Are Seeing in Paris," *Arts and Decoration*, Sept. 1929, 69.

107. Emile Vuillermoz, "Bells versus Umbrellas," *CSM*, 29 June 1929, 6.

108. André Levinson, "Les Ballets de Mme Ida Rubinstein," *Comoedia*, 25 May 1929, 1.

109. Henry Prunières, "Novelties in Paris," *NYT*, 30 June 1929, X6.

110. Rubinstein to BN, undated, 76B/120, BNC.

111. BN to Rubinstein, draft letter, undated, 76B/10, BNC.

112. Baer, *Bronislava Nijinska*, 61.

113. Arnold L. Haskell, *Dancing round the World: Memoirs of an Attempted Escape from Ballet* (London: Gollancz, 1937), 321. Other early manifestations of this "romantic revival" singled out by Stephanie Jordan are Balanchine's *Le Bal* (1929) and *Cotillon* (1932), Mario Praz's *The Romantic Agony*, and Sacheverell Sitwell's biography of Liszt, published in 1934 (*Moving Music: Dialogues with Music in Twentieth-Century Ballet* [London: Dance Books, 2000], 198).

114. Statement of account, Dec. 1928, AJ13/1293, AN. The Ida Rubinstein Collection at the Library of Congress, which contains business as well as personal papers, was processed too late for the author to consult it.

115. Contract between "L'Ente Autonomo del Teatro alla Scala" and Ida Rubinstein, 12 Oct. 1928, former collection of George Verdak.

116. The May 1929 bills and statements are in AJ13/1293, AN. Among the "eleven girls" who were paid ten francs each for taking part in one of the company's performances was the future ballerina Yvette Chauviré.

117. BN, "Balety Idy Rubinshtein," 48/10, BNC. This article, typed on the back of four pages of *L'Art et la vie* letterhead, was written in the spring of 1931.

118. "It is my honor to report to you that I have received 15 pounds through Lloyd's Bank. I hope that you will be so kind to send me the remaining money soon, since I have promised to pay off my loan by the end of May at the latest" (Zenon to BN, 3 Apr. 1929, 77B/18, BNC).

119. BN, draft letter to "Anna" [Teplicka?], 1930, 77B/25, BNC.

120. Prunières, "Novelties in Paris."

121. Hélène Benois was a daughter of Alexandre Benois and an artist in her own right. In 1927 she married the Russian émigré poet Alexandre Braslavsky and was identified on programs as "Mme Braslawsky." For an overview of her life and career, see "Le blog de helene-benois-peintre" by Dimitri Vicheney, http://helene-benois-peintre.over-blog.com/.

122. Rubinstein to BN, undated, 76B/10, BNC.

123. "Diary 1927–29," entry for May 1, 59/1, BNC.

124. Schollar to BN, 7 May [1928], 76A/27, BNC.

125. Tikanova, *La Jeune Fille en bleu*, 95.

126. Ibid., 99.

127. Forrest and Snoke, *Roman Jasinski*, 37.

128. Anatole Vilzak, "Memories of Bronislava Nijinskaia," unpublished manuscript. I am grateful to the late Nancy Van Norman Baer for sharing this with me.

129. "Diary 1927–29," entry for Mar. 1929.

Chapter 11

1. Rouché to BN, 2 May 1929, 76/7, BNC; BN to Rouché, 23 July 1929, L.A.S. Nijinska, Bronislava 10, BM-Opéra.

2. Among them, *Le Petit Nègre*, to Debussy, a solo for Leon Woizikovsky; a pas de trois, *La Jota Aragonesa*, to Saint-Saëns for Felia Doubrovska, Woizikovsky, and Nicholas Zverev. See Baer, *Bronislava Nijinska*, 71; BN, draft letter to Viktor Emilevich [Dandré], 8 Nov. [1929], 68/8, BNC. *Jota aragonesa* was almost certainly the *Pas de trois espagnol* danced by Woizikovsky, Nina Kirsanova, and Lipa Alperova during Pavlova's brief season at Golders Green in December 1929 and credited to Nijinska ("Sitter-Out," *DT*, Jan. 1930, 444).

3. Anton Dolin, *Olga Spessivtzeva: The Sleeping Ballerina*, foreword Marie Rambert (London, 1966; rpt. London: Dance Books, 1974), 59. For the ballet *Paysage Enfantin* that Nijinska choreographed for Spessivtzeva, see "Variety Theatres," *Times*, 30 Apr. 1930, 14; G. E. Fussell, "Spessiva and Mangan: Notes on Decor," *DT*, June 1930, 277. A copy of the Coliseum playbill for "Olga Spessiva and Her Company" for the week of Monday, 28 Apr. 1930, is in 76A/44, BNC. The dancers were Elena Antonova, Joyce Berry, Roman Jasinski, Eugene Lapitzky, Ludovic Matlinsky, Ignacy Matuszewsky, Yurek Shabelevsky, Serge Unger, and Nijinska's daughter Irina (under the name Istomina).

4. A writer and performer with a flamboyant personality and unconventional lifestyle, Pascar grew up in Romania, married in Kiev (where she gave birth to her son, Alexander Lieberman, the future editorial director of Condé-Nast), and after the Revolution, with the backing of Anatoly Lunacharsky, founded the First State Theater for Children in Moscow. In 1926, Nijinska choreographed a program of "*danses mimées*" for Pascar's first Paris recital and four years later staged the movement for Pascar's *Nini (or How a Shopgirl Became a Star)*. For an unflattering memoir by her granddaughter-in-law, see Francine du Plessix Gray, *Them: A Memoir of Parents* (New York: Penguin, 2005).

5. Jean-Louis de Faucigny-Lucinge, *Legendary Parties*, foreword Brooke Astor (New York: Vendome Press, 1987), 68–79.

6. Poulenc to Charles de Noailles, [March 1929] and [late March 1929], in *Correspondence*, 301–2.

7. Richard D. E. Burton, *Francis Poulenc* (Bath: Absolute Press, 2002), 37. Poulenc uses the word "distress" to describe his state of mind in a letter to the singer Claire Croiza (Poulenc to Croiza, *Correspondence*, 308).

8. Poulenc to Croiza, *Correspondence*, 309.

9. Poulenc, *Entretiens avec Claude Rostand*, 80–81.

10. "Diary 1927–29," 12 June 1930, 59/2, BNC. Nijinska made at least two fair copies of her 1927–29 diary (which actually continued into 1930). The earliest version was in pencil, the later ones in ink. There are minor differences among the three versions.

11. Tikanova, *La Jeune Fille en bleu*, 103.

12. Ibid. For the photograph of Ludmila, see Faucigny-Lucinge, *Legendary Parties*, 76. See also Francis Poulenc, *Aubade: Concerto chorégraphique pour piano et dix-huit instruments* (Paris: Salabert, 1930). The orchestral score published in 1931 does not include Poulenc's argument, and the stage directions are less detailed.

13. "Francis Poulenc on His Ballets," 58. Poulenc reiterates his admiration for Nijinska's version of the ballet in "Entretien avec Maurice Ciantar," *Combat*, 14 Nov. 1952, and "Entretien avec André Boll et Maurice Brianchon," *Arts*, 21–27 Nov. 1952, in Poulenc, *J'écris ce qui me chante*, ed. Nicolas Southon (Paris: Fayard, 2011), 609–11.

14. Tikanova, 104; Hervé Lacombe, *Francis Poulenc* (Paris: Fayard, 2013), 343. A printed program is in 16/20, BNC.

15. Ernest Ansermet to Igor Stravinsky, 21 Aug. [1929], in *Correspondance Ernest Ansermet–Igor Strawinsky (1914–1967)*, ed. Claude Tappolet (Geneva: Georg Editeur, 1991), II, 193.

16. See also "Les Ballets Russes de Serge de Diaghilew," a special issue of *La Revue musicale*, 1 Dec. 1930; *Art vivant*, 15 Sept. 1929; the numerous articles by Edwin Evans, Cyril W. Beaumont, Philip J. S. Richardson, and especially Valerian Svetlov in the *Dancing Times* in 1929 and 1930; and Lincoln Kirstein's article, "The Diaghilev Period," *Hound and Horn*, July–Sept. 1930.

17. André Levinson, "La prodigieuse existence de Serge de Diaghilew: un destin hors série," *Comoedia*, 22 Aug. 1929, 1.

18. "Italie: Les funérailles de Diaghilef," *Journal des Débats*, 22 Aug. 1929, 2; "Deuils," *Figaro*, 22 Aug. 1929, 2; *Illiustrirovannaia Rossiia*, 31 Aug. 1929.

19. Robert Craft, "Stravinsky, Diaghilev, and Misia Sert," *BR* 6, no. 4 (1977–78), 77. The Panikhida service was held on August 21, the requiem mass on August 27 ("La mort de Serge de Diaghilew," *Comoedia*, 21 Aug. 1929, 1; "A la mémoire de Serge de Diaghilew," *Comoedia*, 27 Aug. 1929, 1). A second mass was held on 28 Sept. ("Le Spectacle à Paris," *Journal des Débats*, 28 Sept. 1929, 4).

20. "Le Spectacle à Paris," *Journal des Débats*, 6 Sept. 1929, 4; Kochno, *Le Ballet*, 291; Buckle, *George Balanchine*, 54.

21. Judith Chazin-Bennahum, *René Blum and the Ballets Russes: In Search of a Lost Life* (New York: Oxford University Press, 2011), 99–101.

22. Qtd. in García-Márquez, *Massine*, 209.

23. "Autobiographical outline," 34/15, BNC.

24. Jean Rollot, "Les merveilleux ballets russes de Mme Nijinska," *Paris-Soir*, 5 June 1932, 6.

25. BN, draft letter to an unknown correspondent, undated, 77B/25, BNC.

26. Tikanova, *La Jeune Fille en bleu*, 104.

27. Gustave de Pawlowski, "Saison d'Opéra russe: 'Le Prince Igor,'" *Journal*, 29 Jan. 1929, 5.

28. Pierre Maudru, "A l'Opéra russe: Prélude religieux à des Spectacles profanes," *Comoedia*, 27 Jan. 1929, 1.

29. Tikanova recounts the South American débacle in *La Jeune Fille en bleu*, 105.

30. Tikanova, *La Jeune Fille en bleu*, 105. For Tsereteli, see Vicente García-Márquez, *The Ballets Russes: Colonial de Basil's Ballets Russes de Monte Carlo, 1932–1952* (New York: Knopf, 1990), 5; Kathrine Sorley Walker, *De Basil's Ballets Russes* (London: Hutchinson, 1982), 5; Paul du Quenoy, *Stage Fright: Politics and the Performing Arts in Late Imperial Russia* (University Park: Pennsylvania State University Press, 2009), 27.

31. "Philinte," "Au Théâtre des Champs-Elysées. Avant la saison russe d'opéra," *Journal des Débats*, 18 May 1930, 5.

32. See *Mir i iskusstvo*, 1 May 1930, 1–5. Notices of individual performances appeared in subsequent issues and one of Boris Bilinsky's designs for *Ruslan and Ludmila* on the cover of the 1 June issue.

33. Edouard Beaudu, "La Pavlova chez la Nijinska. En regardant danser . . . ," *Intransigeant*, 16 May 1930, 1–2.

34. Henry Malherbe, "Chronique Musicale," *Temps*, 21 May 1930, 3.

35. Ibid.

36. Charles Tenroc, "Premières représentations," *Petit Parisien*, 18 May 1930, 7.

37. Tikanova, *La Jeune Fille en bleu*, 107.

38. Henry Malherbe, "Chronique Musicale," *Temps*, 11 June 1930, 3.

39. Ibid.

40. Tribute dated Paris, 24 May 1930, 75/14, BNC. The artwork is unattributed but is probably by Bilinsky.

41. T. de S., "Acontecimiento artístico en el Kursaal. En función brillantísima 'el Príncipe Igor' logra una representación de apotesis," *El Día* (San Sebastián), 16 Sept. 1930, 16.

42. Zereteli to BN, 4 Aug. 1930, 77B/19, BNC.

43. "Diary 1927–29," 23 Sept. 1929, 59/1.

44. Bechert to BN, 5 Sept. 1929, 70/21, BNC.

45. Schlee to BN, 23 Sept. 1929, 70/21, BNC.

46. Bechert to BN, 29 Oct. 1929, 70/21, BNC.

47. Krauss, cable to Franze, 30 Sept. 1929, OHHSTA, Krauss, 1930, 311.

48. Franze to Krauss, 10 Oct. 1929, OHHSTA, Krauss, 1930, 310.

49. "Diary 1927–29," 4 Nov. 1930.

50. "Ballettmeisterin Bronislava Nijinska, die Schwester Nijinskis, in Wien," *Die Stunde*, 22 Jan. 1930.

51. "Bronislawa Nijinska in Wien. Verhandlungen mit der Wiener Staatsoper," *Neues Wiener Tagblatt*, 21 Jan. 1930, 7.

52. Ibid., 7–8.

53. Ibid., 8.

54. "Die Verhandlungen Frau Nijinskas mit der Staatsoper," *Neues Wiener Tagblatt*, 23 Jan. 1930, 10.
55. "Vom Theater," *Das interessante Blatt*, 30 Jan. 1930, 23.
56. "Introduction," *A View of German Dance in the Weimar Republic*, ed. Valerie Preston-Dunlop and Susanne Lahusen (London: Dance Books, 1990), xv.
57. "On Movement and the School of Movement," in *Schrifttanz*, 55. It appeared as "Von der Bewegung und der Schule der Bewegung" in the April 1930 issue (3–6). A typescript of the German translation, dated Paris, 1930, as well as a copy of the actual issue, is in 48/9, BNC.
58. "On Movement and the School of Movement," 57.
59. Ibid., 58. "Fundamental reform" comes from the chapter on Nijinska in Andrea Amort's Ph.D. thesis, "Die Geschichte des Balletts der Wiener Staatsoper 1918–1942," University of Vienna, 1981. See also Amort, "Free Dance in Interwar Vienna," in *Interwar Vienna: Culture between Tradition and Modernity*, ed. Deborah Holmes and Lisa Silverman (Rochester, NY: Camden House, 2009), 117–42; Wayne Heisler Jr., *The Ballet Collaborations of Richard Strauss* (Rochester, NY: University of Rochester Press, 2009); George Jackson, "Dance and the City," *Dance Chronicle* 33, no. 3 (2010), 465–79.
60. Amort, "Die Geschichte," 139.
61. Contract between Krauss and BN, 23 Jan. 1930, 46/10, BNC.
62. Richard Mittler & Cie. to BN, 1 Apr. 1930, 46/1, BNC.
63. Contract, 23 Jan. 1930.
64. Bechert to BN, 25 Apr., 10 May, 27 May 1930, 70/21, BNC.
65. K. F. D., "The German Dance Convention. From Our Own Correspondent," *DT*, May 1930, 163.
66. "Debüt der neuen Ballettmeisterin Nijinska in der Staatsoper," *Die Stunde*, 15 July 1930.
67. "Angebliche Differenzen mit Ballettmeistern Nijinskaja," *Nueues Wiener Tagblatt*, 21 Aug. 1930, 26; "Was ist mit dem Vertrag der Nijinskaja," *Die Stunde*, 22 Aug. 1930, 7; "Frau Nijinskaja und die Wiener Oper," *Neues Wiener Tagblatt*, 23 Aug. 1930, 8; "Die Affäre der Ballettmeisterin Nijinskaja—Rücktritt; wegen mangelnder Kenntnis der deutschen Sprache," *Neues Wiener Tagblatt*, 29 Aug. 1930, 29; "Pläne der neuen Ballettmeisterin Nijinska," *Die Stunde*, 5 Sept. 1930, BNC.
68. Bechert to BN, 8 Sept. 1930, 70/21, BNC.
69. French translation of an interview with BN, undated, Dossier d'artiste (Bronislava Nijinska), BM-Opéra. This appears to be a translation of "Bronislawa Nijinska ist gestern nach Wien gekommen. Sie beginnt heute mit der Arbeit in der Oper," *Die Stunde*, 30 Sept. 1930, 3.
70. "Hedy Pfundmayr erzählt von ihrem neuen Tanzabend," *Die Stunde*, 28 Sept. 1930.
71. "Clemens Krauss über aktuelle Operndinge," *Die Stunde*, 7 Oct. 1930, 3.
72. BN to Krauss, 18 Oct. 1930, 73/32, BNC. Nijinska's rough Russian draft, "1930 / Hoffopern Theatre Staatsoper. Letter to Director Krauss. Plan for Reform of the School of the Vienna Opera," is in 59/15, BNC. All quotations are from the German translation.
73. Amort, "Die Geschichte," 142.

74. BN to Krauss, 25 Oct. 1930, 73/32. Nijinska's rough Russian draft is in a notebook entitled "Wien 1930," 16/9, BNC.

75. *Das interessante Blatt*, 16 Oct. 1930, 23. Another photo was published in the *Wiener Mittag Zeitung*, 3 Oct. 1930. Both clippings are in Box 121, BNC.

76. Julius Korngold, "Opera-Theater," *Neue Freie Presse*, 17 Oct. 1930, 4. See also "Eine neue Volksoper," *Das kleine Blatt*, 17 Oct. 1930, 9; "Czech Composer's Opera Gets Vienna Ovation," *New-York Herald*, 22 Oct. 1930, Box 121, BNC; "Vom Theater— Jaromir Weinbergers 'Schwanda,'" *Das interessante Blatt*, 23 Oct. 1930, 19, which included several photos. For *Die Stunde*, see Amort, "Die Geschichte," 142.

77. Rubinstein to BN, 27 Aug. 1930, 76/10, BNC.

78. Rubinstein to BN, 13 Oct. 1930, Nijinska Archives.

79. Rubinstein, telegram to BN, 23 Oct. 1930, Nijinska Archives. Nijinska recorded her answer on the envelope.

80. Rubinstein, telegram to BN, 31 Oct. 1930; NS, draft letter to Rubinstein, [31 Oct. 1930], Nijinska Archives.

81. Krauss to BN, 3 Nov. 1930, 76A/47, BNC. The third contract, unsigned by either of the parties, is in 46/10, BNC. It also stipulated a fixed salary of 2,400 schillings the first year, 3,100 the second, and 3,500 the third.

82. Amort, "Die Geschichte," 143.

83. "Bronislawa Nijinska will heute abreisen," *Die Stunde*, 5 Nov. 1930.

84. "Der Konflikt der Madame Nijinska mit der Staatsoper," *Neue Freie Press*, 5 Nov. 1930, 11.

85. Qtd. in Gunhild Schüller, "Bronislava Nijinska, Eine Monographie" (1975), 145. I am grateful to George Jackson for sharing his copy of Schüller's monograph with me.

86. Pichler to BN, 10 Nov. 1930, 75/4, BNC.

87. Schüller, "Bronislava Nijinska," 145.

88. BN, draft letter, undated [early November 1930], 76B/47, BNC.

89. For Viennese dance modernism, see *Alles tanzt: Kosmos Wiener Tanzmoderne*, ed. Andrea Amort, exhibition catalogue, Kunst Historisches Museum, Vienna, 2019.

90. *Journal des Débats*, 9 Nov. 1930, 5.

91. Charles Tenroc, "Théâtre des Champs-Elysées.—*Le Prince Igor*," *Petit Parisien*, 18 Nov. 1930, 5.

92. Charles Tenroc, "Théâtre des Champs-Elysées.—*La Roussalka*," *Petit Parisien*, 23 Dec. 1930, 5; Pierre Maudru, "Les répétitions générales. 'La Roussalka,'" *Comoedia*, 23 Dec. 1930, 2; Jean Prudhomme, "Théâtre des Champs-Elysées.—(Opéra Russe).— La Roussalka," *Matin*, 25 Dec. 1930, 5. Prudhomme mentions that the Bohemian dances were encored.

93. Maudru, "Les répétitions générales," 2.

94. Marc Semenoff, "La Danse. A propos de 'Petrouchka': Les Idées de Mme Nijinska," *Courrier musical*, 15 Dec. 1930, 746. An "instantaneous" color photograph published in *L'Illustration* shows the three puppets hanging over the barre. It is clear from this and the article's other images that the costumes and scenery, although by Benois, were quite different from his designs for the Diaghilev production (Robert de Beauplan, "L'Opéra Russe à Paris," *Illustration*, 14 Feb. 1931, 197–98).

95. Henri de Curzon, "Revue musicale," *Journal des Débats*, 15 Dec. 1930, 4.

96. André Levinson, "La Danse. Rentrée de 'Petrouchka,'" *Candide*, 18 Dec. 1930, 15.

97. Tikanova, *La Jeune Fille en bleu*, 107.

98. Levinson, "La Danse. Rentrée de 'Petrouchka.'" The steps are similar to those Nijinska had choreographed for herself in *Les Biches*.

99. Ibid.

100. Marc Semenoff, "Un Entretien avec Alexandre Benois: sur la manière d'interpréter 'Petrouchka,'" *Courrier musical*, 1 Jan. 1931, 6.

101. Ibid.

102. "Diary 1930–31."

103. Marc Semenoff, "Un entretien avec Mme Nijinska," *Courrier musical*, 1 Apr. 1931, 21.

104. Pierre Michaut, *Le Ballet contemporain 1929–1950* (Paris: Plon, 1950), 22.

105. Ibid., 23.

106. Vuillermoz, "Ballets Russes."

107. Fernand Divoire, "La Danse," *Revue de France*, Mar.–Apr. 1931, 560–61.

108. An architrave is the lowest part of a classical temple above the columns.

109. André Levinson, "Etude sur l'Etude: Variations de danse sur des thèmes de Bach," *Comoedia*, 30 Jan. 1931, 1.

110. André Levinson, "La Danse. Nouveaux ballets russes," *Candide*, 12 Feb. 1931, 13.

111. "Bilans et souhaits lyriques," *Petit Parisien*, 5 Jan. 1931, 2.

112. Levinson, "La Danse. Nouveaux ballets russes."

113. Ibid. The composer Darius Milhaud noted in his review of the season that Nijinska had created "a disciplined phalanx, full of drive and spirit, with a solid technique and great virtuosity, that recalls a bit the happy times once spent with Diaghilev" ("Les spectacles," *Europe Nouvelle*, 7 Feb. 1931, 178).

114. Tikanova, *La Jeune Fille en bleu*, 108. Tikanova incorrectly dates this event four days later.

115. Rubinstein to BN, 11 Dec. 1930; draft of BN's undated response accepting Rubinstein's terms, 76B/10, BNC; "Diary 1930–31."

116. BN, "The Ida Rubinstein Ballet," unpublished manuscript, Nijinska Archives. Although undated, this was written in the spring of 1931 in preparation for Rubinstein's seasons at the Paris Opéra and in London. It is unclear whether Nijinska's article was ever published.

117. Rubinstein to BN, 7 Dec. 1930, Nijinska Archives. Rubinstein's notes and telegrams are in 76B/10, BNC.

118. For a reminiscence of Egorova and her studio in the 1930s, see Oleg Tupine, interviewed by Katy Matheson, 1978, 2–13, *MGZMT 3-428, NYPL.

119. Alexis Dolinoff, interviewed by Amanda Smith, 1979, Part II, 70–73, *MGZMT 5-670, NYPL.

120. "Diary, 1930–31."

121. Jean Chantavoine, "La Semaine musicale," *Ménestrel*, 3 July 1931, 292.

122. André Levinson, "Les Ballets de Mme Ida Rubinstein. 'La Valse,'" *Comoedia*, 27 June 1931, 1.

123. "The Theatres. French Ballets and Plays," *The Times*, 2 July 1931, 12; "Mme. Ida Rubinstein Arrives," *Daily Mail*, 4 July 1931, 12.

124. "Mme. Ida Rubinstein Arrives"; "Madame Ida Rubinstein," *Observer*, 5 July 1931, 10.

125. Richard Capell, "Mme. Rubinstein in London. 'St. Sebastian' at Covent Garden," *Daily Mail*, 7 July 1931, 6.

126. Tikanova, *La Jeune Fille en bleu*, 111–12.

127. E. B., "Ida Rubinstein Season," *MG*, 9 July 1931, 8.

128. "The Sitter Out," *DT*, Aug. 1931, 418.

129. F. Bonavia, "The Close of the London Season," *NYT*, 26 July 1931, X6.

130. Cyril W. Beaumont, *Complete Book of Ballets* (London: Putnam, 1937), 812–13.

131. Interview with Tikanova, 14 Mar. 1993, Paris.

132. "Lis'Ener," "Wireless Notes and Programmes," *MG*, 16 July 1931, 10; "Broadcasting. The Programmes. Henri Sauguet's 'David,'" *Times*, 16 July 1931, 21; "Quelques remarques sur les programmes," *Intransigeant*, 17 Jan. 1931, 6.

133. "Les Londoniens ont accueilli avec enthousiasme les ballets de Mme Ida Rubinstein," *Comoedia*, 24 July 1931, 2.

134. Arnold Haskell, *Balletomania* (London: Gollancz, 1934), 84–86, 216.

135. For *Amphion*'s "living pyramids," see André Levinson, "Les Ballets de Mme Ida Rubinstein. 'Amphion,'" *Comoedia*, 25 June 1931, 2.

136. "Diary, 1930–31."

137. Unger to BN, 29 Aug. 1931, 77A/25, BNC. Roman Jasinski, whom Lapitzky and Unger had taken under their wing at Nijinska's behest because they spoke Polish, witnessed the tragedy. "And then Lapitzky went to swim in the ocean," he told his biographers. "Everyone told him not to go far out because it was dangerous. Big rocks were hidden under the water and the waves were strong; the waves took him up and crashed him down. I remember how Unger searched all night up and down the beach in the dark, calling his name" (Forrest and Snoke, *Roman Jasinski*, 62).

138. Unger to BN, 2 Sept. 1931, 77A/25, BNC.

139. Rubinstein, telegram to BN, 13 Oct. 1931, 76B/10, BNC.

140. Tugal to BN, 26 Oct. 1931, 77A/23, BNC.

141. Anton Dolin, *Ballet Go Round* (London: Michael Joseph, 1938), 41. A copy of the program is in the Reinhardt Archives.

142. "Diary 1931–32."

143. Ibid.

144. Reinhardt to BN, 2 Dec. 1931, 75/50, BNC.

Chapter 12

1. Louis Levy, "Théâtre. Les galas lyriques des Champs-Elysées. Les ballets russes de Nijinska—'Le Barbier de Séville', avec Chaliapine," *Populaire*, 29 Dec. 1933, Box 119, BNC.

2. Diary entry, 12 Oct. 1931, 59/9 and 59/10. On October 25, she writes, "all of a sudden, everything fell through. There is no Opéra Russe."

3. Henri Rebois, "Au Théâtre de Monte-Carlo; Une conversation avec M. René Blum," *Figaro*, 3 Dec. 1931, 8. According to Vicente García-Márquez, Balanchine and Kochno began working with de Basil at the end of the summer although they signed formal contracts only in November and December (5-6).

4. The original 1927–30 diary is in 59/1; the first "clean" copy, *Diaries of Gratuitous Pain*, in 59/2, and the second, *Two Loves: Diaries of Gratuitous Pain*, in 59/3. Her 1930–31 diary, *Rain on My Parnassus, or Love Madness*, with the epigraph by Jacopone da Todi, is in 59/8. The untitled version of her 1931–32 diary is in 59/9, and the version titled *Without Consciousness, Only Heart* in 59/10. Another title she played around with was "Exhalations of a Dancer's Loquacious Body" ("Diary 1927–29," 4 Nov. 1929, 59/2).

5. Joseph Darsky, *Sex and the Singer: Women in Feodor Chaliapin's Life* (New York: Nova Science Publishers, 2014), 44–45.

6. *EM*, 357.

7. See the entries for 18–19, 22, 28 Nov. and 7 Dec. 1928, in "Diary 1927–29," 59/1, BNC.

8. "Diary 1927–29," 30 May 1929.

9. "Diary 1930–31," 8 Nov. 1930, 59/8, BNC.

10. "Diary 1930–31," undated [Dec. 1930].

11. "Diary 1930–31," 22 July 1931, 59/8, BNC.

12. "Diary 1931–32," 10 Nov. and 28 Dec. 1931, 59/10, BNC.

13. García-Márquez, *The Ballets Russes*, 6.

14. "Diary 1931–32," 22 Jan. 1932, 59/10, BNC.

15. Vladimir Ivanovich Pohl (1875–1962) was a pianist and composer; his wife, Anna Mikhailovna, a concert singer. See Vladimir Nabokov, *Letters to Véra*, ed. and trans. Olga Voronina and Brian Boyd (New York: Knopf, 2015), 620–21.

16. Poulenc to BN, [13 Mar. 1932], 75/42, BNC.

17. Laurencin's design, reproduced in the 1934 Théâtre de la Danse/Ballets Russes souvenir program, is quite different from the curtain she designed for Diaghilev in 1924.

18. BN to El'iash, 22 June 1965, 72/25, BNC. El'iash was the author of *Russkaia terpsikhora* (Moscow: Sovetskaia Rossiia, 1965); *Pushkin i baletnyi teatr* (Moscow: Iskusstvo, 1970), and *Avdotia Istomina* (Leningrad: Iskusstvo, 1971).

19. Chagall to BN, [20] Apr. 1932, 71A/9, BNC.

20. The poster is in the Department of Architecture and Design, Museum of Modern Art.

21. Tikanova, *La Jeune Fille en bleu*, 114.

22. Ibid., 115.

23. "Diary 1931–32," 10 Feb. 1932, 59/10, BNC.

24. Margaret Severn, "Dancing with Bronislava Nijinska and Ida Rubinstein," *Dance Chronicle* 11, no. 3 (1988), 333–37.

25. Ibid., 343.

26. "Diary 1931–32," 12 Mar. 1932, 59/10, BNC.

27. Severn, "Dancing with Bronislava Nijinska," 339.

28. Tikanova, *La Jeune Fille en bleu*, 112–13.

29. Grand Concert program, Salle du Trocadero, 10 Apr. 1932, 12/10, BNC; Tikanova, 116; Severn, "Dancing with Bronislava Nijinska," 348–50.

30. Severn, "Dancing with Bronislava Nijinska," 350.

31. Ibid., 347. Nijinska finished *Bolero* on March 20.

32. Ibid., 341.

33. Ibid., 354.

34. Ibid., 342.

35. *Nikitina by Herself*, 113. See also Severn, "Dancing with Bronislava Nijinska," 352; "A l'Opéra-Comique," *Comoedia*, 15 Mar. 1932, 2; "La Danse. Alice Nikitina se retire," *Comoedia*, 21 May 1932, 2; André Levinson, "Le Gala de danses d'Alice Nikitina et Anatole Vilzac," *Comoedia*, 3 July 1932, 1–2.

36. Tikanova, *La Jeune Fille en bleu*, 113; Severn, "Dancing with Bronislava Nijinska," 353–54.

37. Maurice Brillant, "L'Aube musicale. L'enchantement de 'Prince Igor,'" *Aube*, 31 May 1932, 2. For press and reviews see Box 116, BNC.

38. P[ierre] B[ertrand], "La Semaine musicale," *Ménestrel*, 3 June 1932, 251–52.

39. Henry Malherbe, "La Musique," *Temps*, 15 June 1932, 3; Emile Vuillermoz, "La Musique," *Excelsior*, 13 June 1932, 3.

40. Gaston George, "Les Ballets Nijinska à l'Opéra-Comique," *Journal des Théâtres*, 15 July 1932, 46.

41. Maurice Brillant, "L'Aube musicale. Musiques bariolées," *Aube*, 14 June 1932, 2.

42. "Russian Ballet at Two Theatres. Champs-Elysées and Opéra-Comique—Pronounced Successes—Some Startling Changes—Search for Novel Forms of Expression," by The Dramatic Critic, *Daily Mail*, 12 June 1932.

43. Lollii Lvov, "Bronislava Nijinska's Ballets at the Opéra-Comique," *Rossiia i Slavianstvo*, 18 June 1932.

44. For the film comparison, see Brunel, "A l'Opéra-Comique. Ballets Russes." Emile Vuillermoz thought there was much too much going on, and blamed this on a somewhat disconcerting use of "simultaneism." "Twenty dancers execute at the same time in all corners of the stage different feats each of which demands an attentive examination" ("La Musique," *Excelsior*, 13 June 1932, 3).

45. Henry Malherbe, "La Musique," *Temps*, 15 June 1932, 3.

46. "Diary 1931–32," 12 Mar. 1932, 59/10, BNC.

47. Apr. 1932.

48. 21 May 1932.

49. 17 June 1932.

50. Prunières, "Russian Ballet in Paris."

51. Dominique Sordet, "Les Ballets Nijinska," *Action Française*, 17 June 1932, 3.

52. André Levinson, "Les Ballets Russes de Monte-Carlo," *Comoedia*, 20 June 1932, 1–2.

53. Valerian Svetlov, "Nijinska's Ballets," *Vozrozhdenie*, 12 June 1932, 4.

54. Prince Sergei Volkonsky, "Nijinska's Ballets," *Poslednie novosti*, 13 June 1932.

55. Christian Dahl, "Ballets," *Diapason*, 25 July 1932, Box 163, BNC. *Diapason* described itself as "an absolutely independent representative of music, dance, theater, circus, and cinema."

56. Ibid.

57. Ibid.

58. "Diary 1931–32," undated [mid-June 1932], 59/10, BNC.

59. Ibid. Although Nikitina danced in several of Nijinska's works for the Diaghilev company, she was not one of her students.

60. "Vozrozhdenie russkogo baleta: Beseda s V. G. Basilem," *Vozrozhdenie*, 14 June 1932, 4. Prince Sergei Volkonsky wrote two reviews of the Monte Carlo company

in *Poslednie novosti* ("Russkie balety Monte Karlo," 12 June 1932, 4; "Russkie balety Monte Karlo," 14 June 1932, 4).

61. Gabriel-Louis Pruque, "Soirs de Paris. Ballets chez le prince de Beauvau-Craon," *Paris-Midi*, 5 July 1932, 2.

62. Victoria Tennant, *Irina Baronova and the Ballets Russes de Monte Carlo* (Chicago: University of Chicago Press, 2014), 90.

63. "Opéra-Comique Losses. Manager Resigns: Theatre Depression," *MG*, 30 Sept. 1932, 9. For a study of changing mores, see Jacques Rouché, "L'Opéra et les moeurs nouvelles," *Revue des Deux Mondes*, 1 July 1932, 68–84.

64. BN to Rouché, 4 Oct. 1932, L.A.S. Nijinska, Bronislava, 13, BM-Opéra.

65. "Diary 1931–32," 23 July 1932, 59/10, BNC.

66. "Diary 1931–32," 28 June 1932.

67. Unger to BN, 3 Dec. 1932, 77A/25, BNC.

68. Alexis Vlassoff to NS, 14 Nov. 1932, and BN, 15 Nov. 1932, 77A/39, BNC.

69. Théâtre National Populaire to NS, 10 Nov. 1932, and BN, 19, 23, and 29 Nov. 1932, 77A/14, BNC.

70. Tikanova, *Le Jeune Fille en bleu*, 118.

71. BN, draft New Year's letter to Volkoff, undated, 77A/40, BNC.

72. C. G. Crisp, *The Classic French Cinema, 1930–1960* (Bloomington: Indiana University Press, 1993), 166–70.

73. "Un grand film français, réalisé par une grande firme française . . . et qui n'est peut-être pas ce qu'on peut raisonnablement appeler un film français," *Ciné-Déchaîné*, 30 Dec. 1932, Box 116, BNC.

74. Tikanova, *La Jeune Fille en bleu*, 113.

75. Katherine Foshko, "The Paul Dumer Assassination and the Russian Diaspora in Interwar France," *French History* 23, no. 3 (1 Sept. 2009), 392. The law "protecting the native workforce" was published in the *Journal Officiel de la République Française* on 12 Aug. 1932, 8818. The percentage of foreign workers in the various branches of entertainment was published in the *Journal Officiel* on 27 April 1933, 4395–98.

76. Eugen Weber, *The Hollow Years: France in the 1930s* (New York: W. W. Norton, 1994), 91–92.

77. Tikanova, *La Jeune Fille en bleu*, 118–19; contracts between Joseph Gilbert, Teatro Nuevo, Barcelona, and BN, 1 Sept. 1932 and 2 Feb. 1933, 46/10, BNC. For reviews of the tour and other press see Box 116, BNC.

78. J. Stan, "Spectacles," *Eclaireur du soir* (Nice), 31 Jan. 1933.

79. Louis Darves, "La Soirée Niçoise," *Petit Niçois*, 19 Jan. 1933.

80. J. R. de Larios, "En el Nuevo. Debutó la Compañía del Teatro de la Danza de Bronislava Nijinska," *La Noche*, 6 Feb. 1933.

81. G. T., "Bailes rusos en el Teatro Nuevo. Bronislava Nijinska, la sombra de Diaghileff," *Las noticias*, 4 Feb. 1933.

82. Sebastià Gasch, "Els ballets de la Nijinska," *Mirador*, undated, Box 116, BNC.

83. Tikanova, *La Jeune Fille en bleu*, 120.

84. Carmelo A. Zapparrata, "Ottant'anni fa esatti Bronislava Nijinska si esibiva al Grande di Brescia," *Danza & Danza*, Jan.–Feb. 2013, 19; Tikanova, 120–22. For press and the souvenir program for Brescia, see Box 116, BNC.

85. Tikanova, *La Jeune Fille en bleu*, 122.

86. Unger's letters are in 77A/25, BNC.

87. Unger to BN, 1 May 1933. The quotas were published in the *Journal Officiel*, 27 Apr. 1933, 4396–97. According to Article 3 of the 12 Aug. 1932 law, foreigners seeking employment in France needed "special ministerial authorization" (8818). Although the newly triumphant Nazis targeted Jews, they also targeted—albeit to a lesser extent—theater artists and musicians with Slavic and Gallic names. "Nazis Barring Foreign Artists," *Literary Digest*, 25 Feb. 1933, 16.

88. For Unger's comments on Les Ballets 1933 and the Ballets Russes de Monte-Carlo, see his letters of 6 and 14 June 1933 as well as an undated letter written after the premiere of *Scuola di Ballo* on 13 June.

89. Unger to BN, 23 Aug. 1933.

90. Contracts between the Directorio del Teatro Colón and BN, 6 May and 25 July 1933, 46/10, BNC. For Singaevsky's salary of 300 pesos for a five-month period, see "En torno a las actividades del Teatro Colón," *Razón*, 31 July 1933, 24/3, BNC. Unless otherwise noted, all clippings are from this file.

91. In her archives is a list of what she calls "choreographic miniatures," along with their soloists. Nearly all were from her repertory of opera dances and divertissements.

92. Omar Corrado, "Victoria Ocampo y la música: una experiencia social y estética de la modernidad," *Revista Musical Chilena* 61, no. 208 (July–Dec. 2007), 43.

93. "Bronislava Nijinska, Primera Bailarina del Colón, pasó hoy por nuestro puerto," *El Plata*, 7 May 1933; "La Nijinska trae nuevo proyecto de coreografía," *Crítica*, [6?] May 1933; "Rodean a la señora Nijinska un grupo de amigos y alumnas del cuerpo estable del teatro Colón," *Noticias gráficas*, 8 May 1933; "En honor de Madame Nijinska," *Noticias gráficas*, 10 May 1933.

94. Juan Carlos Mendoza, "Política y arte," *Mañana*, 27 May 1933; "El cuerpo de baile del Teatro Colón durante los ensayos," *Prensa*, 28 May 1933; Aguaratá, "Desde la platea del Colón," *Sintonía*, 27 May 1933.

95. "Las bailarinas del Teat. Colón," *Ultima hora*, 4–5 June 1933.

96. "Habla Bronislawa Nijinska, Coreógrafa del Teatro Colón," *Ultima hora*, 9 June 1933.

97. "El 'ballet' triunfa en el escenario del Teatro Colón," *Noticias gráficas*, 11 June 1933.

98. "En torno a las actividades del teatro Colón," *Razón*, 31 July 1933. When the August edition of the *Boletín Municipal* was published, it came out that the Colón had paid Nijinska an additional 8,000 pesos to rent the scenery for her ballets (unidentified clipping, 24/3, BNC).

99. Corrado, "Victoria Ocampo y la música," 45.

100. "Un espectáculo mediocre en el Teatro Colón: las versiones plasticocoreográficas de tres desaguisados musicales," *Razón*, 28 Aug. 1933.

101. "Un espectáculo de danzas en el Colón," *Nación*, 28 Aug. 1933.

102. L.A.G., "Dos novedades coreográficas en el Colón," 25 Sept. 1933.

103. "Desgracias del 'Ballet' en el Teatro Colón," *Crítica*, 10 Sept. 1933.

104. "En el Colón hubo un espectáculo de bailes anoche," *Nación*, 24 Sept. 1933.

105. "En el Teatro Colón se realizó anoche una sesión de coreografía," *Prensa*, 24 Sept. 1933.

106. "La temporada de primavera del Teatro Colón," *Razón*, 12 Sept. 1933.

107. Emilio Basaldúa, "Héctor Basaldúa and the Colón Theater: Thirty Years of Stage Design," *The Journal of Decorative and Propaganda Arts*, 18 (1992), 43. Basaldúa's design is reproduced on page 44. For a stage photograph, see *Historia general de la danza in la Argentina* (Buenos Aires: Fondo Nacional de las Artes, 2008), 64.

108. F. E., "La sombra de Tschaikowsky y el antiguo esplendor del 'ballet russe' se evocan en la nueva obra de Stravinsky, estrenada en el Colón," *Bandera Argentina*, 27 Oct. 1933.

109. Mia Slavenska, unpublished memoir, 117. I am grateful to the ballerina's daughter, Maria Ramas, for allowing me to consult this.

110. L. R. D., "Nijinska et Anton Dollin [*sic*] nous disent . . . ," *Intransigeant*, 24 Dec. 1933, 8.

111. Louis Lévy, "Les galas lyriques des Champs-Elysées," *Populaire*, 29 Dec. 1933, 4.

112. Jean Laurent, "Au Théâtre des Champs-Elysées: Les ballets russes de Nijinska," *Volonté*, 27 Dec. 1933, Box 119, BNC.

113. Ibid.

114. Paul Le Flem, "Les Galas de Danses des Ballets Russes sous la direction de Mme Nijinska," *Comoedia*, 27 Dec. 1933, 1–2. Le Flem, a composer and music critic, began his review: "Trained by a great artist, Madame Nijinska, the Ballets Russes has reappeared on the stage of the Théâtre des Champs-Elysées."

115. Signed contract between BN, "Ballet Mistress," and W. de Basil, "Director of the Ballets Russes de Monte-Carlo," 10 Dec. 1933, 46/10, BNC. The playbills for the Monte Carlo ballet season are in 5/1, BNC.

116. Danilova, *Choura*, 136.

117. A. E. Twysden, *Alexandra Danilova* (London: C. W. Beaumont, 1945), 104.

118. Danilova, *Choura*, 136.

119. Tamara Finch, "My Dancing Years, Part Two," *Dance Chronicle*, 27, no. 2 (2004), 264–65.

120. Kira [Abricossova] Bousloff, interviewed by Michelle Potter, Esso Performing Arts Collection, recorded 28 Aug. 1990, Session 2, National Library of Australia. http://nla.gov.au/nla.obj-216852351/listen.

121. BN, draft letter to an unidentified correspondent about her reactions to Romola Nijinsky's biography of her husband and Arnold Haskell's *Diaghileff*, undated [mid-1930s], 69/23, BNC.

122. For reviews of the season see Box 119, BNC.

123. De Basil to BN, 2 Feb., 17 Mar., and 21 Apr. 1934, 71/48, BNC.

124. Signed contract between Kachouk and BN, 17 May 1934, 46/10, BNC.

125. French translation of the contract between Stoll and BN, 5 June 1934, 76A/41, BNC.

126. Valère, "Petit courrier musical," *Comoedia*, 13 June 1934, 2.

127. "Aff. Nijinska c/o Stoll-London Coliseum Ltd.," English version of a statement summarizing the "affaire Nijinska," undated [late June 1934], 76A/41, BNC.
128. Unger to BN, 15 Feb. 1934, 77A/25, BNC.
129. Tikanova, *La Jeune Fille en bleu*, 126–27.
130. Dolinoff, interviewed by Smith, Part II, 75–79.
131. See, for example, Edouard Beaudu, "La Danse. Au Châtelet.—Le Baiser de la Fée," *L'Intransigeant*, 23 June 1934, 9, and Henry Bénazet, "Premières représentations," *Petit Parisien*, 24 June 1934, 7.
132. Reynaldo Hahn, "Chronique musicale," *Figaro*, 3 July 1934, 5.
133. "La Nijinska Ballets Russes, Théâtre de la Danse" souvenir program, NYPL. The dancers in the main roles were Nijinska (Hamlet); Ruth Chanova (Ophelia), Thomas Armour (Laertes), Igor Schwetzoff (Claudius), Nina Nikitina (Gertrude), Ivan/Jean Rykoff (Horatio), Serge Klimoff (Marcello), Alexis Dolinoff (Player), David Grey (Player), Edmond Linval (Player), Vadim Kochanovsky and Serge Unger (Buffoons).
134. Fernand Divoire, "La Danse," *Revue de France*, 1 Sept. 1934, 178–79.
135. For "Hamlet" and other Liszt music see Boxes 192–96, BNC.
136. Jean Delaincourt, "Ballets de Mme Nijinska. Hamlet (Musique de Liszt)," *Ami du Peuple*, 30 June 1934.
137. BN, draft letter to "Miss Allan," undated [Feb. 1935], 70/1, BNC.
138. Maurice Brillant, "L'Aube musicale. Ophélie en chaussons de danse," *Aube*, 1 July 1934, 2.
139. Ibid.
140. Ibid.
141. Albert Lestray, "Le gala des ballets russes," *Liberté*, 27 June 1934.
142. Henry Malherbe, "La Musique," *Temps*, 4 July 1934, 3.
143. Max Frantel, "Creation of 'Hamlet' par les ballets de Mme Nijinska," *Comoedia*, 28 June 1934, 2.
144. Brillant, "Ophélie en chaussons de danse" and "La Quinzaine théâtrale: Polichinelle, Hamlet, Oedipe," *Ouest-Eclair*, 18 July 1934, 6.
145. Reynaldo Hahn, "Chronique musicale," *Figaro*, 3 July 1934, 5.
146. Tikanova, *Le Jeune Fille en bleu*, 126.
147. "Aff. Nijinska c/o Stoll."
148. BN, telegram to Stoll, 2 July 1934; letter to Stoll, 2 July 1934; Stoll to BN, 2 July 1934, 76A/41, BNC. For public announcement of the canceled season, see "Ballet Season Cancelled," *Daily Telegraph*, 5 July 1934, Anton Dolin Scrapbooks, V&A.
149. Blum to NS, 4 July 1934, 78/5, BNC.
150. BN, draft letters to Anna Teplicka, undated, 69/19, and "Miss Allan," undated [Feb. 1935], 70/1, BNC.
151. Tikanova, *Le Jeune Fille en bleu*, 127.
152. The two "Hamlet" notebooks are in 17/14, BNC.
153. "Un quart d'heure avec le créateur des Ballets russes de Monte-Carlo," *Comoedia*, 10 June 1936, 2.

Chapter 13

1. For BN's 1934 trip to the United States, see the New York Passenger Lists on Ancestry Library (where she is listed as Bronislava Singaevsky). *Nijinsky* was published in London by Victor Gollancz; in New York by Simon & Schuster; and in Paris by Denoël et Steele. For the rougher and more fragmentary of Kirstein's manuscripts at NYPL, see 19/191, Lincoln Kirstein Papers; for the more finished and polished version, see *MGZMB-Res.+830759, Nijinsky, Romola de Pulszky. Kirstein met regularly with Romola between late 1932 and March. 1933 (Martin Duberman, *The Worlds of Lincoln Kirstein* [New York: Knopf, 2007], 143–48).

2. BN, unpublished notes, undated [mid-1930s], 69/23, BNC.

3. Ibid.

4. *Nijinsky*, 52–53; Arnold Haskell, in collaboration with Walter Nouvel, *Diaghileff: His Artistic and Private Life* (London: Gollancz, 1935), 73.

5. "Nijinsky's Sister Hits Biography as 'Fairy Tale,'" *NYHT*, 15 Nov. 1934, 21. See also "Nijinski's Sister Here," *NYT*, 15 Nov. 1934, 24.

6. "Autobiographical outline," 34/15, BNC.

7. Douglas W. Churchill, "Will Shakespeare in the Film City," *NYT*, 2 Dec. 1934, X5. Edwin Schallert, the *Washington Post*'s Hollywood reporter, mentioned "150 coryphees" in "Straight from the Studios," *WP*, 26 Nov. 1934, 14. Rather than Russian, they were probably speaking French.

8. "Terpsichore's High Priestess Lends Her Art to the Cinema!" *WP*, 27 Oct. 1935, SA1; Alice L. Tildesley, "Max Reinhardt Films a Dream," *Sun* (Baltimore), 24 Mar. 1935, T5.

9. This description is based on the Max Reinhardt film released by MGM/UA Home Video (Santa Monica, CA) in 1993. Details about the costumes are from Tildesley, "Max Reinhardt Films a Dream." "Process blue" was a color that the negative did not pick up. See D.W.C., "The Solid Fabric of a Midsummer's Dream," *NYT*, 20 Oct. 1935, X4.

10. "Diary (1932–38)," 59/13, BNC.

11. Léon (Nijinsky) Kochetovsky, notebook, undated [late 1934–early 1935], 68/5, BNC.

12. Léon (Nijinsky) Kochetovsky, handwritten letter in French to BN, undated [Dec. 1934–Jan. 1935], 80/4, BNC.

13. Read Kendall, "Around and About in Hollywood," *LAT*, 3 Jan. 1935, 19.

14. Isabel Morse Jones, "Music and Art," *LAT*, 20 Jan. 1935, A6.

15. Edwin Schallert, "Nijinska, Sister of Famous Dancer, Negotiates," *LAT*, 9 Jan. 1935, 13. On January 8, after a "verbal battle" with Dieterle, Nijinska walked off the set and was replaced by Theilade ("Nijinska Quits WB, Gets Nod from Metro," *Variety*, 15 Jan. 1935, 5).

16. Agreement between Hurok Attractions Inc. and BN, Feb. 1935, 72/72, BNC. The contract described the company as "consisting of not less than thirty-six (36) artists-dancers" and having "a special, extraordinary and unique character, corresponding to reputation of said ballet."

17. BN, notes about Léo, undated [summer 1935], 59/14, BNC.

18. "Diary 1932–38." Many of the entries are undated, so it is difficult to know when she was down to her last dollar. In a letter to her friend Maria Prianishnikova, Nijinska alludes to continuing difficulties. "You don't know the half of what was done and is being done to us. . . . I am run aground here again, worse than in Paris, because there I had my children. . . . [I]n the entire year I have had only two weeks of work in Hollywood. If I could at least get paid for my work—more than half my money is stuck in the hands of those theater crooks" (BN, draft letter to Prianishnikova, undated [winter–spring 1935], 75/63, BNC).

19. Ruth Eleanor Howard, "Nijinska Visits America," *American Dancer*, July 1935, 8. The American Ballet season at the Adelphi Theatre ran from March 1 to March 17.

20. J. D. B., "Feodor Chaliapin Gives Recital at Carnegie Hall," *NYHT*, 4 Mar. 1935, 11; H. T., "Chaliapin Recital Warmly Received," *NYT*, 4 Mar. 1935, 12; "Show by Boris Chaliapin," *NYT*, 8 Mar. 1935, 19.

21. John Martin, "Monte Carlo Ballet Opens Season Here," *NYT*, 21 Mar. 1935, 26, and "Premiere Offered by Ballet Russe," *NYT*, 22 Mar. 1935, 27.

22. Howard, "Nijinska Visits America."

23. Kirstein diary, entry for 2 Apr. 1935, 5/25, Kirstein Papers.

24. Ibid., 12 Apr. 1935.

25. Ibid.

26. Ibid., 2 May 1935.

27. "Dance Notes," *NYHT*, 9 June 1935, E6.

28. "Diary (1932–38)," undated entries.

29. Arnold Haskell, "Balletomane's Log Book. IX.—La Nijinska," *DT*, Sept. 1935, 569.

30. Playbill, Col. W. De Basil's Ballets Russes, Royal Opera House, Covent Garden, 18 July 1935, CAL.

31. Edwin Evans, "Fairy Tale in Ballet. Baron d'Erlanger's 'Elegant' Music," *Daily Mail*, 19 July 1935, 13; "Ballets Russes. 'Les Cent Baisers' at Covent Garden," *Scotsman*, [1]8 July 1936, 17; J. H. M., " 'Les Cent Baisers.' New Ballet at Covent Garden," *MG*, 20 July 1935, 16.

32. Irina Baronova, *Irina: Ballet, Life and Love*, foreword by Clement Crisp (Gainesville: University Press of Florida, 2005), 154.

33. Ibid.

34. Ibid., 155.

35. Sono Osato, *Distant Dances* (New York: Knopf, 1980), 80–81.

36. H[ubert] G[riffith], "A New Russian Ballet. 'Les Cent Baisers.' Baron d'Erlanger's Music. First Rehearsal," *Observer*, 7 July 1935, 10.

37. Baronova, *Irina*, 160–61.

38. Osato, *Distant Dances*, 81.

39. García-Márquez, *The Ballets Russes*, 146.

40. "Sitter Out," "A New Nijinska Ballet," *DT*, Aug. 1935, 464.

41. Caryl Brahms, *Footnotes to the Ballet* (London: Lovat Dickson, 1936), 116; J. H. M., "'Les Cent Baisers.' New Ballet at Covent Garden"; Evans, "Fairy Tale in Ballet."

42. Brahms, *Footnotes to the Ballet*, 118–19.

43. "Souvenir de la création du ballet 'Les Cent Baisers' par les Ballets Russes du Col. W. De Basil," Royal Opera, Covent Garden, 1935, CAL.

44. "Ballet at Covent Garden," *Times*, 18 July 1935, 14; "News in Brief," *Times*, 22 July 1935, 10; "Russian Ballet. Dresses at Covent Garden," *Times*, 25 July 1935, 12; "Onlooker," "Gala Parties for the Ballet," *Daily Mail*, 26 July 1935, 8. The menu and cabaret program for the July 24 "Ballets Russes Souper" are at CAL.

45. Baronova, *Irina*, 171.

46. Ibid., 171–72.

47. John Martin, "Monte Carlo Ballet Opens Season Here," *NYT*, 21 Mar. 1935, 26.

48. "Ballet at Covent Garden. 'Scheherezade,'" *Times*, 20 June 1935, 12. See also "Covent Garden Theatre. The Russian Ballet," *Times*, 12 June 1935, 10; H[orace] H[orsnell], "The Russian Ballet," *Observer*, 16 June 1935, 15; J. H. M., "Covent Garden Ballet: 'Thamar,'" *MG*, 17 Aug. 1935, 10.

49. Haskell, "Balletomane's Log Book," 570.

50. Haskell, *Balletomania*, 86 (*Noces*), 84 (*Biches*), and 217 (Rubinstein).

51. Haskell to BN, 2 Apr. 1928, 72/61, BNC. Haskell hoped that on his next trip to Paris, she would be willing to meet him.

52. Haskell, *Balletomania*, 85–86. This is from chap. 4 ("Monte Carlo–Paris, 1925"). The choreographers are discussed in chap. 7 ("Four Choreographers: Nijinsky-Fokine-Balanchine-Massine").

53. Haskell, *Diaghileff*, 69.

54. Ibid. Chapter 17, "In Search of Lost Youth," covers the years 1922–1929.

55. Arnold L. Haskell, *Ballet: A Complete Guide to Appreciation, History, Aesthetics, Ballets, Dancers* (Harmondsworth, Middlesex: Penguin Books, 1938), 90.

56. Adrian Stokes, *Russian Ballet* (London: Faber & Faber, 1935).

57. Caryl Brahms, "The Choreography," in *Footnotes to the Ballet*, 54.

58. Ibid., 81.

59. John Martin, "Nijinska's Ballet in Premiere Here," *NYT*, 19 Oct. 1935, 20.

60. John Martin, "The Dance: Tina Flade Scores," *NYT*, 21 July 1935, X4.

61. H[ubert] G[riffith], "Farewell to the Ballet. New Works for America," *Observer*, 25 Aug. 1935, 9.

62. "Nijinska's Son Killed. Car Accident in France," *MG*, 6 Sept. 1935, 18. For clippings about the accident, see 24/9, BNC.

63. "Pokhorony syna B. F. Nizhinskoi," *Poslednie novosti*, 8 Sept. 1935, 3. In the draft of a letter probably intended for Léo's father, Alexander Kochetovsky, Nijinska wrote that Irina remained in the hospital for more than a month and had three surgeries to repair her arms (59/7, BNC).

64. V[ladimir] Pol', "Pamiati Levushki Nizhinskago," *Vozrozhdenie*, 8 Sept. 1935, 4.

65. "Certificat d'identité," issued by the Préfecture de Police, 21 June 1935, 46/5, BNC. The Latin, Polish, and Russian versions of Léo's birth certificate all give his middle name as Vaslav, rather than indicating a patronymic. The various documents are in 46/5, BNC.

66. Léon Kochetovsky to BN, undated [1930s], 80/4, BNC. Tsarevich Alexei Nikolaevich died on July 17, 1918, which means the letter was written on July 18. The Ukrainian famine took place in 1932–1933.

67. Léon Kochetovsky to BN, 1 and 19 Mar. 1935, 79/15, BNC.

68. Léon Kochetovsky to BN, 8 Jan. 1935, 79/15, BNC.

69. Léon Kochetovsky to BN, 19 Mar. 1935, 79/15, BNC.

70. Léo's many names underscore his hybrid identity. Leon Vatslav Kochetovskii on his Latin-Russian baptismal certificate and Léon Koczetovsky on his French identity documents, he answered to Levushka (which his mother always called him), signed his letters to her as "Léon" and those to his friends as Léo. He also started to use the Nijinsky family name, signing the menu for a 1934 *souper* as "Léo Nijinsky" and pages from one of his own musical compositions as "Léon Nijinsky"; in his death notices he is usually called Leon Nijinska Kotzkovski. Léo's Kiev baptismal certificate, French translation thereof, and his "Certificat d'Identité," issued 21 June 1935, are in 46/5; the gala menu from Le Grand Vatel, 25 June 1934, in 75/14; his untitled music manuscript, in 214/3, and his letter to Juan Manuel Pradilla C., 21 Oct. 1934, in 79/14, BNC. Most of his letters to Nijinska are in 79/15, BNC.

71. Colonel de Basil, quoted in "Famous Dancer in Crash," *Dundee Courier*, undated [6 Sept. 1935], 24/9, BNC.

72. Léon Kochetovsky to BN, undated (late March 1935), 79/15, BNC.

73. "Diary (1932–38)."

74. BN, draft letter to IN, July 1935, 79/18, BNC. Léo's letters to his mother from Switzerland are in 79/15, BNC. His last surviving letter to her is dated 9 Aug. 1935.

75. Léon Kochetovsky, notebook, undated [summer 1935], 68/5, BNC.

76. "Diary 1932–38," undated entry.

77. G. B., "'Le Songe d'une nuit d'été' est présenté ce soir en gala au Cinéma Marbeuf," *Paris-Soir*, 13 Dec. 1935, 8.

78. Nijinska described the property and its contents in a form for the US immigration authorities filed in the early 1940s. Form TFR-500: Census of Property in Foreign Countries; Series A-I: Summary Report by Individuals, 46/1, BNC.

79. NS, letter to BN, 6 May 1936, 78/16, BNC.

80. Osato, *Distant Dances*, 97.

81. Ibid., 99–100.

82. The pianists were Pauline Gilbert, Hannah Klein, Joan Blair, and M. Alfred Thielecker; the vocal soloists Jeanne Palmer, Helena Schedova, Ivan Velikanoff, and Vasily Romakoff, with the chorus provided by the Art of Musical Russia, Inc.

83. Osato, *Distant Dances*, 101.

84. John Martin, "'Les Noces' Given by Ballet Russe," *NYT*, 21 Apr. 1936, 27.

85. Ibid.

86. Edwin Denby, "Nijinska's 'Noces,'" *Modern Music*, May–June 1936, 44–45.

87. John Martin, "The Dance: Revival of Nijinska's 'Les Noces,'" *NYT*, 3 May 1936, X7.

88. Marcia B. Siegel, *Days on Earth: The Dance of Doris Humphrey* (New Haven: Yale University Press, 1987), 163.

89. The playbills for the 1936 Stravinsky festival are at the Biblioteca Teatro Colón, Buenos Aires.

90. Nijinska's itinerary has been assembled from the Master List of passengers from Miami to San Juan, Puerto Rico, on 23 Apr. 1936, in Ancestry Library; "Bronislava Nijinska cegou ontem ao Rio. A grande bailarina segue hoje para Buenos Aires," *Jornal do Brasil*, 18 Apr. 1936, 13.

91. BN, draft letter to Prianishnikova, undated [spring 1936], 75/63, BNC.

92. "Sitter Out," "*Les Noces* to Be Revived. Stravinsky's Book—Monte Carlo Ballet at the Alhambra," *DT*, June 1936, 243–48. The issue also included a review of the New York revival (David C. Maclay, "Nijinska's Productions for the De Basil Ballet," 256).

93. H[ubert] G[riffith], "Return of the Ballet," *Observer*, 5 Apr. 1936, 12; "Russian Ballet for Covent Garden," *Observer*, 7 June 1936, 13.

94. BN to NS, undated [Apr. 1936].

95. NS to BN, 20 May 1936, 78/16, BNC.

96. "The Heyday of the Ballet," *Times*, 4 July 1936, 12.

97. Constant Lambert, "Why Ballet Is Booming," *Sunday Referee*, 21 June 1936, 16.

98. For reviews of these books, see Marie Rambert, "Experts on the Ballet," *Sunday Times*, 7 June 1936, 8; Arnold Haskell, "Diaghileff and the Ballet," *Sunday Times*, 21 June 1936, 9; "Fifty Years of Ballet. Prince Lievin Looks Back," *Observer*, 21 June 1936, 11; "Books of the Week: The Russian Ballet. Some New Studies," *Times*, 26 June 1936, 10; H[orace] H[orsnell], "Pure Ballet," *Observer*, 2 Aug. 1936, 5. On June 30 the *Times* announced the imminent publication of *The Diary of Vaslav Nijinsky* by Gollancz ("Books to Come," *Times*, 30 June 1936, 21).

99. "Covent Garden. 'The Midnight Sun,' " *Times*, 20 June 1936, 10; "The Sitter Out," *DT*, Aug. 1936, 484.

100. García-Márquez, *Massine*, 243.

101. Ibid., 244.

102. Ibid., 247; "Dramatis Personae," *Observer*, 19 July 1936, 13.

103. "Our London Correspondence," *MG*, 4 June 1936, 8 (for "Stravinsky's cacophonies").

104. Thomas Armour, letter to Margaret Power, Apr. 1936, qtd. in Sorley Walker, *De Basil's Ballets Russes*, 63.

105. Ibid.

106. Bennahum, *René Blum*, 144–45, 176.

107. "Sitter Out," "Nijinska for London. 'Prometheus' at the Wells," *DT*, Nov. 1936, 135.

108. "The King's Theatre, Hammersmith. Markova-Dolin Ballet," 19 May 1937, 12.

109. Anton Dolin, *Ballet Go Round* (London: Michael Joseph Ltd., 1938), 163. Sergeyev was the former Maryinsky *régisseur* who had staged Diaghilev's *Sleeping Princess* (1921), the Paris Opéra's *Giselle* (1924), and several works for the Vic-Wells Ballet directed by Ninette de Valois.

110. The women included Wendy Toye, Susan Salaman, Molly Lake, and Derroda de Moroda. There were also a number of women designers, including Phyllis Dolton and Motley (the corporate name of sisters Margaret Harris, Sophie Harris, and Elizabeth Montgomery Wilmot).

111. Bronislava Nijinska, "Reflections about the Production of *Les Biches* and *Hamlet* in Markova-Dolin Ballets," trans. Lydia Lopokova, *DT*, Feb. 1937, 618. An undated Russian transcript of the essay is in 34/21, BNC.

112. Nijinska, "Reflections about the Production of *Les Biches* and *Hamlet* in Markova-Dolin Ballets," 619.

113. Dolin, *Ballet Go Round*, 198; Tina Sutton, *The Making of Markova: Diaghilev's Baby Ballerina to Groundbreaking Icon* (New York: Pegasus, 2013), 303.

114. Dolin, *Ballet Go Round*, 199.

115. Qtd. in "Bronislava Nijinska: Dancers Speak," *Ballet Review* 18, no. 1 (Spring 1990), 18–19. When the company opened in Hammersmith, Franklin scored a personal success with the trepak. C. B., "Poetry in Motion: Markova's Blue Bird," *Telegraph*, 2 Mar. 1937, Anton Dolin Archive THM 12/15 (hereafter Dolin Archive), Sept. 1936–Sept. 1937, V&A.

116. "King's Theatre. The Markova-Dolin Ballet," *Times*, 9 Mar. 1937, 14.

117. Qtd. in Sutton, *The Making of Markova*, 231.

118. Richard Buckle, "Alice's Wonderland," *Sunday Times*, 7 July 1968, 47.

119. J. M., "Markova Dolin Ballet. 'The Beloved One,'" *MG*, 25 Mar. 1937, 13.

120. Dolin, *Ballet Go Round*, 200. For Nijinska's involvement in the commission, see L. B. Lestocq, Vivian Van Damm Productions, letter to George Kirsta, 3 Feb. 1937, Box 4-122, Georg Kirsta Collection, University of Salzburg. Seventeen of Kirsta's costume designs for *The Beloved One* are at the V&A; several pencil sketches for the scenery are in 16/4, BNC. For Kirsta's letters to Nijinska, see 73/22, BNC. I am grateful to Kirsta's daughter, Alix Kirsta, for clarifying her family's relationship with Nijinska.

121. Arnold L. Haskell, "Romantic Ballet by Nijinska. 'The Beloved One' Revived," *Daily Telegraph*, 11 May 1937, Markova-Dolin Company File, V&A. *The Beloved One* was disliked by critics who felt that the "romantic theme of the nostalgic poet recalling past loves and grief" had been "quite overdone" (J. H. M., "Markova-Dolin Ballet. 'The Beloved One,'" *MG*, 12 May 1937, 20). For an extreme example of this, see A. V. Coton's damning criticism in *A Prejudice for Ballet* ([London: Methuen, 1938], 165–68). Haskell defended the ballet, noting that it was "the first in date of all the recent romantic ballets and in many ways the richest"—the others being Frederick Ashton's *Apparitions* and Massine's *Symphonie Fantastique*, whose choreographers had both taken part in the 1928 season when Nijinska had created the work for Ida Rubinstein (Haskell, "Romantic Ballet by Nijinska").

122. Dolin, *Ballet Go Round*, 279.

123. Ibid., 199.

124. Arnold L. Haskell, "Balletomane's Log Book," *DT*, July 1937, 412.

125. Haskell, *Balletomania*.

126. Arnold L. Haskell, *Dancing around the World* (London: Gollancz, 1937), 264–65.

127. Ibid., 266–67.

128. Ibid., 267.

129. Janina Pudełek, "The Polish Mishaps of Serge Lifar and Bronislava Nijinska," *Dance Chronicle* 27, no. 2 (2004), 206–8.

130. Ibid., 209–10. The title of "director general" was used to describe Szyfman in the Covent Garden playbills (11/5, BNC). For the German, Polish, and Baltic tour dates, see "Les Spectacles des Ballets Polonais dansés en Allemagne en Janvier–Mars 1938" and Irina Nijinska's informal list in 51/4, BNC.

131. Lisa C. Arkin, "Bronislava Nijinska and the Polish Ballet, 1937–1938: Missing Chapter of the Legacy," *Dance Research Journal* 24, no. 2 (Autumn 1992), 2. Szyfman's article, "Powstanie Baletu Polskiegow 1937 roku" (The Beginnings of the Polish Ballet in 1937), is in *Leon Wojcikowski* (Warsaw: Opera Warszawa, 1958), 50–60.

132. Nadine Bouchonnet, Office Théâtral Européen (O.T.E.), to BN, 11 Mar. 1937, 77A/13, BNC.

133. Bouchonnet to BN, 10 Apr. 1937, 77A/13, BNC.

134. Bouchonnet to BN, 20 Apr. 1937, 77A/13, BNC.

135. Szyfman, "Powstanie," 53.

136. Office of the Director, Polish Ballet, to BN, 29 July 1938, 76/33, BNC.

137. BN, draft letter to Anna Teplicka, undated [summer 1937], 77A/11, BNC. A similar draft is in 77/39, BNC.

138. Szyfman, "Powstanie," 55.

139. Ibid.; Pudełek, "Polish Mishaps," 211; Bożena Mamontowicz-Łojek, *Terpsychora i lekkie muzy: Taniec widowiskowy w Polsce w okresie międzywojennym* (Terpsichore, the Light Muse: Theatrical Dance in Poland in the Interwar Period [1918–1939]) (Krakow: Polskie Wydawnictwo Muzyczne, 1972), 60.

140. Nina Novak, with Luisa Himiob, *El ballet, mi vida, mi pasión: Memorias* (S. I., Venezuela: Gráficas ACEA, 2010), 30, 34.

141. Vladimir Dokoudovsky, interviewed by Joan Kramer, 1975–1977, 294–99, *MGZT 5-1083, NYPL.

142. "Danses: Le ballet polonais se prépare à une grande tournée à létranger," *Echo de Varsovie*, 4 Sept. 1937, Dossier d'artiste (Bronislava Nijinska), BM-Opéra; Stanislas Glowacki, "History of the Ballet in Poland," and "How the Polish Ballets Were Created," in "The Polish Ballets" souvenir program (English version), 11/3, BNC.

143. Unidentified clipping, Box 117, BNC.

144. "Terms of Employment for Artists of the Polish National Ballet," 51/2, BNC.

145. Quoted in Arkin, "Bronislava Nijinska and the Polish Ballet," 3.

146. Dokoudovsky oral history, 304.

147. Ibid.

148. Ibid., 305.

149. Ibid., 307; Dolin, *Ballet Go Round*, 208. Wolska had studied privately with Dolin and subsequently joined the Markova-Dolin company, where Nijinska taught her the role of the Hostess in *Les Biches*. After dancing with the Polish Ballet, she joined the de Basil company.

150. Dokoudovsky, interviewed by Kramer, 316–19.

151. The composers were Roman Palester (*The Song of the Soil*), Michal Kondracki (*The Legend of Cracow*), Ludomir Różycki (*The Eternal Apollo*), and Bolesław Woytowicz (*The Recall*); the designers Teresa Roszkowska (*The Legend of Cracow*), Wacław Borowski (*Chopin Concerto* and *The Song of the Earth*), Władysław Daszewski (*The*

Eternal Apollo), and Irena Lorentowicz-Karwowska (*The Recall*). The poet, editor, and diplomat Ludwik Hieronim Morstin wrote the argument for *Legend*; Światopełk Karpiński, another poet-diplomat, the argument for *Apollo*. I have used the London titles, except for *The Song of the Earth*, which appears in the London souvenir program.

152. Joanna Stacewicz-Podlipska, *Ja byłam wolny ptak—O życiu i sztuce Teresy Roszkowskiej* (Warsaw: Instytut Sztuki Polskirj Akademii Nauk, 2012), 259. Several of Roszkowska's designs for the ballet are reproduced in Katarzyna Sanocka, "Projekty scenografii i kostiumów Teresy Roszkowskiej do baletu *Baśń krakowska* Michała Kondrackiego dla Plskiego Baletu Reprezentacyjnego," *Studia Choreologica* 14, 103–17.

153. "Diary (1932–38)," entry for Sept. 1937.

154. BN, draft letter to Teplicka, undated [summer 1937], 77A/39, BNC. A similar draft is in 77A/11, BNC.

155. See "Wacław Borowski," CULTURE.PL (2019), Adam Mickiewicz Institute. https://culture.pl/en/artist/waclaw-borowski.

156. Boulos, "Les Ballets Polonais," *Ce Soir*, 30 Nov. 1937, Box 117, BNC.

157. Szyfman, "Powstanie," 57; Jean-Emile Bayard, "Paris, 19 novembre," *Echo* (Warsaw), 24 Nov. 1937, Box 117, BNC.

158. M.-A. Dabadie, "Bronislava Nijinska dirige, en gants blancs les dernières répétitions des Ballets Polonais," *L'Epoque*, 19 Nov. 1937, 6.

159. "Ambassades," *Figaro*, 25 Nov. 1937, 2; Louis Léon-Martin, "Le gala des ballets polonais fut hier la première grande fête de la saison parisienne," *Paris Midi*, 21 Nov. 1937, Box 117, BNC.

160. L. Franc Scheuer, "Ballet at the Paris Exhibition," *DT*, May 1937, 191.

161. For the use of dance at the Spanish pavilion to support of the anti-fascist cause, see Idoia Murga Castro, *Pintura e danza. Los artistas españoles y el ballet (1916–1962)* (Madrid: CSIC/Instituto de Historia, 2012), 235–49.

162. *Diplomat in Paris, 1936–1939: Papers and Memoirs of Juliusz Łukasiewicz, Ambassador of Poland*, ed. Wacław Jędrzejewicz (New York: Columbia University Press, 1970), xvii–xxi.

163. Serge Lifar, "Souhaits de bienvenue aux Ballets polonais," *Figaro*, 19 Nov. 1937, 4. For press clippings see Box 117, BNC, and the Dossier d'artiste (Bronislava Nijinska), BM-Opéra.

164. Henri Sauguet, "Les Ballets Polonais," *Jour*, 23 Nov. 1937, Box 117, BNC.

165. Emile Vuillermoz, "Les Ballets Polonais," *Excelsior*, 22 Nov. 1937, 7.

166. Reynaldo Hahn, "Les Ballets Polonais," *Figaro*, 25 Nov. 1937, 5.

167. L. Franc Scheuer, "Polish Ballet in Paris. Our Paris Letter," *DT*, Jan. 1938, 522.

168. René Baron, "Les Ballets Polonais," *Revue musicale*, Dec. 1937, 442.

169. "Le vieil abonné," "Les ballets polonais," *Candide*, 25 Nov. 1937, 15.

170. W[acław] Jędrzejewicz to BN, 29 Nov. 1937, 76/33, BNC; Szyfman, "Powstanie," 60.

171. "Sitter Out," "Balance Sheet for 1937: A Summing Up," *DT*, Dec. 1937, 267.

172. "Les Ballets Polonais. At Covent Garden This Week. Madame Nijinska in Command," *Observer*, 12 Dec. 1937, 22.

173. "Polish Ballet," *Sheffield Independent*, 16 Dec 1937, Box 117, BNC.

174. "Talk of the Day," *Evening News*, 17 Dec. 1937, Box 117, BNC.

175. J. H. M., "Polish Ballet," *MG*, 17 Dec. 1937, 15.

176. "Covent Garden Theatre. The Polish Ballet," *Times*, 17 Dec. 1937, 14.

177. H[orace] H[orsnell], "The Polish Ballet," *Observer*, 19 Dec. 1937, 11.

178. "Interesting Polish Ballet. Promise That May Achieve Distinction," *Birmingham Post*, 18 Dec. 1937, Box 117, BNC.

179. W. Mohl, "Lovely Scenes. Polish Ballet Deserves Better Treatment from London," *Evening News*, 18 Dec. 1937, Box 117, BNC.

180. "Cosmo," "Please Mr. Bernard Shaw," *Ipswich Evening Star*, 18 Dec. 1937, Box 117, BNC.

181. See "Interesting Polish Ballet" ("uncompromisingly harsh and modern"); "Covent Garden Theatre. The Polish Ballet," *Times*, 17 Dec. 1937, 14 ("anthropological"); Arnold L. Haskell, " 'The Eternal Apollo.' Polish Ballet at Covent Garden," *Daily Telegraph and Morning Post*, 18 Dec. 1937 ("insignificantly melodious"); E[rnest] N[ewman], "Polish Ballet," *Sunday Times*, 19 Dec. 1937, 5 ("beneath serious consideration").

182. De Valois to Lopokova, undated [1937], LLK/5/215/15, The Papers of Lydia Lopokova Keynes, King's College, Cambridge.

183. For a partial listing, see "Dramatis Personae," *Observer*, 19 Dec. 1937, 11.

184. "Polish Dancers in London. Christmas Season Show at Covent Garden," *Bayswater Chronicle*, 25 Dec. 1937, Box 117, BNC.

185. "Television News. 'Les Ballets Polonais,'" *Southend Pictorial Telegraph*, 1 Jan. 1938, Box 117, BNC.

186. Szyfman to BN, 10 Jan. 1938, 76/33, BNC.

187. Ibid.

188. "Diary (1932–38)," entry for Jan. 1938.

189. *Diplomat in Berlin, 1933–1939: Papers and Memoirs of Józef Lipski, Ambassador of Poland*, ed. Wacław Jędrzejewicz (New York: Columbia University Press, 1968), 339–40.

190. *Die Tagebucher von Joseph Goebbels*, ed. Elke Fröhlich (Munich: K. G. Saur, 2000), Teil I, Band 5 (December 1937–July 1938), 120 (28 Jan. 1938).

191. Szyfman to BN, 10 Jan. 1938; "Diary (1932–38)," entry for Jan. 1938.

192. "Les Spectacles des Ballets Polonais données en Allemagne en Janvier–Mars 1938," 31/4, BNC.

193. Szyfman to BN, 24 Feb. 1938.

194. "Direction des Ballets Polonais," invitation to performances of the Polish Ballet, Wielki Theater, 6–10 Apr. 1938, Box 117, BNC.

195. This list has been compiled from Pudełek, "The Polish Mishaps," 214, and Irina Nijinska's handwritten list in 52/4, BNC. Lviv is now in Ukraine, Vilnius in Lithuania. According to Julian Braunsweg, the Warsaw-born, Paris-based impresario who later founded London Festival Ballet, the "Warsaw opening was successful, but . . . Nijinska insisted on taking the orchestra on tour. Many of the places we visited were no bigger than church halls, and consequently I lost a good deal of

money" (Julian Braunsweg, *Braunsweg's Ballet Scandals: The Life of an Impresario and the Story of Festival Ballet* [London: Allen & Unwin, 1974], 74).

196. Arkin, "Bronislava Nijinska and the Polish Ballet," 8. For an introduction to Stryjeńska's work, see Jerzy Warchałowski, *Zofja Stryjeńska* (Warsaw: Nakład Gebethnera i Wolffa, 1929).

197. Pudełek, "The Polish Mishaps," 215.

198. Ibid.

199. "Diary (1932–38)," entry for 11 Apr. 1938. I am grateful to Dr. Małgorzata Komorowska for suggesting Popławski and directing me to his biography in the *Słownik Biograficzny Teatru Polskiego*.

200. "Diary (1932–38)," entry for 12 Apr. 1938.

201. Ibid., entry for 19 Apr. 1938.

202. See 66/5, BNC.

203. Teplicka to BN, 16 June 1938.

204. Szyfman to BN, 6 July 1938, 76/3, BNC.

205. IN, draft letter in French to Jan Lechoń, 7 Aug. 1938, 76B/33, BNC.

206. Aleksandr Guttry to BN, 23 Aug. 1938, 76/33, BNC.

207. Direction of the Polish Ballet to BN, 1 Sept. 1938, 76/33, BNC.

208. Direction of the Polish Ballet to BN, 16 Sept. 1938, 76B/33, BNC.

209. Copies of the various documents are in 51/2, BNC.

210. BN, draft letter to Kirsta, 1938, 73/22, BNC.

211. "Diary (1932–39)," entry for Jan. 1939.

212. Ibid., entry for 5 June 1939. Anna Teplicka's visit to Louveciennes is commemorated in two snapshots taken in Nijinska's home (94/2, BNC). A sturdy-looking woman with a warm smile and slightly masculine air, Teplicka died during World War II possibly in the Łódź ghetto.

213. Ibid.

214. Nicolà Benois to BN and NS, 15 July 1937 and 6 Oct. 1937, 70/28, BNC.

215. René Blum, telegram to BN, 17 Mar. 1939, and draft response, undated, 70/37, BNC.

216. Nadine Bouchonnet to BN, 4 Mar. 1939, 77A/13, BNC. In the draft of a letter to Anna Teplicka, Nijinska complained that excerpts from *Les Biches* and *Le Train Bleu* were being staged in tandem with the Diaghilev exhibition ("Ballets russes de Diaghilew 1909–1929") organized by Serge Lifar at the Musée des Arts Décoratifs, but she was not consulted. Bouchonnet's offer was presumably in response to this. The exhibition opened on March 27, 1939.

217. Sevastianov to BN, 8 July 1939, 71/34, BNC.

218. Suzana Braga, *Tatiana Leskova: Uma bailarina solta no mundo* (São Paulo: Editora Globo, 2010), 62; John Martin, "The Dance: New Ballets. Reports from Abroad on Works to Be Seen Here Next Season," *NYT*, 16 July 1939, 112.

219. Gordon W. G. Rayner, Ealing Studios Limited, to BN, 20 July 1939, 75/49, BNC.

220. H. G., "The Russian Ballet. Problem of Policy. What of the Future?" *Observer*, 30 July 1939, 10. By mid-August de Basil was reappointed to his old post (H. G., "Future of the Ballet. Permanent Chief Appointed. Col. de Basil as Director. Hopes for Coming Seasons," *Observer*, 13 Aug. 1939, 8).

221. "Our London Correspondence," *MG*, 2 Aug. 1939, 8.

222. *1939 England and Wales Register*, Ancestry Library.

223. "Form TFR-500: Census of Property in Foreign Countries. Series A-1: Summary Report by Individuals," 46/1, BNC; BN to Maurice Quonian, 27 Sept. 1954, 75/46, BNC.

224. BN, draft letter to Prianishnikova, Oct. 1939, 75/63, BNC.

225. *UK, Outward Passenger Lists, 1890–1960, New York, Passenger and Crew Lists (including Castle Garden and Ellis Island, 1820–1957)*, Ancestry Library.

Chapter 14

1. On the "list or manifest of alien passengers," Nijinska is identified as "Bronislava Singaevsky-Nijinska" and Irina as "Irene Kotchetovsky-Nijinska." See Ancestry Library.

2. John Martin, "The Ballet Russe Hailed at Opening," *NYT*, 27 Oct. 1939, 31. See also John Martin, "The Dance: New Season," *NYT*, 17 Sept. 1939, 142; "The Dance: Ballet and the War," *NYT*, 1 Oct. 1939, 142; "The Dance: Ballet List," *NYT*, 15 Oct. 1939, 146.

3. Ann Barzel, "The Ballet Theatre," unidentified clipping, ABT Clippings File, NYPL.

4. Lucius Beebe, "An Introduction to the Ballet Theatre," Ballet Theatre souvenir program, 1940, n.p. Beebe was a longtime columnist for the *New York Herald Tribune*.

5. Ibid.

6. "The Ballet Theatre," flyer for the Center Theatre season, ABT Clippings File, NYPL.

7. Alexander Kahn, Memorandum of Agreement with BN, 5 Nov. 1939, 11/997, ABT Records.

8. John Martin, "The Dance: Miscellany," *NYT*, 10 Dec. 1939, 174.

9. *EM*, 201–2. For the ballet's history, see Ivor Guest, "The Saga of 'La Fille mal Gardée' " (34–57), in *La Fille mal Gardée*, ed. Ivor Guest (London: Dancing Times Ltd., 1960), 58–64; Roland John Wiley, *The Life and Ballets of Lev Ivanov* (Oxford: Clarendon Press, 1997), 73–84.

10. Lillian Moore, " 'La Fille mal Gardée' in America," *DM*, 47. Moore's essay was originally published in Guest's *La Fille mal Gardée*, 58–64.

11. Irina Nijinska and Jean Rawlinson, "Bronislava Nijinska's La Fille Mal Gardée," unpublished typescript, 9, 17/12, BNC. This was probably written in the late 1970s.

12. BN, choreographic sketch for *La Fille Mal Gardée*, undated [1939–1940], BNC, http://www.loc.gov/exhibits/american-ballet-theatre/1940.html#obj003; Dokoudovsky, interviewed by Kramer, 471.

13. Orest Sergievsky, *Memoirs of a Dancer: Shadows, Dreams, Memories* (New York: Dance Horizons, 1979), 161.

14. "The organization is strictly American" is quoted by Walter Terry in one of his advance pieces ("The Ballet Theater," *NYHT*, 31 Dec. 1939, E10). For the company's dancers and repertory during its first twenty years, see Selma Jeanne Cohen and A. J. Pischl, "The American Ballet Theatre: 1940–1960," *Dance Perspectives* 6 (1960).

15. Orest Sergievsky, interviewed by John Gruen, 1977, 15–16, *MGZMT 3-1469, NYPL.

16. Annabelle Lyon, interviewed by Elizabeth Kendall, 1979, 146–47, *MGZMT 3-1861, NYPL.

17. Patricia Bowman, interviewed by John Gruen, 1975, 43–45, *MGZMT 3-395, NYPL.

18. Anatole Chujoy, "The Ballet Arrives," *Dance*, Feb. 1940, 69.

19. Walter Terry, "Dance Comedy Presented by Ballet Theatre," *NYHT*, 20 Jan. 1940, 7.

20. John Martin, "Old Comedy Given by Ballet Theatre," *NYT*, 20 Jan. 1940, 14.

21. "Ballet Theatre Can't Compete, Wants Ballet Russe Unionized," *NYHT*, 22 Mar. 1940, 16. See also "Kirstein Blasts Open Shop," *Dance*, Mar. 1940, 8–9.

22. Pleasant, telegram to BN, 8 Mar. 1940, also his telegram of 26 Feb. 1940, 75/36, BNC.

23. BN, telegram to Pleasant, 10 Mar. 1940, 75/36, BNC.

24. "Ballet Theatre Closes," *Dance*, Mar. 1940, 9. For Ballet Theatre's financial straits, see Alex C. Ewing, *Bravura! Lucia Chase and the American Ballet Theatre* (Gainesville: University Press of Florida, 2009), 68–71, 77–78.

25. For Nijinska's classes see the advertisement in the *American Dancer*, Apr. 1940, 7. One of Lisette's friends in *Fille* was Nico's sister, Rita Charisse.

26. Isabel Morse Jones, "Nijinska Welcomed Here," *LAT*, 3 Feb. 1940, A7.

27. "1940 United States Federal Census," Ancestry Library.

28. Dorathi Bock Pierre, "Bronislava Nijinska," *American Dancer*, Apr. 1940, 39.

29. Reinhardt to BN, 11 Apr. 1940, 75/50, BNC.

30. Ruth Eleanor Howard, "Nijinska Visits America," *American Dancer*, July 1935, 8.

31. Isabel Morse Jones, "Nijinska's Ballets Win High Favor," *LAT*, 31 July 1940, A8. The program for the performance is in 16/20, BNC.

32. Albertina Vitak, "Dance Events Reviewed," *American Dancer*, Oct. 1940, 14, 24.

33. Louella Parsons, "M-G-M Plans Film Career for Ballerina Cyd Charisse," *Charleston* [WV] *Gazette*, 27 June 1948, 5. For biographical information about Charisse (born Tula Ellice Finklea in 1922), see Kassie Dixon's entry in the Handbook of Texas Online (http://www.tshaonline.org/handbook/online/articles/ffi58), published by the Texas State Historical Association.

34. Maria Tallchief, with Larry Kaplan, *Maria Tallchief: America's Prima Ballerina* (New York: Henry Holt, 1997), 16.

35. "Prima Ballerina Maria Tallchief Will Appear at Civic Center in Ballet Russe de Monte Carlo," *Independent Record* [Helena, MT], 1 Jan. 1955, 10.

36. Betty Marie Tallchief to BN, 15 June 1942, 77A/2, BNC.

37. *Maria Tallchief: America's Prima Ballerina*, 20–25.

38. For Marjorie Tallchief, see Virginia Christian, "Tallchief, Marjorie," in *International Dictionary of Ballet*, ed. Martha Bremser (1993).

39. The class lists are in 45/9–10, BNC.

40. For Nijinska's studio addresses, see the "display ads" in the *Los Angeles Times* as well as the letterhead, classified ads, and class schedules in 59/11, BNC. For Nijinska's influence as a teacher, see "New Dance Studio Ready for First of Classes to Start Monday Afternoon," *Walla Walla* [WA] *Union-Bulletin*, 9 Sept. 1945, 6; "Closeups of Ballet Company Coming Here with Mia Slavenska," *Thomasville* [GA] *Times-Enterprise*, 7 Feb. 1948, 4; "Colorful Dance Numbers to Enliven 'Bartered bride,'" *san Antonio*

Express, 26 Aug. 1951, 4; "Ballet Class Registration Set," *New Mexican* [Santa Fe, NM], 11 June 1957, 7.

41. *Maria Tallchief: America's Prima Ballerina*, 76.

42. Allegra Kent, *Allegra Kent, Once a Dancer . . .* (New York: St. Martin's Press, 1997), 29–30.

43. Ibid., 30.

44. Joel Loebenthal, "A Conversation with Robert Barnett," *BR* 41, no. 4 (Winter 2013–2014), 37. For a fuller account, see Robert Barnett, with Cynthia Crain, *On Stage at the Ballet: My Life as a Dancer and Artistic Director* (Jefferson, NC: McFarland, 2019), 37–42. Lists of the school's GI students are in 45/9, BNC.

45. "Bronislava Nijinska: Dancers Speak," 31–32.

46. Kenneth H. Marcus, "'A New Expression for a New People': Race and Ballet in Los Angeles, 1946–1956," *Journal of the West* 44, no. 2 (Spring 2005), 24–25, and a later article, "Dance Moves: An African American Ballet Company in Postwar Los Angeles," *Pacific Historical Review* 83, no. 3 (Aug. 2014), 487–527; Dawn Lille Horwitz, "The New Negro Ballet in Great Britain," in *Dancing Many Drums: Excavations in African American Dance*, ed. Thomas F. DeFrantz (Madison: University of Wisconsin Press, 2002), 317–39.

47. See, for example, the letters to Nina Sirotinine, Lena Antonova, and Henriette Pascar in the notebooks titled "1941–Letters" (61/4) and "My Letters–1942" (61/6), BNC.

48. Nina traveled with her husband Nicola, an engineer, and her daughter, Irene, a fourteen-year old student, on the SS *Aquitania*, which docked in New York on 16 Sept. 1939, "Passenger and Crew Lists, New York," Ancestry Library.

49. BN to Sirotinine, Easter [1940]. I am indebted to Natasha Tower, Nina's granddaughter, for making this and other Nijinska letters available to me, to her mother Irina (Sirotinine) Poutiatine for translating them, and to Norton Owen of Jacob's Pillow for putting Natasha in touch with me.

50. Ibid.

51. BN to Sirotinine, 30 June [1940].

52. BN to Maurice Quonian, 27 Sept. 1954, 75/46, BNC.

53. BN to Sirotinine, 30 June [1940].

54. BN to Sirotinine, 27 Dec. [1940].

55. Ibid.

56. BN to Richard Pleasant, 29 Oct. 1940, 11/997, ABT Records.

57. Gallo to W. B. McCurdy, 23 June 1941; Playbill, Original Ballet Russe, Summer Ballet Festival, 23–29 Aug. [1941]; flyer announcing the 1941–1942 transcontinental tour of the Original Ballet Russe, Gallo Papers, Box 1.

58. H. N. Glickstein to A. Walter Socolow, Esq., 7 Oct. 1941, 76A/39, BNC.

59. Sevastianov, signed contract with BN, 30 June 1941, 17/1758, ABT Records.

60. Margaret Lloyd, "Festival: The Dancer's Holiday," *CSM*, 13 Sept. 1941, 15.

61. Qtd. in Cohen and Pischl, *The American Ballet Theatre*, 23.

62. Walter Terry, "Ballet Theatre Offers Revival of 'Swan Lake,'" *NYHT*, 14 Nov. 1941, 20. The program note read: "A poet seated at a piano relives his past through his music. His muse appears to him. He recalls the village loves of his younger years, the gaiety of

his student days, his encounter with the fatal woman. He banishes that memory with the thought of his muse who reappears only to vanish again" (Ballet Theatre playbill, Constitution Hall, Washington, DC, 15 Jan. 1942, 22/2240, ABT Records).

63. John Martin, "'Beloved' Dance[d] Here First Time," *NYT*, 14 Nov. 1941, 29.

64. "Ballet Theatre to Open 3d N.Y. Season Nov. 12," *NYHT*, 4 Nov. 1941, 18. In 1942 the title of *Fille* was changed yet again, this time becoming *Naughty Lisette*.

65. Walter Terry, "The Ballet," *NYHT*, 16 Nov. 1941, 45.

66. Baronova, *Irina*, 331–32.

67. Rosella Hightower, interviewed by Elizabeth Kendall, 1975, 50, *MGZMT 3-1516, NYPL.

68. Agreement between BN and Virginia Lee (of Ballet Arts and Nimura Studio), 30 Oct. 1941, 46/10, BNC.

69. Ann Whelan, "Madame Nijinsky, Sister of World Famous Vaslav Nijinsky, Visits Friends in Newtown," *Bridgeport Sunday Post*, 19 Apr. 1942, 5. For Andrew Poe (Andrey Pojarsky), as Singaevsky's brother-in-law anglicized his name, see the 1940 census and World War II Draft Registration Card, Ancestry Library. The Russian typescript is in 56/1, the English translation in 48/4–5, BNC.

70. Didier to NS, 31 Oct. and 29 Dec. 1941; BN, letter agreement with Union Associated Publishers, 21 Jan. 1942, and letter to Didier, 12 Feb. 1942, 77A/26, BNC. In the February letter Nijinska uses the title *Diary of a Young Dancer*, which is what I have used as well.

71. Qtd. in "Festival to Depict Dance in America," *NYT*, 11 Mar. 1942, 22. See also "Dance Notes," *NYHT*, 15 Mar. 1942, F10; Walter Terry, "American Festival," *NYHT*, 5 Apr. 1942, E10; "The Dance: Festival Pan," *NYT*, 21 June 1942, X8.

72. "A Great American Dance Festival and University of the Dance," Jacob's Pillow Dance Festival, Summer of 1942, Ted Shawn's Scrapbook, 1942–1954, JPA. Shawn's scrapbook also includes programs for the season's performances.

73. Shawn's letters to Mumaw are at JPA.

74. Nijinska had invited Youshkevitch to reprise her role in *Chopin Concerto* at the Hollywood Bowl. However, the telegram only reached her in the south of France after the Bowl performance had taken place. Nonetheless, on the strength of this telegram, Youshkevitch and her mother received visas from the American consul in Marseilles, which undoubtedly saved their lives, as both were Jewish. Robert Johnson, email to the author, 17 Aug. 2020. The telegram remains in Johnson's collection.

75. Nina Youshkevitch, reminiscence submitted by Robert Johnson on behalf of his mother, 1997, JPA.

76. Ann Hutchinson Guest, email to the author, 9 Apr. 2014.

77. Although Irina (who was nicknamed Bibi) had studied with well-known Russian teachers both in Paris and New York, she never pursued a professional stage career but, instead, enrolled at Radcliffe College and in 1947 married Prince Dimitry Poutiatine. In the 1950s, Bibi began teaching at the Glen Cove, Long Island, studio founded by her maternal aunt Vera (née Lipskaia) and her husband Serge Vladimiroff (Natalia Tower, email to the author, 17 Apr. 2014). Like her sister, Vera had studied with Nijinska at the School of Movement, and with her husband danced in Nijinska's companies in the 1930s.

78. Denham, letter-contract with BN, 11 Sept. 1942, 48/1941. Nijinska later estimated that she had sold the costumes for $40 apiece (BN to Maurice Quonian, 27 Sept. 1954, 75/46, BNC).
79. BN to Denham, 27 July 1942, Denham Records, Folder 1941.
80. BN, letter-contract with Denham, 10 June 1942, and Denham to BN, 16 July 1942, Denham Records, Folder 1941.
81. John Martin, "The Dance: Ballet No. 2," *NYT*, 11 Oct. 1942, X8.
82. Robert Lawrence, "The Ballet," *NYHT*, 13 Oct. 1942, 18.
83. John Martin, "Season Is Opened by Ballet Russe," *NYT*, 13 Oct. 1942, 18.
84. John Martin, "The Dance," *NYT*, 20 Oct. 1942, 24.
85. Edwin Denby, "With the Dancers," *Modern Music* 20, no. 1 (Nov.–Dec. 1942), 54.
86. Isabel Morse Jones, "'Rodeo' Hit of Opening Ballet Night," *LAT*, 28 Nov. 1942, A7; Cassidy, "Chopin Concerto Ballet"; Martin, "The Dance."
87. For Pavlova and Mordkin, see Claudia Cassidy, "Nijinska's 'Snow Maiden' Ballet Is a Refreshing Piece of Work," *CDT*, 29 Dec. 1942, 14, and Margaret Lloyd, "Monte Carlo Troupe Sets New Record," *CSM*, 23 Feb. 1943, 5. Denham approached Nijinska about choreographing the ballet in May 1942, introduced her to Boris Aronson, and worked out a formal agreement within a month. See Denham, letters to Bronislava Nijinska, 27 May and 8 June 1942; and Bronislava Nijinska, letter-contract to Denham, 10 June 1942, Denham Records, Folder 1941, NYPL.
88. Martin, "Season Is Opened by Ballet Russe."
89. John Martin, "The Dance: A New Period?" *NYT*, 1 Nov. 1942, X5.
90. Lloyd, "Monte Carlo Troupe."
91. Cassidy, "Nijinska's 'Snow Maiden' Ballet." For the set and a number of costumes, see the 1942–1943 Ballet Russe de Monte Carlo souvenir program. Additional designs are reproduced in Frank Rich, with Lisa Aronson, *The Theatre Art of Boris Aronson* (New York: Knopf, 1987), 80. Performance photographs by Fred Fehl are in 43/13, Aronson Papers.
92. BN, notes in Russian about *The Snow Maiden*, with an English translation, 43/13, Aronson Papers.
93. John Martin, "The Dance: A New Period?" *NYT*, 1 Nov. 1942, X5.
94. John Martin, "The Dance: Events Ahead," *NYT*, 27 Sept. 1942, X8. See also John Martin, "The Dance: Ballet Plans," *NYT*, 28 June 1942, X8.
95. John Martin, "The Dance: More Ballet," *NYT*, 18 Oct. 1942, X5.
96. Agnes de Mille, *Dance to the Piper* (Boston: Little, Brown, 1951), chap. 25.
97. Isabel Morse Jones, "Ballet Russe Has Spotlight for the Week," *LAT*, 29 Nov. 1942, C6.
98. "Dance Notes," *NYHT*, 15 Nov. 1942, 102.
99. Qtd. in Jack Anderson, *The One and Only: The Ballet Russe de Monte Carlo* (New York: Dance Horizons, 1981), 78.
100. NS to Helscher, 27 Jan. 1943, 2/10, Helscher Papers.
101. Shawn to Helscher, 22 Mar. 1943, 10/15, Helscher Papers.
102. NS to Helscher, 16 Apr. 1943, 2/10, Helscher Papers.
103. Denham to BN, 28 May 1943, Denham Records, Folder 1942; BN, draft-letter to Denham, undated [June 1943], 71/53, BNC. For the back-and-forth over the

contract, see also NS to Denham, 28 June 1943; Denham to BN, 12 July 1943, and to NS, 22 July 1943, Denham Records, Folder 1943.

104. Denham to BN, 19 July 1943, Denham Records, Folder 1943. For the signed agreement, see Denham, letter-contract to BN, 22 Sept. 1943, Denham Records, Folder 1943.

105. John Martin, "The Dance," *NYT*, 20 Oct. 1942, 24.

106. Claudia Cassidy, "Something Old, Something New Is Good Ballet!" *CDT*, 17 Oct. 1943, 27.

107. Ann Barzel, "Ballet Russe de Monte Carlo, Civic Opera House, Chicago, Oct. 15," *Dance News*, Nov. 1943, 3.

108. Anderson, *The One and Only*, 89.

109. Edwin Denby, "The Ballet," *NYHT*, 11 Apr. 1944, 14A.

110. John Martin, "3 New Ballets Presented Here," *NYT*, 11 Apr. 1944, 17. Doris Humphrey's all-Bach program the previous year prompted Martin to write, "Of all musicians, Bach is the least suitable for theatrical presentation. . . . His unique musical completeness makes him likewise unsuitable for dancing of any kind (Nijinska and Balanchine to the contrary notwithstanding), and especially for the so-called modern dance" ("The Dance: Back to Bach," *NYT*, 17 Jan. 1943, X5).

111. Martin, "3 New Ballets"; Martin, "The Dance: A Flock of Premieres," *NYT*, 16 Apr. 1944, X8.

112. Mary Ellen Moylan, interviewed by Doris Hering, 1979, *MGZTC 3-591, NYPL.

113. Margaret Lloyd, "Nijinska's 'Ancient Russia' in First Boston Performance," *CSM*, 10 Mar. 1944, 4.

114. Ann Barzel, "Ballet Season in Review," *Dance News*, Dec. 1943, 3.

115. BN and Singaevsky's correspondence with Denham is in 70/14, 71/53–54, and 78/7, BNC.

116. Bradley's letters to Nijinska are in 70/45, BNC.

117. Ballet Repertory Company, playbill, June 13–15, 1944, Anderson Playbill Collection, Loyola University Chicago, Archives & Special Collections. I am grateful to Sergey Konaev for sharing this with me.

118. Claudia Cassidy, "Chicago Ballet Company Plans Winter Season Here," *CDT*, 5 Sept. 1943, E3.

119. Claudia Cassidy, "Much Promise Shown in Debut of Ballet Group," *CDT*, 30 Nov. 1943, 16. For Mitruk, see Cassidy, "On the Aisle," *CDT*, 14 Nov. 1943, D3.

120. Qtd. in Lucy Key Miller, "Front Views & Profiles," *CDT*, 9 Oct. 1957, B10.

121. Claudia Cassidy, "On the Aisle," *CDT*, 18 June 1944, E3; Lloyd, "Nijinska's 'Ancient Russia' in First Boston Performance."

122. "N. Y. May Have Ballet Repertory," *Dance News*, Oct. 1943, 3. Like Ballet Society (which Balanchine formed with Lincoln Kirstein in 1946), the company was to be on a "non-profit–making basis" and emphasize "freedom of expression and experimentation."

123. See Anderson, *The One and Only*, 90–91, 290–94; John Martin, "The Dance: Ballet de Norway," *NYT*, 3 Sept. 1944, X4; NS to Denham, 1 Mar. 1944, Denham Records, Folder 1944.

124. Agnes de Mille, "The Marquis de Cuevas," *Portrait Gallery* (Boston: Houghton Mifflin, 1990), 110–21.

125. Libidins to BN, 21 Mar. 1944, 74/20, BNC. Nijinska's contract with Libidins, dated October 4, 1943, is in the same folder.

126. Dalí to "Très cher ami," 1943, International Autograph Auctions, Bidspirit Auction, 15 Oct. 2016, Lot 791. For a copy of the letter, see https://ru.bidspirit.com/ui/lotPage/source/search/auction/1552/lot/110992/DALI-SALVADOR-1904-1989-Spanish?lang=en.

127. De Cuevas to Dalí, 22 May 1944, no. 2272, CED.

128. "Salvadore [*sic*] Dali Labeled Real Realist Surrealist," *LAT,* 20 June 1944, A1.

129. De Cuevas to Dalí, 5 July 1944, no. 2233, CED.

130. BN, unsigned contract with Ballet International Incorporated, 15 July 1944, 46/10, BNC.

131. De Cuevas to Salvador and Gala Dalí, 18 July 1944, no. 2222, CED.

132. Ibid.

133. See, for example, "New York Ballet in Fall Planned by De Cuevas," *NYHT*, 20 June 1944, 15; "Ballet Institute Will Open in the Fall," *NYT*, 20 June 1944, 16; Claudia Cassidy, "On the Aisle," *CDT*, 21 June 1944, 19; "New Institute Opens Season in September," *CSM*, 22 June 1944, 4; John Martin, "The Dance: Another Ballet," *NYT*, 23 July 1944, X4; "2 Ballet Groups Announce Plans," *NYT*, 19 Sept. 1944, 26; John Martin, "The Dance: A Deluge of Ballets," *NYT*, 22 Oct. 1944, X4.

134. Joel Lobenthal, *Wilde Times: Patricia Wilde, George Balanchine, and the Rise of New York City Ballet* (Lebanon, NH: ForeEdge, 2016), 37.

135. Ibid.

136. Francisco Monción, interviewed by Peter Conway, 1979, 62–63, *MGZMT 5-959, NYPL. Dollar's ballet, which premiered at the Metropolitan Opera in 1936, was called *Concerto*, then, in 1937, *Classic Ballet*. See Nancy Reynolds, *Repertory in Review*, introd. Lincoln Kirstein (New York: Dial Press, 77), 44.

137. Lucile Marsh, "Ballet International Opens First Season," *DM*, Dec. 1944, 18.

138. Rehearsal schedules, 16–24 Oct., 1/7, Ballet International Records. For Ballet International's Standard Artists' Agreement (Dancers), see Ballet Institute Incorporated and Sergei Ismailoff, 27 Sept. 1944, Folder 5, Ismailoff Papers.

139. Monción, interviewed by Conway, 61.

140. See, for instance, Halsman's photographs of William Dollar and Marie-Jeanne in *Cue*, 28 Oct. 1944, 11; Helen Constantine and John Guelis in "Rehearsing for 'Brahms Variations,'" *NYT*, 29 Oct. 1944, X4; and Nijinska rehearsing André Eglevsky and Viola Essen, *Vogue*, 15 Nov. 1944, 90. See also "Historical Event," *New York Journal-American*, 30 Oct. 1944, 11; Morris Warman, "Ballet International Moves Rehearsals into Its Own Theater," *NYHT*, 21 Oct. 1944, 8A; "Mme. Nijinska and Dalí," *NYHT*, 29 Oct. 1944, C2.

141. "Two Premieres Open the Ballet International," *NYHT*, 31 Oct. 1944, 17A.

142. "International Ballet Debut in New York," *CSM*, 1 Nov. 1944, 4.

143. Apparently, the Marquis had sent bouquets not only to the principals but also to every female member of the corps de ballet ("Ballet International Bows to New York," *Dance News*, Nov. 1944, 1).

144. John Martin, "New Ballet Group Makes World Bow," *NYT*, 31 Oct. 1944, 23; Anatole Chujoy, "Ballet Season in Review," *Dance News*, Nov. 1944, 4. Marcel Vertès was a Hungarian-born artist and illustrator who had designed Fokine's *Bluebeard* (1941) and *Helen of Troy* (1942).

145. See Dawn Lille Horwitz, "Michel Fokine in America, 1919–1942," Ph.D. diss., New York University, 1982. For other versions, see Nancy Brooks Schmitz, "A Profile of Catherine Littlefield, A Pioneer of American Ballet," Ed.D. diss., Temple University, 1986; Ruth Page, *Page by Page*, ed. Andrew Mark Wentink (New York: Dance Horizons, 1978); Stuart Palmer, "The Month in New York," *DT*, May 1934, 125–26; "War Relief Show Attended by 6,200," *NYT*, 22 Feb. 1941, 10; R. P., "Adler, Paul Draper Invade Carnegie Hall," *NYT*, 29 Dec. 1941, 21.

146. John Martin, " 'Memories' Danced at International," *NYT*, 2 Nov. 1944, 23.

147. Marsh, "Ballet International," 20.

148. Edwin Denby, "The Ballet," *NYHT*, 3 Nov. 1944, 15. Born in Tbilisi to an Armenian family that emigrated after the Russian Revolution, Mamoulian became a major American stage and film director. His Broadway credits include *Porgy and Bess* (1935), *Oklahoma!* (1943), and *Carousel* (1945).

149. Program, Ballet International, 30 Oct. 1944, 1/17, BNC.

150. Harriet Johnson, "Ballet International Gets Dalí to Give Its Opening That Touch!" *New York Post*, 31 Oct. 1944, 22.

151. Arthur V. Berger, "New Ballet Group Has Its Premiere," *New York Sun*, 31 Oct. 1944, 20.

152. John Martin, "New Ballet Group Makes World Bow," *NYT*, 31 Oct. 1944, 23.

153. Anatole Chujoy, "Ballet Season in Review," *Dance News*, Nov. 1944, 4.

154. Edwin Denby, "The Ballet," *NYHT*, 31 Oct. 1944, 17A.

155. Marsh, "Ballet International Opens First Season," 20.

156. John Martin, "New Ballet Given by International," *NYT*, 4 Nov. 1944, 18.

157. Ibid.

158. Edwin Denby, "The Ballet: Mechanized Farm," *NYHT*, 4 Nov. 1944, 9A. For "pseudo-Soviet ballet," see Denby, "Soviet Dance Critic on the Aim of Ballet," *NYHT*, 19 Nov. 1944, C2.

159. Edwin Denby, "The Dance: Dancer as Propagandist," *NYHT*, 5 Oct. 1944, 15A.

160. Denby, "Soviet Dance Critic on the Aim of Ballet," Denby quotes long passages from the condensed translation of Slonimsky's article ("Perspectives of the Soviet Ballet") published in *Dance News*, Sept. 1944, 5, 7. Denby's article appeared two weeks after his damning review of *Pictures*.

161. Edwin Denby, "The Ballet: 'Le Bourgeois' Transformed," *NYHT*, 26 Sept. 1944, 14.

162. Elizabeth Savage, "Ballet: International's 2nd Week," *Cue*, 25 Nov. 1944, 17.

163. Marsh, "Ballet International Opens First Season," 18.

164. John Martin, "Ballet Premiere of 'Harvest Time,'" *NYT*, 6 Apr. 1945, 20.

165. Ibid.

166. Edwin Denby, "The Ballet," *NYHT*, 6 Apr. 1945, 13B.

167. Edwin Denby, "The Ballet: Sh! A Little Mistake," *NYHT*, 21 Apr. 1945, 8A.

168. Frank S. Adams, "Wild Crowds Greet News in City While Others Pray," *NYT*, 8 May 1945, 1. Allied troops had entered Paris on August 26, 1944, more than seven months before hostilities in Europe ended. The Pacific War ended August 15, 1945.

169. "Ballet Theatre Presents 'Giselle' at Metropolitan," *NYHT*, 14 Apr. 1945, 11A.

170. BN, letter to Valentina Denham, 5 May 1945, Denham Records, Folder 1945. Nijinska had left the house in the care of an old family friend, Maria Prianishnikova. However, she had allowed Nina's sister, Vera, and her husband Serge Vladimiroff to live there.

171. "Balety B. Nikzhinskoi," *Russkie novosti*, 21 Dec. 1945, 7.

172. Kyra Nijinsky to BN, 12 Mar. 1946, 79/7; Kirsta to BN, 18 Jan. 1946, 73/22, BNC.

173. Crémer to BN, 19 July 1945, 71A/34, BNC.

174. NS to Ismailoff, 30 Jan. 1946, Folder 3, Ismailoff Papers.

175. BN, "Certificado de Turista," issued by the Ministerio de Agricultura, Dirección de inmigración, 4 Apr. 1946; NS, "Visacion 'en tránsito,'" issued by the Consulate General of Chile in Los Angeles, 12 Mar. 1946, 46/1, BNC.

176. For Wallmann's self-aggrandizing and not entirely accurate memoirs, see Margarita Wallmann, *Les Balcons du ciel*, pref. Bernard Gavorty (Paris: Editions Robert Laffont, 1976).

177. *La ciudad de las puertas de oro* had a libretto by Arturo Capdevila and music by Constantino Gaito; *El Pillán*, a libretto by Carlos Enrique Castelli and music by Alfredo Pinto. The libretti, along with a list of unproduced ballets, are in 61/9, BNC. A full set of programs for the 1946 season is in the Library of the Teatro Colón.

178. She arrived in New York on August 9, 1946, after a stopover in Puerto Rico, Ancestry Library.

179. For changes at the Teatro Colón in this period, see María Eugenia Cadús, "La danza escénica en el primer peronismo (1946–1955): Un acercamiento entre la danza y las políticas de Estado," Ph.D. thesis, Facultad de Filosofía y Letras, Universidad de Buenos Aires en Artes.

180. Harlow Robinson, *The Last Impresario: The Life, Times, and Legacy of Sol Hurok* (New York: Viking, 1994), 299–301; Sorley Walker, *De Basil's Ballets Russes*, 139–41; García-Márquez, *The Ballets Russes*, 298.

181. John Martin, "The Dance: Ballets et al," *NYT*, 22 Sept. 1946, X2.

182. BN to de Basil, 9 Feb. 1947, 71/48, BNC; "Ballet Russe Season Will Open Feb. 7," *LAT*, 19 Jan. 1947, B5; "Ballet Russe Auditions Held Here," *LAT*, Feb. 1947, A1.

183. John Martin, "Nijinska Stages Own Ballet Here," *NYT*, 26 Mar. 1947, 31.

184. Ibid.

185. Letter-contract between BN, Markova, and Dolin, signed in New York City on 2 Apr. 1947, 72/12, BNC; John Martin, "The Dance: Novelties," *NYT*, 6 Apr. 1947, X12; Martin, "The Dance: Return," *NYT*, 28 Sept. 1947, X8.

186. Walter Terry, "The Ballet," *NYHT*, 18 Oct. 1947, 8.

187. John Martin, "The Dance: Notes," *NYT*, 10 Aug. 1947, X5.

188. BN, draft letter to Kirsta, undated, 73/22, BNC.

Chapter 15

1. NS to Ismailoff, 21 May 1947, Ismailoff Papers, Folder 3. For background on the company, see Clement Crisp, "Le Grand Ballet du Marquis de Cuevas," *DR* 23, no. 1 (Summer 2005), 1–17; Irène Lidova, "Grand Ballet du Marquis de Cuevas," *IED*, and "De Cuevas, Marquis George," *International Dictionary of Ballet*, ed. Martha Bremser (1993); G[ermaine] P[rudhommeau] and N[athalie] L[ecomte], "Cuevas, marquis George de," and N[athalie] L[ecomte], "Monte-Carlo (Ballets de)," *Larousse Dictionnaire de la Danse*, ed. Philippe Le Moal (Paris: Larousse/Bordas, 1999). For the company's debut in Vichy, see Irène Lidova, "Un Grand Mécène," *Saisons de la Danse*, Feb. 1981, 36, and for an interview with the Marquis, see Jean Montigny, "Hôtes éminents de Paris: le Marquis de Cuevas conquistador de la danse," *Revue des Deux Mondes*, 15 Sept. 1954, 219–32. See also Pierre Daguerre, *Le Marquis de Cuevas* (Paris: Editions Denoël, 1954); Joaquín Edwards Bello, *El marqués de Cuevas y su tiempo*, prologue by Alfonso Calderón (Santiago de Chile: Editorial Nascimento, 1974); Gérard Mannoni, *Le Marquis de Cuevas* (Paris: J. C. Lattès, 2003); and Francisca Antonia Sofía Folch-Couyoumdjian, "The Marquis de Cuevas: Pushing the Boundaries of Self," Ph.D. diss., University of Texas at Austin, 2014.
2. De Cuevas's letters and telegrams to BN are in 71A/37, BNC.
3. Nijinska's first contract, dated July 8, 1947, stipulated that she would be paid a total of $7,000 for restaging *Brahms Variations*, *Les Biches*, and *Pictures at an Exhibition* in addition to choreographing a new ballet to music by Khachaturian during the period commencing July 16, 1947, and ending on or about September 15, 1947, and that if the contract was extended, she would receive an additional $300 per week. Nijinska never choreographed the Khachaturian ballet. De Cuevas, letter-contract with BN, 8 July 1947, 51/11, BNC.
4. For the "Golden Parisian," see Display Ad 8, *NYHT*, 20 Nov. 1953, 9; Beach Conger, "Travel Topics," *NYHT*, 22 Nov. 1953, D18; Paul J. C. Friedlander, "De Luxe Sleeper Plane to Europe," 29 Nov. 1953, X21; Clementine Paddleford, "Luxury Flying Hotel a French World," *NYHT*, 5 June 1954, 11. For Nijinska's flight on 30 July 1954, "U.S. Departing Passenger and Crew Lists, 1914–1966," Ancestry Library; and Helen Murphy, letter to BN, 6 July 1954, 75/14, BNC. Murphy was a New York employee of the Ballet Institute of which the company was a "project."
5. Singaevsky became a US citizen in Los Angeles on November 13, 1949. The name change—from Nicolas Singaevsky to Nicolas Singaevsky Nijinska—was recorded on his naturalization record. See U.S. Naturalization Record Indexes, 1792–1992, California, Ancestry Library. Nicolas Nijinska (or a variant thereof) is how he appears on various travel documents thereafter and in the Social Security Death Index.
6. Lili Cockerille Livingston, *American Indian Ballerinas* (Norman/London: University of Oklahoma Press, 1997), 152.
7. See the 1953–1954, 1954–1955 season souvenir programs and the 1960 souvenir program from the Teatro Municipal de Caracas, 2/3, 8. The Biblioteca Teatro Colón has a complete run of playbills for the company's 1960 season in Buenos Aires. For one of Lidova's many reminiscences of BN and the company, see "Un Grand Mécène," 38.

8. For background on both Hightower and Marjorie Tallchief, see Livingston, *American Indian Ballerinas*.

9. Ibid., 138.

10. Hightower, interviewed by Kendall, 48–49.

11. Ibid., 51–52.

12. Ibid., 54.

13. Ibid.

14. Ibid., 55–56.

15. Ibid., 58–59.

16. Ibid., 61–62.

17. The photograph was published on the cover of the December 1947 issue of the *Dancing Times*.

18. Peter Anastos, "A Conversation with George Skibine," *BR* 10, no. 1 (Spring 1982), 88–89.

19. *Intransigeant*, 8 Nov. 1947 (courtesy of Sue Lonoff de Cuevas). For the dates of performances, see "Programmes," *Combat*, 7 Nov. 1947, 3, and the box advertisement in the same newspaper on 19 Nov. 1947, 2.

20. Maurice Brillant, "'Les Biches' aux Ballets de Monte-Carlo," *Epoque*, 19 Nov. 1947, 2.

21. Lidova, "Un Grand Mécène," 36.

22. Irène Lidova, *Ma Vie avec la danse* (Paris: Editions Plume, 1992), 71.

23. Irina ("Irene K. Nijinska") married Gibbs S. Raetz on February 19, 1946. According to his World War II draft card registration, Raetz was born in Cozad, Nebraska, on December 10, 1919. George Leonard Raetz was born on August 22, 1947; Natalie Iola Raetz on April 10, 1950. Natalie died on December 23, 2011. See Ancestry Library.

24. BN to Denham, 24 Sept. 1948. See also Nijinska's letters to Denham and his wife, Valentina Denham, 5 Sept. 1948, Denham Records, Folder 1945.

25. BN to Denham, 3 Sept. 1945, Denham Records, Folder 1945. Nijinska's lemon grove was actually a seven-acre ranch located at 16412 Chastwick Drive in San Fernando, a city in the northwestern region of Los Angeles County. Purchased in December 1943 for $6,120, the ranch was sold in 1951 for $16,083.95. Bronislava Nijinska and Nicholas Singaevsky, Statements of Income and Expenses, 1940–70, 45/12, BNC.

26. BN to Denham, 4 Aug. 1947, Denham Records, Folder 1945.

27. Ibid. Nijinska was writing from Vichy.

28. Victor-Michel Sager, "Mme Nijinska crée les 'Variations' de Brahms," *Revue de la Danse*, 15 Mar. 1948, n.p.

29. BN to S. J. and Valentina Denham, 5 Sept. 1948. Denham Records, Folder 1945.

30. Martin Cooper, "Ballet," *Spectator*, 1 July 1949, 13.

31. BN to Denham, 5 July 1949, Denham Records, Folder 1946.

32. Crémer to BN, 13 July 1945, 71A/34, BNC.

33. Crémer to NS, 13 Dec. 1949, 71A/34, BNC.

34. Crémer to NS, 6 Apr. 1950, 71A/34, BNC.

35. Crémer to NS, 23 Dec. 1950, 71A/34, BNC.

36. Crémer to NS, 12 May 1951, 71A/34, BNC.

37. Crémer to NS, 3 July 1953; Djabadary to Crémer, 16 July 1953, 71A/34, BNC.

38. Lucienne Frochot to BN, 15 June 1955, 72/27, BNC.

39. Crémer to NS, 28 Dec. 1956, 71A/34, BNC.

40. "Newscast Gives Sister Word of Dancer Death," *LAT*, 9 Apr. 1950, 10.

41. For a detailed description of the funeral, see Cyril Beaumont, "The Funeral of Vaslav Nijinsky," and his appreciation, "Garland for Nijinsky—Artist and Dancer," in *Ballet Annual 1951*, ed. Arnold Haskell (London: Adam and Charles Black, 1951), 106–8 and 47–51, respectively. Among the mourners was the now ninety-year-old Faustin Zenon, who had helped finance Nijinska's Theatre Choréographique.

42. Dolin to BN, 30 June 1950, 72/12, BNC.

43. RN to Bolm, 15 Aug. 1950, Box 1, Bolm Papers.

44. BN to Denham, 12 June 1951, Denham Papers, Folder 1946. Denham's original letter of 1 June 1951 is in 78/7, BNC.

45. For the school, see Chase to BN, 11 Aug. 1951, 71A/14, BNC; John Onysko, letter of agreement with BN, 16 Aug. 1951; for *Schumann Concerto*, letter-contract between Chase and BN, 24 Aug. 1951, 71A/14, BNC; for *Princess Aurora*, letter to BN, 27 Aug. 1951, 11/997, American Ballet Theatre Records (hereafter ABT Records), NYPL. Although Onysko's letter mentions only teaching, Nijinska was actually heading the newly organized Ballet Theatre School. See "Ballet Season Opens Here," *NYHT*, 2 Sept. 1951, D6; "Ballet Theatre Repertory," *NYT*, 9 Sept. 1951, X10; "The Ballet Theatre School," classified ad, *NYHT*, 16 Sept. 1951, D8.

46. Schollar to BN, 14 Aug. 1951, 76A/27, BNC.

47. Gloria B. Strauss, "Craske, Margaret," *IED*; Jennifer Dunning, "Margaret Craske Is Dead at 97; Directed Met Opera Ballet School," *NYT*, 23 Feb. 1990, B5.

48. BN, notebook entry, 8 June 1950, 69/26, BNC.

49. John Martin, "Nijinska's Ballet in Premiere Here," *NYT*, 28 Sept. 1951, 26.

50. Walter Terry, "The Ballet," *NYHT*, 28 Sept. 1951, 17.

51. Ibid.

52. John Martin, "Ballet Theatre Presents 'Princess Aurora,' with Alicia Alonso Dancing the Title Role," *NYT*, 22 Sept. 1951, 9.

53. The lot, identified for tax purposes, as located at "222 Riverdale on Hudson, New York," was purchased in 1951 for $5,650 and sold in 1955 for $6,500 ("Statement of Income & Expenses for the Year of 1955," 45/12, BNC).

54. Richard Holden, email to the author, 17 Apr. 2013.

55. Ibid.

56. Onysko to BN, 30 Nov. 1951, 75/12, BNC. Romola Nijinska, in a letter to Margaret Powers, wrote that Nijinska had resigned from the Ballet Theatre School "because she could not get along with the other teachers and the gossip says 'she pushed a girl during the lesson, the girl fell loosing [sic] her balance,' the girl and parents sued 'the Ballet Theatre' for damages, there was quite a scandal." Romola's letter, dated 25 Jan. 1952, is in the Stiftung John Neumeier, no. 24437.

57. De Cuevas to BN, 8 Aug. 1952, 71A/37, BNC. For *Petrouchka* being one of the Marquise's favorite ballets, see Gérard Mannoni, *Le Marquis de Cuevas* (Paris: J. C. Lattès, 2003), 34.

58. De Cuevas to BN, 8 Sept. 1952, 71A/37, BNC.

59. De Cuevas to BN, 1 Oct. 1952, 71A/37, BNC.

60. In Paris the Fokine repertory was less well known than in London.

61. Mary Clarke, "Poet of the Dance," *Guardian*, 5 Aug. 1998, 12. See also "A l'Empire, Serge Golovine et ses frère et soeur dansent en famille," *Elle*, Apr. 1951, Marquis de Cuevas Company File (hereafter "De Cuevas Company File"), 1951, V&A.

62. Coquelle to BN, (postmarked) 25 Oct. 1952, 71A/30, BNC.

63. "Triomphe slave," unidentified clipping, Nov. 1952, De Cuevas Company File, 1952.

64. Olivier Merlin, "'Petrouchka' aux ballets Cuevas," *Monde*, 7 Nov. 1952, 11.

65. Marie A. Levinson, "Le Grand Ballet de Cuevas, ou La rencontre providentielle Nijinska-Golovine-de Cuevas," *Pour la Danse*, Dec. 1952, n.p.

66. Marie A. Levinson, "Au Grand Ballet de Cuevas: deuxième miracle Nijinska," *Pour la Danse*, Jan. 1953, n.p.

67. Hightower, interviewed by Kendall, 65, 67. "Rosella remains the Goddess of the dance," de Cuevas wrote to Nijinska on 21 Nov. 1952, 71A/37, BNC.

68. André Eglevsky, interviewed by Lillie Rosen, 1975, 45–46, 49, *MGZMT 5-961, NYPL.

69. De Cuevas, letter-contract with BN, 10 Jan. 1953, 71A/37, BNC.

70. The following account draws on material in 26/1, BNC, as well as in the De Cuevas Company File, 1953. Nijinska's invitation is in 51/13, BNC.

71. "2,000 at Marquis' Party," *NYT*, 2 Sept. 1953, 5; "18th Century Is Recreated at Marquis' $100,000 Ball," *NYHT*, 2 Sept. 1953, 1; Folch-Couyoumdjian, "The Marquis de Cuevas," 202; "Rome Denounces De Cuevas' Party," *NYHT*, 3 Sept. 1953, 9; "Cardinal Attacks Biarritz Ball as One of 'Revolting Lavishness,'" *Hartford Courant*, 21 Sept. 1953, 5.

72. See, in particular, Nicole Hirsch's review, "Des grognards, au bonnet à poil ont reçu les invités des ballets de Cuevas au Théâtre de l'Empire," *France-Soir*, [n.d.], and other clippings in De Cuevas Company File, 1953. *L'Ange Gris* had music by Debussy (Suite Bergamasque), choreography by George Skibine, and a scenario by the Marquis. It was conceived as a vehicle for Golovine and the Australian dancer Kathleen Gorham.

73. Olivier Merlin, "La 'première' des ballets Cuevas," *Monde*, 31 Oct. 1953, 8.

74. Dinah Maggie, "Avec le 'Grand Ballet du Marquis de Cuevas': Brillant(s) spectacle(s) de rentrée," *Combat*, [30?] Oct. 1953, De Cuevas Company File, 1953.

75. For the accusation of effeminacy, see Jacques de Rancourt, "Le Festival de Bordeaux a commencé par la danse," unidentified clipping, [May 1953], and especially "Chef-d'oeuvre et grimaces," *Express*, unidentified clipping [Oct. 1953]; for Taras, "Le Ballet s'agite," *Aurore*, unidentified clipping [fall 1953], De Cuevas Company File, 1953.

76. Maure to BN, 5 Feb. 1951, 77B/27, BNC. See also Dolores Starr's letters to BN in 77B/26, BNC.

77. Clement to BN, 15 Feb. 1951, 77B/27, BNC.

78. Maure to BN, 16 Mar. 1951, 77B/27, BNC.

79. Levinson, "Le Grand Ballet de Cuevas."

80. Taina Elg, interviewed by Rachel Straus, 11 Mar. 1992. Elg danced with the Cuevas company in the late 1940s and early 1950s and later studied with Nijinska in California.

81. Marie A. Levinson, "Rentrée du Grand Ballet de Cuevas," *Toute la Danse*, Dec. 1953, n.p.

82. Ibid. Levinson thought the company looked exhausted, especially Marjorie Tallchief, who also looked extremely thin (although all the de Cuevas dancers seemed to be losing weight).

83. De Cuevas to BN, 21 Nov. 1952, 71A/37, BNC.

84. George Zoritch, *Ballet Mystique: Behind the Glamour of the Ballet Russe*, introd. Vladimir Vasiliev, ed. Renée Renouf (Mountain View, CA: Cynara Editions, 2000), 148.

85. Ibid., 149.

86. Mannoni, *Le Marquis de Cuevas*, 174.

87. Alejandrina Escudero, *Felipe Segura: una vida en la danza* (Mexico City: Instituto Nacional de Bellas Artes y Literatura, 1995), 119. The fact that Zoritch had not only attended Irina's wedding in 1946 but also held one of the golden crowns over the married couple makes his behavior especially grievous. For a photograph of him at Irina's wedding, see Robert Johnson, "Irina Nijinska (1913–1991)," *BR* 20, no. 1 (Spring 1992), 33.

88. Katcharoff to BN, 10 Mar. 1954, 73/18, BNC. See also Katcharoff's letters of 29 Oct. and 17 Nov. 1953.

89. Katcharoff to BN, 30 June 1954, 3/18, BNC.

90. De Cuevas, cable to BN, 22 Dec. 1953, 71A/37, BNC.

91. De Cuevas, cable to BN, 2 Feb. 1954, 71A/37, BNC.

92. De Cuevas to BN, 17 Feb. 1954, 71A/37, BNC.

93. De Cuevas, letter-contract with BN, 3 Mar. 1954, 71A/37, BNC.

94. Anastos, "A Conversation with George Skibine," 87.

95. Michael Meylac, *Behind the Scenes at the Ballets Russes: Stories from a Silver Age*, trans. Rosanna Kelly (London/New York: I. B. Taurus, 2018), 250. Although Nijinska's hearing was clearly impaired, she used an Acousticon Hearing Aid beginning in 1947. Deductions for its purchase and repairs are indicated on her tax returns (45/12, BNC).

96. Carlos Carvajal, interview with the author, New York City, 8 Apr. 2015.

97. Anastos, "A Conversation with George Skibine," 90.

98. Françoise Reiss, *Sur la Pointe des pieds: Annales chorégraphiques* (Paris: Editions Lieutier, 1953), 163.

99. "Nijinsky à Paris," *Pour la Danse*, July 1953, n.p. Among the photographs accompanying the article is one of Nijinska.

100. Reiss to BN, 14 June 1953, 75/51, BNC.

101. Reiss, "Bronislava Nijinska," *Sur la Pointe des pieds*, 63. For the School of Movement, see pages 63 and 69.

102. Ibid., 63.

103. Reiss to BN, 14 June 1953, 75/51, BNC.

104. Reiss to BN, 26 July 1954, 75/51, BNC. Nijinska's doubts about the diary's authenticity were vindicated by the publication of the unexpurgated text in the 1990s.

105. Ibid.

106. Françoise Reiss, *Nijinsky, ou La Grâce* (Paris: Editions d'histoire et d'art, Plon, 1957).

107. De Cuevas to BN, 25 Feb. 1954, 71A/37, BNC.

108. BN, draft letter to de Cuevas, 27 Feb. 1954, 71A/37, BNC.

109. Nicole Hirsch, "La rentrée du Ballet de Cuevas. Une vedette à succès: Belinda Wright. Une grande création: le 'Concerto' de Chopin," *France-Soir*, 7 Oct. 1954, 26/3, BNC. Details about the opening come from clippings in the De Cuevas Company File, 1953–54.

110. Emile Vuillermoz, "Rentrée du ballet du marquis de Cuevas au théâtre Sarah-Bernhardt," *Paris-Presse-l'Intransigeant*, [7 Oct. 1954?], 26/3, BNC.

111. Marie Brillant, "Le 'troisième' *Boléro* de Ravel," *Choix*, 19 Nov. 1954, De Cuevas Company File, 1953–54.

112. "Le *Boléro* de Ravel chez le marquis de Cuevas," *Dimanche Matin*, 21 Nov. 1954, De Cuevas Company File, 1953–54.

113. Dinah Maggie, "Au 'Grand Ballet du Marquis de Cuevas': '*Boléro*,'" *Figaro*, 10 Nov. 1954, De Cuevas Company File, 1953–54.

114. De Cuevas, contract with BN, 1 Dec. 1954, 71A/37, BNC.

115. Richard Buckle, "Diaghilev in London," *Observer*, 24 Oct. 1954, 6, and "Diaghilev Lecture Arrangements," *Observer*, 2 Jan. 1955, 7. Because the London version exhibition was presented by the *Observer* newspaper, for which Buckle wrote, the newspaper published weekly lists of the lectures and other special events connected with the exhibition. See also Buckle's exhibition catalogue and his book *In Search of Diaghilev* (New York: Thomas Nelson & Sons, 1956).

116. De Cuevas to BN, 16 Mar. 1955, 71A/37, BNC.

117. Wolkonsky to BN and NS, 21 Mar. 1955, 77B/9, BNC.

118. Wolkonsky to BN, 3 Aug. 1955, 77B/9, BNC.

119. Anastos, "A Conversation with George Skibine," 89.

120. Loan Application and Financial Statement, Glendale Federal Savings and Loan Association, 3 May 1954, 45/2, BNC. The couple's annual tax statements from 1943 to 1968, when Singaevsky died, are in 45/12, BNC. For a description of the house, built in 1954, and details about the land parcel, see the Los Angeles County Assessor Portal.

121. Toumanova to Donald Hutter, 31 Aug. 1981, 77/23, BNC. Hutter was the executive editor of Holt, Rinehart and Winston, which published *Early Memoirs* in 1981. For Toumanova's concert programs in Mexico City, see Margarita Tortajada Quiroz, *75 años de danza en el Palacio de Bellas Artes: Memoria de un Arte y un Recinto Vivos (1934–2009)* (Mexico City: Cenidi Danza/INBA/CONACULA, 2010).

122. Novak, *El ballet, mi vida, mi passión: memorias*, 80. For her family during the war, see 40–51.

123. Ibid., 93.

124. Anderson, *The One and Only*, 173.

125. BN, letter to Denham, 24 Oct. 1957, Denham Records, Folder 1946; Anderson, *The One and Only*, 171.

126. Denham to BN, 12 Nov. 1957, Denham Records, Folder 1946.

127. De Cuevas to BN, 5 May and 5 Sept. 1959; undated contract, with prolongation to August 1, and contract of 1 Aug. 1960, 71A/37, BNC; Mannoni, *Le Marquis de Cuevas*, chap. 8; Maurice Tassart, "Parisians Praise 'Beauty' and 'Swan Lake': Choreography Restored," *CSM*, 18 Feb. 1961, 4.

128. BN, draft letter to de Cuevas, 15 Feb. 1960, 71A/37, BNC.

129. Ofelia Britos de Dobranich, "La hermana del gran Nijinsky está en Buenos Aires," *Vea y lea* [undated clipping] [1960], 30–31, Box 160, BNC.

130. Juan Orrego Salas, "El Ballet Internacional del Marqués de Cuevas," *El Mercurio*, 20 May 1960, 5.

131. "Graves consecuencias del terremoto en la zona sur," *El Mercurio*, 22 May 1960, 29; Mannoni, *Le Marquis de Cuevas*, 92–97. For the company's performances in Mexico City, see Tortajada Quiroz, *75 años de danza en el Palacio de Bellas Artes*, 210. Marie (Krillova) de Fredericksz was the company's chief secretary and tour administrator. See Meylac, *Behind the Scenes*, 211–22.

132. Renzo Massarani, "Música: Ballet Marquês de Cuevas," *Jornal do Brasil*, 5 June 1960, 6.

133. Anastos, "A Conversation with George Skibine," 89.

134. Jack Anderson, "The Fabulous Career of Bronislava Nijinska," *DM*, Aug. 1963, 46.

135. Hightower, interviewed by Kendall, 73. The other Auroras were Nina Vyroubova, Genia Melikova, and Liane Daydé.

136. Ibid., 73–74.

137. "Rosella Hightower—On Stage," JRH Films, YouTube, https://www.youtube.com/watch?v=BV9IXD4lmwc.

138. Guerrico to BN, 7 Aug. 1960, 71A/37, BNC.

139. BN, draft letter to Guerrico, 15 Sept. 1960, 72/55, BNC.

140. De Cuevas to BN, 28 Sept. 1960, 71A/37, BNC.

141. De Cuevas to BN, 17 Oct. 1960, 71A/37, BNC. She returned it a few days later with a note saying that she has "kept it for the work you charged me to do" (BN, draft letter to de Cuevas, 20 Oct. 1960, 71A/37, BNC).

142. Mannoni, *Le Marquis de Cuevas*, 176.

143. Anderson, "The Fabulous Career of Bronislava Nijinska," 46.

144. Livingston, *American Indian Ballerinas*, 159.

145. Hightower, interviewed by Kendall, 72.

146. Mannoni, *Le Marquis de Cuevas*, 175–76; "Bronislava Nijinska: désaccord avec le marquis de Cuevas," unidentified clipping; "Une lettre de Bronislava Nijinska," *Figaro*, 26 Oct. 1960, 26/7, BNC. A copy of Nijinska's original letter, dated 24 Oct. 1960, is in 51/14, BNC. See also Nicole Hirsch to BN, 26 Oct. 1960, 72/66, BNC. Hirsch was the dance critic of the newspaper *France-Soir*.

147. Reviews and other press relating to the production are in 26/7, BNC. Unless otherwise noted, all reviews are from this folder.

148. "Le Marquis de Cuevas a vendu jusqu'à ses derniers biens," *Combat*, 26 Oct. 1960; "Le Marquis de Cuevas: C'est mon dernier ballet. J'y ai tout mis: mon argent, ma santé, ma passion," *France-Soir*, 22 Oct. 1960; Patrick Thévenon, "Le Marquis de Cuevas fait ses adieux à la danse," *Paris-Press-l'Intransigeant*, 27 Sept. 1960.

149. For the premiere, see "La plus belle nuit de Paris," *Paris Jour*, 28 Oct. 1960; "Le Marquis de Cuevas acclamé hier soir," 28 Oct. 1960; Raphaël Valensi, "Emotion et humour hier soir pour le Tout-Paris. Soirée Grand Siècle au Théâtre des Champs-Elysées avec 'La belle au bois dormant,'" unidentified clipping, 28 Oct. 1960.
150. Olivier Merlin, "'La Belle au Bois dormant' par les Ballets Cuevas," *Monde*, 29 Oct. 1960, 13.
151. Jacques Bourgeois, "*La Belle au bois dormant*," *Arts*, unidentified clipping.
152. Grünberg to BN and NS, 23 Dec. 1960, 72/53, BNC.
153. Paravicini to BN, undated [Jan. 1961], 75/40, BNC.
154. "Le Marquis de Cuevas éclate en sanglots: 'Si je dois mourir, je mourrai dans les coulisses,'" unidentified clipping, 5 Nov. 1960.
155. Grünberg to BN and NS, 23 Dec. 1960, 72/53, BNC.
156. BN, draft letter to Marquise de Cuevas, 5 Dec. 1960, 71A/37, BNC. For Nijinska's arrival in New York from Paris on TWA flight 803 on November 19, 1960, see Ancestry Library.
157. Grünberg to BN and NS, 23 Dec. 1960.
158. Statement of Income & Expenses for the Years 1961, 1962, 1963, 45/12; Hooker, Alley & Duncan to BN, 3 Apr. 1961, and BN, draft letter to Hooker, Alley & Duncan, 9 Oct. 1962, 72/66, BNC.
159. BN, draft letter to Hightower, 28 Feb. 1961, 72/65, BNC.
160. Julie Kavanagh, *Nureyev: The Life* (New York: Pantheon, 2007), 147-48.

Chapter 16

1. BN, draft letter to Frederick Ashton, undated [1964], 63/3, BNC.
2. Margaret Harford, "L.A. Ballet Ready for a Great Leap Forward," *LAT*, 7 July 1964, C1.
3. Albert Goldberg, "L.A. Ballet: Let George Do It," *LAT*, 6 Sept. 1964, P1. See also Albert Goldberg, "Ballet—A Leap toward Resident L.A. Company," *LAT*, 12 Aug. 1964, D1.
4. BN, photostatic copy of a letter to the editor-in-chief of the *LAT*, 15 Sept. 1964, 74/28, BNC. Goldberg's interview of 12 Aug. was not actually an interview but an article about the new company's "experimental preview" ("Ballet—A Leap toward Resident L.A. Company").
5. The twists and turns of this story can be followed in the *Los Angeles Times*.
6. Ashton, telegram to BN, 22 Sept. 1964, 70/7, BNC.
7. BN, telegram to Ashton, 23 Sept. 1964, 70/7, BNC.
8. David Vaughan, "Ashton, Frederick," *IED*, 155.
9. Ashton to BN, 1 Oct. 1964, 70/7, BNC.
10. Fernau Hall, *An Anatomy of Ballet* (London: Andrew Melrose, 1953), 139, 162; republished the following year as *World Dance* (New York: A. A. Wyn, 1954). Nijinska shared the "post-expressionist pseudo-classicism" category with Balanchine, Lifar, and Ashton.

11. Peggy van Praagh and Peter Brinson, *The Choreographic Art: An Outline of Its Principles and Craft*, foreword Cyril Beaumont (New York: Knopf, 1963), 76.

12. In May 1954, David Webster, general administrator of London's Royal Opera House, invited Nijinska to produce *Les Biches* for Sadler's Wells's "Diaghilev celebrations" to coincide with the show's opening in Edinburgh in August. Webster added that Ninette de Valois "sincerely hopes you will accept" (Webster, telegram to BN, 4 May 1954, 77B/3, BNC). Nijinska, however, was already committed to staging *Chopin Concerto* for the Marquis de Cuevas so had to turn down the invitation.

13. Anton Dolin, "Les Biches: A Misconception," *DT*, Feb. 1980, 323. In a letter to Nijinska just after the ballet's premiere, he wrote, "I was sure . . . that my words to Ninette and Ashton would bear 'fruit'. Bravo! Bravo! my great friend and teacher." Dolin to BN, 22 Dec. 1964, 72/12, BNC.

14. Julie Kavanagh, *Secret Muses: The Life of Frederick Ashton* (London: Faber & Faber, 1996), 484.

15. Qtd. in ibid.

16. David Vaughan, *Frederick Ashton and His Ballets* (New York: Knopf, 1977), 344.

17. "Nijinska Rehearses," *Illustrated London News*, 21 Nov. 1964, 827.

18. "Nijinska," *Sunday Times*, 8 Nov. 1964, 11.

19. Geraldine Morris, interview with the author, London, 6 Apr. 2011.

20. Ibid.

21. Ibid.

22. "Bronislava Nijinska: Dancers Speak," 16–17.

23. Ibid., 17–18.

24. Ibid., 24.

25. Peter Williams, "Decor," *Dance and Dancers*, Jan. 1965, 17.

26. "Dancing Interpreter," *Daily Telegraph*, 2 Dec. 1964, Covent Garden Production File, Dec. 1964, V&A (hereafter "Production File").

27. Program, Royal Opera House Covent Garden, Wed., 2 Dec. 1964, Production File. "Infinite care" was how Peter Williams described the re-created scenery and costumes ("Decor," 17).

28. Telegrams to BN from Arnold and Vera Haskell, 2 Dec. 1964, 72/61; Ana Ricarda, 2 Dec. 1964, 76A/9; Georgina Parkinson, 2 Dec. 1964, 75/43, BNC.

29. Richard Buckle, "Life on a Blue Sofa," *Sunday Times*, 6 Dec. 1964, 26.

30. James Kennedy, "Les Biches at Covent Garden," *Guardian*, 3 Dec. 1964. See also Clive Barnes, "A Diaghilev Ballet in London," *NYT*, 3 Dec. 1964, 58; Kathleen Crofton, "Nijinska's 'Les Biches' Captivates London," *CSM*, 12 Dec. 1964, 2; BN, draft letter to Ninette de Valois, 17 Dec. 1964, 63/3, BNC.

31. A. V. Coton, "'Les Biches,' a Revival That Wins on Points," *Daily Telegraph*, 3 Dec. 1964, Production File; Kennedy, "Les Biches at Covent Garden"; Clement Crisp, "Les Biches," *Financial Times*, 4 Dec. 1964, 24; "Turkish Delight World. Royal Opera House: *Les Biches*," *Times*, 3 Dec. 1964, 7; Alexander Bland, "A Twenties Thoroughbred," *Observer*, 6 Dec. 1964, 25; Clive Barnes, "Dancing for Fun," *Spectator*, 11 Dec. 1964, 813.

32. Buckle, "Life on a Blue Sofa."

33. Richard Buckle, "Russian Passion, French Taste," *Sunday Times*, 17 Jan. 1965, 43.

34. Ibid.

35. Clive Barnes, "Choreography," *Dance and Dancers*, Jan. 1965, 13.

36. Dinner menu signed by Nijinska, Arnold Haskell, Mary Clarke, G. B. L. Wilson, Nigel Gosling, and others, 72/32, BNC.

37. Jacqueline Harvey to BN, 31 Dec. 1964, 72/60, BNC.

38. Berry to BN, 10 Dec. 1964, 70/28, BNC.

39. BN to Lubov Tchernicheva and Sergei Grigoriev, 20 Jan. 1965, Grigoriev Papers.

40. Rambert to BN, 29 Nov. 1964, 76A/2, BNC.

41. Allen Hughes, "Royal Ballet Offers 'Biches' and 2 Other Works," *NYT*, 30 Apr. 1965, 43. At the first performance *Les Biches* was programmed with *Les Patineurs* and *Marguerite and Armand*; subsequently with *Les Sylphides* and *The Dream*.

42. Albert Goldberg, "Royal Ballet 'Adult' Dances Display Troupe's Versatility," *LAT*, 30 June 1965, C11. For the Shrine Auditorium (23–29 June) and Hollywood Bowl (8–11 July) programs, see the Royal Ballet publicity brochure, Box 108, BNC. For the San Francisco Opera House programs (1–6 July), see "Royal Ballet to Open July 1 at San Francisco Opera House," *Petaluma Argus-Courier*, 26 June 1965, 3.

43. Renouf to BN, 8 July 1965, 75/53, BNC.

44. BN, draft letter to Renouf, 17 July 1965, 75/53, BNC.

45. Renouf, email to the author, 21 July 2015. Renouf's letter to her nephew was written from Chicago and dated 17 Sept. 1965. The Noverre letter is in Box 218, BNC.

46. Anderson, "The Fabulous Career of Bronislava Nijinska," 40.

47. Alexander Bland, "Mixed Revivals," *Observer*, 14 Feb. 1971, 21.

48. Geraldine Morris, *Frederick Ashton's Ballets: Performance, Choreography* (Binsted, Hants: Dance Books, 2012), 59.

49. The phrase is Anatole Vilzak's. Qtd. in Marian Horosko, "Teachers in the Russian Tradition. Part I. Ludmilla Schollar and Anatole Vilzak," *DM*, Apr. 1979, 70.

50. Qtd. in Gruen, *The Private World of Ballet*, 141.

51. Morris interview.

52. Ian Woodward, "Practice Makes Perfect," *London Life*, 2 Apr. 1966, Production File.

53. Program, Royal Opera House Covent Garden, 23 Mar. 1966, Production File.

54. Igor Stravinsky and Robert Craft, *Expositions and Developments* (Garden City, NY: Doubleday, 1962), 115–17.

55. Her article, "Creation of 'Les Noces,'" was ultimately published in *Dance Magazine* (Dec. 1974, 58–61), translated by the team responsible for *Early Memoirs*. A French translation appeared in *Gontcharova et Larionov: Cinquante ans à Saint Germain-des-Près*, ed. Tatiana Loguine (Paris: Klincksieck, 1971), 117–22.

56. "Depth and Warmth in Ballet's Simplicity," *Times*, 24 Mar. 1966, 16.

57. Alexander Bland, "Sacrament of a Nation's Soul," *Observer*, 27 Mar. 1966, 24.

58. James Kennedy, "Les Noces at Covent Garden," *Guardian*, 24 Mar. 1966, Production File.

59. Nicholas Dromgoole, "Still Brand New," *Sunday Telegraph*, 27 Mar. 1966, Production File.

60. Anthony [Asquith] to BN, 24 Mar. 1966, Box 120, BNC.

61. Ashton to BN, 12 May 1966, Box 120, BNC.

62. Clive Barnes, "Dance: Royal Ballet's 'Shadowplay,'" *NYT*, 4 May 1967, 34.

63. Clive Barnes, "Dance": Nijinska's 'Les Noces' Returns," *NYT*, 7 May 1967, 85.

64. Ibid.

65. Clive Barnes, "A Successful Remarriage," *NYT*, 21 Mar. 1967, D16.

66. Daniel Cariaga, "American Ballet Theatre at Pavilion," *Independent* (Long Beach, CA), 8 Mar. 1968, 34.

67. Qtd. in Stephanie Jordan, *Stravinsky Dances: Re-Visions across a Century* (Alton, Hampshire: Dance Books, 2007), 397.

68. Qtd. in Donna Perlmutter, "Guardian of Ballets Keeps Choreographer's Legend Alive," *LAT*, 28 Apr. 1990, F7. Nevertheless, the Robbins version circulated long after the Oakland Ballet (and other companies) produced Nijinska's.

69. Sonia Gaskell, telegrams to BN, 20 and 26 Dec. 1966, and letter, 4 Jan. 1967, 72/32, BNC.

70. Signed contract between De Nederlander Operastichting and BN, 27 Feb. 1967, 46/10, BNC.

71. Gaskell to Nijinska, 4 Jan. 1967.

72. Gaskell to BN, 1 Mar. 1967, 72/32, BNC.

73. Nicolas Nijinska [*sic*], telegram to Gaskell, 21 Mar. 1967, 72/32, BNC.

74. BN, telegram to Sonia Gaskell, 7 Apr. 1967, 72/32, BNC.

75. Gaskell to BN, 10 May 1967, 72/32, BNC.

76. BN, draft letter to Maria Prianishnikova, undated [Oct. 1967], 75/63, BNC.

77. For Milloss, see Patrizia Veroli, *Milloss: Un maestro della coreografia tra espressionismo e classicità* (Lucca: Libreria Musicale Italiana, 1996), and "The Choreography of Aurel Milloss, Part Three: 1967–1988," *Dance Chronicle* 13, no. 3 (1990–91), 368–92.

78. BN, draft letter to Milloss, 10 Aug. 1968, 75/3, BNC. The financial terms outlined in Nijinska's letter, except for the tickets, were written into her contract (19 Sept. 1968, 46/10).

79. "Arts Patron Franz T. Stone Dies at 95; Was Columbus McKinnon President," *Buffalo News*, 2 Sept. 2002 (buffalonews.com > 2002/09/02 > arts-patron-franz-t-stone).

80. Zoom interview with Sandy Applebaum and Lynn Glauber, 2 May 2020, and their email message to the author, 9 May 2020. For a sense of the creative excitement in Buffalo during the 1960s, see Renée Levine Packer, *The Life of Sounds: Evenings for New Music in Buffalo* (New York: Oxford University Press, 2010).

81. I am indebted (in alphabetical order by maiden name) to Sandy Applebaum, Mary Barres (Riggs), Elizabeth Cunliffe, Lynn Glauber (Mandel), Deborah Hess, Anna-Marie Holmes, Michele Lankowski (Brennan), Raymond Lukens, Ruth Perez (Øian), Judy Pyanowski, Francesca Rochberg, Donna Ross, Karl Singletary, Nancy Wozny, and Deborah Zdominsky, who generously assisted me in reconstructing this era of Nijinska's life through interviews, long emails, memorabilia, and suggestions about sources, including the Fulton History database (https://fultonsearch.org/), and by inviting me to attend a Zoom reunion organized by Donna Ross and Deborah Zdobinsky on 24 May 2020.

82. "Ballet Center of Buffalo Slates Sept. 11 Opening," *Buffalo Courier-Express*, 9 Aug. 1967, n.p.; "Auditions Set at School for Dancing Program," *Buffalo Courier-Express*, 11 Aug. 1967, 16; "Announcement: The Ballet Center of Buffalo," *NYT*, 13 Aug. 1967, 102.

83. Advertisement, "The Ballet Center of Buffalo," *Gowanda News and Observer*, 21 Sept. 1967, 2.

84. Bruce Miller, "Outlook Encouraging; The Ballet Center of Buffalo," *DM*, Mar. 1969, 68.

85. Crofton to BN, 17 Mar. [1968], 71A/35, BNC.

86. Ibid.

87. Ibid.

88. Margaret Converse, "Nijinska," *Democrat and Chronicle* (Rochester), 24 Sept. 1970, C1. See also "Professional Advice," *Buffalo Courier-Express*, 27 Sept. 1968, 17, with a photo of Nijinska with Crofton and a student.

89. Converse, "Nijinska," 4C.

90. Margaret Converse, "Ballet in Buffalo of All Places!" *Democrat and Chronicle* (Rochester), 18 Oct. 1970, 26.

91. Telephone interview with Francesca Rochberg, 5 May 2020.

92. Mary Barres Riggs, email to the author, 15 May 2020. In addition I want to thank Sandy Applebaum, Elizabeth Cunliffe, Lynn Glauber, Howard Sayette, and Deborah Hess.

93. Interview with Deborah Hess.

94. Converse, "Nijinska," 1C.

95. Michele Landowski Brennan, email to the author, 1 May 2020.

96. For the Center Ballet of Buffalo program, 5–9 Aug. 1969, see https://archives .jacobspillow.org/index.php/Detail/objects/4974. The Pillow's online archive also includes photographs of *Les Biches* and *Brahms Variations* by John Lindquist and fragments of *Les Biches* filmed by Robert Savage to which music was added in 2018 (https://danceinteractive.jacobspillow.org/center-ballet-buffalo/7161/).

97. Among the other guests was Howard Sayette from the Metropolitan Opera Ballet. Sayette later staged many productions of *Les Noces* and *Les Biches*.

98. FaceTime interview with Anna-Marie Holmes, 30 Apr. 2020.

99. For footage of Anna-Marie and David Holmes, see *Tour en l'Air*, prod. and directed Grant Munro, National Film Board of Canada, 1973. The film also includes very brief clips of the Buffalo dancers rehearsing *Swan Lake* and dressing for the premiere of *Chopin Concerto*.

100. Clive Barnes, "The Re-Emergence of La Nijinska," 3 Aug. 1969, D23.

101. Richard V. Happel, "Buffalo Ballet at Pillow," *Berkshire Eagle*, 6 Aug. 1969, 19.

102. Margo Miller, "Nijinska by Buffalo: New Ballet at the Pillow," *Boston Globe*, 17 Aug. 1969, A29.

103. Anna Kisselgoff, "'Les Biches' Is Offered by Center Ballet of Buffalo," *NYT*, 8 Aug. 1968, 15.

104. Happel, "Buffalo Ballet at Pillow."

105. Kathleen Cannell, "Nijinska, Nijinsky Revivals," *CSM*, 18 Aug. 1969, 10.

106. Miller, "Nijinska by Buffalo."

107. Happel, "Buffalo Ballet at Pillow," and Cannell, "Nijinska, Nijinsky Revivals."

108. Francesca Rochberg's father, the composer George Rochberg, sat in on rehearsals for *Brahms* and was so inspired by the Paganini variations that he composed his

own virtuoso "Caprice Variations" as a kind of homage (interview with Francesca Rochberg).

109. A[rlene] C[roce], "Bronislava Nijinska," *BR* 4, no. 2 (1972), 74.

110. Walter Terry, "From Nadir to Zenith," *Saturday Review*, 6 Sept. 1969, 39.

111. The "Holiday Special" programs, which describe the changes in *Aurora's Wedding*, are in Box 108, BNC. For the poster, see https://www.loc.gov/resource/ihas.200154605.0.

112. Interview with Lynn Glauber. The names of the fairies in the Buffalo production are a combination of the names in *The Sleeping Princess* and in the 1946 Sadler's Wells production of *The Sleeping Beauty*.

113. Mary Barres Riggs, email to the author, 2 May 2020.

114. Interview with Anna-Marie Holmes.

115. Ruth Pérez Øian, email to the author, 29 May 2020.

116. Unfortunately, Cunliffe left Buffalo before transforming the rough score into a more polished one so the ballet could be accurately revived (interview with Elizabeth Cunliffe).

117. Ruth Pérez Øian, email to the author, 29 May 2020.

118. Jean Battey Lewis, "'Quiet' Ballet," *WP*, 29 Aug. 1970, C5; Lewis, "A 'Modest' Dance Debut," *WP*, 26 Aug. 1970, B11. For the program, see 16/20, BNC.

119. Ann Barzel, "Niagara Ballet," *Dance News*, Oct. 1970, 9. Jeanne Armin was a former ABT soloist, and Tatsuo Sakai, a Japanese-trained dancer who had performed in Europe.

120. BN, draft letter to Wollard, undated, 65/2, BNC.

121. John Percival, "Something Good from Buffalo," *Times*, 12 July 1971, 8; Crofton to BN, 1 Oct. 1971, 71A/35, BNC.

122. Crofton to BN, 7 Sept. 1971, 71A/35, BNC.

123. See Linda Chiavaroli, "Regional Ballet Troupe in Works," *Democrat and Chronicle* (Rochester), 14 Jan. 1972, 37; "Festival Ballet Is Disbanding," *Democrat and Chronicle* (Rochester), 28 Apr. 1973, 10; "Buffalo Ballet Folds for Lack of Funds," *Salamanca Republican-Press*, 30 Apr. 1973, 9; "The Ballet Must Go On," *Sun* (Baltimore), 10 Aug. 1979, A14.

124. BN, draft letter to Miara Prianishnikova, Sept. 1967, 63/6, BNC.

125. Lidova to BN, 25 Sept. and 8 Nov. 1970, 77B/17, BNC.

126. Lidova, *Ma Vie*, 230–31. See also Lidova's article, "Ancora una volta, ricordare Venezia," *Ballettoggi*, Nov. 1988, 42–43.

127. "A Venise avec Mme Nijinska," *La Danse*, 98. Undated clipping, Nijinska Archives.

128. Lidova, *Ma Vie*, 232.

129. Ibid. *Les Noces* was given a total of five performances—15, 17, 20, 21, and 23 Jan. 1971 (http://archiviostorico.teatrolafenice.it/scheda_0.php?ID=15968).

130. Ibid. For a photograph memorializing Nijinska's visit to Diaghilev's grave, see https://www.loc.gov/item/ihas.200181814/.

131. Lidova, "Ancora una volta," 43.

132. "Nijinsky's Sister Hits Biography as 'Fairy Tale,'" *NYHT*, 15 Nov. 1934, 21.

133. BN, draft letter to [Elisabeth?] Stenbock-Fermor, 9 June 1959, 62/5, BNC.

134. BN, draft letter to Lifar, 27 June 1967, 63/6, BNC.

135. A group of these photographs is in the collection of the A. A. Bakhrushin State Central Theatre Museum, Moscow.

136. Kalaushin to BN, 15 July 1963, and Nijinska's draft acknowledgment of his thank-you note, 10 Feb. 1964, 73/13, BNC. M. M. Kalaushin was the Museum's director.

137. BN to Eliash, 22 June 1965. See Nikolai El'iash, *Pushkin i baletnyi teatr* (Moscow: Iskusstvo, 1970), 288–93.

138. BN, draft letter to Maria Prianishnikova, undated [Oct. 1967], 75/63, BNC.

139. Roslavleva to BN, 25 June 1967; BN, draft letter to Roslavleva, 23 Aug. 1967; Roslavleva to BN, undated, 76B/3, BNC. The original of Nijinska's August 23 letter, with an excerpt titled "Ballet at the Maryinsky Theater, Petersburg, 1911," from "Diary of a Young Dancer," is in the St. Petersburg Theatre and Ballet, Fond 22, op. 5, Khr. 167. I am grateful to Sergei Konaev for sending me a copy of this material.

140. B. Nizhinskaia, "Petipa Pobedil" (The Triumph of Petipa), in *Marius Petipa: Materialy, Vospominaniia, Stat'i*, ed. A. Nekhendzi (Leningrad: Iskusstvo, 1971), 315–19.

141. BN, letter ("copy") to Krasovskaya, 11–12 Dec. 1967, 34/22, BNC; *EM*, 450. Krasovskaya's *Russkii baletnyi teatr vtoroi poloviny deviatnadtsatogo veka* (Russian Ballet Theater of the Second Half of the Nineteenth Century) was published in Leningrad in 1963.

142. BN to Krasovskaya, 11–12 Dec. 1967. Krasovskaya quotes Nijinska in *Russkii baletnyi teatr nachala XX veka: 1. Khoreografy* (Russian Ballet Theater at the Beginning of the Twentieth Century, vol. 1 Choreographers) (Leningrad: Iskusstvo, 1971–1972), 435, 440–41. For Hodson's use of the material quoted in Krasovskaya, see Millicent Hodson, *Nijinsky's Crime against Grace: Reconstruction Score of the Original Choreography for "Le Sacre du Printemps"* (Stuyvesant, NY: Pendragon Press, 1996), 166–200.

143. Krasovskaya to BN, 21 Dec. 1967, 73/30, BNC.

144. BN, draft letter to Krasovskaya, 1 Jan. 1968, 48/12, BNC.

145. Krasovskaya to BN, 14 Jan. 1968, 73/30, BNC. Krasovskaya's most recent book was *Stat'i o balete* (Essays on Ballet), published in Leningrad in 1967.

146. Krasovskaya to BN, 21 Feb. 1968, 73/30, BNC.

147. Krasovskaya to BN, 25 Apr. 1968, 73/30, BNC.

148. BN, draft letters to Krasovskaya, 10 Apr. 1969 and 26 Nov. 1970, 73/30, BNC.

149. BN, draft letter to Krasovskaya, 9 June [July] 1968, 48/12, BNC. Dolin had recently been in Leningrad where he had seen Baryshnikov dance. "He simply glows," Krasovskaya wrote back, "and glows on everything around him, filling the stage with light" (BN to Krasovskaya, 16 Jan. 1969, 63/3, BNC). Stars of the Bolshoi Ballet performed *Le Spectre de la Rose* in Los Angeles on June 28 and 30.

150. Krasovskaya to BN, 21 Apr. 1971, 48/12, BNC.

151. Krasovskaya to BN, 8 June 1971, 48/12, BNC.

152. Klausner to BN, 20 June and 19 Oct. 1968; BN's draft response, 6 Oct. 1968, 73/41, BNC.

153. Daroff's letters to BN are in 71/43; her draft letters to him in 65/1, BNC.

154. BN, draft letter to Wollard, 1 Nov. 1971, 65/2, BNC. This and other letters in this file are the source of the account that follows. Both Nathalie and her sister Nina Youshkevitch were born in Odessa and settled with their parents in Paris in the early 1920s. Nathalie married Jacques Wolodarsky (formerly Jacob Wolodowsky) in 1930. Both were Jewish, and in 1940 made their way to Lisbon and ultimately New York, where they settled on the Upper West Side.

155. BN, draft letter to Somes and the "Artists of the Royal Ballet," 30 May 1968, 76A/40, BNC.

156. BN, note to NS, 25 Apr. 1968, 78/17, BNC.

157. Krasovskaya to BN, 19 May 1968, 73/30, BNC.

158. BN, draft letter to Krasovskaya, 22 June 1968, 73/30, BNC.

159. BN, draft letter to Prianishnikova, 24 Oct. 1970, 75/63, BNC. Nina Sirotinine died in New York on January 4, 1967.

160. See "Bella Tietz (Schuty)," https://www.geni.com/people/Bella-Tietz/60000000 37504511969; for a memoir by Bella's daughter, Vera Peck née Tietz, see "Some Early Recollections of My Refugee Family," *WW2 People's War: An Archive of World War Two Memories*, 21 Nov. 2005, https://www.bbc.co.uk/history/ww2peopleswar/stories/74/a7159674.shtml.

161. Tietz to BN, undated [27 Mar. 1966], 76A/35, BNC.

162. Tietz to BN, 16 Sept. 1966, 76A/35, BNC.

163. Tietz to BN, 20 Nov. 1966, 76A/35, BNC.

164. Grigorovich to BN, 20 Sept. 1966, 72/52, BNC.

165. Krasovskaya to BN, 21 Feb. 1968, 73/30, BNC.

166. Clive Barnes, "Kirov Ballet Charms London," *Chicago Tribune*, 29 Aug. 1970, A30.

167. Irina Nijinska, postcard to Joseph Rickard, 30 Aug. 1970, Rickard Papers.

168. Krasovskaya to BN, 16 Oct. 1970, 73/30, BNC. According to Baryshnikov he never worked with Nijinska, although she may have rehearsed with Yuri Soloviev (information relayed by Joan Acocella to the author, 17 June 2020).

169. Krivinskaia to BN, 11 Mar. 1968, 73/36, BNC.

170. Ibid.

171. Krivinskaia to BN, 5 June 1968, 73/36, BNC.

172. Krivinskaia to BN, 18 June 1968, 73/36, BNC.

173. Strelkova's letters to BN are in 70/23, BNC.

174. Volkova to BN, 23 Dec. 1968, 77A/42, BNC. One of Singaevsky's sisters, Thais Pojarsky, died in Newtown, Connecticut, in 1968. According to her obituary in the *Bridgeport Telegram*, her survivors, in addition to her husband, Andrew Pojarsky, were a brother, Nicholas Singaevsky of California, and three sisters in Russia (9 Apr. 1968, 36).

175. BN, draft letter to Krivinskaia, undated [1968], 73/36, BNC.

176. Ibid.

177. Krivinskaia to BN, 5 Sept. 1968, 73/36, BNC.

178. Krivinskaia to BN, 5 Jan. 1969, 73/36, BNC.

179. Krivinskaia to BN, 22 Feb. 1970, 73/36, BNC. See also her letter of 22 Apr. 1969 and her undated letter written just after New Year 1970.

180. Krivinskaia to BN, 22 Apr. 1969, 73/36, BNC.
181. Krivinskaia to BN, 5 Jan. 1969, 73/36, BNC.
182. BN, draft letter to Maria Prianishnikova, undated [Nov.–Dec. 1971], 75/63, BNC.
183. Huber, "A Conversation with Irina Nijinska," 39.
184. Interview with Anna-Marie Holmes.
185. See, for instance, Anna Kisselgoff, "Bronislava Nijinska Is Dead at 81," *NYT*, 23 Feb. 1972, 44; Clive Barnes, "Great Dance Figure," *NYT*, 23 Feb. 1972, 44; "Bronislava Nijinska: Choreographer and Dancer," *Times*, 23 Feb. 1972, 14; Jean Battey Lewis, "Bronislava Nijinska, Noted Choreographer," *WP*, 23 Feb. 1972, C6; Richard Buckle, "Princess of Ballet," *Sunday Times*, 27 Feb. 1972, 33.
186. "Ballet Dancer Bronislava Nijinska Dies," *LAT*, 22 Feb. 1972, C3.
187. Oukhtomsky, Letter to the Editor, *LAT*, 26 Feb. 1972, 81/10, BNC; Oukhtomsky, "Bronislava Nijinska: 1891–1972," *LAT*, 26 Mar. 1972, O44.

Selected Bibliography

Published Writings by Bronislava Nijinska

"Creation of 'Les Noces.'" Trans. and introd. Jean M. Serafetinides and Irina Nijinska. *Dance Magazine*, Dec. 1974, 58–61.

"'Dnevnik' (Diary) (1919–1922); Traktat 'Shkola y Teatr Dvizhenii' (The School and Theater of Movement) (1918–1919)." In *Mnemozina: Dokumenty i fakty iz istorii otechestvennogo teatra XX veka*, 297–321. Vol. 6. Ed. V. V. Ivanov. Moscow: Indrik, 2014. This volume also includes letters by Nijinska to S. P. Diaghilev and B. V. Asafiev.

Early Memoirs. Trans. and ed. Irina Nijinska and Jean Rawlinson. Introd. Anna Kisselgoff. New York: Holt, Rinehart and Winston, 1981.

"On Movement and the School of Movement." In *Schrifttanz: A View of German Dance in the Weimar Republic*. Ed. Valerie Preston-Dunlop and Susanne Lahusen. London: Dance Books, 1990, 55–60.

"On Movement and the School of Movement." Trans. Anya Lem and Thelwall Proctor. Ed. Joan Ross Acocella and Lynn Garafola. In Nancy Van Norman Baer, *Bronislava Nijinska: A Dancer's Legacy*. Exhibition catalogue, Fine Arts Museums of San Francisco, 1986, 85–88. Rpt. *Ballet Review* 13, no. 4 (Winter 1986), 75–81.

"Petipa Pobedil" (The Triumph of Petipa). In *Marius Petipa: Materialy, Vospominaniia, Stat'i*. Ed. A. Nekhendzi. Leningrad: Iskusstvo, 1971, 315–19.

"Reflections about the Production of *Les Biches* and *Hamlet* in Markova-Dolin Ballets." *Dancing Times*, Feb. 1937, 617–20.

Books and Dissertations

Amazons of the Avant-Garde: Alexandra Exter, Natalia Goncharova, Liubov Popova, Olga Rozanova, Varvara Stepanova, and Nadezhda Udaltsova. Ed. John E. Bowlt and Matthew Drutt. New York: Guggenheim Museum/Abrams, 2000.

Amort, Andrea. "Die Geschichte des Balletts der Wiener Staatsoper 1918–1942." Ph.D. diss., Vienna, 1981.

Anderson, Jack. *The One and Only: The Ballet Russe de Monte Carlo*. New York: Dance Horizons, 1981.

André Levinson on Dance: Writings from Paris in the Twenties. Ed. and introd. Joan Acocella and Lynn Garafola. Hanover, NH: Wesleyan University Press/University Press of New England, 1991.

Aschengreen, Erik. *Jean Cocteau and the Dance*. Trans. Patricia McAndrew and Per Avsum. Copenhagen: Gyldendah, 1986.

Baer, Nancy Van Norman. *Bronislava Nijinska: A Dancer's Legacy*. Exhibition catalogue, Fine Arts Museums of San Francisco, 1986.

Barnett, Robert, with Cynthia Crain. *On Stage at the Ballet: My Life as a Dancer and Artistic Director.* Jefferson, NC: McFarland, 2019.

Baronova, Irina. *Irina: Ballet, Life and Love.* Foreword Clement Crisp. Gainesville: University Press of Florida, 2005.

Beaumont, Cyril W. *Bookseller at the Ballet: Memoirs 1891–1929.* London: C. W. Beaumont, 1975.

Beaumont, Cyril W. *Complete Book of Ballets.* London: Putnam, 1937.

Bellow, Juliet. *Modernism on Stage: The Ballets Russes and the Parisian Avant-Garde.* Farnham, Surrey/Burlington, VT: Ashgate, 2013.

Benois, Alexandre. *Reminiscences of the Russian Ballet.* Trans. Maria Britnieva. London: Putnam, 1941.

Bernard, Robert, et al. *L'Art du Ballet des origines à nos jours.* Paris: Editions du Tambourinaire, 1952.

Braga, Suzana. *Tatiana Leskova: uma bailarina solta no mundo.* São Paulo: Editora Globo, 2010.

Brahms, Caryl. *Footnotes to the Ballet: A Book for Balletomanes.* London: Lovat Dickson, 1936.

Brodovitch, Alexey. *Ballet.* New York: J. J. Augustin, 1945.

Buckle, Richard. *Diaghilev.* New York: Atheneum, 1979.

Buckle, Richard. *In Search of Diaghilev.* New York: Thomas Nelson & Sons, 1956.

Buckle, Richard. *Nijinsky.* New York: Simon & Schuster, 1971.

Buckle, Richard, with John Taras. *George Balanchine, Ballet Master.* New York: Random House, 1988.

Bunin, Ivan. *Cursed Days: A Diary of Revolution.* Ed., trans., and introd. Thomas Gaiton Marullo. Chicago: Ivan R. Dee, 1998.

Burton, Richard D. E. *Francis Poulenc.* Bath: Absolute Press, 2002.

Caamaño, Roberto. *La historia del Teatro Colón 1908–1968.* Buenos Aires: Editorial Cinetea, 1969.

Cadús, María Eugenia. "La danza escénica en el primer peronismo (1946–1955): Un acercamiento entre la danza y las políticas de Estado." Ph.D. diss., Universidad de Buenos Aires en Artes, 2017.

Carroll, Mark. *Music and Ideology in Cold War Europe.* Cambridge, UK: Cambridge University Press, 2003.

Chaliapin, Feodor. *Man and Mask: Forty Years in the Life of a Singer.* Trans. Phyllis Mégroz. London: Gollancz, 1932.

Charles-Roux, Edmonde. *Chanel: Her Life, Her World—and the Woman behind the Legend She Herself Created.* Trans. Nancy Amphoux. New York: Knopf, 1975.

Chauvelin, Jean, and Nadia Filatoff. *Alexandra Exter.* Chevilly-Larue: Max Milo Editions, 2003.

Chazin-Bennahum, Judith. *René Blum & the Ballets Russes: In Search of a Lost Life.* New York: Oxford University Press, 2011.

Chujoy, Anatole. *The New York City Ballet.* New York: Knopf, 1953.

Cocteau, Jean. *Le Coq et l'Arlequin: Notes autour de la musique.* Paris: Editions de la Sirène, 1918.

Cohen, Selma Jeanne, and S. J. Pischl. *The American Ballet Theatre: 1940–1960. Dance Perspectives* 6.

Coton, A. V. *A Prejudice for Ballet.* London: Methuen, 1938.

Danilova, Alexandra. *Choura: The Memoirs of Alexandra Danilova.* New York: Knopf, 1986.

De la Guardia, Ernesto, and Roberto Herrera. *El Arte lírico en el Teatro Colón (1908–1933)*. Buenos Aires: Zea y Tejero, 1933.

De Mille, Agnes. *Dance to the Piper*. Boston: Little, Brown, 1951.

Denby, Edwin. *Dance Writings*. Ed. Robert Cornfield and William Mackay. New York: Knopf, 1986.

Depaulis, Jacques. *Ida Rubinstein: une inconnue jadis célèbre*. Paris: Honoré Champion, 1995.

The Designs of Léon Bakst for "The Sleeping Princess." London: Benn Brothers, 1923.

De Valois, Ninette. *Come Dance with Me: A Memoir, 1898–1956*. London: H. Hamilton, 1957.

De Valois, Ninette. *Invitation to the Ballet*. London: John Lane, 1937.

De Valois, Ninette. *Step by Step: The Formation of an Establishment*. London: W. H. Allen, 1977.

Divoire, Fernand. *Découvertes sur la danse*. Paris: Editions G. Crès, 1924.

Dolin, Anton. *Ballet Go Round*. London: Michael Joseph, 1938.

Dolin, Anton. *Divertissement*. London: Samson Low, Marston, [1931].

Dolin, Anton. *Last Words: A Final Autobiography*. Ed. Kay Hunter. London: Century Publishing, 1985.

Dolin, Anton. *Olga Spessivtzeva: The Sleeping Ballerina*. Foreword Marie Rambert. London, 1966; rpt. London: Dance Books, 1974.

Dominic, Zoë, and John Gilbert. *Frederick Ashton: A Choreographer and His Ballets*. Chicago: H. Regnery Co., 1971.

Duberman, Martin. *The Worlds of Lincoln Kirstein*. New York: Knopf, 2007.

Duke, Vernon. *Passport to Paris*. Boston: Little, Brown, 1955.

Edwards Bello, Joaquín. *El marqués de Cuevas y su tiempo*. Prologue Alfonso Calderón. Santiago de Chile: Editorial Nascimento, 1974.

El'iash, Nikolai. *Pushkin i baletnyi teatr*. Moscow: Iskusstvo, 1970.

Escudero, Alejandrina. *Felipe Segura: una vida en la danza*. Mexico City: Instituto de Bellas Artes y Literatura, 1995.

Ewing, Alex C. *Bravura! Lucia Chase and the American Ballet Theatre*. Gainesville: University Press of Florida, 2009.

Fitzpatrick, Sheila. *The Commissariat of Enlightenment: Soviet Organization of Education and the Arts under Lunacharsky, October 1917–1921*. Cambridge, UK: Cambridge University Press, 1970.

Fokine: Memoirs of a Ballet Master. Trans. Vitale Fokine. Ed. Anatole Chujoy. Boston: Little, Brown, 1961.

Folch-Couyoumdjian, Antonia Sofía. "The Marquis de Cuevas: Pushing the Boundaries of Self." Ph.D. diss., University of Texas at Austin, 2014.

Forrest, Cheryl, and Georgia Snoke. *Roman Jasinski: A Gypsy Prince from the Ballet Russe*. Tulsa: Tulsa Ballet, 2008.

Francis Poulenc: Selected Correspondence 1915–1963. Trans. and ed. Sidney Buckland. London: Gollancz, 1991.

Franko, Mark. *The Fascist Turn in the Dance of Serge Lifar: Interwar French Ballet and the German Occupation*. New York: Oxford University Press, 2020.

Garafola, Lynn. *Diaghilev's Ballets Russes*. New York: Oxford University Press, 1989.

Garafola, Lynn. *Legacies of Twentieth-Century Dance*. Middletown, CT: Wesleyan University Press, 2005.

Garafola, Lynn. Trans. and ed. *The Diaries of Marius Petipa*. Studies in Dance History 3, no. 1 (Spring 1992).

García-Márquez, Vicente. *The Ballets Russes: Colonel de Basil's Ballets Russes de Monte Carlo 1932–1952*. New York: Knopf, 1990.

García-Márquez, Vicente. *Massine: A Biography*. New York: Knopf, 1995.

Geva, Tamara. *Split Seconds: A Remembrance*. New York: Harper & Row, 1972.

Giovannini, Marta, and Amelia Foglio de Ruíz. *Ballet argentino en el Teatro Colón*. Buenos Aires: Editorial Plus Ultra, 1973.

Gontcharova et Larionov: cinquante ans à Saint Germain-des-Près. Ed. Tatiana Loguine. Paris: Klincksieck, 1971.

Gorboff, Marina. *La Russie fantôme: L'émigration russe de 1920 à 1950*. Lausanne: Editions L'Age d'Homme, 1995.

Gray, Francine du Plessix. *Them: A Memoir of Parents*. New York: Penguin, 2005.

Grigoriev, S. L. *The Diaghilev Ballet 1909–1929*. Trans. and ed. Vera Bowen. London: Constable, 1953.

Guest, Ivor. *Le Ballet de l'Opéra de Paris*. Rev. ed. Pref. Hugues R. Gall. Paris: Opéra National de Paris/Flammarion, 2001.

Guest, Ivor, ed. *La Fille mal Gardée*. London: Dancing Times Ltd., 1960.

Gupta, Maureen Anne. "Diaghilev's *Sleeping Princess* (1921)." Ph.D. diss., Princeton University, 2011.

Gutsche-Miller, Sarah. "Pantomime-Ballet on the Music-Hall Stage: The Popularisation of Classical Ballet in Fin-de-siècle Paris." Ph.D. diss., McGill University, 2010.

Hall, Fernau. *An Anatomy of Ballet*. London: Andrew Melrose, 1953.

Haselbarth, Patty. "Anna Ludmila: The Forgotten Ballerina." Ph.D. diss., Texas Woman's University, 1999.

Haskell, Arnold L. *Balletomania: The Story of an Obsession*. London: Gollancz, 1934.

Haskell, Arnold L. *Dancing around the World: Memoirs of an Attempted Escape from Ballet*. London: Gollancz, 1937.

Haskell, Arnold L., in collaboration with Walter Nouvel. *Diaghileff: His Artistic and Private Life*. London: Gollancz, 1935.

Hennebert, Elisabeth. "'Coureurs de cachet': Histoire des danseurs russes de Paris (1917–1944)." 3 vols. Thèse de Doctorat (Histoire), Université de Paris I, 2002.

Historia general de la danza en la Argentina. Buenos Aires: Fondo Nacional de las artes, 2008.

Hodson, Millicent. *Nijinsky's Crime against Grace: Reconstruction Score of the Original Choreography for "Le Sacre du Printemps."* Stuyvesant, NY: Pendragon Press, 1996.

Hofmann, Andreï, Vladimir Hofmann, and Georgy Khatsenkov. *Les artistes russes hors frontière*. Paris: Musée du Montparnasse, 2010.

Homans, Jennifer. *Apollo's Angels: A History of Ballet*. New York: Random House, 2010.

Horwitz, Dawn Lille. "Michel Fokine in America, 1919–1942." Ph.D. diss., New York University, 1982.

Istoriia "Russkogo Baleta" real'naia i fantasticheskaia v risunkakh, memuarakh i fotografiiakh iz arkhiva Mikhaila Larionova. Moscow: Izdatel'skaia programma "Interrosa," 2009.

Järvinen, Hanna. "The Myth of Genius in Movement. Historical Deconstruction of the Nijinsky Legend." Ph.D. diss., University of Turku, 2003.

Johnston, Robert H. *"New Mecca, New Babylon": Paris and the Russian Exiles, 1920–1945*. Kingston and Montreal: McGill–Queen's University Press, 1988.

Jones, Susan. *Literature, Modernism & Dance*. Oxford: Oxford University Press, 2013.

Jordan, Stephanie. *Moving Music: Dialogues with Music in Twentieth-Century Ballet*. London: Dance Books, 2000.

Jordan, Stephanie. *Stravinsky Dances: Re-Visions across a Century*. Alton, Hants: Dance Books, 2007.

Kaden, Laurie Ann. "Nijinska's Theatre Choréographique Nijinska: The 1925 Tour of English Resort Towns." M.A. thesis, University of California–Riverside, 1988.

Kahan, Sylvia. *Music's Modern Muse: A Life of Winnaretta Singer, Princesse de Polignac*. Rochester, NY: University of Rochester Press, 2003.

Kahnweiler, Daniel-Henry. *Juan Gris: His Life and Work*. Rev. ed. Trans. Douglas Cooper. New York: Abrams, 1969.

Karsavina, Tamara. *Theatre Street: The Reminiscences of Tamara Karsavina*. Foreword J. M. Barrie. London: Heinemann, 1930.

Kavanagh, Julie. *Nureyev: The Life*. New York: Pantheon, 2007.

Kavanagh, Julie. *Secret Muses: The Life of Frederick Ashton*. London: Faber & Faber, 1996.

Kelkel, Manfred. *La Musique de Ballet en France de la Belle Epoque aux Années Folles*. Paris: Librairie Philosophique J. Vrin, 1992.

Kendall, Elizabeth. *Balanchine and the Lost Muse: Revolution and the Making of a Choreographer*. New York: Oxford University Press, 2013.

Kent, Allegra. *Once a Dancer . . . An Autobiography*. New York: St. Martin's Press, 1997.

Kirstein, Lincoln. *Ballet Alphabet: A Primer for Laymen*. New York: Kamin Publishers, 1939.

Kirstein, Lincoln. *Blast at Ballet: A Corrective for the American Audience*. New York: Marstin Press, 1938.

Kirstein, Lincoln. *Dance: A Short History of Classic Theatrical Dancing*. New York: Putnam's, 1935.

Kirstein, Lincoln. *Movement and Metaphor: Four Centuries of Ballet*. New York: Praeger, 1970.

Kochno, Boris. *Diaghilev and the Ballets Russes*. Trans. Adrienne Foulke. New York: Harper & Row, 1970.

Kochno, Boris, with Maria Luz. *Le Ballet*. Paris: Hachette, 1954.

Kovalenko, Georgy. *Alexandra Exter*. Trans. Brian Droitcour. Moscow: Moscow Museum of Modern Art/Maier Publishing, 2010.

Krasovskaia, V. *Russkii baletnyi teatr nachala XX veka*. 2 vols. Leningrad: Iskusstvo, 1971–1972.

Krasovskaya, Vera. *Nijinsky*. Trans. John E. Bowlt. New York: Schirmer Books, 1979.

Krasovskaya, Vera. *Vaganova: A Dance Journey from Petersburg to Leningrad*. Trans. Vera M. Siegel. Foreword Lynn Garafola. Gainesville: University Press of Florida, 2005.

Kurbas, Les. *S'ohodni Ukraïns'koho teatru i Berezil'*. Kharkov: Biblioteka VAPLITE, 1927.

Lacombe, Hervé. *Francis Poulenc*. Paris: Fayard, 2013.

Lee, Michael Edward. "Georges Auric and the Danced Theater, 1919–1924." Ph.D. diss., University of Southern California, 1993.

Levinson, André. *Ballet Old and New*. Trans. Susan Cook Summer. New York: Dance Horizons, 1982.

Levinson, André. *La Danse au Théâtre*. Paris: Bloud & Gay, 1924.

Levinson, André. *La Danse d'aujourd'hui: Etudes, Notes, Portraits*. Paris: Duchartre et Van Buggenhoudt, 1929.

Levinson, André. *Les Visages de la Danse*. Paris: Bernard Grasset, 1933.

Levinson, André. *Serge Lifar: Destin d'un Danseur*. Paris: Bernard Grasset, 1934.

Levitz, Tamara. *Modernist Mysteries: Perséphone*. New York: Oxford University Press, 2012.

Lidova, Irène. *Ma Vie avec la danse*. Paris: Editions Plume, 1992.

Lifar, Serge. *Du temps que j'avais faim*. Paris: Stock, 1935.

Lifar, Serge. *Ma Vie from Kiev to Kiev: An Autobiography*. Trans. James Holman Mason. London: Hutchinson, 1970.

Lifar, Serge. *Les Mémoires d'Icare*. Monaco: Editions Sauret, 1993.

Lifar, Serge. *Serge Diaghilev: His Life, His Work, His Legend—An Intimate Biography*. New York: Putnam, 1940.

Livak, Leonid. *How It Was Done in Paris: Russian Emigré Literature and French Modernism*. Madison: University of Wisconsin Press, 2003.

Livingston, Lili Cockerille. *American Indian Ballerinas*. Norman: University of Oklahoma Press, 1997.

Lloyd, Stephen. *Constant Lambert: Beyond the Rio Grande*. Woodbridge: Boydell Press, 2014.

Lobenthal, Joel. *Patricia Wilde, George Balanchine, and the Rise of New York City Ballet*. Lebanon, NH: ForeEdge/University Press of New England, 2016.

Loeffler, James. *"The Most Musical Nation": Jews and Culture in the Late Russian Empire*. New Haven: Yale University Press, 2006.

Lydia and Maynard: The Letters of Lydia Lopokova and John Maynard Keynes. Ed. Polly Hill and Richard Keynes. London: André Deutsch, 1989.

Macdonald, Nesta. *Diaghilev Observed by Critics in England and the United States, 1911–1929*. New York: Dance Horizons/London: Dance Books, 1975.

Mackrell, Judith. *Bloomsbury Ballerina: Lydia Lopokova, Imperial Dancer and Mrs. John Maynard Keynes*. London: Weidenfeld & Nicolson, 2008.

Mamontowicz-Łojek, Bożena. *Terpsychora i lekkie muzy: Taniec widowiskowy w Polsce w okresie międzywojennym* (Terpsichore, the Light Muse: Theatrical Dance in Poland in the Interwar Period [1918–1939]). Cracow: Polskie Wydawnictwo Muzyczne, 1972.

Manning, Susan. *Ecstasy and the Demon: The Dances of Mary Wigman*. Minneapolis: University of Minnesota Press, 2006.

Mannoni, Gérard. *Le Marquis de Cuevas*. Paris: J. C. Lattès, 2003.

Manso, Carlos. *Maria Ruanova (La verdad de la danza)*. Prologue Serge Lifar. Buenos Aires: Ediciones tres tiempos, 1987.

Marchesseau, Daniel. *Marie Laurencin: cent oeuvres des collections du Musée Marie Laurencin au Japon*. Martigny, Switzerland: Fondation Pierre Gianadda, 1993–1994.

Marius Petipa: Materialy, Vospominaniia, Stat'i. Ed. A. Nekhendzi. Leningrad: Iskusstvo, 1971.

Marquié, Hélène. *Non, la danse n'est pas un truc de filles! Essai sur le genre en danse*. Toulouse: Editions de l'Attribut, 2016.

Massine, Léonide. *My Life in Ballet*. Ed. Phyllis Hartnoll and Robert Rubens. London: Macmillan, 1968.

Mawer, Deborah. *The Ballets of Maurice Ravel: Creation and Interpretation*. Aldershot Hants/Burlington, VT: Ashgate, 2006.

Meisner, Nadine. *Marius Petipa: The Emperor's Ballet Master*. New York: Oxford University Press, 2019.

Meyer-Stabley, Bertrand. *Marie Laurencin*. Paris: Pygmalion, 2011.

Meylac, Michael. *Behind the Scenes at the Ballets Russes: Stories from a Silver Age*. Trans. Rosanna Kelly. London: I. B. Taurus, 2018.

Michaut, Pierre. *Le Ballet Contemporain 1929–1950*. Paris: Plon, 1950.

Milhaud, Darius. *Notes without Music*. New York: Knopf, 1953.

Milner, John. *Kazimir Malevich and the Art of Geometry*. New Haven: Yale University Press, 1996.

Mnemozina: Dokumenty i fakty iz istorii otechestvennogo teatra XX veka. Vol. 6. Ed. V. V. Ivanov. Moscow: Indrik, 2014.

Modernism in Kyiv: Jubilant Experimentation. Ed. Irena R. Makaryk and Virlana Tkacz. Toronto: University of Toronto Press, 2010.

Money, Keith. *Anna Pavlova, Her Life and Art*. New York: Knopf, 1982.

Morris, Geraldine. *Frederick Ashton's Ballets: Performance, Choreography*. Binsted, Hants: Dance Books, 2012.

Morrison, Simon. *The People's Artist: Prokofiev's Soviet Years*. New York: Oxford University Press, 2009.

Murga Castro, Idoia. *Pintura en danza. Los artistas españoles y el ballet (1916–1962)*. Madrid: Consejo Superior de Investigaciones Científicas, Grupo de Investigación de Historia del Arte, Instituto de Historia, 2012.

Nice, David. *Prokofiev: From Russia to the West, 1891–1935*. New Haven: Yale University Press, 2003.

Nijinsky, Romola. *The Last Years of Nijinsky*. London: Gollancz, 1952.

Nijinsky, Romola. *Nijinsky*. Foreword Paul Claudel. New York: Simon & Schuster, 1934.

Nijinsky, Tamara. *Nijinsky and Romola*. London: Bachman & Turner, 1991.

Nikitina by Herself. Trans. Baroness Budberg. London: Allan Wingate, 1959.

Novak, Nina, with Luisa Himiob. *El ballet, mi vida, mi pasión: Memorias*. S. I., Venezuela: Gráficas ACEA, 2010.

Osato, Sono. *Distant Dances*. New York: Knopf, 1980.

Packer, Renée Levine. *The Life of Sounds: Evenings for New Music in Buffalo*. New York: Oxford University Press, 2010.

Page, Ruth. *Page by Page*. Ed. Andrew Mark Wentink. New York: Dance Horizons, 1978.

Paris Modern: The Swedish Ballet 1920–1925. Ed. Nancy Van Norman Baer. Exhibition catalogue, Fine Arts Museums of San Francisco, 1995.

Parton, Anthony. *Goncharova: The Art and Design of Natalia Goncharova*. Woodbridge, Suff: Antique Collectors' Club, 2010.

Parton, Anthony. *Mikhail Larionov and the Russian Avant-Garde*. London: Thames and Hudson, 1993.

Paustovsky, Konstantin. *The Story of a Life*. Trans. Joseph Barnes. New York: Pantheon, 1964.

Peter, Frank-Manuel, and Rainer Stamm, eds. *Die Sacharoffs: Two Dancers within the "Blaue Reiter" Circle*. Cologne: Weinand Verlag, 2002.

Polish Dance Avant-Garde Artists. Stories and Reconstructions. Ed. Joanna Szymajda. Warsaw: Instytut Muzyki i Tańca/Instytut Adama Mickiewicza, 2017.

Poulenc, Francis. *Correspondance 1910–1963*. Ed. Myriam Chimènes. Paris: Fayard, 1994.

Poulenc, Francis. *Entretiens avec Claude Rostand*. Paris: René Julliard, 1954.

Prevots, Naima. *Dance for Export: Cultural Diplomacy and the Cold War*. Hanover, NH: Wesleyan University Press/University Press of New England, 1998.

Raeff, Mark. *Russia Abroad: A Cultural History of the Russian Emigration, 1919–1939*. New York: Oxford University Press, 1990.

Rambert, Marie. *Quicksilver*. London: Macmillan, 1972.

Reiss, Françoise. *Sur la Pointe des pieds: Annales chorégraphiques 1951–1952*. Paris: Edition Revue Adam, 1952.

Rich, Frank, with Lisa Aronson. *The Theatre Art of Boris Aronson*. New York: Knopf, 1987.

Ries, Frank W. D. *The Dance Theatre of Jean Cocteau*. Ann Arbor, MI: UMI Research Press, 1986.

Robinson, Harlow. *The Last Impresario: The Life, Times, and Legacy of Sol Hurok*. New York: Viking, 1994.

Robinson, Harlow. *Russians in Hollywood, Hollywood's Russians:* Biography of an Image. Boston: Northeastern University; Hanover, NH: University Press of New England, 2007.

Romanovsky-Krassinsky, H.S.H. The Princess. *Dancing in Petersburg: The Memoirs of Kschessinska*. Trans. Arnold Haskell. London: Gollancz, 1960.

Roust, Colin. *Georges Auric: A Life in Music and Politics*. New York: Oxford University Press, 2020.

Saunders, Frances Stonor. *The Cultural Cold War: The CIA and the World of Arts and Letters*. New York: New Press, 1999.

Scheijen, Sjeng. *Diaghilev: A Life*. Trans. Jane Hedley-Prôle and S. J. Leinbach. London: Profile Books, 2009.

Schmitz, Nancy Brooks. "A Profile of Catherine Littlefield, A Pioneer of American Ballet." Ed.D. diss., Temple University, 1986.

Schouvaloff, Alexander. *The Art of Ballets Russes: The Serge Lifar Collection of Theater Designs, Costumes, and Paintings at the Wadsworth Atheneum, Hartford, Connecticut*. New Haven: Yale University Press/Wadsworth Atheneum, 1998.

Schrifttanz: A View of German Dance in the Weimar Republic. Ed. Valerie Preston-Dunlop and Susanne Lahusen. London: Dance Books, 1990.

Schüller, Gunhild (also Oberzaucher-Schüller). "Bronislava Nijinska: Eine Monographie." Ph.D. diss., University of Vienna, 1974.

Searcy, Anne. *Ballet in the Cold War: A Soviet-American Exchange*. New York: Oxford University Press, 2019.

Segura Escalona, Felipe. *Nelsy Dambre: Un ballet para México*. Mexico City: Instituto Nacional de Bellas Artes, 1998.

Sergievsky, Orest. *Memoirs of a Dancer: Shadows, Dreams, Memories*. New York: Dance Horizons, 1979.

Sharp, Jane. *Russian Modernism between East and West: Natalia Goncharova and the Moscow Avant-Garde*. Cambridge/New York: Cambridge University Press, 2006.

Shkandrij, Myroslav. *Jews in Ukrainian Literature: Representation and Identity*. New Haven: Yale University Press, 2009.

Sokolova, Lydia. *Dancing for Diaghilev: The Memoirs of Lydia Sokolova*. Ed. Richard Buckle. London: John Murray, 1960.

Sorley Walker, Kathrine. *De Basil's Ballets Russes*. London: Hutchinson, 1982.

Sorley Walker, Kathrine. *Ninette de Valois: Idealist without Illusions*. London: Dance Books, 1987.

Souritz, Elizabeth. *Soviet Choreographers in the 1920s*. Trans. Lynn Visson. Ed., with additional translation, Sally Banes. Durham, NC: Duke University Press, 1990.

Stacewicz-Podlipska, Joanna. *Ja byłam wolny ptak—O życiu i sztuce Teresy Roszkowskiej*. Warsaw: Instytut Sztuki Polskirj Akademii Nauk, 2012.

Stanishevskyi, Iurii. *Baletnyi Teatr Ukrainy: 225 Rokiv Istorii*. Kyiv: Muzychna Ukraina, 2003.

Stanishevskyi, Iurii. *Natsional'nyi akademichnyi teatr opery ta baletu Ukraïny imeni Tarasa Shevchenka: istoriia i suchasnist'*. Kyiv: Muzychna Ukraina, 2002.

Steegmuller, Francis. *Cocteau: A Biography*. Boston: Little, Brown, 1970.

Steichen, James. *Balanchine and Kirstein's American Enterprise*. New York: Oxford University Press, 2019.

Stokes, Adrian. *Russian Ballet*. London: Faber & Faber, 1935.

Stravinsky, Igor. *An Autobiography*. New York: Simon & Schuster, 1936.

Stravinsky, Igor. *Memories and Commentaries*. Garden City, NY: Doubleday, 1960.

Stravinsky, Igor, and Robert Craft. *Expositions and Developments*. Garden City, NY: Doubleday, 1962.

Surits, E. Ia. *Mikhail Mikhailovich Mordkin: Artist baleta*. Moscow: URSS, 2003.

Sutton, Tina. *The Making of Markova: Diaghilev's Baby Ballerina to Groundbreaking Icon*. New York: Pegasus, 2013.

Tairov, Alexander. *Notes of a Director*. Trans. and introd. William Kuhlke. Coral Gables, FL: University of Miami Press, 1969.

Tallchief, Maria, with Larry Kaplan. *Maria Tallchief: America's Prima Ballerina*. New York: Henry Holt, 1997.

Taruskin, Richard. *Stravinsky and the Russian Traditions: A Biography of the Works through "Mavra."* 2 vols. Berkeley: University of California Press, 1996.

Teliakovskii, V. A. *Dnevniki direktora imperatorskikh teatrov, 1906–1909*. Ed. M. G. Svetaeva. Moscow: Artist, Rezhisser, Teatr, 2011.

Teliakovskii, V. A. *Dnevniki direktora imperatorskikh teatrov, 1909–1913*. Ed. M. G. Svetaeva, M. B. L'vova, and Mariia Khalizeva. Moscow: Artist, Rezhisser, Teatr, 2016.

Théâtre Serge de Diaghilew: Les Biches. Paris: Editions des Quatre Chemins, 1924.

Théâtre Serge de Diaghilew: Les Fâcheux. Paris: Editions des Quatre Chemins, 1924.

Tikanova, Nina. *La Jeune Fille en bleu: Pétersbourg-Berlin-Paris*. Lausanne: Editions L'Age d'Homme, 1991.

Tortajada Quiroz, Margarita. *75 años de danza en el Palacio de Bellas Artes: Memoria de un Arte y un Recinto Vivos (1934–2009)*. Mexico City: Denidi Danza/INBA/ CONACULA, 2010.

Ukrainian Modernism: 1910–1930. Kyiv: National Art Museum of the Ukraine, 2006.

Vaillat, Léandre. *Ballets de l'Opéra de Paris (Ballets dans les opéras et nouveaux ballets)*. Paris: Compagnie Française des Arts Graphiques, 1947.

Vaillat, Léandre. *La Danse à l'Opéra de Paris*. Paris: Amiot-Dumont, 1955.

Van Praagh, Peggy, and Peter Brinson. *The Choreographic Art: An Outline of Its Principles and Craft*. Foreword Cyril Beaumont. New York: Knopf, 1963.

Vassiliev, Alexandre. *Beauty in Exile: The Artists, Models, and Nobility Who Fled the Russian Revolution and Influenced the World of Fashion*. Trans. Antonina W. Bouis and Anya Kucharev. New York: Abrams, 2000.

Vaughan, David. *Frederick Ashton and His Ballets*. New York: Knopf, 1977.

Veroli, Patrizia. *Milloss: Un maestro della coreografia tra espressionismo e classicità*. Pref. Roman Vlad. Lucca: Libreria Italiana Musicale, 1996.

Von Geldern, James. *Bolshevik Festivals 1917–1920*. Berkeley: University of California Press, 1993.

Wallmann, Margarita. *Les Balcons du ciel*. Pref. Bernard Gavorty. Paris: Editions Robert Laffont, 1976.

Walsh, Stephen. *Stravinsky: A Creative Spring: Russia and France, 1882–1934*. New York: Knopf, 1999.

Walsh, Stephen. *Stravinsky: The Second Exile: France and America, 1934–1971*. New York: Knopf, 2006.

Wiley, Roland John. *The Life and Ballets of Lev Ivanov*. Oxford: Clarendon Press, 1997.

Wiley, Roland John. *Tchaikovsky's Ballets: Swan Lake, Sleeping Beauty, Nutcracker*. Oxford: Clarendon Press, 1985.

Zlobin, Vladimir. *A Difficult Soul: Zinaida Gippius*. Ed. and introd. Simon Karlinsky. Berkeley: University of California Press, 1980.

Zoritch, George. *Ballet Mystique: Behind the Glamour of the Ballet Russe*. Introd. Vladimir Vasiliev. Ed. Renée Renouf. Mountain View, CA: Cynara Editions, 2000.

Articles and Book Chapters

Amort, Andrea. "Free Dance in Interwar Vienna." In *Interwar Vienna: Culture between Tradition and Modernity*. Ed. Deborah Holmes and Lisa Silverman, 117–42. Rochester, NY: Camden House, 2009.

Anastos, Peter. "A Conversation with George Skibine." *Ballet Review* 10, no. 1 (Spring 1982), 68–97.

Arkin, Lisa C. "Bronislava Nijinska and the Polish Ballet, 1937–1938: Missing Chapter of the Legacy." *Dance Research Journal* 24, no. 2 (Autumn 1992), 1–16.

Auclair, Mathias, and Aurélien Poidevin. "Les Ballets russes et l'Opéra de Paris (1909–1929)." In *Les Ballets Russes*. Ed. Mathias Auclair and Pierre Vidal, 193–216. Paris: Editions Gourcuff Gradenigo, 2009.

"Bronislava Nijinska: Dancers Speak." *Ballet Review* 18, no. 1 (Spring 1990), 15–35.

Corrado, Omar. "Victoria Ocampo y la música: una experiencia social y estética de la modernidad." *Revista Musical Chilena* 61, no. 208 (July–Dec. 2007), 37–68.

Crisp, Clement. "Le Grand Ballet du Marquis de Cuevas." *DR* 23, no. 1 (Summer 2005), 1–17.

Dorris, George. "Léo Staats at the Roxy, 1916–1928." *Dance Research* 13, no. 1 (Summer 1995), 84–99.

Finch, Tamara. "My Dancing Years, Part Two." *Dance Chronicle* 27, no. 2 (2004), 235–73.

Foshko, Katherine. "The Paul Dumer Assassination and the Russian Diaspora in Interwar France." *French History* 23, no. 3 (Sept. 2009), 383–404.

Foster, Andrew. "A Directory of Diaghilev Dancers." *Dance Research* 37, no. 2 (Winter 2019), 181–205.

Garafola, Lynn. "Where Are Ballet's Women Choreographers?" In *Legacies of Twentieth-Century Dance*, 215–28. Middletown, CT: Wesleyan University Press, 2005.

Goncharova, Natalia. "The Metamorphoses of the Ballet 'Les Noces.'" Trans. Mary Chamot. *Leonardo* 12, no. 2 (Spring 1979), 137–43.

Huber, Andrea Grodsky. "A Conversation with Irina Nijinska." *Ballet Review* 20, no. 1 (Spring 1992), 36–60.

Jackson, George. "Dance and the City." *Dance Chronicle* 33, no. 3 (2010), 465–79.

Järvinen, Hanna. "Ballets Russes and Blackface: On Assumptions and Invisibility." *Dance Research Journal* 52, no. 3 (Dec. 2020), 76–96.

Kirstein, Lincoln. "The Diaghilev Period." *Hound and Horn* 3, no. 4 (July–Sept. 1930), 468–501.

Marcus, Kenneth H. "'A New Expression for a New People': Race and Ballet in Los Angeles, 1946–1956." *Journal of the West* 44, no. 2 (Spring 2005), 24–33.

Marcus, Kenneth H. "Dance Moves: An African American Ballet Company in Postwar Los Angeles." *Pacific Historical Review* 83, no. 3 (Aug. 2014), 487–527.

Marquié, Hélène. "Enquête en cours sur Madame Stichel (1856–ap. 1933). " *Recherches en danse* 3 (2015), https://journals.openedition.org/danse/974.

Mazo, Margarita. "Stravinsky's 'Les Noces' and Russian Village Wedding Ritual." *Journal of the American Musicological Society* 43, no. 1 (Spring 1990), 99–142.

Olivesi, Vannina. "Entre plaisir et censure, Marie Taglioni chorégraphe du Second Empire." *CLIO Femmes, Genre, Histoire* 46 (2017), 43–64.

Pritchard, Jane. "Serge Diaghilev's Ballets Russes—An Itinerary. Part I: 1909–1921." *Dance Research* 27, no. 1 (Summer 2009), 108–98.

Pritchard, Jane. "Serge Diaghilev's Ballets Russes—An Itinerary. Part II (1922–9)." *Dance Research* 27, no. 2 (2009), 255–357.

Pritchard, Jane. "Two Letters." In *Following Sir Fred's Steps—Ashton's Legacy*. Ed. Stephanie Jordan and Andrée Grau, 101–14. London: Dance Books, 1996.

Pudełek, Janina. "The Polish Mishaps of Serge Lifar and Bronislava Nijinska." *Dance Chronicle* 27, no. 3 (2004), 199–216.

Sanocka, Katarzyna. "Projekty scenografii i kostiumów Teresy Roszkowskiej do baletu *Baśń krakowska* Michała Kondrackiego dla Polskiego Baletu Reprezentacyjnego." *Studia Choreologica* 14, 103–17.

Severn, Margaret. "Dancing with Bronislava Nijinska and Ida Rubinstein." *Dance Chronicle* 11, no. 3 (1988), 333–64.

Szyfman, Arnold. "Powstanie Baletu Polskiegow 1937 roku." In *Leon Wojcikowski*, 50–60. Warsaw: Opera Warszawa, 1958.

Veroli, Patrizia. "The Choreography of Aurel Milloss, Part Three: 1967–1988." *Dance Chronicle* 13, no. 3 (1990–91), 368–92.

Veroli, Patrizia. "Serge Lifar as a Dance Historian and the Myth of Russian Dance in 'Zarubezhnaia Rossia' (Russia Abroad) 1930–1940." *Dance Research* 32, no. 2 (Winter 2014), 105–43.

Index

Endnotes are indicated with a lowercase n, as in 515n1. Except in their own main headings, Nijinska and Nijinsky have been abbreviated BN (for Bronislava) and VN (for Vaslav). In subheadings, long titles of ballet companies are abbreviated accordng to impresario: "Ballets Russes (Diaghilev)," "Ballets Russes (BN)," and so on, as well as "Ballets Rubinstein" and "Grand Ballet (Cuevas)." Abbreviations for ballet titles are based on initial words as found in main headings: "Apres-midi," "Cent Baisers," and so on. Narrative entries for companies and people are organized chronologically rather than alphabetically.

von Neurath, Baron Constantine, 375
Vorobieva, Anna ("Niusia"): in School of
    Movement, 56; arrest of by Cheka, 69;
    takes over BN's Centro-Studio classes,
    116, 117; in Ballets Rubinstein, 244;
    with Sofia Opera, 47, 322
Vronska, Alice, 322
Vsevolozhsky, Prince Ivan, 80
Vuillemin, Louis, 178
Vuillermoz, Emile: on Ballets Rubinstein,
    254; on *Bolero*, 253, 312; on *Chopin
    Concerto*, 446–47; on *Etude*, 294; on *La
    Valse*, 263; on *Les Noces*, 140; on Polish
    Ballet, 371; on Rubinstein, 259; on *Swan
    Princess*, 256
Vyroubova, Nina, 459

Wagner, Richard, 270, 409
Wales, Prince of, 171
Wallerstein, Lothar, 282, 286, 288
Wallmann, Margarita, 419, 420
Walsh, Stephen, 248
Walter, Bruno, 386
Waltz Academy (Balanchine), 416
Wassilievska, Alexandra, 15
Weinberger, Jaromir, 285
Wells, H. G., 357
Welt des Tänzers, Die (Laban), 66
White, Stanford, 412
"white dress" award, 1
White Guard, The (Bulgakov), 59
Wielki Theater, Warsaw, 365, 376
Wielki Theater School, Warsaw, 244
Wieniawski, Henryk, 417
Wigman, Mary, xxii, 279, 419
Wilde, Patricia, 411, 412
Williams, Peter, 465
Williamson, Malcolm, 469–70
Wilson, G. B. L., 466
Wincenc, Margaret, 476
Winterhalter, Franz, 485
Within the Quota, 176, 548n31
With My Red Fires (Humphrey), 356
Woizikovsky, Leon: in Ballets de Monte-
    Carlo (Blum), 359; BN relinquishes
    Faun role to, 112, 113; in *Comédiens*,

329; competitiveness of with BN,
    329–30; directs de Basil's Australian
    company, 359; in *Fâcheux*, 164; in *Les
    Biches*, 157; in Pavlova company, 569n2;
    replaces BN at Polish Ballet, 365, 379; in
    Train Bleu, 171, 175; undermines BN's
    contributions, xxiii
Wolkonsky, André, 449
Wollard, Nathalie, 489, 615n154
Wolska, Hélène (formerly Bessie Forbes-
    Jones), 368, 588n149
Wood, Christopher, 214, 217
Woodward, Ian, 469
Writing a Woman's Life (Heilbrun), 5
Wusty, Egon, 322
WWII, 418

xenophobia, 210, 212, 319–20, 322, 374,
    376–77, 556n68, 579n87

Yar (Moscow cabaret), 38, 521n31
Yiddish Art Theatre, 401
Youshkevitch, Nina: in Ballets Russes
    (BN), 326, 329; BN on, 364; in *Chopin
    Concerto*, Fig. 48; on Jacob's Pillow, 398,
    595n74; pictured on outing with BN
    family, Fig. 45; in Polish Ballet, 367, 370;
    sister of translates BN memoir, 615n154
Youskevitch, Igor, 400, 433

Zack, Léon, 331
Zajlich, Piotr, 365
Zambelli, Carlotta, 208, 227, 228, 229, 259
Zdobinsky, Deborah, 481
Zenon, Faustin, 26, 201–3, 219,
    237, 603n41
Zéphyr et Flore (Massine), 184, 193
Zerbazon (theatrical agency), 274
Zhabchinskaia, Elena, 34
Zhakhovskaia-Chukhmanenko, Kleopatra
    (Pati). *See* Batueva-Shakhovsky,
    Kleopatra
Zirmaya, Blanca, 232, 233, 238, 323–24
Zmarzlik, Stanislaw, 203, 555n39
Zoritch, George, 440, 605n87
Zverev, Nicholas, 569n2